Authorized Self-Study Guide

Designing for Cisco Internetwork Solutions (DESGN)

Second Edition

Diane Teare

Cisco Press

800 East 96th Street
Indianapolis, IN 46240 USA

Authorized Self-Study Guide
Designing for Cisco Internetwork Solutions (DESGN), Second Edition

Diane Teare

Copyright© 2008 Cisco Systems, Inc.

Published by:
Cisco Press
800 East 96th Street
Indianapolis, IN 46240 USA

Printed in the United States of America

First Printing   October 2007

Library of Congress Cataloging-in-Publication Data:

Teare, Diane.

  Designing for Cisco internetwork solutions (DESGN) / Diane Teare. -- 2nd ed.

     p. cm. -- (Authorized self-study guide)

  Rev. ed. of: CCDA self-study : designing for Cisco internetwork solutions (DESGN) / Diane Teare. c2004.

  "Exam 640-863."

  ISBN-13: 978-1-58705-272-9 (hardcover)

  ISBN-10: 1-58705-272-5 (hardcover)

  1. Computer networks--Examinations--Study guides. 2. Telecommunications engineers--Certification. 3. Internetworking (Telecommunication)--Examinations--Study guides. I. Title. II. Series.

TK5105.5.T418 2008

  004.6--dc22

                            2007032855

ISBN-13: 978-1-58705-272-9

ISBN-10: 1-58705-272-5

Warning and Disclaimer

Trademark Acknowledgments

All terms mentioned in this book that are known to be trademarks or service marks have been appropriately capitalized. Cisco Press or Cisco Systems, Inc., cannot attest to the accuracy of this information. Use of a term in this book should not be regarded as affecting the validity of any trademark or service mark.

Corporate and Government Sales

The publisher offers excellent discounts on this book when ordered in quantity for bulk purchases or special sales, which may include electronic versions and/or custom covers and content particular to your business, training goals, marketing focus, and branding interests. For more information, please contact:

U.S. Corporate and Government Sales
1-800-382-3419
corpsales@pearsontechgroup.com

For sales outside the United States please contact:
International Sales
international@pearsoned.com

Feedback Information

At Cisco Press, our goal is to create in-depth technical books of the highest quality and value. Each book is crafted with care and precision, undergoing rigorous development that involves the unique expertise of members from the professional technical community.

Readers' feedback is a natural continuation of this process. If you have any comments regarding how we could improve the quality of this book, or otherwise alter it to better suit your needs, you can contact us through email at feedback@ciscopress.com. Please make sure to include the book title and ISBN in your message.

We greatly appreciate your assistance.

Publisher: Paul Boger

Associate Publisher: Dave Dusthimer

Executive Editor: Brett Bartow

Managing Editor: Patrick Kanouse

Senior Project Editor: Tonya Simpson

Editorial Assistant: Vanessa Evans

Designer: Louisa Adair

Composition: Mark Shirar

Indexer: Ken Johnson

Cisco Representative: Anthony Wolfenden

Cisco Press Program Manager: Jeff Brady

Development Editor: Eric Stewart

Copy Editor: Mike Henry

Technical Editors: Shawn Boyd and Richard Piquard

Proofreader: Gayle Johnson

Americas Headquarters
Cisco Systems, Inc.
170 West Tasman Drive
San Jose, CA 95134-1706
USA
www.cisco.com
Tel: 408 526-4000
800 553-NETS (6387)
Fax: 408 527-0883

Asia Pacific Headquarters
Cisco Systems, Inc.
168 Robinson Road
#28-01 Capital Tower
Singapore 068912
www.cisco.com
Tel: +65 6317 7777
Fax: +65 6317 7799

Europe Headquarters
Cisco Systems International BV
Haarlerbergpark
Haarlerbergweg 13-19
1101 CH Amsterdam
The Netherlands
www-europe.cisco.com
Tel: +31 0 800 020 0791
Fax: +31 0 20 357 1100

Cisco has more than 200 offices worldwide. Addresses, phone numbers, and fax numbers are listed on the Cisco Website at **www.cisco.com/go/offices.**

About the Author

Diane Teare is a professional in the networking, training, and e-learning fields. She has more than 20 years of experience in designing, implementing, and troubleshooting network hardware and software and has also been involved in teaching, course design, and project management. She has extensive knowledge of network design and routing technologies and is an instructor with one of the largest authorized Cisco Learning Partners. She was recently the Director of e-Learning for the same company, where she was responsible for planning and supporting all the company's e-learning offerings in Canada, including Cisco courses. Diane has a bachelor's degree in applied science in electrical engineering (BASc) and a master's degree in applied science in management science (MASc). She is a certified Cisco instructor and currently holds her CCNP and CCDP certifications. She coauthored the Cisco Press titles *Campus Network Design Fundamentals,* the three editions of *Building Scalable Cisco Internetworks (BSCI),* and *Building Scalable Cisco Networks.* She also edited the first edition of this book and *Designing Cisco Networks.*

About the Technical Reviewers

Shawn Boyd is a senior network consultant for ARP Technologies, Inc. He has worldwide experience in consulting on many different projects, such as security/VoIP for Cisco Systems Israel, intrusion prevention for Top Layer Networks of Boston, and DSL infrastructure rollout for Telus Canada. Shawn is also active in course development and is a certified Cisco instructor with ARP Technologies, Inc., responsible for teaching most of the Cisco curriculum. He has coauthored IT security–related books for Cisco Press and has been a technical editor on a few Cisco Press Self-Study Guides. His background is in network security and design at a service provider level. He has worked for Canada's largest telco providers, performing network designs and implementations, and was lead contact on many large government contracts.

Richard Piquard is a senior network architect for Global Knowledge Network, Inc. He has more than seven years of experience as a certified Cisco instructor, teaching introductory and advanced routing, switching, design, and voice-related courses throughout North America and Europe. Richard has a highly diverse skill set in design and implementation of both Cisco and multivendor environments. His experience in the industry ranges from his military background as the network chief of the Marine Corps Systems Command, Quantico, Virginia, to a field engineer for the Xylan Corporation (Alcatel), Calabasas, California, to a member of a four-person, worldwide network planning and implementation team for the Household Finance Corporation, Chicago.

Dedications

This book is dedicated to my wonderful husband, Allan Mertin, whose optimism inspires me; to our captivating son, Nicholas, and his enthusiastic curiosity and quest for knowledge; to my parents, Syd and Beryl, for their continuous love and support; and to my friends, including "the Girls," for continuing to help me keep my sanity!

Acknowledgments

I would like to thank the many people who helped put this book together, including the following:

The Cisco Press team—Brett Bartow, the executive editor, for driving this book through the process, and his continued support over the years. Vanessa Evans was instrumental in organizing the logistics and administration. Eric Stewart, the development editor, has been invaluable in producing a high-quality manuscript. I would also like to thank Tonya Simpson for her excellent work in shepherding this book through the editorial process. Thanks also to Richard Froom, Balaji Sivasubramanian, and Erum Frahim, the authors of Cisco Press's *Building Cisco Multilayer Switched Networks (BCMSN),* Fourth Edition.

The Cisco Systems team—Many thanks to the members of the team who developed the latest version of the DESGN course. The team included two people from Chesapeake Netcraftsmen: Carole Warner Reece and Peter Welcher. Members of the team from Cisco Systems included Dennis Masters, Dwayne Fields, Pat Lao, Bill Chadwick, Bob Eckoff, Bob Ligett, Drew Blair, and the project manager, Dan Stern.

The technical reviewers—I would like to thank the technical reviewers of this book, Shawn Boyd and Richard Piquard, for their comprehensive, detailed review and beneficial input.

My family—Of course, this book would not have been possible without the constant understanding and tolerance of my family, who have lived through the many weekends and nights it took to complete it. Special thanks to Nicholas for always making sure I got lots of hugs!

This Book Is Safari Enabled

The Safari® Enabled icon on the cover of your favorite technology book means the book is available through Safari Bookshelf. When you buy this book, you get free access to the online edition for 45 days.

Safari Bookshelf is an electronic reference library that lets you easily search thousands of technical books, find code samples, download chapters, and access technical information whenever and wherever you need it.

To gain 45-day Safari Enabled access to this book:

- Go to http://www.ciscopress.com/safarienabled.
- Complete the brief registration form.
- Enter the coupon code FNNP-QHIM-XSJX-XALZ-9PE4.

If you have difficulty registering on Safari Bookshelf or accessing the online edition, please e-mail customer-service@safaribooksonline.com.

Contents at a Glance

Contents

Icons Used in This Book

 Access Point

 Cisco Unified Communications Manager

 Router

 Bridge

 Hub

 DSU/CSU

 Cisco IP Phone

 H.323 Device

 PBX

 Catalyst Switch

 Multilayer Switch

 ATM Switch

 ISDN/Frame Relay Switch

 Content Switch

 Voice-Enabled Router

 Router with Firewall

 Communication Server

 Gateway

 Access Server

 Phone

 Netflow Router

 VPN Concentrator

 Network Management Appliance

 DSLAM

 Wide Area Application Engine

 WiSM

 Optical Services Router

Lightweight Double Radio Access Point

 WLAN Controller

 PC with Software

 Terminal

 File Server

 Web Server

 Cisco Works Workstation

 Modem

 PC

 Printer

 Laptop

 Cisco Security MARS

 NAC Appliance

 PIX Security Appliance

Network Cloud

 Cisco MDS 9000 SSM

 Optical Transport

 NAS

 InfiniBand

 WAFS

 IDS

 Token Ring

 FDDI

Line: Ethernet

Line: Serial

Line: Switched Serial

Wireless Connection

Command Syntax Conventions

The conventions used to present command syntax in this book are the same conventions used in the IOS Command Reference. The Command Reference describes these conventions as follows:

- **Boldface** indicates commands and keywords that are entered literally as shown. In actual configuration examples and output (not general command syntax), boldface indicates commands that are manually input by the user (such as a **show** command).

- *Italics* indicate arguments for which you supply actual values.

- Vertical bars (l) separate alternative, mutually exclusive elements.

- Square brackets [ ] indicate optional elements.

- Braces { } indicate a required choice.

- Braces within brackets [{ }] indicate a required choice within an optional element.

Foreword

Cisco Certification Self-Study Guides are excellent self-study resources for networking professionals to maintain and increase internetworking skills and to prepare for Cisco Career Certification exams. Cisco Career Certifications are recognized worldwide and provide valuable, measurable rewards to networking professionals and their employers.

Cisco Press exam certification guides and preparation materials offer exceptional—and flexible—access to the knowledge and information required to stay current in one's field of expertise, or to gain new skills. Whether used to increase internetworking skills or as a supplement to a formal certification preparation course, these materials offer networking professionals the information and knowledge required to perform on-the-job tasks proficiently.

Developed in conjunction with the Cisco certifications and training team, Cisco Press books are the only self-study books authorized by Cisco. They offer students a series of exam practice tools and resource materials to help ensure that learners fully grasp the concepts and information presented.

Additional authorized Cisco instructor-led courses, e-learning, labs, and simulations are available exclusively from Cisco Learning Solutions Partners worldwide. To learn more, visit http://www.cisco.com/go/training/.

I hope you will find this guide to be an essential part of your exam preparation and professional development, as well as a valuable addition to your personal library.

Drew Rosen
Manager, Learning and Development
Learning@Cisco
September 2007

Introduction

Modern networks are both extremely complex and critical to business success. As organizational processes continue to increase the requirements for bandwidth, reliability, and functionality from their networks, network designers are challenged to rapidly develop and evolve networks that use new protocols and technologies. Network designers are also challenged to stay current with the internetworking industry's constant and rapid changes. Designing robust, reliable, scalable networks is a necessary skill for network operators and designers in the modern organizational environment.

This book teaches you how to design enterprise networks. You will learn about network design in the context of the Cisco Service Oriented Network Architecture (SONA) architectural framework and Enterprise Architecture. Specific topics include campus and data center infrastructure, remote connectivity, IP addressing design, routing protocol selection, designing voice networks, wireless network design, and including security in your designs.

An ongoing case study and chapter-ending review questions illustrate and help solidify the concepts presented in this book.

This book provides you with the knowledge and skills you need to achieve associate-level competency in network design. It starts you down the path to attaining your CCDA certification, because it provides in-depth information to help you prepare for the DESGN exam.

DESGN is the first step in the design curriculum that supports the Cisco network design certification track. This book focuses on the technology and methods currently available.

Objectives of This Book

The goal of this book is to provide you with the knowledge you need to gather internetworking requirements, identify solutions, and design the network infrastructure and services to ensure basic functionality, using the principles of hierarchical network design to structure and modularize a converged enterprise network design. Design tasks might include understanding the design methodology; structuring and modularizing the network design using the Cisco Enterprise Architecture; designing the Enterprise Campus, Enterprise Data Center, Enterprise Edge, and remote modules as needed; designing an addressing plan and selecting suitable routing protocols; designing basic voice transport across the network; designing a basic wireless solution; and evaluating security solutions.

Who Should Read This Book

This book is intended for network and sales engineers who are involved in network design, planning, and implementation, and for those who plan to take the 640-863 DESGN exam toward the CCDA certification. This book provides in-depth study material for that exam. To fully benefit from this book, you should have the following prerequisite skills:

- CCNA–level knowledge (or CCNA certification), which can best be achieved by completing the related CCNA courses and using CCNA books from Cisco Press. You can find more information on the CCNA certification at http://www.cisco.com/go/ccna/.

- Knowledge of wireless networking, quality of service (QoS), and multilayer switching is highly recommended. The level equivalent to that covered in the Building Cisco Multilayer Switched Networks (BCMSN) course or the book *Building Cisco Multilayer Switched Networks (BCMSN)*, Fourth Edition (Richard Froom, Balaji Sivasubramanian, Erum Frahim, Cisco Press, 2007) is appropriate.

> **NOTE** We assume that you understand the wireless networking material in the Cisco Press book just mentioned. In Chapter 9, we include some material from that book as an introduction to wireless technology. Refer to the Cisco Press BCMSN book for more detailed information.

- Practical experience deploying and operating networks based on Cisco network devices and the Cisco IOS.

Summary of the Contents

The chapters and appendixes of this book are as follows:

- Chapter 1, "Network Fundamentals Review," introduces some fundamental concepts and terminology that are the foundation for the material in the rest of the book.

- Chapter 2, "Applying a Methodology to Network Design," introduces the Cisco vision of intelligent networks and the Service Oriented Network Architecture (SONA) architectural framework. The lifecycle of a network and a network design methodology based on the lifecycle are presented, and each phase of the network design process is explored in detail.

- Chapter 3, "Structuring and Modularizing the Network," introduces a modular hierarchical approach to network design, the Cisco Enterprise Architecture. The chapter includes a detailed description of services within modular networks. Network management protocols and features are also discussed.

- Chapter 4, "Designing Basic Campus and Data Center Networks," examines the design of the Enterprise Campus and Enterprise Data Center network infrastructure.

- Chapter 5, "Designing Remote Connectivity," discusses WAN technologies and design considerations. This chapter describes the Enterprise WAN and metropolitan-area network (MAN) architectures and the Enterprise Branch and Teleworker architectures and discusses the selection of WAN hardware and software components.

- Chapter 6, "Designing IP Addressing in the Network," discusses the design of an IP version 4 (IPv4) addressing scheme. The chapter also introduces IP version 6 (IPv6) and discusses IPv4-to-IPv6 migration strategies.

- Chapter 7, "Selecting Routing Protocols for the Network," describes considerations for selecting the most appropriate network routing protocol. The chapter discusses why certain protocols are suitable for specific modules in the Enterprise Architecture. It concludes with a description of some advanced routing protocol deployment features, including redistribution, filtering, and summarization.

- Chapter 8, "Voice Network Design Considerations," introduces voice design principles and provides guidelines for a successful integrated network deployment. It begins with an overview of traditional voice architectures and features and continues with a discussion of integrated voice architectures, including VoIP and IP telephony.

- Chapter 9, "Wireless Network Design Considerations," introduces the Cisco Unified Wireless Network (UWN) architecture and discusses wireless design principles. The chapter introduces wireless technologies and explores considerations when designing Cisco UWNs in enterprise environments.

- Chapter 10, "Evaluating Security Solutions for the Network," describes network security, including threats and risks, and network security policies. The Cisco Self-Defending Network strategy for designing network security is explored, and Cisco network security solutions for enterprise networks are discussed.

- Appendix A, "Answers to Review Questions and Case Studies," contains answers to the review questions and case studies that appear at the end of the chapters.

- Appendix B, "IPv4 Supplement," provides job aids and supplementary information intended for your use when working with IPv4 addresses. Topics include an IP addressing and subnetting job aid, a decimal-to-binary conversion chart, IPv4 addressing review, and IPv4 access lists.

- Appendix C, "Open Systems Interconnection (OSI) Reference Model," is a brief overview of the OSI seven-layer model.

- Appendix D, "Network Address Translation," contains information about Cisco's implementation of Network Address Translation (NAT) and port address translation (PAT).

- "Acronyms and Abbreviations" spells out the abbreviations, acronyms, and initialisms used in this book.

Case Studies and Review Questions

Starting in Chapter 2, each chapter concludes with a case study on Acme County Medical Center (ACMC) Hospital, a fictitious small county hospital in the United States, to help you evaluate your understanding of the concepts presented. In each task of the case study, you act as a network design consultant and make creative proposals to accomplish the customer's business needs. The final goal of each case study is a paper solution. Also starting in Chapter 2, each chapter also includes review questions on the subjects covered in that chapter so that you can test your knowledge.

To find out how you did and what material you might need to study further, you can compare your answers to those provided in Appendix A. Note that for each case study task, Appendix A provides a solution based on the assumptions made. There is no claim that the provided solution is the best or only solution. Your solution might be more appropriate for the assumptions you made. The provided solution allows you to understand the author's reasoning and offers you a means of comparing and contrasting your solution.

What's New in This Edition

This book is an update to *CCDA Self-Study: Designing for Cisco Internetwork Solutions (DESGN),* ISBN 1-58705-141-9. This second edition reflects changes to the DESGN course. The following are the major changes between editions:

- Every chapter has been rewritten. Some material that was removed from the main portion of the previous edition because of course changes has been put in sidebars, as appropriate. The appendixes have been modified and updated to reflect the book's content.

- The methodology used throughout the book is now based on Cisco's SONA framework and Enterprise architectures.

- New topics include the design of the data center and the design of teleworker and branch offices.

- A new chapter on wireless network design, Chapter 9, has been included.

- Chapter 1 has been enhanced to include a more thorough review of networking fundamentals and to reflect new prerequisite material.

- Some information on IP addressing in the main body of the first edition has been moved to Appendix B.

- Chapter 10 includes details of Cisco network security solutions and the Cisco Self-Defending Network strategy.

- The information about network management has been condensed and moved to Chapter 3.

- The case study is new and includes a more thorough examination of network design issues. Simulation output is no longer included.

Author's Notes, Key Points, Sidebars, and Cautions

The notes, key points, and sidebars found in this book provide extra information on a subject.

KEY POINT | The key points highlight information that is important for understanding the topic at hand and specific points of interest.

Resources for Further Study

Within each chapter are references to other resources that provide you with further information on specific topics. For more information about Cisco exams, training, and certifications, refer to the Training and Events area on the Cisco website at http://www.cisco.com/web/learning/index.html.

NOTE The website references in this book were accurate at the time of writing; however, they might have since changed. If a URL is unavailable, you might try conducting a search using the title as keywords in your favorite search engine.

This chapter describes the fundamental concepts that relate to networks and includes the following sections:

- Introduction to Networks

- Protocols and the OSI Model

- LANs and WANs

- Network Devices

- Introduction to the TCP/IP Suite

- Routing

- Addressing

- Switching Types

- Spanning Tree Protocol

- Virtual LANs

- Comprehensive Example

- Summary

CHAPTER 1

Network Fundamentals Review

The goal of this chapter is to introduce some fundamental concepts and terminology that are the foundation for the other material in the book. After a brief introduction to networks in general, we delve into the communication protocols that are used by network devices; this necessarily includes a discussion of the infamous Open Systems Interconnection (OSI) model. LANs and WANs are described, as are the various devices found in a network. This is followed by an introduction to TCP/IP, used extensively in the Internet. Routing and addressing, including IP addresses, are explored. The two types of switching—Layer 2 and Layer 3 switching—are described. Spanning Tree Protocol (STP) and its operation are introduced, followed by a discussion of VLANs. The chapter concludes with a comprehensive example, tying together many of the concepts covered. You are encouraged to review any of the material in this chapter that you are not familiar with before reading the rest of the book, because these ideas are critical to understanding the more complex technologies covered in the other chapters.

Introduction to Networks

In the 1960s and 1970s, before the PC was invented, a company would typically have only one central computer: a mainframe. Users connected to the mainframe through terminals on their desks. These terminals had no intelligence of their own—their only function was to display a text-based user interface provided by the mainframe. For this reason, they were usually called *dumb terminals*. The only network was the connection between the terminals and the mainframe.

In 1981, the IBM PC was released—an event that changed the industry significantly. The PC had intelligence of its own, allowing users to do tasks on their desktops that previously required a mainframe. Networks were introduced to interconnect these distributed PCs.

The term *network* is used in many ways. For example, people network with one another, telephones are networked in the public telephone system, and data networks connect different computers. These uses of the term have a common thread: Networks make it possible for people or devices to communicate with each other.

A *data network* is a network that allows computers to exchange data. The simplest data network is two PCs connected through a cable. However, most data networks connect many devices.

An *internetwork* is a collection of individual networks connected by networking devices and that function as a single large network. The public Internet is the most common example—it is a single network that connects millions of computers. *Internetworking* refers to the industry and products that are involved in the design, implementation, and administration of internetworks.

The first networks were LANs; they enabled multiple users in a relatively small geographic area to exchange files and messages and to access shared resources such as printers and disk storage. WANs were introduced to interconnect these LANs so that geographically dispersed users could also share information. The "LANs and WANs" section later in this chapter further describes these two types of networks.

> **NOTE**   The "Acronyms and Abbreviations" appendix near the end of the book lists many of the acronyms that appear in this book.

Protocols and the OSI Model

This section describes the OSI model and protocols used in internetworking. As an introduction, imagine that you are in Toronto and you want to send an e-mail to your friend in San Francisco. Successfully sending and receiving e-mail involves doing many things, including the following:

■   You must type the message in your e-mail application.

■   You must address the message in your e-mail application.

■   You must click the **Send** button in your e-mail application to start sending the message.

■   You must use the correct type of connections and wires to connect your PC to your local network.

■   Your PC must put the data on the wire.

■   Your PC must be able to connect to the Internet, and you must provide any necessary login information.

■   Network devices must find the best path through the Internet so that the e-mail is received by the right person.

The following section introduces the OSI model, a model that describes all these communication functions and their relationships with each other.

The OSI Model

The ISO standards committee created a list of all the network functions required for sending data (such as an e-mail) and divided them into seven categories. This model is known as the *OSI seven-layer* model. The OSI seven-layer model was released in 1984; it is illustrated in Figure 1-1.

Figure 1-1   *Each of the Seven Layers of the OSI Model Represents Functions Required for Communication*

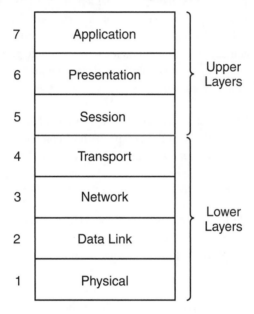

NOTE   You might also have heard people talk about OSI Layers 8 and 9. Although they are not official, Layer 8 is commonly known as the political layer, and Layer 9 is the religious layer. These lightheartedly represent all the other issues you might encounter in an IT project.

KEY POINT   The OSI model represents everything that must happen to send data. The important thing to remember is that the OSI model does not specify *how* these things are to be done, just *what* needs to be done. Different protocols can implement these functions differently. For example, the open-standard Internet Protocol (IP) and Novell's Internetwork Packet Exchange (IPX) protocol are different implementations of the network layer.

As also shown in Figure 1-1, the seven layers can be thought of in two groups: the upper layers and the lower layers. The term *upper layers* often refers to Layers 5 through 7, and the term *lower layers* often refers to Layers 1 through 4, although this terminology is relative. The term *upper layer* also refers to any layer above another layer.

The upper layers are concerned with application issues—for example, the interface to the user and the format of the data. The lower layers are concerned with transport issues—for example, how the data traverses the network and the physical characteristics of that network.

Protocols

A *protocol* is a set of rules. The OSI model provides a framework for the *communication protocols* used between computers. Just as we need rules of the road—for example, so that we know that a red light means stop and a green light means go—computers also need to agree on a set of rules to successfully communicate. Two computers must use the same protocol to communicate. Computers that try to use different protocols would be analogous to speaking in Italian to someone who understands only English—it would not work.

Many different networking protocols are in use, in a variety of categories. For example, *LAN* and *WAN protocols* (at the lower two OSI layers) specify how communication is accomplished across various media types. *Routed protocols* (at Layer 3) specify the data's format and how it is carried throughout a network, and *routing protocols* (some of which also operate at Layer 3) specify how routers communicate with one another to indicate the best paths through the network.

KEY POINT | Many *protocol suites* define various protocols that correspond to the functions defined in the seven OSI layers, including routed protocols, a selection of routing protocols, applications, and so forth. Protocol suites are also known as *protocol stacks*.

The most widely used network protocol suite today is the TCP/IP suite, named after two of the protocols within the suite. This network protocol suite is used in many places, including the backbone of the Internet and within organization's networks. Novell's NetWare, Apple Corporation's AppleTalk, and IBM's System Network Architecture are other examples of network protocol suites.

KEY POINT | The OSI protocol suite is yet another suite. Although the OSI protocol suite uses the same names for its seven layers as the OSI seven-layer model does, the two OSI items are different—one is a protocol suite, and the other is the model that is used as a point of reference for all of the protocol suites.

The OSI Layers

The following sections briefly describe each of the seven layers of the OSI model, starting at the lowest layer. Appendix C, "Open System Interconnection (OSI) Reference Model," delves deeper into the details of the OSI model.

Physical Layer—Layer 1

The OSI physical layer defines specifications such as the electrical and mechanical conditions necessary for activating, maintaining, and deactivating the physical link between devices. Specifications include voltage levels, maximum cable lengths, connector types, and maximum data rates. The physical layer is concerned with the binary transmission of data. This binary data is represented as *bits* (which is short for *binary digits*). A bit has a single binary value, either 0 or 1.

Data Link Layer—Layer 2

Layer 2, the data link layer, defines the format of data that is to be transmitted across the physical network. It indicates how the physical medium is accessed, including physical addressing, error handling, and flow control. The data link layer sends frames of data; different media have different types of frames.

KEY POINT | A *frame* is a defined set of data that includes addressing and control information and is transmitted between network devices. A frame can contain a header field (in front of the data) and a trailer field (after the data); these two fields are said to "frame" the data.

For LANs, the Institute of Electrical and Electronics Engineers (IEEE) split Layer 2 into two sublayers: Logical Link Control (LLC) and Media Access Control (MAC).

The LLC sublayer (defined by the IEEE 802.2 specification) allows multiple network layer (Layer 3) protocols to communicate over the same physical data link by allowing the Layer 3 protocol to be specified in the LLC portion of the frame.

Some examples of MAC sublayer protocols are IEEE 802.3 Ethernet and IEEE 802.5 Token Ring. The MAC sublayer specifies the *physical* MAC address that uniquely identifies a device on a network. Each frame that is sent specifies a destination MAC address; only the device with that MAC address should receive and process the frame. Each frame also includes the MAC address of the frame's source.

NOTE   You might be interested in some IEEE trivia: The IEEE 802 committee was formed in February (the second month) of 1980, and thus was called "802." The IEEE 802.3 standard, for example, was ratified in the IEEE annex building 3 in Geneva at that time.

Network Layer—Layer 3

The network layer is responsible for routing, which allows data to be properly forwarded across a logical internetwork (consisting of multiple physical networks). *Logical* network addresses (as opposed to physical MAC addresses) are specified at Layer 3. Layer 3 protocols include routed and routing protocols. The routing protocols determine the best path that should be used to forward the routed data through the internetwork to its destination.

The network layer sends *datagrams* (or *packets*); different routed protocols have different types of datagrams.

KEY POINT	A *datagram* is a defined set of data that includes addressing and control information and is routed between the data's source and destination.

If a datagram needs to be sent across a network that can handle only a certain amount of data at a time, the datagram can be fragmented into multiple packets and then reassembled at the destination. Therefore, a *datagram* is a unit of data, whereas a *packet* is what physically goes on the network. If no fragmentation is required, a packet is a datagram; the two terms are often used interchangeably.

Transport Layer—Layer 4

Layer 4, the transport layer, is concerned with end-to-end connections between the source and the destination. The transport layer provides network services to the upper layers.

Connection-oriented reliable transport establishes a logical connection and uses sequence numbers to ensure that all data is received at the destination. Connectionless best-effort transport just sends the data and relies on upper-layer error detection mechanisms to report and correct problems. Reliable transport has more overhead than best-effort transport.

KEY POINT	*Best-effort delivery* means that the protocol will *not check* to see whether the data was delivered intact; a higher-level protocol, or the end user, must confirm that the data was delivered correctly

Multiplexing allows many applications to use the same physical connection. For example, data is tagged with a number that identifies the application from which it came. Both sides of the connection then can interpret the data in the same way.

The transport layer sends segments.

KEY POINT	A *segment* is a defined set of data that includes control information and is sent between the transport layers of the sender and receiver of the data.

Upper Layers—Layers 5 Through 7

From the lower layers' perspective, the three upper layers represent the data that must be transmitted from the source to the destination; the network typically neither knows nor cares about the contents of these layers. For completeness, the following briefly describes the functions of these layers:

- The session layer, Layer 5, is responsible for establishing, maintaining, and terminating communication sessions between applications running on different hosts.

- The presentation layer, Layer 6, specifies the format, data structure, coding, compression, and other ways of representing the data to ensure that information sent from one host's application layer can be read by the destination host.

- Finally, the application layer, Layer 7, is the closest to the end user; it interacts directly with software applications that need to communicate over the network.

KEY POINT | The OSI application layer is not the application itself; rather, the OSI application layer provides the communication services to the application.

For example, your e-mail application might use two OSI application layer protocols— Simple Mail Transfer Protocol (SMTP) and Post Office Protocol version 3 (POP3)—to send and retrieve e-mail messages.

Communication Among OSI Layers

This section describes how communication among the seven OSI layers is accomplished. When you send an e-mail from Toronto to your friend in San Francisco, you can think of your e-mail application sending a message to the e-mail application on your friend's computer. In OSI model terms, information is exchanged between peer OSI layers—the application layer on your computer is communicating with the application layer on your friend's computer. However, to accomplish this, the e-mail must go through all the other layers on your computer; for example, it must have the correct network layer address, be put in the correct frame type, and so on. The e-mail must then go over the network, and then go back through all the layers on your friend's computer, until it finally arrives at your friend's e-mail application.

Control information from each layer is added to the e-mail data before it passes to lower layers; this control information is necessary to allow the data to go through the network properly. Thus, the data at each layer is *encapsulated*, or wrapped in, the information appropriate for that layer, including addressing and error checking. The right side of Figure 1-2 illustrates the following encapsulation process:

- At Layer 4, the e-mail is encapsulated in a segment.

- At Layer 3, this segment is encapsulated in a packet.

- At Layer 2, this packet is encapsulated in a frame.

- Finally, at Layer 1, the frame is sent out on the wire (or air, if wireless is used) in bits.

Figure 1-2   *Data Is Encapsulated as It Goes Down Through the Layers and Is Unencapsulated as It Goes Up*

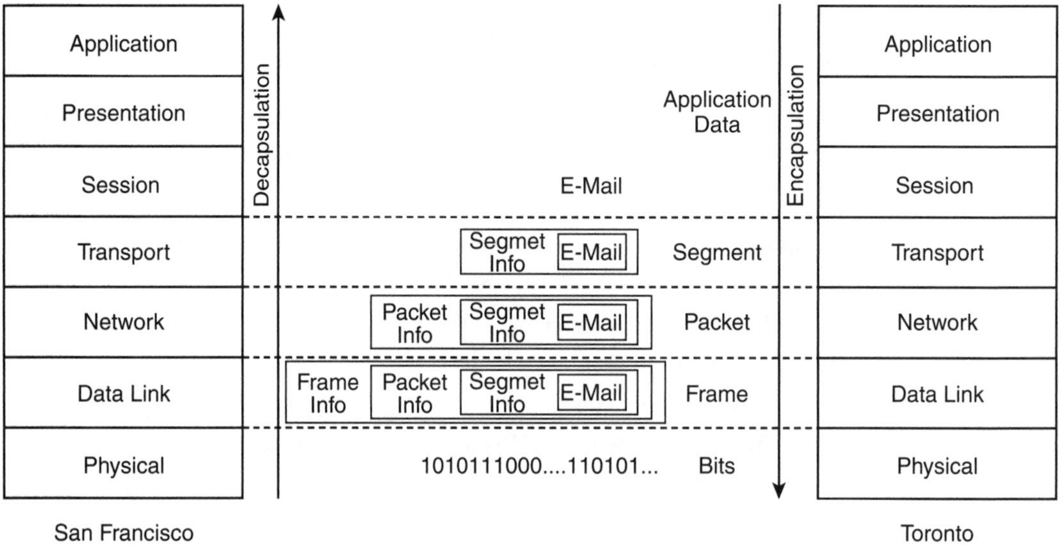

The grouping of data used to exchange information at a particular OSI layer is known as a *protocol data unit (PDU)*. Thus, the PDU at Layer 4 is a segment, at Layer 3 is a packet, and at Layer 2 is a frame.

Notice how the overall size of the information increases as the data goes down through the lower layers. When data is received at the other end of the network, this additional information is analyzed and then removed as the data is passed to the higher layers toward the application layer. In other words, the data is *unencapsulated,* or unwrapped; this process is shown on the left side of Figure 1-2.

> **NOTE**   Cisco sometimes uses the word *decapsulate* instead of unencapsulate.

> **NOTE**   For simplicity, Figure 1-2 shows only two systems, one in San Francisco and one in Toronto, and does not show the details of e-mail protocols or e-mail servers. Later sections in this chapter describe what happens when intermediate devices, such as routers, are encountered between the two systems.

At each layer, different protocols are available. For example, the packets sent by IP are different from those sent by IPX because different protocols (rules) must be followed. Both sides of peer layers that are communicating must support the same protocol.

LANs and WANs

LANs were first used between PCs when users needed to connect with other PCs in the same building to share resources. A *LAN* is a high-speed, yet relatively inexpensive, network that allows connected computers to communicate. LANs have limited reach (hence the term *local-area* network), typically less than a few hundred meters, so they can connect only devices in the same room or building, or possibly within the same campus.

A LAN is an always-on connection—in other words, you don't have to dial up or otherwise connect to it when you want to send some data. LANs also usually belong to the organization in which they are deployed, so no incremental cost is typically associated with sending data. A variety of LAN technologies are available, some of which are shown in the center of Figure 1-3 and briefly described here:

■ Ethernet and IEEE 802.3, running at 10 megabits per second (Mbps), use a carrier sense multiple access collision detect (CSMA/CD) technology. When a CSMA/CD device has data to send, it listens to see whether any of the other devices on the wire (multiple access) are transmitting (carrier sense). If no other device is transmitting, this device starts to send its data, listening all the time in case another device erroneously starts to send data (collision detect).

■ Fast Ethernet (at 100 Mbps), covered by the IEEE 802.3u specification, also uses the CSMA/CD technology.

■ Gigabit Ethernet (running at 1 gigabit per second [Gbps]) is covered by the IEEE 802.3z and 802.3ab specifications and uses the CSMA/CD technology.

■ Wireless LAN (WLAN) standards, defined by the IEEE 802.11 specifications, are capable of speeds up to 54 Mbps under the 802.11g specification. (A new standard, 802.11n, planned to be ratified in 2007, will be capable of higher speeds.) WLANs use a carrier sense multiple access collision *avoidance* (CSMA/CA) mechanism (versus the CSMA/CD mechanism used by the wired Ethernet standards).

Figure 1-3   *A Variety of LAN and WAN Standards*

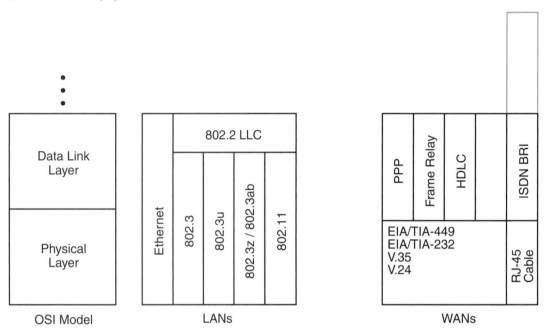

WANs interconnect devices that are usually connected to LANs and are located over a relatively broad geographic area (hence the term *wide-area* network). Compared to a LAN, a typical WAN is slower, requires a connection request when you want to send data, and usually belongs to another organization (called a *service provider*). You pay the service provider a fee (known as a *tariff*) for the use of the WAN; this fee could be a fixed monthly amount, or it could be variable based on usage and distance.

Just as you find many types of LANs, many types of WANs are also available, some of which are illustrated on the right side of Figure 1-3. Like LANs, WANs function at the lower two layers of the OSI model. A few, such as ISDN, also function at Layer 3. The service you use depends on many factors, including what is available where you are and, of course, the cost of the service. Some of the common WAN technologies include the following:

■ **Packet-switched network**: A network that shares the service provider's facilities. The service provider creates permanent virtual circuits and switched virtual circuits that deliver data between subscribers' sites. Frame Relay is an example of a packet-switched network.

■ **Leased line**: A point-to-point connection reserved for transmission. Common data link layer protocols used in this case are PPP and High-Level Data Link Control (HDLC).

- **Circuit-switched network**: A physical path reserved for the duration of the connection between two points. ISDN Basic Rate Interface (BRI) is an example of this type of network.

Two other technologies, digital subscriber line (DSL) and cable, connect residential and business premises to service providers' premises:

- **DSL**: Uses unused bandwidth on traditional copper telephone lines to deliver traffic at higher speeds than traditional modems allow. The most common DSL implementation is asymmetric DSL (ADSL). It is called *asymmetric* because the download speed is faster than the upload speed, reflecting the needs of most users and more efficiently using the available bandwidth on standard two-wire telephone lines. ADSL allows regular telephone traffic to simultaneously share the line with high-speed data traffic so that only one telephone line is required to support both high-speed Internet and normal telephone services.

- **Cable**: Uses unused bandwidth on cable television networks to deliver data at higher speeds than traditional modems allow.

NOTE   These and other WAN technologies are discussed in Chapter 5, "Designing Remote Connectivity."

Network Devices

The main devices that interconnect networks are hubs, switches, and routers, as described in the following sections.

NOTE   Many other devices can be used in networks to provide specific functionality; these devices are introduced in the appropriate chapters in this book. For example, security devices, including firewalls, are discussed in Chapter 10, "Evaluating Security Solutions for the Network."

Terminology: Domains, Bandwidth, Unicast, Broadcast, and Multicast

The following is some terminology related to the operation of network devices:

- A *domain* is a specific part of a network.

- *Bandwidth* is the amount of data that can be carried across a network in a given time period.

- *Unicast data* is data meant for a specific device.

- *Broadcast data* is data meant for all devices; a special broadcast address indicates this.

- *Multicast data* is data destined for a specific group of devices; again, a special address indicates this.

- A *bandwidth domain,* known as a *collision domain* for Ethernet LANs, includes all devices that share the same bandwidth.

- A *broadcast domain* includes all devices that receive each others' broadcasts (and multicasts).

Devices in the same bandwidth domain are also in the same broadcast domain; however, devices in the same broadcast domain can be in different bandwidth domains.

Hubs

A typical Ethernet LAN uses unshielded twisted-pair (UTP) cables with RJ-45 connectors (which are slightly bigger than telephone RJ-11 connectors). Because these cables have only two ends, you need an intermediary device to connect more than two computers. That device is a hub.

A hub works at Layer 1 and connects multiple devices so that they are logically all on one LAN.

Physical Interfaces and Ports

The physical connection point on a network device—a hub, switch, or router—is called an *interface* or a *port.*

Don't confuse this definition of *port* with the application layer *port numbers* discussed in the "TCP/IP Transport Layer Protocols" section later in this chapter.

A hub has no intelligence—it sends all data received on any port to all the other ports. Consequently, devices connected through a hub receive everything that the other devices send, whether or not it was meant for them. This is analogous to being in a room with lots of people—if you speak, everyone can hear you. If more than one person speaks at a time, everyone just hears noise.

All devices connected to a hub are in one collision domain and one broadcast domain.

> **NOTE**   A hub just repeats all the data received on any port to all the other ports; thus, hubs are also known as *repeaters.*

Switches

Just as having many people in a room trying to speak can result in nobody hearing anything intelligible, using hubs in anything but a small network is not efficient. To improve performance,

LANs are usually divided into multiple smaller LANs interconnected by a Layer 2 LAN switch. The devices connected to a switch again appear as they are all on one LAN, but this time, multiple conversations between devices connected through the switch can happen simultaneously.

> **NOTE** This section discusses Layer 2 LAN switches. The later section "Switching Types" introduces Layer 3 switching.

LAN switches are Layer 2 devices and have some intelligence—they send data to a port only if the data needs to go there. A device connected to a switch port does not receive any of the information addressed to devices on other ports. Therefore, the main advantage of using a switch instead of a hub is that the traffic received by a device is reduced because only frames addressed to a specific device are forwarded to the port on which that device is connected.

Switches read the source and destination MAC addresses in the frames and therefore can keep track of who is where, and who is talking to whom, and send data only where it needs to go. However, if the switch receives a frame whose destination address indicates that it is a broadcast (information meant for everyone) or multicast (information meant for a group), by default it sends the frame out all ports (except for the one on which it was received).

All devices connected to one switch port are in the same collision domain, but devices connected to different ports are in different collision domains. By default, all devices connected to a switch are in the same broadcast domain.

Switches Versus Bridges

You might have also heard of bridges. Switches and bridges are logically equivalent. The main differences are as follows:

- Switches are significantly faster because they switch in hardware, whereas bridges switch in software.

- Switches can interconnect LANs of unlike bandwidth. A 10-Mbps Ethernet LAN and a 100-Mbps Ethernet LAN, for example, can be connected using a switch. In contrast, all the ports on a bridge support one type of media.

- Switches typically have more ports than bridges.

- Modern switches have additional features not found on bridges; these features are described in later chapters.

Switches do not allow devices on different logical LANs to communicate with each other; this requires a router, as described in the next section.

Routers

A *router* goes one step further than a switch. It is a Layer 3 device that has much more intelligence than a hub or switch. By using logical Layer 3 addresses, routers allow devices on different LANs to communicate with each other and with distant devices—for example, those connected through the Internet or through a WAN. Examples of logical Layer 3 addresses include TCP/IP's IP addresses and Novell's IPX addresses.

A device connected to a router does not receive any of the information meant just for devices on other ports, or broadcasts (destined for all networks) from devices on other ports.

The router reads the source and destination logical addresses in the packets and therefore keeps track of who is where, and who is talking to whom, and sends data only where it needs to go. It supports communication between LANs, but it blocks broadcasts (destined for all networks).

All devices connected to one router port are in the same collision domain, but devices connected to different ports are in different collision domains.

All the devices connected to one router port are in the same broadcast domain, but devices connected to different ports are in different broadcast domains. Routers block broadcasts (destined for *all* networks) and multicasts by default; routers forward only *unicast* packets (destined for a specific device) and packets of a special type called *directed broadcasts.*

> **NOTE**   IP multicast technology, which enables multicast packets to be sent throughout a network, is described in Chapter 4, "Designing Basic Campus and Data Center Networks."

> **NOTE**   An IP-directed broadcast is an IP packet that is destined for all devices on an IP subnet. IP subnets are described in the "Addressing" section later in this chapter.

The fact that a router does not forward broadcasts (destined for all networks) is a significant difference between a router and a switch, and it helps control the amount of traffic on the network. For example, many protocols, such as IP, might use broadcasts for routing protocol advertisements, discovering servers, and so on. These broadcasts are a necessary part of local LAN traffic, but they are not required on other LANs and can even overwhelm slower WANs. Routers can generate broadcasts themselves if necessary (for example, to send a routing protocol advertisement), but do not pass on a received broadcast.

Routing operation is discussed further in the "Routing" section, later in this chapter.

NOTE   The concepts of unicast, multicast, and broadcast apply to Layer 2 and Layer 3 separately. Although a router does not forward any type of frame, it can forward a unicast, multicast, or directed broadcast packet that it received in a frame. A switch, however, can forward a unicast, multicast, or broadcast frame.

Introduction to the TCP/IP Suite

As mentioned earlier, TCP/IP is the most widely used protocol suite. The relationship between the five layers of the TCP/IP protocol suite and the seven layers of the OSI model is illustrated in Figure 1-4.

Figure 1-4   *TCP/IP Protocol Suite*

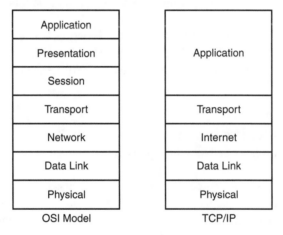

The five layers of the TCP/IP suite are the application layer, transport layer, Internet layer, data link layer, and physical layer.

NOTE   The data link and physical layers are sometimes grouped as one layer, called the *network interface layer*.

The TCP/IP application layer includes the functionality of the OSI application, presentation, and session layers. Applications defined in the TCP/IP suite include the following:

- **FTP and Trivial File Transfer Protocol (TFTP)**: Transfer files between devices.

- **SMTP and POP3**: Provide e-mail services.

- **HTTP**: Transfers information to and from a World Wide Web server through web browser software.

- **Telnet**: Emulates a terminal to connect to devices.

- **Domain Name System (DNS)**: Translates network device names into network addresses and vice versa.

- **Simple Network Management Protocol (SNMP)**: Used for network management, including setting threshold values and reporting network errors.

- **Dynamic Host Configuration Protocol (DHCP)**: Assigns dynamic IP addressing information to devices as they require it.

The transport layer and Internet layer protocols are detailed in the following sections.

The data link and physical layers can support a wide variety of LANs and WANs (including those discussed in the "LANs and WANs" section, earlier in this chapter). A data link layer protocol related to the TCP/IP suite is described in the later "TCP/IP-Related Data Link Layer Protocol" section.

TCP/IP Transport Layer Protocols

The TCP/IP transport layer includes the following two protocols:

- **Transmission Control Protocol (TCP)**: Provides connection-oriented, end-to-end reliable transmission. Before sending any data, TCP on the source device establishes a connection with TCP on the destination device, ensuring that both sides are synchronized. Data is acknowledged; any data not received properly is retransmitted. FTP is an example of an application that uses TCP to guarantee that the data sent from one device to another is received successfully.

- **User Datagram Protocol (UDP)**: Provides connectionless, best-effort unacknowledged data transmission. In other words, UDP does not ensure that all the segments arrive at the destination undamaged. UDP does not have the overhead of TCP related to establishing the connection and acknowledging the data. However, this means that upper-layer protocols or the user must determine whether all the data arrived successfully, and retransmit if necessary. TFTP is an example of an application that uses UDP. When all the segments have arrived at the destination, TFTP computes the file check sequence and reports the results to the user. If an error occurs, the user must send the entire file again.

NOTE   DNS is an example of an application layer protocol that may use either TCP or UDP, depending on the function it is performing.

TCP and UDP, being at the transport layer, send segments. Figure 1-5 illustrates the fields in a UDP segment and in a TCP segment.

Figure 1-5 *UDP Segment Headers Contain at Least 8 Bytes, Whereas TCP Segment Headers Contain at Least 20 Bytes*

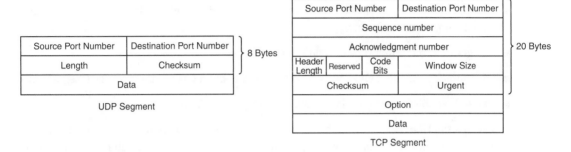

The UDP segment fields are as follows:

■ **Source and destination port numbers** (16 bits each): Identify the upper-layer protocol (the application) in the sending and receiving devices.

■ **Length** (16 bits): The total number of 32-bit words in the header and the data.

■ **Checksum** (16 bits): The checksum of the header and data fields, used to ensure that the segment is received correctly.

■ **Data** (variable length): The upper-layer data (the application data).

The TCP segment fields are as follows:

■ **Source and destination port numbers** (16 bits each): Identify the upper-layer protocol (the application) in the sending and receiving hosts.

■ **Sequence and acknowledgment numbers** (32 bits each): Ensure the correct order of the received data and that the data reached the destination.

■ **Header length** (4 bits): The number of 32-bit words in the header.

■ **Reserved** (6 bits): For future use, set to 0.

■ **Code bits** (6 bits): Indicates different types of segments. For example, the SYN (synchronize) bit is used for setting up a session, the ACK (acknowledge) bit is used for acknowledging a segment, and the FIN (finish) bit is used for closing a session.

- **Window size** (16 bits): The number of octets that the receiving device is willing to accept before it must send an acknowledgment.

NOTE   An *octet* is 8 bits of data.

- **Checksum** (16 bits): The checksum of the header and data fields, used to ensure that the segment is received correctly.

- **Urgent** (16 bits): Indicates the end of urgent data.

- **Option** (0 or 32 bits): Only one option is currently defined: the maximum TCP segment size.

- **Data** (variable): The upper-layer data (the application data).

Notice that the UDP header is much smaller than the TCP header. UDP does not need the sequencing, acknowledgment, or windowing fields, because it does not establish and maintain connections.

Port number operation, which is the same for both TCP and UDP, is described in the next section. Following that section, the operation of sequence and acknowledgment numbers and windowing are described; these are crucial to understanding TCP operation.

Port Numbers

KEY POINT   TCP and UDP use protocol *port numbers* to distinguish among multiple applications that are running on a single device.

Well-known, or standardized, port numbers are assigned to applications so that different implementations of the TCP/IP protocol suite can interoperate. Well-known port numbers are numbers up to 1023; examples include the following:

- **FTP**: TCP port 20 (data) and port 21 (control)

- **TFTP**: UDP port 69

- **SMTP**: TCP port 25

- **POP3**: TCP port 110

- **HTTP**: TCP port 80

- **Telnet**: TCP port 23

- **DNS**: TCP and UDP port 53

- **SNMP**: UDP port 161

Port numbers from 1024 through 49151 are called *registered port numbers;* these are registered for use by other applications. The dynamic ports numbers are those from 49152 through 65535; these can be dynamically assigned by hosts as source port numbers when they create and end sessions.

For example, Figure 1-6 illustrates a device in Toronto that is opening a Telnet session (TCP port 23) with a device in London. Note that the source port from Toronto is 50051. Toronto records this Telnet session with London as port 50051 to distinguish it from any other Telnet sessions it might have running (because simultaneous multiple Telnet sessions can be running on a device). The London device receives port number 23 and therefore knows that this is a Telnet session. In its reply, it uses a destination port of 50051, which Toronto knows is the Telnet session it opened with London.

Figure 1-6   *Source and Destination Port Numbers Indicate the Application Being Used*

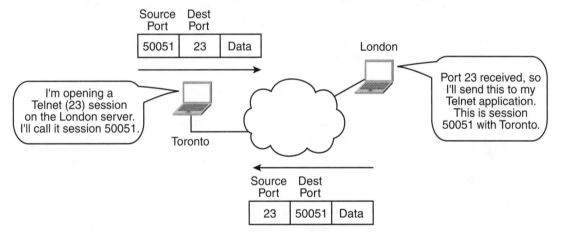

TCP Sequencing, Acknowledgment, and Windowing

To illustrate TCP operation, this section follows a TCP session as it is established, data is sent, and the session is closed.

KEY POINT | A TCP connection is established by a process called a *three-way handshake.* This process uses the SYN and ACK bits (in the code bits field in the TCP segment) as well as the sequence and acknowledgment number fields.

The TCP three-way handshake is shown in Figure 1-7.

Figure 1-7   *Three-Way Handshake Establishes a TCP Session*

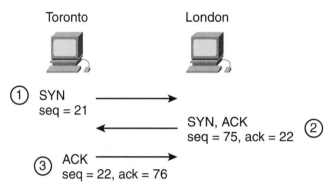

In this example, a user in Toronto wants to establish a TCP session with a device in London to start a Telnet session. The first step in the handshake involves the initiator, Toronto, sending a segment with the SYN bit set—this indicates that it wants to start a session and synchronize with London. This segment also includes the initial sequence number that Toronto is using—21 in this example.

Assuming that the device in London is willing to establish the session, it returns a segment that also has the SYN bit set. In addition, this segment has the ACK bit set because London is acknowledging that it successfully received a segment from Toronto. The acknowledgment number is set to 22, indicating that London is now expecting to receive segment 22 and therefore that it successfully received number 21. This is known as an *expectational acknowledgment.* The new segment includes the initial sequence number that London is using—75 in this example.

Finally, Toronto replies with an acknowledgment segment, sequence number 22 (as London is expecting), and acknowledgment number 76, indicating that it is now expecting number 76 and therefore has successfully received number 75. The session is now established, and data can be exchanged between Toronto and London.

> **NOTE**   The sequence and acknowledgment numbers specify octet numbers, not segment numbers. For ease of illustration, this example assumes that a segment is 1 octet of data. This is not the case in real life, but it simplifies the example so that the concepts are easier to understand.

The window size field in the segment controls the flow of the session. It indicates how many octets a device is willing to accept before it must send an acknowledgment. Because each host can have different flow restrictions (for example, one host might be very busy and therefore require that a smaller amount of data be sent at one time), each side of the session can have different window sizes, as illustrated in Figure 1-8.

Figure 1-8 *Window Size Indicates the Number of Octets a Device Is Willing to Accept Before It Sends an Acknowledgment*

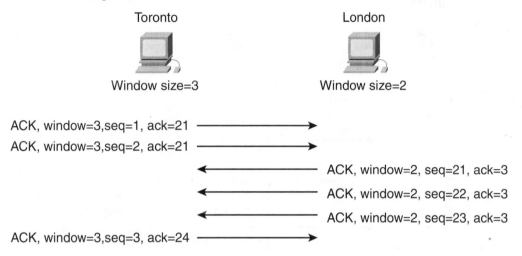

In this example, the window size on Toronto is set to 3, and on London it is set to 2. When Toronto sends data to London, it can send 2 octets before it must wait for an acknowledgment. When London sends data to Toronto, it can send 3 octets before it must wait for an acknowledgment.

> **NOTE**   The window size specifies the number of octets that can be sent, not the number of segments. For ease of illustration, this example assumes that a segment is 1 octet of data. This is not the case in real life, but it again simplifies the example so that the concepts are easier to understand. The window sizes shown in the example are also small for ease of explanation. In reality, the window size would be much larger, allowing a lot of data to be sent between acknowledgments.

After all the data for the session is sent, the session can be closed. The process is similar to how it was established, using a handshake. In this case, four steps are used, as illustrated in Figure 1-9.

In this example, Toronto wants to close its Telnet session with London. The first step in the handshake involves Toronto sending a segment with the FIN bit set, indicating that it wants to finish the session. This segment also includes the sequence number that Toronto is currently using—107 in this example.

Figure 1-9 *Four-Way Handshake Closes a TCP Session*

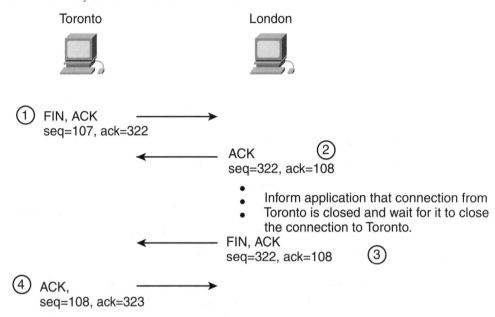

London immediately acknowledges the request. This segment has the ACK bit set with the acknowledgment number set to 108, indicating that London successfully received number 107. This segment includes the sequence number that London is currently using—322 in this example. London then informs its Telnet application that half of the session, the connection from Toronto, is now closed.

When the application on the London device requests that the other half of the connection (to Toronto) be closed, London sends a new segment with the FIN bit set, indicating that it wants to close the session.

Finally, Toronto replies with an acknowledgment segment with acknowledgment number 323 (indicating that it has successfully received number 322). The session is now closed in both directions.

TCP/IP Internet Layer Protocols

The TCP/IP Internet layer corresponds to the OSI network layer and includes the IP-routed protocol, as well as a protocol for message and error reporting.

Protocols

The protocols at this layer include the following:

- **IP**: Provides connectionless, best-effort delivery of datagrams through the network. A unique IP address—a logical address—is assigned to each interface of each device in the network. IP and IP addresses are introduced later in this chapter and are described in more detail in Appendix B, "IPv4 Supplement."

> **NOTE**   Two versions of IP currently exist: IP version 4 (IPv4) and the emerging IP version 6 (IPv6). In this book, the term *IP* refers to IPv4. IPv6 is introduced in Chapter 6, "Designing IP Addressing in the Network."

- **Internet Control Message Protocol (ICMP)**: Sends messages and error reports through the network. For example, the ping application included in most TCP/IP protocol suites sends an ICMP echo message to a destination, which then replies with an ICMP echo reply message. Ping provides confirmation that the destination can be reached and gives a measure of how long packets are taking to travel between the source and destination.

> **NOTE**   These protocols are all at the TCP/IP Internet layer, corresponding to the OSI model network layer, Layer 3. They run on top of the TCP/IP physical and data link layers, Layers 1 and 2.

> **NOTE**   You might have heard people refer to IP as a "LAN protocol"; this is because they configure IP on PCs that are attached to LANs. However, IP is, in fact, a network layer protocol—it runs on top of any LAN or WAN.

IP Datagrams

Figure 1-10 illustrates the fields of an IP datagram.

Figure 1-10 *An IP Datagram Contains at Least 20 Bytes*

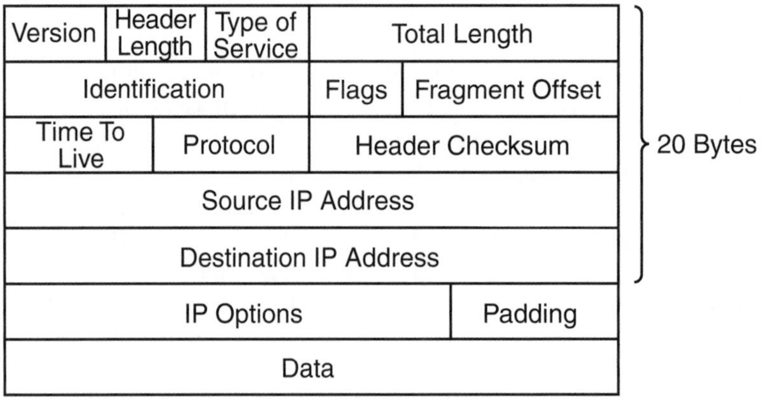

The IP datagram fields are as follows:

■ **Version** (4 bits): Identifies the IP version—in this case, version 4.

■ **Header length** (4 bits): The number of 32-bit words in the header (including the options).

■ **Type of service (ToS)** (8 bits): Specifies how the datagram should be handled within the network. These bits mark traffic for a specific quality of service (QoS), which is further described in Chapter 4.

■ **Total length** (16 bits): The total number of octets in the header and data fields.

■ **Identification** (16 bits), **flags** (3 bits), and **fragment offset** (13 bits): Handle cases where a large datagram must be fragmented—split into multiple packets—to go through a network that cannot handle datagrams of that size.

■ **Time to Live (TTL)** (8 bits): Ensures that datagrams do not loop endlessly in the network; this field must be decremented by 1 by each router that the datagram passes through.

■ **Protocol** (8 bits): Indicates the upper-layer (Layer 4, the transport layer) protocol that the data is for. Therefore, this field might indicate the type of segment that the datagram is carrying, similar to how the port number field in the UDP and TCP segments indicates the type of application that the segment is carrying. A protocol number of 6 means that the datagram is carrying a TCP segment, whereas a protocol number of 17 means that the datagram is carrying a UDP segment. The protocol may have other values, such as a value indicating that traffic from a specific routing protocol is being carried inside the datagram.

■ **Header checksum** (16 bits): Ensures that the header is received correctly.

- **Source and destination IP addresses** (32 bits each): Logical IP addresses assigned to the source and destination of the datagram, respectively. IP addresses are introduced later in this chapter, in the "Addressing" section.

- **IP options and padding** (variable length; 0 or a multiple of 32 bits): Used for network testing and debugging.

- **Data** (variable): The upper-layer (transport layer) data.

TCP/IP-Related Data Link Layer Protocol

The TCP/IP data link layer corresponds to the OSI data link layer. It includes the Address Resolution Protocol (ARP) to request the MAC address (the data link layer physical address) for a given IP address. The returned MAC address is used as the destination address in the frames that encapsulate the packets of data being routed to the destination IP address.

Routing

This section examines how routers work and introduces routing tables and routing protocols. Routers work at the OSI model network layer. The main functions of a router are first to determine the best path that each packet should take to get to its destination and second to send the packet on its way. Sending the packet out the appropriate interface, along the best path, is also called *switching the packet* because the packet is encapsulated in a new frame, with the appropriate framing information.

Therefore, a router's job is much like that of a worker at a post office. The postal worker looks at the address label on the letter (the network layer address on the packet), determines which way the letter (the packet) should be sent, and then sends it. The comparison between the post office and a router is illustrated in Figure 1-11.

Figure 1-11   *A Router Behaves Much Like a Worker at a Post Office*

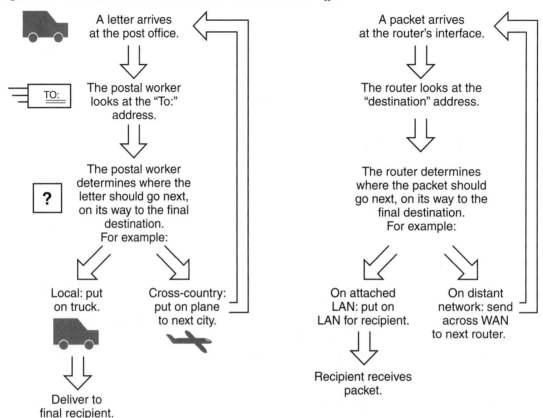

> **NOTE**   This discussion of routers is concerned with the traditional role of routers in a network, at the OSI model network layer. Routers are now taking on more functions—for example, in QoS and security areas; these other functions are described in the relevant chapters throughout this book.

Routers Work at the Lower Three OSI Layers

The router doesn't care what is in the higher layers—what kind of data is in the packet. The router is just responsible for sending the packet the correct way. The router does have to be concerned with the data link and physical layers, though, because it might have to receive and send data on different media. For example, a packet received on an Ethernet LAN might have to be sent out on a Frame Relay WAN, requiring the router to know how to communicate on both these types of media. In terms of layers, therefore, a router unencapsulates received data up to the network layer and then encapsulates the data again into the appropriate frame and bit types. This process is illustrated in Figure 1-12, where the PC on the left is sending data to the PC on the right. The routers have determined that the path marked with the arrows is the best path between the PCs.

Figure 1-12 *Router Works at the Network Layer*

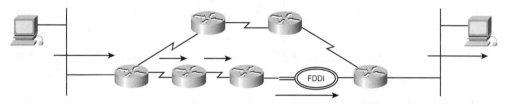

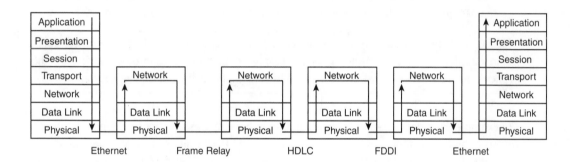

In this figure, notice that only the two PCs care about the upper layers, whereas all the routers in the path concern themselves with only the lower three layers.

Routing Tables

To determine the best path on which to send a packet, a router must know where the packet's destination network is.

KEY POINT   Routers learn about networks by being physically connected to them or by learning about them either from other routers or from a network administrator. Routes configured by network administrators are known as *static routes* because they are hard-coded in the router and remain there—static—until the administrator removes them. Routes to which a router is physically connected are known as *directly connected routes.* Routers learn routes from other routers by using a routing protocol.

However routes are learned, routers keep the best path (or multiple best paths) to each destination in a *routing table*. A routing table contains a list of all the networks that a router knows how to reach. For each network, the routing table typically contains the following items:

■ How the route to the network was learned (for example, statically or by using a routing protocol).

■ The network address of the router from which the route to the network was learned (if applicable).

■ The interface (port) on the router through which the network can be reached.

■ The metric of the route. The metric is a measurement, such as the number of other routers that the path goes through, that routing protocols use when determining the best path.

> **NOTE** The path that the router determines is the *best* depends on the routing protocol in use. For example, some routing protocols define *best* as the path that goes through the fewest other routers (the fewest hops), whereas others define *best* as the path with the highest bandwidth.

For example, in the network shown in Figure 1-13, the metric used is hops—the number of other routers between this router and the destination network. Both routers know about all three networks. Router X, on the left, knows about networks A and B because it is connected to them (hence the metric of 0) and knows about network C from Router Y (hence the metric of 1). Router Y, on the right, knows about networks B and C because it is connected to them (hence the metric of 0) and knows about network A from Router X (hence the metric of 1).

Figure 1-13 *Routers Keep Routing Information in Routing Tables*

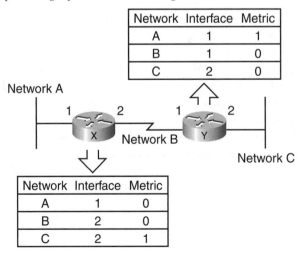

Routing Protocols

Routers use routing protocols to exchange routing information. *Routing protocols* allow routers to learn from other routers the networks that are available so that data can be sent in the correct direction. Remember that two routers communicating with each other must use the same routing protocol or they can't understand each other.

The TCP/IP protocol suite includes the following routing protocols:

■ Routing Information Protocol (RIP), versions 1 and 2 (RIPv1 and RIPv2)

■ Enhanced Interior Gateway Routing Protocol (EIGRP)

■ Open Shortest Path First (OSPF)

■ Integrated Intermediate System-to-Intermediate System (IS-IS)

■ Border Gateway Protocol (BGP) Version 4 (BGP-4)

> **NOTE**   These routing protocols are discussed further in Chapter 7, "Selecting Routing Protocols for the Network."

The previous sections introduced the basics of routing and how routers learn about the available networks so that data can be sent along the correct path. Routers look at the packet's destination address to determine where the packet is going so that they can then select the best route to get the packet there. The following section discusses these addresses.

Addressing

This section describes physical and network layer addressing and how routers use these addresses. The section concludes with a brief introduction to IP addressing.

Physical Addresses

MAC addresses were discussed earlier; recall that these are at the data link layer and are considered physical addresses. When a network interface card is manufactured, it is assigned an address—called a *burned-in address* (BIA)—that doesn't change when the network card is installed in a device and is moved from one network to another. Typically, this BIA is copied to interface memory and is used as the interface's MAC address. MAC addresses are analogous to Social Insurance numbers or Social Security numbers—one is assigned to each person, and the numbers don't change when that person moves to a new house. These numbers are associated with the physical person, not where the person lives.

> **NOTE** Some organizations set the MAC addresses of their devices to something other than the BIA (for example, based on the location of the device in the network) for management purposes.

> **KEY POINT** The BIA is a 48-bit value. The upper 24 bits are an Organizational Unique Identifier (OUI) representing the vendor that makes the device. The lower 24 bits are a unique value for that OUI, typically the device's serial number.

> **NOTE** The top 2 bits of the BIA are not actually part of the OUI. The seventh bit in a BIA is referred to as the *universal/locally administered (U/L)* bit; it identifies whether the address has been locally or universally assigned. The eighth bit in the BIA is the *individual/group (I/G)* bit; it identifies whether the address is for an individual device or a group.

Knowing the MAC address assigned to a PC or to a router's interface doesn't tell you anything about where it is or what network it is attached to—it can't help a router determine the best way to send data to it. For that you need logical network layer addresses; they are assigned when a device is installed on a network and should be changed when the device is moved.

Logical Addresses

When you send a letter to someone, you have to know that person's postal address. Because every postal address in the world is unique, you can potentially send a letter to anyone in the world. Postal addresses are logical and hierarchical—for example, they include the country, province/state, street, and building/house number. The top portion of Figure 1-14 illustrates Main Street with various houses. All these houses have one portion of their address in common—Main Street—and one portion that is unique—their house number.

> **KEY POINT** Network layer addresses are also logical and hierarchical, and they are either defined statically by an administrator or obtained automatically from a server. They have two main parts: the network that the device is on (similar to the street, city, province, and so on) and the device number on that network (similar to the building number).

Figure 1-14   *Network Layer Addresses Are Similar to Postal Addresses*

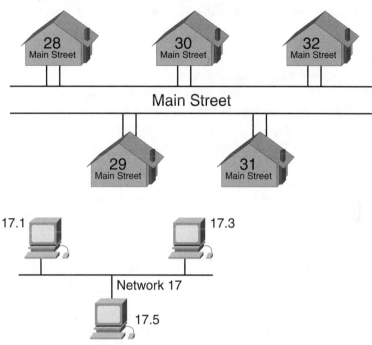

The lower portion of Figure 1-14 illustrates a network, 17, with various PCs on it. All these PCs have one portion of their address in common—17—and one part that is unique—their device number. Devices on the same logical network must share the same network portion of their address and have different device portions.

Routing and Network Layer Addresses

A router typically looks at only the network portion of a destination address. It compares the network portion to its routing table, and if it finds a match, it sends the packet out the appropriate interface, toward its destination.

A router needs to concern itself only with the device portion of a destination address if it is directly connected to the same network as the destination. In this case, the router must send the packet directly to the appropriate device, and it needs to use the entire destination address for this. A router on a LAN uses ARP to determine the MAC address of the device with that IP address and then creates an appropriate frame with that MAC address as the destination MAC address.

IP Addresses

IP addresses are network layer addresses. As you saw earlier, IP addresses are 32-bit numbers. As shown in Figure 1-15, the 32 bits are usually written in *dotted-decimal notation*—they are grouped into 4 octets (8 bits each), separated by dots, and each octet is represented in decimal format. Each bit in the octet has a binary weight (the highest is 128 and the next is 64, followed by 32, 16, 8, 4, 2, and 1). Thus, the minimum value for an octet is 0, and the maximum decimal value for an octet is 255.

Figure 1-15 *32-Bit IPv4 Addresses Are Written in Dotted-Decimal Notation*

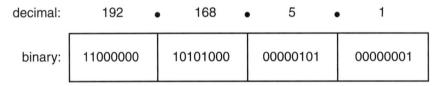

NOTE   The maximum value of an octet is when all 8 bits are binary 1. The decimal value of an octet is calculated by adding all the weighted bits—in this case, 128 + 64 + 32 + 16 + 8 + 4 + 2 + 1 = 255.

NOTE   Appendix B details how to convert between decimal and binary formats and vice versa and provides a decimal-to-binary conversion chart. Appendix B also includes further details on IPv4 addressing.

IP Address Classes

IPv4 addresses are categorized into five classes: A, B, C, D, and E. Only Class A, B, and C addresses are used for addressing devices; Class D is used for multicast groups, and Class E is reserved for experimental use.

The first octet of an IPv4 address defines which class it is in, as illustrated in Table 1-1 for Class A, B, and C addresses. The address class determines which part of the address represents the network bits (N) and which part represents the host bits (H), as shown in this table. The number of networks available in each class and the number of hosts per network are also shown.

Table 1-1   *IP Address Classes A, B, and C Are Available for Addressing Devices*

Class	Format*	Higher-Order Bits	Address Range	Number of Networks	Number of Hosts per Network
A	N.H.H.H	0	1.0.0.0 to 126.0.0.0	126	16,777,214
B	N.N.H.H	10	128.0.0.0 to 191.255.0.0	16,386	65,534
C	N.N.N.H	110	192.0.0.0 to 223.255.255.0	2,097,152	254

*N=network number bits; H=host number bits

> **NOTE**   Class A addresses are any addresses that have the higher-order bit set to 0; this would include 0 through 127 in the first octet. However, network 0.0.0.0 is reserved, and network 127.0.0.0 (any address starting with decimal 127) is reserved for loopback functionality. Therefore, the first octet of Class A addresses ranges from 1 to 126.

> **NOTE**   Class D addresses have higher-order bits 1110 and are in the range of 224.0.0.0 to 239.255.255.255. Class E addresses have higher-order bits 1111 and are in the range of 240.0.0.0 to 255.255.255.255.

For example, 192.168.5.1 is a Class C address. Therefore, it is in the format N.N.N.H—the network part is 192.168.5 and the host part is 1.

Private and Public IP Addresses

The IPv4 address space is divided into public and private sections. Private addresses are reserved addresses to be used only internally within a company's network, not on the Internet. When you want to send anything on the Internet, private addresses must be mapped to a company's external registered address. Public IPv4 addresses are provided for external communication.

KEY POINT | RFC 1918, *Address Allocation for Private Internets*, defines the private IPv4 addresses as follows:

- 10.0.0.0 to 10.255.255.255

- 172.16.0.0 to 172.31.255.255

- 192.168.0.0 to 192.168.255.255

The remaining addresses are public addresses.

> **NOTE** Internet RFC documents are written definitions of the Internet's protocols and policies. A complete list and the documents themselves can be found at http://www.rfc-editor.org/rfc.html.

Note that all the IP addresses used in this book are private addresses, to avoid publishing anyone's registered address.

Subnets

As illustrated in Table 1-1, Class A addresses have little use in a normal organization—most companies would not want one network with more than 16 million PCs on it! This would not be physically possible or desirable. Because of this limitation on addresses when only their class is considered (called *classful addressing*) and the finite number of such addresses, subnets were introduced by RFC 950, *Internet Standard Subnetting Procedure*.

Class A, B, and C addresses can be divided into smaller networks, called *subnetworks* or *subnets*, resulting in a larger number of possible networks, each with fewer host addresses available than the original network.

The addresses used for the subnets are created by borrowing bits from the host field and using them as subnet bits; a subnet mask indicates which bits have been borrowed. A *subnet mask* is a 32-bit value associated with an IP address to specify which bits in the address represent network and subnet bits and which represent host bits. Using subnet masks creates a three-level hierarchy: network, subnet, and host.

KEY POINT	In binary format, a subnet mask bit of 1 indicates that the corresponding bit in the IP address is a network or subnet bit, and a subnet mask bit of 0 indicates that the corresponding bit in the IP address is a host bit.
	Subnet bits come from the higher-order (leftmost) bits of the host field; therefore, the 1s in the subnet mask are contiguous.

The default subnet masks for Class A, B, and C addresses are shown Table 1-2.

Table 1-2 *IP Address Default Subnet Masks*

Class	Default Mask in Binary Format	Default Mask in Decimal Format
A	11111111.00000000.00000000.00000000	255.0.0.0
B	11111111.11111111.00000000.00000000	255.255.0.0
C	11111111.11111111.11111111.00000000	255.255.255.0

When all of an address's host bits are 0, the address is for the subnet itself (sometimes called *the wire*). When all of an address's host bits are 1, the address is the directed broadcast address for that subnet (in other words, for all the devices on that subnet).

NOTE   An *IP-directed broadcast* is an IP packet destined for all devices on an IP subnet. When the directed broadcast originates from a device on another subnet, routers that are not directly connected to the destination subnet forward the IP-directed broadcast in the same way they would forward unicast IP packets destined for a host on that subnet.

On Cisco routers, the **ip directed-broadcast** interface command controls what the last router in the path, the one connected to the destination subnet, does with a directed broadcast packet. If **ip directed-broadcast** is enabled on the interface, the router changes the directed broadcast to a broadcast and sends the packet, encapsulated in a Layer 2 broadcast frame, onto the subnet. However, if the **no ip directed-broadcast** command is configured on the interface, directed broadcasts destined for the subnet to which that interface is attached are dropped. In Cisco IOS version 12.0, the default for this command was changed to **no ip directed-broadcast**.

KEY POINT	The formula 2^s calculates the number of subnets created, where s is the number of subnet bits (the number of bits borrowed from the host field).
	The formula $2^h - 2$ calculates the number of host addresses available on each subnet, where h is the number of host bits.

For example, 10.0.0.0 is a Class A address with a default subnet mask of 255.0.0.0, indicating 8 network bits and 24 host bits. If you want to use 8 of the host bits as subnet bits instead, you would use a subnet mask of 11111111.11111111.00000000.00000000, which is 255.255.0.0 in decimal format. You could then use the 8 subnet bits to address 256 subnets. Each of these subnets could support up to 65,534 hosts. The address of one of the subnets is 10.1.0.0; the broadcast address on this subnet is 10.1.255.255.

Another way of indicating the subnet mask is to use a prefix. A *prefix* is a slash (/) followed by a numeral that is the number of bits in the network and subnet portion of the address—in other words, the number of contiguous 1s that would be in the subnet mask. For example, the subnet mask of 255.255.240.0 is 11111111.11111111.11110000.00000000 in binary format, which is 20 1s followed by 12 0s. Therefore, the prefix would be /20 for the 20 bits of network and subnet information, the number of 1s in the mask.

IP addressing is further explored in Appendix B; IP address planning is discussed in Chapter 6.

Switching Types

Switches were initially introduced to provide higher-performance connectivity than hubs because switches define multiple collision domains. Switches have always been able to process data at a faster rate than routers because the switching functionality is implemented in hardware—in Application-Specific Integrated Circuits (ASIC)—rather than in software, which is how routing has traditionally been implemented. However, switching was initially restricted to the examination of Layer 2 frames. With the advent of more powerful ASICs, switches can now process Layer 3 packets, and even the contents of those packets, at high speeds.

The following sections first examine the operation of traditional Layer 2 switching. Layer 3 switching—which is really routing in hardware—is then explored.

Layer 2 Switching

KEY POINT Layer 2 LAN switches segment a network into multiple collision domains and interconnect devices within a workgroup, such as a group of PCs.

The heart of a Layer 2 switch is its MAC address table, also known as its content-addressable memory. This table contains a list of the MAC addresses that are reachable through each switch port. Recall that a physical MAC address uniquely identifies a device on a network. When a switch is first powered up, its MAC address table is empty, as shown in Figure 1-16.

Figure 1-16 *The MAC Address Table Is Initially Empty*

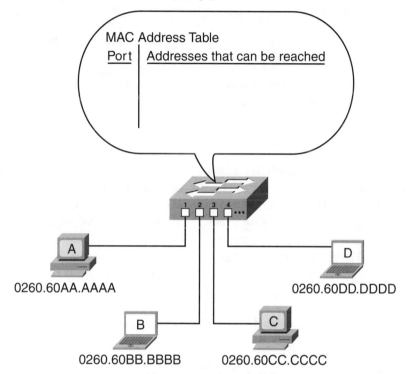

In this sample network, consider what happens when device A sends a frame destined for device D. The switch receives the frame on port 1 (from device A). Recall that a frame includes the MAC address of the source device and the MAC address of the destination device. Because the switch does not yet know where device D is, the switch must *flood* the frame out of all the other ports; therefore, the switch sends the frame out of ports 2, 3, and 4. This means that devices B, C, and D all receive the frame. Only device D, however, recognizes its MAC address as the destination address in the frame; it is the only device on which the CPU is interrupted to further process the frame.

KEY POINT Broadcast and multicast frames are, by default, flooded to all ports of a Layer 2 switch other than the incoming port. The same is true for unicast frames destined for any device not in the MAC address table.

In the meantime, the switch now knows that device A can be reached on port 1 because the switch received a frame from device A on port 1; the switch therefore puts the MAC address of device A in its MAC address table for port 1. This process is called *learning*—the switch is learning all the MAC addresses it can reach.

KEY POINT A switch uses the frame's *destination* MAC address to determine the port to which it sends the frame.

A switch uses the frame's *source* MAC address to populate its MAC address table; the switch eavesdrops on the conversation between devices to learn which devices can be reached on which ports.

At some point, device D is likely to reply to device A. At that time, the switch receives a frame from device D on port 4; the switch records this information in its MAC address table as part of its learning process. This time, the switch knows where the destination, device A, is; the switch therefore forwards the frame only out of port 1. This process is called *filtering*—the switch sends the frames out of only the port through which they need to go, when the switch knows which port that is, rather than flooding them out of every port. This reduces the traffic on the other ports and reduces the interruptions that the other devices experience. Over time, the switch learns where all the devices are, and the MAC address table is fully populated, as shown in Figure 1-17.

Figure 1-17   *The Switch Learns Where All the Devices Are and Populates Its MAC Address Table*

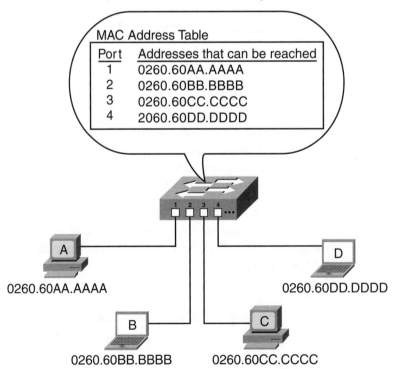

The filtering process also means that multiple simultaneous conversations can occur between different devices. For example, if device A and device B want to communicate, the switch sends their data between ports 1 and 2; no traffic goes on ports 3 or 4. At the same time, devices C and D can communicate on ports 3 and 4 without interfering with the traffic on ports 1 and 2. Consequently, the network's overall throughput has increased dramatically.

The MAC address table is kept in the switch's memory and has a finite size (depending on the specific switch used). If many devices are attached to the switch, the switch might not have room for an entry for every one, so the table entries time out after a period of not being used. As a result, the most active devices are always in the table.

MAC addresses can also be statically configured in the MAC address table, and you can specify a maximum number of addresses allowed per port. One advantage of static addresses is that less flooding occurs, both when the switch first comes up and because of not aging out the addresses. However, this also means that if a device is moved, the switch configuration must be changed. A related feature available in some switches is the capability to *sticky-learn* addresses—the address is dynamically learned, as described earlier, but is then automatically entered as a static command in the switch configuration. Limiting the number of addresses per port to one and statically configuring those addresses can ensure that only specific devices are permitted access to the network; this feature is particularly useful when addresses are sticky-learned.

Layer 3 Switching

KEY POINT | A Layer 3 switch is really a router with some of the functions implemented in hardware to improve performance. In other words, some of the OSI model network layer routing functions are performed in high-performance ASICs rather than in software.

The functions performed by routers (as described in the earlier "Routing" section) can be CPU-intensive. Offloading the switching of the packet to hardware can result in a significant increase in performance.

A Layer 3 switch performs all the same functions as a router; the differences are in the physical implementation of the device rather than in the functions it performs. Therefore, functionally, the terms *router* and *Layer 3 switch* are synonymous.

Layer 4 switching is an extension of Layer 3 switching that includes examination of the contents of the Layer 3 packet. For example, the protocol number in the IP packet header (as described in the "IP Datagrams" section) indicates which transport layer protocol (for example, TCP or UDP) is being used, and the port number in the TCP or UDP segment indicates the application being used (as described in the "TCP/IP Transport Layer Protocols" section). Switching based on the protocol and port numbers can ensure, for example, that certain types of traffic get higher priority on the network or take a specific path.

Within Cisco switches, Layer 3 switching can be implemented in two different ways—through multilayer switching or through Cisco Express Forwarding, as described in Chapter 4.

Spanning Tree Protocol

KEY POINT STP is a Layer 2 protocol that prevents logical loops in switched networks that have redundant links.

The following sections examine why such a protocol is needed in Layer 2 networks. STP terminology and operation are then introduced.

Redundancy in Layer 2 Switched Networks

Redundancy in a network, such as that shown in Figure 1-18, is desirable so that communication can still take place if a link or device fails. For example, if switch X in this figure stopped functioning, devices A and B could still communicate through switch Y. However, in a switched network, redundancy can cause problems.

Figure 1-18 *Redundancy in a Switched Network Can Cause Problems*

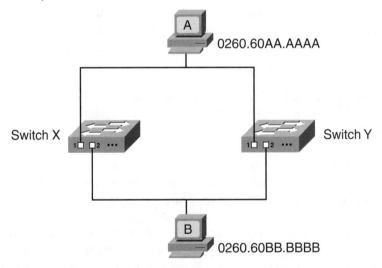

The first type of problem occurs if a broadcast frame is sent on the network. For example, consider what happens when device A in Figure 1-18 sends an ARP request to find the MAC address of device B. The ARP request is sent as a broadcast. Both switch X and switch Y receive the broadcast; for now, consider just the one received by switch X, on its port 1. Switch X floods the broadcast to all its other connected ports; in this case, it floods it to port 2. Device B can see the broadcast, but so can switch Y, on its port 2; switch Y floods the broadcast to its port 1. This broadcast is received by switch X on its port 1; switch X floods it to its port 2, and so forth. The broadcast continues to loop around the network, consuming bandwidth and processing power. This situation is called a *broadcast storm*.

The second problem that can occur in redundant topologies is that devices can receive multiple copies of the same frame. For example, assume that neither of the switches in Figure 1-18 has learned where device B is located. When device A sends data destined for device B, switch X and switch Y both flood the data to the lower LAN, and device B receives two copies of the same frame. This might be a problem for device B, depending on what it is and how it is programmed to handle such a situation.

The third difficulty that can occur in a redundant situation is within the switch itself—the MAC address table can change rapidly and contain wrong information. Again referring to Figure 1-18, consider what happens when neither switch has learned where device A or B is located, and device A sends data to device B. Each switch learns that device A is on its port 1, and each records this in its MAC address table. Because the switches don't yet know where device B is, they flood the frame—in this case, on their port 2. Each switch then receives the frame from the other switch on its port 2. This frame has device A's MAC address in the source address field; therefore, both switches now learn that device A is on their port 2. As a result, the MAC address table is overwritten. Not only does the MAC address table have incorrect information (device A is actually connected to port 1, not port 2, of both switches), but because the table changes rapidly, it might be considered unstable.

To overcome these problems, you must have a way to logically disable part of the redundant network for regular traffic while maintaining redundancy for the case when an error occurs. STP does just that.

STP Terminology and Operation

The following sections introduce the IEEE 802.1d STP terminology and operation.

STP Terminology

STP terminology can best be explained by examining how a sample network, such as the one shown in Figure 1-19, operates.

Figure 1-19 *STP Chooses the Port to Block*

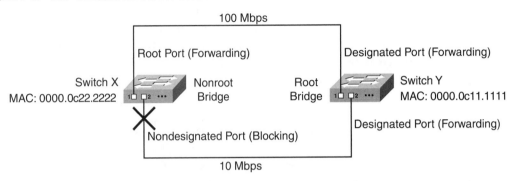

Within an STP network, one switch is elected as the *root bridge*—it is at the root of the spanning tree. All other switches calculate their best path to the root bridge. Their alternative paths are put in the blocking state. These alternative paths are logically disabled from the perspective of regular traffic, but the switches still communicate with each other on these paths so that the alternative paths can be unblocked in case an error occurs on the best path.

All switches running STP (it is turned on by default in Cisco switches) send out Bridge Protocol Data Units (BPDU). Switches running STP use BPDUs to exchange information with neighboring switches. One of the fields in the BPDU is the bridge identifier (ID); it comprises a 2-octet bridge priority and a 6-octet MAC address. STP uses the bridge ID to elect the root bridge—the switch with the lowest bridge ID is the root bridge. If all bridge priorities are left at their default values, the switch with the lowest MAC address therefore becomes the root bridge. In Figure 1-19, switch Y is elected as the root bridge.

All the ports on the root bridge are called *designated ports,* and they are all in the *forwarding state*—that is, they can send and receive data. The STP states are described in the next section.

On all *nonroot bridges,* one port becomes the *root port,* and it is also in the forwarding state. The *root port* is the one with the lowest cost to the root. The cost of each link is by default inversely proportional to the link's bandwidth, so the port with the fastest total path from the switch to the root bridge is selected as the root port on that switch. In Figure 1-19, port 1 on switch X is the root port for that switch because it is the fastest way to the root bridge.

NOTE   If multiple ports on a switch have the same fastest total path costs to the root bridge, STP considers other BPDU fields. STP looks first at the bridge IDs in the received BPDUs (the bridge IDs of the next switch in the path to the root bridge); the port that received the BPDU with the lowest bridge ID becomes the root port. If these bridge IDs are also equal, the port ID breaks the tie; the port with the lower port ID becomes the root port. The port ID field includes a port priority and a port index, which is the port number. Therefore, if the port priorities are the same (for example, if they are left at their default value), the lower port number becomes the root port.

Each LAN segment must have one designated port. It is on the switch that has the lowest cost to the root bridge (or, if the costs are equal, the port on the switch with the lowest bridge ID is chosen), and it is in the forwarding state. In Figure 1-19, the root bridge has designated ports on both segments, so no more are required.

NOTE   The root bridge sends configuration BPDUs on all its ports periodically—every 2 seconds, by default. These configuration BPDUs include STP timers, therefore ensuring that all switches in the network use the same timers. On each LAN segment, the switch that has the designated port forwards the configuration BPDUs to the segment; every switch in the network therefore receives these BPDUs on its root port.

All ports on a LAN segment that are not root ports or designated ports are called *nondesignated ports* and transition to the blocking state—they do not send data, so the redundant topology is logically disabled. In Figure 1-19, port 2 on switch X is the nondesignated port, and it is in the blocking state. Blocking ports do, however, listen for BPDUs.

If a failure happens—for example, if a designated port or a root bridge fails—the switches send topology change BPDUs and recalculate the spanning tree. The new spanning tree does not include the failed port or switch, and the ports that were previously blocking might now be in the forwarding state. This is how STP supports the redundancy in a switched network.

STP States

Figure 1-20 illustrates the various STP port states.

Figure 1-20 *A Port Can Transition Among STP States*

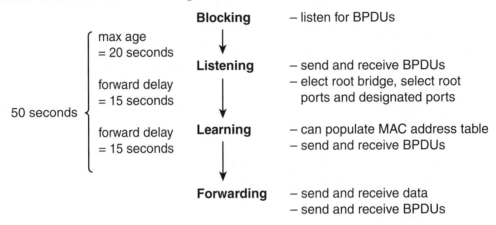

When a port initially comes up, it is put in the blocking state, in which it listens for BPDUs and then transitions to the listening state. A blocking port in an operational network can also transition to the listening state if it does not hear any BPDUs for the *max-age time* (a default of 20 seconds). While in the listening state, the switch can send and receive BPDUs but not data. The root bridge and the various final states of all the ports are determined in this state.

If the port is chosen as the root port on a switch, or as a designated port on a segment, that port transitions to the learning state after the listening state. In the learning state, the port still cannot send data, but it can start to populate its MAC address table if any data is received. The length of time spent in each of the listening and learning states is dictated by the value of the *forward-delay* parameter, which is 15 seconds by default. After the learning state, the port transitions to the forwarding state, in which it can operate normally. Alternatively, if in the listening state the port is not chosen as a root port or designated port, it becomes a nondesignated port and transitions back to the blocking state.

KEY POINT Do not confuse the STP learning state with the learning process that the switch goes through to populate its MAC address table. The STP learning state is a transitory state. Although a switch can learn MAC addresses from data frames received on its ports that are in the STP learning state, it does not forward those frames. In a stable network, switch ports are in either the forwarding or blocking state. Ports in the blocking state do not listen to data frames and therefore do not contribute to the switch's MAC address table. Ports in the forwarding state do, of course, listen to (and forward) data frames, and those frames populate the switch's MAC address table.

Several features and enhancements to STP are implemented on Cisco switches to help to reduce the convergence time—the time it takes for all the switches in a network to agree on the network's topology after that topology has changed.

Rapid STP

Rapid STP (RSTP) is defined by IEEE 802.1w. RSTP incorporates many of the Cisco enhancements to STP, resulting in faster convergence. Switches in an RSTP environment converge quickly by communicating with each other and determining which links can forward, rather than just waiting for the timers to transition the ports among the various states. RSTP ports take on different roles than STP ports. The RSTP roles are root, designated, alternate, backup, and disabled. RSTP port states are also different from STP port states. The RSTP states are discarding, learning, and forwarding. RSTP is compatible with STP. For example, 802.1w alternate and backup port states correspond to the 802.1d blocking port state.

Virtual LANs

As noted earlier, a broadcast domain includes all devices that receive each others' broadcasts (and multicasts). All the devices connected to one router port are in the same broadcast domain. Routers block broadcasts (destined for *all* networks) and multicasts by default; routers forward only *unicast* packets (destined for a specific device) and packets of a special type called *directed broadcasts.* Typically, you think of a broadcast domain as being a physical wire, a LAN. But a broadcast domain can also be a VLAN, a logical construct that can include multiple physical LAN segments.

> **KEY POINT** The Cisco definition of VLANs is very clear: "[A] group of devices on one or more LANs that are configured (using management software) so that they can communicate as if they were attached to the same wire, when in fact they are located on a number of different LAN segments. Because VLANs are based on logical instead of physical connections, they are extremely flexible." This definition is from "Virtual LANs/VLAN Trunking Protocol (VLANs/VTP)," available at http://www.cisco.com/en/US/tech/tk389/tk689/tsd_technology_support_protocol_home.html.

Figure 1-21 illustrates the VLAN concept. On the left side of the figure, three individual physical LANs are shown, one each for Engineering, Accounting, and Marketing. These LANs contain workstations—E1, E2, A1, A2, M1, and M2—and servers—ES, AS, and MS. Instead of physical LANs, an enterprise can use VLANs, as shown on the right side of the figure. With VLANs, members of each department can be physically located anywhere, yet still be logically connected with their own workgroup. Therefore, in the VLAN configuration, all the devices attached to VLAN E (Engineering) share the same broadcast domain, the devices attached to VLAN A (Accounting) share a separate broadcast domain, and the devices attached to VLAN M

(Marketing) share a third broadcast domain. Figure 1-21 also illustrates how VLANs can span multiple switches; the link between the two switches in the figure carries traffic from all three of the VLANs and is called a *trunk*.

Figure 1-21 *A VLAN Is a Logical Implementation of a Physical LAN*

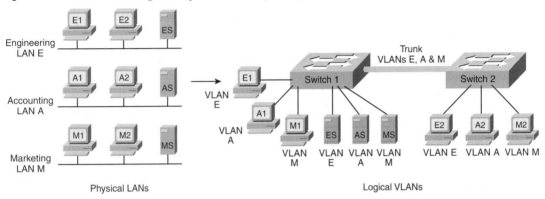

VLAN Membership

KEY POINT | A switch port that is not a trunk can belong to only one VLAN at a time. You can either statically or dynamically configure which VLAN a port belongs to.

Static port membership means that the network administrator configures which VLAN the port belongs to, regardless of the devices attached to it. This means that after you have configured the ports, you must ensure that the devices attaching to the switch are plugged into the correct port, and if they move, you must reconfigure the switch.

Alternatively, you can configure dynamic VLAN membership. Some static configuration is still required, but this time, it is on a separate device called a *VLAN Membership Policy Server (VMPS)*. The VMPS could be a separate server, or it could be a higher-end switch that contains the VMPS information. VMPS information consists of a MAC address–to–VLAN map. As a result, ports are assigned to VLANs based on the MAC address of the device connected to the port. When you move a device from one port to another port (either on the same switch or on another switch in the network), the switch dynamically assigns the new port to the proper VLAN for that device by consulting the VMPS.

Trunks

As mentioned earlier, a port that carries data from multiple VLANs is called a *trunk*. A trunk port can be on a switch, a router, or a server. A trunk port can use one of two protocols: Inter-Switch Link (ISL) or IEEE 802.1Q.

ISL is a Cisco-proprietary trunking protocol that involves encapsulating the data frame between an ISL header and trailer. The header is 26 bytes long; the trailer is a 4-byte cyclic redundancy check that is added after the data frame. A 15-bit VLAN ID field is included in the header to identify the VLAN that the traffic is for. (Only the lower 10 bits of this field are used, thus supporting 1024 VLANs.)

The 802.1Q protocol is an IEEE standard protocol in which the trunking information is encoded within a Tag field inserted inside the frame header itself. Trunks using the 802.1Q protocol define a native VLAN. Traffic for the native VLAN is not tagged; it is carried across the trunk unchanged. Consequently, end-user stations that don't understand trunking can communicate with other devices directly over an 802.1Q trunk as long as they are on the native VLAN. The native VLAN must be defined to be the same VLAN on both sides of the trunk. Within the Tag field, the 802.1Q VLAN ID field is 12 bits long, allowing up to 4096 VLANs to be defined. The Tag field also includes a 3-bit 802.1p user priority field; these bits are used as class of service (CoS) bits for QoS marking. (Chapter 4 describes QoS.)

The two types of trunks are not compatible with each other, so both ends of a trunk must be defined with the same trunk type.

> **NOTE**   Multiple switch ports can be logically combined so that they appear as one higher-performance port. Cisco does this with its EtherChannel technology, combining multiple Fast Ethernet or Gigabit Ethernet links. Trunks can be implemented on both individual ports and on these EtherChannel ports.

STP and VLANs

Cisco developed per-VLAN spanning tree (PVST) so that switches can have one instance of STP running per VLAN, allowing redundant physical links within the network to be used for different VLANs and thus reducing the load on individual links. PVST is illustrated in Figure 1-22.

Figure 1-22 *PVST Allows Redundant Physical Links to Be Used for Different VLANs*

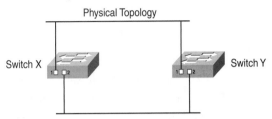

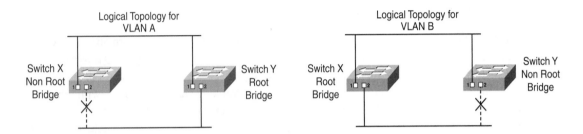

The top diagram in Figure 1-22 shows the physical topology of the network, with switches X and Y redundantly connected. In the lower-left diagram, switch Y has been selected as the root bridge for VLAN A, leaving port 2 on switch X in the blocking state. In contrast, the lower-right diagram shows that switch X has been selected as the root bridge for VLAN B, leaving port 2 on switch Y in the blocking state. With this configuration, traffic is shared across all links, with traffic for VLAN A traveling to the lower LAN on switch Y's port 2, whereas traffic for VLAN B traveling to the lower LAN goes out switch X's port 2.

PVST works only over ISL trunks. However, Cisco extended this functionality for 802.1Q trunks with the PVST+ protocol. Before this became available, 802.1Q trunks supported only Common Spanning Tree, with one instance of STP running for all VLANs.

Multiple-Instance STP (MISTP) is an IEEE standard (802.1s) that uses RSTP and allows several VLANs to be grouped into a single spanning-tree instance. Each instance is independent of the other instances so that a link can forward for one group of VLANs while blocking for other VLANs. MISTP therefore allows traffic to be shared across all the links in the network, but it reduces the number of STP instances that would be required if PVST/PVST+ were implemented.

Rapid per-VLAN Spanning Tree Plus (RPVST+) is a Cisco enhancement of RSTP, using PVST+.

Inter-VLAN Routing

KEY POINT | Just like devices on different LANs, those on different VLANs require a Layer 3 mechanism (a router or a Layer 3 switch) to communicate with each other.

A Layer 3 device can be connected to a switched network in two ways: by using multiple physical interfaces or through a single interface configured as a trunk. These two connection methods are shown in Figure 1-23. The diagram on the left illustrates a router with three physical connections to the switch; each physical connection carries traffic from only one VLAN.

Figure 1-23 *A Router, Using Either Multiple Physical Interfaces or a Trunk, Is Required for Communication Among VLANs*

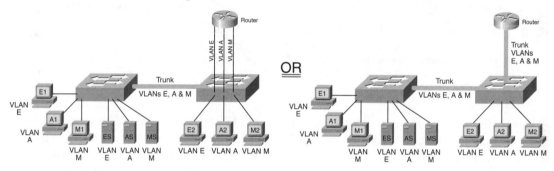

The diagram on the right illustrates a router with one physical connection to the switch. The interfaces on the switch and the router have been configured as trunks; therefore, multiple logical connections exist between the two devices. When a router is connected to a switch through a trunk, it is sometimes called a "router on a stick," because it has only one physical interface (a stick) to the switch.

Each interface between the switch and the Layer 3 device, whether physical interfaces or logical interfaces within a trunk, is in a separate VLAN and therefore in a separate subnet for IP networks.

Comprehensive Example

This section presents a comprehensive example, tying together many of the concepts covered in the rest of this chapter. Figure 1-24 illustrates the network used in this example.

Figure 1-24 *PC1 in New York Is Sending FTP Data to FS1 in London*

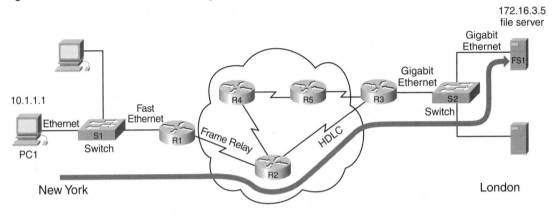

In this network, PC1, located in New York, has an FTP connection with the file server FS1 in London. PC1 is transferring a file, using FTP, to FS1. The path between PC1 and FS1 goes through switch S1; routers R1, R2, and R3; and switch S2, as illustrated by the thick line in the figure. The routers have communicated, using a routing protocol, to determine the best path between network 10.0.0.0 and network 172.16.0.0. PC1 has an IP address of 10.1.1.1, and FS1 has an IP address of 172.16.3.5. When PC1 first needed to send data to a device on another network, it sent an ARP request; its default gateway, R1, replied with its own MAC address, which PC1 keeps in its memory.

FTP data is now being sent from PC1 to FS1. Figure 1-25 shows how this data flows within the devices in the network, and what the data looks like at each point within the network.

Figure 1-25 *Data Is Encapsulated and Unencapsulated as It Flows Through the Network*

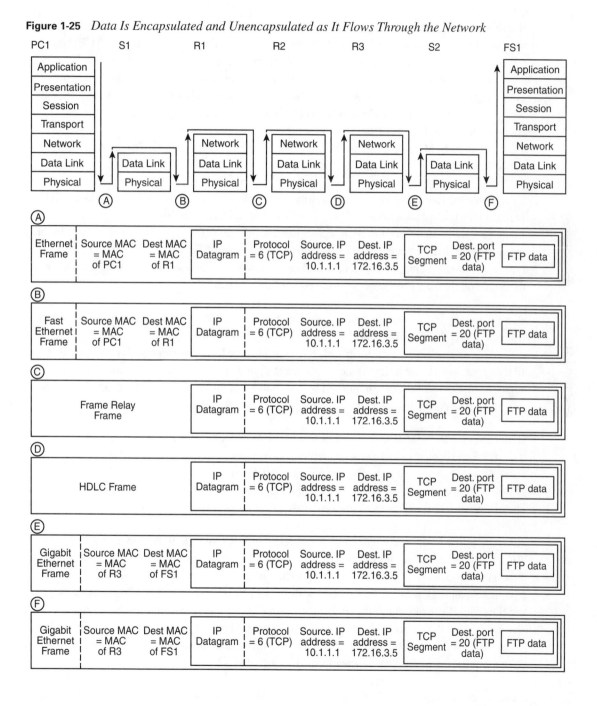

Starting at the left of Figure 1-25, PC1 prepares the data for transport across the network, and the resulting frame is shown as point A in the figure. PC1 encapsulates the FTP data in a TCP segment; the destination port field of the segment is set to 20, indicating that it contains FTP data. This TCP segment is then encapsulated in an IP datagram. The protocol number of the datagram is set to 6, indicating that it contains a TCP segment. The source IP address is set to PC1's address, 10.1.1.1, whereas the destination IP address is set to FS1's address, 172.16.3.5. The IP datagram is encapsulated in an Ethernet frame, with the source MAC address set to PC1's MAC address and the destination MAC address set to R1's MAC address. PC1 then puts the frame on the Ethernet network, and the bits arrive at S1.

S1 receives the frame and looks at the destination MAC address—it is R1's MAC address. S1 looks in its MAC address table and sees that this MAC address is on its Fast Ethernet port. Therefore, S1 encapsulates the IP datagram in a Fast Ethernet frame, as shown at point B in the figure. Notice that the source and destination MAC addresses have not changed in this new frame type, and that the datagram, segment, and data all remain untouched by the switch. S1 then puts the frame on the Fast Ethernet network, and the bits arrive at R1.

R1 receives the frame, and because it is destined for R1's MAC address, R1 unencapsulates the frame to Layer 3. R1 looks at the destination IP address 172.16.3.5 and compares it to its routing table. This network is accessible through R2, over a Frame Relay network, so R1 encapsulates the IP datagram in a Frame Relay frame, as shown at point C in the figure. Notice that the datagram, segment, and data all remain untouched by the router, but the frame type has changed. R1 then puts the frame on the Frame Relay network, and the bits arrive at R2.

R2 receives the frame and unencapsulates it to Layer 3. R2 looks at the destination IP address 172.16.3.5 and compares it to its routing table. This network is accessible through R3, over an HDLC network, so R2 encapsulates the IP datagram in an HDLC frame, as shown at point D in the figure. Notice that the datagram, segment, and data all remain untouched by the router, but the frame type has changed again. R2 then puts the frame on the HDLC network, and the bits arrive at R3.

R3 receives the frame and unencapsulates it to Layer 3. R3 looks at the destination IP address 172.16.3.5 and compares it to its routing table. This network is accessible through its Gigabit Ethernet interface—it is directly connected to that network. When R3 first needed to send data to FS1, it sent an ARP request; FS1 replied with its own MAC address, which R3 keeps in its memory. So, R3 encapsulates the IP datagram in a Gigabit Ethernet frame, as shown at point E in the figure, with the source MAC address set to its own address and the destination MAC address set to FS1's address. Notice that the datagram, segment, and data all remain untouched by the router, but the frame type has changed. The bits arrive at S2.

S2 receives the frame and looks at the destination MAC address—it is FS1's MAC address. S2 looks in its MAC address table and sees that this MAC address is on another one of its Gigabit Ethernet ports. Therefore, the IP datagram can stay in a Gigabit Ethernet frame, as shown at point

F in the figure. Notice that the source and destination MAC addresses have not changed in this frame, and that the datagram, segment, and data all remain untouched by the switch. S2 then puts the frame on the other Gigabit Ethernet network, and the bits arrive at FS1. FS1 receives the frame, and because it is destined for FS1's MAC address, FS1 unencapsulates the frame to Layer 3. FS1 looks at the destination IP address and determines that it is its own address. Therefore, FS1 unencapsulates the segment and the FTP data and then sends it to its FTP application. The FTP data is now at its destination.

KEY POINT | At each communication layer, the same protocol must be used at each side of a connection.

For example, PC1 is sending data to FS1 using FTP, so both PC1 and FS1 must support FTP at the application layer. If they don't, the session will fail, and data will not be sent.

Note, however, that the FTP data can go through many different types of media—Layers 1 and 2—on its way to FS1. The devices (switches, routers, PC, and file server) all unencapsulate up to at least Layer 2; thus, both sides of each connection between these devices must support the same Layers 1 and 2. For example, if PC1 supported only Ethernet and S1 supported only Fast Ethernet, they would not be able to communicate. Because S1 has an Ethernet port, it can connect to PC1 and then convert the data to send out on its Fast Ethernet port.

Summary

In this chapter, you learned about fundamental networking concepts; these concepts form a solid foundation for understanding the rest of this book. The following topics were explored:

- Introduction to networks

- Discussion of networking protocols and the OSI model, a key component of networking and the basis of modern protocol suites

- LANs and WANs

- Network devices, including hubs, switches, and routers

- Introduction to the TCP/IP suite and a discussion of the IP, TCP, and UDP protocols

- Routing, including an introduction to routing protocols

- Addressing, including MAC and IP addresses

- Layer 2 and Layer 3 switching

- Use and operation of STP in Layer 2 networks

- Concept and operation of VLANs

- Comprehensive example illustrating the encapsulation and unencapsulation processes

This chapter introduces a network design methodology and presents guidelines for building an effective network design solution. It includes the following sections:

- The Cisco Service Oriented Network Architecture

- Network Design Methodology

- Identifying Customer Requirements

- Characterizing the Existing Network and Sites

- Using the Top-Down Approach to Network Design

- The Design Implementation Process

- Summary

- References

- Case Study: ACMC Hospital Network Upgrade

- Review Questions

CHAPTER 2

Applying a Methodology to Network Design

This chapter begins with an introduction to the Cisco vision of intelligent networks and the Service Oriented Network Architecture (SONA) architectural framework. The lifecycle of a network and a network design methodology based on the lifecycle are presented. Each phase of the network design process is explored in detail, starting with how to identify customer requirements, including organizational and technical goals and constraints. Because many customers build on an existing network and at existing sites, this chapter also presents methods of characterizing that existing network and those sites. A top-down approach to design and structured design principles is presented. The design process includes a discussion about building a prototype or pilot and the appropriate content of a design specification. The chapter concludes with a discussion of the design implementation process.

The Cisco Service Oriented Network Architecture

The extremely rich variety of application-level business solutions available today and the need to integrate these applications drives the need for a new network architecture. This section introduces the Cisco vision and framework that enable customers to build a more intelligent network infrastructure. the Cisco SONA architectural framework shifts the view of the network from a pure traffic transport-oriented view toward a service- and application-oriented view.

Business Drivers for a New Network Architecture

New business requirements, the growth of applications, and the evolution of IT combine to drive the need for a new network architecture. In today's business environment, intense competition and time-to-market pressures are prompting enterprises to look for new IT solutions that can help them better respond to market and customer demands. Consumers are asking for new products and service offerings—and they want them fast. They are also demanding improved customer service, enhanced customization flexibility, and greater security, all at a lower cost.

Modern networks connect multiple resources and information assets within the organization as well as provide access to external resources. In this environment, the IT model has evolved from mainframes, to client/server models, to Internet applications, as illustrated in Figure 2-1. The Cisco vision of the next phase of IT evolution is a real-time infrastructure that integrates the network and the applications as one system.

Figure 2-1 *IT Evolution from Connectivity to Intelligent Systems*

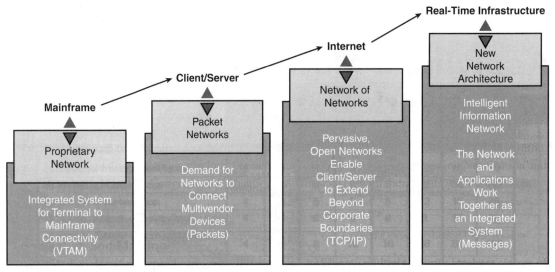

Organizations are finding that networking is no longer just about connectivity; rather, network intelligence is starting to play a role in improving business performance and processes. Intelligence enhances the network's role as a foundation for enabling communication, collaboration, and business success. With increased awareness of the applications that operate on the network foundation, the network becomes an active participant in applications, network management, business systems, and services to enable them to work better.

The network is the common single element that connects and enables *all* components of the IT infrastructure.

Organizations need their networks to evolve to intelligent systems that participate actively in the delivery of applications to effectively reach the goals of improved productivity, reduced time to market, greater revenue, lower expenses, and stronger customer relationships. An effective network provides the foundation for transforming business practices.

Intelligence in the Network

Integrating intelligence into the network involves aligning network and business requirements. To accommodate today's and tomorrow's network requirements, the Cisco vision of the future includes the Intelligent Information Network (IIN), a strategy that addresses how the network is integrated with businesses and business priorities. This vision encompasses the following features:

- **Integration of networked resources and information assets that have been largely unlinked**: The modern converged networks with integrated voice, video, and data require that IT departments (and other departments traditionally responsible for other technologies) more closely link the IT infrastructure with the network.

- **Intelligence across multiple products and infrastructure layers**: The intelligence built in to each component of the network is extended networkwide and applies end-to-end.

- **Active participation of the network in the delivery of services and applications**: With added intelligence, it is possible for the network to actively manage, monitor, and optimize service and application delivery across the entire IT environment.

KEY POINT The intelligent network offers much more than basic connectivity, bandwidth for users, and access to applications. It offers end-to-end functionality and centralized, unified control that promotes true business transparency and agility.

With this technology vision, Cisco is helping organizations address new IT challenges, such as the deployment of service-oriented architectures, web services, and virtualization (as described in the upcoming Phase 2 bullet). This vision offers an evolutionary approach that consists of three phases in which functionality can be added to the infrastructure as required. The three phases are illustrated in Figure 2-2 and described as follows:

- **Phase 1: Integrated transport**: Everything (data, voice, and video) consolidates onto an IP network for secure network convergence. By integrating data, voice, and video transport into a single standards-based modular network, organizations can simplify network management and generate enterprisewide efficiencies. Network convergence also lays the foundation for a new class of IP-enabled applications, now known as Cisco Unified Communications solutions.

NOTE *Cisco Unified Communications* is the name, launched in March 2006, for the entire range of what were previously known as *Cisco IP communications* products. These include all call control, conferencing, voice mail and messaging, customer contact, IP phone, video telephony, videoconferencing, rich media clients, and voice application products.

- **Phase 2: Integrated services**: When the network infrastructure is converged, IT resources can be pooled and shared, or *virtualized*, to flexibly address the changing needs of the organization. By extending this virtualization concept to encompass server, storage, and network elements, an organization can transparently use all its resources more efficiently. Business continuity is also enhanced because in the event of a local systems failure, shared resources across the intelligent network can provide needed services.

- **Phase 3: Integrated applications**: This phase focuses on making the network application-aware so that it can optimize application performance and more efficiently deliver networked applications to users. In addition to capabilities such as content caching, load balancing, and application-level security, application network services make it possible for the network to simplify the application infrastructure by integrating intelligent application message handling, optimization, and security into the existing network.

Figure 2-2 *Intelligence in the Network*

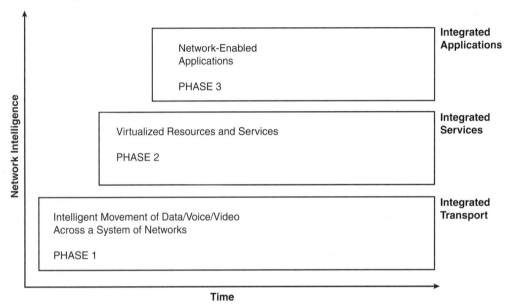

NOTE   You can access the IIN home page at http://www.cisco.com/go/iin.

NOTE   The IT industry is currently deploying Phase 2 integrated services. With Application-Oriented Networking technology, Cisco has entered Phase 3, and the industry is starting to define Phase 3 integrated applications.

Cisco SONA Framework

The Cisco SONA is an architectural framework that illustrates how to build integrated systems and guides the evolution of enterprises toward more intelligent networks. Using the SONA framework, enterprises can improve flexibility and increase efficiency by optimizing applications, business processes, and resources to enable IT to have a greater effect on business.

The SONA framework leverages the extensive product-line services, proven architectures, and experience of Cisco and its partners to help enterprises achieve their business goals.

The SONA framework, shown in Figure 2-3, shows how integrated systems can allow a dynamic, flexible architecture and provide for operational efficiency through standardization and virtualization.

Figure 2-3   *Cisco SONA Framework*

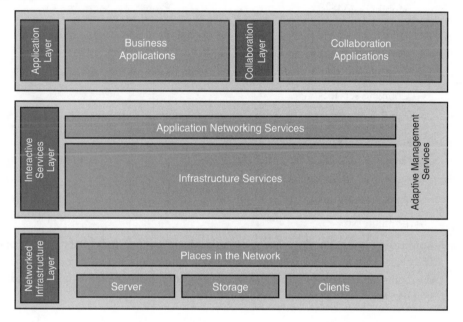

<table>
<tr><td>KEY POINT</td><td>In the SONA framework, the network is the common element that connects and enables all components of the IT infrastructure.</td></tr>
</table>

The SONA framework defines the following three layers:

- **Networked Infrastructure layer**: Where all the IT resources are interconnected across a converged network foundation. The IT resources include servers, storage, and clients. The Networked Infrastructure layer represents how these resources exist in different places in the network, including the campus, branch, data center, enterprise edge, WAN, metropolitan-area network (MAN), and with the teleworker. The objective of this layer is to provide connectivity, anywhere and anytime.

  The Networked Infrastructure layer includes the network devices and links to connect servers, storage, and clients in different places in the network.

- **Interactive Services layer**: Includes both application networking services and infrastructure services. This layer enables efficient allocation of resources to applications and business processes delivered through the networked infrastructure. This layer includes the following services:

  — Voice and collaboration services

  — Mobility services

  — Wireless services

  — Security and identity services

  — Storage services

  — Compute services

  — Application networking services (content networking services)

  — Network infrastructure virtualization

  — Adaptive network management services

  — Quality of service (QoS)

  — High availability

  — IP multicast

- **Application layer**: This layer includes business applications and collaboration applications. The objective of this layer is to meet business requirements and achieve efficiencies by leveraging the interactive services layer. This layer includes the following collaborative applications:

  — Instant messaging

  — Cisco Unified Contact Center

  — Cisco Unity (unified messaging)

  — Cisco IP Communicator and Cisco Unified IP Phones

  — Cisco Unified MeetingPlace

  — Video delivery using Cisco Digital Media System

  — IP telephony

NOTE The preceding lists include *voice* as an infrastructure service and *IP telephony* as an application. Note that some Cisco documentation uses the term *IP telephony* to describe the infrastructure service supported by other services, such as voice. To avoid ambiguity, the term *IP telephony* is used in this book to describe the network application supported by other services, such as voice.

Figure 2-4 illustrates some of these SONA offerings within each of the layers.

Figure 2-4 *Cisco SONA Offerings*

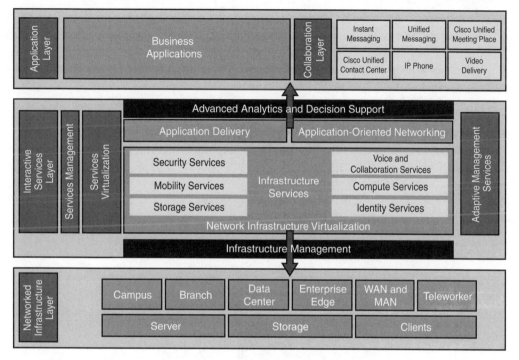

NOTE   You can access the SONA home page at http://www.cisco.com/go/sona.

The benefits of SONA include the following:

- **Functionality**: Supports the organizational requirements.

- **Scalability**: Supports growth and expansion of organizational tasks by separating functions and products into layers; this separation makes it easier to grow the network.

- **Availability**: Provides the necessary services, reliably, anywhere, anytime.

- **Performance**: Provides the desired responsiveness, throughput, and utilization on a per-application basis through the network infrastructure and services.

- **Manageability**: Provides control, performance monitoring, and fault detection.

- **Efficiency**: Provides the required network services and infrastructure with reasonable operational costs and appropriate capital investment on a migration path to a more intelligent network, through step-by-step network services growth.

- **Security**: Provides for an effective balance between usability and security while protecting information assets and infrastructure from inside and outside threats.

Network Design Methodology

The network design methodology presented in this section is derived from the Cisco Prepare, Plan, Design, Implement, Operate, and Optimize (PPDIOO) methodology, which reflects a network's lifecycle. The following sections describe the PPDIOO phases and their relation to the network design methodology, and the benefits of the lifecycle approach to network design. Subsequent sections explain the design methodology in detail.

Design as an Integral Part of the PPDIOO Methodology

The PPDIOO network lifecycle, illustrated in Figure 2-5, reflects the phases of a standard network's lifecycle. As shown in this figure, the PPDIOO lifecycle phases are separate, yet closely related.

Figure 2-5 *PPDIOO Network Lifecycle Influences Design*

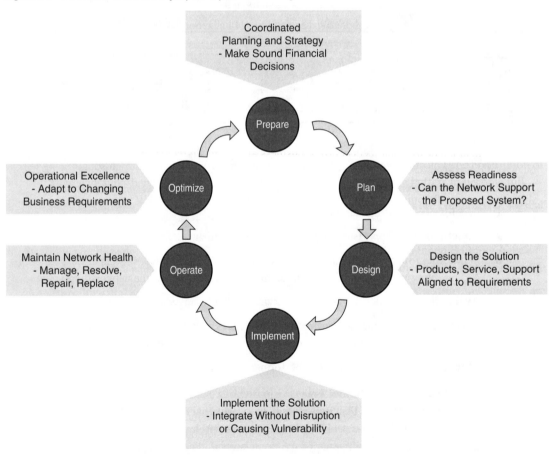

The following describes each PPDIOO phase:

- **Prepare phase**: The Prepare phase involves establishing the organizational (business) requirements, developing a network strategy, and proposing a high-level conceptual architecture, identifying technologies that can best support the architecture. Financial justification for the network strategy is established by assessing the business case for the proposed architecture.

- **Plan phase**: This phase involves identifying the network requirements, which are based on the goals for the network, where the network will be installed, who will require which network services, and so forth. The Plan phase also involves assessing the sites where the network will be installed and any existing networks, and performing a gap analysis to determine if the existing system infrastructure, sites, and operational environment can support the proposed system. A project plan helps manage the tasks, responsibilities, critical milestones, and resources required to implement the changes to the network. The project plan should align with the scope, cost, and resource parameters established in the original business requirements. The output of this phase is a set of network requirements.

- **Design phase**: The initial requirements determined in the Plan phase drive the network design specialists' activities. These specialists design the network according to those initial requirements, incorporating any additional data gathered during network analysis and network audit (when upgrading an existing network) and through discussion with managers and network users. The network design specification that is produced is a comprehensive detailed design that meets current business and technical requirements and incorporates specifications to support availability, reliability, security, scalability, and performance. This design specification provides the basis for the implementation activities.

- **Implement phase**: Implementation and verification begins after the design has been approved. The network and any additional components are built according to the design specifications, with the goal of integrating devices without disrupting the existing network or creating points of vulnerability.

- **Operate phase**: Operation is the final test of the design's appropriateness. The Operate phase involves maintaining network health through day-to-day operations, which might include maintaining high availability and reducing expenses. The fault detection and correction and performance monitoring that occur in daily operations provide initial data for the network lifecycle's Optimize phase.

- **Optimize phase**: The Optimize phase is based on proactive network management, the goal of which is to identify and resolve issues before real problems arise and the organization is affected. Reactive fault detection and correction (troubleshooting) are necessary when proactive management cannot predict and mitigate the failures. In the PPDIOO process, the

Optimize phase might lead to network redesign if too many network problems or errors arise, if performance does not meet expectations, or if new applications are identified to support organizational and technical requirements.

Although Design is one of the six PPDIOO phases, all the other phases influence design decisions, and the Design phase interacts closely with them, as follows:

■ The requirements derived from the Prepare and Plan phases are the basis for network design.

■ The Implement phase includes the initial verification of the design on the actual network.

■ During the Operate and Optimize phases, the final decision is made about the appropriateness of the design, based on network analysis and any problems that arise. The network might have to be redesigned to correct any discovered errors.

Benefits of the Lifecycle Approach to Network Design

The network lifecycle approach provides many benefits, including the following:

■ **Lowering the total cost of network ownership**:
  — Identifying and validating technology requirements
  — Planning for infrastructure changes and resource requirements
  — Developing a sound network design aligned with technical requirements and business goals
  — Accelerating successful implementation
  — Improving the efficiency of the network and of the staff supporting it
  — Reducing operating expenses by improving the efficiency of operation processes and tools

■ **Increasing network availability**:
  — Assessing the state of the network's security and its ability to support the proposed design
  — Specifying the correct set of hardware and software releases and keeping them operational and current
  — Producing a sound operational design and validating network operation
  — Staging and testing the proposed system before deployment
  — Improving staff skills
  — Proactively monitoring the system and assessing availability trends and alerts
  — Proactively identifying security breaches and defining remediation plans

■ **Improving business agility**:

— Establishing business requirements and technology strategies

— Readying sites to support the system to be implemented

— Integrating technical requirements and business goals into a detailed design and demonstrating that the network is functioning as specified

— Expertly installing, configuring, and integrating system components

— Continually enhancing performance

■ **Accelerating access to applications and services**:

— Assessing and improving operational preparedness to support current and planned network technologies and services

— Improving service-delivery efficiency and effectiveness by increasing availability, resource capacity, and performance

— Improving the availability, reliability, and stability of the network and the applications running on it

— Managing and resolving problems affecting the system and keeping software applications current

Design Methodology

When working in an environment that requires creative production on a tight schedule—for example, when designing an internetwork—using a methodology can be helpful. A *methodology* is a documented, systematic way of doing something.

Following a design methodology can have many advantages:

■ It ensures that no step is missed when the process is followed.

■ It provides a framework for the design process deliverables.

■ It encourages consistency in the creative process, enabling network designers to set appropriate deadlines and maintain customer and manager satisfaction.

■ It allows customers and managers to validate that the designers have thought about how to meet their requirements.

The design methodology presented here includes three basic steps; some of the design methodology steps are intrinsic to the PPDIOO Design phase, whereas other steps are related to other PPDIOO phases:

Step 1   **Identify customer requirements**: In this step, which is typically completed during the PPDIOO Prepare phase, key decision makers identify the initial requirements. Based on these requirements, a high-level conceptual architecture is proposed.

Step 2   **Characterize the existing network and sites**: The Plan phase involves characterizing sites and assessing any existing networks, and performing a gap analysis to determine whether the existing system infrastructure, sites, and operational environment can support the proposed system. Characterization of the existing network and sites includes site and network audit and network analysis. During the network audit, the existing network is thoroughly checked for integrity and quality. During the network analysis, network behavior (traffic, congestion, and so forth) is analyzed.

Step 3   **Design the network topology and solutions**: In this step, the detailed design of the network is created. Decisions are made about networked infrastructure, infrastructure services, and applications. The data for making these decisions is gathered during the first two steps.

A pilot or prototype network might be constructed to verify the correctness of the design and to identify and correct any problems as a proof of concept before implementing the entire network.

A detailed design document is also written during this step; it includes information that has been documented in the previous steps.

When the design is complete, the design implementation process is executed; this process includes the following steps:

Step 1   **Plan the implementation**: During this step, the implementation procedures are prepared in advance to expedite and clarify the actual implementation. Cost assessment is also undertaken at this time. This step is performed during the PPDIOO Design phase.

Step 2   **Implement and verify the design**: The actual implementation and verification of the design take place during this step by building a network. This step maps directly to the Implement phase of the PPDIOO methodology.

NOTE   A pilot or prototype network verifies the design somewhat; however, the design is not truly verified until it is actually implemented.

Step 3   **Monitor and optionally redesign**: The network is put into operation after it is built. During operation, the network is constantly monitored and checked for errors. If troubleshooting problems become too frequent or even impossible to manage, a network redesign might be required; this can be avoided if all previous steps have been completed properly. This step is, in fact, a part of the Operate and Optimize phases of the PPDIOO methodology.

The remaining sections in this chapter detail each of the design methodology steps, followed by a brief discussion of the implementation process steps.

Identifying Customer Requirements

As the organization's network grows, so does the organization's dependency on the network and the applications that use it. Network-accessible organizational data and mission-critical applications that are essential to the organization's operations depend on network availability.

To design a network that meets customers' needs, the organizational goals, organizational constraints, technical goals, and technical constraints must be identified. This section describes the process of determining which applications and network services already exist and which ones are planned, along with associated organizational and technical goals and constraints. We begin by explaining how to assess the scope of the design project. After gathering all customer requirements, the designer must identify and obtain any missing information and reassess the scope of the design project to develop a comprehensive understanding of the customer's needs.

Assessing the Scope of a Network Design Project

When assessing the scope of a network design, consider the following:

■ Whether the design is for a new network or is a modification of an existing network.

■ Whether the design is for an entire enterprise network, a subset of the network, or a single segment or module. For example, the designer must ascertain whether the design is for a set of Campus LANs, a WAN, or a remote-access network.

■ Whether the design addresses a single function or the network's entire functionality.

Examples of designs that would involve the entire network include one in which all branch office LANs are upgraded to support Fast Ethernet, and a migration from traditional Private Branch Exchange (PBX)–based telephony to an IP telephony solution. A project to reduce bottlenecks on a slow WAN is an example that would likely affect only the WAN. Adding wireless client mobility or provisioning core redundancy are designs that would likely affect only the campus.

The Open Systems Interconnection (OSI) reference model is important during the design phase. The network designer should review the project scope from the protocol layer perspective and decide whether the design is needed for only the network layer, or if other layers are also involved. For example:

■ The network layer includes the routing and addressing design.

■ The application layer includes the design of application data transport (such as transporting voice).

■ The physical and data link layers include decisions about the connection types and the technologies to be used, such as Gigabit Ethernet, Asynchronous Transfer Mode, and Frame Relay.

> **NOTE**   Appendix C, "Open System Interconnection (OSI) Reference Model," details the seven layers of the OSI reference model.

Table 2-1 exhibits sample results of assessing the scope of design for a sample enterprise, Corporation X.

Table 2-1   *Corporation X Network Design Scope Assessment*

Scope of Design	Comments
Entire network	The backbone at the central office needs to be redesigned. All branch offices' LANs will be upgraded to Fast Ethernet technology.
Network layer	Introduction of private IP addresses requires a new addressing plan. Certain LANs must also be segmented. Routing must be redesigned to support the new addressing plan and to provide greater reliability and redundancy.
Data link layer	The central office backbone and some branch offices require redundant equipment and redundant links are needed. The organization also requires a campus wireless radio frequency (RF) site survey to determine mobility deployment options and equipment scope.

Identifying Required Information

Determining requirements includes extracting initial requirements from the customer and then refining these with other data that has been collected from the organization.

Extracting Initial Requirements

Initial design requirements are typically extracted from the Request for Proposal (RFP) or Request for Information (RFI) documents that the customer issues. An RFP is a formal request to vendors for proposals that meet the requirements that the document identifies. An RFI is typically a less formal document an organization issues to solicit ideas and information from vendors about a specific project.

The first step in the design process should be predocumenting (sifting, processing, reordering, translating, and so forth) the design requirements and reviewing them with the customer for verification and approval, obtaining direct customer input, in either oral or written form. Figure 2-6 illustrates an iterative approach to developing the design requirements document.

Figure 2-6   *Iterative Approach to Identifying Customer Requirements*

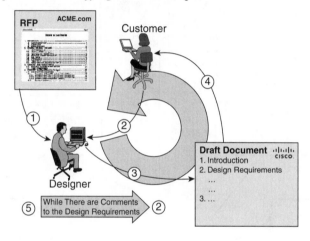

Figure 2-6 illustrates the following steps:

Step 1   Extract the initial customer requirements (from the RFP or RFI).

Step 2   Query the customer for a verbal description of the initial requirements.

Step 3   Produce a draft document that describes the design requirements.

Step 4   Verify the design requirements with the customer, and obtain customer approval.

Step 5   Revise the document as necessary to eliminate errors and omissions.

Steps 2 to 5 are repeated if the customer has additional comments about the draft document.

Gathering Network Requirements

As illustrated in Figure 2-7, the process of gathering requirements can be broken down into five steps. During these steps (which are sometimes called milestones), the designer discusses the project with the customer's staff to determine and gather the necessary data, including appropriate documentation.

Figure 2-7   *Gathering Data for Design Requirements*

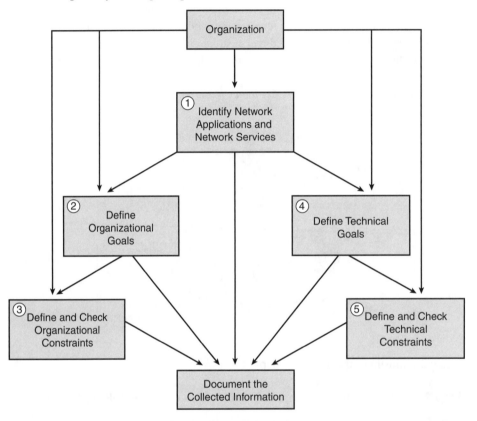

As shown in Figure 2-7, the steps are as follows:

Step 1   Identify the planned network applications and network services.

Step 2   Determine the organizational goals.

Step 3   Determine the possible organizational constraints.

Step 4   Determine the technical goals.

Step 5   Determine the technical constraints that must be taken into account.

These steps provide the designer with data that must be carefully interpreted, analyzed, and presented to support the design proposal. Throughout these steps, the designer takes thorough notes, produces documentation, and presents the findings to the customer for further discussion.

The process is not unidirectional; the designer might return to a step and make additional inquiries about issues as they arise during the design process. The next five sections detail these steps.

Planned Applications and Network Services

The designer must determine which applications the customer is planning to use and the importance of each of these applications. Using a table helps organize and categorize the applications and services planned; the table should contain the following information:

- **Planned application types**: Include e-mail, groupware (tools that aid group work), voice networking, web browsing, video on demand (VoD), databases, file sharing and transfer, computer-aided manufacturing, and so forth.

- **Applications**: Specific applications that will be used, such as Microsoft Internet Explorer, Cisco Unified MeetingPlace, and so forth.

- **Level of importance**: The importance of the applications—whether critical or important or not important—is noted.

- **Comments**: Additional notes taken during the data-gathering process.

Table 2-2 shows an example of data gathered about the planned applications for the sample company, Corporation X.

Table 2-2 *Corporation X's Planned Applications*

Application Type	Application	Level of Importance (Critical, Important, Not Important)	Comments
E-mail	Microsoft Office Outlook	Important	
Groupware	Cisco Unified MeetingPlace	Important	Need to be able to share presentations and applications during remote meetings
Web browsing	Microsoft Internet Explorer, Netscape Navigator, Opera	Important	
Video on demand	Cisco Digital Media System	Critical	
Database	Oracle	Critical	All data storage is based on Oracle
Customer support applications	Custom applications	Critical	

NOTE The Cisco Digital Media System is an enhanced system that can be used in place of the Cisco Internet Protocol Television (IP/TV) products; Cisco has announced the end-of-sale and end-of-life dates for the Cisco IP/TV 3400 Series products. See http://www.cisco.com/en/US/netsol/ns620/networking_solutions_white_paper0900aecd80537d33.shtml for more details.

NOTE Information on the Opera browser is available at http://www.opera.com/.

The planned infrastructure services table is similar to the planned application table. It lists infrastructure services that are planned for the network and additional comments about those services.

Recall that infrastructure services include security, QoS, network management, high availability, and IP multicast. Software distribution, backup, directory services, host naming, and user authentication and authorization are examples of other services and solutions that are deployed to support a typical organization's many applications. Table 2-3 shows sample data that was gathered about the infrastructure services planned for the sample company, Corporation X.

Table 2-3 *Corporation X's Planned Infrastructure Services*

Service	Comments
Security	Deploy security systematically: Firewall technology to protect the internal network; virus-scanning application to check incoming traffic for viruses; intrusion detection and prevention systems to protect from and inform about possible outside intrusions. Consider the use of authentication, authorization, and accounting systems to ensure that only authenticated and authorized users have access to specific services.
QoS	Implementation of QoS to prioritize more important and more delay-sensitive traffic over less important traffic (higher priority for voice and database traffic; lower priority for HTTP traffic).
Network management	Introduction and installation of centralized network management tools (such as HP OpenView with CiscoWorks applications) for easier and more efficient network management.
High availability	Use redundant paths and terminate connections on different network devices to eliminate single points of failure.
IP multicast	Introduction of IP multicast services needed for the introduction of videoconferencing and e-learning solutions.
Voice	Company wants to migrate to IP telephony.
Mobility	Need mobility for employees and guest access for clients.

Organizational Goals

Every design project should begin by determining the organizational goals that are to be achieved. The criteria for success must be determined, and the consequences of a failure understood.

Network designers are often eager to start by analyzing the technical goals before considering the organizational goals and constraints. However, detailed attention to organizational goals and constraints is important for a project's success. In discussions about organizational goals, the designer obtains knowledge about the customer's expectations of the design's positive outcomes for the organization. Both short- and long-term goals should be identified. This organization-centered approach allows the network to become a strategic asset and competitive weapon for the customer.

Preliminary research on the organization's activities, products, processes, services, market, suppliers, competitive advantages, and structure enhances the positioning of the technologies and products to be used in the network.

This is an opportunity to determine what is important to the customer. Some sample questions a designer might ask to help determine organizational goals include the following:

- What are you trying to accomplish with this project?

- What business challenges are you currently facing?

- What are the consequences of *not* resolving these issues?

- How would you measure or quantify success if you could fix or correct the identified problems and issues?

- What applications are most critical to your organization?

- What is the major objective of this project?

- What is driving the change?

- Do you need to support any government or safety or legal mandates?

- What are your main concerns with the implementation of a new solution?

- What technologies or services are needed to support your objectives?

- What other technology projects and business initiatives will affect your group in the next two to five years?

- What skill sets does your technical staff currently have?

- What is your goal for return on investment?

Organizational goals differ from organization to organization. The following are some typical goals that commercial organizations might have:

- Increase the operation's generated revenue and profitability. A new design should reduce costs in certain segments and propel growth in others. The network designer should discuss with the customer any expectations about how the new network will influence revenues and profits.

- Shorten development cycles and enhance productivity by improving internal data availability and interdepartmental communications.

- Improve customer support and offer additional customer services that can expedite reaction to customer needs and improve customer satisfaction.

- Open the organization's information infrastructure to all key stakeholders (prospects, investors, customers, partners, suppliers, and employees), and build relationships and information accessibility to a new level.

NOTE Similar, though not identical, goals are common to governmental, charitable, religious, and educational organizations. Most of these entities focus on using available resources effectively to attain the organization's goals and objectives. In not-for-profit organizations, key measures are typically stated in terms of cost containment, service quality, service expansion, and resource deployment. This section emphasizes the deployment of networks in commercial organizations as an example of the type of research required for establishing the network requirements.

To illustrate the importance of considering organizational goals in a network design, consider two manufacturing enterprises that are contemplating network updates. Enterprise A's main reason for change is to improve customer satisfaction. It has received many complaints that customer information is difficult to obtain and understand, and there is a need for online ordering capability. In contrast, Enterprise B is driven by the need to reduce costs—this is a mandate from its CEO. When design decisions are made, these goals will most likely result in different outcomes. For example, Enterprise A might choose to implement an integrated product information database with e-commerce capability, whereas Enterprise B might not see the value of investing in this technology.

Following are examples of the types of data that can be gathered about some common organizational goals:

■ **Increase competitiveness**: List competitive organizations and their advantages and weaknesses. Note possible improvements that might increase competitiveness or effectiveness.

■ **Reduce costs**: Reducing operational costs can result in increased profitability (even without a revenue increase) or increased services with the same revenue. List current expenses to help determine where costs could be reduced.

■ **Improve customer support**: Customer support services help provide a competitive advantage. List current customer support services, with comments about possible and desired improvements.

■ **Add new customer services**: List current customer services, and note future and desired (requested) services.

Table 2-4 presents data gathered about the organizational goals of a sample company, Corporation X.

Table 2-4 *Corporation X's Organizational Goals*

Organizational Goal	Gathered Data (Current Situation)	Comments
Increase competitiveness	Corporation Y	Better products
	Corporation Z	Reduced costs
Reduce cost	Repeating tasks—entering data multiple times, time-consuming tasks	Single data-entry point Easy-to-learn applications Simple data exchange
Improve customer support	Order tracking and technical support is done by individuals	Introduction of web-based order tracking and web-based tools for customer technical support
Add new customer services	Current services: Telephone and fax orders, and telephone and fax confirmation	Secure web-based ordering Secure web-based confirmations

Organizational Constraints

When assessing organizational goals, it is important to analyze any organizational constraints that might affect the network design. Some sample questions the designer might ask to help determine organizational constraints include the following:

- What in your current processes works well?

- What in your current processes does not work well?

- Which processes are labor-intensive?

- What are the barriers for implementation in your organization?

- What are your major concerns with the implementation of a new solution?

- What financial and timing elements must be considered?

- What projects already have budget approval?

- Are other planned technology projects and business initiatives compatible with your current infrastructure and technology solutions?

- What qualifications does your current staff have? Do you plan to hire more staff? If so, for what roles?

- Do you have a budget for technical development for your staff?

- Are there any policies in place that might affect the project?

Typical constraints include the following:

- **Budget**: Reduced budgets or limited resources often force network designers to implement an affordable solution rather than the best technical solution. This usually entails some compromises in availability, manageability, performance, and scalability. The budget must include all equipment purchases, software licenses, maintenance agreements, staff training, and so forth. Budget is often the final decision point for design elements, selected equipment, and so on. The designer must know how much money is available to invest in a solid design. It also useful to know the areas in which the network can be compromised to meet budget requirements.

- **Personnel**: The availability of trained personnel within the organization might be a design consideration. Organizations might not have enough trained personnel, or they might not have enough personnel. Familiarity with both the equipment and technologies speeds deployment and reduces cost, and trained technicians must be available to verify that all network elements are working. Therefore, the designer must know the number and availability of operations personnel, their expertise, and possible training requirements. Additional constraints might be imposed if the organization is outsourcing network management. The designer must consider the network's implementation and maintenance phases, which require adequately trained staff.

■ **Policies**: Organizations have different policies about protocols, standards, vendors, and applications; to design the network successfully, the designer must understand these policies. For example, the designer should determine customer policies related to single-vendor or multivendor platforms; an end-to-end single-vendor solution might be a benefit, because compatibility issues do not restrain the network. As another example, many organizations, such as government agencies (for example, defense departments), often have strict policies preventing implementation of proprietary protocols.

■ **Schedule**: The organization's executive management must discuss and approve the project schedule to avoid possible disagreements about deadlines. For example, the introduction of new network applications often drives the new network design; the implementation time frames for new applications are often tightly connected and therefore influence the available time for network design.

Table 2-5 shows organizational constraints and accompanying data that has been collected for a sample company, Corporation X.

Table 2-5 *Corporation X's Organizational Constraints*

Organizational Constraint	Gathered Data (Current Situation)	Comments
Budget	$650,000	Budget can be extended by a maximum of $78,000
Personnel	Two engineers with college degrees and Cisco Certified Network Associate (CCNA) certifications for network maintenance; one has Cisco Certified Network Professional (CCNP) certification Three engineers for various operating systems and applications maintenance	Plans to hire additional engineers for network maintenance; need technical development plan for staff
Policy	Prefers a single vendor and standardized protocols	Current equipment is Cisco; prefers to stay with Cisco
Schedule	Plans to introduce various new applications in the next nine months	New applications that will be introduced shortly are videoconferencing, groupware, and IP telephony

Technical Goals

The technical goals of the project must also be determined before the design starts. Some sample questions the designer might ask to help determine technical goals include the following:

- What are your technology priorities?

- How does your technology budgeting process work?

- What infrastructure issues exist or will exist related to your applications rollouts?

- What skill sets does your technical staff need to acquire?

- Does your current network have any performance issues?

- Which portions of your network are considered mission-critical?

- Do you anticipate significant growth in the number of network users over the next few years?

- How is your network managed now?

The following list describes some common technical goals:

- **Improve network performance**: An increase in the number of users and the introduction of new applications might degrade network performance, especially responsiveness and throughput. The first goal of network redesign is usually to increase performance—for example, by upgrading the speed of links or by partitioning the network into smaller segments.

> **NOTE** *Performance* is a general term that includes responsiveness, throughput, and resource utilization. The users of networked applications and their managers are usually most sensitive to responsiveness issues; speed is of the essence. The network system's managers often look to throughput as a measure of effectiveness in meeting the organization's needs. Executives who have capital budget responsibility tend to evaluate resource utilization as a measure of economic efficiency. It is important to consider the audience when presenting performance information.

- **Improve security and reliability of mission-critical applications and data**: Increased threats from both inside and outside the enterprise network require the most up-to-date security rules and technologies to avoid disruptions of network operation.

- **Decrease expected downtime and related expenses**: When a network failure occurs, downtime must be minimal, and the network must respond quickly to minimize related costs.

- **Modernize outdated technologies**: The emergence of new network technologies and applications demands regular updates to and replacement of outdated equipment and technologies.

■ **Improve scalability of the network**: Networks must be designed to provide for upgrades and future growth.

■ **Simplify network management**: Simplify network management functions so that they are easy to use and easily understood.

Using a table helps the designer identify technical goals. Different goals have different levels of importance, which the customer should determine. One way of expressing the level of importance is with percentages: Specific technical goals are rated in importance on a scale from 1 to 100, with the sum totaling 100; this scale provides direction for the designer when choosing equipment, protocols, features, and so forth.

Table 2-6 depicts the desired technical goals that were gathered for the sample company, Corporation X, along with their importance rating and additional comments. In this example, the designer sees that the customer places great importance on availability, scalability, and performance; this suggests that the network design should include redundant equipment, redundant paths, use of high-speed links, and so forth.

Table 2-6 *Corporation X's Technical Goals*

Technical Goals	Importance	Comments
Performance	20	Important in the central site, less important in branch offices
Security	15	The critical data transactions must be secure
Availability	25	Should be 99.9%
Adaptability (to new technologies)	10	
Scalability	25	The network must be scalable
Manageability	5	
	Total 100	

Technical Constraints

Network designers might face various technical constraints during the design process. Some sample questions the designer might ask to help determine technical constraints include the following:

■ How do you determine your technology priorities?

■ Do you have a technology refresh process? If so, is that an obstacle, or does it support the proposed project?

■ What urgent technical problems require immediate resolution or mitigation?

■ Do you have a plan for technical development for your staff in specific areas?

■ Do any applications require special network features (protocols and so forth)?

Good network design addresses constraints by identifying possible trade-offs, such as the following:

■ **Existing equipment**: The network design process is usually progressive; legacy equipment must coexist with new equipment.

■ **Bandwidth availability**: Insufficient bandwidth in parts of the network where the bandwidth cannot be increased because of technical constraints must be resolved by other means.

■ **Application compatibility**: If the new network is not being introduced at the same time as new applications, the design must provide compatibility with old applications.

■ **Lack of qualified personnel**: Lack of qualified personnel suggests that the designer must consider the need for additional training; otherwise, certain features might have to be dropped. For example, if the network proposal includes the use of IP telephony but the network administrators are not proficient in IP telephony, it might be necessary to propose an alternative solution.

Using a table can facilitate the process of gathering technical constraints. The designer identifies the technical constraints and notes the current situation and the necessary changes that are required to mitigate a certain constraint.

Table 2-7 presents sample technical constraints gathered for Corporation X. Under existing equipment, the designer notes that the coaxial cabling in the LAN's physical cabling plant still exists and comments that twisted pair and fiber optics should replace it. The bandwidth availability indicates that the WAN service provider does not have any other available links; the organization should consider changing to another service provider. Application compatibility suggests that the designer should take care when choosing equipment.

Table 2-7 *Technical Constraints for Corporation X*

Technical Constraints	Gathered Data (Current Situation)	Comments
Existing equipment	Coaxial cable	The cabling must be replaced with twisted pair to the desktop, and fiber optics for uplinks and in the core
Bandwidth availability	64-kbps WAN link	Upgrade bandwidth; change to another service provider because the current one does not have any other links to offer
Application compatibility	IP version 6 (IPv6)-based applications	New network equipment must support IPv6

Characterizing the Existing Network and Sites

The second step of the design methodology is characterizing the existing network and sites. Information collected and documented in this step is important, because the design might depend on the existing network's hardware, software, and link capacity.

In many cases, a network already exists and the new design relies on restructuring and upgrading the existing network and sites. Even when a network does not exist, the sites that will be networked still should be examined. The following sections present insights into the process of examining an existing network and sites and describe the tools used to gather the data, assess the network, and analyze the network. A checklist to assess the network's health is presented. Guidelines for creating a summary report are introduced. The discussion concludes with the draft design document and estimates of the time required to complete the entire characterization process.

The first step in characterizing the existing network and sites is to gather as much information about them as possible, typically based on the following input:

Step 1   **Customer input**: Review existing documentation about the network, and use verbal input from the customer to obtain a first impression about the network. Although this step is mandatory, it is usually insufficient, and some results might be incorrect.

Step 2   **Network audit**: Perform a network audit, also called an *assessment*, which reveals details of the network and augments the customer's description.

Step 3   **Traffic analysis**: If possible, use traffic analysis to provide information about the applications and protocols used and to reveal any shortcomings in the network.

> **NOTE**   Although traffic analysis is a good idea in principle, it is often too costly in terms of time and effort to do in practice.

The following sections describe each of these steps and the tools used.

Customer Input

Customer input includes all pertinent network and site documentation. Some items the designer could request, depending on the scope of the project, include the following:

■   Site contact information (especially needed if remote deployments are planned)

■   Existing network infrastructure (from physical diagrams and documents, and site surveys as needed), including the following:

— Locations and types of servers, including a list of network applications supported

— Locations and types of network devices

— Cabling that is currently in place, including network interface connection tables and worksheets

— Wiring closet locations

— Environmental controls, including heating, ventilation, and air conditioning requirements, and filtration

— Locations of telephone service demarcation points

— WAN speeds and locations of the WAN connection feeds

— Locations of power receptacles, and availability of additional receptacles and power sources

■ Existing network infrastructure from logical topology diagrams, including the addressing scheme and routing protocols in use, and the infrastructure services supported, such as voice, storage, and wireless services

■ Information about the expected network functionality

This documentation should allow the designer to determine information about the planned and existing network and sites, including the following:

■ **Network topology**: Includes devices, physical and logical links, external connections, bandwidth of connections, frame types (data link encapsulations), IP addressing, routing protocols, and so forth.

■ **Network services**: Includes security, QoS, high availability, voice, storage, wireless, and so forth.

■ **Network applications**: Examples include unified messaging and video delivery.

All this information should be included in the design document; it also forms the basis for breaking the network into modules.

Sample Site Contact Information

Site contact information is especially important for projects involving remote deployments when equipment delivery and installations must be coordinated. The customer might provide all the necessary site contact information, or the designer might have to conduct a physical site audit to obtain the necessary information.

While at the site, the designer can also obtain other information; for example, power availability can be determined by examining the existing wiring closets. Digital pictures taken by a remote site contact can help in getting a quick sense of the remote environment. Table 2-8 illustrates a sample site contact form.

Table 2-8   *Sample Site Contact Form*

1. What is the site location/name?	
2. What is the site address?	
3. What is the shipping address?	
4. Who is the site contact?	Name: Title: Telephone Number: Cell Phone Number: Fax Number: Pager Number: E-mail address: Out-of-Hours Contact Number:
5. Is this site owned and maintained by the customer?	Yes/No
6. Is this a staffed site?	Yes/No
7. What are the hours of operation?	
8. What are the building and room access procedures?	
9. Are there any special security/safety procedures?	Yes/No What are they?
10. Are there any union/labor requirements or procedures?	Yes/No What are they?
11. What are the locations of the equipment cabinets and racks?	Floor: Room: Position:

Sample High-Level Network Diagram

Figure 2-8 shows the high-level topology of a sample network, provided by a customer.

Figure 2-8 *Sample Customer-Provided High-Level Network Diagram*

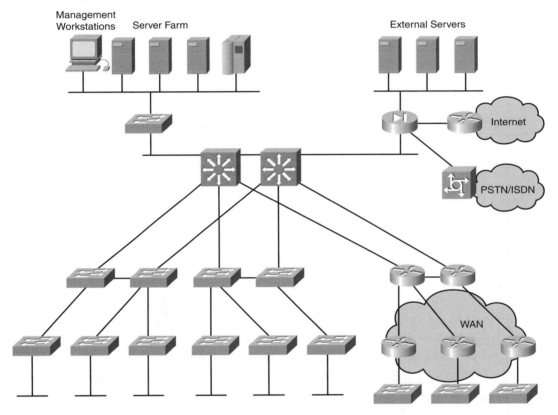

With only this diagram, many questions remain about the network and the expected network functionality, including the following:

■ What is the IP addressing scheme?

■ What level of redundancy or high availability currently exists in the network?

■ What level of redundancy or high availability is required in the new network?

■ What are the details of the security design?

■ What types of links are in the network?

■ What are the link speeds?

- What are the planned Layer 2 and Layer 3 topologies?

- How is connectivity provided to remote sites?

- What network infrastructure services are in use, such as voice and video, and what is planned?

- Are existing wireless devices in place, or are any wireless deployments planned?

- What routing protocols are in use?

- Are there any server farm or remote data center connectivity requirements?

- What network management tools are in place?

It is important to get as much information as possible about the existing situation before commencing design.

Auditing or Assessing the Existing Network

A network audit or assessment is the second step in acquiring information about an existing network. The auditing process starts by consolidating existing information the customer provides. Up-to-date information can be gathered from the existing management software used by the customer. If the customer has insufficient tools, the designer can choose to temporarily introduce additional software tools; if they prove useful, these tools can be used in the network permanently (during the Operate and Optimize phases). An audit provides details such as the following:

- A list of network devices

- Hardware specifications and versions, and software versions of network devices

- Configurations of network devices

- Output of various auditing tools to verify and augment the existing documentation

- Link, CPU, and memory utilization of network devices

- A list of unused ports, modules, and slots in network devices, to be used to understand whether the network is expandable

Figure 2-9 illustrates three different sources of information that can be used in the auditing process: existing documentation, existing tools, and new tools.

Figure 2-9 *Network Audit Information Sources*

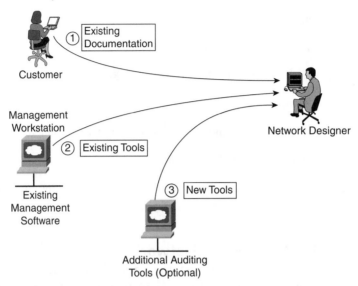

The auditing process might require minor (temporary) network changes. Automated auditing should be used in large networks for which a manual approach would take too much time. However, the audit process balances both detail and effort to produce as much information as needed or possible. For example, it should not require that a large set of CPU-heavy auditing tools be purchased and installed in the customer network to collect configurations of network devices. The auditing process is typically performed from a central location, such as a location in a secure environment that has access to all network devices.

Figure 2-10 illustrates sample information that a manual or automated auditing process collects from the network management workstation. The auditing process should collect all information relevant to the redesign. The same process should be used for all network devices affected by the design.

Figure 2-10 *Sample Information Collected During a Network Audit*

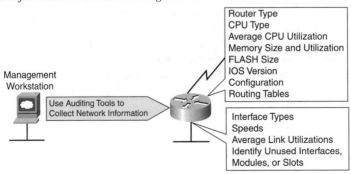

Tools for Assessing the Network

A small network can be assessed without special tools. Monitoring commands can be used to collect relevant information on a small number of network devices. The approach can be semi-automated by introducing scripting tools to execute the monitoring commands automatically.

In large networks, a manual auditing approach is too time-consuming and less reliable. The following are some special tools that can be used to collect the relevant information from the network devices:

- CiscoWorks to map a network and collect various types of information (such as network topology, hardware and software versions, configurations, and so on).

- Third-party tools such as WhatsUp Professional from Ipswitch, SNMPc from Castle Rock Computing, open-source Cacti (which is a successor to the popular Multi Router Traffic Grapher), NetMRI from Netcordia, and NetVoyant from NetQoS.

- Other vendors' tools to collect relevant information from equipment manufactured by those vendors.

- Other tools can help characterize the existing environment. For example, instead of a full wireless site survey, it can be helpful to conduct a brief RF sample of the environment using enterprise-level tools. Such tools include AirMagnet Survey PRO (to perform an RF site survey), Cognio Spectrum Expert (a spectrum analysis tool), and laptop applications such as AiroPeek from WildPackets (network analyzer software that supports decoding of wireless data packets) and the Cisco Aironet Site Survey Utility. Wireless networks are described in detail in Chapter 9, "Wireless Network Design Considerations."

Assessment Tool Information

Information on the aforementioned tools can be found at the following locations:

- CiscoWorks: http://www.cisco.com/

- WhatsUp Professional: http://www.ipswitch.com/

- SNMPc: http://www.castlerock.com/

- Cacti: http://www.cacti.net/

- NetMRI: http://www.netcordia.com/

- NetVoyant: http://www.netqos.com/

- AirMagnet Survey PRO: http://www.airmagnet.com/

- Spectrum Expert: http://www.cognio.com/

■ AiroPeek: http://www.wildpackets.com/

■ Cisco Aironet Site Survey Utility: http://www.cisco.com/

Manual Information Collection Examples

The auditing process can be performed manually on relatively small networks using various monitoring commands. Figure 2-11 illustrates three different types of network devices, information to be collected, and commands that can be used to obtain the information:

■ On Cisco routers that run Cisco IOS software, the **show tech-support** command usually displays all information about the router. **show processes cpu** can be used to determine CPU use, and **show processes memory** can be used to determine memory usage.

■ On Cisco switches that run Cisco Catalyst Operating System (CatOS) software, the most useful commands vary, depending on the version of the software. Useful commands might include **show version**, **show running-config**, or **show tech-support**, if available.

■ On Cisco Secure PIX Security Appliances, the **show version** and **write terminal** (to see the configuration) commands are useful.

Figure 2-11 *Collecting Audit Information on Cisco Devices*

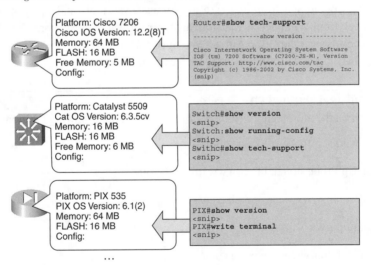

Many other commands are available on Cisco devices to determine relevant information.

> **NOTE** If older equipment or older versions of the Cisco IOS are being used, the capability of the network to support new services might be affected.

Example 2-1 illustrates sample output from the **show processes cpu** command on a Cisco router.

Example 2-1 show processes cpu *Command Output*

```
Router#show processes cpu


CPU utilization for five seconds: 24%/20%; one minute: 45%; five minutes: 40%
 PID Runtime(ms)    Invoked     uSecs    5Sec    1Min    5Min  TTY  Process
   1        2464     468381         5   0.00%   0.00%   0.00%    0  Load Meter
   2          44         44      1000   0.16%   0.04%   0.01%   66  Virtual Exec
   3           0          2         0   0.00%   0.00%   0.00%    0  IpSecMibTopN
   4     6326689     513354     12324   0.00%   0.25%   0.27%    0  Check heaps
   5           0          1         0   0.00%   0.00%   0.00%    0  Chunk Manager
   6          60         58      1034   0.00%   0.00%   0.00%    0  Pool Manager
   7           0          2         0   0.00%   0.00%   0.00%    0  Timers
   8           0         12         0   0.00%   0.00%   0.00%    0  Serial Backgroun
   9        2139     468342         4   0.00%   0.00%   0.00%    0  ALARM_TRIGGER_SC
  10        3851      78081        49   0.00%   0.00%   0.00%    0  Environmental mo
  11        4768      44092       108   0.00%   0.00%   0.00%    0  ARP Input
  12        4408      19865       221   0.00%   0.00%   0.00%    0  DDR Timers
  13           4          2      2000   0.00%   0.00%   0.00%    0  Dialer event
  14          16          2      8000   0.00%   0.00%   0.00%    0  Entity MIB API
  15           0          1         0   0.00%   0.00%   0.00%    0  SERIAL A'detect
  16           0          1         0   0.00%   0.00%   0.00%    0  Critical Bkgnd
  17       57284     377088       151   0.00%   0.00%   0.00%    0  Net Background
  18       15916      59331       268   0.00%   0.00%   0.00%    0  Logger

<more>
```

The output in Example 2-1 displays information about the network device CPU utilization, which is important for describing the network's health. Table 2-9 describes the **show processes cpu** command output's fields and descriptions.

Table 2-9 **show processes cpu** *Command Output Description*

Field	Description
CPU utilization	CPU utilization for the last: Five seconds—The first number in the ratio indicates the total CPU utilization; the second number in the ratio indicates the percentage of CPU time that was spent at the interrupt level One minute—Total CPU utilization for the last minute Five minutes—Total CPU utilization for the last 5 minutes
PID	The process ID
Runtime (ms)	CPU time, expressed in milliseconds, that the process has used
Invoked	The number of times the process has been invoked
uSecs	Microseconds of CPU time for each process invocation
5Sec	CPU utilization by task in the last 5 seconds
1Min	CPU utilization by task in the last minute
5Min	CPU utilization by task in the last 5 minutes
TTY	Terminal that controls the process
Process	Name of the process

Example 2-2 illustrates sample output from the **show processes memory** command on a Cisco router.

Example 2-2 **show processes memory** *Command Output*

```
Router#show process memory
Total: 26859400, Used: 8974380, Free: 17885020
 PID TTY  Allocated      Freed    Holding    Getbufs    Retbufs Process
   0   0      88464       1848    6169940          0          0 *Init*
   0   0        428    1987364        428          0          0 *Sched*
   0   0  116119836  105508736     487908     373944      55296 *Dead*
   1   0        284        284       3868          0          0 Load Meter
   2  66       5340       1080      17128          0          0 Virtual Exec
   3   0        668        284       7252          0          0 IpSecMibTopN
   4   0          0          0       6868          0          0 Check heaps
   5   0         96          0       6964          0          0 Chunk Manager
   6   0      17420     231276       6964       5388     254912 Pool Manager
   7   0        284        284       6868          0          0 Timers
   8   0        284        284       6868          0          0 Serial Background
```

Example 2-2   **show processes memory** *Command Output (Continued)*

```
 9   0          0          0       6868          0          0 ALARM_TRIGGER_SC
10   0        284        284       6868          0          0 Environmental mo
11   0        316    3799360       7184          0          0 ARP Input
12   0    2547784    1033916       7372       6804          0 DDR Timers
13   0        284        284      12868          0          0 Dialer event
14   0      10744       2284      15328          0          0 Entity MIB API
15   0         96          0       6964          0          0 SERIAL A'detect
16   0         96          0       6964          0          0 Critical Bkgnd
17   0      23412       2632      15404          0          0 Net Background
<more>
```

Table 2-10 describes the **show processes memory** command output's fields and descriptions.

Table 2-10   **show processes memory** *Command Output Description*

Field	Description
Total	Total amount of held memory
Used	Total amount of used memory
Free	Total amount of free memory
PID	Process ID
TTY	Terminal that controls the process
Allocated	Bytes of memory allocated by the process
Freed	Bytes of memory freed by the process, regardless of who originally allocated it
Holding	Amount of memory currently allocated to the process
Getbufs	Number of times the process has requested a packet buffer
Retbufs	Number of times the process has relinquished a packet buffer
Process	Process name *Init*: System initialization *Sched*: The scheduler *Dead*: Processes that are now dead as a group
Total (not shown in Example 2-2)	Total amount of memory held by all processes

Automatic Information Collection Examples

Figure 2-12 is a screen shot from the open-source Cacti application showing a list of devices found in the network.

Figure 2-12 *Cacti Device List Example*

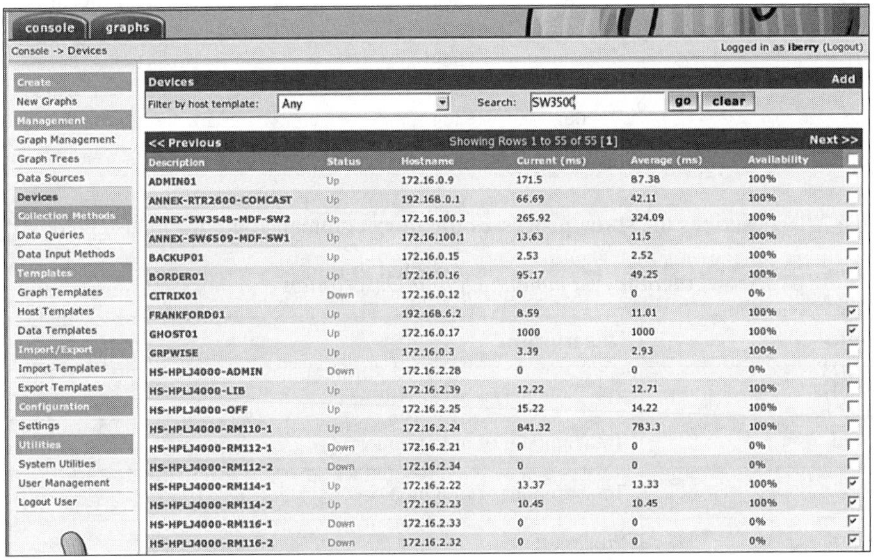

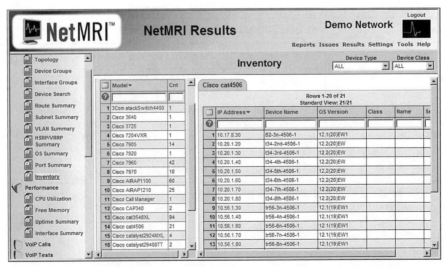

Figure 2-13 is a screen shot from the NetMRI appliance from Netcordia. The inventory results are expanded to show the Cisco Cat4506 devices, including IP addresses, device names, and operating system versions.

Figure 2-13 *NetMRI Inventory Example*

Analyzing Network Traffic and Applications

Traffic analysis is the third step in characterizing a network. Traffic analysis verifies the set of applications and protocols used in the network and determines the applications' traffic patterns. It might reveal any additional applications or protocols running on the network. Each discovered application and protocol should be described in the following terms:

- Importance to the customer

- QoS-related requirements

- Security-related requirements

- Scope (in other words, the network modules in which the application or protocol is used)

Use the following interactive approach, illustrated in Figure 2-14, to create a list of applications and protocols used in the network:

Step 1   Use customer input to list expected applications.

Step 2   Use traffic analyzers to verify the customer's list of applications.

Step 3   Present the customer with the new list of applications, and discuss discrepancies.

Step 4   Generate the final list of applications and their requirements (importance, QoS, security), as defined by the customer.

Figure 2-14   *Use an Interactive Traffic Analysis Process*

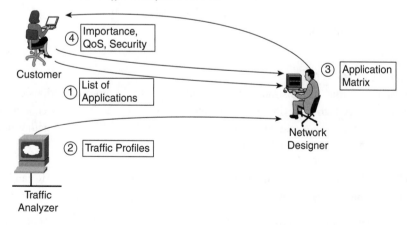

For example, the following information was collected about a fictitious application:

- Name: Application #8

- Description: Accounting software

- Protocol: Transmission Control Protocol (TCP) port 5151

- Servers: 2

- Clients: 50

- Scope: Campus

- Importance: High

- Avg. Rate: 50 kbps with 10-second bursts to 1 megabit per second (Mbps)

Assume that a customer requirement concerns QoS on a WAN connection with limited bandwidth. In this case, the information collected is relevant because it describes the following:

- The application (TCP port 5151), which is required for performing classification

- The importance of the application; this information is useful for evaluating how much bandwidth should be allocated to the application

- The current bandwidth consumption according to the present QoS implementation

Note, however, that this information might not be relevant should the customer requirement instead concern a secure and resilient Internet connection. In that case, it might be necessary to gather additional information.

Tools for Analyzing Traffic

Tools used for traffic analysis range from manual identification of applications using Cisco IOS software commands to those in which dedicated software- or hardware-based analyzers capture live packets or use the Simple Network Management Protocol (SNMP) to gather interface information. Analysis tools include the following:

- **Cisco IOS Network-Based Application Recognition (NBAR)**: NBAR can be used to identify the presence of well-known applications and protocols in the network.

- **Cisco IOS NetFlow technology**: NetFlow is an integral part of Cisco IOS software that collects and measures data as it enters specific routers or switch interfaces. NetFlow allows the identification of lesser-known applications because it gathers information about every flow. This information can be collected manually using the Cisco IOS software **show ip cache flow** command. Alternatively, Cisco Network Service (CNS) NetFlow Collection Engine (NFC) allows automatic information gathering of each flow in the network segment.

- **Third-party hardware or software-based products**: Can be used to analyze traffic in different subnets of the network. Examples include the following:

  — The open-source Cacti (http://www.cacti.net/)

  — Network General Sniffer (http://www.sniffer.com/)

  — WildPackets EtherPeek and AiroPeek (http://www.wildpackets.com/)

  — SolarWinds Orion (http://www.solarwindssoftware.com/)

  — Wireshark (http://www.wireshark.org/)

- Remote monitoring probes can also be used to support traffic analysis.

The following sections include examples of some of these tools.

NBAR

Cisco IOS NBAR is a classification engine that recognizes a wide variety of applications, including web-based and other difficult-to-classify protocols, which utilize dynamic TCP and User Datagram Protocol (UDP) port assignments. Other QoS tools within the network can be configured to invoke services for a specific application that is recognized and classified by NBAR, ensuring that network resources are used efficiently.

QoS

The purpose of QoS is to provide appropriate network resources (such as bandwidth, delay, jitter, and packet loss) to applications. QoS maximizes the return on network infrastructure investments by ensuring that mission-critical applications receive the required performance and that noncritical applications do not hamper the performance of critical applications. QoS is deployed by defining application classes or categories. These classes are defined using various classification techniques, such as NBAR, that are available in Cisco IOS software. After these classes are defined and configured, the desired QoS features—such as marking, congestion management, congestion avoidance, link efficiency mechanisms, or policing and shaping—can be applied to the classified traffic to provide the appropriate network resources among the defined classes. Therefore, classification is an important first step in configuring QoS in a network infrastructure.

NOTE   Further details about NBAR can be found at http://www.cisco.com/en/US/products/ps6616/products_ios_protocol_group_home.html.

Example 2-3 is sample output of the Cisco IOS NBAR **show ip nbar protocol-discovery** command. This command shows the statistics gathered by the NBAR Protocol Discovery feature, which provides an easy way to discover application protocols that are transiting an interface. The Protocol Discovery feature discovers any protocol traffic supported by NBAR and can be used to monitor both input and output traffic. This command displays statistics for all interfaces on which the Protocol Discovery feature is currently enabled. The default output of this command includes the average 30-second bit rate (in bits per second), input byte count, input packet count, and protocol name.

Example 2-3 **show ip nbar protocol-discovery** *Command Output*

```
Router#show ip nbar protocol-discovery
FastEthernet0/0.2
                      Input                   Output
    Protocol          Packet Count            Packet Count
                      Byte Count              Byte Count
                      30 second bit rate (bps) 30 second bit rate(bps)
    . . . . . . . . . . . . . .  . . . . . . . . . . . . . . .  . . . . . . . . . . . . .
    http              46384                   79364
                      5073520                 64042528
                      305                     1655

    secure-http       2762                    2886
                      429195                  1486350
                      0                       0
    snmp              143                     10676
                      17573                   1679322
                      0                       0
    telnet            1272                    12147
                      122284                  988834
                      0                       0
    ntp               5383                    0
                      624428                  0
                      0                       0
    dns               305                     235
                      31573                   55690
                      50                      120
```

NetFlow

NetFlow switching provides network administrators with access to detailed recording information from their data networks. NetFlow also provides a highly efficient mechanism with which to process security access lists without paying as much of a performance penalty as other available switching methods incur.

Cisco Network Service NetFlow Collection technology provides the base for applications, including network traffic accounting, usage-based network billing, network planning, network monitoring, outbound marketing, and data-mining capabilities for both service provider and enterprise customers. Cisco provides a set of NFC applications that collect NetFlow export data, perform data volume reduction and post-processing, and give end-user applications easy access to NFC data. NFC also provides measurement-based QoS by capturing the traffic classification or precedence associated with each flow, enabling differentiated charging based on QoS. NFC is supported on HPUX, Solaris, Linux, and the Cisco CNS Programmable Network Family product. Chapter 3, "Structuring and Modularizing the Network," discusses NetFlow technology in more detail.

Example 2-4 provides sample output from the Cisco IOS **show ip cache flow** command, illustrating statistics gathered by the NetFlow switching feature. By analyzing NetFlow data, a designer can identify the cause of congestion, determine the class of service for each user and application, and identify the traffic's source and destination network. NetFlow allows extremely granular and accurate traffic measurements and high-level aggregated traffic collection.

Example 2-4 **show ip cache flow** *Command Output*

```
Router#show ip cache flow

IP packet size distribution (12718M total packets):
   1-32   64   96  128  160  192  224  256  288  320  352  384  416  448  480
   .000 .554 .042 .017 .015 .009 .009 .009 .013 .030 .006 .007 .005 .004 .004

   512  544  576 1024 1536 2048 2560 3072 3584 4096 4608
   .003 .007 .139 .019 .098 .000 .000 .000 .000 .000 .000

IP Flow Switching Cache, 4456448 bytes
  65509 active, 27 inactive, 820628747 added
  955454490 ager polls, 0 flow alloc failures
  Exporting flows to 1.1.15.1 (2057)
  820563238 flows exported in 34485239 udp datagrams, 0 failed
  last clearing of statistics 00:00:03

Protocol         Total   Flows   Packets Bytes   Packets Active(Sec) Idle(Sec)
--------         Flows   /Sec    /Flow   /Pkt    /Sec    /Flow       /Flow
TCP-Telnet      2656855   4.3        86     78   372.3      49.6       27.6
TCP-FTP         5900082   9.5         9     71    86.8      11.4       33.1
TCP-FTPD        3200453   5.1       193    461  1006.3      45.8       33.4
TCP-WWW       546778274 887.3        12    325 11170.8       8.0       32.3
TCP-SMTP       25536863  41.4        21    283   876.5      10.9       31.3
TCP-BGP           24520   0.0        28    216     1.1      26.2       39.0
TCP-other      49148540  79.7        47    338  3752.6      30.7       32.2
UDP-DNS       117240379 190.2         3    112   570.8       7.5       34.7
UDP-NTP         9378269  15.2         1     76    16.2       2.2       38.7
```

continues

Example 2-4 **show ip cache flow** *Command Output (Continued)*

```
UDP-TFTP          8077    0.0      3   62     0.0    9.7    33.2
UDP-Frag         51161    0.0     14  322     1.2   11.0    39.4
ICMP          14837957   24.0      5  224   125.8   12.1    34.3
IP-other         77406    0.1     47  259     5.9   52.4    27.0
...
Total:       820563238 1331.7     15  304 20633.0    9.8    33.0
```

Table 2-11 provides the **show ip cache flow** command output's fields and descriptions.

Table 2-11 **show ip cache flow** *Command Output Description*

Field	Description
bytes	Number of bytes of memory used by the NetFlow cache
active	Number of active flows in the NetFlow cache at the time this command was executed
inactive	Number of flow buffers allocated in the NetFlow cache
added	Number of flows created since the start of the summary period
ager polls	Number of times the NetFlow code looked at the cache to expire entries
flow alloc failures	Number of times the NetFlow code tried to allocate a flow but could not
Exporting flows	IP address and UDP port number of the workstation to which flows are exported
flows exported	Total number of flows exported and the total number of UDP datagrams sent
failed	Number of flows that the router could not export
last clearing of statistics	Standard time output (hh:mm:ss) since the **clear ip flow stats** command was executed
The activity by each protocol display field descriptions are as follows:	
Protocol	IP protocol and the well-known port number (as documented at http://www.iana.org/)
Total Flows	Number of flows for this protocol since the last time statistics were cleared
Flows/Sec	Average number of flows seen for this protocol, per second
Packets/Flow	Average number of packets in the flows seen for this protocol
Bytes/Pkt	Average number of bytes in the packets seen for this protocol
Packets/Sec	Average number of packets for this protocol, per second

Table 2-11   **show ip cache flow** *Command Output Description (Continued)*

Field	Description
Active(Sec)/Flow	Sum of all the seconds from the first packet to the last packet of an expired flow
Idle(Sec)/Flow	Sum of all the seconds from the last packet seen in each non-expired flow

Other Network Analysis Tools Examples

Figure 2-15 shows sample output from the Cacti tool, illustrating the daily throughput on a link in Dallas.

Figure 2-15   *Cacti Can Display Daily Traffic*

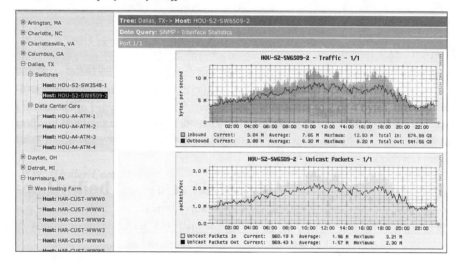

Figure 2-16 is a sample utilization table from the SolarWinds Orion tool, illustrating the current percentage utilization on the top 25 interfaces.

Figure 2-16 *SolarWinds Orion Tool Can Display Utilization*

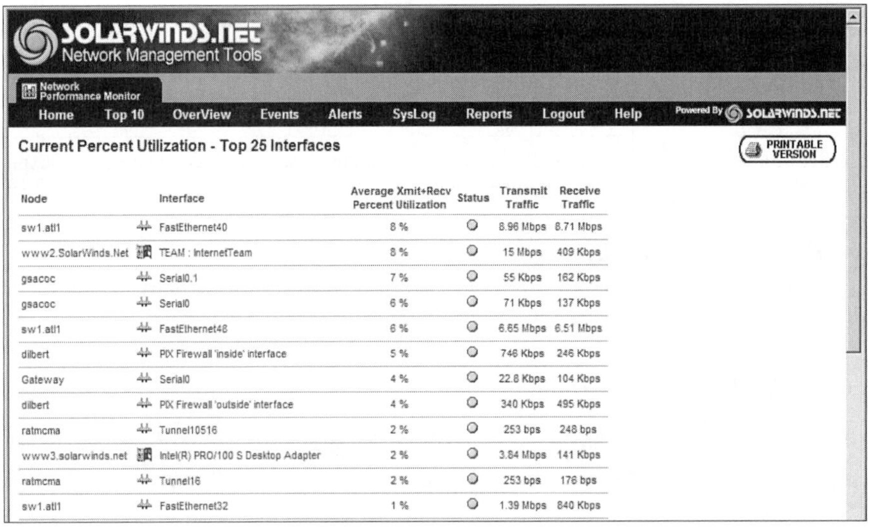

Current Percent Utilization - Top 25 Interfaces

Node	Interface	Average Xmit+Recv Percent Utilization	Status	Transmit Traffic	Receive Traffic
sw1.atl1	FastEthernet40	8 %		8.96 Mbps	8.71 Mbps
www2.SolarWinds.Net	TEAM : InternetTeam	8 %		15 Mbps	409 Kbps
gsacoc	Serial0.1	7 %		55 Kbps	162 Kbps
gsacoc	Serial0	6 %		71 Kbps	137 Kbps
sw1.atl1	FastEthernet48	6 %		6.65 Mbps	6.51 Mbps
dilbert	PIX Firewall 'inside' interface	5 %		746 Kbps	246 Kbps
Gateway	Serial0	4 %		22.8 Kbps	104 Kbps
dilbert	PIX Firewall 'outside' interface	4 %		340 Kbps	495 Kbps
ratmcma	Tunnel10516	2 %		253 bps	248 bps
www3.solarwinds.net	Intel(R) PRO/100 S Desktop Adapter	2 %		3.84 Mbps	141 Kbps
ratmcma	Tunnel16	2 %		253 bps	176 bps
sw1.atl1	FastEthernet32	1 %		1.39 Mbps	840 Kbps

Network Health Checklist

Based on the data gathered from the customer's network, the designer should check off any items that are true in the following Network Health Checklist. On a healthy network, it should be possible to check off all the items.

Note that these guidelines are only approximations. Exact thresholds depend on the type of traffic, applications, internetworking devices, topology, and criteria for accepting network performance. As every good engineer knows, the answer to most network performance questions (and most questions in general) is "It depends."

- ☐ No shared Ethernet segments are saturated (no more than 40 percent network utilization).
- ☐ No WAN links are saturated (no more than 70 percent network utilization).
- ☐ The response time is generally less than 100 milliseconds (1 millisecond = 1/1000 of a second; 100 milliseconds = 1/10 of a second).
- ☐ No segments have more than 20 percent broadcasts or multicasts.
- ☐ No segments have more than one cyclic redundancy check error per million bytes of data.
- ☐ On the Ethernet segments, less than 0.1 percent of the packets result in collisions.
- ☐ The Cisco routers are not overutilized (the 5-minute CPU utilization is no more than 75 percent).

☐   The number of output queue drops has not exceeded 100 in an hour on any Cisco router.

☐   The number of input queue drops has not exceeded 50 in an hour on any Cisco router.

☐   The number of buffer misses has not exceeded 25 in an hour on any Cisco router.

☐   The number of ignored packets has not exceeded 10 in an hour on any interface on a Cisco router.

The designer should also document any concerns about the existing network's health and its ability to support growth.

Summary Report

The result of the network characterization process is a summary report that describes the network's health. The customer input, network audit, and traffic analysis should provide enough information to identify possible problems in the existing network. The collected information must be collated into a concise summary report that identifies the following:

■   Features required in the network

■   Possible drawbacks of and problems in the existing network

■   Actions needed to support the new network's requirements and features

With this information, the designer should be able to propose hardware and software upgrades to support the customer requirements or to influence a change in requirements. Example 2-5 presents a sample summary report that identifies different aspects of a network infrastructure.

Example 2-5   *Sample Summary Report*

```
The network uses 895 routers:
-655 routers use Cisco IOS software version 12.3 or later
-221 routers use Cisco IOS software version 12.1(15)
-19 routers use Cisco IOS software version 12.0(25)


Requirement: QoS congestion management (queuing) required in the WAN
Identified problem:
-Cisco IOS software version 12.0 does not support new queuing technologies
-15 out of 19 routers with Cisco IOS software 12.0 are in the WAN
-12 out of 15 routers do not have enough memory to upgrade to Cisco IOS
software version 12.3 or later
-5 out of 15 routers do not have enough flash memory to upgrade to Cisco IOS
software version 12.3 or later


Recommended action:
-12 memory upgrades to 64 Megabytes (MB), 5 FLASH upgrades to 16MB
Alternatives:
```

continues

Example 2-5 *Sample Summary Report (Continued)*

```
-Replace hardware as well as software to support queuing
-Find an alternative mechanism for that part of the network
-Find an alternative mechanism and use it instead of queuing
-Evaluate the consequences of not implementing the required feature in that part of the
network
```

The summary report conclusions should identify the existing infrastructure's shortcomings. In Example 2-5, QoS congestion management (queuing) is required. However, the designer has identified that Cisco IOS software version 12.0 does not support the newest queuing technologies. In addition, some routers do not have enough RAM and flash memory for an upgrade.

Summary report recommendations relate the existing network and the customer requirements. These recommendations can be used to propose upgrading of hardware and software to support the required features or modifying the customer requirements. In this example, options include evaluating the necessity of the queuing requirement in the WAN.

Creating a Draft Design Document

After thoroughly examining the existing network, the designer creates a draft design document. Figure 2-17 illustrates a draft design document's index (not yet fully developed), including the section that describes the existing network. The "Design Requirements" and "Existing Network Infrastructure" chapters of the design document are closely related—examining the existing network can result in changes to the design requirements. Data from both chapters directly influences the network's design.

Figure 2-17 *Draft Design Document Index*

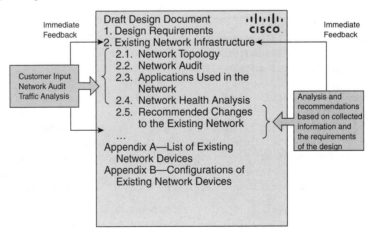

Typical draft documentation for an existing network should include the following items:

■ Logical (Layer 3) topology map or maps. Divide the topology into network modules if the network is too large to fit into one topology map.

■ Physical (Layer 1) topology map or maps.

■ The network audit results, including the types of traffic in the network, the traffic congestion points, the suboptimal traffic paths, and so on.

■ A summary section describing the major network services used in the existing network, such as Open Shortest Path First (OSPF), Border Gateway Protocol (BGP), and Internet Protocol Security (IPsec).

■ A summary description of applications and overlay services used in the network.

■ A summary description of issues that might affect the design or the established design requirements.

■ A list of existing network devices, with the platform and software versions.

■ Configurations of existing network devices, usually attached as either a separate document or an appendix to the design document.

Time Estimates for Performing Network Characterization

This section provides some guidelines to estimate how long it may take to characterize the network. The time required to characterize a network varies significantly, depending on factors such as the following:

■ The experience of the network engineer

■ The quality of documentation provided by the customer and the quality of the communication with the customer

■ The size and complexity of network

■ The efficiency of network management and discovery tools

■ Whether or not the network devices are carefully managed via SNMP

■ How much information is needed for the scope of the project

Figure 2-18 provides a range of time estimates, in hours, for the characterization of networks in a variety of sizes. These estimates assume a highly skilled (Cisco Certified Internet Expert level) network engineer with efficient automated tools for network discovery and performance gathering, and a network in which the devices communicate with SNMP. The network characterization includes strategic evaluation and possible network redesign.

Figure 2-18 *Network Characterization Estimates (in Hours)*

	Small Network 1-20 Switches/ Routers		Medium Network 20-200 Switches/ Routers		Large Network 200-800 Switches/ Routers		Very Large Network >800 Switches/ Routers	
a) Interview management team	4	4	8	8	12	12	16	16
b) Interview network team	4	4	6	6	8	12	24	24
c) Review documentation	4	4	6	6	8	12	16	16
d) Set up network discovery tool	4	4	6	6	8	8	16	16
e) Resolve SNMP access and similar problems	4	4	8	16	16	48	80	160
f) Allow tools to gather data	Variable		Variable		Variable		Variable	
g) Analyze captured data	4	8	16	16	24	24	40	40
h) Prepare high-level Layer 3 diagrams	4	4	4	8	8	16	16	32
i) Prepare report stating conclusions	16	16	32	32	48	48	80	80
j) Incremental effort to prepare network diagrams	Not Included		Not Included		Not Included		Not Included	
Total estimated manpower, in hours	44 - 48		86 - 98		132 - 180		288 - 384	

The steps in Figure 2-18 are as follows:

a. Interviewing the management team to gather goals and constraints.

b. Interviewing the network team, and gathering goals, constraints, documentation, and diagrams.

c. Reviewing documentation and diagrams, and clarifying items with the site team.

d. Setting up the network discovery tool, which typically involves using automated discovery or entering a device list or IP address range into the tool; verifying that the tool has found most routers and switches; and starting to collect performance data.

e. Resolving SNMP access and similar problems if devices have not been very carefully managed in the past.

f. Allowing the discovery tool to gather data. The time for this step will vary depending on network, and should include seasonal or cyclical factors, but generally one week of data is sufficient. The network engineer typically does not need to oversee this process.

g. Analyzing the captured data; minimizing the time required is dependent on using efficient tools.

h. Preparing high-level (Layer 3) diagrams of the proposed network.

i. Preparing the report of conclusions and recommendations.

> **NOTE**   These estimates do not include the time needed to prepare detailed network diagrams if the customer does not supply them.

Consequently, network characterization typically takes from one to many weeks of effort, depending on the size and complexity of the network and the other factors mentioned at the beginning of this section.

Using the Top-Down Approach to Network Design

After establishing the organizational requirements and documenting the existing network, the designer is ready to design a network solution. This section first discusses the top-down approach to network design. Decision tables and structured design are described, and the section includes a brief discussion of the types of network design tools that might be used. The section concludes with a discussion about building a pilot or prototype, and the contents of a detailed design document.

The Top-Down Approach to Network Design

Designing a large or even medium-sized network can be a complex project. Procedures have been developed to facilitate the design process by dividing it into smaller, more manageable steps. Identifying the separate steps or tasks ensures a smooth process and reduces potential risks.

A *top-down design* allows the designer to "see the big picture" before getting to the details. Top-down design clarifies the design goals and initiates the design from the perspective of the required applications. The top-down approach adapts the physical infrastructure to the needs of the applications. Network devices are chosen only after a thorough requirements analysis. Structured design practices should be integrated with the top-down approach, especially in very complex networks.

In contrast to top-down design, the network design approach in which network devices and technologies are selected first is called *bottom-up*, or *connect-the-dots*. This approach often results in an inappropriate network for the required services and is primarily used when a very quick response to the design request is needed. With a bottom-up approach, the risk of having to redesign the network is high.

Guidelines for producing a top-down design include the following:

- Thoroughly analyze the customer's requirements.

- Initiate the design from the top of the OSI model. In other words, define the upper OSI layers (application, presentation, and session) first, and then define the lower OSI layers (transport, network, data link, and physical)—the infrastructure (routers, switches, and media) that is required.

- Gather additional data about the network (protocol behavior, scalability requirements, additional requirements from the customer, and so forth) that might influence the logical and physical design. Adapt the design to the new data, as required.

Top-Down Approach Compared to Bottom-Up Approach

A top-down approach to design has many benefits compared to a bottom-up approach, including the following:

- Incorporating the customer organization's requirements

- Providing the customer and the designer with the "big picture" of the desired network

- Providing a design that is appropriate for both current requirements and future development

The disadvantage of the top-down approach is that it is more time-consuming than the bottom-up approach; it necessitates a requirement analysis so that the design can be adapted to the identified needs.

A benefit of the bottom-up approach—selecting the devices and technologies and then moving toward services and applications—is that it allows a quick response to a design request. This design approach facilitates designs based on the designer's previous experience.

The major disadvantage of the bottom-up approach is that it can result in an inappropriate design, leading to costly redesign.

Top-Down Design Example

Consider an example that uses the basics of the top-down approach when designing an IP telephony network solution. In this example, the customer requires a network that can support IP telephony. IP telephony permits the use of the same network resources for both data and voice transport, thus reducing the costs of having two separate networks. To achieve this, the network must support Voice over IP (VoIP) technology; this first step in the design process is illustrated in Figure 2-19.

Figure 2-19   *A Voice over IP Network Is Required for IP Telephony*

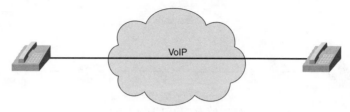

Figure 2-20 illustrates the addition of an IP-based network, which is required to support VoIP. The network includes IP-enabled routers and other devices not shown in the figure. The IP network's delay is also managed; to achieve this, specific QoS mechanisms are also implemented in the network, as indicated in Figure 2-20.

Figure 2-20   *IP and QoS Are Required for VoIP*

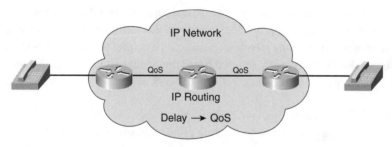

Figure 2-21 illustrates the addition of the call monitoring and management function. This function was previously overlooked because such functions were traditionally handled by a PBX on a separate voice network; during the top-down design, it became clear that this function is necessary. A Cisco Unified Communications Manager is therefore placed inside the network to manage and monitor IP telephone calls.

> **NOTE**   Cisco Unified Communications Manager is a server-based application that establishes and maintains signaling and control for IP telephone sessions.
>
> IP telephony is described further in Chapter 8, "Voice Network Design Considerations."

Figure 2-21 *Cisco Unified Communications Manager Is Required for Monitoring and Managing VoIP Calls*

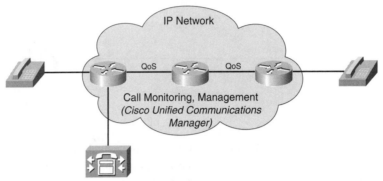

Decision Tables in Network Design

Decision tables are used for making systematic decisions when there are multiple solutions or options to a network issue or problem. Decision tables facilitate the selection of the most appropriate option from many possibilities and can be helpful for justifying why a certain solution was chosen. Options are usually selected based on the highest level of compliance with given requirements. Basic guidelines for creating a network design decision table include the following:

Step 1   Determine the network building block about which decisions will be made (the physical topology, routing protocol, security implementation, and so on).

Step 2   Collect possible options for each decision. Be certain to include all options (or as many as possible) to obtain maximum value from the decision table. A thorough survey of the existing state of technology and considerable knowledge are needed to include all options.

Step 3   Create a table of the possible options and the given requirements. Include the relevant parameters or properties.

Step 4   Match the given requirements with the specific properties of the given options.

Step 5   Select the most appropriate option—the option with the most matches—if all requirements are treated equally. However, if some requirements are considered more important than others, implement a weighting system such that each of the requirements is assigned a weight that is proportional to its importance in the decision-making process.

Figure 2-22 is an example of a decision table for selecting a routing protocol based on multiple criteria. In this example, several routing protocols are considered as possible options: OSPF,

Intermediate System–to–Intermediate System (IS-IS), Enhanced Interior Gateway Routing Protocol (EIGRP), and BGP. Five required parameters are listed, along with an indication of how well the routing protocols comply with these parameters. As indicated in the figure, the chosen protocol should include the following properties:

- It should support a large network. All the protocols being considered meet this requirement.

- It must be Enterprise-focused, rather than Internet service provider–focused. BGP was designed to support interconnecting networks of autonomous systems; it is not optimized for use in the enterprise. IS-IS is typically deployed in service provider environments, rather than in enterprises.

- Support for variable-length subnet mask (VLSM) is required. All the protocols being considered support VLSM.

- It must be supported on Cisco routers, which is the case for all the protocols being considered.

- Network support staff should have a good knowledge of the chosen protocol to enable them to troubleshoot the network. In this case, the network support staff are knowledgeable about EIGRP, but not about OSPF, IS-IS, or BGP.

NOTE   All requirements in this example have the same level of importance, so no weights are used.

Based on the stated requirements, EIGRP is the routing protocol of choice in this example.

Figure 2-22 *Sample Decision Table for Routing Protocol Selection*

Options Parameters	EIGRP	OSPF	IS-IS	BGP	Required Network Parameters
Size of Network (Small/Medium/ Large/Very Large)	Large	Large	Very Large	Very Large	Large
Enterprise-Focused (Yes/No)	Yes	Yes	No	No	Yes
Support for VLSM (Yes/No)	Yes	Yes	Yes	Yes	Yes
Supports Cisco Routers (Yes/No)	Yes	Yes	Yes	Yes	Yes
Network Support Staff Knowledge (Good/Fair/Poor)	Good	Fair	Poor	Poor	Good

Structured Design

The output of the design should be a model of the complete system. The top-down approach is highly recommended. Rather than focusing on the network components, technologies, or protocols, instead focus on the business goals, technical objectives, and existing and future network applications and services.

Structured design focuses on a systematic approach, dividing the design task into related, less complex components, as follows:

■ First, identify the applications needed to support the customer's requirements.

■ Next, identify the applications' logical connectivity requirements, with a focus on the necessary infrastructure services and network infrastructure.

■ Split the network functionally to develop the network infrastructure and hierarchy requirements.

NOTE   This book uses the Cisco Enterprise Architecture to provide consistent infrastructure modularization, as described in Chapter 3.

■ Design each of the functional elements separately, yet in relation to other elements. For example, the network infrastructure and infrastructure services designs are tightly connected; they are both bound to the same logical, physical, and functional models. Use the top-down approach during all designs.

After identifying the connectivity requirements, the designer works on each of the functional module's details. The network infrastructure and infrastructure services are composed of logical structures. Each of these structures (such as addressing, routing protocols, QoS, security, and so forth) must be designed separately, but in close relation to other structures, with a goal of creating one homogenous network.

Some logical structures are more closely related than others. Network infrastructure elements are more closely related to each other than to infrastructure services, and infrastructure services are more closely related to each other than to network infrastructure elements. For example, physical topology and addressing design are very closely related, whereas addressing and QoS design are not.

Several approaches to physically structuring a network module exist. The most common approach is a three-layer hierarchical structure: core, distribution, and access. In this approach, three separate, yet related, physical structures are developed instead of a single, large network, resulting in meaningful and functionally homogeneous elements within each layer. Selecting the functionality and required technologies is easier when it is applied to separate structured network elements than when it is applied to the complex network.

> **NOTE**   Chapter 3 discusses the hierarchical model in detail.

Figure 2-23 is an example of how a network design can be divided into smaller, yet related sections using structured design practices.

Figure 2-23   *Structured Design Example*

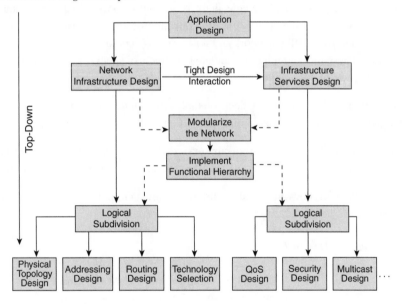

In this example, network infrastructure design and infrastructure services design are tightly connected; both are bound to the same logical, physical, and functional models. These elements are subdivided logically. The network infrastructure design is subdivided into physical topology design, addressing design, routing design, and technology selection. The infrastructure services design is subdivided into QoS design, security design, and multicast design. All design phases use the top-down approach.

Network Design Tools

Several types of tools can be used to ease the task of designing a complex modern network, including the following:

- **Network modeling tools**: Network modeling tools are helpful when a lot of input design information (such as customer requirements, network audit and analysis results, and so on) exists. Network modeling tools enable modeling of both simple and complex networks. The tools process the information provided and return a proposed configuration, which can be modified and reprocessed to add redundant links, support additional sites, and so forth.

- **Strategic analysis tools**: Strategic analysis or what-if tools help designers and other people who are working on the design (engineers, technologists, and business and marketing professionals) to develop network and service plans, including detailed technical and business analysis. These tools attempt to calculate the effects of specific network components through simulated scenarios.

- **Decision tables**: As discussed, decision tables are manual tools for choosing specific network characteristics from multiple options, based on required parameters.

- **Simulation and verification tools or services**: These tools or services are used to verify the acquired design, thereby lessening the need for a pilot network implementation.

Figure 2-24 illustrates how the initial requirements information is processed with network design tools to produce a network design.

Figure 2-24   *Using Network Design Tools*

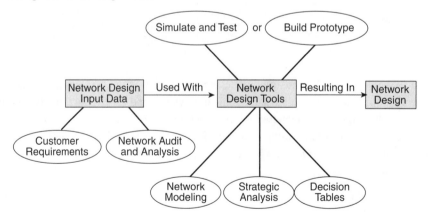

To verify a network design that was produced with the help of network modeling tools, strategic analysis tools, and decision tables, either use simulation and test tools or build a pilot or prototype network. The pilot or prototype network also creates a proof of concept that confirms the appropriateness of the design implementation plan.

Building a Prototype or Pilot Network

It is often desirable to verify a design before implementation. A design can be tested in an existing, or live, network—this is called a pilot—or, preferably, in a prototype network that does not affect the existing network. A successful design implementation in either a pilot or prototype network can be used as a proof of concept in preparation for full implementation and can be used as input to the implementation steps.

KEY POINT | A pilot network tests and verifies the design before the network is launched, or is a subset of the existing network in which the design is tested.

A pilot network is normally used when the design is for a completely new network; pilots can also be used for designs that add to an existing network.

A prototype network tests and verifies a redesign in an isolated network, before it is applied to the existing network. A prototype network is usually used to verify designs that must be implemented on an existing network infrastructure.

It is important that the pilot or prototype test the design, including the customer's most important stated requirements. For example, if a key requirement is minimal response time for remote users, ensure that the prototype or pilot verifies that the maximum acceptable response time is not exceeded.

A prototype or pilot implementation can have one of two results:

- **Success**: This result is usually enough to prove the design concept.

- **Failure**: This result is normally used to correct the design; the prototype or pilot phase is then repeated. In the case of small deviations, the design can be corrected and tested in the prototype or pilot network immediately.

Figure 2-25 is a sample topology subset of a planned network. The highlighted areas indicate the parts of the network involved in a redesign. This part of the topology is implemented first in a prototype to verify the design.

Figure 2-25 *A Prototype Network*

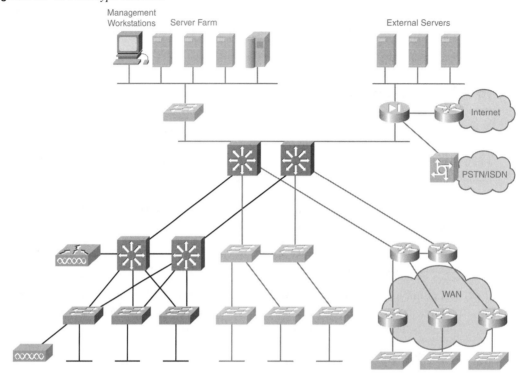

Documenting the Design

A design document lists the design requirements, documents the existing network and the network design, identifies the proof-of-concept strategy and results, and details the implementation plan. The final design document structure should be similar to the one in Figure 2-26, which includes the following:

- **Introduction**: Every design document should include an introduction to present the main reasons leading to the network design or redesign.

- **Design requirements**: Also a mandatory part of any design document, this section includes the organization's requirements and design goals that must be fulfilled.

- **Existing network infrastructure**: This section is required only for a network redesign. The subsections document the results of the existing network characterization steps.

- **Design**: This section is an essential part of the design document and identifies the design and implementation details. The design details documented will obviously differ depending on the type of design project (whether it is a completely new network, a network redesign, or simply a new service introduction, for example), but they typically include the topology, addressing, and design. Implementation details, such as configuration templates and exact configurations of network devices, are included to ease the implementation process.

- **Proof of concept**: This section describes the pilot or prototype network verification and test results.

- **Implementation plan**: This section provides the implementation details that technical staff need to carry out as quickly and smoothly as possible, without requiring the presence of the designer.

- **Appendixes**: The appendixes usually include lists and, optionally, configurations of existing network devices.

Figure 2-26 *Sample Design Document*

```
Design Document Index         cisco.
1. Introduction
2. Design Requirements
3. Existing Network Infrastructure
   3.1. Network topology
   3.2. Network audit
   3.3. Applications used in the
        network
   3.4. Network health analysis
   3.5. Recommended changes to the
        existing network
4. Design
   4.1. Design summary
   4.2. Design details
      4.2.1. Topology design
      4.2.2. Addressing design
      4.2.3. EIGRP design
      4.2.4. Security design
   ...
```

```
   4.3. Implementation details
      4.3.1. Configuration templates
             for campus devices
      4.3.2. Configuration templates
             for WAN devices
   ...
5. Proof of Concept
   5.1. Pilot or prototype network
   5.2. Test results
6. Implementation Plan
   6.1. Summary
   6.2. Implementation steps

Appendix A—List of existing network
devices
Appendix B—Configurations of
existing network devices
```

The Design Implementation Process

After the design is complete, the design implementation process is executed.

Planning a Design Implementation

Planning and documenting the design implementation is the first step in this process. The design implementation description should be as detailed as possible. The more detailed the design documentation, the less knowledgeable the network engineer must be to implement the design. Very complex implementation steps usually require that the designer carry out the implementation, whereas other staff members (or another company) can perform well-documented, detailed implementation steps.

Implementation must consider the possibility of a failure, even after a successful pilot or prototype network test. The plan should therefore include a test at every step and a rollback plan to revert to the original setup if a problem occurs. List implementation steps and estimated times in a table.

If a design is composed of multiple complex implementation steps, plan to implement each step separately rather than all at once. In case of failure, incremental implementation reduces troubleshooting and reduces the time needed to revert to a previous state. Implementation of a network design consists of several phases (install hardware, configure systems, launch into production, and so forth). Each phase consists of several steps, and the documentation for each step should contain the following:

- Description of the step

- References to design documents

- Detailed implementation guidelines

- Detailed rollback guidelines in case of failure

- Estimated time necessary for implementation

Figure 2-27 illustrates a sample implementation plan summary.

Figure 2-27   *Sample Summary Design Implementation Plan*

	Date Time	Description	Implementation Details	Complete
Phase 3	04/02/2007	Install campus hardware	Section 6.2.3	✓
Step 1		Connect switches	Section 6.2.3.1	✓
Step 2		Install routers	Section 6.2.3.2	✓
Step 3		Complete cabling	Section 6.2.3.3	✓
Step 4		Verify data link layer	Section 6.2.3.4	✓
Phase 4	04/03/2007	Configure campus hardware	Section 6.2.4	
Step 1		Configure VLANs		
Step 2		Configure IP addressing	Section 6.2.4.1	
Step 3		Configure routing	Section 6.2.4.2	
Step 4		Verify connectivity	Section 6.2.4.3	
Phase 5	04/02/2007	Launch campus updates into production	Section 6.2.4.4 Section 6.2.5	
Step 1	...	Complete connections to existing network	Section 6.2.5.1	
Step 2		Verify connectivity	Section 6.2.5.2	

In Figure 2-27, each step of the implementation phase is briefly described, with references to the detailed implementation plan for further details. The detailed implementation plan section should describe precisely what needs to be accomplished.

Figure 2-28 provides a detailed description of an implementation step. It describes the configuration of EIGRP on 50 routers in the network and lists the two major components of the step (in the per-router configuration procedure).

Figure 2-28 *Sample Detailed Design Implementation Step*

- Section 6.2.7.3, "Configure routing protocols in the WAN network module":
  - Number of routers involved is 50.
  - Use template from section 4.2.3, "EIGRP details."
  - Per router configuration:
    - Use **passive-interface** command on all nonbackbone LANs. (See section 4.2.3, "EIGRP details")
    - Use summarization according to the design. (See section 4.2.3, "EIGRP details," and section 4.2.2, "Addressing details")
  - Estimated time is 10 minutes per router.
  - Roll-back procedure: Remove EIGRP configuration on all routers.

The reference to the design document is useful for retrieving the details about the EIGRP implementation.

Implementing and Verifying the Design

Successful implementation of the pilot or prototype network might have already concluded work on the design. However, implementation is the designed network's first actual test. Even if a pilot or prototype network was used as a proof of concept, only the actual implementation reveals any design weaknesses. The design's final confirmation is the full, live network implementation. As part of the implementation phase, the designer assists with the design verification and takes remedial actions, if necessary.

The design document should include a list of checks to be performed both during the pilot or prototype phase and during the implementation, to ensure that the network is functioning as required.

Monitoring and Redesigning the Network

The network is put into operation after it is built. During operation, the network is constantly monitored and checked for errors and problems. A network redesign might be required if troubleshooting problems become too frequent or even impossible to manage. For example, at least a partial redesign might be necessary if the new network is consistently congested. Solutions might include increasing bandwidth, adding filters, upgrading to devices with more capacity, moving servers that are in high use, and so forth. Hopefully this scenario can be avoided if all previous design steps have been completed properly.

Summary

In this chapter you learned about the principles of network design, with a focus on the following topics:

- The three phases of the Cisco SONA architectural framework: integrated transport, services, and applications

- The three layers of the Cisco SONA architectural framework: networked infrastructure, interactive (infrastructure) services, and application

- The PPDIOO network lifecycle

- The network design methodology based on this lifecycle, which has three basic steps:

   — Identify customer requirements

   — Characterize the existing network and sites

   — Design the network topology

- The design implementation process, which also has three basic steps:

   — Plan the implementation

   — Implement and verify the design

   — Monitor and optionally redesign

References

For additional information, see the following resources:

- Service Oriented Network Architecture Introduction, http://www.cisco.com/go/sona/

- Lifecycle Services Strategy Introduction, http://www.cisco.com/en/US/products/ps6890/serv_category_home.html

- Oppenheimer, P. *Top-Down Network Design*, Second Edition. Indianapolis: Cisco Press, 2004.

Case Study: ACMC Hospital Network Upgrade

This case study analyzes the network infrastructure of Acme County Medical Center (ACMC) Hospital, a fictitious small county hospital in the United States. This same case study is used throughout the remainder of the book so that you can continue to evaluate your understanding of the concepts presented.

Case Study General Instructions

Use the scenarios, information, and parameters provided at each task of the ongoing case study. If you encounter ambiguities, make reasonable assumptions and proceed. For all tasks, use the initial customer scenario and build on the solutions provided thus far. You can use any and all documentation, books, white papers, and so on.

In each step, you act as a network design consultant. Make creative proposals to accomplish the customer's business needs. Justify your ideas when they differ from the provided solutions. Use any design strategies you feel are appropriate. The final goal of each case study is a paper solution.

Appendix A, "Answers to Review Questions and Case Studies," provides a solution for each step based on assumptions made. There is no claim that the provided solution is the best or only solution. Your solution might be more appropriate for the assumptions you made. The provided solution helps you understand the author's reasoning and allows you to compare and contrast your solution.

In this case study, you develop a high-level design for the ACMC Hospital network.

Case Study Scenario

This case study analyzes the network infrastructure of ACMC Hospital, a fictitious small county hospital. The hospital has provided you with a short description of the current situation and its plans. As a network designer, it is your job to identify all the organization's requirements and data that will allow you to provide an effective solution.

Organizational Facts

ACMC Hospital is a medium-sized regional hospital located in Acme County, with approximately 500 staff members supporting up to 1000 patients. The hospital is interested in updating its main facility (which uses equipment from various vendors) in its Layer 2 campus. You are meeting to define the client's requirements.

ACMC has 15 buildings in total on the campus, plus 5 small remote clinics. There are two main hospital buildings and an auxiliary building. The two main buildings have seven floors each, with four wiring closets per floor. The auxiliary building—the Children's Place—is connected to the two main buildings; the switches from these three buildings are connected with fiber connections in a ring. The Children's Place has three floors, with three wiring closets per floor. The other 12 campus buildings are smaller office and support facilities, with 10 to 40 people per building, located on one or two floors.

The network architect is new to the hospital. The hospital is aggressively expanding its clinic and alternative emergency room presence within Acme County. Due to population growth in general, plans to enlarge the main campus are also under way. The hospital is doing fairly well financially. It wants to selectively deploy cutting-edge technology for better patient care and high productivity. Management is tired of network downtime and slowness affecting patient care. Network manageability is important because ACMC has a tradition of basing operations on small support staffs with high productivity. ACMC's upgrade timeframe is 6 to 12 months.

Current Situation

The current network uses inexpensive switches from several vendors, purchased over time. They comply with various standards, depending on when they were purchased. The switches are not SNMP-manageable, although a small amount of information is available from each switch via the web or command-line interface.

Within each of the three main buildings is a main switch. One floor switch from each floor connects to the main switch. The other switches connect either directly to the floor switch or via a daisy chain of switches, depending on which was most convenient at the time.

The small outlying buildings have one or two 24-port switches. One of these connects back to one of the main building switches via fiber. If there is a second switch, it connects via the first switch.

Currently, the staff VLAN spans the entire campus. No Layer 3 switching is present. The address space is 172.16.0.0 /16. Addresses are coded sequentially into PCs as they are deployed. Staff members have been meaning to deploy DHCP but have not had the time.

The applications that the organization is currently running include standard office applications, plus some specialized medical tools running over IP. Radiology, Oncology, and other departments do medical imaging. As these departments acquire new tools, they are adding real-time motion to the highly detailed medical images, requiring large amounts of bandwidth. All the new servers are capable of using Gigabit or Gigabit EtherChannel connectivity.

Many servers are currently located in various closets. Many lack uninterrupted power supplies or proper environmental controls. A staff member has to roll a tape backup cart to each server closet to back up each server. There are about 40 centrally located servers in one raised floor "server room," and 30 other servers distributed around the campus near their users. The server room takes up part of the first floor of Main Building 1, along with the cafeteria and other non-networked areas.

Hospital Support Services has been experimenting with workstations on wheels (WoW). Moving these and plugging them into an Ethernet jack is just not working very well.

The WAN uses 56-kbps links to three of the remote clinics and dialup connectivity to the other two. The one router uses static routing that was configured by a previous network designer.

The staff members have frequently complained about slow response times. There appears to be severe congestion of the LAN, especially at peak hours. The staff provided you with a copy of its recent network diagram, which is shown in Figure 2-29.

Figure 2-29 *ACMC Network Diagram Provided by the Customer*

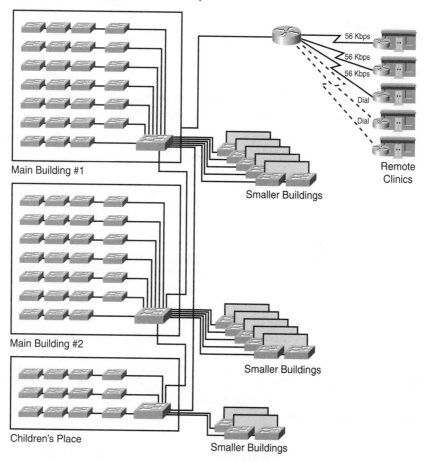

You believe that the current situation does not provide for future growth, high reliability, and ease of management.

Plans and Requirements

The introduction of new applications will result in an additional load on the links to the remote clinics. The expected tighter integration and growth of remote offices will even further increase the traffic load on the WAN links. The hospital would like to upgrade the WAN infrastructure to provide sufficient bandwidth between the remote clinics and headquarters and, at the same time, find a solution for better convergence during network failures. The company is aware of the drawbacks of its current IP addressing scheme and is seeking a better solution.

The hospital must comply with the U.S. Health Insurance Portability and Accountability Act (HIPAA).

Case Study Questions

Complete the following steps:

Step 1   Document ACMC's requirements.

Step 2   Document any information that you think is missing from the case study scenario and that you consider necessary for the design.

Before beginning the design, you will need this information. Assume that you have talked to the customer about the missing information, and document any assumptions you make. You don't need to assume that all the missing information is provided by the customer; some might never be available. However, you do need to assume answers for your critical questions.

NOTE   Further information is provided in the case studies in subsequent chapters, as relevant for that chapter. Thus, not all the information is provided in these answers.

Step 3   Outline the major design areas that you feel need to be addressed when designing the solution for this scenario. List the tasks, and provide a brief comment for each.

NOTE   There are many ways, other than those provided in our answer, in which this customer's network could be improved. Further information is provided in the case studies in subsequent chapters, and other options are discussed, as relevant for that chapter.

Review Questions

Answer the following questions, and then refer to Appendix A for the answers.

1. What features are included in the Cisco vision of an intelligent network?

2. Describe the three phases of evolving to an intelligent information network.

3. Describe the three layers of the SONA framework.

4. Name some of the benefits of using the SONA framework.

5. Match the PPDIOO network lifecycle phases with their correct descriptions.

   Phases:

   a. Prepare phase

   b. Plan phase

   c. Design phase

   d. Implement phase

   e. Operate phase

   f. Optimize phase

   1. The network is built

   2. A network design specification is produced

   3. Includes fault detection and correction and performance monitoring

   4. Network requirements are identified

   5. Business requirements and strategy related to the network are established

   6. Based on proactive management of the network

6. During which PPDIOO phase is the initial design verification performed?

7. What are the three basic steps of the design methodology?

8. What steps are needed to implement a design?

9. List some determinants of the scope of a design project.

10. What steps are involved in gathering network requirements?

11. Corporation X is planning to introduce new systems for its employees, including e-learning, groupware, videoconferencing, and an alternative telephone service to reduce its operational costs. Which of the following is a planned application?

    a. E-mail

    b. IP multicast

    c. Cisco Unified MeetingPlace

    d. Quality of service

12. What are some typical organizational goals?

13. Corporation X is currently spending $7000 per month for telephony services provided by its local phone company. The new IP telephony equipment costs $40,000, and the operating costs are $2000 per month. When will the introduction of IP telephony pay for itself?

    a. After eight months.

    b. After five months.

    c. After one year.

    d. It will not pay for itself.

14. List some common organizational constraints.

15. Explain why a schedule might be a design constraint.

16. Users typically think of network performance in terms of what?

    a. Throughput

    b. Responsiveness

    c. Resource utilization

17. How might bandwidth be a technical constraint for a network design?

18. How does traffic analysis help in the characterization of a network?

19. List some site contact information that would be important for projects involving remote deployments when equipment delivery and installations must be coordinated.

20. True or false: The auditing process should never require any changes in the network?

21. List some tools that can be used in the network assessment process.

22. Which command can be used to determine memory usage on a Cisco router?

    a. **show processes memory**

    b. **show processes cpu**

    c. **show memory utilization**

    d. **show version**

23. Which command displays packet size distribution and activity by protocol on a Cisco router?

   a. **show ip nbar protocol-discovery**

   b. **show ip interface**

   c. **show version**

   d. **show ip cache flow**

24. What is the difference between a saturated Ethernet segment and a saturated WAN link?

25. The network health summary report includes recommendations that _____.

   a. relate the existing network and the customer requirements

   b. are based on the customer requirements

   c. are used to sell more boxes

26. True or false: Characterization of a network can typically be completed in a few hours.

27. With a top-down design: (choose three)

   a. The design adapts the physical infrastructure to the requirements.

   b. The design adapts the requirements to the physical infrastructure.

   c. Network devices are chosen after requirement analysis.

   d. Network devices are selected first.

   e. The risk of having to redesign the network is high.

   f. The risk of having to redesign the network is low.

28. What are the layers in the three-layer hierarchical structure?

   a. Core, distribution, and desktop

   b. Core, distribution, and access

   c. Core, routing, and access

   d. Backbone, routing, and access

29. What types of tools can be used during the network design process?

30. What is the difference between a pilot and a prototype?

31. What sections are included in a typical final design document?

32. What items should be included in the documentation for a network design implementation plan?

33. Why is the network designer involved in the implementation phase?

34. What might necessitate a redesign of the network?

This chapter introduces a modular hierarchical approach to network design, the Cisco Enterprise Architecture. This chapter includes the following sections:

- Network Hierarchy

- Using a Modular Approach to Network Design

- Services Within Modular Networks

- Network Management Protocols and Features

- Summary

- References

- Case Study: ACMC Hospital Modularity

- Review Questions

CHAPTER 3

Structuring and Modularizing the Network

This chapter introduces a modular hierarchical approach to network design, the Cisco Enterprise Architecture. The chapter begins with a discussion of the hierarchical network structure. The next section introduces network modularization and discusses the details of the Cisco Enterprise Architecture. Following that are a detailed description of services within modular networks, and a discussion of network management protocols and features.

Network Hierarchy

This section explains the hierarchical network model, which is composed of the access, distribution, and core layers. The functions generally associated with each of these layers are discussed, as is the most common approach to designing a hierarchical network.

Historically used in the design of enterprise local-area network and wide-area network data networks, this model works equally well within the functional modules of the Cisco Enterprise Architecture. These modules are discussed later in this chapter, in the section "Using a Modular Approach to Network Design."

Hierarchical Network Model

The hierarchical network model provides a framework that network designers can use to help ensure that the network is flexible and easy to implement and troubleshoot.

Hierarchical Network Design Layers

As shown in Figure 3-1, the hierarchical network design model consists of three layers:

- The access layer provides local and remote workgroup or user access to the network.

- The distribution layer provides policy-based connectivity.

- The core (or backbone) layer provides high-speed transport to satisfy the connectivity and transport needs of the distribution layer devices.

Figure 3-1 *Hierarchical Model's Three Layers*

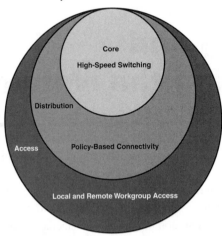

Each hierarchical layer focuses on specific functions, thereby allowing the network designer to choose the right systems and features based on their function within the model. This approach helps provide more accurate capacity planning and minimize total costs. Figure 3-2 illustrates a sample network showing the mapping to the hierarchical model's three layers.

Figure 3-2 *Sample Network Designed Using the Hierarchical Model*

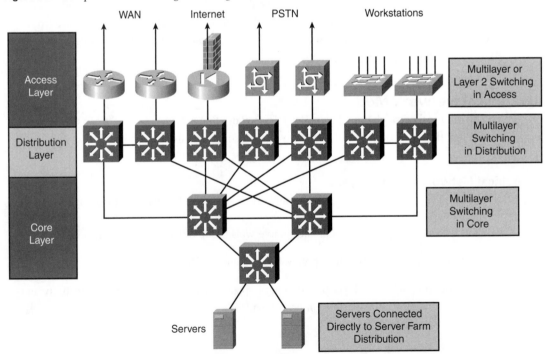

You do not have to implement the hierarchical layers as distinct physical entities; they are defined to aid successful network design and to represent functionality that must exist within a network. The actual manner in which you implement the layers depends on the needs of the network you are designing. Each layer can be implemented in routers or switches, represented by physical media, or combined in a single device. A particular layer can be omitted, but hierarchy should be maintained for optimum performance. The following sections detail the functionality of the three layers and the devices used to implement them.

Access Layer Functionality

This section describes the access layer functions and the interaction of the access layer with the distribution layer and local or remote users.

The Role of the Access Layer

The access layer is the concentration point at which clients access the network. Access layer devices control traffic by localizing service requests to the access media.

The purpose of the access layer is to grant user access to network resources. Following are the access layer's characteristics:

- In the campus environment, the access layer typically incorporates switched LAN devices with ports that provide connectivity for workstations and servers.

- In the WAN environment, the access layer for teleworkers or remote sites provides access to the corporate network across some wide-area technology, such as Frame Relay, Multiprotocol Label Switching (MPLS), Integrated Services Digital Network, leased lines, Digital Subscriber Line (DSL) over traditional telephone copper lines, or coaxial cable.

- So as not to compromise network integrity, access is granted only to authenticated users or devices (such as those with physical address or logical name authentication). For example, the devices at the access layer must detect whether a telecommuter who is dialing in is legitimate, yet they must require minimal authentication steps for the telecommuter.

Layer 2 and Multilayer Switching in the Access Layer

Access can be provided to end users as part of either a Layer 2 (L2) switching environment or a multilayer switching environment.

> **NOTE**   In this book, the term *multilayer switching* denotes a switch's generic capability to use information at different protocol layers as part of the switching process; the term *Layer 3 switching* is a synonym for multilayer switching in this context.
>
> Cisco switches implement the use of protocol information from multiple layers in the switching process in two different ways. The first way is *multilayer switching (MLS)* and the second way is *Cisco Express Forwarding (CEF)*. MLS and CEF are described further in Chapter 4, "Designing Basic Campus and Data Center Networks."

Using Layer 2 Switching in the Access Layer

Access to local workstations and servers can be provided using shared or switched media LANs; VLANs may be used to segment the switched LANs. Each LAN or VLAN is a single broadcast domain.

The access layer aggregates end-user switched 10/100 ports and provides Fast Ethernet, Fast EtherChannel, and Gigabit Ethernet uplinks to the distribution layer to satisfy connectivity requirements and reduce the size of the broadcast domains. You can deploy multiple VLANs, each with its own IP subnet and its own instance of Spanning Tree Protocol (STP) providing alternative paths in case of failure. In this case, Layer 2 trunking (typically using the Institute for Electrical and Electronic Engineers [IEEE] 802.1Q trunking protocol) is used between the access layer switches and the distribution layer switches, with per-VLAN STP on each uplink for load balancing and redundancy, and with a distribution layer multilayer switch providing the inter-VLAN communication for the access layer.

> **NOTE**   Chapter 4 discusses STP further.

> **KEY POINT**   A recommended best practice is to implement one VLAN—thus supporting one IP subnet—per access switch and to connect the access switches to the distribution switches with Layer 3 links rather than with trunks.

> **NOTE**   In small networks, the access layer is often collapsed into the distribution layer; in other words, one device might handle all functions of the access and distribution layers.

KEY POINT | Using the Rapid Spanning Tree Protocol (RSTP) is a recommended best practice in the enterprise. RSTP is an evolution of the IEEE 802.1d STP standard and provides faster spanning-tree convergence after a topology change.

When RSTP cannot be implemented, Cisco IOS STP features such as UplinkFast, PortFast, and BackboneFast can be used to provide equivalent convergence improvements. These features are described as follows:

- **UplinkFast**: Enables faster failover on an access layer switch on which dual uplinks connect to the distribution layer. The failover time is reduced by unblocking the blocked uplink port on a switch immediately after root port failure, thereby transitioning it to the forwarding state immediately, without transitioning the port through the listening and learning states.

- **BackboneFast**: If a link fails on the way to the root switch but is not directly connected to the local switch, BackboneFast reduces the convergence time from 50 seconds to between 20 and 30 seconds.

- **PortFast**: Enables switch ports connected to nonswitch devices (such as workstations) to immediately enter the spanning-tree forwarding state, thereby bypassing the listening and learning states, when they come up. Ports connected only to an end-user device do not have bridging loops, so it is safe to go directly to the forwarding state, significantly reducing the time it takes before the port is usable.

NOTE   Chapter 4 discusses other STP features.

Using Multilayer Switching in the Access Layer

The most common design for remote users is to use multilayer switches or routers. A multilayer switch, or router, is the boundary for broadcast domains and is necessary for communicating between broadcast domains (including VLANs). Access routers provide access to remote office environments using various wide-area technologies combined with multilayer features, such as route propagation, packet filtering, authentication, security, Quality of Service (QoS), and so on. These technologies allow the network to be optimized to satisfy a particular user's needs. In a dialup connection environment, dial-on-demand routing (DDR) and static routing can be used to control costs.

Access Layer Example

Figure 3-3 illustrates a sample network in which the campus access layer aggregates end users and provides uplinks to the distribution layer. The access layer switches are dual-attached to the distribution layer switches for high availability.

Figure 3-3 *Access Layer Connectivity in a Campus LAN*

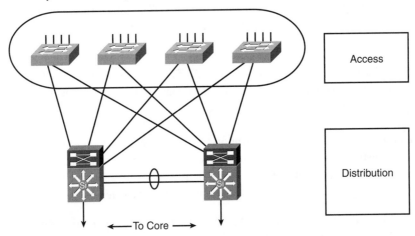

The access layer can support convergence, high availability, security, QoS, and IP multicast. Some services found at the access layer include establishing a QoS trust boundary, broadcast suppression, and Internet Group Management Protocol (IGMP) snooping.

Distribution Layer Functionality

This section describes distribution layer functions and the interaction of the distribution layer with the core and access layers.

The Role of the Distribution Layer

The *distribution layer* represents both a separation between the access and core layers and a connection point between the diverse access sites and the core layer. The distribution layer determines department or workgroup access and provides policy-based connectivity.

Following are the characteristics of the distribution layer:

■ Distribution layer devices control access to resources that are available at the core layer and must therefore use bandwidth efficiently.

■ In a campus environment, the distribution layer aggregates wiring closet bandwidth by concentrating multiple low-speed access links into a high-speed core link and using switches to segment workgroups and isolate network problems to prevent them from affecting the core layer.

■ Similarly, in a WAN environment, the distribution layer aggregates WAN connections at the edge of the campus and provides policy-based connectivity.

- This layer provides redundant connections for access devices. Redundant connections also provide the opportunity to load-balance between devices.

- The distribution layer represents a routing boundary between the access and core layers and is where routing and packet manipulation are performed.

- The distribution layer allows the core layer to connect diverse sites while maintaining high performance. To maintain good performance in the core, the distribution layer can redistribute between bandwidth-intensive access-layer routing protocols and optimized core routing protocols. Route filtering is also implemented at the distribution layer.

- The distribution layer can summarize routes from the access layer to improve routing protocol performance. For some networks, the distribution layer offers a default route to access-layer routers and runs dynamic routing protocols only when communicating with core routers.

- The distribution layer connects network services to the access layer and implements policies for QoS, security, traffic loading, and routing. For example, the distribution layer addresses different protocols' QoS needs by implementing policy-based traffic control to isolate backbone and local environments. Policy-based traffic control prioritizes traffic to ensure the best performance for the most time-critical and time-dependent applications.

- The distribution layer is often the layer that terminates access layer VLANs (broadcast domains); however, this can also be done at the access layer.

- This layer provides any media transitions (for example, between Ethernet and ATM) that must occur.

Policy-Based Connectivity

Policy-based connectivity means implementing the policies of the organization (as described in Chapter 2, "Applying a Methodology to Network Design"). Methods for implementing policies include the following:

- Filtering by source or destination address

- Filtering based on input or output ports

- Hiding internal network numbers by route filtering

- Providing specific static routes rather than using routes from a dynamic routing protocol

- Security (for example, certain packets might not be allowed into a specific part of the network)

- QoS mechanisms (for example, the precedence and type of service [ToS] values in IP packet headers can be set in routers to leverage queuing mechanisms to prioritize traffic)

Distribution Layer Example

Figure 3-4 shows a sample network with various features of the distribution layer highlighted.

Figure 3-4 *Example of Distribution Layer Features*

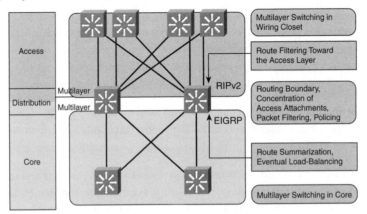

Following are the characteristics of the distribution layer in the routed campus network shown in Figure 3-4:

- Multilayer switching is used toward the access layer (and, in this case, within the access layer).

- Multilayer switching is performed in the distribution layer and extended toward the core layer.

- The distribution layer performs two-way route redistribution to exchange the routes between the Routing Information Protocol version 2 (RIPv2) and Enhanced Interior Gateway Routing Protocol (EIGRP) routing processes.

- Route filtering is configured on the interfaces toward the access layer.

- Route summarization is configured on the interfaces toward the core layer.

- The distribution layer contains highly redundant connectivity, both toward the access layer and toward the core layer.

Core Layer Functionality

This section describes core layer functions and the interaction of the core layer with the distribution layer.

The Role of the Core Layer

The function of the core layer is to provide fast and efficient data transport. Characteristics of the core layer include the following:

■ The core layer is a high-speed backbone that should be designed to switch packets as quickly as possible to optimize communication transport within the network.

■ Because the core is critical for connectivity, core layer devices are expected to provide a high level of availability and reliability. A fault-tolerant network design ensures that failures do not have a major impact on network connectivity. The core must be able to accommodate failures by rerouting traffic and responding quickly to changes in network topology. The core must provide a high level of redundancy. A full mesh is strongly suggested, and at least a well-connected partial mesh with multiple paths from each device is required.

■ The core layer should not perform any packet manipulation, such as checking access lists or filtering, which would slow down the switching of packets.

■ The core layer must be manageable.

■ The core devices must be able to implement scalable protocols and technologies, and provide alternative paths and load balancing.

Switching in the Core Layer

Layer 2 switching or multilayer switching (routing) can be used in the core layer. Because core devices are responsible for accommodating failures by rerouting traffic and responding quickly to network topology changes, and because performance for routing in the core with a multilayer switch incurs no cost, most implementations have multilayer switching in the core layer. The core layer can then more readily implement scalable protocols and technologies, and provide alternate paths and load balancing.

Figure 3-5 shows an example of Layer 2 switching in the campus core.

Figure 3-5 *Layer 2 Switching in the Campus Core*

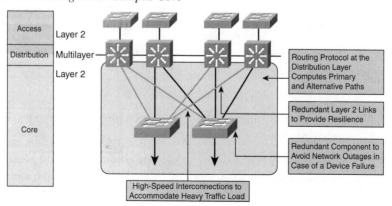

In Figure 3-5, a typical packet between access sites follows these steps:

Step 1   The packet is Layer 2–switched toward a distribution switch.

Step 2   The distribution switch performs multilayer switching toward a core interface.

Step 3   The packet is Layer 2–switched across the LAN core.

Step 4   The receiving distribution switch performs multilayer switching toward an access layer LAN.

Step 5   The packet is Layer 2–switched across the access layer LAN to the destination host.

Figure 3-6 shows an example of multilayer switching in the campus core.

Figure 3-6   *Multilayer Switching in the Campus Core*

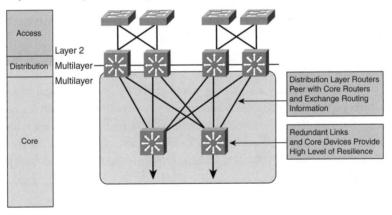

In Figure 3-6, a typical packet between access sites follows these steps:

Step 1   The packet is Layer 2–switched toward a distribution switch.

Step 2   The distribution switch performs multilayer switching toward a core interface.

Step 3   The packet is multilayer-switched across the LAN core.

Step 4   The receiving distribution switch performs multilayer switching toward an access LAN.

Step 5   The packet is Layer 2–switched across the access layer LAN to the destination host.

Hierarchical Routing in the WAN

Figure 3-7 shows an example of hierarchical routing in the WAN portion of a network.

Figure 3-7 *Hierarchical Routing in the WAN*

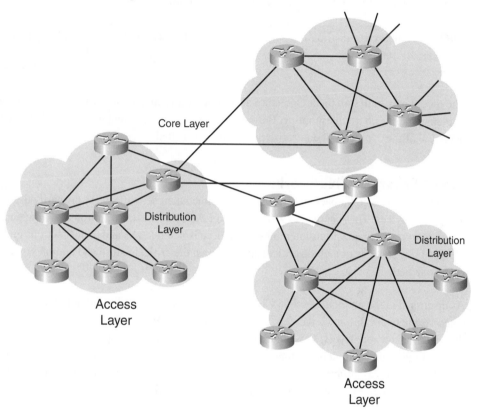

In Figure 3-7, a typical packet between access sites follows these steps:

Step 1   The packet is Layer 3–forwarded toward the distribution router.

Step 2   The distribution router forwards the packet toward a core interface.

Step 3   The packet is forwarded across the WAN core.

Step 4   The receiving distribution router forwards the packet toward the appropriate access layer router.

Step 5   The packet is Layer 3–forwarded to the destination host's access layer LAN.

Using a Modular Approach to Network Design

This section expands on the Cisco Service-Oriented Network Architecture (SONA) framework described in Chapter 2 and explores the six modules of the Cisco Enterprise Architecture, with an emphasis on the network infrastructure design considerations.

> **NOTE**   The access, distribution, and core layers can appear within each module of the Cisco Enterprise Architecture.

The modularity built into the architecture allows flexibility in network design and facilitates implementation and troubleshooting. Before the details of the architecture itself are introduced, an overview of the evolution of enterprise networks is provided.

Evolution of Enterprise Networks

You do not have to go far back in history to find a time when networks were primarily used for file and print services. These networks were isolated LANs that were built throughout the enterprise organization. As organizations interconnected, these isolated LANs and their functions grew from file and print services to include critical applications; the critical nature and complexity of the enterprise networks also grew.

As discussed in the previous section, Cisco introduced the hierarchical model to divide the enterprise network design (separately for both campus and WAN networks) into the access, distribution, and core layers. This solution has several weaknesses, especially for large networks, which are difficult to implement, manage, and, particularly, troubleshoot. Networks became complex, and it was difficult to evaluate a network solution end-to-end through the network. The hierarchical model does not scale well to these large networks.

An efficient method of solving and scaling a complex task is to break it into smaller, more specialized tasks. Networks can easily be broken down smaller because they have natural physical, logical, and functional boundaries. If they are sufficiently large to require additional design or operational separation, these specialized functional modules can then be designed hierarchically with the access, distribution, and core layers.

The Cisco Enterprise Architecture does just that: It reduces the enterprise network into further physical, logical, and functional boundaries, to scale the hierarchical model. Now, rather than designing networks using only the hierarchical model, networks can be designed using this Cisco Enterprise Architecture, with hierarchy (access, distribution, and core) included in the various modules, as required.

Designing with this Cisco Enterprise Architecture is not much different from what is already used in practice; it formalizes current practice. There have always been separate hierarchies for the campus (with access, distribution, and core) and for the WAN (the remote office was the access layer, the regional office provided the distribution layer, and the headquarters was the core). The hierarchies tied together at the campus backbone. The Cisco Enterprise Architecture extends the concept of hierarchy from the original two modules: Campus and WAN.

Cisco SONA Framework

As illustrated in Figure 3-8, the Cisco SONA provides an enterprise-wide framework that integrates the entire network—campus, data center, enterprise edge, WAN, branches, and teleworkers—offering staff secure access to the tools, processes, and services they require.

Figure 3-8 *Cisco SONA Framework*

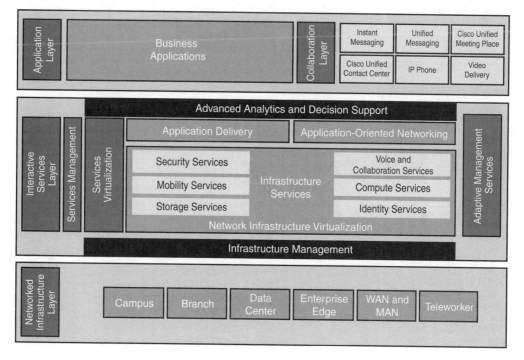

The modules of the Cisco Enterprise Architecture represent focused views of each of the places in the network described in the SONA framework. Each module has a distinct network infrastructure and distinct services; network applications extend between the modules.

Functional Areas of the Cisco Enterprise Architecture

At the first layer of modularity in the Cisco Enterprise Architecture, the entire network is divided into functional *components*—functional areas that contain network modules—while still maintaining the hierarchical concept of the core-distribution-access layers within the network modules as needed.

> **NOTE** The access, distribution, and core layers can appear in any functional area or module of the Cisco Enterprise Architecture.

The Cisco Enterprise Architecture comprises the following six major functional areas (also called *modules*):

- Enterprise Campus

- Enterprise Edge

- Service Provider

- Enterprise Branch

- Enterprise Data Center

- Enterprise Teleworker

KEY POINT An enterprise does not implement the modules in the Service Provider functional area; they are necessary for enabling communication with other networks.

> **NOTE** The Cisco SONA Enterprise Edge and the WAN and metropolitan-area network (MAN) modules are represented as one functional area in the Cisco Enterprise Architecture, the Enterprise Edge.

Figure 3-9 illustrates the modules within the Cisco Enterprise Architecture.

Figure 3-9 *Cisco Enterprise Architecture*

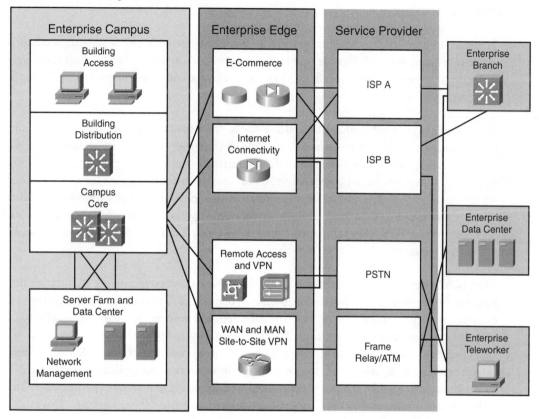

NOTE   Figure 3-9 is reproduced on the inside back cover of this book for your reference.

The Cisco Enterprise Campus Architecture combines a core infrastructure of intelligent switching and routing with tightly integrated productivity-enhancing technologies, including Cisco Unified Communications, mobility, and advanced security. The architecture provides the enterprise with high availability through a resilient multilayer design, redundant hardware and software features, and automatic procedures for reconfiguring network paths when failures occur. IP multicast capabilities provide optimized bandwidth consumption, and QoS features ensure that real-time traffic (such as voice, video, or critical data) is not dropped or delayed. Integrated security protects against and mitigates the impact of worms, viruses, and other attacks on the network, including at the switch port level. For example, the Cisco enterprise-wide architecture extends support for security standards, such as the IEEE 802.1X port-based network access control standard and the Extensible Authentication Protocol. It also provides the flexibility to add Internet Protocol Security (IPsec) and MPLS virtual private networks (VPN), identity and access management, and

VLANs to compartmentalize access. These features help improve performance and security while decreasing costs.

The Cisco Enterprise Edge Architecture offers connectivity to voice, video, and data services outside the enterprise. This module enables the enterprise to use Internet and partner resources, and provide resources for its customers. QoS, service levels, and security are the main issues in the Enterprise Edge.

The Cisco Enterprise WAN and MAN and Site-to-Site VPN module is part of the Enterprise Edge. It offers the convergence of voice, video, and data services over a single Cisco Unified Communications network, which enables the enterprise to span large geographic areas in a cost-effective manner. QoS, granular service levels, and comprehensive encryption options help ensure the secure delivery of high-quality corporate voice, video, and data resources to all corporate sites, enabling staff to work productively and efficiently wherever they are located. Security is provided with multiservice VPNs (both IPsec and MPLS) over Layer 2 or Layer 3 WANs, hub-and-spoke, or full-mesh topologies.

The Cisco Enterprise Data Center Architecture is a cohesive, adaptive network architecture that supports requirements for consolidation, business continuance, and security while enabling emerging service-oriented architectures, virtualization, and on-demand computing. Staff, suppliers, and customers can be provided with secure access to applications and resources, simplifying and streamlining management and significantly reducing overhead. Redundant data centers provide backup using synchronous and asynchronous data and application replication. The network and devices offer server and application load balancing to maximize performance. This architecture allows the enterprise to scale without major changes to the infrastructure. This module can be located either at the campus as a server farm or at a remote facility.

The Cisco Enterprise Branch Architecture allows enterprises to extend head-office applications and services (such as security, Cisco Unified Communications, and advanced application performance) to thousands of remote locations and users or to a small group of branches. Cisco integrates security, switching, network analysis, caching, and converged voice and video services into a series of integrated services routers (ISR) in the branch so that the enterprises can deploy new services without buying new routers. This architecture provides secure access to voice, mission-critical data, and video applications—anywhere, anytime. Advanced routing, VPNs, redundant WAN links, application content caching, and local IP telephony call processing features are available with high levels of resilience for all the branch offices. An optimized network leverages the WAN and LAN to reduce traffic and save bandwidth and operational expenses. The enterprise can easily support branch offices with the capability to centrally configure, monitor, and manage devices located at remote sites, including tools, such as Cisco AutoQoS and the Cisco Router and Security Device Manager graphical user interface QoS wizard, which proactively resolve congestion and bandwidth issues before they affect network performance.

The Cisco Enterprise Teleworker Architecture allows enterprises to securely deliver voice and data services to remote small or home offices (known as small office, home office [SOHO]) over a standard broadband access service, providing a business-resiliency solution for the enterprise and a flexible work environment for employees. Centralized management minimizes the IT support costs, and robust integrated security mitigates the unique security challenges of this environment. Integrated security and identity-based networking services enable the enterprise to extend campus security policies to the teleworker. Staff can securely log in to the network over an always-on VPN and gain access to authorized applications and services from a single cost-effective platform. Productivity can be further enhanced by adding an IP phone, thereby providing cost-effective access to a centralized IP communications system with voice and unified messaging services.

> **NOTE**   Each of these modules has specific requirements and performs specific roles in the network; note that their sizes in Figure 3-9 are not meant to reflect their scale in a real network.

This architecture allows network designers to focus on only a selected module and its functions. Designers can describe each network application and service on a per-module basis and validate each as part of the complete enterprise network design. Modules can be added to achieve scalability if necessary; for example, an organization can add more Enterprise Campus modules if it has more than one campus.

Guidelines for Creating an Enterprise Network

When creating an Enterprise network, divide the network into appropriate areas, where the Enterprise Campus includes all devices and connections within the main Campus location; the Enterprise Edge covers all communications with remote locations and the Internet from the perspective of the Enterprise Campus; and the remote modules include the remote branches, teleworkers, and the remote data center. Define clear boundaries between each of the areas.

> **NOTE**   Depending on the network, an enterprise can have multiple campus locations. A location that might be a remote branch from the perspective of a central campus location might locally use the Cisco Enterprise Campus Architecture.

Figure 3-10 shows an example of dividing a network into an Enterprise Campus area, an Enterprise Edge area, and some remote areas.

Figure 3-10 *Sample Network Divided into Functional Areas*

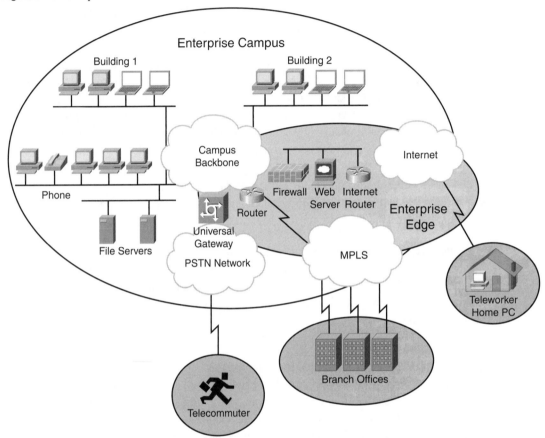

The following sections provide additional details about each of the functional areas and their modules.

Enterprise Campus Modules

This section introduces the Enterprise Campus functional area and describes the purpose of each module therein. It also discusses connections with other modules.

An *enterprise campus* site is a large site that is often the corporate headquarters or a major office. Regional offices, SOHOs, and mobile workers might have to connect to the central campus for data and information. As illustrated in Figure 3-11, the Enterprise Campus functional area includes the Campus Infrastructure module and, typically, a Server Farm module.

Figure 3-11 *Enterprise Campus Functional Area*

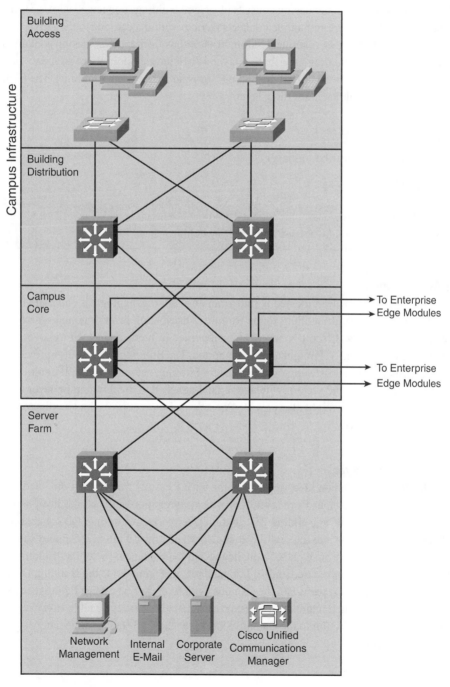

Campus Infrastructure Module

The Campus Infrastructure design consists of several buildings connected across a Campus Core. The Campus Infrastructure module connects devices within a campus to the Server Farm and Enterprise Edge modules. A single building in a Campus Infrastructure design contains a Building Access layer and a Building Distribution layer. When more buildings are added to the Campus Infrastructure, a backbone or Campus Core layer is added between buildings. The Campus Infrastructure module includes three layers:

- The Building Access layer

- The Building Distribution layer

- The Campus Core layer

> **NOTE**   In the most general model, the Building Access layer uses Layer 2 switching, and the Building Distribution layer uses multilayer switching.

Building Access Layer

The Building Access layer, located within a campus building, aggregates end users from different workgroups and provides uplinks to the Building Distribution layer. It contains end-user devices such as workstations, Cisco IP phones, and networked printers, connected to Layer 2 access switches; VLANs and STP might also be supported. The Building Access layer provides important services, such as broadcast suppression, protocol filtering, network access, IP multicast, and QoS. For high availability, the access switches are dual-attached to the distribution layer switches. The Building Access layer might also provide Power over Ethernet (PoE) and auxiliary VLANs to support voice services.

Building Distribution Layer

The Building Distribution layer aggregates the wiring closets within a building and provides connectivity to the Campus Core layer. It provides aggregation of the access layer networks using multilayer switching. The Building Distribution layer performs routing, QoS, and access control. Requests for data flow into the multilayer switches and onward into the Campus Core layer; responses follow the reverse path. Redundancy and load balancing with the Building Access and Campus Core layer are recommended. For example, in Figure 3-11, the Building Distribution layer has two equal-cost paths into the Campus Core layer, providing fast failure recovery because each distribution switch maintains two equal-cost paths in its routing table to every destination network. If one connection to the Campus Core layer fails, all routes immediately switch over to the remaining path.

Campus Core Layer

The Campus Core layer is the core layer of the Campus Infrastructure module. Within the Enterprise Campus functional area, this high-performance, switched backbone connects the buildings and various parts of the campus. Specifically, this layer interconnects the Building Distribution layer with the Server Farm and the Enterprise Edge modules.

The Campus Core layer of the Campus Infrastructure module provides redundant and fast-converging connectivity between buildings and with the Server Farm and Enterprise Edge modules. It routes and switches traffic as quickly as possible from one module to another. This module usually uses multilayer switches for high-throughput functions with added routing, QoS, and security features.

Server Farm Module

A high-capacity, centralized server farm module provides users with internal server resources. In addition, it typically supports network management services for the enterprise, including monitoring, logging, and troubleshooting, and other common management features from end to end.

The Server Farm module typically contains internal e-mail and other corporate servers that provide internal users with application, file, print, e-mail, and Domain Name System (DNS) services. As shown in Figure 3-11, because access to these servers is vital, as a best practice, they are typically connected to two different switches to enable full redundancy or load sharing. Moreover, the Server Farm module switches are cross-connected with the Campus Core layer switches, thereby enabling high reliability and availability of all servers in the Server Farm module.

The network management system performs system logging, network monitoring, and general configuration management functions. For management purposes, an out-of-band network connection (a network on which no production traffic travels) to all network components is recommended. For locations where an out-of-band network is impossible (because of geographic or system-related issues), the network management system uses the production network.

Network management can provide configuration management for nearly all devices in the network, using a combination of the following two technologies:

■ Cisco IOS routers can act as terminal servers to provide a dedicated management network segment to the console ports on the Cisco devices throughout the enterprise by using a reverse-Telnet function.

- More extensive management features (software changes, content updates, log and alarm aggregation, and Simple Network Management Protocol [SNMP] management) can be provided through the dedicated out-of-band management network segment.

> **NOTE**   These Server Farm attributes also apply to a remote Data Center module.

Enterprise Campus Guidelines

Follow these guidelines for creating the modules within an Enterprise Campus functional area:

Step 1   Select modules within the campus that act as buildings with access and distribution layers.

Step 2   Determine the locations and the number of access switches and their uplinks to distribution layer switches.

Step 3   Select the appropriate distribution layer switches, taking into account the number of access layer switches and end users. Use at least two distribution layer switches for redundancy.

Step 4   Consider two uplink connections from each access layer switch to the two distribution layer switches.

Step 5   Determine where servers are or will be located, and design the Server Farm module with at least two distribution layer switches that connect all servers for full redundancy. Include out-of-band network management connections to all critical devices in the campus network.

Step 6   Design the Campus Infrastructure module's Campus Core layer using at least two switches and provide for the expected traffic volume between modules.

Step 7   Interconnect all modules of the Enterprise Campus with the Campus Infrastructure module's Campus Core layer in a redundant manner.

Enterprise Edge Modules

This section describes the components of the Enterprise Edge and explains the importance of each module. The Enterprise Edge infrastructure modules aggregate the connectivity from the various elements outside the campus—using various services and WAN technologies as needed, typically provisioned from service providers—and route the traffic into the Campus Core layer. The Enterprise Edge modules perform security functions when enterprise resources connect across public networks and the Internet. As shown in Figure 3-12 and in the following list, the Enterprise Edge functional area is composed of four main modules:

- **E-commerce module**: The E-commerce module includes the devices and services necessary for an organization to provide e-commerce applications.

- **Internet Connectivity module**: The Internet Connectivity module provides enterprise users with Internet access.

- **Remote Access and VPN module**: This module terminates VPN traffic and dial-in connections from external users.

- **WAN and MAN and Site-to-Site VPN module**: This module provides connectivity between remote sites and the central site over various WAN technologies.

Figure 3-12 *Enterprise Edge Functional Area*

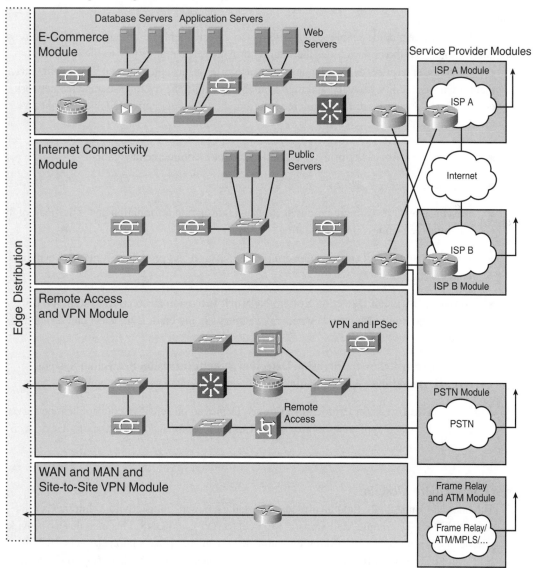

These modules connect to the Campus Core directly or through an optional Edge Distribution module. The optional Edge Distribution module aggregates the connectivity from the various elements at the enterprise edge and routes the traffic into the Campus Core layer. In addition, the Edge Distribution module acts as a boundary between the Enterprise Campus and the Enterprise Edge and is the last line of defense against external attacks; its structure is similar to that of the Building Distribution layer.

The following sections detail each of the four main Enterprise Edge modules.

E-commerce Module

The E-commerce module enables enterprises to successfully deploy e-commerce applications and take advantage of the opportunities the Internet provides. The majority of traffic is initiated external to the enterprise. All e-commerce transactions pass through a series of intelligent services that provide scalability, security, and high availability within the overall e-commerce network design. To build a successful e-commerce solution, the following network devices might be included:

- **Web servers**: Act as the primary user interface for e-commerce navigation

- **Application servers**: Host the various applications

- **Database servers**: Contain the application and transaction information that is the heart of the e-commerce business implementation

- **Firewalls or firewall routers**: Govern communication and provide security between the system's various users

- **Network Intrusion Detection System/Network Intrusion Protection System (NIDS/ NIPS) appliances**: Monitor key network segments in the module to detect and respond to attacks against the network

- **Multilayer switch with Intrusion Detection System/Intrusion Protection System (IDS/IPS) modules**: Provide traffic transport and integrated security monitoring

- **Host-Based Intrusion Protection Systems**: Deployed on sensitive core application servers and on dedicated appliances to provide real-time reporting and prevention of attacks as an extra layer of defense

Internet Connectivity Module

The Internet Connectivity module provides internal users with connectivity to Internet services, such as HTTP, FTP, Simple Mail Transfer Protocol (SMTP), and DNS. This module also provides Internet users with access to information published on an enterprise's public servers, such as HTTP and FTP servers. Internet session initiation is typically from inside the enterprise toward the Internet. Additionally, this module accepts VPN traffic from remote users and remote sites and forwards it to the Remote Access and VPN module, where VPN termination takes place. The Internet Connectivity module is not designed to serve e-commerce applications. Major components used in the Internet Connectivity module include the following:

- **SMTP mail servers**: Act as a relay between the Internet and the intranet mail servers.

- **DNS servers**: Serve as the authoritative external DNS server for the enterprise and relay internal DNS requests to the Internet.

- **Public servers (for example, FTP and HTTP):** Provide public information about the organization. Each server on the public services segment contains host-based intrusion detection systems (HIDS) to monitor against any rogue activity at the operating system level and in common server applications including HTTP, FTP, and SMTP.

- **Firewalls or firewall routers**: Provide network-level protection of resources, provide stateful filtering of traffic, and forward VPN traffic from remote sites and users for termination.

- **Edge routers**: Provide basic filtering and multilayer connectivity to the Internet.

Remote Access and VPN Module

The Remote Access and VPN module terminates remote access traffic and VPN traffic that the Internet Connectivity Module forwards from remote users and remote sites. It also uses the Internet Connectivity module to initiate VPN connections to remote sites. Furthermore, the module terminates dial-in connections received through the public switched telephone network (PSTN) and, after successful authentication, grants dial-in users access to the network. Major components used in the Remote Access and VPN module include the following:

- **Dial-in access concentrators**: Terminate dial-in connections and authenticate individual users

- **Cisco Adaptive Security Appliances (ASA)**: Terminate IPsec tunnels, authenticate individual remote users, and provide firewall and intrusion prevention services

- **Firewalls**: Provide network-level protection of resources and stateful filtering of traffic, provide differentiated security for remote access users, authenticate trusted remote sites, and provide connectivity using IPsec tunnels

- **NIDS appliances**: Provide Layer 4 to Layer 7 monitoring of key network segments in the module

WAN and MAN and Site-to-Site VPN Module

The WAN and MAN and Site-to-Site VPN module uses various WAN technologies, including site-to-site VPNs, to route traffic between remote sites and the central site. In addition to traditional media (such as leased lines) and circuit-switched data-link technologies (such as Frame Relay and ATM), this module can use more recent WAN physical layer technologies, including Synchronous Optical Network/Synchronous Digital Hierarchy (SDH), cable, DSL, MPLS, Metro Ethernet, wireless, and service provider VPNs. This module incorporates all Cisco devices that support these WAN technologies, and routing, access control, and QoS mechanisms. Although security is not as critical when all links are owned by the enterprise, it should be considered in the network design.

KEY POINT | The WAN and MAN and Site-to-Site VPN module does not include the WAN connections or links; it provides only the *interfaces* to the WAN.

Enterprise Edge Guidelines

Follow these guidelines for creating the modules within the Enterprise Edge functional area:

Step 1   Create the E-commerce module (for business-to-business or business-to-customer scenarios) when customers or partners require Internet access to business applications and database servers. Deploy a high-security policy that allows customers to access predefined servers and services yet restricts all other operations.

Step 2   Determine the connections from the corporate network into the Internet, and assign them to the Internet Connectivity module. This module should implement security to prevent any unauthorized access from the Internet to the internal network. Public web servers reside in this module or the E-commerce module.

Step 3   Design the Remote Access and VPN module if the enterprise requires VPN connections or dial-in for accessing the internal network from the outside world. Implement a security policy in this module; users should not be able to access the internal network directly without authentication and authorization. The VPN sessions use connectivity from the Internet Connectivity module.

Step 4   Determine which part of the edge is used exclusively for permanent connections to remote locations (such as branch offices), and assign it to the WAN and MAN and Site-to-Site VPN module. All WAN devices supporting Frame Relay, ATM, cable, MPLS, leased lines, SONET/SDH, and so on, are located here.

Service Provider Modules

Figure 3-13 shows the modules within the Service Provider functional area. The enterprise itself does not implement these modules; however, they are necessary to enable communication with other networks, using a variety of WAN technologies, and with Internet service providers (ISP). The modules within the Service Provider functional area are as follows:

- Internet Service Provider module

- PSTN module

- Frame Relay/ATM module

Figure 3-13 *Service Provider Functional Area*

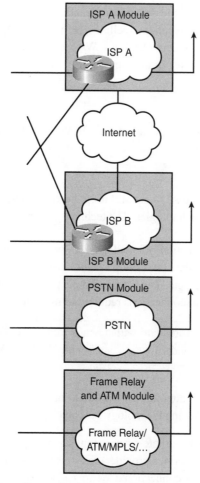

The following sections describe each of these modules.

Internet Service Provider Module

The Internet Service Provider module represents enterprise IP connectivity to an ISP network for basic access to the Internet or for enabling Enterprise Edge services, such as those in the E-commerce, Remote Access and VPN, and Internet Connectivity modules. Enterprises can connect to two or more ISPs to provide redundant connections to the Internet. The physical connection between the ISP and the enterprise can use any of the WAN technologies.

PSTN Module

> **KEY POINT** | The PSTN module represents all *nonpermanent* WAN connections.

The PSTN module represents the dialup infrastructure for accessing the enterprise network using ISDN, analog, and wireless telephony (cellular) technologies. Enterprises can also use this infrastructure to back up existing WAN links; WAN backup connections are generally established on demand and torn down after an idle timeout.

Frame Relay/ATM Module

> **KEY POINT** | The Frame Relay/ATM module covers all WAN technologies for *permanent* connectivity with remote locations.

Traditional Frame Relay and ATM are still used; however, despite the module's name, it also represents many modern technologies. The technologies in this module include the following:

- Frame Relay is a connection-oriented, packet-switching technology designed to efficiently transmit data traffic at data rates of up to those used by E3 and T3 connections. Its capability to connect multiple remote sites across a single physical connection reduces the number of point-to-point physical connections required to link sites.

> **NOTE**   E3 is a European standard with a bandwidth of 34.368 megabits per second (Mbps). T3 is a North American standard with a bandwidth of 44.736 Mbps.

- ATM is a higher-speed alternative to Frame Relay. It is a high-performance, cell-oriented, switching and multiplexing technology for carrying different types of traffic.

- Leased lines provide the simplest permanent point-to-point connection between two remote locations. The carrier (service provider) reserves point-to-point links for the customer's private use. Because the connection does not carry anyone else's communications, the carrier can ensure a given level of quality. The fee for the connection is typically a fixed monthly rate.

- SONET/SDH are standards for transmission over optical networks. Europe uses SDH, whereas North America uses SONET.

- Cable technology uses existing coaxial cable TV cables. Coupled with cable modems, this technology provides much greater bandwidth than telephone lines and can be used to achieve extremely fast access to the Internet or enterprise network.

- DSL uses existing twisted-pair telephone lines to transport high-bandwidth data, such as voice, data, and video. DSL is sometimes referred to as *last-mile technology* because it is used only for connections from a telephone switching station (at a service provider) to a home or office, not between switching stations. DSL is used by telecommuters to access enterprise networks; however, more and more companies are migrating from traditional Frame Relay to DSL technology using VPNs because of its cost efficiency.

- Wireless bridging technology interconnects remote LANs using point-to-point signal transmissions that go through the air over a terrestrial radio or microwave platform, rather than through copper or fiber cables. Wireless bridging requires neither satellite feeds nor local phone service. One of the advantages of bridged wireless is its capability to connect users in remote areas without having to install new cables. However, this technology is limited to shorter distances, and weather conditions can degrade its performance.

- MPLS combines the advantages of multilayer routing with the benefits of Layer 2 switching. With MPLS, labels are assigned to each packet at the edge of the network. Rather than examining the IP packet header information, MPLS nodes use this label to determine how to process the data, resulting in a faster, more scalable, and more flexible WAN solution.

NOTE   Chapter 5, "Designing Remote Connectivity," discusses WANs in more detail.

Remote Enterprise Modules

The three modules supporting remote enterprise locations are the Enterprise Branch, the Enterprise Data Center, and the Enterprise Teleworker.

Enterprise Branch Module

The Enterprise Branch module extends the enterprise by providing each location with a resilient network architecture with integrated security, Cisco Unified Communications, and wireless mobility.

A branch office generally accommodates employees who have a compelling reason to be located away from the central site, such as a regional sales office. A branch office is sometimes called a *remote site*, *remote office*, or *sales office*. Branch office users must be able to connect to the central site to access company information. Therefore, they benefit from high-speed Internet access, VPN connectivity to corporate intranets, telecommuting capabilities for work-at-home employees, videoconferencing, and economical PSTN-quality voice and fax calls over managed IP networks. The Enterprise Branch module typically uses a simplified version of the Campus Infrastructure module design.

Enterprise Data Center Module

The Enterprise Data Center module has an architecture that is similar to the campus Server Farm module discussed earlier. The Enterprise Data Center network architecture allows the network to evolve into a platform that enhances the application, server, and storage solutions and equips organizations to manage increased security, cost, and regulatory requirements while providing the ability to respond quickly to changing business environments. The Enterprise Data Center module may include the following components:

■ **At the networked infrastructure layer**: Gigabit Ethernet, 10-Gigabit Ethernet, or InfiniBand connections, with storage switching and optical transport devices

NOTE InfiniBand is a high-speed switched fabric mesh technology.

■ **At the interactive services layer**: Services include storage fabric services, computer services, security services, and application optimization services

■ **At the management layer**: Tools include Fabric Manager (for element and network management) and Cisco VFrame (for server and service provisioning)

The remote Enterprise Data Center module also needs highly available WAN connectivity with business continuance capabilities to integrate it with the rest of the Cisco Enterprise Architecture. The Server Farm module in the campus can leverage the WAN connectivity of the campus core, but the remote Enterprise Data Center must implement its own WAN connectivity.

Enterprise Teleworker Module

The Enterprise Teleworker module provides people in geographically dispersed locations, such as home offices or hotels, with highly secure access to central-site applications and network services.

The Enterprise Teleworker module supports a small office with one to several employees or the home office of a telecommuter. Telecommuters might also be mobile users—people who need access while traveling or who do not work at a fixed company site.

Depending on the amount of use and the WAN services available, telecommuters working from home tend to use broadband or dialup services. Mobile users tend to access the company network using a broadband Internet service and the VPN client software on their laptops or via an asynchronous dialup connection through the telephone company. Telecommuters working from home might also use a VPN tunnel gateway router for encrypted data and voice traffic to and from the company intranet. These solutions provide simple and safe access for teleworkers to the corporate network site, according to the needs of the users at the sites.

The Cisco Teleworker solution provides an easy-to-deploy, centrally managed solution that addresses both the workers' mobility needs and the enterprise's needs for lower operational costs, security, productivity, business resiliency, and business responsiveness. Small ISRs form the backbone of the Enterprise Teleworker architecture. An optional IP phone can be provided to take advantage of a centralized Cisco Unified Communications system.

Services Within Modular Networks

Businesses that operate large enterprise networks strive to create an enterprise-wide networked infrastructure and interactive services to serve as a solid foundation for business and collaborative applications. This section explores some of the interactive services with respect to the modules that form the Cisco Enterprise Architecture.

KEY POINT | A network service is a supporting and necessary service, but not an ultimate solution. For example, security and QoS are not ultimate goals for a network; they are necessary to enable other services and applications and are therefore classified as network services. However, IP telephony might be an ultimate goal of a network and is therefore a network *application* (or *solution*), rather than a service.

Interactive Services

Since the inception of packet-based communications, networks have always offered a forwarding service. Forwarding is the fundamental activity within an internetwork. In IP, this forwarding service was built on the assumption that end nodes in the network were intelligent, and that the network core did not have intelligence. With advances in networking software and hardware, the network can offer an increasingly rich, intelligent set of mechanisms for forwarding information. Interactive services add intelligence to the network infrastructure, beyond simply moving a datagram between two points.

For example, through intelligent network classification, the network distinguishes and identifies traffic based on application content and context. Advanced network services use the traffic classification to regulate performance, ensure security, facilitate delivery, and improve manageability.

Network applications such as IP telephony support the entire enterprise network environment— from the teleworker to the campus to the data center. These applications are enabled by critical network services and provide a common set of capabilities to support the application's networkwide requirements, including security, high availability, reliability, flexibility, responsiveness, and compliancy.

Recall the layers of the Cisco SONA framework, illustrated in Figure 3-14. The SONA interactive services layer includes both application networking services and infrastructure services.

Figure 3-14   *Cisco SONA Framework*

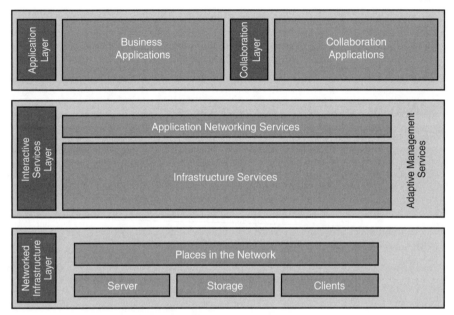

For example, the following infrastructure services (shown earlier in Figure 3-8) enhance classic network functions to support today's applications environments by mapping the application's requirements to the resources that they require from the network:

- **Security services**: Ensure that all aspects of the network are secure, from devices connecting to the network to secured transport to data theft prevention

- **Mobility services**: Allow users to access network resources regardless of their physical location

- **Storage services**: Provide distributed and virtual storage across the infrastructure

- **Voice and collaboration services**: Deliver the foundation by which voice can be carried across the network, such as security and high availability

- **Compute services**: Connect and virtualize compute resources based on the application

- **Identity services**: Map resources and policies to the user and device

Examples of network services imbedded in the infrastructure services include the following:

- **Network management**: Includes LAN management for advanced management of multilayer switches; routed WAN management for monitoring, traffic management, and access control to administer the routed infrastructure of multiservice networks; service management for managing and monitoring service level agreements (SLAs); and VPN security management for optimizing VPN performance and security administration.

- **High availability**: Ensures end-to-end availability for services, clients, and sessions. Implementation includes reliable, fault-tolerant network devices to automatically identify and overcome failures, and resilient network technologies.

- **QoS**: Manages the delay, delay variation (jitter), bandwidth availability, and packet loss parameters of a network to meet the diverse needs of voice, video, and data applications. QoS features provide value-added functionality, such as network-based application recognition for classifying traffic on an application basis, Cisco IOS IP SLAs (previously called the *service assurance agent*) for end-to-end QoS measurements, Resource Reservation Protocol signaling for admission control and reservation of resources, and a variety of configurable queue insertion and servicing functions.

- **IP multicasting**: Provides bandwidth-conserving technology that reduces network traffic by delivering a single stream of information intended for many recipients through the transport network. Multicasting enables distribution of videoconferencing, corporate communications, distance learning, software, and other applications. Multicast packets are replicated only as necessary by Cisco routers enabled with Protocol Independent Multicast and other supporting multicast protocols that result in the most efficient delivery of data to multiple receivers.

To support network applications efficiently, deploy the underlying infrastructure services in some or all modules of the enterprise network as required. These design elements can be replicated simply to other enterprise network modules as the network changes. As a result, modularization to small subsets of the overall network simplifies the network design and often reduces the network's cost and complexity.

The following sections explore some of the infrastructure services and application networking services. Network management services are described in the "Network Management Protocols and Features" section later in this chapter.

Security Services in a Modular Network Design

KEY POINT | Security is an infrastructure service that increases the network's integrity by protecting network resources and users from internal and external threats.

Without a full understanding of the threats involved, network security deployments tend to be incorrectly configured, too focused on security devices, or lacking appropriate threat response options.

Security both in the Enterprise Campus (internal security) and at the Enterprise Edge (from external threats) is important. An enterprise should include several layers of protection so that a breach at one layer or in one network module does not mean that other layers or modules are also compromised; Cisco calls deploying layered security *defense-in-depth*.

Internal Security

Strongly protecting the internal Enterprise Campus by including security functions in each individual element is important for the following reasons:

■ If the security established at the Enterprise Edge fails, an unprotected Enterprise Campus is vulnerable. Deploying several layers of security increases the protection of the Enterprise Campus, where the most strategic assets usually reside.

■ Relying on physical security is not enough. For example, as a visitor to the organization, a potential attacker could gain physical access to devices in the Enterprise Campus.

■ Often external access does not stop at the Enterprise Edge; some applications require at least indirect access to the Enterprise Campus resources. Strong security must protect access to these resources.

Figure 3-15 shows how internal security can be designed into the Cisco Enterprise Architecture.

Figure 3-15 *Designing Internal Security into the Network*

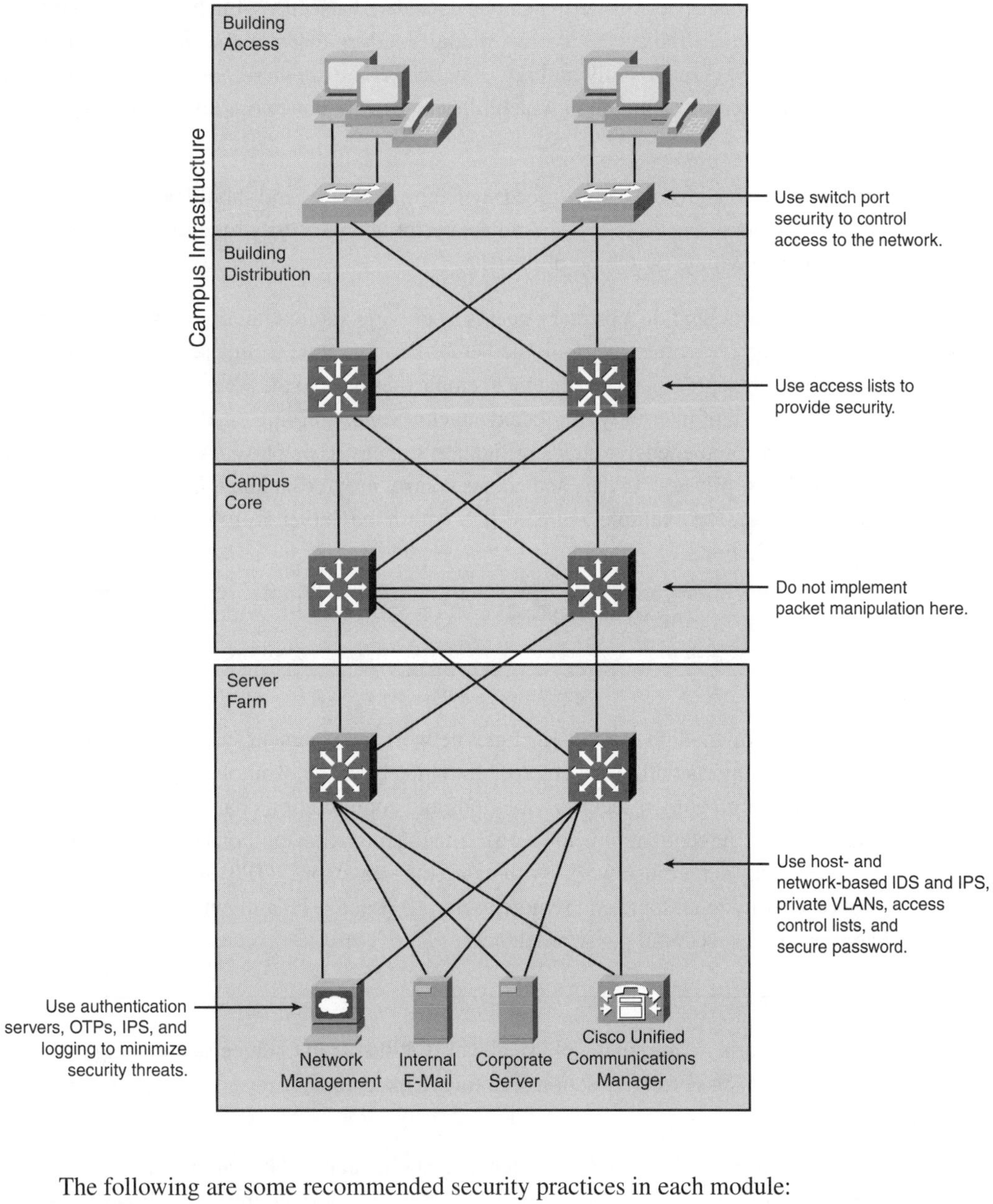

The following are some recommended security practices in each module:

- At the Building Access layer, access is controlled at the port level using the data link layer information. Some examples are filtering based on media access control addresses and IEEE 802.1X port authentication.

- The Building Distribution layer performs filtering to keep unnecessary traffic from the Campus Core. This packet filtering can be considered a security function because it does prevent some undesired access to other modules. Given that switches in the Building Distribution layer are typically multilayer switches (and are therefore Layer 3–aware), this is the first place on the data path in which filtering based on network layer information can be performed.

- The Campus Core layer is a high-speed switching backbone and should be designed to switch packets as quickly as possible; it should not perform any security functions, because doing so would slow down the switching of packets.

- The Server Farm module's primary goal is to provide application services to end users and devices. Enterprises often overlook the Server Farm module from a security perspective. Given the high degree of access that most employees have to these servers, they often become the primary goal of internally originated attacks. Simply relying on effective passwords does not provide a comprehensive attack mitigation strategy. Using host-based and network-based IPSs and IDSs, private VLANs, and access control provides a much more comprehensive attack response. For example, onboard IDS within the Server Farm's multilayer switches inspects traffic flows.

> **NOTE** Private VLANs provide Layer 2 isolation between ports within the same broadcast domain.

- The Server Farm module typically includes network management systems to securely manage all devices and hosts within the enterprise architecture. For example, syslog provides important information on security violations and configuration changes by logging security-related events (authentication and so on). An authentication, authorization, and accounting (AAA) security server also works with a one-time password (OTP) server to provide a high level of security to all local and remote users. AAA and OTP authentication reduces the likelihood of a successful password attack.

IPS and IDS

IDSs act like an alarm system in the physical world. When an IDS detects something it considers an attack, it either takes corrective action or notifies a management system so that an administrator can take action.

HIDSs work by intercepting operating system and application calls on an individual host and can also operate via after-the-fact analysis of local log files. The former approach allows better attack prevention, and the latter approach is a more passive attack-response role.

Because of their specific role, HIDSs are often more effective at preventing specific attacks than NIDSs, which usually issue an alert only on discovering an attack. However, this specificity does not allow the perspective of the overall network; this is where NIDS excels.

Intrusion prevention solutions form a core element of a successful security solution because they detect and block attacks, including worms, network viruses, and other malware through inline intrusion prevention, innovative technology, and identification of malicious network activity.

Network-based IPS solutions protect the network by helping detect, classify, and stop threats, including worms, spyware or adware, network viruses, and application abuse. Host-based IPS solutions protect server and desktop computing systems by identifying threats and preventing malicious behavior.

This information was derived from the *SAFE Blueprint for Small, Midsize, and Remote-User Networks,* available at http://www.cisco.com/go/safe/, and the *Cisco Intrusion Prevention System Introduction,* available at http://www.cisco.com/en/US/products/sw/secursw/ps2113/index.html.

Authentication, Authorization, and Accounting

AAA is a crucial aspect of network security that should be considered during the network design. An AAA server handles the following:

- **Authentication—*Who?*** Authentication checks the user's identity, typically through a username and password combination.

- **Authorization—*What?*** After the user is authenticated, the AAA server dictates what activity the user is allowed to perform on the network.

- **Accounting—*When?*** The AAA server can record the length of the session, the services accessed during the session, and so forth.

The principles of strong authentication should be included in the user authentication. *Strong authentication* refers to the two-factor authentication method in which users are authenticated using two of the following factors:

- **Something you know**: Such as a password or personal identification number (PIN)

- **Something you have**: Such as an access card, bank card, or token

- **Something you are**: For example, some biometrics, such as a retina print or fingerprint

- **Something you do**: Such as your handwriting, including the style, pressure applied, and so forth

As an example, when accessing an automated teller machine, strong authentication is enforced because a bank card (something you have) and a PIN (something you know) are used.

Tokens are key-chain-sized devices that show OTPs, one at a time, in a predefined order. The OTP is displayed on the token's small LCD, typically for 1 minute, before the next password in the sequence appears. The token is synchronized with a token server, which has the same predefined list of passcodes for that one user. Therefore, at any given time, only one valid password exists between the server and a token.

This information was derived from Cisco Press's *Campus Network Design Fundamentals* by Diane Teare and Catherine Paquet, 2006.

External Threats

When designing security in an enterprise network, the Enterprise Edge is the first line of defense at which potential outside attacks can be stopped. The Enterprise Edge is like a wall with small doors and strong guards that efficiently control any access. The following four attack methods are commonly used in attempts to compromise the integrity of the enterprise network from the outside:

- **IP spoofing**: An IP spoofing attack occurs when a hacker uses a trusted computer to launch an attack from inside or outside the network. The hacker uses either an IP address that is in the range of a network's trusted IP addresses or a trusted external IP address that provides access to specified resources on the network. IP spoofing attacks often lead to other types of attacks. For example, a hacker might launch a denial of service (DoS) attack using spoofed source addresses to hide his identity.

- **Password attacks**: Using a packet sniffer to determine usernames and passwords is a simple password attack; however, the term *password attack* usually refers to repeated brute-force attempts to identify username and password information. Trojan horse programs are another method that can be used to determine this information. A hacker might also use IP spoofing as a first step in a system attack by violating a trust relationship based on source IP addresses. First, however, the system would have to be configured to bypass password authentication so that only a username is required.

- **DoS attacks**: DoS attacks focus on making a service unavailable for normal use and are typically accomplished by exhausting some resource limitation on the network or within an operating system or application.

- **Application layer attacks**: Application layer attacks typically exploit well-known weaknesses in common software programs to gain access to a computer.

DoS Attacks

DoS attacks are different from most other attacks because they are not generally targeted at gaining access to a network or its information. Rather, these attacks focus on making a service unavailable for normal use. They are typically accomplished by exhausting some resource limitation on the network or within an operating system or application.

When involving specific network server applications, such as a web server or an FTP server, these attacks focus on acquiring and keeping open all the available connections supported by that server, thereby effectively locking out valid users of the server or service. DoS attacks are also implemented using common Internet protocols, such as TCP and Internet Control Message Protocol (ICMP).

Rather than exploiting a software bug or security hole, most DoS attacks exploit a weakness in the overall architecture of the system being attacked. However, some attacks compromise a network's performance by flooding the network with undesired and often useless network packets and by providing false information about the status of network resources. This type of attack is often the most difficult to prevent, because it requires coordinating with the upstream network provider. If traffic meant to consume the available bandwidth is not stopped there, denying it at the point of entry into your network does little good, because the available bandwidth has already been consumed. When this type of attack is launched from many different systems at the same time, it is often referred to as a *distributed denial of service attack*.

This information was derived from the *SAFE Blueprint for Small, Midsize, and Remote-User Networks*, available at http://www.cisco.com/go/safe/.

Application Layer Attacks

Hackers perform application layer attacks using several different methods. One of the most common methods is exploiting well-known weaknesses in software commonly found on servers, such as SMTP, HTTP, and FTP. By exploiting these weaknesses, hackers gain access to a computer with the permissions of the account that runs the application—usually a privileged system-level account. These application layer attacks are often widely publicized in an effort to allow administrators to rectify the problem with a patch. Unfortunately, many hackers also subscribe to these same informative mailing lists and therefore learn about the attack at the same time (if they have not discovered it already).

The primary problem with application-layer attacks is that they often use ports that are allowed through a firewall. For example, a hacker who executes a known vulnerability against a web server often uses TCP port 80 in the attack. A firewall needs to allow access on that port because the web server serves pages to users using port 80. From a firewall's perspective, the attack appears as merely standard port 80 traffic.

This information was derived from the *SAFE Blueprint for Small, Midsize, and Remote-User Networks*, available at http://www.cisco.com/go/safe/.

Figure 3-16 shows these four attack methods and how they relate to the Enterprise Edge modules.

Figure 3-16 *External Threats*

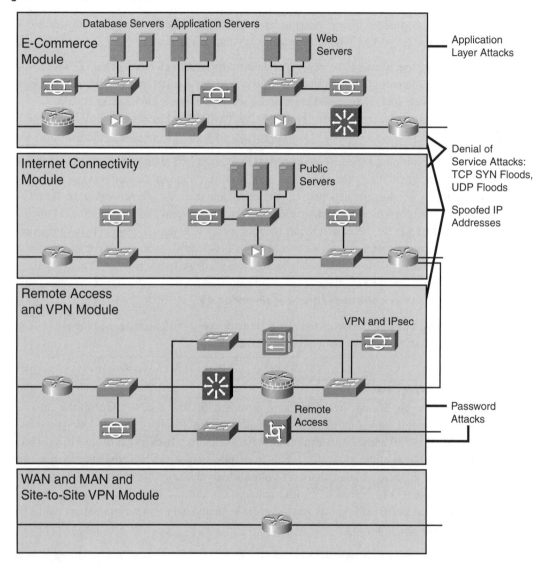

Because of the complexity of network applications, access control must be extremely granular and flexible yet still provide strong security. Tight borders between outside and inside cannot be defined, because interactions are continuously taking place between the Enterprise Edge and

Enterprise Campus. The ease of use of the network applications and resources must be balanced against the security measures imposed on the network users.

> **NOTE** Chapter 10, "Evaluating Security Solutions for the Network," covers security in the network in more detail.

High-Availability Services in a Modular Network Design

Most enterprise networks carry mission-critical information. Organizations that run such networks are usually interested in protecting the integrity of that information. Along with security, these organizations expect the internetworking platforms to offer a sufficient level of resilience.

This section introduces another network infrastructure service: high availability. To ensure adequate connectivity for mission-critical applications, high availability is an essential component of an enterprise environment.

Designing High Availability into a Network

Redundant network designs duplicate network links and devices, eliminating single points of failure on the network. The goal is to duplicate components whose failure could disable critical applications.

Because redundancy is expensive to deploy and maintain, redundant topologies should be implemented with care. Redundancy adds complexity to the network topology and to network addressing and routing. The level of redundancy should meet the organization's availability and affordability requirements.

KEY POINT | Before selecting redundant design solutions, analyze the business and technical goals and constraints to establish the required availability and affordability.

Critical applications, systems, internetworking devices, and links must be identified. Analyze the risk tolerance and the consequences of *not* implementing redundancy, and ensure that you consider the trade-offs of redundancy versus cost and simplicity versus complexity. Duplicate any component whose failure could disable critical applications.

Redundancy is not provided by simply duplicating all links. Unless all devices are completely fault-tolerant, redundant links should terminate at different devices; otherwise, devices that are not fault-tolerant become single points of failure.

KEY POINT | Because many other modules access the Server Farm and Campus Core modules, they typically require higher availability than other modules.

The following types of redundancy may be used in the modules of an enterprise:

■ Device redundancy, including card and port redundancy

■ Redundant physical connections to critical workstations and servers

■ Route redundancy

■ Link redundancy

■ Power redundancy, including redundant power supplies integral to the network devices and redundant power to the building's physical plant

KEY POINT | The key requirement in redundancy is to provide alternative paths for mission-critical applications. Simply making the backbone fault-tolerant does not ensure high availability. For example, if communication on a local segment is disrupted for any reason, that information will not reach the backbone. End-to-end high availability is possible only when redundancy is deployed throughout the internetwork.

High Availability in the Server Farm

Improving the reliability of critical workstations and servers usually depends on the hardware and operating system software in use. Some common ways of connecting include the following:

■ **Single attachment**: When a workstation or server has traffic to send to a station that is not local, it must know the address of a router on its network segment. If that router fails, the workstation or server needs a mechanism to discover an alternative router. If the workstation or server has a single attachment, it needs a Layer 3 mechanism to dynamically find an alternative router; therefore, the single-attachment method is not recommended. The available mechanisms include Address Resolution Protocol (ARP), Router Discovery Protocol (RDP), routing protocols (such as Routing Information Protocol [RIP]), Hot Standby Router Protocol (HSRP), Gateway Load Balancing Protocol (GLBP), and Virtual Router Redundancy Protocol (VRRP). These router discovery methods are described in the "Router Discovery" sidebar on the next page.

■ **Attachment through a redundant transceiver**: Physical redundancy with a redundant transceiver attachment is suitable in environments where the workstation hardware or software does not support redundant attachment options.

■ **Attachment through redundant network interface cards (NIC)**: Some environments (for example, most UNIX servers) support a redundant attachment through dual NICs (primary and backup); the device driver represents this attachment as a single interface to the operating system.

- **Fast EtherChannel or Gigabit EtherChannel port bundles**: Fast EtherChannel and Gigabit EtherChannel port bundles group multiple Fast or Gigabit Ethernet ports into a single logical transmission path between a switch and a router, host, or another switch. STP treats this EtherChannel as one logical link. The switch distributes frames across the ports in an EtherChannel. This load balancing was originally done based only on MAC addresses; however, newer implementations can also load-balance based on IP addresses or Layer 4 port numbers. Source, destination, or source and destination addresses or port numbers can be used. If a port within an EtherChannel fails, traffic previously carried over the failed port reverts to the remaining ports within the EtherChannel.

Router Discovery

When a workstation has traffic to send to a station that is not local, the workstation has many possible ways of discovering the address of a router on its network segment, including the following:

- **Explicit configuration**: Most IP workstations must be configured with a default router's IP address, called the *default gateway*.

  If the workstation's default router becomes unavailable, the workstation must be reconfigured with a different router's address. Some IP stacks enable multiple default routers to be configured, but many IP stacks do not support this.

- **ARP**: Some IP workstations send an ARP frame to find a remote station. A router running proxy ARP responds with its own data link layer address; Cisco routers run proxy ARP by default.

- **RDP**: RFC 1256, *ICMP Router Discovery Messages*, specifies an extension to ICMP that allows an IP workstation and router to run RDP to allow the workstation to learn a router's address. With RDP, each router periodically multicasts a router advertisement from each of its interfaces, thereby announcing the IP address of that interface. Hosts discover the addresses of their neighboring routers simply by listening for these advertisements. When a host starts up, it multicasts a router solicitation to ask for immediate advertisements rather than waiting for the next periodic one to arrive.

NOTE   RFCs are available at http://www.cis.ohio-state.edu/cs/Services/rfc/index.html.

- **Routing protocol**: An IP workstation can run RIP in passive, rather than active, mode to learn about routers. (*Active mode* means that the station sends RIP packets every 30 seconds; *passive mode* means that the station just listens for RIP packets but does not send any.) Alternatively, some workstations run the Open Shortest Path First (OSPF) protocol.

- **HSRP**: The Cisco HSRP provides a way for IP workstations to continue communicating even if their default router becomes unavailable. HSRP works by creating a virtual router that has its own IP and MAC addresses. The workstations use this virtual router as their default router.

HSRP routers on a LAN communicate among themselves to designate one router as active and one as standby. The active router sends periodic hello messages. The other HSRP routers listen for the hello messages. If the active router fails and the other HSRP routers stop receiving hello messages, the standby router takes over and becomes the active router. Because the new active router assumes the virtual router's IP and MAC addresses, end nodes do not see any change; they continue to send packets to the virtual router's MAC address, and the new active router delivers those packets. HSRP also works with proxy ARP: When an active HSRP router receives an ARP request for a node that is not on the local LAN, the router replies with the virtual router's MAC address rather than its own. If the router that originally sent the ARP reply later loses its connection, the new active router still delivers the traffic.

■ **GLBP**: GLBP is similar to HSRP, but it allows packet sharing between redundant routers in a group. GLBP provides load balancing over multiple routers (gateways) using a single virtual IP address and multiple virtual MAC addresses. Each host is configured with the same virtual IP address for its default gateway, and all routers in the virtual router group participate in forwarding packets.

■ **VRRP**: VRRP is an election protocol that dynamically assigns responsibility for one or more virtual routers to the VRRP routers on a LAN, allowing several routers on a multiaccess link to use the same virtual IP address. A VRRP router is configured to run the VRRP protocol in conjunction with one or more other routers attached to a LAN. In a VRRP configuration, one router is elected as the virtual router master, with the other routers acting as backups in case the virtual router master fails.

Figure 3-17 shows a server-to-switch connection implemented with a redundant transceiver.

Figure 3-17 *Physical Redundancy: Redundant Transceiver*

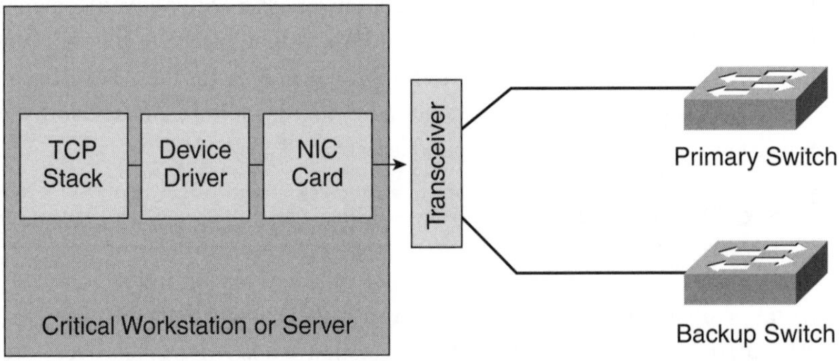

The redundant transceiver has two uplink ports that are usually connected to two access switches. The transceiver activates the backup port after it detects a link failure (carrier loss) on the primary port. The redundant transceiver can detect only physical layer failures; it cannot detect failures inside the switch or failures beyond the first switch. This type of redundancy is most often implemented on servers.

In Figure 3-18, the installation of an additional interface card in the server provides redundancy.

Figure 3-18 *Physical Redundancy: Redundant NICs*

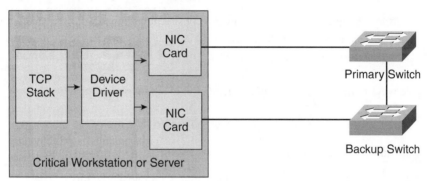

In this case, the device driver presents the configured NIC cards as a single interface (one IP address) to the operating system. If the primary link dies, the backup card activates. The two NICs might use a common MAC address, or they might use two distinct MAC addresses and send gratuitous ARP messages to provide proper IP-to-MAC address mapping on the switches when the backup interface card activates. With a redundant NIC, a VLAN shared between the two access switches is required to support the single IP address on the two server links.

> **NOTE**   The workstation sends gratuitous ARP messages to update the ARP tables and the forwarding tables on attached neighboring nodes (in this example, the Layer 2 switches).

Designing Route Redundancy

Redundant routes have two purposes:

- To minimize the effect of link failures

- To minimize the effect of an internetworking device failure

Redundant routes might also be used for load balancing when all routes are up.

Load Balancing

By default, the Cisco IOS balances between a maximum of four equal-cost paths for IP. Using the **maximum-paths** *maximum-path* router configuration command, you can request that up to 16 equally good routes be kept in the routing table (set *maximum-path* to 1 to disable load balancing).

When a packet is process-switched, load balancing over equal-cost paths occurs on a per-packet basis. When packets are fast-switched, load balancing over equal-cost paths is on a per-destination basis.

To support load balancing, keep the bandwidth consistent within a layer of the hierarchical model so that all paths have the same metric. Cisco's EIGRP includes the variance feature to load-balance traffic across multiple routes that have different metrics.

Possible ways to make the connection redundant include the following:

■   Parallel physical links between switches and routers

■   Backup LAN and WAN links (for example, DDR backup for a leased line)

The following are possible ways to make the network redundant:

■   A full mesh to provide complete redundancy and good performance

■   A partial mesh, which is less expensive and more scalable

The common approach when designing route redundancy is to implement partial redundancy by using a partial mesh instead of a full mesh and backup links to the alternative device. This protects only the most vital parts of the network, such as the links between the layers and concentration devices.

A full-mesh design forms any-to-any connectivity and is ideal for connecting a reasonably small number of devices. However, as the network topology grows, the number of links required to maintain a full mesh increases exponentially. (The number of links in a full mesh is $n(n-1)/2$, where n is the number of routers.) As the number of router peers increases, the bandwidth and CPU resources devoted to processing routing updates and service requests also increase.

A partial-mesh network is similar to the full-mesh network with some of its connections removed. A partial-mesh backbone might be appropriate for a campus network in which traffic predominantly goes into one centralized Server Farm module.

Figure 3-19 illustrates an example of route redundancy in a campus. In this example, the access layer switches are fully meshed with the distribution layer switches. If a link or distribution switch fails, an access layer switch can still communicate with the distribution layer. The multilayer switches select the primary and backup paths between the access and distribution layers based on the link's metric as computed by the routing protocol algorithm in use. The best path is placed in the forwarding table, and, in the case of equal-cost paths, load sharing takes place.

Figure 3-19 *Campus Infrastructure Redundancy Example*

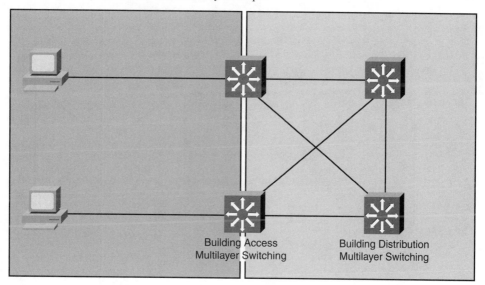

Building Access
Multilayer Switching

Building Distribution
Multilayer Switching

> **NOTE**   Chapter 7, "Selecting Routing Protocols for the Network," discusses routing protocols in detail.

Designing Link Redundancy

It is often necessary to provision redundant media in locations where mission-critical application traffic travels. In Layer 2–switched networks, redundant links are permitted as long as STP is running. STP guarantees one, and only one, active path within a broadcast domain, avoiding problems such as *broadcast storms* (when a broadcast continuously loops). The redundant path automatically activates when the active path goes down.

Because WAN links are often critical pieces of the internetwork, redundant media are often deployed in WAN environments. As is the case in Figure 3-20, where a Frame Relay circuit is used in parallel with a backup IPsec connection over the Internet, backup links can use different technologies. It is important that the backup provide sufficient capacity to meet the critical requirements if the primary route fails.

Figure 3-20 *Example of Enterprise Edge Link Redundancy*

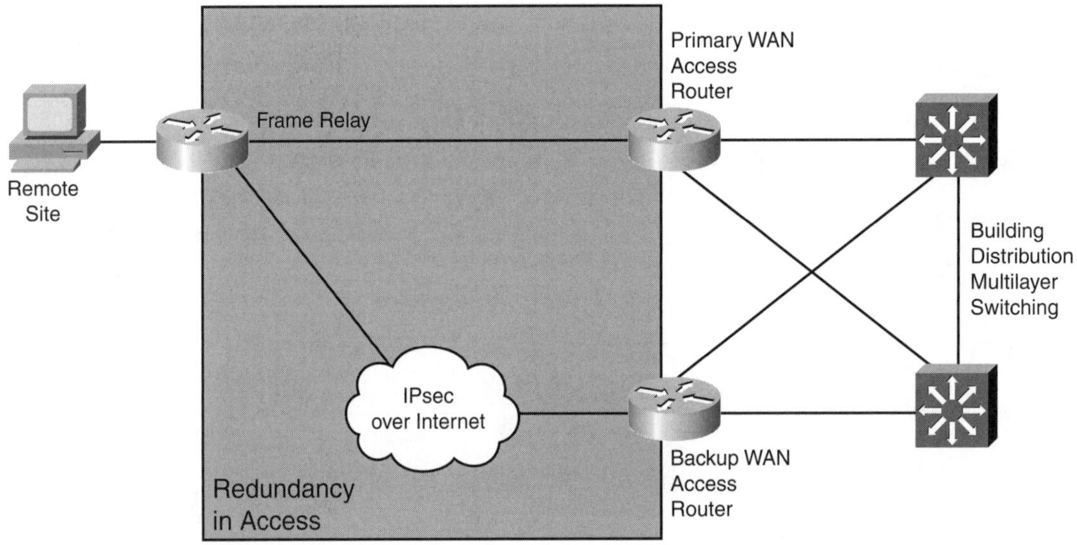

Backup links can be always-on or become active when a primary link goes down or becomes congested.

Backup Links

Backup links often use a different technology. For example, a leased line can be parallel with a backup IPsec connection over the Internet.

Using a floating static route, specify that the backup route has a higher administrative distance (used by Cisco routers to select which routing information to use) than the primary route learned from the routing protocol in use. Doing so ensures that the backup link is not used unless the primary route goes down.

When provisioning backup links, learn as much as possible about the actual physical circuit routing. Different carriers sometimes use the same facilities, meaning that your backup path is susceptible to the same failures as your primary path. Do some investigative work to ensure that the backup really is a backup.

Backup links can be used for load balancing and channel aggregation. *Channel aggregation* means that a router can bring up multiple channels (such as ISDN B channels) as bandwidth requirements increase.

Cisco supports the Multilink Point-to-Point Protocol (MLP), also referred to as *MPPP*, which is an Internet Engineering Task Force (IETF) standard for ISDN B channel (or asynchronous serial interface) aggregation. MLP does not specify how a router should accomplish the decision-making process to bring up extra channels. Instead, it seeks to ensure that packets arrive in sequence at the receiving router. The data is encapsulated within PPP, and the datagram is given a sequence number. At the receiving router, PPP uses this sequence number to re-create the original data stream. Multiple channels appear as one logical link to upper-layer protocols.

Voice Services in a Modular Network Design

To ensure successful implementation of voice applications, network designers must consider the enterprise services and infrastructure, and its configuration. For example, to support VoIP, the underlying IP infrastructure must be functioning and robust. In other words, don't even think of adding voice to a network experiencing other problems such as congestion or network failures.

Two Voice Implementations

Voice transport is a general term that can be divided into the following two implementations:

- **VoIP**: VoIP uses voice-enabled routers to convert analog voice into IP packets or packetized digital voice channels and route those packets between corresponding locations. Users do not often notice that VoIP is implemented in the network—they use their traditional phones, which are connected to a PBX. However, the PBX is not connected to the PSTN or to another PBX, but to a voice-enabled router that is an entry point to VoIP. Voice-enabled routers can also terminate IP phones using Session Initiation Protocol for call control and signaling.

- **IP telephony**: For IP telephony, traditional phones are replaced with IP phones. A server for call control and signaling, such as a Cisco Unified Communications Manager, is also used. The IP phone itself performs voice-to-IP conversion, and no voice-enabled routers are required within the enterprise network. However, if a connection to the PSTN is required, a voice-enabled router or other gateway in the Enterprise Edge is added where calls are forwarded to the PSTN.

> **NOTE** Earlier names for the Cisco Unified Communications Manager include Cisco CallManager and Cisco Unified CallManager.

Both implementations require properly designed networks. Using a modular approach in a voice transport design is especially important because of the voice sensitivity to delay and the complexity of troubleshooting voice networks. All Cisco Enterprise Architecture modules are involved in voice transport design.

IP Telephony Components

An IP telephony network contains four main voice-specific components:

- **IP phones**: IP phones are used to place calls in an IP telephony network. They perform voice-to-IP (and vice versa) coding and compression using special hardware. IP phones offer services such as user directory lookups and Internet access. The phones are active network devices that require power to operate; power is supplied through the LAN connection using PoE or with an external power supply.

- **Switches with inline power**: Switches with inline power (PoE) enable the modular wiring closet infrastructure to provide centralized power for Cisco IP telephony networks. These switches are similar to traditional switches, with an added option to provide power to the LAN ports where IP phones are connected. The switches also perform some basic QoS tasks, such as packet classification, which is required for prioritizing voice through the network.

- **Call-processing manager**: The call-processing manager, such as a Cisco Unified Communications Manager, provides central call control and configuration management for IP phones. It provides the core functionality to initialize IP telephony devices and to perform call setup and call routing throughout the network. Cisco Unified Communications Manager can be clustered to provide a distributed, scalable, and highly available IP telephony model. Adding more servers to a cluster of servers provides more capacity to the system.

- **Voice gateway**: Voice gateways, also called *voice-enabled routers* or *voice-enabled switches*, provide voice services such as voice-to-IP coding and compression, PSTN access, IP packet routing, backup call processing, and voice services. Backup call processing allows voice gateways to take over call processing in case the primary call-processing manager fails. Voice gateways typically support a subset of the call-processing functionality supported by the Cisco Unified Communications Manager.

Other components of an IP telephony network include a robust IP network, voice messaging and applications, and digital signal processor resources to process voice functions in hardware, which is much faster than doing it in software. These components are located throughout the enterprise network, as illustrated in Figure 3-21.

Figure 3-21   *IP Telephony Components*

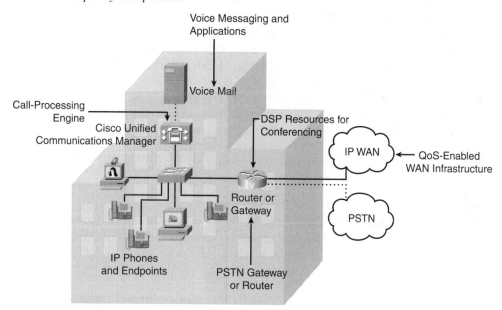

Modular Approach in Voice Network Design

Implementing voice requires deploying delay-sensitive services from end to end in all enterprise network modules. Use the modular approach to simplify design, implementation, and especially troubleshooting. Voice implementation requires some modifications to the existing enterprise network infrastructure in terms of performance, capacity, and availability because it is an end-to-end solution. For example, clients (IP phones) are located in the Building Access layer, and the call-processing manager is located in the Server Farm module; therefore, all modules in the enterprise network are involved in voice processing and must be adequately considered. Voice affects the various modules of the network as follows:

■ **Building Access layer**: IP phones and end-user computers are attached to Layer 2 switches here. Switches provide power to the IP phones and provide QoS packet classification and marking, which is essential for proper voice packet manipulation through the network.

■ **Building Distribution layer**: This layer performs packet reclassifications if the Building Access layer is unable to classify packets or is not within the trusted boundary. It aggregates Building Access layer switches (wiring closets) and provides redundant uplinks to the Campus Core layer.

- **Campus Core layer**: The Campus Core layer forms the network's core. All enterprise network modules are attached to it; therefore, virtually all traffic between application servers and clients traverses the Campus Core. With the advent of wire-speed multilayer gigabit switching devices, LAN backbones have migrated to switched gigabit architectures that combine all the benefits of routing with wire-speed packet forwarding.

- **Server Farm module**: This module includes multilayer switches with redundant connections to redundant Cisco Unified Communications Managers, which are essential for providing high availability and reliability.

- **Enterprise Edge**: The Enterprise Edge extends IP telephony from the Enterprise Campus to remote locations via WANs, the PSTN, and the Internet.

Figure 3-22 shows the voice network solution in the Cisco Enterprise Architecture. It illustrates how a call is initiated on an IP phone, how the call setup goes through the Cisco Unified Communications Manager, and how the end-to-end session between two IP phones is established. Note that Cisco Unified Communications Manager is involved in only the call setup.

Figure 3-22 *Voice Transport Example*

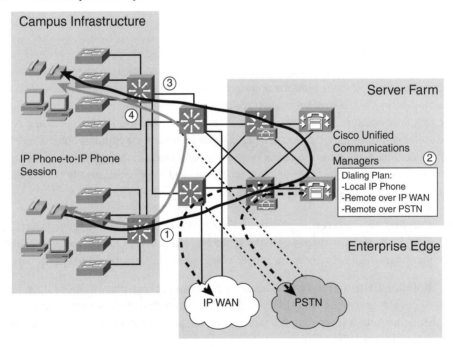

Calls destined for remote locations traverse the Enterprise Edge through the WAN and MAN and Site-to-Site VPN module or through the Remote Access and VPN module. Calls destined for public phone numbers on the PSTN are routed over the Enterprise Edge through the Remote Access and VPN module. Calls between IP phones traverse the Building Access, Building Distribution, and Campus Core layers, and the Server Farm module. Although call setup uses all these modules, speech employs only the Building Access, Building Distribution, and, in some cases, the Campus Core layers.

Evaluating the Existing Data Infrastructure for Voice Design

When designing IP telephony, designers must document and evaluate the existing data infrastructure in each enterprise module to help determine upgrade requirements. Items to consider include the following:

- **Performance**: Enhanced infrastructure for additional bandwidth, consistent performance, or higher availability, if required, might be necessary for the converging environment. Performance evaluation includes analyzing network maps, device inventory information, and network baseline information. Links and devices such as those with high peak or busy-hour use might have to be upgraded to provide sufficient capacity for the additional voice traffic. Devices with high CPU use, high backplane use, high memory use, queuing drops, or buffer misses might have to be upgraded.

- **Availability**: Redundancy in all network modules should be reviewed to ensure that the network can meet the recommended IP telephony availability goals with the current or new network design.

- **Features**: Examine the router and switch characteristics—including the chassis, module, and software version—to determine the IP telephony feature capabilities in the existing environment.

- **Capacity**: Evaluate the overall network capacity and the impact of IP telephony on a module-by-module basis to ensure that the network meets capacity requirements and that there is no adverse impact on the existing network and application requirements.

- **Power**: Assess the power requirements of the new network infrastructure, ensuring that the additional devices will not oversubscribe existing power. Consider taking advantage of PoE capabilities in devices.

NOTE   Chapter 8, "Voice Network Design Considerations," covers voice in detail.

Wireless Services in a Modular Network

A wireless LAN (WLAN) supports mobile clients connecting to the enterprise network. The mobile clients do not have a physical connection to the network because WLANs replace the Layer 1 traditional wired network (usually Category 5 cable) with radio frequency (RF) transmissions through the air. WLANs are for local networks, either in-building, line-of-sight outdoor bridging applications, or a combination of both.

In a wireless network, many issues can arise to prevent the RF signal from reaching all parts of the facility, including multipath distortion, hidden node problems, interference from other wireless sources, and near/far issues. A site survey helps find the regions where these issues occur by defining the contours of RF coverage in a particular facility, discovering regions where multipath distortion can occur, areas where RF interference is high, and finding solutions to eliminate such issues.

Privacy and security issues must also be considered in a wireless network. Because WLANs are typically connected to the wired network, all the modules within the enterprise infrastructure must be considered to ensure the success of a wireless deployment.

Centralized WLAN Components

As illustrated in Figure 3-23, the four main components in a centralized WLAN deployment are as follows:

- **End-user devices**: A PC or other end-user device in the access layer uses a wireless NIC to connect to an access point (AP) using radio waves.

- **Wireless APs**: APs, typically in the access layer, are shared devices that function similar to a hub. Cisco APs can be either lightweight or autonomous.

  Lightweight APs are used in centralized WLAN deployments. A lightweight AP receives control and configuration from a WLAN controller (WLC) with which it is associated, providing a centralized point of management and reducing the security concern of a stolen AP. An autonomous AP has a local configuration and requires local management, which might make consistent configurations difficult and add to the cost of network management.

- **WLC**: A WLC provides management and support for wireless services such as roaming. The WLC is typically in the core layer of an enterprise network.

- **Existing switched and routed wired network**: The wireless APs connect to the wired enterprise network.

Figure 3-23   *Centralized WLAN Components*

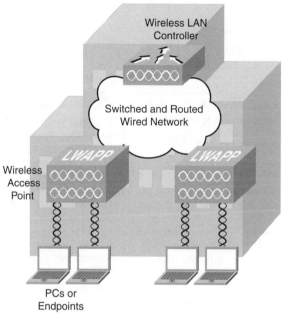

NOTE   WLANs are described further in Chapter 9, "Wireless Network Design Considerations."

Application Networking Services in a Modular Network Design

Traditional networks handled static web pages, e-mail, and routine client/server traffic. Today, enterprise networks must handle more sophisticated types of network applications that include voice and video. Examples include voice transport, videoconferencing, online training, and audio and video broadcasts. Applications place increasing demands on IT infrastructures as they evolve into highly visible services that represent the face of the business to internal and external audiences.

The large amount and variety of data requires that the modern network be *application-aware*—in other words, be aware of the content carried across it to optimally handle that content. It is no longer enough simply to add more bandwidth as needs grow. Networks have had to become smarter. A new role is emerging for the network as a provider of application infrastructure services that extend the value of applications, either by improving delivery of content to users and other applications or by offloading infrastructure functions that today burden development and operations teams. Application Networking Services (ANS) provide this intelligence.

ANS Examples

Table 3-1 illustrates some sample application deployment issues that many IT managers face today and how ANS resolves these issues.

Table 3-1 *Examples of Application Deployment Issues and Solutions*

Sample Deployment Issue	Sample ANS Solution
Consolidation of data centers results in remote employees having slower access to centrally managed applications	Wide-area application services in the branch office that compress, cache, and optimize content for remote users so that they experience LAN-like responsiveness
A new web-based ordering system experiences a high proportion of abandoned orders because of poor responsiveness during the checkout process	Optimization of web streams being sent to an e-commerce portal, which reduces latency, suppresses unnecessary reloading of web objects, and offloads low-level tasks from the web server
Business partners need immediate and secure electronic access to information held in back-office applications, such as shipment information	Security and remote connectivity services that automatically validate a partner's request, route it to the appropriate back-office application, and encrypt and prioritize the response
A purchasing application needs to log and track orders over a certain value for compliance purposes	Application messaging service that intercepts purchase orders, locates the value, and logs large orders to a database according to business policy rules

ANS Components

Figure 3-24 illustrates an example of ANS deployed in offices connected over a WAN, providing LAN-like performance to users in the branch, regional, and remote offices. ANS components are deployed symmetrically in the data center and the distant offices. The ANS components in this example are as follows:

- **Cisco Wide Area Application Services (WAAS) software**: Cisco WAAS software gives remote offices LAN-like access to centrally hosted applications, servers, storage, and multimedia.

- **Cisco Wide Area Application Engine (WAE) appliance**: Cisco WAE appliances provide high-performance global LAN-like access to enterprise applications and data. WAEs use either WAAS or Application and Content Networking System [ACNS] software. WAEs help consolidate storage, servers, and so forth in the corporate data center, with only low-cost, easy-to-maintain network appliances in distant offices.

Each Cisco WAE device can be managed using the embedded command-line interface, the device Web GUI, or the Cisco WAAS Central Manager GUI. The Cisco WAAS Central Manager runs on Cisco WAE appliances and can be configured for high availability by deploying a pair of Cisco WAEs as central managers. The two central manager WAEs automatically share configuration and monitoring data.

- **Cisco 2600/3600/3700 Series Content Engine Module**: Content Engine Modules can be deployed in the data center or branch offices to optimize WAN bandwidth, accelerate deployment of mission-critical web applications, add web content security, and deliver live and on-demand business video.

Figure 3-24 *ANS Components in a WAN Environment*

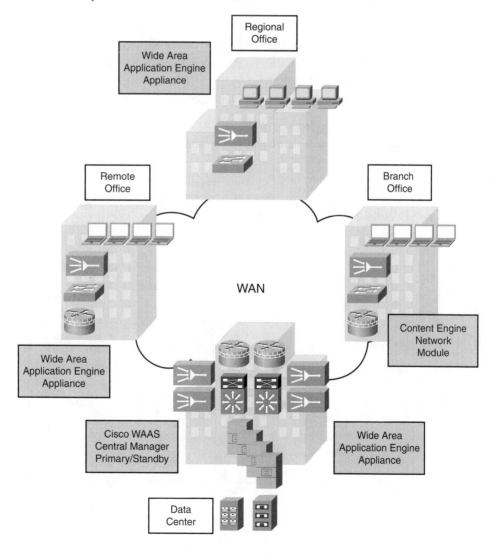

> **NOTE**   Further details on ANS are available at http://www.cisco.com/go/applicationservices/.

Network Management Protocols and Features

Proper network management is a critical component of an efficient network. Network administrators need tools to monitor the functionality of the network devices, the connections between them, and the services they provide. SNMP has become the de facto standard for use in network management solutions and is tightly connected with remote monitoring (RMON) and Management Information Bases (MIB). Each managed device in the network has several variables that quantify the state of the device. You can monitor managed devices by reading the values of these variables, and you can control managed devices by writing values into these variables.

This section introduces SNMP and describes the differences between SNMP versions 1, 2, and 3. The role of MIBs in SNMP and RMON monitoring is described, and Cisco's network discovery protocol, Cisco Discovery Protocol (CDP), is introduced. The section concludes with a description of methods for gathering network statistics.

Network Management Architecture

Figure 3-25 illustrates a generic network management architecture.

Figure 3-25   *Network Management Architecture*

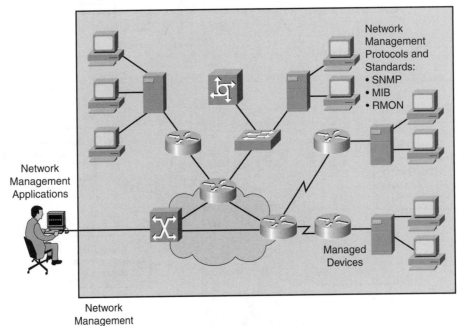

The network management architecture consists of the following:

- **Network management system (NMS)**: A system that executes applications that monitor and control managed devices. NMSs provide the bulk of the processing and memory resources that are required for network management.

- **Network management protocol**: A protocol that facilitates the exchange of management information between the NMS and managed devices, including SNMP, MIB, and RMON.

- **Managed devices**: A device (such as a router) managed by an NMS.

- **Management agents**: Software, on managed devices, that collects and stores management information, including SNMP agents and RMON agents.

- **Management information**: Data that is of interest to a device's management, usually stored in MIBs.

A variety of network management applications can be used on a network management system; the choice depends on the network platform (such as the hardware or operating system). The management information resides on network devices; management agents that reside on the device collect and store data in a standardized data definition structure known as the *MIB*.

The network management application uses SNMP or other network management protocols to retrieve the data that the management agents collect. The retrieved data is typically processed and prepared for display with a GUI, which allows the operator to use a graphical representation of the network to control managed devices and program the network management application.

Protocols and Standards

Several protocols are used within the network management architecture.

KEY POINT

SNMP is the simplest network management protocol. SNMP version 1 (SNMPv1) was extended to SNMP version 2 (SNMPv2) with its variants, which were further extended with SNMP version 3 (SNMPv3).

The MIB is a detailed definition of the information on a network device and is accessible through a network management protocol, such as SNMP.

RMON is an extension of the MIB. The MIB typically provides only static information about the managed device; the RMON agent collects specific groups of statistics for long-term trend analysis.

> **NOTE** The ISO network management model defines the following five functional areas of network management (which are abbreviated as *FCAPS*): fault management, configuration management, accounting management, performance management, and security management.
>
> The FCAPS model and these functional areas are rarely implemented in a single enterprise-wide network management system. A typical enterprise uses a variety of network infrastructure and service elements managed by element-specific network management systems.

> **NOTE** Information on specific management systems for technologies such as voice, security, and wireless are provided in the relevant chapters in this book.

The following sections discuss SNMP, MIB, and RMON in detail.

SNMP

SNMP has become the de facto standard for network management. SNMP is a simple solution that requires little code to implement, which enables vendors to easily build SNMP agents for their products. In addition, SNMP is often the foundation of the network management architecture. SNMP defines how management information is exchanged between network management applications and management agents. Figure 3-26 shows the terms used in SNMP; they are described as follows:

- **Manager**: The manager, a network management application in an NMS, periodically polls the SNMP agents that reside on managed devices for the data, thereby enabling information to be displayed using a GUI on the NMS. A disadvantage of periodic SNMP polling is the possible delay between when an event occurs and when it is collected by the NMS; there is a trade-off between polling frequency and bandwidth usage.

- **Protocol**: SNMP is a protocol for message exchange. It uses the User Datagram Protocol (UDP) transport mechanism to send and retrieve management information, such as MIB variables.

- **Managed device**: A device (such as a router) managed by the manager.

- **Management agents**: SNMP management agents reside on managed devices to collect and store a range of information about the device and its operation, respond to the manager's requests, and generate traps to inform the manager about certain events. SNMP traps are sent by management agents to the NMS when certain events occur. Trap notifications could result in substantial network and agent resource savings by eliminating the need for some SNMP polling requests.

■ **MIB**: The management agent collects data and stores it locally in the MIB, a database of objects about the device. Community strings, which are similar to passwords, control access to the MIB. To access or set MIB variables, the user must specify the appropriate read or write community string; otherwise, access is denied.

Figure 3-26 *NMP Is a Protocol for Management Information Exchange*

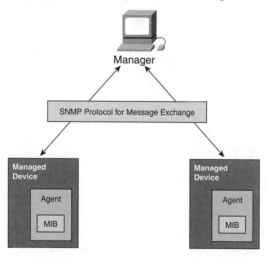

SNMPv1

The initial version of SNMP, SNMPv1 is defined in RFC 1157, *Simple Network Management Protocol (SNMP)*. The protocol's simplicity is apparent by the set of operations that are available. Figure 3-27 shows the basic SNMP messages, which the manager uses to transfer data from agents that reside on managed devices. These messages are described as follows:

■ **Get Request**: Used by the manager to request a specific MIB variable from the agent.

■ **Get Next Request**: Used after the initial get request to retrieve the next object instance from a table or list.

■ **Set Request**: Used to set a MIB variable on an agent.

■ **Get Response**: Used by an agent to respond to a manager's Get Request or Get Next Request message.

■ **Trap**: Used by an agent to transmit an unsolicited alarm to the manager. A Trap message is sent when specific conditions occur, such as a change in the state of a device, a device or component failure, or an agent initialization or restart.

Figure 3-27 *SNMPv1 Message Types*

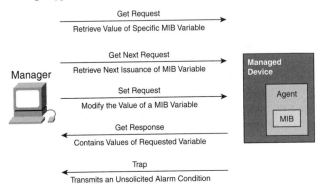

SNMPv2

SNMPv2 is a revised protocol that includes performance and manager-to-manager communication improvements to SNMP. SNMPv2 was introduced with RFC 1441, *Introduction to version 2 of the Internet-standard Network Management Framework*, but members of the IETF subcommittee could not agree on several sections of the SNMPv2 specification (primarily the protocol's security and administrative needs). Several attempts to achieve acceptance of SNMPv2 have been made by releasing experimental modified versions, commonly known as SNMPv2*, SNMPv2, SNMPv2u, SNMPv1+, and SNMPv1.5, which do not contain the disputed parts.

Community-based SNMPv2 (or SNMPv2c), which is defined in RFC 1901, *Introduction to Community-based SNMPv2*, is referred to as SNMPv2 because it is the most common implementation. The "c" stands for *community-based security* because SNMPv2c uses the same community strings as SNMPv1 for read and write access. SNMPv2 changes include the introduction of the following two new message types:

■ **GetBulk message type**: Used for retrieving large amounts of data, such as tables. This message reduces repetitive requests and replies, thereby improving performance.

■ **InformRequest**: Used to alert the SNMP manager of a specific condition. Unlike unacknowledged trap messages, InformRequest messages are acknowledged. A managed device sends an InformRequest to the NMS; the NMS acknowledges the receipt of the message by sending a Response message back to the managed device.

Another improvement of SNMPv2 over SNMPv1 is the addition of new data types with 64-bit counters because 32-bit counters were quickly overflowed by fast network interfaces.

On Cisco routers, Cisco IOS software release 11.3 and later versions implement SNMPv2. However, neither SNMPv1 nor SNMPv2 offers security features. Specifically, SNMPv1 and SNMPv2 can neither authenticate the source of a management message nor encrypt the message.

Because of the lack of security features, many SNMPv1 and SNMPv2 implementations are limited to a read-only capability, reducing their usefulness to that of a network monitor.

SNMPv3

SNMPv3 is the latest SNMP version to become a full standard. Its introduction has moved SNMPv1 and SNMPv2 to historic status. SNMPv3, which is described in RFCs 3410 through 3415, adds methods to ensure the secure transmission of critical data to and from managed devices. Table 3-2 lists these RFCs. Note that these RFCs make RFCs 2271 through 2275 and RFCs 2570 through 2575 obsolete.

Table 3-2 *SNMPv3 Proposed Standards Documents*

RFC Number	Title of RFC
3410	Introduction and Applicability Statements for Internet-Standard Management Framework
3411	An Architecture for Describing Simple Network Management Protocol (SNMP) Management Frameworks
3412	Message Processing and Dispatching for the Simple Network Management Protocol (SNMP)
3413	Simple Network Management Protocol (SNMP) Applications
3414	User-based Security Model (USM) for Version 3 of the Simple Network Management Protocol (SNMPv3)
3415	View-based Access Control Model (VACM) for the Simple Network Management Protocol (SNMP)

SNMPv3 introduces the following three security levels:

- **NoAuthNoPriv**: Without authentication and without privacy (encryption).

- **AuthNoPriv**: With authentication but without privacy. Authentication is based on Hash-Based Message Authentication Code-Message Digest 5 or HMAC-Secure Hash Algorithm algorithms.

- **AuthPriv**: With authentication as described earlier and privacy using the 56-bit Cipher-Block Chaining-Data Encryption Standard encryption standard.

Security levels can be specified per user or per group of users via direct interaction with the managed device or via SNMP operations. Security levels determine which SNMP objects a user can access for reading, writing, or creating, and the list of notifications that users can receive. On Cisco routers, Cisco IOS software release 12.0 and later versions implement SNMPv3.

MIB

> **KEY POINT** | A MIB is a collection of managed objects. A MIB stores information, which is collected by the local management agent, on a managed device for later retrieval by a network management protocol.

Each object in a MIB has a unique identifier that network management applications use to identify and retrieve the value of the specific object. The MIB has a tree-like structure in which similar objects are grouped under the same branch of the MIB tree. For example, different interface counters are grouped under the MIB tree's interfaces branch.

Internet MIB Hierarchy

As shown in Figure 3-28, the MIB structure is logically represented by a tree hierarchy. The root of the tree is unnamed and splits into three main branches: Consultative Committee for International Telegraph and Telephone (CCITT), ISO, and joint ISO/CCITT.

These branches and those that fall below each category are identified with short text strings and integers. Text strings describe object names, whereas integers form object identifiers that allow software to create compact, encoded representations of the names. The *object identifier* in the Internet MIB hierarchy is the sequence of numeric labels on the nodes along a path from the root to the object. The Internet standard MIB is represented by the object identifier 1.3.6.1.2.1, which can also be expressed as iso.org.dod.internet.mgmt.mib.

Figure 3-28   *Internet MIB Hierarchy*

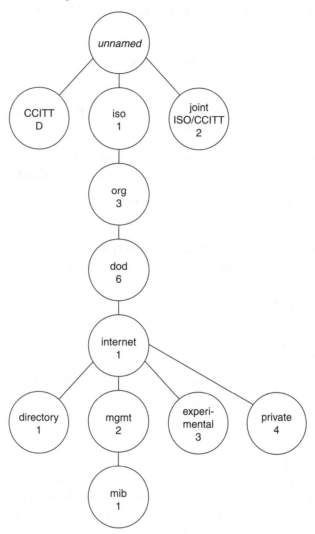

This information was adapted from the *Cisco Management Information Base (MIB) User Quick Reference*, which is available at http://www.cisco.com/univercd/cc/td/doc/product/software/ios112/mbook/index.htm.

Standard MIBs are defined in various RFCs. For example, RFC 1213, *Management Information Base for Network Management of TCP/IP-based internets: MIB-II*, defines the TCP/IP MIB.

In addition to standard MIBs, vendors can obtain their own branch of the MIB subtree and create custom managed objects under that branch. A Cisco router MIB uses both standard and private managed objects.

A Cisco router's MIB tree contains several defined standard managed objects, including from the following groups:

■ Interface group (including interface description, type, physical address, counts of incoming and outgoing packets, and so forth)

■ IP group (including whether the device is acting as an IP gateway, the number of input packets, the number of packets discarded because of error, and so forth)

■ ICMP group (including the number of ICMP messages received, the number of messages with errors, and so forth)

The Cisco private section of the MIB tree contains private managed objects, which were introduced by Cisco, such as the following objects for routers:

■ Small, medium, large, and huge buffers

■ Primary and secondary memory

■ Proprietary protocols

Private definitions of managed objects must be compiled into the NMS before they can be used; the result is output that is more descriptive, with variables and events that can be referred to by name.

MIB-II

MIB-II is an extension of the original MIB (which is now called *MIB-I*) and is defined by RFC 1213. MIB-II supports a number of new protocols and provides more detailed, structured information. It remains compatible with the previous version, which is why MIB-II retains the same object identifier as MIB-I (1.3.6.1.2.1).

The location of MIB-II objects is under the iso.org.dod.internet.mgmt subtree, where the top-level MIB objects are defined as follows (definitions of these objects can be found in RFC 1213):

■ System (1)

■ Interfaces (2)

■ Address Translation (3)

■ IP (4)

- ICMP (5)

- TCP (6)

- UDP (7)

- EGP (8)

- Transmission (10)

- SNMP (11)

Although the MIB-II definition is an improvement over MIB-I, the following unresolved issues exist:

- MIB-II is still a *device-centric* solution, meaning that its focus is on individual devices, not the entire network or data flows.

- MIB-II is *poll-based*, meaning that data is stored in managed devices and a management system must request (poll) it via the management protocol; the data is not sent automatically.

Cisco MIB

The Cisco private MIB definitions are under the Cisco MIB subtree (1.3.6.1.4.1.9 or iso.org.dod.internet.private.enterprise.cisco). Cisco MIB definitions supported on Cisco devices are available at http://www.cisco.com/public/mibs/.

The Cisco private MIB subtree contains three subtrees: Local (2), Temporary (3), and CiscoMgmt (9). The Local (2) subtree contains MIB objects defined before Cisco IOS software release 10.2; these MIB objects are implemented in the SNMPv1 Structure of Management Information (SMI). The SMI defines the structure of data that resides within MIB-managed objects. Beginning with Cisco IOS software release 10.2, however, Cisco MIBs are defined according to the SNMPv2 SMI and are placed in the CiscoMgmt subtree (9). The variables in the temporary subtree are subject to change for each Cisco IOS software release.

MIB Polling Guidelines

Monitoring networks using SNMP requires that the NMS poll each managed device on a periodic basis to determine its status. Frequently polling many devices or MIB variables on a device across a network to a central NMS might result in performance issues, including congestion on slower links or at the NMS connection, or overwhelming the NMS resources when processing all the collected data. The following are recommended polling guidelines:

- Restrict polling to only those MIB variables necessary for analysis.

- Analyze and use the data collected; do not collect data if it is not analyzed.

- Increase polling intervals (in other words, reduce the number of polls per period) over low-bandwidth links.

- For larger networks, consider deploying management domains, a distributed model for deploying an NMS. Management domains permit polling to be more local to the managed devices. As a result, they reduce overall management traffic across the network and the potential for one failed device or link to interrupt management visibility to the remaining network. Aggregated management data might still be centralized when management domains are used. This model is particularly appropriate for networks that already have separate administrative domains or where large campuses or portions of the network are separated by slower WAN links.

- Leverage nonpolling mechanisms such as SNMP traps, RMON, and syslog (as described in later sections of this chapter).

MIB Example

Figure 3-29 depicts SNMP MIB variable retrieval in action.

Figure 3-29 *SNMP MIB Variable Retrieval*

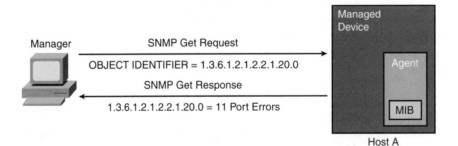

— Base format to retrieve the number of errors on an interface

iso	org	dod	internet	mgmt	mib	interface	ifTable	ifEntry	ifOutErrors
1	3	6	1	2	1	2	2	1	20

— Specific format to retrieve the number of errors on first interface

iso	org	dod	internet	mgmt	mib	interface	ifTable	ifEntry	ifOutErrors	Instance
1	3	6	1	2	1	2	2	1	20	0

Manager

SNMP Get Request

OBJECT IDENTIFIER = 1.3.6.1.2.1.2.2.1.20.0

SNMP Get Response

1.3.6.1.2.1.2.2.1.20.0 = 11 Port Errors

Managed Device

Agent

MIB

Host A

In this example, the network manager wants to retrieve the number of errors on the first interface. Starting with interface number 0, the valid range for interface numbers is *0* through *the maximum number of ports minus one*. The manager creates the SNMP Get Request message with reference to the MIB variable 1.3.6.1.2.1.2.2.1.20.0, which represents interface outgoing errors on interface

0. The agent creates the SNMP Get Response message in response to the manager's request. The response includes the value of the referenced variable. In the example, the agent returned value is 11, indicating that there were 11 outgoing errors on that interface.

RMON

KEY POINT RMON is a MIB that provides support for proactive management of LAN traffic.

The RMON standard allows packet and traffic patterns on LAN segments to be monitored. RMON tracks the following items:

- Number of packets

- Packet sizes

- Broadcasts

- Network utilization

- Errors and conditions, such as Ethernet collisions

- Statistics for hosts, including errors generated by hosts, busiest hosts, and which hosts communicate with each other

RMON features include historical views of RMON statistics based on user-defined sample intervals, alarms that are based on user-defined thresholds, and packet capture based on user-defined filters.

NOTE RMON is defined as a portion of the MIB II database. RFC 2819, *Remote Network Monitoring Management Information Base*, defines the objects for managing remote network monitoring devices. RFC 1513, *Token Ring Extensions to the Remote Network Monitoring MIB*, defines extensions to the RMON MIB for managing IEEE 802.5 Token Ring networks.

KEY POINT Without RMON, a MIB could be used to check the device's network performance. However, doing so would lead to a large amount of bandwidth required for management traffic. By using RMON, the managed device itself (via its RMON agent) collects and stores the data that would otherwise be retrieved from the MIB frequently.

RMON agents can reside in routers, switches, hubs, servers, hosts, or dedicated RMON probes. Because RMON can collect a lot of data, dedicated RMON probes are often used on routers and switches instead of enabling RMON agents on these devices. Performance thresholds can be set and reported on if the threshold is breached; this helps reduce management traffic. RMON provides effective network fault diagnosis, performance tuning, and planning for network upgrades.

RMON1

> **KEY POINT** | RMON1 works on the data link layer (with MAC addresses) and provides aggregate LAN traffic statistics and analysis for remote LAN segments.

Because RMON agents must look at every frame on the network, they might cause performance problems on a managed device. The agent's performance can be classified based on processing power and memory.

> **NOTE** The RMON MIB is 1.3.6.1.2.1.16 (iso.ord.dod.internet.mgmt.mib.rmon).

RMON1 Groups

RMON agents gather nine groups of statistics, ten including Token Ring, which are forwarded to a manager on request, usually via SNMP. As summarized in Figure 3-30, RMON1 agents can implement some or all of the following groups:

- **Statistics**: Contains statistics such as packets sent, bytes sent, broadcast packets, multicast packets, CRC errors, runts, giants, fragments, jabbers, collisions, and so forth, for each monitored interface on the device.

- **History**: Used to store periodic statistical samples for later retrieval.

- **Alarm**: Used to set specific thresholds for managed objects and to trigger an event on crossing the threshold (this requires an Events group).

- **Host**: Contains statistics associated with each host discovered on the network.

- **Host Top N**: Contains statistics for hosts that top a list ordered by one of their observed variables.

- **Matrix**: Contains statistics for conversations between sets of two addresses, including the number of packets or bytes exchanged between two hosts.

- **Filters**: Contains rules for data packet filters; data packets matched by these rules generate events or are stored locally in a Packet Capture group.

■ **Packet Capture**: Contains data packets that match rules set in the Filters group.

■ **Events**: Controls the generation and notification of events from this device.

■ **TokenRing**: Contains the following Token Ring Extensions:

— **Ring Station**—Detailed statistics on individual stations

— **Ring Station Order**—Ordered list of stations currently on the ring

— **Ring Station Configuration**—Configuration information and insertion/removal data on each station

— **Source Routing**—Statistics on source routing, such as hop counts

Figure 3-30 *RMON1 Groups*

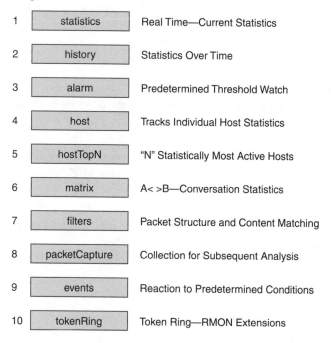

1	statistics	Real Time—Current Statistics
2	history	Statistics Over Time
3	alarm	Predetermined Threshold Watch
4	host	Tracks Individual Host Statistics
5	hostTopN	"N" Statistically Most Active Hosts
6	matrix	A< >B—Conversation Statistics
7	filters	Packet Structure and Content Matching
8	packetCapture	Collection for Subsequent Analysis
9	events	Reaction to Predetermined Conditions
10	tokenRing	Token Ring—RMON Extensions

RMON1 and RMON2

RMON1 only provides visibility into the data link and the physical layers; potential problems that occur at the higher layers still require other capture and decode tools. Because of RMON1's limitations, RMON2 was developed to extend functionality to upper-layer protocols. As illustrated in Figure 3-31, RMON2 provides full network visibility from the network layer through to the application layer.

Figure 3-31 *RMON2 Is an Extension of RMON1*

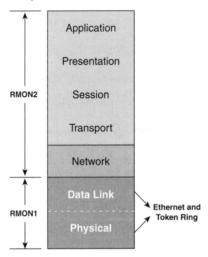

KEY | RMON2 is not a replacement for RMON1, but an extension of it. RMON2 extends
POINT | RMON1 by adding nine more groups that provide visibility to the upper layers.

With visibility into the upper-layer protocols, the network manager can monitor any upper-layer protocol traffic for any device or subnet in addition to the MAC layer traffic.

RMON2 allows the collection of statistics beyond a specific segment's MAC layer and provides an end-to-end view of network conversations per protocol. The network manager can view conversations at the network and application layers. Therefore, traffic generated by a specific host or even a specific application (for example, a Telnet client or a web browser) on that host can be observed.

RMON2 Groups

Figure 3-32 illustrates the RMON groups that were added when RMON2 was introduced. They include the following:

- **Protocol Directory**: Provides the list of protocols that the device supports

- **Protocol Distribution**: Contains traffic statistics for each supported protocol

- **Address Mapping**: Contains network layer-to-MAC layer address mappings

- **Network Layer Host**: Contains statistics for the network layer traffic to or from each host

- **Network Layer Matrix**: Contains network layer traffic statistics for conversations between pairs of hosts

- **Application Layer Host**: Contains statistics for the application layer traffic to or from each host

- **Application Layer Matrix**: Contains application layer traffic statistics for conversations between pairs of hosts

- **User History Collection**: Contains periodic samples of user-specified variables

- **Probe Configuration**: Provides a standard way of remotely configuring probe parameters, such as trap destination and out-of-band management

Figure 3-32 *RMON2 Groups Extend RMON1 Groups*

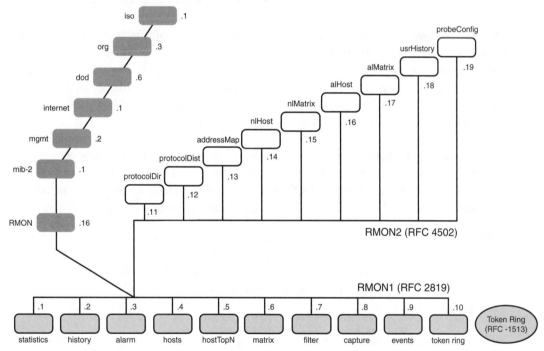

> **NOTE**   See RFC 3577, *Introduction to the Remote Monitoring (RMON) Family of MIB Modules*, for a description of RMON1, RMON2, and pointers to many of the RFCs describing extensions to RMON.

NetFlow

Cisco NetFlow is a measurement technology that measures flows that pass through Cisco devices.

> **NOTE**   NetFlow was originally implemented only on larger devices; it is now available on other devices, including ISRs.

NetFlow answers the questions of what, when, where, and how traffic is flowing in the network. NetFlow data can be exported to network management applications to further process the information, providing tables and graphs for accounting and billing or as an aid for network planning. The key components of NetFlow are the NetFlow cache or data source that stores IP flow information and the NetFlow export or transport mechanism that sends NetFlow data to a network management collector, such as the NetFlow Collection Engine.

NetFlow-collected data serves as the basis for a set of applications, including network traffic accounting, usage-based network billing, network planning, and network monitoring. NetFlow also provides the measurement base for QoS applications: It captures the traffic classification (or precedence) associated with each flow, thereby enabling differentiated charging based on QoS.

KEY POINT   A *network flow* is a unidirectional sequence of packets between source and destination endpoints. Network flows are highly granular; both IP address and transport layer application port numbers identify flow endpoints. NetFlow also identifies the flows by IP protocol type, ToS, and the input interface identifier.

Non-NetFlow–enabled switching handles incoming packets independently, with separate serial tasks for switching, security services (access control lists [ACL]), and traffic measurements that are applied to each packet. Processing is applied only to a flow's first packet with NetFlow-enabled switching; information from the first packet is used to build an entry in the NetFlow cache. Subsequent packets in the flow are handled via a single, streamlined task that handles switching, security services, and data collection concurrently. Multilayer switches support multilayer NetFlow.

Therefore, NetFlow services capitalize on the network traffic's flow nature to provide detailed data collection with minimal impact on router performance and to efficiently process ACLs for packet filtering and security services. Figure 3-33 illustrates the NetFlow infrastructure.

Figure 3-33 *NetFlow Infrastructure*

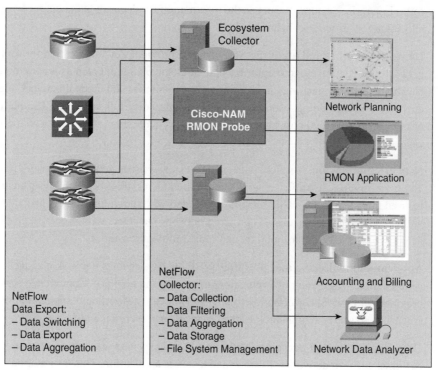

NetFlow can be configured to export data to a *flow collector*, a device that provides NetFlow export data filtering and aggregation capabilities, such as the NetFlow Collection Engine. Expired flows are grouped into NetFlow Export datagrams for export from the NetFlow-enabled device.

The focus of NetFlow used to be on IP flow information; this is changing with the Cisco implementation of a generic export transport format. NetFlow version 9 (v9) export format is a flexible and extensible export format that is now on the IETF standards track in the IP Flow Information Export (IPFIX) working group. IPFIX export is a new generic data transport capability within Cisco routers. It can be used to transport performance information from a router or switch, including Layer 2 information, security detection and identification information, IP version 6 (IPv6), multicast, MPLS, and Border Gateway Protocol (BGP) information, and so forth. NetFlow enables several key customer applications, including the following:

- **Accounting and billing**: Because flow data includes details such as IP addresses, packet and byte counts, time stamps, and application port numbers, NetFlow data provides fine-grained metering for highly flexible and detailed resource utilization accounting. For example, service providers can use this information to migrate from single-fee, flat-rate billing to more flexible charging mechanisms based on time of day, bandwidth usage, application usage, QoS, and so forth. Enterprise customers can use the information for departmental cost recovery or cost allocation for resource utilization.

■ **Network planning and analysis**: NetFlow data provides key information for sophisticated network architecture tools to optimize both strategic planning (such as whom to peer with, backbone upgrade planning, and routing policy planning) and tactical network engineering decisions (such as adding resources to routers or upgrading link capacity). This has the benefit of minimizing the total cost of network operations while maximizing network performance, capacity, and reliability.

■ **Network monitoring**: NetFlow data enables extensive near-real-time network monitoring. To provide aggregate traffic- or application-based views, flow-based analysis techniques can be used to visualize the traffic patterns associated with individual routers and switches on a networkwide basis. This analysis provides network managers with proactive problem detection, efficient troubleshooting, and rapid problem resolution.

■ **Application monitoring and profiling**: NetFlow data enables network managers to gain a detailed, time-based view of application usage over the network. Content and service providers can use this information to plan and allocate network and application resources (such as web server sizing and location) to meet customer demands.

■ **User monitoring and profiling**: NetFlow data enables network managers to understand customer and user network utilization and resource application. This information can be used to plan efficiently; allocate access, backbone, and application resources; and detect and resolve potential security and policy violations.

■ **NetFlow data warehousing and data mining**: In support of proactive marketing and customer service programs, NetFlow data or the information derived from it can be warehoused for later retrieval and analysis. For example, you can determine which applications and services are being used by internal and external users and target them for improved service. This is especially useful for service providers, because NetFlow data enables them to create a wider range of offered services. For example, a service provider can easily determine the traffic characteristics of various services and, based on this data, provide new services to the users. An example of such a service is VoIP, which requires QoS adjustment; the service provider might charge users for this service.

NetFlow Versus RMON Information Gathering

NetFlow can be configured on individual interfaces, thereby providing information on traffic that passes through those interfaces and collecting the following types of information:

■ Source and destination interfaces and IP addresses

- Input and output interface numbers

- TCP/UDP source port and destination ports

- Number of bytes and packets in the flow

- Source and destination autonomous system numbers (for BGP)

- Time of day

- IP ToS

Compared to using SNMP with RMON MIB, NetFlow's information-gathering benefits include greater detail of collected data, data time-stamping, support for various data per interface, and greater scalability to a large number of interfaces (RMON is also limited by the size of its memory table). NetFlow's performance impact is much lower than RMON's, and external probes are not required.

CDP

KEY POINT | *CDP* is a Cisco-proprietary protocol that operates between Cisco devices at the data link layer. CDP information is sent only between directly connected Cisco devices; a Cisco device never forwards a CDP frame.

CDP enables systems that support different network layer protocols to communicate and enables other Cisco devices on the network to be discovered. CDP provides a summary of directly connected switches, routers, and other Cisco devices.

CDP is a media- and protocol-independent protocol that is enabled by default on each supported interface of Cisco devices (such as routers, access servers, and switches). The physical media must support Subnetwork Access Protocol encapsulation. Figure 3-34 illustrates the relationship between CDP and other protocols.

Figure 3-34 *CDP Runs at the Data Link Layer and Enables the Discovery of Directly Connected Cisco Devices*

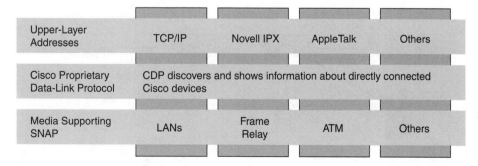

CDP Information

Information in CDP frames includes the following:

- **Device ID**: The name of the neighbor device and either the MAC address or the serial number of the device.

- **Local Interface**: The local (on this device) interface connected to the discovered neighbor.

- **Holdtime**: The remaining amount of time (in seconds) that the local device holds the CDP advertisement from a sending device before discarding it.

- **Capability List**: The type of device discovered (R—Router, T—Trans Bridge, B—Source Route Bridge, S—Switch, H—Host, I—IGMP, r—Repeater).

- **Platform**: The device's product type.

- **Port Identifier (ID)**: The port (interface) number on the discovered neighbor on which the advertisement is sent. This is the interface on the neighbor device to which the local device is connected.

- **Address List**: All network layer protocol addresses configured on the interface (or, in the case of protocols configured globally, on the device). Examples include IP, Internetwork Packet Exchange, and DECnet.

How CDP Works

As illustrated in Figure 3-35, CDP information is sent only between directly connected Cisco devices. In this figure, the person connected to Switch A can see the router and the two switches directly attached to Switch A; other devices are not visible via CDP. For example, the person would have to log in to Switch B to see Router C with CDP.

Figure 3-35 *CDP Provides Information About Neighboring Cisco Devices*

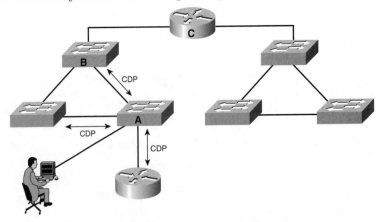

KEY POINT | Cisco devices never forward a CDP frame.

CDP is a hello-based protocol, and all Cisco devices that run CDP periodically advertise their attributes to their neighbors using a multicast address. These frames advertise a time-to-live value (the holdtime, in seconds) that indicates how long the information must be retained before it can be discarded. CDP frames are sent with a time-to-live value that is nonzero after an interface is enabled. A time-to-live value of 0 is sent immediately before an interface is shut down, allowing other devices to quickly discover lost neighbors.

Cisco devices receive CDP frames and cache the received information; it is then available to be sent to the NMS via SNMP. If any information changes from the last received frame, the new information is cached and the previous information is discarded, even if its time-to-live value has not yet expired.

CDP is on by default and operates on any operational interface. However, CDP can be disabled on an interface or globally on a device. Consequently, some caveats are indicated:

■ Do not run CDP on links that you do not want discovered, such as Internet connections.

■ Do not run CDP on links that do not go to Cisco devices.

For security reasons, block SNMP access to CDP data (or any other data) from outside your network and from subnets other than the management station subnet.

Syslog Accounting

A system message and error reporting service is an essential component of any operating system. The syslog system message service provides a means for the system and its running processes to report system state information to a network manager.

Cisco devices produce syslog messages as a result of network events. Every syslog message contains a time stamp (if enabled), severity level, and facility.

Example 3-1 shows samples of syslog messages produced by the Cisco IOS software. The most common messages are those that a device produces upon exiting configuration mode, and the link up and down messages. If ACL logging is configured, the device generates syslog messages when packets match the ACL condition. ACL logging can be useful to detect packets that are denied access based on the security policy that is set by an ACL.

Example 3-1 *Syslog Messages*

```
20:11:31: %SYS-5- CONFIG I: Configured from console by console

20:11:57: %LINK-5-CHANGED: Interface FastEthernet0/0, changed state to administratively
down
20:11:58: %LINEPROTO-5-UPDOWN: Line protocol on Interface FastEthernet0/0, changed state
to down

20:12:04: %LINK-3-UPDOWN: Interface FastEthernet0/0, changed state to up
20:12:06: %LINEPROTO-5-UPDOWN: Line protocol on Interface FastEthernet0/0, changed state
to up
20:13:53: %SEC-6-IPACCESSLOGP: list internet-inbound denied udp 66.56.16.77(1029) -
> 63.78.199.4(161), 1 packet
20:14:26: %MLS-5-MLSENABLED:IP Multilayer switching is enabled
20:14:26: %MLS-5-NDEDISABLED: Netflow  Data Export disabled
20:14:26: %SYS-5-MOD_OK:Module 1 is online
20:15:47: %SYS-5-MOD_OK:Module 3 is online
20:15:42: %SYS-5-MOD_OK:Module 6 is online
20:16:27: %PAGP-5-PORTTOSTP:Port 3/1 joined bridge port 3/1
20:16:28: %PAGP-5-PORTTOSTP:Port 3/2 joined bridge port 3/2
```

Syslog messages contain up to 80 characters; a percent sign (%) follows the optional sequence number or time-stamp information if configured. Syslog messages are structured as follows:

    seq no:timestamp: %facility-severity-MNEMONIC:description

The following parameters are used in the syslog messages:

■ A sequence number appears on the syslog message if the **service sequence-numbers** global configuration command is configured.

■ The time stamp shows the date and time of the message or event if the **service timestamps log** [**datetime** | **log**] global configuration command is configured. The time stamp can have one of three formats:

— *mm/dd hh:mm:ss*

— *hh:mm:ss* (for short uptimes)

— *d h* (for long uptimes)

- **Facility**: A code consisting of two or more uppercase letters that indicate the facility to which the message refers. Syslog facilities are service identifiers used to identify and categorize system state data for error and event message reporting. A facility can be a hardware device, a protocol, or a module of the system software. The Cisco IOS software has more than 500 different facilities; the following are the most common:

  — IP

  — OSPF (OSPF protocol)

  — SYS (operating system)

  — IPsec (IP Security)

  — RSP (Route Switch Processor)

  — IF (interface)

  — LINK (data link messages)

  Other facilities include CDP, QoS, RADIUS, multicast (MCAST), MLS, TCP, VLAN trunking protocol (VTP), Telnet, and trivial file transfer protocol (TFTP).

- **Severity**: A single-digit code (from 0 to 7) that reflects the severity of the condition; the lower the number, the more serious the situation. Syslog defines the following severity levels:

  — Emergency (Level 0, which is the highest level)

  — Alert (Level 1)

  — Critical (Level 2)

  — Error (Level 3)

  — Warning (Level 4)

  — Notice (Level 5)

  — Informational (Level 6)

  — Debugging (Level 7)

- **Mnemonic**: A code that uniquely identifies the error message.

- **Description**: A text string that describes the condition. This portion of the message sometimes contains detailed information about the event, including port numbers, network addresses, or addresses that correspond to locations in the system memory address space.

NOTE For more syslog information, see http://www.cisco.com/univercd/cc/td/doc/product/ software/ios124/124sup/124sms/index.htm.

Syslog Distributed Architecture

Figure 3-36 illustrates the syslog distributed architecture.

Figure 3-36 *Syslog Distributed Architecture*

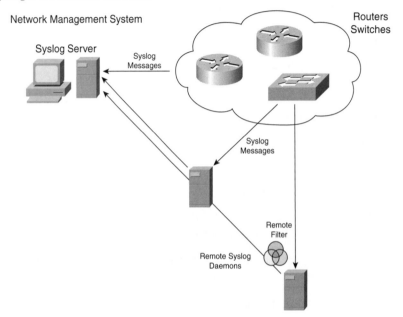

Syslog messages are sent to the console session by default. A device must be configured to send syslog messages elsewhere; the configuration includes the address of the NMS or another device. Network devices can be configured to send syslog messages directly to the NMS or to the remote network host on which a syslog analyzer is installed. A syslog analyzer conserves bandwidth on WAN links because the analyzer usually applies different filters and sends only the predefined subset of all syslog messages it receives. The analyzer filters and periodically forwards messages to the central NMS. For example, the analyzer could filter ACL logging data from other router or switch syslog entries to ensure that the ACL logging data does not overwhelm the syslog reporting tool.

The Syslog Analyzer is a CiscoWorks Resource Manager Essentials application that supports a distributed syslog server architecture for localized collection, filtering, aggregation, and forwarding of syslog data to a central syslog server for further processing and analysis. The Syslog Analyzer also supports reporting functions to automatically parse the log data into predefined or custom formats for ease of use and readability.

When it receives a syslog message, the NMS applies filters to remove unwanted messages. Filters can also be applied to perform actions based on the received syslog message, such as paging or e-mailing the network manager.

Syslog data can consume large amounts of network bandwidth and might require a very large storage capacity based on the number of devices sending syslog messages, the syslog facility and severity levels set for each, and any error conditions that may trigger excessive log messages. Therefore, it is important to enable logging only for network facilities of particular interest and to set the appropriate severity level to provide sufficient, but not excessive, detail.

KEY POINT If the collected data will not be analyzed, do not collect it.

Selectively filter and aggregate syslog data that the distributed or centralized syslog servers receive based on the requirements.

Summary

In this chapter, you learned about modularizing the network, with a focus on the following topics:

- The hierarchical network model's three layers: access, distribution, and core

- The Cisco SONA framework that integrates the enterprise-wide network

- The Cisco Enterprise Architecture functional areas:

    — Enterprise Campus: Including the Campus Infrastructure module (composed of the Campus Core layer, the Building Distribution layer, and the Building Access layer) and the Server farm module

    — Enterprise Edge: Including the E-commerce module, the Internet Connectivity module, the Remote Access and VPN module, and the WAN and MAN and Site-to-Site VPN module

    — Service Provider: Including the Internet Service Provider module, the PSTN module, and the Frame Relay/ATM module

    — Enterprise Branch

    — Enterprise Data Center

    — Enterprise Teleworker

- The infrastructure services and application networking services used within the Cisco Enterprise Architecture modules

- Security services to protect network resources and users from internal and external threats

- High-availability services to ensure adequate connectivity for mission-critical applications

- Voice services to support VoIP and IP telephony

- Wireless services to support mobile clients connecting to the enterprise network

- ANS to make the network aware of the content carried across it and to optimally handle that content

- Network management protocols and features, including SNMP, MIBs, RMON, NetFlow, CDP, and syslog

References

See the following resources for additional information:

- "Service-Oriented Network Architecture: Introduction," http://www.cisco.com/go/sona/

- *Top-Down Network Design,* Second Edition, Priscilla Oppenheimer, Cisco Press, 2004

- "Internetworking Design Basics," Cisco Internetwork Design Guide, http://www.cisco.com/univercd/cc/td/doc/cisintwk/idg4/nd2002.htm

- "SAFE Blueprint for Small, Midsize, and Remote-User Networks," http://www.cisco.com/go/safe/

- "Enterprise Architectures: Introduction," http://www.cisco.com/en/US/netsol/ns517/networking_solutions_market_segment_solutions_home.html

- *NetFlow Services Solutions Guide*, http://www.cisco.com/en/US/products/sw/netmgtsw/ps1964/products_implementation_design_guide09186a00800d6a11.html

Case Study: ACMC Hospital Modularity

This case study is a continuation of the ACMC Hospital case study introduced in Chapter 2.

Case Study General Instructions

Use the scenarios, information, and parameters provided at each task of the ongoing case study. If you encounter ambiguities, make reasonable assumptions and proceed. For all tasks, use the initial customer scenario and build on the solutions provided thus far. You can use any and all documentation, books, white papers, and so on.

In each step, you act as a network design consultant. Make creative proposals to accomplish the customer's business needs. Justify your ideas when they differ from the provided solutions. Use any design strategies you feel are appropriate. The final goal of each case study is a paper solution.

Appendix A, "Answers to Review Questions and Case Studies," provides a solution for each step based on assumptions made. There is no claim that the provided solution is the best or only solution. Your solution might be more appropriate for the assumptions you made. The provided solution helps you understand the author's reasoning and allows you to compare and contrast your solution.

In this case study, you apply the Cisco Enterprise Architecture to the ACMC Hospital network requirements and develop a high-level view of the planned network hierarchy. Complete the following steps:

Step 1   Consider each of the functional areas of the Cisco Enterprise Architecture:

- Enterprise Campus: Including the Campus Infrastructure module (composed of the Campus Core layer, the Building Distribution layer, and the Building Access layer) and the Server farm module

- Enterprise Edge: Including the E-commerce module, the Internet Connectivity module, the WAN and MAN and Site-to-Site VPN module, and the Remote Access and VPN module

- Enterprise Branch

- Enterprise Data Center

- Enterprise Teleworker

Mark up the existing network diagram, provided in Figure 3-37, indicating where each of the modules would be at a high level.

Figure 3-37   *Existing ACMC Hospital Network*

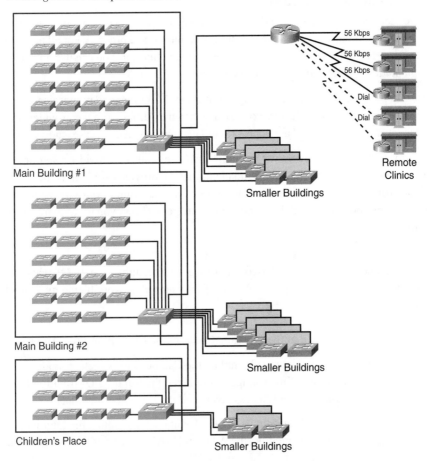

Step 2   List some key considerations or functions for each of the modules in the Cisco Enterprise Architecture. Indicate whether each module is used in the ACMC Hospital network.

Step 3   Since the time initial discussions with ACMC occurred, the following additional requirements have surfaced:

- The staff needs Internet access for purchasing supplies and reviewing research documents and new medical products.

- There has been some discussion about allowing employees to telecommute.

- ACMC has a web server for a patient communications and community relations service called "Text a Nurse." This for-fee service allows a patient to send a text message to the hospital, requesting medical advice.

How does this new information change the design? Incorporate the changes into your high-level design, and update the list of modules and considerations.

Step 4   Which of the following infrastructure or network services are immediately applicable to your design?

- Security services

- Voice services

- Wireless

- Network management

- High availability

- QoS

- Multicast

Are there specific locations or modules where some of these services are particularly relevant?

Step 5   Indicate where redundancy should be supported in the design.

Review Questions

Answer the following questions, and then refer to Appendix A for the answers.

1. Figure 3-38 presents a sample hierarchically structured network. Some of the devices are marked with letters. Map the marked devices to the access, distribution, and core layers in this figure.

2. Describe the role of each layer in the hierarchical network model.

3. True or false: Each layer in the hierarchical network model must be implemented with distinct physical devices.

4. Which two statements are true?

   a. UplinkFast immediately unblocks a blocked port after root port failure.

   b. PortFast immediately puts a port into the forwarding state.

   c. UplinkFast immediately puts a port into the forwarding state.

   d. PortFast immediately unblocks a blocked port after root port failure.

5. What features of a multilayer switch could be used in the access layer?

6. Which layer in the hierarchical model provides media translation?

Figure 3-38 *Hierarchical Network*

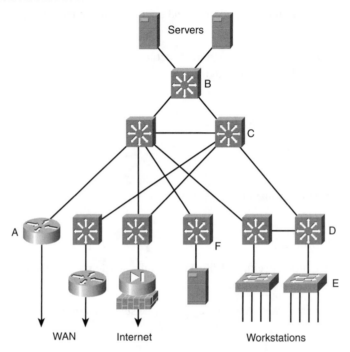

7. Why might the distribution layer need to redistribute between routing protocols?

8. What are three roles of the hierarchical model's core layer?

    a. Provide fast and efficient data transport

    b. Provide maximum availability and reliability

    c. Provide access to the corporate network via some wide-area technology

    d. Implement security policies

    e. Delineate broadcast domains

    f. Implement scalable routing protocols

9. What is a benefit of using multilayer switching in the core network layer?

10. What are the six major functional areas in the Cisco Enterprise Architecture?

11. What are the modules and layers within the Enterprise Campus functional area?

12. The Enterprise Edge functional area includes which modules?

13. The Service Provider functional area is composed of which modules?

14. Which module of the Cisco Enterprise Architecture includes wireless bridging connectivity to remote locations?

15. What is an advantage of using the Cisco Enterprise Architecture?

16. What is the Campus Core layer's role?

17. Indicate which types of devices would be found in each of these modules (note that some devices are found in more than one module).

   Modules:

   ■ E-commerce module

   ■ Internet Connectivity module

   ■ Remote Access and VPN module

   Devices:

   ■ Web servers

   ■ SMTP mail servers

   ■ Firewalls

   ■ Network Intrusion Detection System (NIDS) appliances

   ■ DNS servers

   ■ ASAs

   ■ Public FTP servers

18. What is the role of the Service Provider functional area?

19. Which other module has a design similar to that of the Enterprise Branch module?

20. Which other module has an architecture similar to that of the Enterprise Data Center module?

21. Which module of the Cisco Enterprise Architecture provides telecommuter connectivity?

22. The SONA interactive services layer includes both _____ services and _____ services.

23. How can the Server Farm module be involved in an organization's internal security?

24. High availability from end to end is possible only when _____ is deployed throughout the internetwork.

25. What is the purpose of designing route redundancy in a network?

26. A full-mesh design is ideal for connecting a _____ number of devices.

    a. small

    b. large

27. True or false: Backup links can use different technologies.

28. What components are required for IP telephony?

29. What role does the Building Access layer play in voice transportation?

30. What should you consider when evaluating an existing data infrastructure for IP telephony?

31. What are the main components of a centralized WLAN deployment?

32. What is a Cisco WAE appliance?

33. What is a network management agent?

34. How does an SNMPv1 manager request a list of data?

35. How does an SNMPv2 manager request a list of data?

36. What is the MIB structure?

37. How are private MIB definitions supported?

38. What are the RMON1 groups?

39. What groups are added to the RMON1 groups by RMON2?

40. How does RMON simplify proactive network management?

41. What is a NetFlow network flow?

42. How does NetFlow compare to RMON?

43. At which layer does CDP work?

44. Two routers are connected via Frame Relay, but ping is not working between them. How could CDP help troubleshoot this situation?

45. What are the syslog severity levels?

46. What syslog severity level is indicated by the messages in Example 3-2?

Example 3-2 *Sample Message for Question 46*

```
20:11:58: %LINEPROTO-5-UPDOWN: Line protocol on Interface FastEthernet0/0, changed state
to down
20:12:04: %LINK-3-UPDOWN: Interface FastEthernet0/0, changed state to up
```

This chapter introduces general campus switching and data center design considerations. It includes the following sections:

- Campus Design Considerations

- Enterprise Campus Design

- Enterprise Data Center Design Considerations

- Summary

- References

- Case Study: ACMC Hospital Network Campus Design

- Review Questions

CHAPTER 4

Designing Basic Campus and Data Center Networks

The availability of multigigabit campus switches gives customers the opportunity to build extremely high-performance, high-reliability networks—if they follow correct network design approaches. Unfortunately, some alternative network design approaches can result in a network that has lower performance, reliability, and manageability.

This chapter describes a hierarchical modular design approach called multilayer design. This chapter examines the designs of the Enterprise Campus and the Enterprise Data Center network infrastructures. First, it addresses general campus design considerations, followed by a discussion of the design of each of the modules and layers within the Enterprise Campus. The chapter concludes with an introduction to design considerations for the Enterprise Data Center.

Campus Design Considerations

The multilayer approach to campus network design combines data link layer and multilayer switching to achieve robust, highly available campus networks. This section discusses factors to consider in a Campus LAN design.

Designing an Enterprise Campus

The Enterprise Campus network is the foundation for enabling business applications, enhancing productivity, and providing a multitude of services to end users. The following three characteristics should be considered when designing the campus network:

- **Network application characteristics**: The organizational requirements, services, and applications place stringent requirements on a campus network solution—for example, in terms of bandwidth and delay.

- **Environmental characteristics**: The network's environment includes its geography and the transmission media used.

  — The physical environment of the building or buildings influences the design, as do the number of, distribution of, and distance between the network nodes (including end users, hosts, and network devices). Other factors include space, power, and heating, ventilation, and air conditioning support for the network devices.

— Cabling is one of the biggest long-term investments in network deployment. Therefore, transmission media selection depends not only on the required bandwidth and distances, but also on the emerging technologies that might be deployed over the same infrastructure in the future.

■ **Infrastructure device characteristics**: The characteristics of the network devices selected influence the design (for example, they determine the network's flexibility) and contribute to the overall delay. Trade-offs between data link layer switching—based on media access control (MAC) addresses—and multilayer switching—based on network layer addresses, transport layer, and application awareness—need to be considered.

— High availability and high throughput are requirements that might require consideration throughout the infrastructure.

— Most Enterprise Campus designs use a combination of data link layer switching in the access layer and multilayer switching in the distribution and core layers.

The following sections examine these factors.

Network Application Characteristics and Considerations

The network application's characteristics and requirements influence the design in many ways. The applications that are critical to the organization, and the network demands of these applications, determine enterprise traffic patterns inside the Enterprise Campus network, which influences bandwidth usage, response times, and the selection of the transmission medium.

Different types of application communication result in varying network demands. The following sections review four types of application communication:

■ Peer-peer

■ Client–local server

■ Client–Server Farm

■ Client–Enterprise Edge server

Peer-Peer Applications

From the network designer's perspective, peer-peer applications include applications in which the majority of network traffic passes from one network edge device to another through the organization's network, as shown in Figure 4-1. Typical peer-peer applications include the following:

■ **Instant messaging**: After the connection is established, the conversation is directly between two peers.

- **IP phone calls**: Two peers establish communication with the help of an IP telephony manager; however, the conversation occurs directly between the two peers when the connection is established. The network requirements of IP phone calls are strict because of the need for quality of service (QoS) treatment to minimize delay and variation in delay (jitter).

> **NOTE** QoS is discussed in the later section "QoS Considerations in LAN Switches."

- **File sharing**: Some operating systems and applications require direct access to data on other workstations.

- **Videoconference systems**: Videoconferencing is similar to IP telephony; however, the network requirements are usually higher, particularly related to bandwidth consumption and QoS.

Figure 4-1 *Peer-Peer Applications*

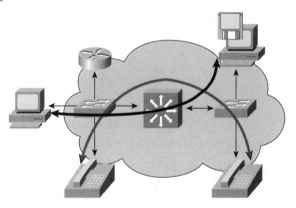

Client–Local Server Applications

Historically, clients and servers were attached to a network device on the same LAN segment and followed the 80/20 workgroup rule for client/server applications. This rule indicates that 80 percent of the traffic is local to the LAN segment and 20 percent leaves the segment.

With increased traffic on the corporate network and a relatively fixed location for users, an organization might split the network into several isolated segments, as shown in Figure 4-2. Each of these segments has its own servers, known as *local servers*, for its application. In this scenario, servers and users are located in the same VLAN, and department administrators manage and control the servers. The majority of department traffic occurs in the same segment, but some data exchange (to a different VLAN) happens over the campus backbone. The bandwidth requirements for traffic passing to another segment typically are not crucial. For example, traffic to the Internet goes through a common segment and has lower performance requirements than traffic to the local segment servers.

Figure 4-2 *Client–Local Server Application*

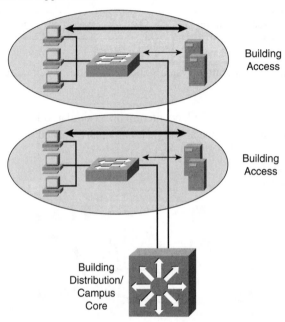

Client–Server Farm Applications

Large organizations require their users to have fast, reliable, and controlled access to critical applications.

Because high-performance multilayer switches have an insignificant switch delay, and because of the reduced cost of network bandwidth, locating the servers centrally rather than in the workgroup is technically feasible and reduces support costs.

To fulfill these demands and keep administrative costs down, the servers are located in a common Server Farm, as shown in Figure 4-3. Using a Server Farm requires a network infrastructure that is highly resilient (providing security) and redundant (providing high availability) and that provides adequate throughput. High-end LAN switches with the fastest LAN technologies, such as Gigabit Ethernet, are typically deployed in such an environment.

Figure 4-3 *Client–Server Farm Application*

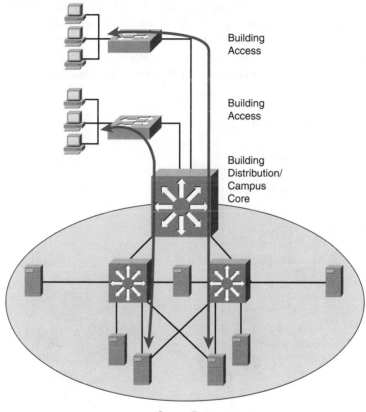

In a large organization, application traffic might have to pass across more than one wiring closet, LAN, or VLAN to reach servers in a Server Farm. Client–Server Farm applications apply the 20/80 rule, where only 20 percent of the traffic remains on the local LAN segment, and 80 percent leaves the segment to reach centralized servers, the Internet, and so on. Such applications include the following:

■ Organizational mail servers (such as Microsoft Exchange)

■ Common file servers (such as Microsoft and Sun)

■ Common database servers for organizational applications (such as Oracle)

Client–Enterprise Edge Applications

As shown in Figure 4-4, client–Enterprise Edge applications use servers on the Enterprise Edge to exchange data between the organization and its public servers. The most important issues between the Enterprise Campus network and the Enterprise Edge are security and high availability; data exchange with external entities must be in constant operation. Applications installed on the Enterprise Edge can be crucial to organizational process flow; therefore, any outages can increase costs.

Figure 4-4 *Client–Enterprise Edge Application*

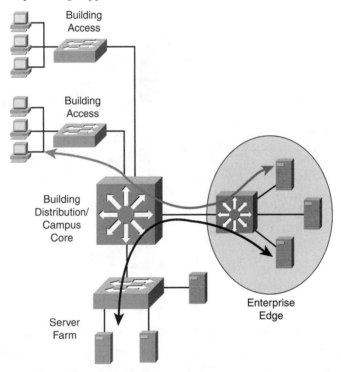

Typical Enterprise Edge applications are based on web technologies. Examples of these application types—such as external mail and DNS servers and public web servers—can be found in any organization.

Organizations that support their partnerships through e-commerce applications also place their e-commerce servers into the Enterprise Edge. Communication with these servers is vital because of the two-way replication of data. As a result, high redundancy and resiliency of the network, along with security, are the most important requirements for these applications.

Application Requirements

Table 4-1 lists the types of application communication and compares their requirements with respect to some important network parameters. The following sections discuss these parameters.

Table 4-1 *Network Application Requirements*

Parameter	Peer-Peer		Client–Local Server	Client–Server Farm	Client–Enterprise Edge Servers
Connectivity type	Shared	Switched	Switched	Switched	Switched
Total required throughput	Low	Medium to high	Medium	High	Medium
High availability	Low	Low	Medium	High	High
Total network cost	Low	Low	Medium	High	Medium

Connectivity

The wide use of LAN switching at Layer 2 has revolutionized local-area networking and has resulted in increased performance and more bandwidth for satisfying the requirements of new organizational applications. LAN switches provide this performance benefit by increasing bandwidth and throughput for workgroups and local servers.

> **NOTE** Using shared media for peer-to-peer communication is suitable only in a limited scope, typically when the number of client workstations is very low (for example, with four or fewer workstations in small home offices).

Throughput

The required throughput varies from application to application. An application that exchanges data between users in the workgroup usually does not require a high throughput network infrastructure. However, organizational-level applications usually require a high-capacity link to the servers, which are usually located in the Server Farm.

> **NOTE** Peer-peer communication, especially in the case of frequent file transfers, could be intensive, and the total throughput requirements can be high.

Applications located on servers in the Enterprise Edge are normally not as bandwidth-consuming as applications in the Server Farm, but they might require high availability and security features.

High Availability

The high availability of an application is a function of the application and the entire network between a client workstation and a server located in the network. Although the network design primarily determines the network's availability, the individual components' mean time between failures (MTBF) is a factor. Redundancy in the Building Distribution and Campus Core layers is recommended.

Total Network Cost

Depending on the application and the resulting network infrastructure, the cost varies from low in a peer-peer environment to high in a network with redundancy in the Building Distribution, Campus Core, and Server Farm. In addition to the cost of duplicate components for redundancy, costs include the cables, routers, switches, software, and so forth.

Environmental Characteristics and Considerations

The campus environment, including the location of the network nodes, the distance between the nodes, and the transmission media used, influences the network topology. This section examines these considerations.

Network Geography Considerations

The location of Enterprise Campus nodes and the distances between them determine the network's geography.

Nodes, including end-user workstations and servers, can be located in one or multiple buildings. Based on the location of nodes and the distance between them, the network designer decides which technology should interconnect them based on the required maximum speed, distance, and so forth.

Consider the following structures with respect to the network geography:

- Intrabuilding

- Interbuilding

- Distant remote building

These geographic structures, described in the following sections, serve as guides to help determine Enterprise Campus transmission media and the logical modularization of the Enterprise Campus network.

Intrabuilding Structure

An intrabuilding campus network structure provides connectivity for all end nodes located in the same building and gives them access to the network resources. The Building Access and Building Distribution layers are typically located in the same building.

User workstations are usually attached to the Building Access switches in the floor wiring closet with twisted-pair copper cables. Wireless LANs (WLAN) can also be used to provide intrabuilding connectivity, enabling users to establish and maintain a wireless network connection throughout—or between—buildings, without the limitations of wires or cables.

> **NOTE**   WLANs are covered in Chapter 9, "Wireless Network Design Considerations."

Access layer switches usually connect to the Building Distribution switches over optical fiber, providing better transmission performance and less sensitivity to environmental disturbances than copper. Depending on the connectivity requirements to resources in other parts of the campus, the Building Distribution switches may be connected to Campus Core switches.

Interbuilding Structure

As shown in Figure 4-5, an interbuilding network structure provides connectivity between the individual campus buildings' central switches (in the Building Distribution and/or Campus Core layers). These buildings are usually in close proximity, typically only a few hundred meters to a few kilometers apart.

Figure 4-5   *Interbuilding Network Structure*

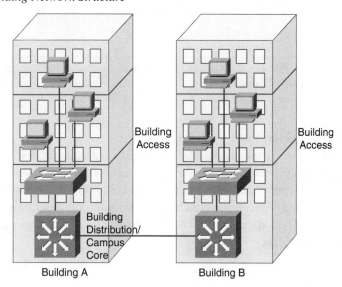

Because the nodes in all campus buildings usually share common devices such as servers, the demand for high-speed connectivity between the buildings is high. Within a campus, companies might deploy their own physical transmission media. To provide high throughput without excessive interference from environmental conditions, optical fiber is the medium of choice between the buildings.

Depending on the connectivity requirements to resources in other parts of the campus, the Building Distribution switches might be connected to Campus Core switches.

Distant Remote Building Structure

When connecting buildings at distances that exceed a few kilometers (but still within a metropolitan area), the most important factor to consider is the physical media. The speed and cost of the network infrastructure depend heavily on the media selection.

If the bandwidth requirements are higher than the physical connectivity options can support, the network designer must identify the organization's critical applications and then select the equipment that supports intelligent network services—such as QoS and filtering capabilities—that allow optimal use of the bandwidth.

Some companies might own their media, such as fiber, microwave, or copper lines. However, if the organization does not own physical transmission media to certain remote locations, the Enterprise Campus must connect through the Enterprise Edge using connectivity options from public service providers, such as traditional WAN links or Metro Ethernet.

The risk of downtime and the service level agreements available from the service providers must also be considered. For example, inexpensive but unreliable and slowly repaired fiber is not desirable for mission-critical applications.

> **NOTE**   Chapter 5, "Designing Remote Connectivity," includes further discussion of connecting remote locations.

Transmission Media Considerations

An Enterprise Campus can use various physical media to interconnect devices. The type of cable is an important consideration when deploying a new network or upgrading an existing one. Cabling infrastructure represents a long-term investment—it is usually installed to last for ten years or more. The cost of the medium (including installation costs) and the available budget must be considered in addition to the technical characteristics such as signal attenuation and electromagnetic interference.

A network designer must be aware of physical media characteristics, because they influence the maximum distance permitted between devices and the network's maximum transmission speed. Twisted-pair cables (copper), optical cables (fiber), and wireless (satellite, microwave, and Institute of Electrical and Electronics Engineers [IEEE] 802.11 LANs) are the most common physical transmission media used in modern networks.

Copper

Twisted-pair cables consist of four pairs of isolated wires that are wrapped together in plastic cable. With unshielded twisted-pair (UTP), no additional foil or wire is wrapped around the core wires. This makes these wires less expensive, but also less immune to external electromagnetic influences than shielded twisted-pair cables. Twisted-pair cabling is widely used to interconnect workstations, servers, or other devices from their network interface card (NIC) to the network connector at a wall outlet.

The characteristics of twisted-pair cable depend on the quality of the material from which they are made. As a result, twisted-pair cables are sorted into categories. Category 5 or greater is recommended for speeds of 100 megabits per second (Mbps) or higher. Category 6 is recommended for Gigabit Ethernet. Because of the possibility of signal attenuation in the wires, the maximum cable length is usually limited to 100 meters. One reason for this length limitation is collision detection. If one PC starts to transmit and another PC is more than 100 meters away, the second PC might not detect the signal on the wire and could therefore start to transmit at the same time, causing a collision on the wire.

One of the main considerations in network cabling design is electromagnetic interference. Due to high susceptibility to interference, twisted pair is not suitable for use in environments with electromagnetic influences. Similarly, twisted pair is not appropriate for environments that can be affected by the interference created by the cable itself.

> **NOTE**   Some security issues are also associated with electromagnetic interference. Hackers with access to the cabling infrastructure might eavesdrop on the traffic carried across UTP, because these cables emit electromagnetic signals that can be detected.

Distances longer than 100 meters may require Long-Reach Ethernet (LRE). LRE is Cisco-proprietary technology that runs on voice-grade copper wires; it allows higher distances than traditional Ethernet and is used as an access technology in WANs. Chapter 5 further describes LRE.

Optical Fiber

Typical requirements that lead to the selection of optical fiber cable as a transmission medium include distances longer than 100 meters and immunity to electromagnetic interference. Different types of optical cable exist; the two main types are multimode (MM) and single-mode (SM).

Multimode fiber is optical fiber that carries multiple light waves or modes concurrently, each at a slightly different reflection angle within the optical fiber core. Because modes tend to disperse over longer lengths (modal dispersion), MM fiber transmission is used for relatively short distances. Typically, LEDs are used with MM fiber. The typical diameter of an MM fiber is 50 or 62.5 micrometers.

Single-mode (also known as *monomode*) *fiber* is optical fiber that carries a single wave (or laser) of light. Lasers are typically used with SM fiber. The typical diameter of an SM fiber core is between 2 and 10 micrometers. Single-mode fiber limits dispersion and loss of light, and therefore allows for higher transmission speeds, but it is more expensive than multimode fiber.

Both MM and SM cables have lower loss of signal than copper cable. Therefore, optical cables allow longer distances between devices. Optical fiber cable has precise production and installation requirements; therefore, it costs more than twisted-pair cable.

Optical fiber requires a precise technique for cable coupling. Even a small deviation from the ideal position of optical connectors can result in either a loss of signal or a large number of frame losses. Careful attention during optical fiber installation is imperative because of the traffic's high sensitivity to coupling misalignment. In environments where the cable does not consist of a single fiber from point to point, coupling is required, and loss of signal can easily occur.

Wireless

The inherent nature of wireless is that it does not require wires to carry information across geographic areas that are otherwise prohibitive to connect. WLANs can either replace a traditional wired network or extend its reach and capabilities. In-building WLAN equipment includes access points (AP) that perform functions similar to wired networking hubs, and PC client adapters. APs are distributed throughout a building to expand range and functionality for wireless clients. Wireless bridges and APs can also be used for interbuilding connectivity and outdoor wireless client access.

Wireless clients supporting IEEE 802.11g allow speeds of up to 54 Mbps in the 2.4-GHz band over a range of about 100 feet. The IEEE 802.11b standard supports speeds of up to 11 Mbps in the 2.4-GHz band. The IEEE 802.11a standard supports speeds of up to 54 Mbps in the 5-GHz band.

NOTE   Wireless issues are discussed further in Chapter 9.

Transmission Media Comparison

Table 4-2 presents various characteristics of the transmission media types.

Table 4-2   *Transmission Media Type Characteristics*

Parameter	Copper Twisted Pair	MM Fiber	SM Fiber	Wireless
Distance (range)	Up to 100 meters	Up to 2 kilometers (km) (Fast Ethernet) Up to 550 m (Gigabit Ethernet) Up to 300 m (10 Gigabit Ethernet)	Up to 10 km (Fast Ethernet) Up to 5 km (Gigabit Ethernet) Up to 80 km (10 Gigabit Ethernet)	Up to 500 m at 1 Mbps
Bandwidth	Up to 10 Gigabits per second (Gbps)	Up to 10 Gbps	Up to 10 Gbps or higher	Up to 54 Mbps[1]
Price	Inexpensive	Moderate	Moderate to expensive	Moderate
Deployment area	Wiring closet	Internode or interbuilding	Internode or interbuilding	Internode or interbuilding

[1]Wireless is half-duplex, so effective bandwidth will be no more than half of this rate.

The parameters listed in Table 4-2 are as follows:

- **Distance**: The maximum distance between network devices (such as workstations, servers, printers, and IP phones) and network nodes, and between network nodes. The distances supported with fiber vary, depending on whether it supports Fast Ethernet or Gigabit Ethernet, the type of fiber used, and the fiber interface used.

- **Bandwidth**: The required bandwidth in a particular segment of the network, or the connection speed between the nodes inside or outside the building.

NOTE   The wireless throughput is significantly less than its maximum data rate due to the half-duplex nature of radio frequency technology.

- **Price**: Along with the price of the medium, the installation cost must be considered. For example, fiber installation costs are significantly higher than copper installation costs because of strict requirements for optical cable coupling.

- **Deployment area**: Indicates whether wiring is for wiring closet only (where users access the network), for internode, or for interbuilding connections.

When deploying devices in an area with high electrical or magnetic interference—for example, in an industrial environment—you must pay special attention to media selection. In such environments, the disturbances might interfere with data transfer and therefore result in an increased number of frame errors. Electrical grounding can isolate some external disturbance, but the additional wiring increases costs. Fiber- optic installation is the only reasonable solution for such networks.

Cabling Example

Figure 4-6 illustrates a typical campus network structure. End devices such as workstations, IP phones, and printers are no more than 100 m away from the LAN switch. UTP wiring can easily handle the required distance and speed; it is also easy to set up, and the price-performance ratio is reasonable.

Figure 4-6 *Campus Networks Use Many Different Types of Cables*

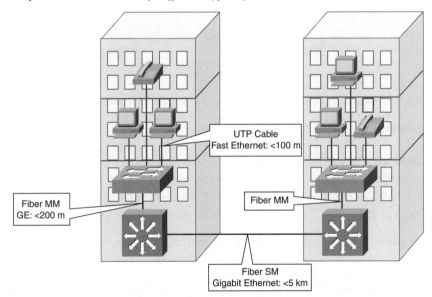

NOTE The distances shown in the figure are for a sample network; however, the maximum distance supported varies depending on the fiber interface used.

Optical fiber cables handle the higher speeds and distances that may be required among switch devices. MM optical cable is usually satisfactory inside the building. Depending on distance, organizations use MM or SM optical for interbuilding communication cable. If the distances are short (up to 500 m), MM fiber is a more reasonable solution for speeds up to 1 Gbps.

However, an organization can install SM fiber if its requirements are for longer distances, or if there are plans for future higher speeds (for example, 10 Gbps).

> **NOTE**   Selecting the less expensive type of fiber might satisfy a customer's current needs, but this fiber might not meet the needs of future upgrades or equipment replacement. Replacing cable can be very expensive. Planning with future requirements in mind might result in higher initial costs but lower costs in the long run.

Infrastructure Device Characteristics and Considerations

Network end-user devices are commonly connected using switched technology rather than using a shared media segment. Switched technology provides dedicated network bandwidth for each device on the network. Switched networks can support network infrastructure services, such as QoS, security, and management; a shared media segment cannot support these features.

In the past, LAN switches were Layer 2–only devices. Data link layer (Layer 2) switching supports multiple simultaneous frame flows. Multilayer switching performs packet switching and several functions at Layer 3 and at higher Open Systems Interconnection (OSI) layers and can effectively replace routers in the LAN switched environment. Deciding whether to deploy pure data link layer switches or multilayer switches in the enterprise network is not a trivial decision. It requires a full understanding of the network topology and user demands.

KEY POINT   The difference between data link layer and multilayer switching is the type of information used inside the frame to determine the correct output interface.

Data link layer switching forwards frames based on data link layer information (the MAC address), whereas multilayer switching forwards frames based on network layer information (such as IP address).

Multilayer switching is hardware-based switching and routing integrated into a single platform. See the upcoming "Multilayer Switching and Cisco Express Forwarding" section for implementation details.

When deciding on the type of switch to use and the features to be deployed in a network, consider the following factors:

- **Infrastructure service capabilities**: The network services that the organization requires (IP multicast, QoS, and so on).

- **Size of the network segments**: How the network is segmented and how many end devices will be connected, based on traffic characteristics.

- **Convergence time**: The maximum amount of time the network will be unavailable in the event of network outages.

- **Cost**: The budget for the network infrastructure. Note that multilayer switches are typically more expensive than their Layer 2 counterparts; however, multilayer functionality can be obtained by adding cards and software to a modular Layer 2 switch.

The following sections examine the following infrastructure characteristics: convergence time, multilayer switching and Cisco Express Forwarding, IP multicast, QoS, and load sharing.

Convergence Time

Loop-prevention mechanisms in a Layer 2 topology cause the Spanning Tree Protocol (STP) to take between 30 and 50 seconds to converge. To eliminate STP convergence issues in the Campus Core, all the links connecting core switches should be routed links, not VLAN trunks. This also limits the broadcast and failure domains.

> **NOTE**   STP tools are covered in the section "The Cisco STP Toolkit" later in this chapter.

In the case where multilayer switching is deployed everywhere, convergence is within seconds (depending on the routing protocol implemented) because all the devices detect their connected link failure immediately and act on it promptly (sending respective routing updates).

In a mixed Layer 2 and Layer 3 environment, the convergence time depends not only on the Layer 3 factors (including routing protocol timers such as hold-time and neighbor loss detection), but also on the STP convergence.

Using multilayer switching in a structured design reduces the scope of spanning-tree domains. It is common to use a routing protocol, such as Enhanced Interior Gateway Routing Protocol (EIGRP) or Open Shortest Path First (OSPF), to handle load balancing, redundancy, and recovery in the Campus Core.

Multilayer Switching and Cisco Express Forwarding

As noted in Chapter 3, "Structuring and Modularizing the Network," in this book the term *multilayer switching* denotes a switch's generic capability to use information at different protocol layers as part of the switching process; the term *Layer 3 switching* is a synonym for multilayer switching in this context.

The use of protocol information from multiple layers in the switching process is implemented in two different ways within Cisco switches. The first way is called *multilayer switching (MLS)*, and the second way is called *Cisco Express Forwarding*.

Multilayer Switching

Multilayer switching, as its name implies, allows switching to take place at different protocol layers. Switching can be performed only on Layers 2 and 3, or it can also include Layer 4. MLS is based on network flows.

> **KEY POINT**
> A *network flow* is a unidirectional sequence of packets between a source and a destination. Flows can be very specific. For example, a network flow can be identified by source and destination IP addresses, protocol numbers, and port numbers as well as the interface on which the packet enters the switch.

The three major components of MLS are as follows:

- **MLS Route Processor (MLS-RP)**: The MLS-enabled router that performs the traditional function of routing between subnets

- **MLS Switching Engine (MLS-SE)**: The MLS-enabled switch that can offload some of the packet-switching functionality from the MLS-RP

- **Multilayer Switching Protocol (MLSP)**: Used by the MLS-RP and the MLS-SE to communicate with each other

> **KEY POINT**
> MLS allows communication between two devices that are in different VLANs (on different subnets), that are connected to the same MLS-SE, and that share a common MLS-RP. The communication bypasses the MLS-RP and instead uses the MLS-SE to relay the packets, thus improving overall performance.

MLS History

Pure MLS is an older technique used on the Catalyst 5500 switches with a Route Switch Module (manually configured as the MLS-RP) and a Supervisor Engine III with a NetFlow Feature Card (manually configured as the MLS-SE). The first packet of a flow is routed by the MLS-RP, whereas the MLS-SE records (caches) all flow, or header, information; all subsequent packets in the identical flow are hardware-switched by the MLS-SE.

Most of Cisco's modern multilayer switches use Cisco Express Forwarding–based multilayer switching (as described in the next section), using hardware integrated in the switch platform.

Cisco Express Forwarding

Cisco Express Forwarding, like MLS, aims to speed the data routing and forwarding process in a network. However, the two methods use different approaches.

Cisco Express Forwarding uses two components to optimize the lookup of the information required to route packets: the Forwarding Information Base (FIB) for the Layer 3 information and the adjacency table for the Layer 2 information.

Cisco Express Forwarding creates an FIB by maintaining a copy of the forwarding information contained in the IP routing table. The information is indexed, so it is quick to search for matching entries as packets are processed. Whenever the routing table changes, the FIB is also changed so that it always contains up-to-date paths. A separate routing cache is not required.

The adjacency table contains Layer 2 frame header information, including next-hop addresses, for all FIB entries. Each FIB entry can point to multiple adjacency table entries—for example, if two paths exist between devices for load balancing.

After a packet is processed and the route is determined from the FIB, the Layer 2 next-hop and header information is retrieved from the adjacency table, and the new frame is created to encapsulate the packet.

Cisco Express Forwarding can be enabled on a router (for example, on a Cisco 7600 Series router) or on a switch with Layer 3 functionality (such as the Catalyst 6500 Series switch).

NOTE Not all Catalyst switches support Cisco Express Forwarding. See the specific product documentation on the Cisco website for device support information.

IP Multicast

A traditional IP network is not efficient when sending the same data to many locations; the data is sent in unicast packets and therefore is replicated on the network for each destination. For example, if a CEO's annual video address is sent out on a company's network for all employees to watch, the same data stream must be replicated for each employee. Obviously, this would consume many resources, including precious WAN bandwidth.

IP multicast technology enables networks to send data to a group of destinations in the most efficient way. The data is sent from the source as one stream; this single data stream travels as far as it can in the network. Devices replicate the data only if they need to send it out on multiple interfaces to reach all members of the destination group.

Multicast groups are identified by Class D IP addresses, which are in the range from 224.0.0.0 to 239.255.255.255. IP multicast involves some new protocols for network devices, including two for informing network devices which hosts require which multicast data stream and one for determining the best way to route multicast traffic. These three protocols are described in the following sections.

Internet Group Management Protocol and Cisco Group Management Protocol

Internet Group Management Protocol (IGMP) is used between hosts and their local routers. Hosts register with the router to join (and leave) specific multicast groups; the router then knows that it needs to forward the data stream destined for a specific multicast group to the registered hosts.

In a typical network, hosts are not directly connected to routers but are connected to a Layer 2 switch, which is in turn connected to the router. IGMP is a network layer (Layer 3) protocol. Consequently, Layer 2 switches do not participate in IGMP and therefore are not aware of which hosts attached to them might be part of a particular multicast group. By default, Layer 2 switches flood multicast frames to all ports (except the port from which the frame originated), which means that all multicast traffic received by a switch would be sent out on all ports, even if only one device on one port required the data stream. Cisco therefore developed Cisco Group Management Protocol (CGMP), which is used between switches and routers. The routers tell each of their directly connected switches about IGMP registrations that were received from hosts through the switch—in other words, from hosts accessible through the switch. The switch then forwards the multicast traffic only to ports that those requesting hosts are on, rather than flooding the data to all ports. Switches, including non-Cisco switches, can alternatively use *IGMP snooping* to eavesdrop on the IGMP messages sent between routers and hosts to learn similar information.

Figure 4-7 illustrates the interaction of these two protocols. Hosts A and D register, using IGMP, to join the multicast group to receive data from the server. The router informs both switches of these registrations using CGMP. When the router forwards the multicast data to the hosts, the switches ensure that the data goes out of only the ports on which hosts A and D are connected. The ports on which hosts B and C are connected do not receive the multicast data.

Figure 4-7   *IGMP and CGMP Tell Network Devices Which Hosts Want Which Multicast Data*

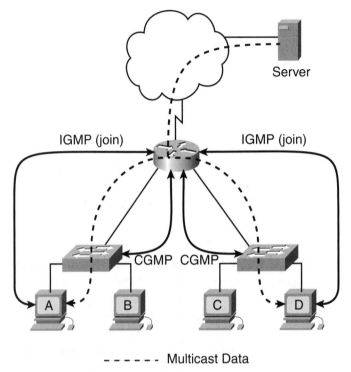

Protocol-Independent Multicast Routing Protocol

Protocol-Independent Multicast (PIM) is used by routers that forward multicast packets. The *protocol-independent* part of the name indicates that PIM is independent of the unicast routing protocol (for example, EIGRP or OSPF) running in the network. PIM uses the normal routing table, populated by the unicast routing protocol, in its multicast routing calculations.

> **NOTE**   EIGRP, OSPF, and so forth are called *unicast routing protocols* because they are used to create and maintain unicast routing information in the routing table. Recall, though, that they use multicast packets (or broadcast packets in some protocols) to send their routing update traffic. Note that a variant of OSPF, called multicast OSPF, supports multicast routing; Cisco routers do not support multicast OSPF.

Unlike other routing protocols, no routing updates are sent between PIM routers.

When a router forwards a unicast packet, it looks up the destination address in its routing table and forwards the packet out of the appropriate interface. However, when forwarding a multicast packet, the router might have to forward the packet out of multiple interfaces, toward all the receiving hosts. Multicast-enabled routers use PIM to dynamically create distribution trees that control the path that IP multicast traffic takes through the network to deliver traffic to all receivers.

The following two types of distribution trees exist:

- **Source tree**: A source tree is created for each source sending to each multicast group. The source tree has its root at the source and has branches through the network to the receivers.

- **Shared tree**: A shared tree is a single tree that is shared between all sources for each multicast group. The shared tree has a single common root, called a *rendezvous point (RP)*.

Multicast routers consider the source address of the multicast packet as well as the destination address, and they use the distribution tree to forward the packet away from the source and toward the destination. Forwarding multicast traffic away from the source, rather than to the receiver, is called *Reverse Path Forwarding (RPF)*. To avoid routing loops, RPF uses the unicast routing table to determine the upstream (toward the source) and downstream (away from the source) neighbors and ensures that only one interface on the router is considered to be an incoming interface for data from a specific source. For example, data received on one router interface and forwarded out another interface can loop around the network and come back into the same router on a different interface; RPF ensures that this data is not forwarded again.

PIM operates in one of the following two modes:

- **Sparse mode**: This mode uses a "pull" model to send multicast traffic. Sparse mode uses a shared tree and therefore requires an RP to be defined. Sources register with the RP. Routers along the path from active receivers that have explicitly requested to join a specific multicast group register to join that group. These routers calculate, using the unicast routing table, whether they have a better metric to the RP or to the source itself; they forward the join message to the device with the better metric.

- **Dense mode**: This mode uses a "push" model that floods multicast traffic to the entire network. Dense mode uses source trees. Routers that have no need for the data (because they are not connected to receivers that want the data or to other routers that want it) request that the tree be pruned so that they no longer receive the data.

QoS Considerations in LAN Switches

A campus network transports many types of applications and data, which might include high-quality video and delay-sensitive data (such as real-time voice). Bandwidth-intensive applications enhance many business processes but might also stretch network capabilities and resources.

Networks must provide secure, predictable, measurable, and sometimes guaranteed services. Achieving the required QoS by managing delay, delay variation (jitter), bandwidth, and packet loss parameters on a network can be the key to a successful end-to-end business solution. QoS mechanisms are techniques used to manage network resources.

The assumption that a high-capacity, nonblocking switch with multigigabit backplanes never needs QoS is incorrect. Many networks or individual network elements are oversubscribed; it is easy to create scenarios in which congestion can potentially occur and that therefore require some form of QoS. The sum of the bandwidths on all ports on a switch where end devices are connected is usually greater than that of the uplink port; when the access ports are fully used, congestion on the uplink port is unavoidable. Uplinks from the Building Access layer to the Building Distribution layer, or from the Building Distribution layer to the Campus Core layer, most often require QoS. Depending on traffic flow and uplink oversubscription, bandwidth is managed with QoS mechanisms on the Building Access, Building Distribution, or even Campus Core switches.

QoS Mechanisms

QoS mechanisms or tools implemented on LAN switches include the following:

- **Classification and marking**: Packet *classification* is the process of partitioning traffic into multiple priority levels, or classes of service. Information in the frame or packet header is inspected, and the frame's priority is determined. *Marking* is the process of changing the priority or class of service (CoS) setting within a frame or packet to indicate its classification.

  For IEEE 802.1Q frames, the 3 user priority bits in the Tag field—commonly referred to as the 802.1p bits—are used as CoS bits. However, Layer 2 markings are not useful as end-to-end QoS indicators, because the medium often changes throughout a network (for example, from Ethernet to a Frame Relay WAN). Thus, Layer 3 markings are required to support end-to-end QoS.

  For IPv4, Layer 3 marking can be done using the 8-bit type of service (ToS) field in the packet header. Originally, only the first 3 bits were used; these bits are called the *IP Precedence bits*. Because 3 bits can specify only eight marking values, IP precedence does not allow a granular classification of traffic. Thus, more bits are now used: the first 6 bits in the TOS field are now known as the *DiffServ Code Point (DSCP) bits*.

> **NOTE**   Two models exist for deploying end-to-end QoS in a network for traffic that is not suitable for best-effort service: Integrated Services (IntServ) and Differentiated Services (DiffServ). *End-to-end QoS* means that the network provides the level of service required by traffic throughout the entire network, from one end to the other.
>
> With IntServ, an application requests services from the network, and the network devices confirm that they can meet the request, before any data is sent. The data from the application is considered a flow of packets.
>
> In contrast, with DiffServ, each packet is marked as it enters the network based on the type of traffic that it contains. The network devices then use this marking to determine how to handle the packet as it travels through the network. The DSCP bits are used to implement the DiffServ model.

- **Congestion management: Queuing**: Queuing separates traffic into various queues or buffers; the marking in the frame or packet can be used to determine which queue traffic goes in. A network interface is often congested (even at high speeds, transient congestion is observed); queuing techniques ensure that traffic from the critical applications is forwarded appropriately. For example, real-time applications such as VoIP and stock trading might have to be forwarded with the least latency and jitter.

- **Congestion Management: Scheduling**: Scheduling is the process that determines the order in which queues are serviced.

- **Policing and shaping**: Policing and shaping tools identify traffic that violates some threshold level and reduces a stream of data to a predetermined rate or level. Traffic shaping buffers the frames for a short time. Policing simply drops or lowers the priority of the frame that is out of profile.

> **NOTE**   Later chapters in this book describe two other QoS mechanisms: congestion avoidance and link efficiency techniques.

QoS in LAN Switches

When configuring QoS features, classify the specific network traffic, prioritize and mark it according to its relative importance, and use congestion management and policing and shaping techniques to provide preferential treatment. Implementing QoS in the network makes network performance more predictable and bandwidth use more effective. Figure 4-8 illustrates where the various categories of QoS may be implemented in LAN switches.

Figure 4-8 *QoS in LAN Switches*

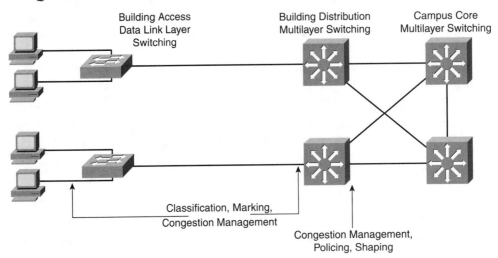

Data link layer switches are commonly used in the Building Access layer. Because they do not have knowledge of Layer 3 or higher information, these switches provide QoS classification and marking based only on the switch's input port or MAC address. For example, traffic from a particular host can be defined as high-priority traffic on the uplink port. Multilayer switches may be used in the Building Access layer if Layer 3 services are required.

Building Distribution layer, Campus Core layer, and Server Farm switches are typically multilayer switches and can provide QoS selectively—not only on a port basis, but also according to higher-layer parameters, such as IP addresses, port numbers, or QoS bits in the IP packet. These switches make QoS classification more selective by differentiating the traffic based on the application. QoS in distribution and core switches must be provided in both directions of traffic flow. The policing for certain traffic is usually implemented on the distribution layer switches.

Load Sharing in Layer 2 and Layer 3 Switches

Layer 2 and Layer 3 switches handle load sharing differently.

Layer 2 Load Sharing

Because Layer 2 switches are aware of only MAC addresses, they cannot perform any intelligent load sharing. In an environment characterized by multiple VLANs per access switch and more than one connection to the uplink switch, the solution is to put all uplink connections into trunks (Inter-Switch Link [ISL] or IEEE 802.1Q). Each trunk carries all VLANs; however, without additional configuration, the STP protocol disables all nonprimary uplink ports. This configuration might result in a bandwidth shortage, because the traffic for all the VLANs passes through the same link. To overcome this problem, the STP parameters must be configured to carry some VLANs across one uplink and the rest of the VLANs across the other uplink. For example, one uplink could be configured to carry the VLANs with odd numbers, whereas the other uplink would be configured to carry the VLANs with even numbers.

> **NOTE**   Some options related to STP are described in the "Building Access Layer Design Considerations" section on the next page.

Layer 3 Load Sharing

Layer 3–capable switches can perform load sharing based on IP addresses, either per packet or per destination-source IP pair.

The advantage of Layer 3 IP load sharing is that links are used more proportionately than with Layer 2 load sharing, which is based on VLANs only. For example, the traffic in one VLAN can be very heavy, while the traffic in another VLAN is very low; in this case, per-VLAN load sharing by using even and odd VLANs is not appropriate. Due to the dynamic nature of organizational applications, Layer 3 load sharing is more appropriate. Layer 3 allows for dynamic adaptation to link utilization and depends on the routing protocol design. Layer 3 switches also support Layer 2 load sharing, so they can still apply per-VLAN load sharing while connected to other Layer 2 switches.

Enterprise Campus Design

As discussed in Chapter 3, the Enterprise Campus functional area is divided into the following modules:

- Campus Infrastructure—This module includes three layers:
  - The Building Access layer
  - The Building Distribution layer
  - The Campus Core layer
- Server Farm
- Edge Distribution (optional)

This section discusses the design of each of the layers and modules within the Enterprise Campus and identifies best practices related to the design of each.

Enterprise Campus Requirements

As shown in Table 4-3, each Enterprise Campus module has different requirements. For example, this table illustrates how modules located closer to the users require a higher degree of scalability so that the Campus network can be expanded in the future without redesigning the complete network. For example, adding new workstations to a network should result in neither high investment cost nor performance degradations.

Table 4-3 *Enterprise Campus Design Requirements*

Requirement	Building Access	Building Distribution	Campus Core	Server Farm	Edge Distribution
Technology	Data link layer or multilayer switched	Multilayer switched	Multilayer switched	Multilayer switched	Multilayer switched
Scalability	High	Medium	Low	Medium	Low
High availability	Medium	Medium	High	High	Medium
Performance	Medium	Medium	High	High	Medium
Cost per port	Low	Medium	High	High	Medium

End users (in the Building Access layer) usually do not require high performance or high availability, but these features are crucial to the Campus Core layer and the Server Farm module.

The price per port increases with increased performance and availability. The Campus Core and Server Farm require a guarantee of higher throughput so they can handle all traffic flows and not introduce additional delays or drops to the network traffic.

The Edge Distribution module does not require the same performance as in the Campus Core. However, it can require other features and functionalities that increase the overall cost.

Building Access Layer Design Considerations

When implementing the campus infrastructure's Building Access layer, consider the following questions:

■ How many users or host ports are currently required in the wiring closet, and how many will it require in the future? Should the switches be fixed or modular configuration?

■ How many ports are available for end-user connectivity at the walls of the buildings?

■ How many access switches are not located in wiring closets?

- What cabling is currently available in the wiring closet, and what cabling options exist for uplink connectivity?

- What data link layer performance does the node need?

- What level of redundancy is needed?

- What is the required link capacity to the Building Distribution layer switches?

- How will VLANs and STP be deployed? Will there be a single VLAN, or several VLANs per access switch? Will the VLANs on the switch be unique or spread across multiple switches? The latter design was common a few years ago, but today end-to-end VLANs (also called *campuswide VLANs*) are not desirable.

- Are additional features, such as port security, multicast traffic management, and QoS (such as traffic classification based on ports), required?

Based on the answers to these questions, select the devices that satisfy the Building Access layer's requirements. The Building Access layer should maintain the simplicity of traditional LAN switching, with the support of basic network intelligent services and business applications.

KEY POINT | The following are best-practice recommendations for optimal Building Access layer design:

- Manage VLANs and STP

- Manage trunks between switches

- Manage default Port Aggregation Protocol (PAgP) settings

- Consider implementing routing

These recommendations are described in the following sections.

Managing VLANs and STP

This section details best-practice recommendations related to VLANs and STP.

Limit VLANs to a Single Wiring Closet Whenever Possible

As a best practice, limit VLANs to a single wiring closet whenever possible.

> **NOTE**   Cisco (and other vendors) use the term *local VLAN* to refer to a VLAN that is limited to a single wiring closet.

Avoid Using STP if Possible

STP is defined in IEEE 802.1d. Avoid requiring any type of STP (including Rapid STP [RSTP]) by design for the most deterministic and highly available network topology that is predictable and bounded and has reliably tuned convergence.

For example, the behavior of Layer 2 environments (using STP) and Layer 3 environments (using a routing protocol) are different under "soft failure" conditions, when keepalive messages are lost. In an STP environment, if bridge protocol data units (BPDU) are lost, the network fails in an "open" state, forwarding traffic with unknown destinations on all ports, potentially causing broadcast storms.

In contrast, routing environments fail "closed," dropping routing neighbor relationships, breaking connectivity, and isolating the soft failed devices.

Another reason to avoid using STP is for load balancing: If there are two redundant links, STP by default uses only one of the links, while routing protocols by default use both.

If STP Is Required, Use RSTP with Per-VLAN Spanning Tree Plus

Cisco developed Per-VLAN Spanning Tree (PVST) so that switches can have one instance of STP running per VLAN, allowing redundant physical links within the network to be used for different VLANs and thus reducing the load on individual links. PVST works only over ISL trunks. However, Cisco extended this functionality for 802.1Q trunks with the Per-VLAN Spanning Tree Plus (PVST+) protocol. Before this became available, 802.1Q trunks supported only Common Spanning Tree (CST), with one instance of STP running for all VLANs.

Multiple-Instance STP (MISTP) is an IEEE standard (802.1s) that uses RSTP and allows several VLANs to be grouped into a single spanning-tree instance. Each instance is independent of the other instances so that a link can forward for one group of VLANs while blocking for other VLANs. MISTP therefore allows traffic to be shared across all the links in the network, but it reduces the number of STP instances that would be required if PVST/PVST+ were implemented.

RSTP is defined by IEEE 802.1w. RPVST+ is a Cisco enhancement of RSTP. As a best practice, if STP must be used, use RPVST+.

> **NOTE** When Cisco documentation refers to implementing RSTP, it is referring to RPVST+.

The Cisco RPVST+ implementation is far superior to 802.1d STP and even PVST+ from a convergence perspective. It greatly improves the convergence times for any VLAN on which a link comes up, and it greatly improves the convergence time compared to BackboneFast (as described in the next section) for any indirect link failures.

Two other STP-related recommendations are as follows:

- If a network includes non-Cisco switches, isolate the different STP domains with Layer 3 routing to avoid STP compatibility issues.

- Even if the recommended design does not depend on STP to resolve link or node failure events, use STP in Layer 2 designs to protect against user-side loops. A loop can be introduced on the user-facing access layer ports in many ways, such as wiring mistakes, misconfigured end stations, or malicious users. STP is required to ensure a loop-free topology and to protect the rest of the network from problems created in the access layer.

NOTE   Some security personnel have recommended disabling STP at the network edge. Cisco does not recommend this practice, however, because the risk of lost connectivity without STP is far greater than any STP information that might be revealed.

The Cisco STP Toolkit

The Cisco STP toolkit provides tools to better manage STP when RSTP+ is not available:

- **PortFast**: Used for ports to which end-user stations or servers are directly connected. When PortFast is enabled, there is no delay in passing traffic, because the switch immediately puts the port in STP forwarding state, skipping the listening and learning states. Two additional measures that prevent potential STP loops are associated with the PortFast feature:

  — **BPDU Guard**: PortFast transitions the port into the STP forwarding state immediately on linkup. Because the port still participates in STP, the potential for an STP loop exists if some device attached to that port also runs STP. The BPDU Guard feature enforces the STP domain borders and keeps the active topology predictable. If the port receives a BPDU, the port is transitioned into *errdisable state* (meaning that it was disabled due to an error), and an error message is reported.

NOTE   Additional information on the errdisable state is available in *Recovering from errDisable Port State on the CatOS Platforms*, at http://www.cisco.com/en/US/tech/tk389/ tk214/technologies_tech_note09186a0080093dcb.shtml.

  — **BPDU Filtering**: This feature blocks PortFast-enabled, nontrunk ports from transmitting BPDUs. STP does not run on these ports. BPDU filtering is not recommended, because it effectively disables STP at the edge and can lead to STP loops.

- **UplinkFast**: If the link on a switch to the root switch goes down and the blocked link is directly connected to the same switch, UplinkFast enables the switch to put a redundant port (path) into the forwarding state immediately, typically resulting in convergence of 3 to 5 seconds after a link failure.

- **BackboneFast**: If a link on the way to the root switch fails but is *not* directly connected to the same switch (in other words, it is an indirect failure), BackboneFast reduces the convergence time by max_age (which is 20 seconds by default), from 50 seconds to approximately 30 seconds. When this feature is used, it must be enabled on all switches in the STP domain.

- **STP Loop Guard**: When one of the blocking ports in a physically redundant topology stops receiving BPDUs, usually STP creates a potential loop by moving the port to forwarding state. With the STP Loop Guard feature enabled, and if a blocking port no longer receives BPDUs, that port is moved into the STP loop-inconsistent blocking state instead of the listening/learning/forwarding state. This feature avoids loops in the network that result from unidirectional or other software failures.

- **RootGuard**: The RootGuard feature prevents external switches from becoming the root. RootGuard should be enabled on all ports where the root bridge should *not* appear; this feature ensures that the port on which RootGuard is enabled is the designated port. If a *superior* BPDU (a BPDU with a lower bridge ID than that of the current root bridge) is received on a RootGuard-enabled port, the port is placed in a root-inconsistent state—the equivalent of the listening state.

- **BPDU Skew Detection**: This feature allows the switch to keep track of late-arriving BPDUs (by default, BPDUs are sent every 2 seconds) and notify the administrator via Syslog messages. Skew detection generates a report for every port on which BPDU has ever arrived late (this is known as *skewed* arrival). Report messages are rate-limited (one message every 60 seconds) to protect the CPU.

- **Unidirectional Link Detection (UDLD)**: A unidirectional link occurs whenever traffic transmitted by the local switch over a link is received by the neighbor but traffic transmitted from the neighbor is not received by the local device. If the STP process that runs on the switch with a blocking port stops receiving BPDUs from its upstream (designated) switch on that port, STP eventually ages out the STP information for this port and moves it to the forwarding state. If the link is unidirectional, this action would create an STP loop. UDLD is a Layer 2 protocol that works with the Layer 1 mechanisms to determine a link's physical status. If the port does not see its own device/port ID in the incoming UDLD packets for a specific duration, the link is considered unidirectional from the Layer 2 perspective. After UDLD detects the unidirectional link, the respective port is disabled, and an error message is generated.

NOTE PortFast, Loop Guard, RootGuard, and BPDU Guard are also supported for RPVST+.

As an example of the use of these features, consider when a switch running a version of STP is introduced into an operating network. This might not always cause a problem, such as when the switch is connected in a conference room to temporarily provide additional ports for connectivity. However, sometimes this is undesirable, such as when the switch that is added has been configured to become the STP root for the VLANs to which it is attached. BDPU Guard and RootGuard are tools that can protect against these situations. BDPU Guard requires operator intervention if an unauthorized switch is connected to the network, and RootGuard protects against a switch configured in a way that would cause STP to reconverge when it is being connected to the network.

Managing Trunks Between Switches

Trunks are typically deployed on the interconnection between the Building Access and Building Distribution layers. There are several best practices to implement with regard to trunks.

Trunk Mode and Encapsulation

As a best practice when configuring trunks, set Dynamic Trunking Protocol (DTP) to **desirable** on one side and **desirable** (with the **negotiate** option) one the other side to support DTP protocol (encapsulation) negotiation.

> **NOTE**   Although turning DTP to **on** and **on** with the **no negotiate** option could save seconds of outage when restoring a failed link or node, with this configuration DTP does not actively monitor the state of the trunk, and a misconfigured trunk is not easily identified.

> **NOTE**   The specific commands used to configure trunking vary; refer to your switch's documentation for details.

Manually Pruning VLANs

Another best practice is to manually prune unused VLANs from trunked interfaces to avoid broadcast propagation. Cisco recommends not using automatic VLAN pruning; manual pruning provides stricter control. As mentioned, campuswide or access layer–wide VLANs are no longer recommended, so VLAN pruning is less of an issue than it used to be.

VTP Transparent Mode

VTP transparent mode should be used as a best practice because hierarchical networks have little need for a shared common VLAN database. Using VTP transparent mode decreases the potential for operational error.

Trunking on Ports

Trunking should be disabled on ports to which hosts will be attached so that host devices do not need to negotiate trunk status. This practice speeds up PortFast and is a security measure to prevent VLAN hopping.

Managing Default PAgP Settings

Fast EtherChannel and Gigabit EtherChannel solutions group several parallel links between LAN switches into a channel that is seen as a single link from the Layer 2 perspective. Two protocols handle automatic EtherChannel formation: PAgP, which is Cisco-proprietary, and the Link Aggregation Control Protocol (LACP), which is standardized and defined in IEEE 802.3ad.

When connecting a Cisco IOS software device to a Catalyst operating system device using PAgP, make sure that the PAgP settings used to establish EtherChannels are coordinated; the defaults are different for a Cisco IOS software device and a Catalyst operating system device. As a best practice, Catalyst operating system devices should have PAgP set to **off** when connecting to a Cisco IOS software device if EtherChannels are not configured. If EtherChannel/PAgP is used, set both sides of the interconnection to **desirable**.

Implementing Routing in the Building Access Layer

Although not as widely deployed in the Building Access layer, a routing protocol, such as EIGRP, when properly tuned, can achieve better convergence results than Layer 2 and Layer 3 boundary hierarchical designs that rely on STP. However, adding routing does result in some additional complexities, including uplink IP addressing and subnetting, and loss of flexibility.

Figure 4-9 illustrates a sample network with Layer 3 routing in both the Building Access and Building Distribution layers. In this figure, equal-cost Layer 3 load balancing is performed on all links (although EIGRP could perform unequal-cost load balancing). STP is not run, and a first-hop redundancy protocol (such as Hot Standby Router Protocol [HSRP]) is not required. VLANs cannot span across the multilayer switch.

Figure 4-9 *Layer 3 Access-to-Distribution Layer Interconnection*

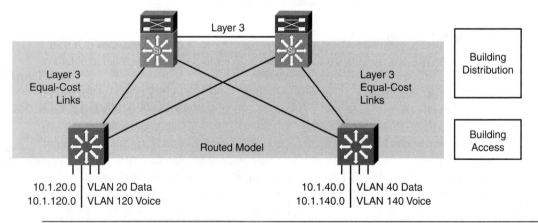

NOTE HSRP and other first-hop redundancy protocols are discussed in the "Using First-Hop Redundancy Protocols" section.

Building Distribution Layer Design Considerations

The Building Distribution layer aggregates the Building Access layer, segments workgroups, and isolates segments from failures and broadcast storms. This layer implements many policies based on access lists and QoS settings. The Building Distribution layer can protect the Campus Core network from any impact of Building Access layer problems by implementing all the organization's policies.

When implementing the Building Distribution layer, consider the following questions:

- How many devices will each Building Distribution switch handle?

- What type and level of redundancy are required?

- How many uplinks are needed?

- What speed do the uplinks need to be to the building core switches?

- What cabling is currently available in the wiring closet, and what cabling options exist for uplink connectivity?

- As network services are introduced, can the network continue to deliver high performance for all its applications, such as video on demand, IP multicast, or IP telephony?

The network designer must pay special attention to the following network characteristics:

- **Performance**: Building Distribution switches should provide wire-speed performance on all ports. This feature is important because of Building Access layer aggregation on one side and high-speed connectivity of the Campus Core module on the other side. Future expansions with additional ports or modules can result in an overloaded switch if it is not selected properly.

- **Redundancy**: Redundant Building Distribution layer switches and redundant connections to the Campus Core should be implemented. Using equal-cost redundant connections to the core supports fast convergence and avoids routing black holes. Network bandwidth and capacity should be engineered to withstand node or link failure.

   When redundant switches cannot be implemented in the Campus Core and Building Distribution layers, redundant supervisors and the Stateful Switchover (SSO) and Nonstop Forwarding (NSF) technologies can provide significant resiliency improvements. These technologies result in 1 to 3 seconds of outage in a failover, which is less than the time needed to replace a supervisor and recover its configuration. Depending on the switch platform, full-image In Service Software Upgrade (ISSU) technology might be available such that the complete Cisco IOS software image can be upgraded without taking the switch or network out of service, maximizing network availability.

- **Infrastructure services**: Building Distribution switches should not only support fast multilayer switching, but should also incorporate network services such as high availability, QoS, security, and policy enforcement.

  Expanding and/or reconfiguring distribution layer devices must be easy and efficient. These devices must support the required management features.

With the correct selection of Building Distribution layer switches, the network designer can easily add new Building Access modules.

KEY POINT | Multilayer switches are usually preferred as the Building Distribution layer switches, because this layer must usually support network services, such as QoS and traffic filtering.

KEY POINT | The following are best-practice recommendations for optimal Building Distribution layer design:

- Use first-hop redundancy protocols.

- Deploy Layer 3 routing protocols between the Building Distribution switches and Campus Core switches.

- If required, Building Distribution switches should support VLANs that span multiple Building Access layer switches.

The following sections describe these recommendations.

Using First-Hop Redundancy Protocols

If Layer 2 is used between the Building Access switch and the Building Distribution switch, convergence time when a link or node fails depends on default gateway redundancy and failover time. Building Distribution switches typically provide first-hop redundancy (default gateway redundancy) using HSRP, Gateway Load-Balancing Protocol (GLBP), or Virtual Router Redundancy Protocol (VRRP).

This redundancy allows a network to recover from the failure of the device acting as the default gateway for end nodes on a physical segment. Uplink tracking should also be implemented with the first-hop redundancy protocol.

HSRP or GLBP timers can be reliably tuned to achieve subsecond (800 to 900 ms) convergence for link or node failure in the boundary between Layer 2 and Layer 3 in the Building Distribution layer.

In Cisco deployments, HSRP is typically used as the default gateway redundancy protocol. VRRP is an Internet Engineering Task Force (IETF) standards-based method of providing default gateway redundancy. More deployments are starting to use GLBP because it supports load balancing on the uplinks from the access layer to the distribution layer, as well as first-hop redundancy and failure protection.

As shown in Figure 4-10, this model supports a recommended Layer 3 point-to-point interconnection between distribution switches.

Figure 4-10 *Layer 3 Distribution Switch Interconnection*

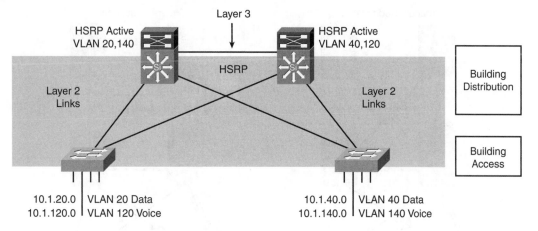

No VLANs span the Building Access layer switches across the distribution switches, so from an STP perspective, both access layer uplinks are forwarding, and no STP convergence is required if uplink failure occurs. The only convergence dependencies are the default gateway and return path route selection across the Layer 3 distribution-to-distribution link.

> **NOTE**   Notice in Figure 4-10 that the Layer 2 VLAN number is mapped to the Layer 3 subnet for ease of management.

If Layer 3 is used to the Building Access switch, the default gateway is at the multilayer Building Access switch, and a first-hop redundancy protocol is not needed.

Deploying Layer 3 Routing Protocols Between Building Distribution and Campus Core Switches

Routing protocols between the Building Distribution switches and the Campus Core switches support fast, deterministic convergence for the distribution layer across redundant links.

Convergence based on the up or down state of a point-to-point physical link is faster than timer-based nondeterministic convergence. Instead of indirect neighbor or route loss detection using hellos and dead timers, physical link loss indicates that a path is unusable; all traffic is rerouted to the alternative equal-cost path.

For optimum distribution-to-core layer convergence, build redundant *triangles*, not *squares*, to take advantage of equal-cost redundant paths for the best deterministic convergence. Figure 4-11 illustrates the difference.

Figure 4-11 *Redundant Triangles Versus Redundant Squares*

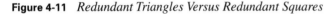

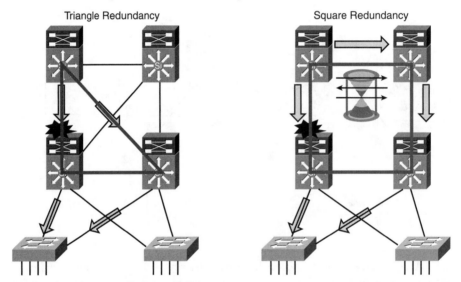

On the left of Figure 4-11, the multilayer switches are connected redundantly with a triangle of links that have Layer 3 equal costs. Because the links have equal costs, they appear in the routing table (and by default will be used for load balancing). If one of the links or distribution layer devices fails, convergence is extremely fast, because the failure is detected in hardware and there is no need for the routing protocol to recalculate a new path; it just continues to use one of the paths already in its routing table. In contrast, on the right of Figure 4-11, only one path is active by default, and link or device failure requires the routing protocol to recalculate a new route to converge.

Other related recommended practices are as follows:

■ Establish routing protocol peer relationships only on links that you want to use as transit links.

■ Summarize routes from the Building Distribution layer into the Campus Core layer.

Supporting VLANs That Span Multiple Building Access Layer Switches

In a less-than-optimal design where VLANs span multiple Building Access layer switches, the Building Distribution switches must be linked by a Layer 2 connection, or the Building Access layer switches must be connected via trunks.

This design is more complex than when the Building Distribution switches are interconnected with Layer 3. STP convergence is required if an uplink failure occurs.

As shown in Figure 4-12, the following are recommendations for use in this (suboptimal) design:

- Use RPVST+ as the version of STP.

- Provide a Layer 2 link between the two Building Distribution switches to avoid unexpected traffic paths and multiple convergence events.

- If you choose to load-balance VLANs across uplinks, be sure to place the HSRP primary and the RPVST+ root on the same Building Distribution layer switch to avoid using the interdistribution switch link for transit.

Figure 4-12 *Layer 2 Building Distribution Switch Interconnection*

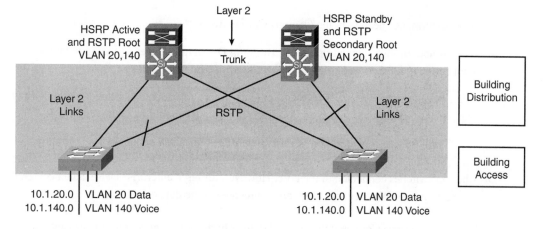

Campus Core Design Considerations

Low price per port and high port density can govern switch choice for wiring closet environments, but high-performance wire-rate multilayer switching drives the Campus Core design.

Using Campus Core switches reduces the number of connections between the Building Distribution layer switches and simplifies the integration of the Server Farm module and Enterprise Edge modules. Campus Core switches are primarily focused on wire-speed forwarding on all interfaces and are differentiated by the level of performance achieved per port rather than by high port densities.

KEY POINT | As a recommended practice, deploy a dedicated Campus Core layer to connect three or more buildings in the Enterprise Campus, or four or more pairs of Building Distribution switches in a very large campus.

Campus Core switches are typically multilayer switches.

Using a Campus Core makes scaling the network easier. For example, with a Campus Core, new Building Distribution switches only need connectivity to the core rather than full-mesh connectivity to all other Building Distribution switches.

NOTE   Not all campus implementations need a Campus Core. As discussed in the upcoming "Small and Medium Campus Design Options" section, the Campus Core and Building Distribution layers can be combined at the Building Distribution layer in a smaller campus.

Issues to consider in a Campus Core layer design include the following:

- The performance needed in the Campus Core network.

- The number of high-capacity ports for Building Distribution layer aggregation and connection to the Server Farm module or Enterprise Edge modules.

- High availability and redundancy requirements. To provide adequate redundancy, at least two separate switches (ideally located in different buildings) should be deployed.

Another Campus Core consideration is Enterprise Edge and WAN connectivity. For many organizations, the Campus Core provides Enterprise Edge and WAN connectivity through Edge Distribution switches connected to the core. However, for large enterprises with a data center, the Enterprise Edge and WAN connectivity are aggregated at the data center module.

Typically, the Campus Core switches should deliver high-performance, multilayer switching solutions for the Enterprise Campus and should address requirements for the following:

- Gigabit density

- Data and voice integration

- LAN, WAN, and metropolitan area network (MAN) convergence

- Scalability

- High availability

- Intelligent multilayer switching in the Campus Core, and to the Building Distribution and Server Farm environments

Large Campus Design

For a large campus, the most flexible and scalable Campus Core layer consists of dual multilayer switches, as illustrated in Figure 4-13.

Figure 4-13 *Large Campus Multilayer Switched Campus Core Design*

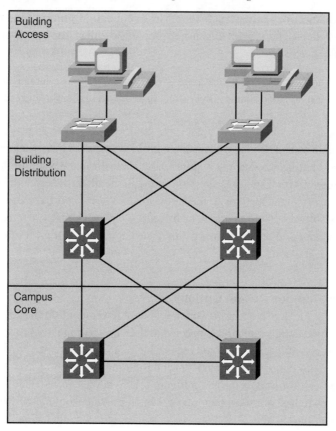

Multilayer-switched Campus Core layers have several best-practice features:

- **Reduced multilayer switch peering (routing adjacencies)**: Each multilayer Building Distribution switch connects to only two multilayer Campus Core switches, using a redundant triangle configuration. This implementation simplifies any-to-any connectivity between Building Distribution and Campus Core switches and is scalable to an arbitrarily large size. It also supports redundancy and load sharing.

- **Topology with no spanning-tree loops**: No STP activity exists in the Campus Core or on the Building Distribution links to the Campus Core layer, because all the links are Layer 3 (routed) links. Arbitrary topologies are supported by the routing protocol used in the Campus Core layer. Because the core is routed, it also provides multicast and broadcast control.

- **Improved network infrastructure services support**: Multilayer Campus Core switches provide better support for intelligent network services than data link layer core switches could support.

This design maintains two equal-cost paths to every destination network. Thus, recovery from any link failure is fast and load sharing is possible, resulting in higher throughput in the Campus Core layer.

One of the main considerations when using multilayer switches in the Campus Core is switching performance. Multilayer switching requires more sophisticated devices for high-speed packet routing. Modern Layer 3 switches support routing in the hardware, even though the hardware might not support all the features. If the hardware does not support a selected feature, it must be performed in software; this can dramatically reduce the data transfer. For example, access lists might not be processed in the hardware if they have too many entries, resulting in switch performance degradation.

Small and Medium Campus Design Options

A small campus (or large branch) network might have fewer than 200 end devices, and the network servers and workstations might be connected to the same wiring closet. Because switches in a small campus network design may not require high-end switching performance or much scaling capability, in many cases, the Campus Core and Building Distribution layers can be combined into a single layer, as illustrated on the left of Figure 4-14. This design can scale to only a few Building Access layer switches. A low-end multilayer switch provides routing services closer to the end user when multiple VLANs exist. For a very small office, one low-end multilayer switch may support the LAN access requirements for the entire office.

Figure 4-14 *Small and Medium Campus Design Options*

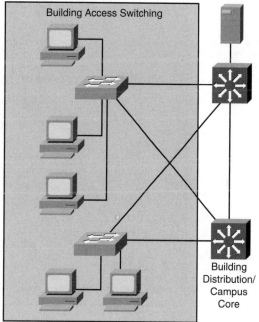

For a medium-sized campus with 200 to 1000 end devices, the network infrastructure typically consists of Building Access layer switches with uplinks to Building Distribution/Campus Core multilayer switches that can support the performance requirements of a medium-sized campus network. If redundancy is required, redundant multilayer switches connect to the Building Access switches, providing full link redundancy, as illustrated on the right of Figure 4-14.

NOTE   Branch and teleworker infrastructure considerations are described further in Chapter 5.

Edge Distribution at the Campus Core

As mentioned in Chapter 3, the Enterprise Edge modules connect to the Campus Core directly or through an optional Edge Distribution module, as illustrated in Figure 4-15.

Figure 4-15 *Edge Distribution Design*

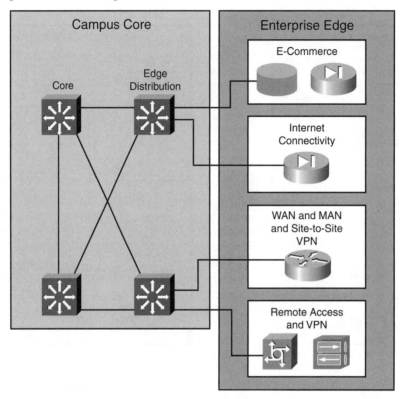

The Edge Distribution multilayer switches filter and route traffic into the Campus Core, aggregate Enterprise Edge connectivity, and provide advanced services.

Switching speed is not as important as security in the Edge Distribution module, which isolates and controls access to devices that are located in the Enterprise Edge modules (for example, servers in an E-commerce module or public servers in an Internet Connectivity module). These servers are closer to the external users and therefore introduce a higher risk to the internal campus. To protect the Campus Core from threats, the switches in the Edge Distribution module must protect the campus from the following attacks:

■ **Unauthorized access**: All connections from the Edge Distribution module that pass through the Campus Core must be verified against the user and the user's rights. Filtering mechanisms must provide granular control over specific edge subnets and their capability to reach areas within the campus.

- **IP spoofing**: IP spoofing is a hacker technique for impersonating the identity of another user by using that user's IP address. Denial of service (DoS) attacks use IP spoofing to generate requests to servers, using the stolen IP address as a source. The server therefore does not respond to the original source, but it does respond to the stolen IP address. A significant amount of this type of traffic causes the attacked server to be unavailable, thereby interrupting business. DoS attacks are a problem because they are difficult to detect and defend against; attackers can use a valid internal IP address for the source address of IP packets that produce the attack.

- **Network reconnaissance**: Network reconnaissance (or discovery) sends packets into the network and collects responses from the network devices. These responses provide basic information about the internal network topology. Network intruders use this approach to find out about network devices and the services that run on them.

  Therefore, filtering traffic from network reconnaissance mechanisms before it enters the enterprise network can be crucial. Traffic that is not essential must be limited to prevent a hacker from performing network reconnaissance.

- **Packet sniffers**: Packet sniffers are devices that monitor and capture the traffic in the network and might be used by hackers. Packets belonging to the same broadcast domain are vulnerable to capture by packet sniffers, especially if the packets are broadcast or multicast. Because most of the traffic to and from the Edge Distribution module is business-critical, corporations cannot afford this type of security lapse. Multilayer switches can prevent such an occurrence.

The Edge Distribution devices provide the last line of defense for all external traffic that is destined for the Campus Infrastructure module. In terms of overall functionality, the Edge Distribution switches are similar to the Building Distribution layer switches. Both use access control to filter traffic, although the Edge Distribution switches can rely on the Enterprise Edge modules to provide additional security. Both modules use multilayer switching to achieve high performance, but the Edge Distribution module can provide additional security functions because its performance requirements might not be as high.

When the enterprise includes a significant data center rather than a simple server farm, remote connectivity and performance requirements are more stringent. Edge Distribution switches can be located in the data center, giving remote users easier access to corporate resources. Appropriate security concerns need to be addressed in this module.

Server Placement

Within a campus network, servers may be placed locally in the Building Access or Building Distribution layer, or attached directly to the Campus Core. Centralized servers are typically grouped into a server farm located in the Enterprise Campus or in a separate data center.

Servers Directly Attached to Building Access or Building Distribution Layer Switches

If a server is local to a certain workgroup that corresponds to one VLAN, and all workgroup members and the server are attached to a Building Access layer switch, most of the traffic to the server is local to the workgroup. If required, an access list at the Building Distribution layer switch could hide these servers from the enterprise.

In some midsize networks, building-level servers that communicate with clients in different VLANs, but that are still within the same physical building, can be connected to Building Distribution layer switches.

Servers Directly Attached to the Campus Core

The Campus Core generally transports traffic quickly, without any limitations. Servers in a medium-sized campus can be connected directly to Campus Core switches, making the servers closer to the users than if the servers were in a Server Farm, as illustrated in Figure 4-16. However, ports are typically limited in the Campus Core switches. Policy-based control (QoS and access control lists [ACL]) for accessing the servers is implemented in the Building Distribution layer, rather than in the Campus Core.

Figure 4-16 *Servers Directly Attached to the Campus Core in a Medium-Sized Network*

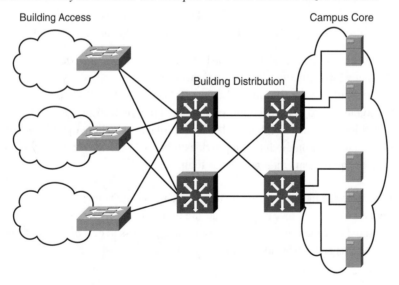

Servers in a Server Farm Module

Larger enterprises may have moderate or large server deployments. For enterprises with moderate server requirements, common servers are located in a separate Server Farm module connected to the Campus Core layer using multilayer server distribution switches, as illustrated in Figure 4-17.

Because of high traffic load, the servers are usually Gigabit Ethernet–attached to the Server Farm switches. Access lists at the Server Farm module's multilayer distribution switches implement the controlled access to these servers. Redundant distribution switches in a Server Farm module and solutions such as the HSRP and GLBP provide fast failover. The Server Farm module distribution switches also keep all server-to-server traffic off the Campus Core.

Figure 4-17   *Server Farm in a Large Network*

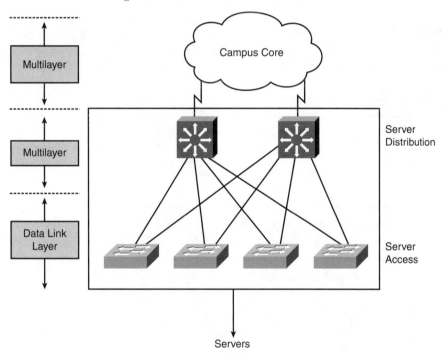

Rather than being installed on only one server, modern applications are distributed among several servers. This approach improves application availability and responsiveness. Therefore, placing servers in a common group (in the Server Farm module) and using intelligent multilayer switches provide the applications and servers with the required scalability, availability, responsiveness, throughput, and security.

For a large enterprise with a significant number of servers, a separate data center, possibly in a remote location, is often implemented. Design considerations for an Enterprise Data Center are discussed in the later "Enterprise Data Center Design Considerations" section.

Server Farm Design Guidelines

As shown in Figure 4-18, the Server Farm can be implemented as a high-capacity building block attached to the Campus Core using a modular design approach. One of the main concerns with the Server Farm module is that it receives the majority of the traffic from the entire campus. Random frame drops can result because the uplink ports on switches are frequently oversubscribed. To guarantee that no random frame drops occur for business-critical applications, the network designer should apply QoS mechanisms to the server links.

> **NOTE** *Switch oversubscription* occurs when a switch allows more ports (bandwidth) in the chassis than the switch's hardware can transfer through its internal structure.

Figure 4-18 *Sample Server Farm Design*

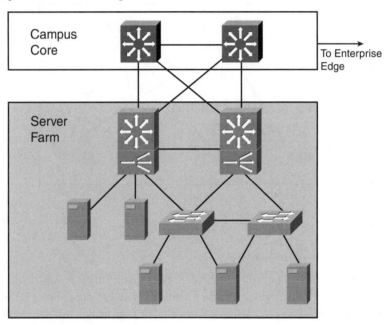

The Server Farm design should ensure that the Server Farm uplink ports are not as oversubscribed as the uplink ports on the switches in the Building Access or Building Distribution layers. For example, if the campus consists of a few Building Distribution layers connected to the Campus Core layer with Gigabit Ethernet, attach the Server Farm module to the Campus Core layer with either a 10-Gigabit Ethernet or multiple Gigabit Ethernet links.

The switch performance and the bandwidth of the links from the Server Farm to the Campus Core are not the only considerations. You must also evaluate the server's capabilities. Although server manufacturers support a variety of NIC connection rates (such as Gigabit Ethernet), the underlying network operating system might not be able to transmit at the maximum line capacity. As such, oversubscription ratios can be raised, reducing the Server Farm's overall cost.

Server Connectivity Options

Servers can be connected in several different ways. For example, a server can attach by one or two Fast Ethernet connections. If the server is dual-attached (dual-NIC redundancy), one interface can be active while the other is in hot standby. Installing multiple single-port NICs or multiport NICs in the servers extends dual homing past the Server Farm module switches to the server itself. Servers needing redundancy can be connected with dual-NIC homing in the access layer or a NIC that supports EtherChannel. With the dual-homing NIC, a VLAN or trunk is needed between the two access switches to support the single IP address on the two server links to two separate switches.

Within the Server Farm module, multiple VLANs can be used to create multiple policy domains as required. If one particular server has a unique access policy, a unique VLAN and subnet can be created for that server. If a group of servers has a common access policy, the entire group can be placed in a common VLAN and subnet. ACLs can be applied on the interfaces of the multilayer switches.

Several other solutions are available to improve server responsiveness and evenly distribute the load to them. For example, Figure 4-18 includes content switches that provide a robust front end for the Server Farm by performing functions such as load balancing of user requests across the Server Farm to achieve optimal performance, scalability, and content availability.

The Effect of Applications on Switch Performance

Server Farm design requires that you consider the average frequency at which packets are generated and the packets' average size. These parameters are based on the enterprise applications' traffic patterns and number of users of the applications.

Interactive applications, such as conferencing, tend to generate high packet rates with small packet sizes. In terms of application bandwidth, the packets-per-second limitation of the multilayer switches might be more critical than the throughput (in Mbps). In contrast, applications that involve large movements of data, such as file repositories, transmit a high percentage of full-length (large) packets. For these applications, uplink bandwidth and oversubscription ratios become key factors in the overall design. Actual switching capacities and bandwidths vary based on the mix of applications.

Enterprise Data Center Design Considerations

This section describes general Enterprise Data Center design considerations and provides an overview of the general technologies and models used in an Enterprise Data Center.

The Enterprise Data Center

This section describes technology and trends influencing the Enterprise Data Center. For large enterprises with a significant number of servers, a dedicated Enterprise Data Center provides employees, partners, and customers with access to data and resources to effectively work, collaborate, and interact. Historically, most Enterprise Data Centers grew rapidly as organizational requirements expanded. Applications were implemented as needed, often resulting in underutilized, isolated infrastructure silos. Each silo was designed based on the specific application being deployed, so a typical data center supported a broad assortment of operating systems, computing platforms, and storage systems, resulting in various application "islands" that were difficult to change or expand and expensive to manage, integrate, secure, and back up.

This *server*-centric data center model is evolving to a *service*-centric model, as illustrated in Figure 4-19. This evolution includes the following:

■ The deployment of virtual machine software, such as VMware and Xen, which breaks the one-to-one relationship between applications and the server hardware and operating system on which they run. Virtual machine software allows multiple applications to run on a single server, independent of each other and of the underlying operating system.

> **NOTE** VMware information is available at http://www.vmware.com/. Xen information is available at http://www.xensource.com/.

■ The removal of storage from the server, consolidating it in storage pools. Networked storage (such as storage area networks [SAN]) allows easier management, provisioning, improved utilization, and consistent recovery practices.

■ The creation of pools of one-way, two-way, or four-way servers that can be pooled and provisioned, on demand.

> **NOTE** One-way servers have a single processor, two-way servers have two processors, and four-way servers have four processors.

■ The consolidation of I/O resources so that the I/O can be pooled and provisioned on demand for connectivity to other servers, storage, and LAN pools.

Figure 4-19 *Evolution from Server-Centric to Service-Centric Data Center*

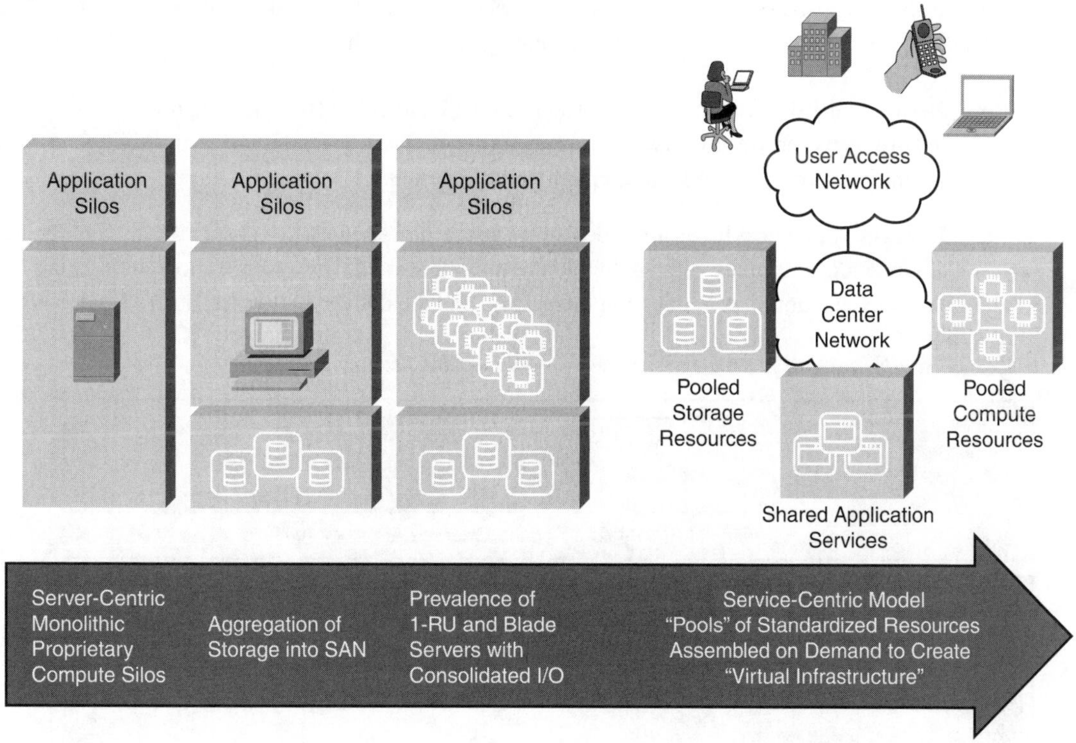

The resulting service-centric data center has pooled compute, storage, and I/O resources that are provisioned to support applications over the data center network. Because the network touches and can control all the components, the network can be used to integrate all the applications and services; network technology actively participates in the delivery of applications to end users.

The Cisco Enterprise Data Center Architecture Framework

The consolidation and virtualization of data center resources requires a highly scalable, resilient, secure data center network foundation.

As described in Chapter 2, "Applying a Methodology to Network Design," the Cisco Service-Oriented Network Architecture (SONA) framework defines how enterprises can evolve toward intelligence in the network that optimizes applications, business processes, and resources. The Cisco Enterprise Data Center Architecture, based on SONA, provides organizations with a framework to address immediate data center demands for consolidation and business continuance while enabling emerging service-oriented architectures (SOA), virtualization, and on-demand computing technologies in the data center.

The Cisco Enterprise Data Center Architecture, as illustrated in Figure 4-20, aligns data center resources with business applications and provides multiple resources to end users in an enterprise. The Cisco Enterprise Data Center Architecture has the following layers:

- **Networked Infrastructure layer**: Meets all the bandwidth, latency, and protocol requirements for user-to-server, server-to-server, and server-to-storage connectivity and communications in a modular, hierarchical infrastructure.

- **Interactive Services layer**: Provides the infrastructure services that ensure the fast and secure alignment of resources with application requirements and Cisco Application Networking Services that optimize application integration and the delivery of applications to end users.

Figure 4-20 *Cisco Enterprise Data Center Network Architecture Framework*

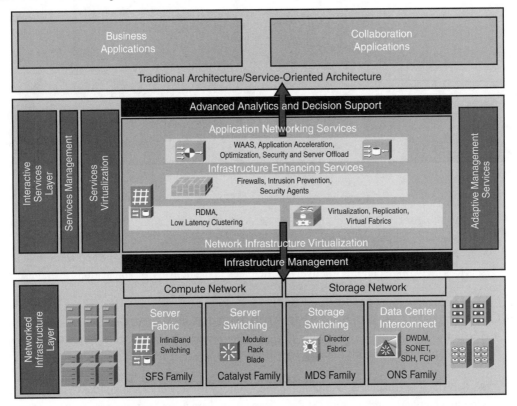

WAAS = Wide-Area Application Services; RDMA = Remote Data Memory Access; SFS = Server Fabric Switching; MDS = Multilayer Directors and Fabric Switches; ONS = Optical Networking Solutions; DWDM = Dense Wave Division Multiplexing; SONET = Synchronous Optical Network; SDH = Synchronous Digital Hierarchy; FCIP = Fiber Channel over IP

The Cisco Enterprise Data Center Architecture provides a scalable foundation that allows data centers to host a variety of legacy and emerging systems and technologies, including the following:

- **N-tier applications**: Secure network zones support two, three, or *n*-tier application environments with techniques that optimize application availability and server and storage utilization.

- **Web applications**: Application acceleration and server optimization technologies provide improved scalability and delivery of web applications to end users, wherever they are.

- **Blade servers**: As self-contained servers, blade servers, housed in a blade enclosure, have all the functional components required to be considered computers but have reduced physical components, so they require less space, power, and so forth. The Cisco Enterprise Data Center Architecture provides an intelligent network foundation using integrated Ethernet and InfiniBand switching technology that helps optimize blade server availability, security, and performance.

- **Clustering, high-performance computing and grid**: The Cisco high-performance data, server, and storage switching solutions, whether based on Ethernet, InfiniBand, or Fiber Channel, enable the deployment of data- and I/O-intensive applications that make use of these distributed compute and storage architectures.

- **SOA and web service**: The Cisco Enterprise Data Center Architecture facilitates the reliable, secure, and rapid deployment of an SOA by enabling dynamic deployment and scaling of secure infrastructures and by enhancing application integration with message-based services.

- **Mainframe computing**: Cisco offers a comprehensive set of technologies supporting Systems Network Architecture (SNA), SNA-to-IP migration, fiber connection, and native IP mainframe services.

The Cisco Enterprise Data Center Architecture is supported by networking technologies and solutions that allow organizations to evolve their data center infrastructures through the following phases:

- **Consolidation**: Integration of network, server, application, and storage services into a shared infrastructure enhances scalability and manageability while reducing cost and complexity.

- **Virtualization**: Network-enabled virtualization of computing and storage resources and virtual network services increase utilization and adaptability while reducing overall costs.

- **Automation**: Dynamic monitoring, provisioning, and orchestration of data center infrastructure resources resulting from changing loads, disruptions, or attacks increases overall IT agility while minimizing operational requirements.

Figure 4-21 illustrates a sample high-performance data center network topology that requires many technologies and connectivity options among applications and data centers. This network topology provides connectivity services for networked elements within the data center, such as servers and storage, as well as to external users or other data centers.

Figure 4-21   *Sample Data Center Network Topology*

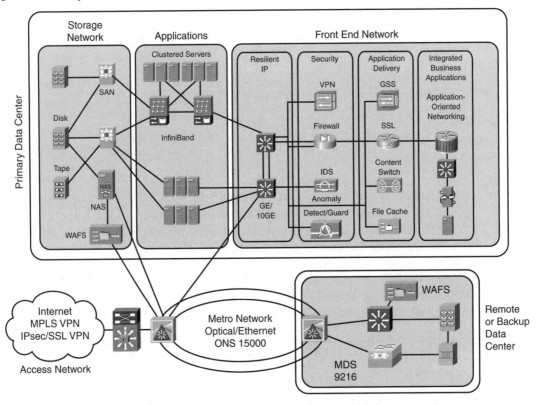

NAS = Network Attached Storage; WAFS = Wide-Area File Services; GE = Gigabit Ethernet; VPN = Virtual Private Network; IDS = intrusion detection system; GSS = Global Site Selector; SSL = Secure Sockets Layer

Enterprise Data Center Infrastructure

Figure 4-22 shows a typical large Enterprise Data Center infrastructure design. The design follows the Cisco multilayer infrastructure architecture, including core, aggregation, and access layers.

> **NOTE**   In the Enterprise Data Center, the distribution layer is known as the *aggregation* layer.

Figure 4-22   *Sample Data Center Infrastructure*

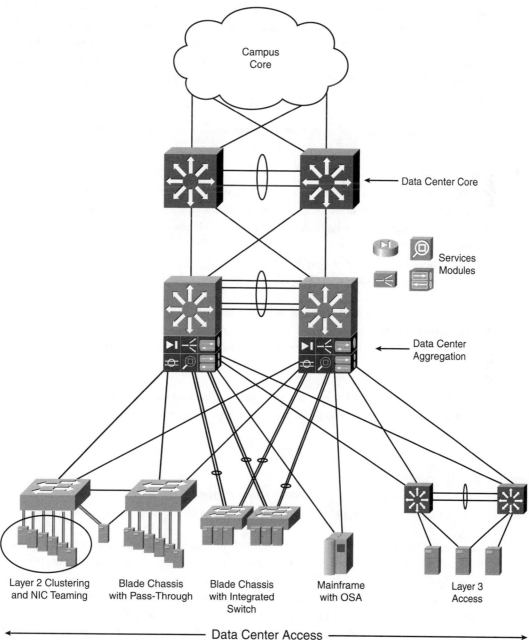

OSA = Open Systems Adapter

The data center infrastructure must provide port density and Layer 2 and Layer 3 connectivity for servers at the access layer, while supporting security services provided by ACLs, firewalls, and intrusion detection systems (IDS) at the data center aggregation layer. It must support Server Farm services, such as content switching, caching, and Secure Sockets Layer (SSL) offloading while integrating with multitier Server Farms, mainframes, and mainframe services (such as TN3270, load balancing, and SSL offloading). Network devices are often deployed in redundant pairs to avoid a single point of failure.

The following sections describe the three layers of the Enterprise Data Center infrastructure.

Data Center Access Layer

The Data Center Access layer provides Layer 2, Layer 3, and mainframe connectivity. The design of the Data Center Access layer varies depending on whether Layer 2 or Layer 3 access switches are used; it is typically built with high-performance, low-latency Layer 2 switches, allowing better sharing of service devices across multiple servers and allowing the use of Layer 2 clustering, which requires the servers to be Layer 2–adjacent. With Layer 2 access switches, the default gateway for the servers can be configured at the access or aggregation layer.

Servers can be single- or dual-attached; with dual-attached NICs in the servers, a VLAN or trunk is required between the two redundant access layer switches to support having a single IP address on the two server links to two separate switches. The default gateway is implemented at the access layer.

A mix of both Layer 2 and Layer 3 access switches using one rack unit (1RU) and modular platforms results in a flexible solution and allows application environments to be optimally positioned.

Data Center Aggregation Layer

The Data Center Aggregation (distribution) layer aggregates the uplinks from the access layer to the Data Center Core layer and is the critical point for control and application services.

Security and application service devices (such as load-balancing devices, SSL offloading devices, firewalls, and IDS devices) provide Layer 4 through Layer 7 services and are often deployed as a module in the aggregation layer. This highly flexible design takes advantage of economies of scale by lowering the total cost of ownership (TCO) and reducing complexity by reducing the number of components to configure and manage. Service devices deployed at the aggregation layer are shared among all the servers, whereas service devices deployed at the access layer benefit only the servers that are directly attached to the specific access switch.

Although Layer 2 at the aggregation (distribution) layer is tolerated for legacy designs, new designs should have Layer 2 only at the Data Center Access layer. With Layer 2 at the Data Center Aggregation layer, physical loops in the topology would have to be managed by STP; in this case, as for other designs, RPVST+ is a recommended best practice to ensure a logically loop-free topology over the physical topology.

The Data Center Aggregation layer typically provides Layer 3 connectivity from the data center to the core and maintains the connection and session state for redundancy. Depending on the requirements and the design, the boundary between Layer 2 and Layer 3 at the Data Center Aggregation layer can be in the multilayer switches, the firewalls, or the content-switching devices in the aggregation layer. Depending on the data center applications, the aggregation layer might also need to support a large STP processing load.

Data Center Core Layer

Implementing a Data Center Core layer is a best practice for large data centers. The following should be taken into consideration when determining whether a core is appropriate:

- **10-Gigabit Ethernet density**: Without a Data Center Core, will there be enough 10-Gigabit Ethernet ports on the Campus Core switch pair to support both the campus Building Distribution layer and the Data Center Aggregation layer?

- **Administrative domains and policies**: Separate campus and data center cores help isolate the campus Building Distribution layers from Data Center Aggregation layers for troubleshooting, maintenance, administration, and implementation of policies (using QoS and ACLs).

- **Anticipation of future development**: The impact that could result from implementing a separate Data Center Core layer at a later date might make it worthwhile to install it at the beginning.

The data center typically connects to the Campus Core using Layer 3 links. The data center network addresses are summarized into the Campus Core, and the Campus Core injects a default route into the data center network. Key Data Center Core layer characteristics include the following:

- A distributed forwarding architecture

- Low-latency switching

- 10-Gigabit Ethernet scalability

- Scalable IP multicast support

Density and Scalability of Servers

Some scaling issues in the data center relate to the physical environment.

The most common access layer in enterprises today is based on the modular chassis Cisco Catalyst 6500 or 4500 Series switches. This topology has also proven to be a very scalable method of building Server Farms that provide high-density, high-speed uplinks and redundant power and processors. Although this approach has been very successful, it results in challenges when used in Enterprise Data Center environments. The typical Enterprise Data Center experiences high growth in the sheer number of servers; at the same time, server density has been improved with 1RU and blade server solutions. Three particular challenges result from this trend:

■ **Cable bulk**: Typically, three to four interfaces are connected on a server. With a higher density of servers per rack, cable routing and management can become quite difficult.

■ **Power**: The increased density of components in a rack is driving a need for a larger power feed to the rack. Many data centers do not have the power capacity at the server rows to support this increase.

■ **Cooling**: The number of cables lying under the raised floor and the cable bulk at the cabinet base entry is blocking the airflow required to cool equipment in the racks. At the same time, the servers in the rack require more cooling volume because of their higher density.

These challenges have forced customers to find alternative solutions by spacing cabinets, modifying cable routes, or other means, including not deploying high-density server solutions. Another way that customers seek to solve some of these problems is by using a rack-based switching solution. Using 1RU top-of-rack switches keeps the server interface cables in the cabinet, reducing the amount of cabling in the floor and thus reducing the cabling and cooling issues. Another option is to place Cisco Catalyst 6500 Series switches like bookends near the ends of the row of racks so that there are fewer switches to manage.

Summary

In this chapter you learned about campus and data center network design, with a focus on the following topics:

■ The effects of the characteristics of the following on the campus network design:

— Application: Including peer-peer, client–local server, client–Server Farm, and client–Enterprise Edge server

— Environment: Including the location of the network nodes, the distance between the nodes, and the transmission media used

— Infrastructure devices: Including Layer 2 or multilayer switching, convergence time, type of multilayer switching, IP multicast, QoS, and load sharing

- The design considerations and recommended practices for the Building Access layer, the Building Distribution layer, the Campus Core layer, the optional Edge Distribution module, and the Server Farm module.

- Enterprise Data Center module design considerations, including an introduction to the general technologies and models used in Enterprise Data Center design.

References

For additional information, refer to the following resources:

- Cisco Systems, Inc., Introduction to Gigabit Ethernet, http://www.cisco.com/en/US/tech/tk389/tk214/tech_brief09186a0080091a8a.html

- Cisco Systems, Inc., Ethernet Introduction, http://www.cisco.com/en/US/tech/tk389/tk214/tsd_technology_support_protocol_home.html

- Cisco Systems, Inc., SAFE Blueprint Introduction, http://www.cisco.com/go/safe

- Cisco Systems, Inc., Designing a Campus Network for High Availability, http://www.cisco.com/application/pdf/en/us/guest/netsol/ns432/c649/cdccont_0900aecd801a8a2d.pdf

- Cisco Systems, Inc., Enterprise Data Center: Introduction, http://www.cisco.com/en/US/netsol/ns340/ns394/ns224/networking_solutions_packages_list.html

- Cisco Systems, Inc., Cisco Data Center Network Architecture and Solutions Overview, http://www.cisco.com/application/pdf/en/us/guest/netsol/ns377/c643/cdccont_0900aecd802c9a4f.pdf

- Cisco Systems, Inc., Switches: Compare Products and Solutions, http://www.cisco.com/en/US/products/hw/switches/products_category_buyers_guide.html

- Szigeti and Hattingh, *End-to-End QoS Network Design: Quality of Service in LANs, WANs, and VPNs*, Indianapolis, Cisco Press, 2004.

- Cisco Systems, Inc., Spanning Tree Protocol: Introduction, http://www.cisco.com/en/US/tech/tk389/tk621/tsd_technology_support_protocol_home.html

Case Study: ACMC Hospital Network Campus Design

This case study is a continuation of the ACMC Hospital case study introduced in Chapter 2.

Case Study General Instructions

Use the scenarios, information, and parameters provided at each task of the ongoing case study. If you encounter ambiguities, make reasonable assumptions and proceed. For all tasks, use the initial customer scenario and build on the solutions provided thus far. You can use any and all documentation, books, white papers, and so on.

In each step, you act as a network design consultant. Make creative proposals to accomplish the customer's business needs. Justify your ideas when they differ from the provided solutions. Use any design strategies you feel are appropriate. The final goal of each case study is a paper solution.

Appendix A, "Answers to Review Questions and Case Studies," provides a solution for each step based on assumptions made. There is no claim that the provided solution is the best or only solution. Your solution might be more appropriate for the assumptions you made. The provided solution helps you understand the author's reasoning and allows you to compare and contrast your solution.

In this case study you create a high-level design for the Cisco Enterprise Campus Architecture of the ACMC Hospital network.

Case Study Additional Information

Figure 4-23 identifies the device counts throughout the ACMC campus.

Assume that each building needs as many spare ports as there are people. Each patient room or staff position has two jacks, and spare server ports should be provided to allow for migration of all servers to the Server Farm.

The hospital has 500 staff members and 1000 patients.

Each floor of the main buildings has about 75 people, except for the first floor of Main Building 1, which has only the Server Farm with 40 servers. Each floor of the Children's Place has 60 people. Buildings A through D have 10 people each, buildings E through J have 20 people each, and buildings K through L have 40 each.

Assume that the hospital has structured cabling with plenty of MM fiber in the risers and plenty of fiber between buildings. If there is not enough fiber, either the hospital will have to install the fiber or the design will have to be modified for the existing cabling; produce an ideal design before making any adjustments.

Figure 4-23   *Case Study: ACMC Campus Device Counts*

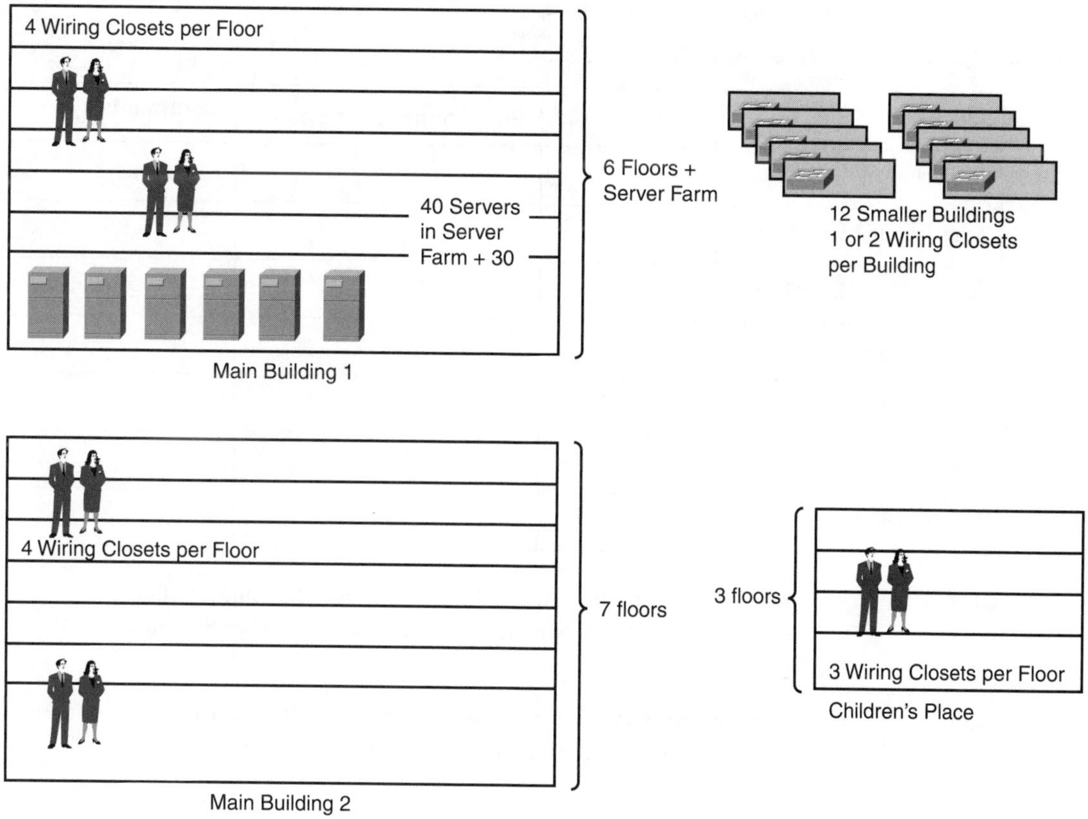

Case Study Questions

Complete the following steps:

Step 1   Determine the location, quantity, and size of the required Campus Core switch or switches and what connections are required within the core and to the distribution layer.

Step 2   Determine the location of required Building Distribution layer switches or whether a collapsed core/distribution approach makes more sense. In a design with distribution layer switches, determine their location and size, how they connect to the Campus Core, and the use of VLANs versus Layer 3 switching.

Step 3   Determine the location and size of the required Building Access layer switches, and complete Table 4-4.

Table 4-4 *Building Access Layer Port Counts by Location*

Location	Port Counts	Port Counts with Spares	Comments
Main building 1, per floor			
Main building Server Farm			
Main building 2, per floor			
Children's Place, per floor			
Buildings A–D			
Buildings E–J			
Buildings K–L			

Step 4   Determine how the Building Access layer switches will connect to the Building Distribution layer switches (or to the combined distribution/core switches).

Step 5   Determine how the Server Farm should be connected. If Server Farm access or distribution switches are used, determine how they will connect to each other and to the core.

Step 6   Does any other information need to be included in your final design?

Step 7   Determine appropriate Cisco switch models for each part of your campus design.

The following links might be helpful (note that these links were correct at the time this book was published):

- The Cisco switch main page at http://www.cisco.com/en/US/products/hw/switches/index.html

- The Cisco switch comparison page at http://www.cisco.com/en/US/products/hw/switches/products_category_buyers_guide.html

- The Cisco Product Quick Reference Guide at http://www.cisco.com/warp/public/752/qrg/index.shtml

- The Cisco Catalyst Switch Solution Finder at http://www.cisco.com/en/US/partner/products/hw/switches/products_promotion0900aecd8050364f.html

Step 8   (Optional) Use the Cisco Dynamic Configuration Tool to configure one or more of the switches in your design. The Cisco Dynamic Configuration Tool is available at the following link: http://www.cisco.com/en/US/ordering/or13/or8/ordering_ordering_help_dynamic_configuration_tool_launch.html. (Note that a valid username and password on www.cisco.com are required to access this tool.)

Figure 4-24 displays a screen shot showing the options available for a Catalyst 6506 switch.

Figure 4-24   *Cisco Dynamic Configuration Tool Screen Output*

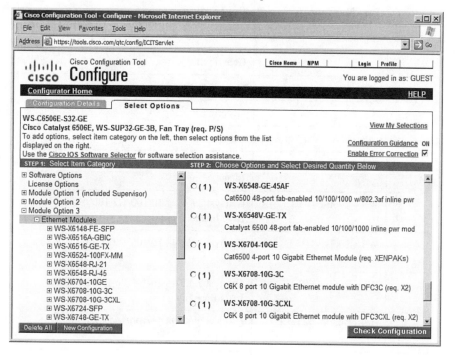

Selecting the options for devices is easier and faster if you use only a few switch models repeatedly in your design, possibly with different numbers of blades in them.

NOTE   There are not many options for the smaller switches in the Cisco Dynamic Configuration Tool.

Step 9　(Optional) Develop a bill of materials (BOM) listing switch models, numbers, prices, and total price.

Creating a BOM can be time-consuming; you might want to use the Sample Price List provided in Table 4-5 for this exercise. Note that the prices shown in this table are not actual equipment prices; they are loosely derived from Cisco list prices at the time of publication and are provided for your convenience.

Table 4-5　*Case Study: Sample Price List*

Category	Part Number	Description	Fictional Price
Port Transceiver Modules			
		Generic SFP	$400
		Generic GBIC	$400
		Generic LR Xenpack	$4000
Cisco Catalyst 2960 Series Workgroup Switches			
	WS-C2960-24TC-L	Catalyst 2960 24 10/100 + 2T/SFP LAN Base Image	$2500
	WS-C2960-24TT-L	Catalyst 2960 24 10/100 + 2 1000BT LAN Base Image	$1300
	WS-C2960-48TC-L	Catalyst 2960 48 10/100 + 2T/SFP LAN Base Image	$4500
	WS-C2960-48TT-L	Catalyst 2960 48 10/100 Ports + 2 1000BT LAN Base Image	$2500
	WS-C2960G-24TC-L	Catalyst 2960 24 10/100/1000, 4T/SFP LAN Base Image	$3300
	WS-C2960G-48TC-L	Catalyst 2960 48 10/100/1000, 4T/SFP LAN Base Image	$6000
Cisco Catalyst 3560 Series			
	WS-C3560G-48TS-S	Catalyst 3560 48 10/100/1000T + 4 SFP Standard Image	$8000
	WS-C3560G-24TS-S	Catalyst 3560 24 10/100/1000T + 4 SFP Standard Image	$4800

Table 4-5   *Case Study: Sample Price List (Continued)*

Category	Part Number	Description	Fictional Price
	WS-C3560-48TS-S	Catalyst 3560 48 10/100 + 4 SFP Standard Image	$5000
	WS-C3560-24TS-S	Catalyst 3560 24 10/100 + 2 SFP Standard Image	$3000
Cisco IOS Upgrades for the Catalyst 3560 (EMI = Layer 3 image)			
	CD-3560-EMI=	Enhanced Multilayer Image upgrade for 3560 10/100 models	$2000
	CD-3560G-EMI=	Enhanced Multilayer Image upgrade for 3560 GE models	$4000
Cisco Catalyst 3750 Series 10/100/1000, GE, 10GE Workgroup Switches			
	WS-C3750G-24T-S	Catalyst 3750 24 10/100/1000T Standard Multilayer Image	$6000
	WS-C3750G-24TS-S1U	Catalyst 3750 24 10/100/1000 + 4 SFP Standard Multilayer;1RU	$7000
	WS-C3750G-48TS-S	Catalyst 3750 48 10/100/1000T + 4 SFP Standard Multilayer	$14,000
	WS-C3750G-16TD-S	Catalyst 3750 16 10/100/1000BT+ 10GE (requires XENPAK) Standard Image	$12,000
	WS-C3750G-12S-S	Catalyst 3750 12 SFP Standard Multilayer Image	$8000
Cisco Catalyst 3750 Series 10/100 Workgroup Switches			
	WS-C3750-24TS-S	Catalyst 3750 24 10/100 + 2 SFP Standard Multilayer Image	$4000
	WS-C3750-48TS-S	Catalyst 3750 48 10/100 + 4 SFP Standard Multilayer Image	$7000
Cisco IOS Upgrades for the Catalyst 3750			
	CD-3750-EMI=	Enhanced Multilayer Image upgrade for 3750 FE models	$2000
	CD-3750G-EMI=	Enhanced Multilayer Image upgrade for 24-port 3750 GE models	$4000

continues

Table 4-5   *Case Study: Sample Price List (Continued)*

Category	Part Number	Description	Fictional Price
	CD-3750G-48EMI=	Enhanced Multilayer Image upgrade for 48-port 3750 GE models	$8000
	3750-AISK9-LIC-B=	Advanced IP Services upgrade for 3750 FE models running SMI	$5000
	3750G-AISK9-LIC-B=	Advanced IP Services upgrade for 3750 GE models running SMI	$7000
	3750G48-AISK9LC-B=	Advanced IP Services upgrade for 3750G-48 models running SMI	$11,000
Cisco Catalyst 4948 Switches			
	WS-C4948-S	Catalyst 4948, IPB software, 48-port 10/100/1000+4 SFP, 1 AC power supply	$10,500
	WS-C4948-E	Catalyst 4948, ES software, 48-port 10/100/1000+4 SFP, 1 AC power supply	$14,500
	WS-C4948-10GE-S	Catalyst 4948, IPB software, 48*10/100/1000+2*10GE(X2), 1 AC power supply	$17,500
	WS-C4948-10GE-E	Catalyst 4948, ES Image, 48*10/100/1000+2*10GE(X2), 1 AC power supply	$21,500
Cisco Catalyst 4948 Software			
	S49L3K9-12220EWA	Cisco Catalyst 4948 IOS Standard Layer 3 3DES (RIP, St. Routes, IPX, AT)	$0
	S49L3EK9-12220EWA	Cisco Catalyst 4948 IOS Enhanced Layer 3 3DES (OSPF, EIGRP, IS-IS, BGP)	$4000
	S49ESK9-12225SG	Cisco Catalyst 4900 IOS Enterprise Services SSH	$4000
Cisco Catalyst 4500—Chassis			
	WS-C4510R	Catalyst 4500 Chassis (10-slot), fan, no power supply, Redundant Supervisor Capable	$12,500
	WS-C4507R	Catalyst 4500 Chassis (7-slot), fan, no power supply, Redundant Supervisor Capable	$10,000
	WS-C4506	Catalyst 4500 Chassis (6-slot), fan, no power supply	$5000

Table 4-5   *Case Study: Sample Price List (Continued)*

Category	Part Number	Description	Fictional Price
	WS-C4503	Catalyst 4500 Chassis (3-slot),fan, no power supply	$1000
	WS-C4506-S2+96	Catalyst 4506 Bundle, 1x 1000AC, 1x S2+, 2x WS-X4148-RJ	$16,800
	WS-C4503-S2+48	Catalyst 4503 Bundle, 1x 1000AC, 1x S2+, 1x WS-X4148-RJ	$10,000
Cisco Catalyst 4500 Non-PoE Power Supplies			
	PWR-C45-1400AC	Catalyst 4500 1400W AC Power Supply (Data Only)	$1500
	PWR-C45-1000AC	Catalyst 4500 1000W AC Power Supply (Data Only)	$1000
Cisco Catalyst 4500 Supervisor Engines			
	WS-X4516-10GE	Catalyst 4500 Supervisor V-10GE, 2x10GE (X2) and 4x1GE (SFP)	$20,000
	WS-X4516-10GE/2	Catalyst 45xxR Supervisor V-10GE, 2x10GE (X2) or 4x1GE (SFP)	$20,000
	WS-X4516	Catalyst 4500 Supervisor V (2 GE), Console (RJ-45)	$16,500
	WS-X4515	Catalyst 4500 Supervisor IV (2 GE), Console (RJ-45)	$12,000
	WS-X4013+10GE	Catalyst 4500 Supervisor II+10GE, 2x10GE (X2), and 4x1GE (SFP)	$12,000
	WS-X4013+	Catalyst 4500 Supervisor II-Plus (IOS), 2GE, Console (RJ-45)	$6000
	WS-X4013+TS	Catalyst 4503 Supervisor II-Plus-TS, 12 10/100/1000 PoE+8 SFP slots	$6000
Cisco Catalyst 4500 10/100 Linecards			
	WS-X4148-RJ	Catalyst 4500 10/100 Auto Module, 48-Ports (RJ-45)	$4500
	WS-X4124-RJ45	Catalyst 4500 10/100 Module, 24-Ports (RJ-45)	$2500

continues

Table 4-5 *Case Study: Sample Price List (Continued)*

Category	Part Number	Description	Fictional Price
	WS-X4148-RJ21	Catalyst 4500 10/100 Module, 48-Ports Telco (4xRJ21)	$4500
	WS-X4232-GB-RJ	Catalyst 4500 32-10/100 (RJ-45), 2-GE (GBIC)	$4500
	WS-X4232-RJ-XX	Catalyst 4500 10/100 Module, 32-ports (RJ-45) + Modular uplinks	$3500
Cisco Catalyst 4500 10/100/1000 Linecards			
	WS-X4548-GB-RJ45	Catalyst 4500 Enhanced 48-Port 10BASE-T, 100BASE-T, 1000BASE-T (RJ-45)	$500
	WS-X4506-GB-T	Catalyst 4500 6-Port 10/100/1000 PoE or SFP (Optional)	$3500
	WS-X4448-GB-RJ45	Catalyst 4500 48-Port 10/100/1000 Module (RJ-45)	$6000
	WS-X4424-GB-RJ45	Catalyst 4500 24-port 10/100/1000 Module (RJ-45)	$3500
Cisco Catalyst 4500 1000 Base-X GE Linecards			
	WS-X4306-GB	Catalyst 4500 Gigabit Ethernet Module, 6-Ports (GBIC)	$3000
	WS-X4506-GB-T	Catalyst 4500 6-Port 10/100/1000 PoE or SFP (Optional)	$3500
	WS-X4302-GB	Catalyst 4500 Gigabit Ethernet Module, 2-Ports (GBIC)	$1000
	WS-X4418-GB	Catalyst 4500 GE Module, Server Switching 18-Ports (GBIC)	$10,000
	WS-X4448-GB-SFP	Catalyst 4500 48-Port 1000BASE-X (SFPs Optional)	$16,500
Cisco Catalyst 4500 Series Supervisor IOS Software Options			
	S4KL3-12220EWA	Cisco IOS Basic Layer 3 Catalyst 4500 Supervisor 2+/4/5 (RIP, St. Routes, IPX, AT)	$0
	S4KL3E-12220EWA	Cisco IOS Enhanced Layer 3 Catalyst 4500 Supervisor 4/5 (OSPF, EIGRP, IS-IS)	$10,000

Table 4-5 *Case Study: Sample Price List (Continued)*

Category	Part Number	Description	Fictional Price
Cisco Catalyst 6500 Series Supervisor 32-GE Bundles—Top Sellers			
	WS-C6503E-S32-GE	Cisco Catalyst 6503E, WS-SUP32-GE-3B, Fan Tray (requires power supply)	$13,000
	WS-C6504E-S32-GE	6504-E Chassis + Fan Tray + Supervisor 32-GE	$13,000
	WS-C6506E-S32-GE	Cisco Catalyst 6506E, WS-Supervisor 32-GE-3B, Fan Tray (requires power supply)	$16,000
	WS-C6509E-S32-GE	Cisco Catalyst 6509E, WS-Supervisor 32-GE-3B, Fan Tray (requires power supply)	$20,000
	WS-C6513-S32-GE	Cisco Catalyst 6513, WS-Supervisor 32-GE-3B, Fan Tray (requires power supply)	$26,000
Cisco Catalyst 6500 Series Supervisor 32-10GE Bundles—Top Sellers			
	WS-C6503E-S32-10GE	Cat6503E chassis, WS-Supervisor 32-10GE-3B, Fan Tray (requires power supply)	$23,000
	WS-C6504E-S32-10GE	6504-E Chassis + Fan Tray + Supervisor 32-10GE	$23,000
	WS-C6506E-S32-10GE	Cat6506E chassis, WS-Supervisor 32-10GE-3B, Fan Tray (requires power supply)	$26,000
	WS-C6509E-S32-10GE	Cat6509E chassis, WS-Supervisor 32-10GE-3B, Fan Tray (requires power supply)	$30,000
Cisco Catalyst 6500 Series AC Power Supplies—Top Sellers			
	PWR-2700-AC/4	2700W AC power supply for Cisco 7604/6504-E	$3000
	WS-CAC-3000W	Catalyst 6500 3000W AC power supply	$3000
	WS-CAC-6000W	Cat6500 6000W AC power supply	$5000
Cisco Catalyst 6500 Series 10 Gigabit Ethernet—Top Sellers			
	WS-X6704-10GE	Cat6500 4-port 10 Gigabit Ethernet Module (requires XENPAKs)	$20,000
	S-67-10GE-C2	Cat6500, 1x6704-10 GE, 1xWS-F6700-DFC3B, 2xXENPAK-10GB-SR=	$33,500

continues

Table 4-5 *Case Study: Sample Price List (Continued)*

Category	Part Number	Description	Fictional Price
Cisco Catalyst 6500 Series Gigabit Ethernet—Top Sellers			
	WS-X6408A-GBIC	Catalyst 6000 8-port GE, Enhanced QoS (requires GBICs)	$10,000
	WS-X6516A-GBIC	Catalyst 6500 16-port Gigabit Ethernet Module, fabric-enabled (requires GBICs)	$15,000
	WS-X6724-SFP	Catalyst 6500 24-port Gigabit Ethernet Module, fabric-enabled (requires SFPs)	$15,000
	WS-X6748-SFP	Catalyst 6500 48-port Gigabit Ethernet Module, fabric-enabled (requires SFPs)	$25,000
Cisco Catalyst 6500 Series 10/100/1000—Top Sellers			
	WS-X6148A-GE-TX	Catalyst 6500 48-port 10/100/1000 with Jumbo Frame, RJ-45	$7000
	WS-X6548-GE-TX	Catalyst 6500 48-port fabric-enabled 10/100/1000 Module	$12,000
	WS-X6748-GE-TX	Catalyst 6500 48-port 10/100/1000 GE Module: fabric-enabled, RJ-45	$15,000
Cisco Catalyst 6500 Series 10/100—Top Sellers			
	WS-X6148A-RJ-45	Catalyst 6500 48-port 10/100 with TDR, upgradable to PoE 802.3af	$6000
	WS-X6148-RJ-21	Catalyst 6500 48-port 10/100 upgradable to voice, RJ-21	$6000
	WS-X6196-RJ-21	Catalyst 6500 96-port 10/100 upgradable to PoE 802.3af	$10,500
Cisco Catalyst 6500 Series Supervisor 32 Cisco IOS—Top Sellers			
	S323IBK9-12218SXF	Cisco Catalyst 6000 IP Base SSH	$0
	S323ESK9-12218SXF	Cisco Catalyst 6000 Enterprise Services SSH	$10,000
	S323AEK9-12218SXF	Cisco Catalyst 6000 Advanced Enterprise Services SSH	$15,000

NOTE   For other options not listed in Table 4-5, assume a 5 to 10 percent upgrade charge from components shown. For example, if PoE is desired on upgradeable modules, include an upgrade charge of 10 percent per module.

Review Questions

Answer the following questions, and then refer to Appendix A for the answers.

1. What characteristics must you consider when designing a campus network?

2. What are the most important network requirements for client–Enterprise Edge application communication?

3. List examples of applications that would be appropriate to reside in a Server Farm.

4. A company keeps all its servers and workstations within one building. What geographic design structure should you choose?

5. Describe how interbuilding and distant remote network geographic structures are different.

6. What is the difference between the 80/20 rule and the 20/80 rule?

7. What type of cable would you recommend for connecting two switches that are 115 m apart?

8. Compare the range and bandwidth specifications of copper twisted pair, MM fiber, SM fiber, and wireless.

9. Fill in Table 4-6 for the IEEE 802.11 wireless standards.

Table 4-6   *IEEE 802.11 Wireless Standards*

Standard	Frequency Band	Maximum Bandwidth
802.11a		
802.11b		
802.11g		

10. What is the difference between data link layer and multilayer switching?

11. What is a network flow?

12. What applications might require the network to handle multicast traffic?

13. A company is using video on demand, which uses IP multicast as part of its distance-learning program. The routers are configured for IP multicast. Taking into account that the majority of the LAN switches are Layer 2 switches, which protocol should be enabled on the LAN switches to reduce flooding?

14. What is PIM?

15. Why might QoS mechanisms be required on a LAN switch?

16. Which parts of the Enterprise Campus typically have both high availability and high performance requirements?

17. A link between the Building Distribution and Campus Core is oversubscribed, but it carries mission-critical data along with Internet traffic. How would you ensure that the mission-critical applications are not adversely affected by the bandwidth limitations?

18. A corporate network is spread over four floors. Each floor has a Layer 2 switch and more than one VLAN. One connection from each floor leads to the basement, where all WAN connections are terminated and all servers are located. Traffic between VLANs is essential. What type of device should be used in the basement?

19. What are the recommended best practices related to managing VLANs and STP in the Building Access layer?

20. What functions does the Building Distribution layer provide?

21. As a recommended practice, when should a dedicated Campus Core layer be deployed?

22. An organization requires a highly available core network and uses IP telephony for all its voice communication, both internal and external. Which devices and topology would you recommend for the Campus Core design?

23. What is the function of the Edge Distribution module?

24. A company has mission-critical applications hosted on common servers that are accessible to selected employees throughout the company's multiple buildings. Where and how would you recommend that these servers be placed within the network?

25. Describe how the Enterprise Data Center has evolved to a service-centric model from a server-centric model.

26. An organization evolves its data center infrastructure; put the following phases of evolution in the correct order:

- Virtualization

- Consolidation

- Automation

27. What is the purpose of the Data Center aggregation layer?

28. When determining whether to implement a Core layer within a Data Center design, what factors should you consider?

This chapter discusses wide-area network technologies and design, and includes the following sections:

CHAPTER 5

Designing Remote Connectivity

This chapter discusses the WAN function that provides access to remote sites and the outside world. It details WAN technologies and WAN design considerations. The chapter explores how these technologies are used, including for remote access, with virtual private networks (VPN), for backup, and how the Internet is used as a backup WAN.

This chapter describes the Enterprise WAN and metropolitan-area network (MAN) architecture, and the Enterprise Branch and Teleworker architectures. The selection of WAN hardware and software components is also discussed.

Enterprise Edge WAN Technologies

This section introduces the concept of the WAN, beginning with the definition of a WAN and the types of WAN interconnections. Various WAN technologies are described. The section concludes with a discussion of WAN pricing and contract considerations.

Introduction to WANs

This section defines a WAN and describes its primary design objectives.

> **KEY POINT** A *WAN* is a data communications network that covers a relatively broad geographic area. A WAN typically uses the transmission facilities provided by service providers (SP) (also called *carriers*), such as telephone companies.

Switches, or concentrators, connect the WAN links, relay information through the WAN, and enable the services it provides. A network provider often charges users a fee, called a tariff, for the services provided by the WAN. Therefore, WAN communication is often known as a service.

Recall that the purpose of the Cisco Enterprise architecture is to modularize the enterprise network. All WAN connections are concentrated in a single functional area: the Enterprise Edge. A WAN provides the Enterprise Edge with access to remote sites and the outside world. Using various Layer 2 and Layer 3 technologies, WANs operate between the Enterprise Edge and the Service Provider Edge.

Designing a WAN is a challenging task. The first design step is to understand the WAN's networking requirements, which are driven by two primary goals:

■ **Service level agreement (SLA)**: Networks carry application information between computers. If the applications are not available to network users, the network fails to achieve its design objectives. Organizations need to define the level of service, such as bandwidth, allowed latency, packet loss, and so forth, that is acceptable for the applications running across the WAN.

■ **Cost of investment and usage**: WAN designs are always subject to budget limitations. Selecting the right type of WAN technology is critical to providing reliable services for end-user applications in a cost-effective and efficient manner.

Flowing from these goals are the following objectives of an effective WAN design:

■ A well-designed WAN must reflect the goals, characteristics, and policies of an organization.

■ The selected WAN technology should be sufficient for current and, to some extent, future application requirements.

■ The associated costs of investment and usage should stay within the budget limits.

WAN Interconnections

Figure 5-1 illustrates the three ways that WAN technologies connect the Enterprise Edge modules with the outside world, represented by the service provider network. Typically, the intent is to provide the following connections:

■ Connectivity between the Enterprise Edge modules and the Internet Service Provider (ISP) Edge module

■ Connectivity between Enterprise sites across the ISP network

■ Connectivity between Enterprise sites across the SP or public switched telephone network (PSTN) carrier network

WAN connections can be point-to-point between two locations or connections to a multipoint WAN service offering, such as a Frame Relay or Multiprotocol Label Switching (MPLS) network.

> **NOTE** The available service provider offerings often limit designers and thus directly affect the WAN selection process. Review the availability of offerings from multiple service providers to support your WAN design.

Figure 5-1 *Different Types of WAN Connections Are Appropriate for Different Uses*

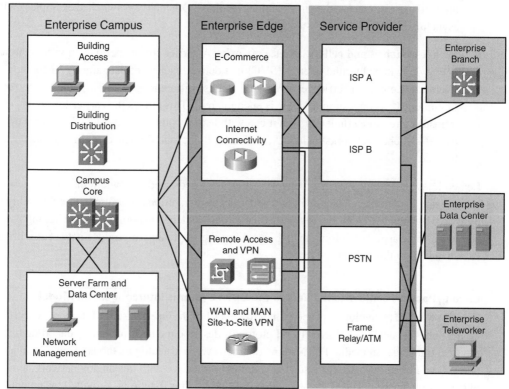

One of the main issues in WAN connections is selecting the appropriate physical WAN technology. The following sections discuss WAN technologies, starting with traditional WAN technologies.

Traditional WAN Technologies

Traditional WAN technologies include the following:

- **Leased lines**: Point-to-point connections indefinitely reserved for transmissions, rather than used only when transmission is required. The carrier establishes the connection either by dedicating a physical wire or by delegating a channel using frequency division multiplexing or time-division multiplexing (TDM). Leased-line connections usually use synchronous transmission.

- **Circuit-switched networks**: A type of network that, for the duration of the connection, obtains and dedicates a physical path for a single connection between two network endpoints. Ordinary voice phone service over the PSTN is circuit-switched; the telephone company reserves a specific physical path to the number being called for the call's duration. During that time, no one else can use the physical lines involved. Other circuit-switched examples include asynchronous serial transmission and ISDN.

■ **Packet-switched and cell-switched networks**: A carrier creates permanent virtual circuits (PVC) or switched virtual circuits (SVC) that deliver packets of data among customer sites. Users share common carrier resources and can use different paths through the WAN (for example, when congestion or delay is encountered). This allows the carrier to use its infrastructure more efficiently than it can with leased point-to-point links. Examples of packet-switched networks include X.25, Frame Relay, and Switched Multimegabit Data Service.

Leased lines and circuit-switched networks offer users dedicated bandwidth that other users cannot take. In contrast, packet-switched networks have traditionally offered more flexibility and used network bandwidth more efficiently than circuit-switched networks. Cell switching combines some aspects of circuit switching and packet switching to produce networks with low latency and high throughput.

Circuit-/Packet-/Cell-Switched Versus the Open Systems Interconnection Model

Circuit-switched technologies properly fit into Layer 1 of the Open Systems Interconnection (OSI) model—the physical layer. Layer 1 OSI protocols describe methods for binary encoding on physical transmission media. PSTN networks, however, use analog methods to encode data on a phone line. For a network device such as a router to interface with this analog network, a means of converting binary-encoded data to analog is required. This function is provided by a modulator/ demodulator (modem). ISDN networks, on the other hand, are digital (the "D" in ISDN stands for "digital"). There is no need to convert from digital to analog, so devices adapt to an ISDN network using not a modem, but a terminal adapter.

In contrast, packet- and cell-switched networks operate at the data link layer (Layer 2) of the OSI model. As such, they use protocols that define methods to control access to the physical layer, allowing many conversations to multiplex over the same physical transmission medium. This is achieved by framing the binary transmission at Layer 2 and providing addressing to identify the endpoints of the data link. Virtual circuits (either permanent or switched) provide logical paths between the endpoints in the same way that circuit-switched technologies create a physical path.

Packet-Switched Network Topologies

As shown in Figure 5-2, packet-switched networks use three basic topologies: star, full mesh, and partial mesh.

Figure 5-2   *Three Topologies for Packet-Switched Networks*

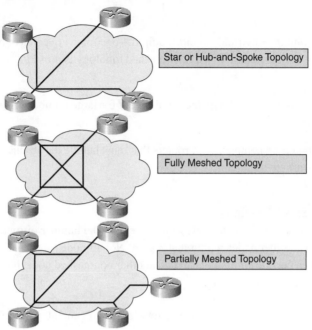

Star Topology

A *star topology* (also called a *hub-and-spoke topology*) features a single internetworking *hub* (for example, a central router) that provides access from remote networks into the core router. Communication between remote networks is possible only through the core router. The advantages of a star approach are simplified management and minimized tariff costs, which result from the low number of circuits. However, the disadvantages are significant, including the following:

- The central router (the hub) is a single point of failure.

- The central router limits overall performance for access to centralized resources because all traffic intended for the centralized resources or for the other regional routers goes through this single device.

- The topology is not scalable.

Fully Meshed Topology

In a *fully meshed topology*, each routing node on the periphery of a given packet-switching network has a direct path to every other node, providing any-to-any connectivity. The key rationale for creating a fully meshed environment is to provide a high level of redundancy; however, a fully meshed topology is not scalable to large packet-switched networks. Key issues include the following:

■ The large number of virtual circuits required—one for every connection between routers. The number of circuits required in a fully meshed topology is $n(n-1)/2$, where n is the number of routers.

■ The problems associated with the requirement for large numbers of packet and broadcast replications.

■ The configuration complexity of routers that must handle the absence of multicast support in nonbroadcast environments.

Partially Meshed Topology

A *partially meshed topology* reduces, within a region, the number of routers that have direct connections to all other nodes within that region. Not all nodes are connected to all other nodes; for a nonmeshed node to communicate with another nonmeshed node, it must send traffic through one of the fully connected routers.

There are many forms of partially meshed topologies. In general, partially meshed approaches provide the best balance for regional topologies in terms of the number of virtual circuits, redundancy, and performance.

WAN Transport Technologies

Table 5-1 compares various WAN technologies, based on the main factors that influence technology selection. This table provides typical baseline characteristics to help you compare the performance and features offered by different technologies. Often, the offerings of the service provider limit your technology decisions.

> **NOTE**   Some WAN technology characteristics differ between service providers; Table 5-1 is meant to illustrate typical characteristics.

Table 5-1   *WAN Transport Technology Comparison*

Technology[1]	Bandwidth	Latency and Jitter	Connect Time	Tariff	Initial Cost	Reliability
TDM (leased line)	M	L	L	M	M	M
ISDN	L	M/H	M	M	L	M
Frame Relay	L	L	L	M	M	M

Table 5-1   *WAN Transport Technology Comparison (Continued)*

Technology[1]	Bandwidth	Latency and Jitter	Connect Time	Tariff	Initial Cost	Reliability
ATM	M/H	L	L	M	M	H
MPLS	M/H	L	L	M	M	H
Metro Ethernet	M/H	L	L	M	M	H
DSL	L/M[2]	M/H	L	L	L	M
Cable modem	L/M[2]	M/H	L	L	M	L
Wireless	L/M	M/H	L	L	M	L
SONET/SDH	H	L	L	M	H	H
DWDM	H	L	L	M	H	H
Dark fiber	H	L	L	M	H	H

L = low, M = medium, H = high

[1] Nonstandard acronyms are expanded within the text of the chapter

[2] Unbalanced (asymmetric) transmit and receive

These technologies are introduced in the following sections.

TDM (Leased Lines)

> **KEY POINT**   TDM is a type of digital multiplexing in which pulses representing bits from two or more channels are interleaved, on a time basis. Rather than using bandwidth only as required, TDM indefinitely reserves point-to-point connection bandwidth for transmissions.

The base channel bandwidth is 64 kilobits per second (kbps), also known as *digital signal level 0 (DS0)*. 64 kbps is the bandwidth required for an uncompressed digitized phone conversation.

DS0 Rate

Standard speech is typically below 4000 hertz (Hz); analog speech is therefore filtered at 4000 Hz before being sampled. The Nyquist theorem states that a signal should be sampled at a rate at least two times the input frequency to obtain a quality representation of the signal. Therefore, the input analog signal is sampled at 8000 times per second.

Each of the samples is encoded into 8-bit octets. The DS0 rate is therefore 8000 samples per second times 8 bits per sample, which results in 64,000 bits per second, or 64 kbps.

For example, a North American T1 circuit is made up of 24 channels, each at 64 kbps, resulting in a bandwidth of 1.544 megabits per second (Mbps). A T3 circuit has 672 channels and runs at 44.736 Mbps. Corresponding European standards are the E1 standard, supporting 30 channels at 2.048 Mbps, and the E3 standard, supporting 480 channels at 34.368 Mbps.

A carrier establishes a connection in a TDM network by dedicating a channel for a specific connection. In contrast, packet-switched networks traditionally offer the service provider more flexibility and use network bandwidth more efficiently than TDM networks because the network resources are shared dynamically and subscribers are charged on the basis of their network use.

ISDN

ISDN is a system of digital phone connections that has been available as a communications standard since 1984. This system allows voice and data to be transmitted simultaneously across the world using end-to-end digital connectivity.

> **KEY POINT** ISDN connectivity offers increased bandwidth, reduced call setup time, reduced latency, and lower signal-to-noise ratios, compared to analog dialup.

However, because the industry is moving toward using broadband technologies—such as Digital Subscriber Line (DSL), cable, and public wireless—to IP security (IPsec) VPNs, ISDN presents an effective solution only for remote-user applications where broadband technologies are not available.

> **NOTE**   Analog modem dialup, also called plain old telephone service (POTS), provides data connectivity over the PSTN using analog modems. Dialup supports relatively low-speed connections, compared to broadband technologies. Dialup point-to-point service is typically no longer a cost-effective solution for WAN connectivity. It might be cost-effective only as a backup access solution for Internet connectivity in teleworker environments.

Frame Relay

Frame Relay is an example of a packet-switched technology for connecting devices on a WAN that has been deployed since the late 1980s. Frame Relay is an industry-standard networking protocol that handles multiple virtual circuits (VC) using a derivation of High-Level Data Link Control (HDLC) encapsulation between connected devices.

> **KEY POINT** Frame Relay networks transfer data using one of two connection types:
>
>   ■ PVCs, which are permanent connections.
>
>   ■ SVCs, which are temporary connections created for each data transfer and then terminated when the data transfer is complete. SVCs are not widely used.

Asynchronous Transfer Mode

KEY | ATM uses cell-switching technology to transmit fixed-sized (53-byte) cells.
POINT

Each ATM cell can be processed asynchronously (relative to other related cells), queued, and multiplexed over the transmission path. ATM provides support for multiple Quality of Service (QoS) classes to meet delay and loss requirements.

MPLS

MPLS is an Internet Engineering Task Force (IETF) standard architecture that combines the advantages of Layer 3 routing with the benefits of Layer 2 switching.

KEY | With MPLS, short fixed-length labels are assigned to each packet at the edge of the
POINT | network. Rather than examining the IP packet header information, MPLS nodes use this label to determine how to process the data.

This process results in a faster, more scalable, and more flexible WAN solution. The MPLS standards evolved from the efforts of many companies, including Cisco's tag-switching technology.

MPLS enables scalable VPNs, end-to-end QoS, and other IP services that allow efficient utilization of existing networks with simpler configuration and management and quicker fault correction.

MPLS Operation

MPLS is a connection-oriented technology whose operation is based on a label attached to each packet as it enters the MPLS network. A label identifies a flow of packets (for example, voice traffic between two nodes), also called a Forwarding Equivalence Class (FEC). An FEC is a grouping of packets; packets belonging to the same FEC receive the same treatment in the network. The FEC can be determined by various parameters, including source or destination IP address or port numbers, IP protocol, IP precedence, or Layer 2 circuit identifier. Therefore, the FEC can define the flow's QoS requirements. In addition, appropriate queuing and discard policies can be applied for FECs.

The MPLS network nodes, called *Label-Switched Routers (LSR)*, use the label to determine the packet's next hop. The LSRs do not need to examine the packet's IP header; rather, they forward it based on the label.

After a path has been established, packets destined for the same endpoint with the same requirements can be forwarded based on these labels without a routing decision at every hop.

Labels usually correspond to Layer 3 destination addresses, which makes MPLS equivalent to destination-based routing.

A *Label-Switched Path (LSP)* must be defined for each FEC before packets can be sent. It is important to note that labels are locally significant to each MPLS node only; therefore, the nodes must communicate what label to use for each FEC. One of two protocols is used for this communication: the *Label Distribution Protocol* or an enhanced version of the Resource Reservation Protocol. An interior routing protocol, such as Open Shortest Path First (OSPF) or Enhanced Interior Gateway Routing Protocol (EIGRP), is also used within the MPLS network to exchange routing information.

A unique feature of MPLS is its capability to perform label stacking, in which multiple labels can be carried in a packet. The top label, which is the last one in, is always processed first. Label stacking enables multiple LSPs to be aggregated, thereby creating tunnels through multiple levels of an MPLS network.

An MPLS label is a 32-bit field placed between a packet's data link layer header and its IP header. Figure 5-3 illustrates the flow of two packets through an MPLS network.

Figure 5-3 *Labels Are Used to Assign a Path for a Packet Flow Through an MPLS Network*

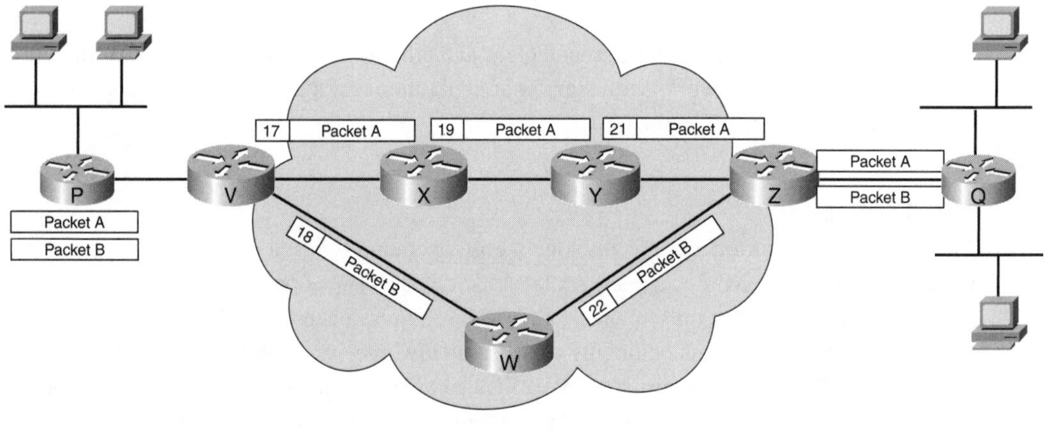

> **NOTE** The links shown in Figure 5-3 are meant to be generic; thus, they do not represent any particular type of interface.

In Figure 5-3, each of the MPLS nodes has previously communicated the labels it uses for each of the defined FECs to its neighboring nodes. Packet A and Packet B represent different flows; for example, Packet A might be from an FTP session, whereas Packet B is from a voice conversation. Without MPLS, these packets would take the same route through the network.

For Packets A and B, Router V is the *ingress edge LSR*—that is, the point at which the packets enter the network. Router V examines each packet and determines the appropriate FEC. Packet A is assigned label 17 and is sent to Router X; Packet B is assigned label 18 and is sent to Router W. As each LSR receives a labeled packet, it removes the label, locates the label in its table, applies the appropriate outgoing label, and forwards the packet to the next LSR in the LSP. When the packets reach Router Z (the *egress edge LSR*, or the point at which the packets leave the MPLS network), Router Z removes the label and forwards the packets appropriately, based on its IP routing table.

KEY POINT | Packets sent between the same endpoints might belong to different MPLS FECs, and therefore might flow through different paths in the network.

MPLS Services

The following are some of the most common services provided by MPLS:

- **Traffic engineering**: MPLS allows traffic to be directed through a specific path, which might be different from the least-cost path determined by the IP routing protocol. This ability to define routes and resource utilization is known as *traffic engineering*.

- **QoS support**: MPLS creates a connection-oriented network for IP traffic, thereby providing the foundation for QoS traffic controls. For example, it might provide guaranteed bandwidth to specific traffic between two locations.

- **Fast reroute (FRR)**: Because FRR allows extremely quick recovery from node or link failure, it prevents applications from timing out and losing data.

- **MPLS VPNs**: MPLS VPNs are much easier to deploy than traditional VPNs. They scale easily with increasing numbers of routes and customers and provide the same level of privacy as Layer 2 technologies. MPLS VPNs can also support nonunique IP addresses in various locations; for example, two organizations that use the 10.0.0.0 private address space can be supported simultaneously. MPLS VPNs are described in the later "Peer-to-Peer VPNs" section.

- **Multiprotocol support**: MPLS can be used in an ATM network, a Frame Relay network, or a pure IP-based Internet. MPLS can be used to carry many kinds of traffic, including IP packets, and native ATM, SONET, and Ethernet frames.

The key for the designer of an MPLS WAN is to minimize routing decisions and maximize MPLS switching use.

Metro Ethernet

KEY POINT | Metro Ethernet uses Ethernet technology to deliver cost-effective, high-speed connectivity for MAN and WAN applications.

Service providers offer Metro Ethernet services to deliver converged voice, video, and data networking. Metro Ethernet provides a data-optimized connectivity solution for the MAN and WAN based on Ethernet technology widely deployed within the enterprise LAN. It also supports high-performance networks in the metropolitan area, meeting the increasing need for faster data speeds and more stringent QoS requirements.

Where traditional TDM access is rigid, complex, and costly to provision, Metro Ethernet services provide scalable bandwidth in flexible increments, simplified management, and faster and lower-cost provisioning. This simple, easy-to-use technology appeals to customers who are already using Ethernet on their LANs.

DSL Technologies

DSL delivers high bandwidth over traditional telephone copper lines. It works by way of two modems at either end of the wire. Like dialup, cable, wireless, and T1, DSL is a transmission technology that enables SPs to deliver a wide variety of services to their customers. These can include premium, high-speed Internet and intranet access, voice, VPNs, videoconferencing, and video on demand.

Basic DSL Implementations

The term *xDSL* covers a variety of similar forms of DSL. The two basic DSL categories are Asymmetric DSL (ADSL) and Symmetric DSL (SDSL). ADSL can be used only over short distances (typically less than 2 km).

KEY POINT | ADSL is the most common variety of DSL. Because ADSL operates at frequencies (from 100 kilohertz [kHz] to 1.1 megahertz [MHz]) that are above the voice channel (300 to 3400 Hz), ADSL allows PSTN telephony services concurrently on the same line.

With ADSL, traffic moves upstream and downstream at different speeds. For example, data that travels from the Internet to the end-user computer (*downstream*) could be moving at 1.5 Mbps, while data traveling from the end-user computer to the Internet (*upstream*) could be traveling at

384 kbps. ADSL can also be provisioned for symmetric operation, making it a viable residential and home office solution.

KEY POINT *Downstream* refers to data that travels from the Internet to the end-user computer.

Upstream refers to data that travels from the end-user computer to the Internet.

KEY POINT With SDSL, traffic in either direction travels at the same speed over a single copper twisted pair.

The use of a single twisted pair limits the operating range of SDSL to 10,000 feet (3048.8 meters). Unlike ADSL, SDSL does not allow concurrent PSTN telephony services on the same line. SDSL is a viable business solution and an excellent choice for running applications such as web and e-mail servers.

NOTE   SDSL is sometimes referred to as *single-pair DSL.*

Other Implementations of DSL

Other forms of DSL include the following:

- ISDN DSL (IDSL) is similar to ISDN.

- High-data-rate DSL (HDSL) delivers 1.544 Mbps of bandwidth each way (symmetric) over two pairs of copper twisted wire (data travels over two pairs of wires instead of one). HDSL does not support PSTN. Because HDSL provides T1 speed, telephone companies use it to provision local access to T1 services whenever possible. The operating range of HDSL is limited to 12,000 feet (3658.5 meters).

- HDSL-2 (second generation of HDSL) is a full-rate-only symmetric service that is different from HDSL because it exists over a single twisted-pair wire. HDSL-2 was conceived specifically to provide spectral compatibility with ADSL.

- G.SHDSL combines the best of SDSL and HDSL-2. The standard defines multirates, like SDSL, but provides the spectral compatibility of HDSL-2.

- Very-high-data-rate DSL (VDSL) is an extremely fast asymmetric DSL technology that delivers 13 to 52 Mbps downstream and 1.5 to 2.3 Mbps upstream of data, and PSTN services, over a single twisted copper pair of wires. The operating range of VDSL is limited to 1,000 to 4,500 feet (304.8 to 1,372 meters).

The next section walks through an example of ADSL architecture and design.

ADSL Architecture and Design

Figure 5-4 illustrates a typical ADSL service architecture. The network consists of Customer Premises Equipment (CPE), the Network Access Provider (NAP), and the Network Service Provider (NSP), as follows:

- CPE refers to an end-user workstation, such as a PC, together with an ADSL modem or an ADSL transceiver unit remote terminal (ATU-R).

- The NAP provides ADSL line termination by using DSL access multiplexers (DSLAM).

- The DSLAM forwards traffic to the NSP, the local access concentrator, which is used for Layer 3 termination.

Figure 5-4 *Sample ADSL Architecture*

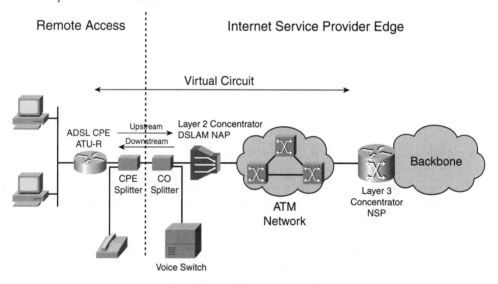

An ADSL circuit connects an ADSL modem on each end of a twisted-pair telephone line. This creates three information channels:

- Medium-speed downstream channel

- Low-speed upstream channel

- Basic telephone service channel

Filters, or splitters, split off the basic telephone service channel from the digital modem, guaranteeing uninterrupted basic telephone service even if ADSL fails. Figure 5-5 illustrates a typical ADSL network, including (from left to right) customer workstations and PCs on a LAN, CPE (ADSL routers), a DSLAM on an ATM transport network, an NSP concentrator, and both packet and ATM core networks. Two very popular point-to-point protocol (PPP) implementations exist in ADSL designs: PPP over ATM (PPPoA) and PPP over Ethernet (PPPoE) .

Figure 5-5 *ADSL Point-to-Point Protocol Implementations*

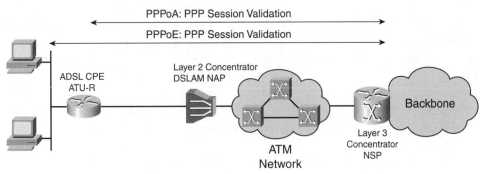

In the PPPoA architecture, the CPE acts as an Ethernet-to-WAN router, and the PPP session is established between the CPE and the Layer 3 access concentrator (the NSP). A PPPoA implementation involves configuring the CPE with PPP authentication information (login and password).

In the PPPoE architecture, the CPE acts as an Ethernet-to-WAN bridge, and the PPP session is established between the end user's PC or PPPoE router and the Layer 3 access concentrator (the NSP). The client initiates a PPP session by encapsulating PPP frames into an Ethernet frame and then bridging the frame (over ATM/DSL) to the gateway router (the NSP). From this point, the PPP sessions are established, authenticated, and addressed. The client receives its IP address using PPP negotiation from the termination point (the NSP).

Long Reach Ethernet Technology

KEY POINT   Long Reach Ethernet (LRE) is Cisco-proprietary technology that allows greater distances than traditional Ethernet and is a WAN access technology. LRE technology enables the use of Ethernet over existing, unconditioned, telephone-grade wire (copper twisted pair) using DSL coding and digital modulation techniques.

LRE technology allows Ethernet LAN transmissions to coexist with POTS, ISDN, or advanced PBX signaling services over the same pair of ordinary copper wires. LRE technology uses coding and digital modulation techniques from the DSL world in conjunction with Ethernet, the most popular LAN protocol.

An LRE system provides a point-to-point transmission that can deliver a symmetrical, full-duplex, raw data rate of up to 15 Mbps over distances of up to 1 mile (1.6 km). The channel's speed decreases with distance.

Cable Technology

KEY POINT | The cable technology for data transport uses coaxial cable media over cable distribution systems. The cable network is a high-speed copper platform that supports analog and digital video services over coaxial cables.

This technology is a good option for environments where cable television is widely deployed. Cable service providers support both residential and commercial customers.

Figure 5-6 illustrates some of the components used to transmit data and voice on a cable network. The Universal Broadband Router (uBR), also referred to as the Cable Modem Termination System (CMTS), provides high-speed data connectivity and is deployed at the cable company's headend. The uBR forwards data upstream to connect with either the PSTN or the Internet. The cable modem, also referred to as the cable access router, at the customer location offers support for transmission of voice, modem, and fax calls over the TCP/IP cable network.

Figure 5-6 *Data and Voice over IP over Cable*

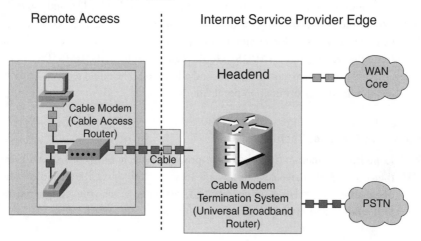

Cable modems are installed at the customer premises to support small businesses, branch offices, and corporate telecommuters.

The uBR is designed to be installed at a cable operator's headend facility or distribution hub and to function as the CMTS for subscriber-end devices.

The Data over Cable Service Interface Specification (DOCSIS) Radio Frequency (RF) Interface Specification defines the interface between the cable modem and the CMTS, and the data-over-cable procedures that the equipment must support.

Upstream and Downstream Data Flow

A data service is delivered to a subscriber through channels in a coaxial or optical fiber cable to a cable modem installed externally or internally to a subscriber's computer or television set. One television channel is used for upstream signals from the cable modem to the CMTS, and another channel is used for downstream signals from the CMTS to the cable modem.

When a CMTS receives signals from a cable modem, it converts these signals into IP packets that are then sent to an IP router for transmission across the Internet. When a CMTS sends signals to a cable modem, it modulates the downstream signals for transmission across the cable, or across the optical fiber and cable, to the cable modem. All cable modems can communicate with the CMTS, but not with other cable modems on the line.

The actual bandwidth for Internet service over a cable TV line is shared 27 Mbps on the download path to the subscriber, with about 2.5 Mbps of shared bandwidth for interactive responses in the other direction.

CATV Transmission

Before converting to their respective channel assignments in the downstream frequency domain, signals from broadcasters and satellite services are descrambled. Video signals are converted from optical signals to electrical signals and then are amplified and forwarded downstream over coaxial cable for distribution to the cable operator's customers.

Wireless Technologies

KEY POINT | With wireless technologies, networks do not have the limitations of wires or cables; instead, electromagnetic waves carry the RF signals.

Common examples of wireless equipment include cellular phones and pagers, global positioning systems, cordless computer peripherals, satellite television, and wireless LANs (WLAN). As shown in Figure 5-7, wireless implementations include the following:

- **Bridged wireless**: Designed to connect two or more networks, typically located in different buildings, at high data rates for data-intensive, line-of-sight applications. A series of wireless bridges or routers connect discrete, distant sites into a single LAN, interconnecting hard-to-wire sites, noncontiguous floors, satellite offices, school or corporate campus settings, temporary networks, and warehouses.

- **Mobile wireless**: Includes cellular voice and data applications. Wireless technology usage increased with the introduction of digital services on wireless. Second- and third-generation mobile phones offer better connectivity and higher speeds. Mobile wireless technologies include the following:

  - **Global System for Mobile (GSM)**: GSM is a digital mobile radio standard that uses time division multiple access (TDMA) technology. It allows eight simultaneous calls on the same frequency, in three different bands: 900, 1800, and 1900 MHz. The transfer data rate is 9.6 kbps. One of the unique benefits of the GSM service is its international roaming capability, a result of roaming agreements established among the various operators.

  - **General Packet Radio Service (GPRS)**: GPRS extends the capability of GSM and supports intermittent and bursty data transfer. Speeds offered to the client are in the range of ISDN speeds (64 kbps to 128 kbps).

  - **Universal Mobile Telephone Service (UMTS)**: UTMS is a so-called *third-generation (3G) broadband*, packet-based transmission of text, digitized voice, video, and multimedia at data rates up to 2 Mbps. UMTS offers a consistent set of services to mobile computer and phone users, regardless of their location in the world.

  - **Code Division Multiple Access (CDMA)**: CDMA is a spread-spectrum technology that assigns a code to each conversation; individual conversations are encoded in a pseudo-random digital sequence.

- **WLAN**: Developed because of demand for LAN connections over the air and often used for intrabuilding communication. WLAN technology can replace a traditional wired network or extend its reach and capabilities. WLANs cover a growing range of applications, such as guest access and voice, and support services, such as advanced security and location of wireless devices.

  The IEEE 802.11g standard supports speeds of up to 54 Mbps in the 2.4-GHz band.
  The IEEE 802.11b standard supports speeds of up to 11 Mbps in the 2.4-GHz band.
  The IEEE 802.11a standard supports speeds of up to 54 Mbps in the 5-GHz band.

Figure 5-7   *Three Wireless Implementations*

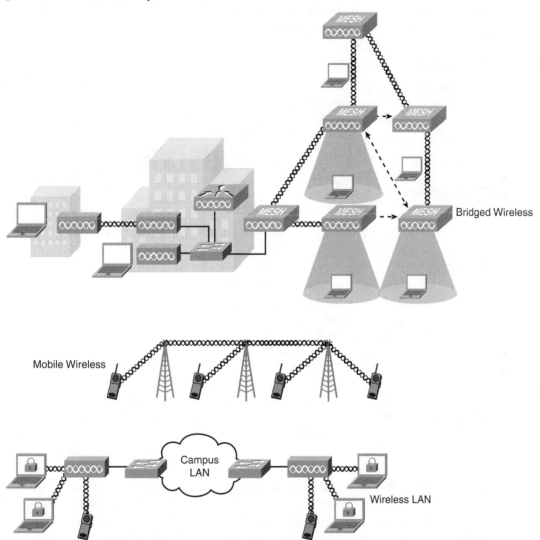

NOTE   Wireless networks are discussed further in Chapter 9, "Wireless Network Design Considerations."

Synchronous Optical Network and Synchronous Digital Hierarchy

Synchronous Optical Network/Synchronous Digital Hierarchy (SONET/SDH) is a circuit-based bandwidth-efficient technology. SONET/SDH establishes high-speed circuits using TDM frames in ring topologies over an optical infrastructure, as illustrated in Figure 5-8. It results in guaranteed bandwidth, regardless of actual usage. Common bit rates are 155 Mbps and 622 Mbps, with a current maximum of 10 Gigabits per second (Gbps).

Figure 5-8 *SONET/SDH*

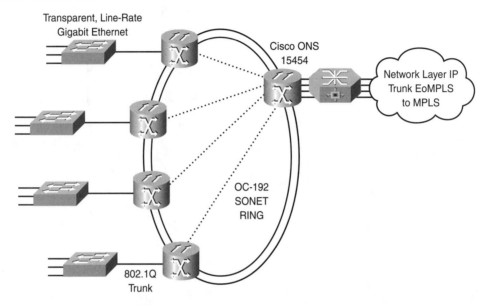

KEY POINT	SONET is an ANSI specification. SDH is the SONET-equivalent specification proposed by the ITU. Whereas European carriers use SDH widely, North American, Asian, and Pacific Rim carriers use SONET more frequently.

SONET/SDH rings support two IP encapsulations for user interfaces: ATM, and Packet over SONET/SDH (POS), which sends native IP packets directly over SONET/SDH frames. SONET/SDH rings provide major innovations for transport and have important capabilities, such as proactive performance monitoring and automatic recovery (self-healing) via an automatic protection switching mechanism. These capabilities increase their reliability to cope with system faults. Failure of a single SONET/SDH link or a network element does not lead to failure of the entire network.

Optical carrier (OC) rates are the digital hierarchies of the SONET standard, supporting the following speeds:

- OC-1 = 51.85 Mbps

- OC-3 = 155.52 Mbps

- OC-12 = 622.08 Mbps

- OC-24 = 1.244 Gbps

- OC-48 = 2.488 Gbps

- OC-192 = 9.952 Gbps

- OC-255 = 13.21 Gbps

Dense Wavelength Division Multiplexing

Dense Wavelength Division Multiplexing (DWDM), illustrated in Figure 5-9, increases bandwidth on an optical medium.

KEY POINT | DWDM increases the available bandwidth on a single strand of fiber by using multichannel signaling.

Figure 5-9 *DWDM*

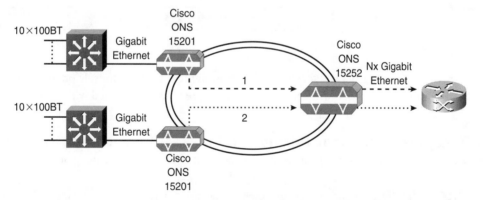

DWDM is a crucial component of optical networks. It maximizes the use of installed fiber cable and allows new services to be provisioned efficiently over existing infrastructure. Flexible add and drop modules allow individual channels to be dropped and inserted along a route. An open architecture system allows the connection of a variety of devices, including SONET terminals, ATM switches, and IP routers. DWDM is also used inside the SONET/SDH ring.

Dark Fiber

> **KEY POINT** | *Dark fiber* refers to fiber-optic cables leased from an SP and connected to a company's own infrastructure.

Dark fiber use is illustrated in Figure 5-10. The framing for the dark fiber is provided by the company's devices and does not have to be SONET/SDH. As a result, the dark-fiber connection eliminates the need for SONET/SDH multiplexers, which are required in SONET/SDH rings. The edge devices connect directly over the site-to-site dark fiber using a Layer 2 encapsulation such as Gigabit Ethernet. When such connectivity is used to transmit data over significantly long distances, regenerators or DWDM concentrators are inserted into the link to maintain signal integrity and provide appropriate jitter control.

Figure 5-10 *Dark Fiber*

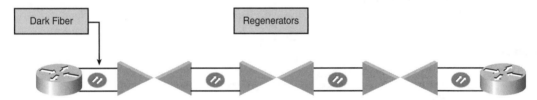

Depending on the carrier and location, dark fiber might be available for sale on the wholesale market for both metro and wide-area links at prices previously associated with leased-line rental.

WAN Transport Technology Pricing and Contract Considerations

This section discusses pricing and contract considerations for WAN technologies.

> **NOTE** The pricing, time frame, and contract details provided here are examples from the United States market. Organizations in other countries might have different experiences. However, the items in this section should be considered when implementing a WAN.
>
> Service and pricing options between carriers should be compared and negotiated, depending on competition in the area.

Historically, WAN transport costs include an access circuit charge and, for TDM, a distance-sensitive rate. Some carriers have dropped or reduced distance-based factors as TDM circuits have become a commodity.

A service provider might need 60 days or more to provision access circuits. The higher the bandwidth, the more lead time it might take to install.

Metro Ethernet might not be available everywhere, and the lead times could be long. Construction and associated fees might be required when provisioning the fiber access.

For Frame Relay and ATM, typical charges include a combination of an access circuit charge (per-PVC) and possibly per-bandwidth (committed information rate [CIR] or minimum information rate [MIR]) charges. Some carriers have simplified these rates by charging based on the access circuit and then setting CIR or MIR to half that speed; this technique allows bursts to two times the guaranteed rate.

Frame Relay might be generally available up to T3 speeds. However, in some cases, the trunks between Frame Relay switches is T3 speed and the service providers do not want to offer T3 access circuits because all the bandwidth would be utilized.

For MPLS VPNs, pricing generally is set to compete with Frame Relay and ATM. Some providers encourage customers to move to MPLS VPN by offering lower prices than for Frame Relay and ATM. Other service providers price MPLS VPNs somewhat higher than Frame Relay or ATM because they include a routing service.

Tariffed commercial services typically are available at published rates and are subject to certain restrictions. Some carriers are moving toward unpublished rates, allowing more flexibility in options and charges.

In general, the time needed to contract a WAN circuit in a standard carrier package is on the order of one month or so. If you choose to negotiate an SLA, expect six months or more of discussions with the service provider, and include your legal department. You might not be able to influence many changes in the SLA unless you represent a very large customer.

Contract periods are usually in the range of one to five years. Because the telecommunications industry is changing quickly, enterprises generally do not want to get locked into a long-term contract. Escape clauses in case of merger or poor performance might help mitigate the business risks of long-term contracts.

For dark fiber, contract periods are generally for 20 years. One option to consider is the right of *nonreversion*, meaning that no matter what happens to the provider, the fiber is yours to use for the full 20 years, protecting the enterprise in case of a service provider merger, bankruptcy, and so on. The process and responsibility to repair the fiber when necessary should also be defined in the contract.

WAN Design

This section describes the WAN design methodology and the application and technical requirement aspects of WAN design. The different possibilities for WAN ownership are discussed. WAN bandwidth optimization techniques are described.

The methodology espoused here follows the guidelines of the Prepare-Plan-Design-Implement-Operate-Optimize (PPDIOO) methodology introduced in Chapter 2, "Applying a Methodology to Network Design." The network designer should follow these steps when planning and designing the Enterprise Edge based on the PPDIOO methodology:

Step 1   **Analyzing customer requirements**: The initial step in the design methodology is to analyze the requirements of the network and its users, including the type of applications, the traffic volume, and traffic patterns. User needs continually change in response to changing business conditions and changing technology. For example, as more voice and video-based network applications become available, there is pressure to increase network bandwidth.

Step 2   **Characterizing the existing network and sites**: The second step is to analyze the existing networking infrastructure and sites, including the technology used and the location of hosts, servers, terminals, and other end nodes. Together with the network's physical description, the analysis should evaluate the possibility of extending the network to support new sites, new features, or the reallocation of existing nodes. For example, the future integration of data and telephone systems requires considerable changes in the network's configuration. In this case, a detailed evaluation of current options is important.

Step 3   **Designing the network topology and solutions**: The final step in the design methodology is to develop the overall network topology and its appropriate services, based on the availability of technology, and taking into account the projected traffic pattern, technology performance constraints, and network reliability. The design document describes a set of discrete functions performed by the Enterprise Edge modules and the expected level of service provided by each selected technology, as dictated by the SP.

Planning and designing WAN networks involves a number of trade-offs, including the following:

- Application aspects of the requirements driven by the performance analysis

- Technical aspects of the requirements dealing with the geographic regulations and the effectiveness of the selected technology

- Cost aspects of the requirements; costs include those of the equipment and of the owned or leased media or communication channel

NOTE   WAN connections are typically characterized by the cost of leasing WAN infrastructure and transmission media from an SP. WAN designs must therefore trade off between the cost of bandwidth and the bandwidth efficiency.

The network's design should also be adaptable for the inclusion of future technologies and should not include any design elements that limit the adoption of new technologies as they become available. There might be trade-offs between these considerations and cost throughout the network design and implementation. For example, many new internetworks are rapidly adopting VoIP technology. Network designs should be able to support this technology without requiring a substantial upgrade by provisioning hardware and software that have options for expansion and upgradeability.

Application Requirements of WAN Design

Just as application requirements drive the Enterprise Campus design (as illustrated in Chapter 4, "Designing Basic Campus and Data Center Networks"), they also affect the Enterprise Edge WAN design. Application availability is a key user requirement; the chief components of application availability are response time, throughput, packet loss, and reliability. Table 5-2 analyzes these components, which are discussed in the following sections.

Table 5-2   *Application Requirements on the WAN*

Requirement	Data File Transfer	Data Interactive Application	Real-Time Voice	Real-Time Video
Response time	Reasonable	Within a second	150 ms of one-way delay with low jitter	Minimum delay and jitter
Throughput	High	Low	Low	High
Packet loss tolerance	Medium	Low	Low	Medium
Downtime (high reliability has low downtime)	Reasonable	Low	Low	Minimum
	← Zero downtime for mission-critical applications →			

Response Time

> **KEY POINT** *Response time* is the time between a user request (such as the entry of a command or keystroke) and the host system's command execution or response delivery.

Users accept response times up to some limit, at which point user satisfaction declines. Applications for which fast response time is considered critical include interactive online services, such as point-of-sale machines.

> **NOTE** Voice and video applications use the terms *delay* and *jitter*, respectively, to express the responsiveness of the line and the variation in the delays.

Throughput

> **KEY POINT** In data transmission, *throughput* is the amount of data moved successfully from one place to another in a given time period.

Applications that put high-volume traffic onto the network have more effect on throughput than interactive end-to-end connections. Throughput-intensive applications typically involve file-transfer activities that usually have low response-time requirements and can often be scheduled at times when response-time-sensitive traffic is low (such as after normal work hours). This could be accomplished via time-based access lists, for example.

Packet Loss

> **KEY POINT** In telecommunication transmission, packet loss is expressed as a *bit error rate (BER)*, which is the percentage of bits that have errors, relative to the total number of bits received in a transmission.

BER is usually expressed as 10 to a negative power. For example, a transmission might have a BER of 10 to the minus 6 (10^{-6}), meaning that 1 bit out of 1,000,000 bits transmitted was in error. The BER indicates how frequently a packet or other data unit must be retransmitted because of an error. A BER that is too high might indicate that a slower data rate could improve the overall transmission time for a given amount of transmitted data; in other words, a slower data rate can reduce the BER, thereby lowering the number of packets that must be re-sent.

Reliability

Although reliability is always important, some applications have requirements that exceed typical needs. Financial services, securities exchanges, and emergency, police, and military operations are examples of organizations that require nearly 100 percent uptime for critical applications. These situations imply a requirement for a high level of hardware and topological redundancy. Determining the cost of any downtime is essential for determining the relative importance of the network's reliability.

Technical Requirements: Maximum Offered Traffic

The goal of every WAN design should be to optimize link performance in terms of offered traffic, link utilization, and response time. To optimize link performance, the designer must balance between end-user and network manager requirements, which are usually diametrically opposed. End users usually require minimum application response times over a WAN link, whereas the network manager's goal is to maximize the link utilization; WAN resources have finite capacity.

Response time problems typically affect only users. For example, it probably does not matter to the network manager if query results are returned 120 ms sooner rather than later. Response time is a thermometer of usability for users. Users perceive the data processing experience in terms of how quickly they can get their screen to update. They view the data processing world in terms of response time and do not usually care about link utilization. The graphs in Figure 5-11 illustrate the response time and link utilization relative to the offered traffic. The response time increases with the offered traffic, until it reaches an unacceptable point for the end user. Similarly, the link utilization increases with the offered traffic to the point that the link becomes saturated. The designer's goal is to determine the maximum offered traffic that is acceptable to both the end user and the network manager.

Figure 5-11   *Determining the Maximum Offered Traffic*

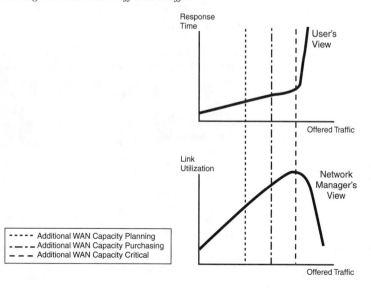

However, planning for additional WAN capacity should occur much earlier than the critical point—usually at about 50% link utilization. Additional bandwidth purchasing should start at about 60% utilization; if the link utilization reaches 75%, increasing the capacity is critical.

Technical Requirements: Bandwidth

> **KEY POINT** *Bandwidth* is the amount of data transmitted or received per unit time, such as 100 Mbps.

In a qualitative sense, the required bandwidth is proportional to the data's complexity for a given level of system performance. For example, downloading a photograph in 1 second takes more bandwidth than downloading a page of text in 1 second. Large sound files, computer programs, and animated videos require even more bandwidth for acceptable system performance. One of the main issues involved in WAN connections is the selection of appropriate technologies that provide sufficient bandwidth. Table 5-3 illustrates the ranges of bandwidths commonly supported by the given technologies.

Table 5-3 *WAN Physical Media Bandwidths*

WAN Media Type	Bandwidth			
	<= 1.5/2 Mbps (Low)	From 1.5/2 Mbps to 45/34 Mbps (Medium)	From 45/34 Mbps to 100 Mbps (High)	From 100 Mbps to 10 Gbps (Higher)
Copper	Serial or asynchronous serial, ISDN, TDM (DS0, E1/ T1), X25, Frame Relay, ADSL	LRE (up to 15 Mbps), ADSL (8 Mbps downstream)		
Fiber		Ethernet, TDM (T3/ E3)	Fast Ethernet, ATM over SONET/SDH, POS[1]	Gigabit Ethernet, 10 Gigabit Ethernet, ATM over SONET/ SDH, POS
Coaxial		Shared bandwidth; 27 Mbps downstream, 2.5 Mbps upstream		
2.4 or 5 GHz WAN Wireless		Varies, based on distance and RF quality		

[1] POS = Packet over SONET/SDH

Bandwidth is inexpensive in the LAN, where connectivity is typically limited only by hardware, implementation, and ongoing maintenance costs. In the WAN, bandwidth has typically been the overriding cost, and delay-sensitive traffic such as voice has remained separate from data. However, new applications and the economics of supporting them are forcing these conventions to change.

Evaluating the Cost-Effectiveness of WAN Ownership

In the WAN environment, the following usually represent fixed costs:

- Equipment purchases, such as modems, channel service unit/data service units, and router interfaces

- Circuit and service provisioning

- Network-management tools and platforms

Recurring costs include the monthly circuit fees from the SP and the WAN's support and maintenance, including any network management center personnel.

From an ownership perspective, WAN links can be thought of in the following three categories:

- **Private**: A private WAN uses private transmission systems to connect distant LANs. The owner of a private WAN must buy, configure, and maintain the physical layer connectivity (such as copper, fiber, wireless, and coaxial) and the terminal equipment required to connect locations. This makes private WANs expensive to build, labor-intensive to maintain, and difficult to reconfigure for constantly changing business needs. The advantages of using a private WAN might include higher levels of security and transmission quality.

> **NOTE**   When the WAN media and devices are privately owned, transmission quality is not necessarily improved, nor is reliability necessarily higher.

- **Leased**: A leased WAN uses dedicated bandwidth from a carrier company, with either private or leased terminal equipment. The provider provisions the circuit and provides the maintenance. However, the company pays for the allocated bandwidth whether or not it is used, and operating costs tend to be high. Some examples include TDM and SONET circuits.

- **Shared**: A shared WAN shares the physical resources with many users. Carriers offer a variety of circuit- or packet-switching transport networks, such as MPLS and Frame Relay. The provider provisions the circuit and provides the maintenance. Linking LANs and private

WANs into shared network services is a trade-off among cost, performance, and security. An ideal design optimizes the cost advantages of shared network services with a company's performance and security requirements.

> **NOTE** Circuits often span regional or national boundaries, meaning that several SPs handle a connection in the toll network. In these cases, devices the subscriber owns (private) and devices the carrier leases to or shares with the subscriber determine the path.

Optimizing Bandwidth in a WAN

It is expensive to transmit data over a WAN. Therefore, one of many different techniques—such as data compression, bandwidth combination, tuning window size, congestion management (queuing and scheduling), congestion avoidance, and traffic shaping and policing—can be used to optimize bandwidth usage and improve overall performance. The following sections describe these techniques.

Data Compression

KEY POINT | *Compression* is the reduction of data size to save transmission time.

Compression enables more efficient use of the available WAN bandwidth, which is often limited and is generally a bottleneck. Compression allows higher throughput because it squeezes packet size and therefore increases the amount of data that can be sent through a transmission resource in a given time period. Compression can be of an entire packet, of the header only, or of the payload only. Payload compression is performed on a Layer 2 frame's payload and therefore compresses the entire Layer 3 packet.

You can easily measure the success of these solutions using compression ratio and platform latency. However, although compression might seem like a viable WAN bandwidth optimization feature, it might not always be appropriate. Cisco IOS software compression support includes the following data software compression types:

- FRF.9 Frame Relay Payload Compression

- Link Access Procedure Balanced payload compression using the Lempel-Ziv Stack (LZS) algorithm, which is commonly referred to as the Stacker (STAC) or Predictor algorithm

- HDLC using LZS

- X.25 payload compression of encapsulated traffic

- PPP using Predictor

- Van Jacobson header compression for TCP/IP (conforms to RFC 1144)

- Microsoft Point-to-Point Compression

Compression Techniques

The basic function of data compression is to reduce the size of a frame of data to be transmitted over a network link. Data compression algorithms use two types of encoding techniques, statistical and dictionary:

- *Statistical compression*, which uses a fixed, usually nonadaptive encoding method, is best applied to a single application where the data is relatively consistent and predictable. Because the traffic on internetworks is neither consistent nor predictable, statistical algorithms are usually not suitable for data compression implementations on routers.

- An example of *dictionary compression* is the Lempel-Ziv algorithm, which is based on a dynamically encoded dictionary that replaces a continuous stream of characters with codes. The symbols represented by the codes are stored in memory in a dictionary-style list. This approach is more responsive to variations in data than statistical compression.

Cisco internetworking devices use the Stacker (abbreviated as STAC) and Predictor data compression algorithms. Developed by STAC Electronics, STAC is based on the Lempel-Ziv algorithm. The Cisco IOS software uses an optimized version of STAC that provides good compression ratios but requires many CPU cycles to perform compression.

The Predictor compression algorithm tries to predict the next sequence of characters in the data stream by using an index to look up a sequence in the compression dictionary. It then examines the next sequence in the data stream to see whether it matches. If so, that sequence replaces the looked-up sequence in the dictionary. If not, the algorithm locates the next character sequence in the index, and the process begins again. The index updates itself by hashing a few of the most recent character sequences from the input stream.

The Predictor data compression algorithm was obtained from the public domain and optimized by Cisco engineers. It uses CPU cycles more efficiently than STAC does, but it also requires more memory.

Real-Time Transport Protocol and Compression

Real-Time Transport Protocol (RTP) is used for carrying packetized audio and video traffic over an IP network. RTP is not intended for data traffic, which uses TCP or User Datagram Protocol. RTP provides end-to-end network transport functions intended for applications that have real-time transmission requirements such as audio, video, or simulation data over multicast or unicast network services. Because RTP header compression (cRTP) compresses the voice headers from 40 bytes to 2 or 4 bytes, it offers significant bandwidth savings. cRTP is also referred to as *Compressed Real-Time Transfer Protocol*.

Hardware-assisted data compression achieves the same goal as software-based data compression, except that it accelerates compression rates by offloading the task from the main CPU to specialized compression circuits. Compression is implemented in compression hardware that is installed in a system slot.

Impact of Compression and Encryption on Router Performance

System performance can be affected when compression or encryption is performed in software rather than hardware. Perform the following operations to determine whether these services are stressing a router's CPU:

- Use the **show processes** Cisco IOS software command to obtain a baseline reading before enabling encryption or compression.

- Enable the service, and use the **show processes** command again to assess the difference.

Cisco recommends that you disable compression or encryption if the router CPU load exceeds 40 percent, and that you disable compression if encryption is enabled. Also, do not enable compression on your routers if the files being sent across the network are already compressed (such as zip files).

Bandwidth Combination

PPP is commonly used to establish a direct connection between two devices; PPP is a Layer 2 protocol for connection over synchronous and asynchronous circuits. For example, PPP is used when connecting computers using serial cables, phone lines, trunk lines, cellular telephones, specialized radio links, or fiber-optic links. As mentioned earlier, ISPs use PPP for customer dial-up access to the Internet. An encapsulated form of PPP (PPPoE or PPPoA) is commonly used in a similar role with DSL Internet service.

Multilink PPP (MLP) logically connects multiple links between two systems, as needed, to provide extra bandwidth. The bandwidths of two or more physical communication links, such as analog modems, ISDN, and other analog or digital links, are logically aggregated, resulting in an increase in overall throughput. MLP is based on the IETF standard RFC 1990, *The PPP Multilink Protocol (MP)*.

Window Size

KEY POINT | *Window size* is the maximum number of frames (or amount of data) the sender can transmit before it must wait for an acknowledgment. The *current window* is defined as the number of frames (or amount of data) that can be sent at the current time; this is always less than or equal to the window size.

Window size is an important tuning factor for achieving high throughput on a WAN link. The acknowledgment procedure confirms the correct delivery of the data to the recipient. Acknowledgment procedures can be implemented at any protocol layer. They are particularly important in a protocol layer that provides reliability, such as hop-by-hop acknowledgment in a reliable link protocol or end-to-end acknowledgment in a transport protocol (for example, TCP). This form of data acknowledgment provides a means of self-clocking the network, such that a steady-state flow of data between the connection's two endpoints is possible.

For example, if the TCP window size is set to 8192 octets, the sender must stop after sending 8192 octets in the event that the receiver does not send an acknowledgment. This might be unacceptable for long (high-latency) WAN links with significant delays, in which the transmitter would waste the majority of its time waiting. The more acknowledgments (because of a smaller window size) and the longer the distance, the lower the throughput. Therefore, on highly reliable WAN links that do not require many acknowledgments, the window size should be adjusted to a higher value to enable maximum throughput. However, the risk is frequent retransmissions in the case of poor-quality links, which can dramatically reduce the throughput. Adjustable windows and equipment that can adapt to line conditions are strongly recommended.

Selective ACK

The TCP selective acknowledgment mechanism, which is defined in RFC 2018, *TCP Selective Acknowledgment Options,* helps overcome the limitations of the TCP acknowledgments. TCP performance can be affected if multiple packets are lost from one window of data; a TCP sender learns about only one lost packet per round trip. With selective acknowledgment enabled (using the **ip tcp selective-ack** global configuration command in Cisco IOS), the receiver returns selective acknowledgment packets to the sender, informing the sender about data that has been received. The sender can then resend only the missing data segments.

This feature is used only when multiple packets drop from a TCP window. Performance is not affected when the feature is enabled but not used.

Queuing to Improve Link Utilization

To improve link utilization, Cisco has developed QoS techniques to avoid temporary congestion and to provide preferential treatment for critical applications. QoS mechanisms such as queuing and scheduling, policing (limiting) the access rate, and traffic shaping enable network operators to deploy and operate large-scale networks that efficiently handle both bandwidth-hungry (such as multimedia and web traffic) and mission-critical applications (such as host-based applications).

KEY POINT	QoS does not create bandwidth; rather, QoS optimizes the use of existing resources, including bandwidth.

If WAN links are constantly congested, either the network requires greater bandwidth or compression should be used.

QoS queuing strategies are unnecessary if WAN links are never congested.

Congestion management includes two separate processes: queuing, which separates traffic into various queues or buffers, and scheduling, which decides from which queue traffic is to be sent next.

Queuing allows network administrators to manage the varying demands of applications on networks and routers. When positioning the role of queuing in networks, the primary issue is the duration of congestion.

KEY POINT	Queuing is configured on outbound interfaces and is appropriate for cases in which WAN links are congested from time to time.

Following are the two types of queues:

- **Hardware queue**: Uses a FIFO strategy, which is necessary for the interface drivers to transmit packets one by one. The hardware queue is sometimes referred to as the *transmit queue* or *TxQ*.

- **Software queue**: Schedules packets into the hardware queue based on the QoS requirements. The following sections discuss the following types of queuing: weighted fair queuing (WFQ), priority queuing (PQ), custom queuing (CQ), class-based WFQ (CBWFQ), and low-latency queuing (LLQ) .

WFQ

WFQ handles the problems inherent in queuing schemes on a FIFO basis. WFQ assesses the size of each message and ensures that high-volume senders do not force low-volume senders out of the queue. WFQ sorts different traffic flows into separate streams, or conversation sessions, and alternately dispatches them. The algorithm also solves the problem of round-trip delay variability. When high-volume conversations are active, their transfer rates and interarrival periods are quite predictable.

WFQ is enabled by default on most low-speed serial interfaces (with speeds at or below 2.048 Mbps) on Cisco routers. (Faster links use a FIFO queue by default.) This makes it very easy to configure (there are few adjustable parameters) but does not allow much control over which traffic takes priority.

PQ

PQ is useful for time-sensitive, mission-critical protocols (such as IBM Systems Network Architecture traffic). PQ works by establishing four interface output queues (high, medium, normal, and low), each serving a different level of priority; queues are configurable for queue type, traffic assignment, and size. The dispatching algorithm begins servicing a queue only when all higher-priority queues are empty. This way, PQ ensures that the most important traffic placed in the higher-level queues gets through first, at the expense of all other traffic types. As shown in Figure 5-12, the high-priority queue is always emptied before the lower-priority queues are serviced. Traffic can be assigned to the various queues based on protocol, port number, or other criteria. Because priority queuing requires extra processing, you should not recommend it unless it is necessary.

Figure 5-12   *Priority Queuing Has Four Queues; the High-Priority Queue Is Always Emptied First*

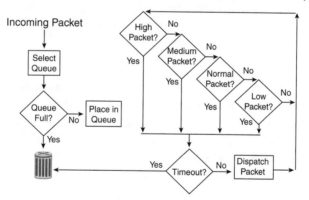

CQ

CQ is a different approach for prioritizing traffic. Like PQ, traffic can be assigned to various queues based on protocol, port number, or other criteria. However, CQ handles the queues in a round-robin fashion.

CQ works by establishing up to 16 interface output queues that are configurable in terms of type, traffic assignment, and size. CQ specifies the transmission window size of each queue in bytes. When the appropriate number of frames is transmitted from a queue, the transmission window size is reached, and the next queue is checked. CQ is a less drastic solution for mission-critical applications than PQ because it guarantees some level of service to all traffic.

CQ is fairer than PQ, but PQ is more powerful for prioritizing a mission-critical protocol. For example, with CQ, you can prioritize a particular protocol by assigning it more queue space; however, it will never monopolize the bandwidth. Figure 5-13 illustrates the custom queuing process.

Figure 5-13 *Custom Queuing Services Each Queue in a Round-Robin Fashion*

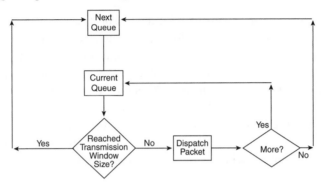

Like PQ, CQ causes the router to perform extra processing. Do not recommend CQ unless you have determined that one or more protocols need special processing.

CBWFQ

CBWFQ allows you to define a traffic class and then assign characteristics to it. For example, you can designate the minimum bandwidth delivered to the class during congestion. CBWFQ extends the standard WFQ functionality to provide support for user-defined traffic classes. With CBWFQ, traffic classes are defined based on match criteria, including protocols, access control lists (ACL), and input interfaces. Packets that satisfy the match criteria for a class constitute the traffic for that class. A queue is reserved for each class, and traffic that belongs to a class is directed to the queue for that class.

After a class has been defined according to its match criteria, you can assign it characteristics, including bandwidth, weight, and maximum queue packet limit. The bandwidth assigned to a class is the guaranteed bandwidth delivered to the class during times of congestion.

The queue packet limit is the maximum number of packets allowed to accumulate in the queue for the class. Packets that belong to a class are subject to the bandwidth and queue limits that characterize the class.

For CBWFQ, the weight for a packet that belongs to a specific class derives from the bandwidth assigned to the class during configuration. Therefore, the bandwidth assigned to the packets of a class determines the order in which packets are sent. All packets are serviced fairly, based on weight; no class of packets may be granted strict priority. This scheme poses problems for voice traffic, which is largely intolerant of delay and variation in delay.

LLQ

LLQ brings strict PQ to CBWFQ; it is a combination of PQ and CBWFQ. Strict PQ allows delay-sensitive data such as voice to be dequeued and sent first (before packets in other queues are dequeued), giving delay-sensitive data preferential treatment over other traffic. Without LLQ, CBWFQ provides WFQ based on defined classes with no strict priority queue available for real-time traffic.

Congestion Avoidance

Congestion-avoidance techniques monitor network traffic loads so that congestion can be anticipated and avoided before it becomes problematic. If congestion-avoidance techniques are *not* used and interface queues become full, packets trying to enter the queue are discarded, regardless of what traffic they hold. This is known as *tail drop*—packets arriving after the tail of the queue are dropped.

> **KEY POINT** | Congestion-avoidance techniques allow packets from streams identified as being eligible for early discard (those with lower priority) to be dropped when the queue is getting full.

Congestion avoidance works well with TCP-based traffic. TCP has a built-in flow control mechanism so that when a source detects a dropped packet, the source slows its transmission.

Weighted random early detection (WRED) is the Cisco implementation of the random early detection (RED) mechanism. RED randomly drops packets when the queue gets to a specified level (when it is nearing full). RED is designed to work with TCP traffic: When TCP packets are dropped, TCP's flow-control mechanism slows the transmission rate and then progressively begins to increase it again. Therefore, RED results in sources slowing down and hopefully avoiding congestion.

WRED extends RED by using the IP precedence bits in the IP packet header to determine which traffic should be dropped; the drop-selection process is weighted by the IP precedence. Similarly, Differentiated Services Code Point (DSCP)–based WRED uses the DSCP value in the IP packet header in the drop-selection process. WRED selectively discards lower-priority traffic when the interface begins to get congested.

Starting in IOS Release 12.2(8)T, Cisco implemented an extension to WRED called explicit *congestion notification (ECN)*. ECN is defined in RFC 3168, *The Addition of Explicit Congestion Notification (ECN) to IP*, and it uses the lower 2 bits in the ToS byte. Devices use these two ECN bits to communicate that they are experiencing congestion. When ECN is in use, it marks packets as experiencing congestion (rather than dropping them) if the senders are ECN-capable and the queue has not yet reached its maximum threshold. If the queue does reach the maximum, packets are dropped, as they would be without ECN.

Traffic Shaping and Policing to Rate-Limit Traffic Classes

Traffic shaping and traffic policing, illustrated in Figure 5-14, also referred to as *committed access rate*, are similar mechanisms in that both inspect traffic and take action based on the various characteristics of that traffic. These characteristics can be based on whether the traffic is over or under a given rate, or is based on some bits in the IP packet header, such as the DSCP or IP precedence.

Figure 5-14 *Policing Drops Excess Traffic, Whereas Shaping Delays It*

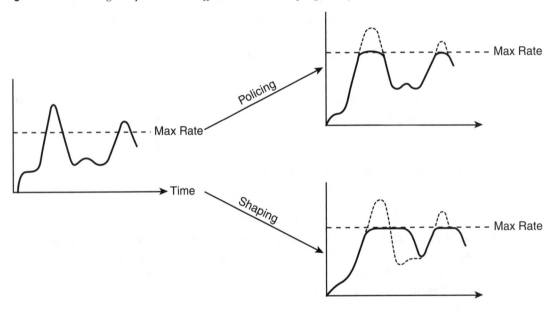

KEY POINT *Policing* either discards the packet or modifies some aspect of it, such as its IP precedence, when the policing agent determines that the packet meets a given criterion.

For example, an enterprise's policy management scheme could deem the traffic generated by a particular resource (such as the first 100 kbps) as first-class traffic, so it receives a top priority marking. Traffic above the first 100 kbps generated by that same resource could drop to a lower priority class or be discarded altogether. Similarly, all incoming streaming Moving Picture Experts

Group (MPEG)-1 Audio Layer 3 (MP3) traffic could be limited to, for example, 10 percent of all available bandwidth so that it does not starve other applications.

| **KEY POINT** | By comparison, *traffic shaping* attempts to adjust the transmission rate of packets that match a certain criterion. |

Topologies that have high-speed links (such as a central site) feeding into lower-speed links (such as a remote or branch site) often experience bottlenecks at the remote end because of the speed mismatch. Traffic shaping helps eliminate the bottleneck situation by throttling back traffic volume at the source end. It reduces the flow of outbound traffic from a router interface by holding packets in a buffer and releasing them at a preconfigured rate; routers can be configured to transmit at a lower bit rate than the interface bit rate.

One common use of traffic shaping in the enterprise is to smooth the flow of traffic across a single link toward a service provider transport network to ensure compliance with the traffic contract, avoiding service provider policing at the receiving end. Traffic shaping reduces the bursty nature of the transmitted data and is most useful when the contract rate is less than the line rate. Traffic shaping can also respond to signaled congestion from the transport network when the traffic rates exceed the contract rate.

Token Bucket

A term you might encounter related to traffic shaping and policing is a *token bucket*. In the token bucket analogy, tokens are put into the bucket at a certain rate, and the bucket itself has a specified capacity. If the bucket fills to capacity, newly arriving tokens are discarded. Each token is permission for the source to send a certain number of bits into the network. To send a packet, the shaper or policer must remove from the bucket a number of tokens equal in representation to the packet size.

If not enough tokens are in the bucket to send a packet, the packet either waits until the bucket has enough tokens or the packet is discarded or marked down. If the bucket is already full of tokens, incoming tokens overflow and are not available to future packets. Consequently, at any time, the largest burst a source can send into the network is roughly proportional to the size of the bucket.

Note that the token bucket mechanism used for traffic shaping has both a token bucket and a data buffer, or queue; if it did not have a data buffer, it would be a policer. For traffic shaping, arriving packets that cannot be sent immediately are delayed in the data buffer.

The information in this sidebar was derived from the *Cisco IOS Quality of Service Solutions Configuration Guide, Release 12.2*, available at http://www.cisco.com/en/US/products/sw/iosswrel/ps1835/products_configuration_guide_book09186a00800c5e31.html.

Using WAN Technologies

Numerous WAN technologies exist today, and new technologies are constantly emerging. The most appropriate WAN selection usually results in high efficiency and leads to customer satisfaction. The network designer must be aware of all possible WAN design choices while taking into account customer requirements. This section describes the use of various WAN technologies, including the following:

■ Remote access

■ VPNs

■ WAN backup

■ The Internet as a backup WAN

Remote Access Network Design

When you're designing remote-access networks for teleworkers and traveling employees, the type of connection drives the technology selection, such as whether to choose a data link or a network layer connection. By analyzing the application requirements and service provider offerings, you can choose the most suitable of a wide range of remote-access technologies. Typical remote-access requirements include the following:

■ Data link layer WAN technologies from remote sites to the Enterprise Edge network. Investment and operating costs are the main issues.

■ Low- to medium-volume data file transfer and interactive traffic.

■ Increasing need to support voice services.

Remote access to the Enterprise Edge network is typically provided over permanent connections for remote teleworkers through a dedicated circuit or a provisioned service, or on-demand connections for traveling workers.

Remote-access technology selections include dialup (both analog and digital), DSL, cable, and hot-spot wireless service.

Dial-on-Demand Routing

Dial-on-demand routing is a technique whereby a router can dynamically initiate and close a circuit-switched session when transmitting end-station demands. A router is configured to consider certain traffic interesting (such as traffic from a particular protocol) and other traffic uninteresting. When the router receives interesting traffic destined for a remote network, a circuit is established, and the traffic is transmitted normally. If the router receives uninteresting traffic and a circuit is already established, that traffic is also transmitted normally. The router maintains an idle timer that is reset only when it receives interesting traffic. If the router does not receive any interesting traffic before the idle timer expires, the circuit is terminated. Likewise, if the router receives uninteresting traffic and no circuit exists, the router drops the traffic.

VPN Design

> **KEY POINT** | A *VPN* is connectivity deployed on a shared infrastructure with the same policies, security, and performance as a private network, but typically with lower total cost of ownership.

The infrastructure used can be the Internet, an IP infrastructure, or any WAN infrastructure, such as a Frame Relay network or an ATM WAN.

The following sections discuss these topics:

- VPN applications

- VPN connectivity options

- VPN benefits

VPN Applications

VPNs can be grouped according to their applications:

- **Access VPN**: Access VPNs provide access to a corporate intranet (or extranet) over a shared infrastructure and have the same policies as a private network. Remote-access connectivity is through dial-up, ISDN, DSL, wireless, or cable technologies. Access VPNs enable businesses to outsource their dial or other broadband remote access connections without compromising their security policy.

  The two access VPN architectures are client-initiated and Network Access Server (NAS)–initiated connections. With client-initiated VPNs, users establish an encrypted IP tunnel from their PCs across an SP's shared network to their corporate network. With NAS-initiated VPNs, the tunnel is initiated from the NAS; in this scenario, remote users dial into the local SP point of presence (POP), and the SP initiates a secure, encrypted tunnel to the corporate network.

- **Intranet VPN**: Intranet VPNs link remote offices by extending the corporate network across a shared infrastructure. The intranet VPN services are typically based on extending the basic remote-access VPN to other corporate offices across the Internet or across the SP's IP backbone. Note that there are no performance guarantees with VPNs across the Internet—no one organization is responsible for the performance of the Internet. The main benefits of intranet VPNs are reduced WAN infrastructure needs, which result in lower ongoing leased-line, Frame Relay, or other WAN charges, and operational savings.

■ **Extranet VPN**: Extranet VPNs extend the connectivity to business partners, suppliers, and customers across the Internet or an SP's network. The security policy becomes very important at this point; for example, the company does not want a hacker to spoof any orders from a business partner. The main benefits of an extranet VPN are the ease of securely connecting a business partner as needed, and the ease of severing the connection with the business partner (partner today, competitor tomorrow), which becomes as simple as shutting down the VPN tunnel. Very granular rules can be created for what traffic is shared with the peer network in the extranet.

VPN Connectivity Options

The following sections describe three connectivity options that provide IP access through VPNs:

■ Overlay VPNs

■ Virtual private dial-up networks (VPDN)

■ Peer-to-peer VPNs

Overlay VPNs

With overlay VPNs, the provider's infrastructure provides virtual point-to-point links between customer sites. Overlay VPNs are implemented with a number of technologies, including traditional Layer 1 and Layer 2 technologies (such as ISDN, SONET/SDH, Frame Relay, and ATM) overlaid with modern Layer 3 IP-based solutions (such as Generic Routing Encapsulation [GRE] and IPsec).

From the Layer 3 perspective, the provider network is invisible: The customer routers are linked with emulated point-to-point links. The routing protocol runs directly between routers that establish routing adjacencies and exchange routing information. The provider is not aware of customer routing and does not have any information about customer routes. The provider's only responsibility is the point-to-point data transport between customer sites. Although they are well known and easy to implement, overlay VPNs are more difficult to operate and have higher maintenance costs for the following reasons:

■ Every individual virtual circuit must be provisioned.

■ Optimum routing between customer sites requires a full mesh of virtual circuits between sites.

■ Bandwidth must be provisioned on a site-to-site basis.

The concept of VPNs was introduced early in the emergence of data communications with technologies such as X.25 and Frame Relay. These technologies use virtual circuits to establish the end-to-end connection over a shared SP infrastructure. In the case of overlay VPNs, emulated point-to-point links replace the dedicated links, and the provider infrastructure is statistically shared. Overlay VPNs enable the provider to offer the connectivity for a lower price and result in lower operational costs.

Figure 5-15 illustrates an overlay VPN. The router on the left (in the Enterprise Edge module) has one physical connection to the SP, with two virtual circuits provisioned. Virtual Circuit 1 (VC #1) provides connectivity to the router on the top right. Virtual Circuit 2 (VC #2) provides connectivity to the branch office router on the bottom right.

Figure 5-15 *Overlay VPNs Extend the Enterprise Network*

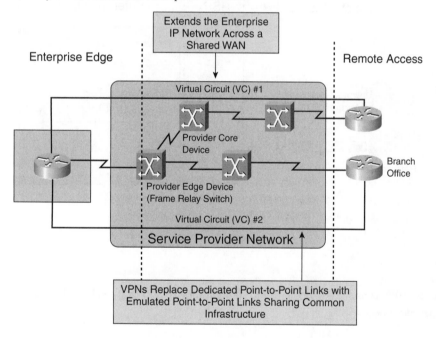

VPDNs

VPDNs enable an enterprise to configure secure networks that rely on an ISP for connectivity. With VPDNs, the customers use a provider's dial-in (or other type of connectivity) infrastructure for their private connections. A VPDN can be used with any available access technology. Ubiquity is important, meaning that VPDNs should work with any technology, including a modem, ISDN, xDSL, or cable connections.

The ISP agrees to forward the company's traffic from the ISP's POP to a company-run home gateway. Network configuration and security remain in the client's control. The SP supplies a virtual tunnel between the company's sites using Cisco Layer 2 Forwarding, point-to-point tunneling, or IETF Layer 2 Tunneling Protocol (L2TP) tunnels.

Figure 5-16 illustrates a VPDN. In this figure, the ISP terminates the dialup connections at the L2TP Access Concentrator (LAC) and forwards traffic through dynamically established tunnels to a remote access server called the L2TP Network Server (LNS). A VPDN provides potential operations and infrastructure cost savings because a company can outsource its dialup equipment, thereby avoiding the costs of being in the remote access server business.

Figure 5-16 *VPDN for Remote Access*

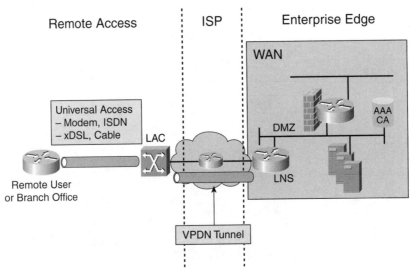

Access VPN connectivity involves the configuration of VPDN tunnels. Following are the two types of tunnels:

- The client PC initiates *voluntary tunnels*. The client dials into the SP network, a PPP session is established, and the user logs on to the SP network. The client then runs the VPN software to establish a tunnel to the network server.

- *Compulsory tunnels* require SP participation and awareness, giving the client no influence over tunnel selection. The client still dials in and establishes a PPP session, but the SP (not the client) establishes the tunnel to the network server.

Peer-to-Peer VPNs

In a peer-to-peer VPN, the provider actively participates in customer routing.

Traditional peer-to-peer VPNs are implemented with packet filters on shared provider edge (PE) routers, or with dedicated per-customer PE routers. In addition to high maintenance costs for the packet filter approach or equipment costs for the dedicated per-customer PE-router approach, both methods require the customer to accept the provider-assigned address space or to use public IP addresses in the private customer network.

Modern *MPLS VPNs* provide all the benefits of peer-to-peer VPNs and alleviate most of the peer-to-peer VPN drawbacks such as the need for common customer addresses. Overlapping addresses, which are usually the result of companies using private addressing, are one of the major obstacles to successful peer-to-peer VPN implementations. MPLS VPNs solve this problem by giving each VPN its own routing and forwarding table in the router, thus effectively creating virtual routers for each customer.

> **NOTE**   RFC 4364, *BGP/MPLS IP Virtual Private Networks (VPNs)*, defines MPLS VPNs.

With MPLS VPNs, networks are learned via static route configuration or with a routing protocol such as OSPF, EIGRP, Routing Information Protocol (RIP) version 2 (RIPv2), or Border Gateway Protocol (BGP) from other internal routers. As described in the earlier "MPLS" section, MPLS uses a label to identify a flow of packets. MPLS VPNs use an additional label to specify the VPN and the corresponding VPN destination network, allowing for overlapping addresses between VPNs.

Benefits of VPNs

The benefits of using VPNs include the following:

- **Flexibility**: VPNs offer flexibility because site-to-site and remote-access connections can be set up quickly and over existing infrastructure to extend the network to remote users. Extranet connectivity for business partners is also a possibility. A variety of security policies can be provisioned in a VPN, thereby enabling flexible interconnection of different security domains.

- **Scalability**: VPNs allow an organization to leverage and extend the classic WAN to more remote and external users. VPNs offer scalability over large areas because IP transport is universally available. This arrangement reduces the number of physical connections and simplifies the underlying structure of a customer's WAN.

- **Lower network communication cost**: Lower cost is a primary reason for migrating from traditional connectivity options to a VPN connection. Reduced dialup and dedicated bandwidth infrastructure and service provider costs make VPNs attractive. Customers can reuse existing links and take advantage of the statistical packet multiplexing features.

WAN Backup Strategies

This section describes various backup options for providing alternative paths for remote access. WAN links are relatively unreliable compared to LAN links and often are much slower than the LANs to which they connect. This combination of uncertain reliability, lack of speed, and high importance makes WAN links good candidates for redundancy to achieve high availability.

Branch offices should experience minimum downtime in case of primary link failure. A backup connection can be established, either via dialup or by using permanent connections. The main WAN backup options are as follows:

- Dial backup routing

- Permanent secondary WAN link

- Shadow PVC

The following sections describe these options.

Dial Backup Routing

Dial backup routing is a way of using a dialup service for backup purposes. In this scenario, the switched circuit provides the backup service for another type of circuit, such as point-to-point or Frame Relay. The router initiates the dial backup line when it detects a failure on the primary circuit. The dial backup line provides WAN connectivity until the primary circuit is restored, at which time the dial backup connection terminates.

Permanent Secondary WAN Link

Deploying an additional permanent WAN link between each remote office and the central office makes the network more fault-tolerant. This solution offers the following two advantages:

- **Provides a backup link**: The backup link is used if a primary link that connects any remote office with the central office fails. Routers automatically route around failed WAN links by using floating static routes and routing protocols, such as EIGRP and OSPF. If one link fails, the router recalculates and sends all traffic through another link, allowing applications to proceed if a WAN link fails, thereby improving application availability.

> **NOTE**   A *floating* static route is one that appears in the routing table only when the primary route goes away. The administrative distance of the static route is configured to be higher than the administrative distance of the primary route, and it "floats" above the primary route until the primary route is no longer available.

- **Increased bandwidth**: Both the primary and secondary links can be used simultaneously because they are permanent. The routing protocol automatically performs load balancing between two parallel links with equal costs (or unequal costs if EIGRP is used). The resulting increased bandwidth decreases response times.

Cost is the primary disadvantage of duplicating WAN links to each remote office. For example, in addition to new equipment, including new WAN router interfaces, a large star network with 20 remote sites might need 20 new virtual circuits.

In Figure 5-17, the connections between the Enterprise Edge and remote sites use permanent primary and secondary WAN links for redundancy. A routing protocol, such as EIGRP, that supports load balancing over unequal paths on either a per-packet or per-destination basis is used to increase the utilization of the backup link.

Figure 5-17 *Permanent Secondary WAN Link*

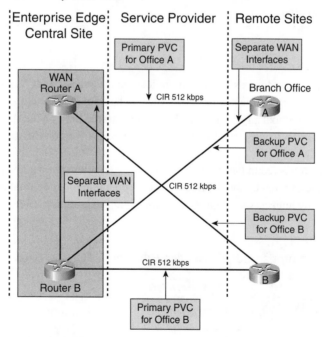

If the WAN connections are relatively slow (less than 56 kbps), per-packet load balancing should be used. Load balancing occurs on a per-destination basis when fast switching is enabled, which is appropriate on WAN connections faster than 56 kbps.

Switching Modes: Process, Fast, and Other Modes

During process switching, the router examines the incoming packet and looks up the Layer 3 address in the routing table, which is located in main memory, to associate this address with a destination network or subnet. Process switching is a scheduled process performed by the system processor. Compared to other switching modes, process switching is slow because of the latency caused by scheduling and the latency within the process itself.

With fast switching, an incoming packet matches an entry in the fast-switching cache (also called the *route cache*), which is located in main memory. This cache is populated when the first packet to the destination is process-switched. Fast switching is done via asynchronous interrupts, which are handled in real time and result in higher throughput.

Other switching modes are available on some routers (including Autonomous Switching, Silicon Switching, Optimum Switching, Distributed Switching, and NetFlow Switching). Cisco Express Forwarding (CEF) technology, described in Chapter 4, is the latest advance in Cisco IOS switching capabilities for IP.

Shadow PVC

With shadow PVCs, as long as the maximum load on the shadow PVC does not exceed a certain rate (such as one-fourth of the primary speed) while the primary PVC is available, the SP provides a secondary PVC without any additional charge. If the traffic limit on the shadow PVC is exceeded while the primary PVC is up, the SP charges for the excess load on the shadow PVC.

Figure 5-18 illustrates redundant connections between remotes sites and the Enterprise Edge using the shadow PVCs offered by the SP. Because of the potential for additional costs, the routers must avoid sending any unnecessary data (except, for example, routing traffic) over the shadow PVC.

Figure 5-18 *Shadow PVC*

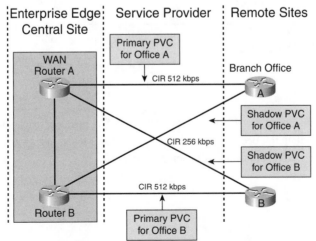

The Internet as a WAN Backup Technology

This section describes the Internet as an alternative option for a failed WAN connection. This type of connection is considered best-effort and does not guarantee any bandwidth. Common methods for connecting noncontiguous private networks over a public IP network include the following:

- IP routing without constraints

- GRE tunnels

- IPsec tunnels

The following sections describe these methods.

IP Routing Without Constraints

When relying on the Internet to provide a backup for branch offices, a company must fully cooperate with the ISP and announce its networks. The backup network—the Internet—therefore becomes aware of the company's data, because it is sent unencrypted.

Layer 3 Tunneling with GRE and IPsec

Layer 3 tunneling uses a Layer 3 protocol to transport over another Layer 3 network. Typically, Layer 3 tunneling is used either to connect two noncontiguous parts of a non-IP network over an IP network or to connect two IP networks over a backbone IP network, possibly hiding the IP addressing details of the two networks from the backbone IP network. Following are the two Layer 3 tunneling methods for connecting noncontiguous private networks over a public IP network:

- **GRE**: A protocol developed by Cisco that encapsulates a wide variety of packet types inside IP tunnels. GRE is designed for generic tunneling of protocols. In the Cisco IOS, GRE tunnels IP over IP, which can be useful when building a small-scale IP VPN network that does not require substantial security.

  GRE enables simple and flexible deployment of basic IP VPNs. Deployment is easy; however, tunnel provisioning is not very scalable in a full-mesh network because every point-to-point association must be defined separately. The packet payload is not protected against sniffing and unauthorized changes (no encryption is used), and no sender authentication occurs.

  Using GRE tunnels as a mechanism for backup links has several drawbacks, including administrative overhead, scaling to large numbers of tunnels, and processing overhead of the GRE encapsulation.

- **IPsec**: IPsec is both a tunnel encapsulation protocol and a security protocol. IPsec provides security for the transmission of sensitive information over unprotected networks (such as the Internet) by encrypting the tunnel's data. IPsec acts as the network layer in tunneling or transport mode and protects and authenticates IP packets between participating IPsec devices. Following are some features of IPsec:

  — **Data confidentiality**: An IPsec sender can encrypt packets before transmitting them across a network.

  — **Data integrity**: An IPsec receiver can authenticate packets sent by an IPsec sender to ensure that the data has not been altered during transmission.

  — **Data origin authentication**: An IPsec receiver can authenticate the source of the sent IPsec packets. This service depends on the data integrity service.

  — **Anti-replay**: An IPsec receiver can detect and reject replay by rejecting old or duplicate packets.

  — **Easy deployment**: IPsec can be deployed with no change to the intermediate systems (the ISP backbone) and no change to existing applications (it is transparent to applications).

  — **Internet Key Exchange (IKE)**: IPsec uses IKE for automated key management.

  — **Public Key Infrastructure (PKI)**: IPsec is interoperable with PKI.

IPsec can be combined with GRE tunnels to provide security in GRE tunnels; for example, the GRE payload (the IP packet) would be encrypted.

NOTE   Routing protocols cannot be run over IPsec tunnels because there is no standard for IPsec to encrypt the broadcast or multicast packets used by IP routing protocols. Instead of using IPsec tunnels with routing protocols, use GRE tunnels with IPsec as the security protocol. GRE tunnels encapsulate the original IP packet—whether it is unicast, multicast, or broadcast—within a unicast packet, destined for the other end of the GRE tunnel.

IPsec and IKE

Because it is standards-based, IPsec allows Cisco devices to interoperate with other non-Cisco IPsec-compliant networking devices, including PCs and servers. IPsec also allows the use of digital certificates using the IKE protocol and certification authorities (CA). A *digital certificate* contains information to identify a user or device, such as the name, serial number, company, or IP address. It also contains a copy of the device's public key. The CA, which is a third party that the receiver explicitly trusts to validate identities and create digital certificates, signs the certificate. When using digital certificates, each device is enrolled with a CA. When two devices want to communicate, they exchange certificates and digitally sign data to authenticate each other. Manual exchange and verification of keys are not required.

When a new device is added to the network, it must simply enroll with a CA; none of the other devices need modification. When the new device attempts an IPsec connection, certificates are automatically exchanged, and the device can be authenticated.

Figure 5-19 illustrates two noncontiguous networks connected over a point-to-point logical link with a backup implemented over an IP network using a GRE IP tunnel. Such tunnels are configured between a source (ingress) router and a destination (egress) router and are visible as interfaces on each router.

Figure 5-19 *Backup GRE Tunnel over a Public IP Network*

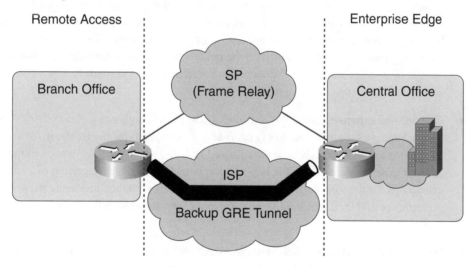

Data to be forwarded across the tunnel is already formatted in a packet, encapsulated in the standard IP packet header. This packet is further encapsulated with a new GRE header and placed into the tunnel with the destination IP address set to the tunnel endpoint, the new next hop. When the GRE packet reaches the tunnel endpoint, the GRE header is stripped away and the packet continues to be forwarded to the destination with the original IP packet header.

Enterprise Edge WAN and MAN Architecture

Recall from Chapter 3, "Structuring and Modularizing the Network," that the Cisco Service-Oriented Network Architecture (SONA) Enterprise Edge and the WAN and MAN modules are represented as the Enterprise Edge functional area of the Cisco Enterprise Architectures. This section describes the Enterprise Edge WAN and MAN architectures and technologies.

Enterprise Edge WAN and MAN Considerations

When selecting Enterprise Edge technologies, consider the following factors:

- **Support for network growth**: Enterprises that anticipate significant growth should choose a technology that allows the network to grow with their business. WAN technologies with high support for network growth make it possible to add new branches or remote offices with minimal configuration at existing sites, thus minimizing the costs and IT staff requirements for such changes. WAN technologies with lower support for network growth require significantly more time, effort, and cost to expand the network.

- **Appropriate availability**: Businesses heavily affected by even the smallest disruption in network communications should consider high availability an important characteristic when choosing a connectivity technology. Highly available technologies provide inherent redundancy where no single point of failure exists in the network. Lower-availability technologies can still dynamically recover from a network disruption in a short time period, but this minor disruption might be too costly for some businesses. Technologies that do not inherently provide high availability can be made more available through redundancy in design, by using products with redundant characteristics such as multiple WAN connections, and by using backup power supplies.

- **Operational expenses**: Some WAN technologies result in higher costs than others. A private-line technology such as Frame Relay or ATM, for example, typically results in higher carrier fees than a technology such as an IPsec-based IP VPN, which takes advantage of the public Internet to help reduce costs. It is important to note, however, that migrating to a particular technology for the sole purpose of reducing carrier fees, without considering network performance and QoS, can limit support for some advanced technologies such as voice and video.

- **Operational complexity**: Cisco MAN and WAN technologies have varying levels of inherent technical complexity, so the level of technical expertise required within the enterprise also varies. In most cases, businesses can upgrade their MAN or WAN and take advantage of the expertise of the existing IT staff, requiring minimal training. When an enterprise wants to maintain greater control over its network by taking on responsibilities usually borne by an SP, extensive IT training could be required to successfully deploy and manage a particular WAN technology.

- **Voice and video support**: Most Cisco MAN and WAN technologies support QoS, which helps enable advanced applications such as voice and video over the network. In cases where a WAN technology uses an SP with a Cisco QoS-certified multiservice IP VPN, an adequate level of QoS is assured to support voice and video traffic. In cases where the public Internet is used as the WAN connection, however, QoS cannot always be guaranteed, and a high-bandwidth broadband connection might be required for small offices, teleworkers, and remote contact center agents using voice and video communications.

- **Effort and equipment cost to migrate from private connectivity**: When an enterprise is migrating from private connectivity to another technology, it is important to evaluate the short- and long-term costs and benefits of this migration. In many cases, this is accomplished with minimal investment in equipment, time, and IT staffing. In some instances, however, this migration requires a significant short-term investment, not only in new equipment, but also in IT training. Such an investment might also provide long-term increased cost savings, lower operational expenditures, and increased productivity.

- **Network segmentation support**: Network segmentation means supporting a single network that is logically segmented. One advantage of network segmentation is that it reduces expenditures associated with equipment and maintenance, network administration, and network carrier charges as compared to separate physical networks. Another advantage is increased security; segmentation can help isolate departments or limit partners' access to the corporate network.

Cisco Enterprise MAN and WAN Architecture Technologies

The Cisco Enterprise MAN and WAN architecture employs a number of MAN and WAN technologies engineered and optimized to interoperate as a contiguous system, providing the integrated QoS, network security, reliability, and manageability required to support a variety of advanced business applications and services. These technologies include a number of secure alternatives to traditional private WAN connectivity and help increase network scalability and reduce monthly carrier fees. The Cisco Enterprise MAN and WAN architecture includes the following technologies, as summarized in Table 5-4:

- **Private WAN**: Private connectivity takes advantage of existing Frame Relay, ATM, or other connections. To provide an additional level of security when connecting sites, strong encryption (using Digital Encryption Standard [DES], Triple DES [3DES], and Advanced Encryption Standard [AES]) can be added. A private WAN is ideally suited for an enterprise with moderate growth expectations, where relatively few new branches or remote offices will be deployed over the coming years. Businesses that require secure, dedicated, and reliable connectivity for compliance with information privacy standards, and that also require support for advanced applications such as voice and video, benefit from encrypted private connectivity. However, this technology can result in relatively high recurring monthly carrier fees and is not the preferred technology for extending connectivity to teleworkers and remote call agents. An enterprise might choose encrypted private connectivity to network its larger branch offices, but opt for other technologies, such as a VPN, to connect remote users and smaller sites.

- **ISP service (site-to-site and remote-access IPsec VPN)**: These technologies take advantage of the ubiquity of public and private IP networks. The use of strong encryption standards (DES, 3DES, and AES) makes this WAN option more secure than traditional private connectivity and makes it compliant with the many new information security regulations imposed on government and industry groups (such as healthcare and finance). When implemented over the public Internet, IPsec VPNs are best suited for businesses that require basic data connectivity. However, if support for delay-sensitive, advanced applications such as voice and video is required, an IPsec VPN should be implemented over an SP's private network where an adequate level of QoS is assured to support voice and video traffic. Relatively low monthly carrier fees make this technology appropriate for businesses seeking to connect a high number of teleworkers, remote contact center agents, or small remote offices over a geographically dispersed area.

- **SP MPLS and IP VPN**: A network-based IP VPN is similar in many ways to private connectivity, but with added flexibility, scalability, and reach. The any-to-any nature of an MPLS-enabled IP VPN (any branch can be networked to any branch), combined with its comprehensive QoS for voice and video traffic, suits the needs of many enterprises, especially those with high growth expectations, where many new branches and remote offices will be added over the next few years. The secure, reliable connectivity and relatively lower carrier fees that are inherent in this technology make a network-based IP VPN a good choice for businesses looking to use a managed service solution to connect branches, remote offices, teleworkers, and remote call agents.

- **Self-deployed MPLS**: Self-deployed MPLS is a network segmentation technique that allows enterprises to logically segment the network. Self-deployed MPLS is typically reserved for very large enterprises or an SP willing to make a significant investment in network equipment and training, and for those that have an IT staff that is comfortable with a high degree of technical complexity.

Table 5-4 *Cisco Enterprise WAN and MAN Architecture Comparison*

	Private WAN	ISP Service (Site-to-Site and Remote-Access IPsec VPN)	SP MPLS and IP VPN	Self-Deployed MPLS
Secure transport	IPsec (optional)	IPsec (mandatory)	IPsec (mandatory)	IPsec (mandatory)
High availability	Excellent	Good	Excellent	Excellent
Multicast	Good	Good	Good	Excellent
Voice and video support	Excellent	Low	Excellent	Excellent
Scalable network growth	Moderate	Good	Excellent	Excellent
Easily shared WAN links	Moderate	Moderate	Moderate	Excellent

Table 5-4   *Cisco Enterprise WAN and MAN Architecture Comparison (Continued)*

	Private WAN	ISP Service (Site-to-Site and Remote-Access IPsec VPN)	SP MPLS and IP VPN	Self-Deployed MPLS
Operational costs	High	Low	Moderate; depends on transport	Moderate to high
Network control	High	Moderate	Moderate	High
Effort to migrate from private WAN	Low	Moderate	Moderate	High

Enterprises can use a combination of these technologies to support their remote connectivity requirements. Figure 5-20 shows a sample implementation of a combination of three technologies in a healthcare environment.

Figure 5-20   *Sample Cisco WAN Architectures in a Healthcare Environment*

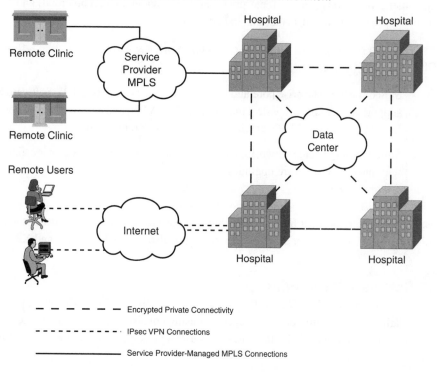

Selecting Enterprise Edge Components

After identifying the remote connectivity requirements and architecture, you are ready to select the individual WAN components.

Hardware Selection

When selecting hardware, use the vendor documentation to evaluate the WAN hardware components. The selection process typically considers the function and features of the particular devices, including their port densities, packet throughput, expandability capabilities, and readiness to provide redundant connections.

Software Selection

The next step is to select the appropriate software features; when using Cisco equipment, the software is the Cisco IOS. As illustrated in Figure 5-21, the Cisco IOS Software has been optimized for different markets, network roles, and platforms. Cisco IOS Software meets the requirements of various markets (enterprise, service provider, and commercial) and places in the network (access, core and distribution, and edge).

KEY POINT | Suited for access layer devices, Cisco IOS Software T releases support advanced technology business solutions.

Suited for the enterprise core and service provider edge, Cisco IOS Software S releases support voice transport, video, multicast, MPLS VPN, and advanced technologies, such as Layer 2 and Layer 3 VPN and integrated services architecture.

Suited for large-scale networks, Cisco IOS Software XR releases provide high availability with in-service software upgrades.

Cisco IOS software product lines share a common base of technologies. Most of the features available in the T releases for a given technology are also available in the S and XR releases.

Cisco IOS Software Packaging

Cisco is migrating to using *Cisco IOS Packaging* to simplify the image-selection process by consolidating the total number of packages and using consistent package names across all hardware products. Figure 5-22 illustrates the various packages available with Cisco IOS packaging.

Figure 5-21 *Cisco IOS Software in the Network*

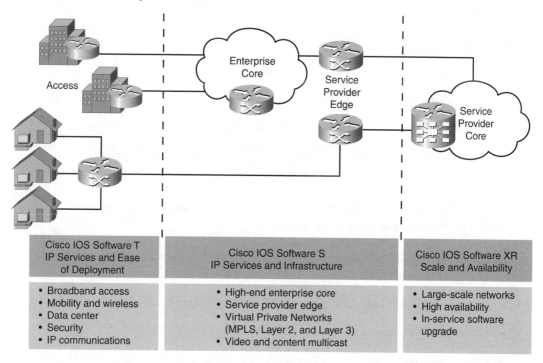

Cisco IOS Software T IP Services and Ease of Deployment	Cisco IOS Software S IP Services and Infrastructure	Cisco IOS Software XR Scale and Availability

• Broadband access
• Mobility and wireless
• Data center
• Security
• IP communications
	• High-end enterprise core
	• Service provider edge
	• Virtual Private Networks
	  (MPLS, Layer 2, and Layer 3)
	• Video and content multicast
		• Large-scale networks
		• High availability
		• In-service software
		  upgrade

Figure 5-22 *Cisco IOS Packaging*

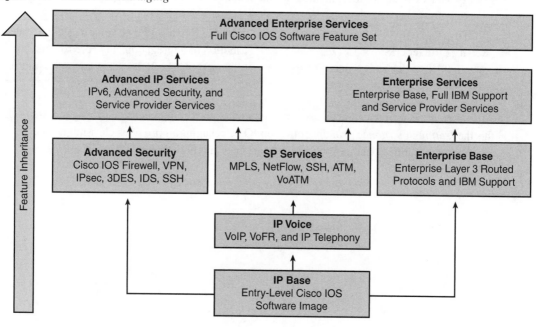

Four packages have been designed to satisfy the requirements in *base service* categories; they are as follows:

- **IP Base**: Supports IP data

- **IP Voice**: Supports converged voice and data

- **Advanced Security**: Provides security and VPN

- **Enterprise Base**: Provides enterprise Layer 3 protocols and IBM support

> **NOTE**   The features of the lower-tier packages are included in the higher-tier packages.

Three additional premium packages offer new Cisco IOS Software feature combinations that address more complex network requirements:

- **SP Services**: Adds SP features, including MPLS, ATM, Secure Shell (SSH) and NetFlow, to the IP Voice package

- **Advanced IP Services**: Adds advanced SP services to the Advanced Security package

- **Enterprise Services**: Adds advanced SP services to the Enterprise Base package

Advanced Enterprise Services, which integrates support for all routing protocols with voice, security, and VPN capabilities, includes all the features of the other packages.

> **NOTE**   Cisco IOS Packaging is available for Cisco IOS Release 12.3 on some Cisco Integrated Services Routers (ISR). Most Cisco access, distribution or aggregation, and core routers, and other hardware that runs Cisco IOS software, will support Cisco IOS Packaging in the future.

After a feature is introduced, it is also included in the more comprehensive packages. Cisco calls this the *feature inheritance principle* of Cisco IOS Packaging; it provides clear migration, clarifying the feature content of the various packages and how they relate to one another.

Cisco IOS Packaging Technology Segmentation

Table 5-5 illustrates some of the technologies supported in the various Cisco IOS packages.

Table 5-5 *Cisco IOS Packaging Technology Segmentation*

	Data Connectivity	VoIP and VoFR[1]	ATM, VoATM[2], MPLS	AppleTalk, IPX[3], IBM Protocols	Firewall, IDS[4], VPN
IP Base	X				
IP Voice	X	X			
Advanced Security	X				X
Enterprise Base	X			X	
SP Services	X	X	X		
Advanced IP Services	X	X	X		X
Enterprise Services	X	X	X	X	
Advanced Enterprise Services	X	X	X	X	X

[1] VoFR = Voice over Frame Relay

[2] VoATM = Voice over ATM

[3] IPX = Internetwork Packet Exchange

[4] IDS = Intrusion Detection System

KEY POINT Use the Cisco Feature Navigator at http://www.cisco.com/go/fn/ to quickly find the right Cisco IOS and Catalyst operating system software release for the features that you want to run on your network.

Comparing the Functions of Cisco Router Platforms and Software Families

Table 5-6 compares the functions of the Cisco router platforms and the software families that support them.

NOTE The specific router platforms and software releases available will change over time; refer to http://www.cisco.com/ for the latest information.

Table 5-6   *Comparing Cisco Router Platforms and Software Features*

Hardware	Software	Function
800, 1800, 2800, 3800, 7200	Cisco IOS T Releases 12.3, 12.4, 12.3T, 12.4T	Supports access routing platforms, providing fast, scalable delivery of mission-critical enterprise applications
7200, 7301, 7304, 7500, 10000	Cisco IOS S Release 12.2SB	Delivers midrange broadband and leased-line aggregation for Enterprise and SP Edge networks
7600	Cisco IOS S Release 12.2SR	Delivers high-end Ethernet LAN switching for Enterprise access, distribution, core, and data center deployments, and high-end Metro Ethernet for the SP Edge
12000, CRS-1	Cisco IOS XR	Provides massive scale, continuous system availability, and service flexibility for SP core and edge (takes advantage of the massively distributed processing capabilities of the Cisco CRS-1 and the Cisco 12000)

Comparing the Functions of Multilayer Switch Platforms and Software Families

Table 5-7 compares the functions of the Cisco multilayer switch platforms and the software families that support them.

> **NOTE**   The specific multilayer switch platforms and software releases available will change over time; refer to http://www.cisco.com/ for the latest information.

Table 5-7   *Comparing Cisco Multilayer Switch Platforms and Software Features*

Hardware	Software	Function
800, 1800, 2800, 3800, 7200	Cisco IOS S Release 12.2SE	Provides low-end to midrange Ethernet LAN switching for Enterprise access and distribution deployments
4500, 4900	Cisco IOS S Release 12.2SG	Provides midrange Ethernet LAN switching for Enterprise access and distribution deployments in the campus, and supports Metro Ethernet
6500	Cisco IOS S Release 12.2SX	Delivers high-end Ethernet LAN switching for Enterprise access, distribution, core, and data center deployments, and high-end Metro Ethernet for the SP Edge

Enterprise Branch and Teleworker Design

This section describes design considerations for the Enterprise Branch and Enterprise Teleworker architectures.

Enterprise Branch Architecture

Recall that the Cisco Enterprise Architecture, based on the Cisco SONA, includes branch modules that focus on the remote places in the network. Enterprises are seeking opportunities to protect, optimize, and grow their businesses by increasing security; consolidating voice, video, and data onto a single IP network; and investing in applications that will improve productivity and operating efficiencies. These services provide enterprises with new opportunities to reduce costs, improve productivity, and safeguard information assets in all their locations.

The Cisco Enterprise Branch architecture takes into account the services that enterprises want to deploy at their endpoints, no matter how far away the endpoints are or how they are connected. Figure 5-23 illustrates how branch services relate to the other parts of the Cisco Enterprise architectures.

> **NOTE**   Teleworker architecture is covered in the later "Enterprise Teleworker (Branch of One) Design" section.

Figure 5-23   *Enterprise Branch Services*

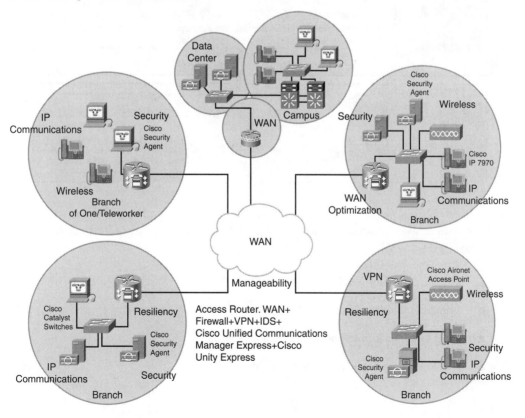

The Cisco Enterprise Branch Architecture, illustrated in Figure 5-24, is an integrated, flexible, and secure framework for extending headquarters applications in real time to remote sites. The Cisco Enterprise Branch Architecture applies the SONA framework to the smaller scale of a branch location.

Figure 5-24 *Enterprise Branch Architecture*

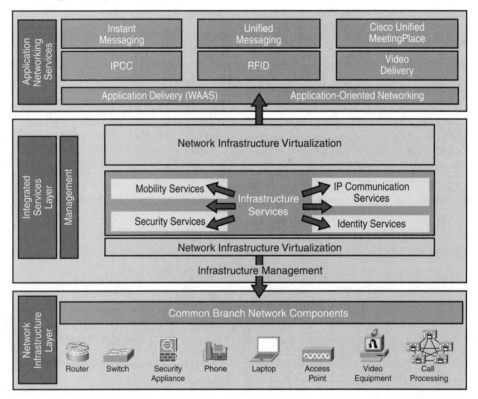

Common network components that might be implemented in the Enterprise Branch include the following:

■ Routers providing WAN edge connectivity

■ Switches providing the LAN infrastructure

■ Security appliances defending the branch devices

■ Wireless access points for device mobility

- Call-processing and video equipment for IP telephony and video support

- End-user devices, including IP phones and computers

Enterprise Branch Design

Requirements differ with the size of the branch offices. Consider to the following questions when designing the Enterprise Branch:

- How many branch locations need to be supported?

- How many existing devices (including end users, hosts, and network infrastructure) are to be supported at each location? The number of devices supported is limited by the physical number of ports available.

- How much growth is expected at each location, and therefore what level of scalability is required?

- What are the high availability requirements at each location?

- What level of security is required in the design? Should security be managed locally or through the central location?

- Are there any requirements for local server farms or networks between the internal network and the external network (for example, in a demilitarized zone [DMZ])?

- Should network management be supported locally or via the central location?

- What wireless services are needed, and how will they be used by the clients? What effect will the network and the environment have on the wireless devices?

- What is the approximate budget available?

KEY POINT | Branch offices can be categorized based on the number of users:

- **Small office**: Up to 50 users, using a single-tier design

- **Medium office**: Between 50 and 100 users, using a dual-tier design

- **Large office**: Between 100 and 200 users, using a three-tier design

The number of devices, high availability, scalability, and migration to advanced services requirements also influence the model adopted. The design models for each of these types of branches are described in the following sections.

Each of the designs in the following sections suggests using an ISR (such as the 2800 series routers) at the WAN edge, which provides various voice, security, and data services that are integrated with the LAN infrastructure. Depending on the specific ISR edge router chosen, the interfaces and modules available include the following:

■   Integrated LAN interfaces (10/100/1000 Mbps)

■   High-speed WAN interface card (HWIC) slots

■   Network modules

■   Embedded security

Alternatively, Cisco multiservice routers (such as the 2600 series routers) can be used.

Small Branch Office Design

Small branch office designs combine an ISR access router with Layer 2 switching and end-user devices, phones, printers, and so forth; a typical design is illustrated in Figure 5-25.

Figure 5-25 *Typical Small Branch Office Design*

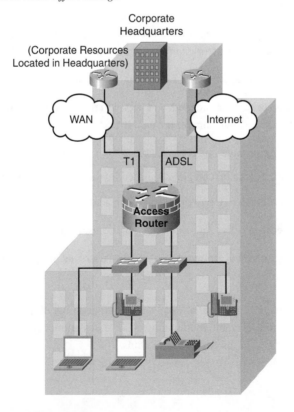

ISR and Switch Connections

The ISR connects with Layer 2 switch ports in one of the following three ways:

- **Integrated switching within the ISR (or multiservice router)**: This option has a lower port density that supports from 16 to 48 client devices on either a Cisco EtherSwitch network module or a Cisco EtherSwitch service module. It provides a one-box solution that offers ease of management. Depending on the module, the integrated switch ports might provide power to end devices using Power over Ethernet (PoE).

- **Trunked network interface on the ISR to external access switches**: In this case, there is no link redundancy between the access switches and the ISR. The access switches might provide power to end devices using PoE.

- **Logical EtherChannel interface between the ISR and access switches**: This approach uses an EtherSwitch module in the ISR configured as an EtherChannel. Link redundancy is provided to the access layer switches over the EtherChannel. The access switches might provide power to end devices using PoE.

If redundant access layer links and higher-bandwidth uplinks are required, only the third option, with higher-performance devices, can be used. The choice of the edge router also depends on the voice and VPN support needed.

The access switch provides Layer 2 services, and the Cisco ISR provides Layer 3 services such as Dynamic Host Configuration Protocol (DHCP), firewall, and Network Address Translation.

The 2811 ISR or larger ISR is suggested. Both the Cisco 2821 and 2851 ISRs support two integrated 10/100/1000 routed (Layer 3) interfaces and have one slot for a network module. The Cisco 2821 ISR supports the 16-port EtherSwitch network module and the 24-port EtherSwitch service module. The Cisco 2851, 3825, and 3845 ISRs can support the high-density 48-port EtherSwitch service module.

Typical access switches include the Cisco Catalyst 2960, 3560, and 3750 Series switches.

To keep manageability simple, the topology has no loops; however, spanning tree must be enabled and configured to protect the network from any accidental loops. As is the case in the Enterprise Campus, the recommended spanning-tree protocol is Rapid Per-VLAN Spanning Tree Plus for all Layer 2 deployments in a branch office environment.

The ISR is the default gateway for each VLAN configured in the topology, and all Layer 3 configurations are done on the ISR. The access switches must be configured with an IP address for management purposes.

WAN Services

WAN services are typically provided by a T1 primary link. The Internet is used as a WAN backup, accessed by an ADSL connection.

Network Services

The EIGRP routing protocol is used. High availability across the WAN is provided by a floating static route across the ADSL Internet connection.

QoS mechanisms used include traffic shaping and policing, and the implementation of a scavenger class of traffic (applied on both the switch and the ISR).

QoS Classes

As mentioned in Chapter 4, end-to-end QoS is provided for IP version 4 using Layer 3 QoS marking in the 8-bit Type of Service (ToS) field in the packet header. Originally, only the first 3 bits were used; these bits are called the IP Precedence bits. Because 3 bits can specify only eight marking values, IP precedence does not allow a granular classification of traffic. Thus, more bits are now used: The first 6 bits in the TOS field are now known as the *DSCP bits*.

Cisco has created a QoS Baseline that provides recommendations to ensure that its products, and the designs and deployments that use them, are consistent in terms of QoS. Although the QoS Baseline document itself is internal to Cisco, it includes an 11-class classification scheme that can be used for enterprises. The classes of traffic in the QoS Baseline are defined as follows:

- **IP Routing class**: This class is for IP routing protocol traffic such as EIGRP, OSPF, and so forth.

- **Voice class**: This class is for VoIP bearer traffic (the conversation traffic), not for the associated signaling traffic, which would go in the Call Signaling class.

- **Interactive Video class**: This class is for IP videoconferencing traffic.

- **Streaming Video class**: This class is for either unicast or multicast unidirectional video.

- **Mission-Critical Data class**: This class is intended for a subset of the Transactional Data applications that are most significant to the business. The applications in this class are different for every organization.

- **Call Signaling class**: This class is intended for voice and video-signaling traffic.

- **Transactional Data class**: This class is intended for user-interactive applications such as database access, transactions, and interactive messaging.

- **Network Management class**: This class is intended for traffic from network management protocols, such as Simple Network Management Protocol.

- **Bulk Data class**: This class is intended for background, noninteractive traffic, such as large file transfers, content distribution, database synchronization, backup operations, and e-mail.

- **Scavenger class**: This class is based on an Internet 2 draft that defines a "less-than-Best-Effort" service. If a link becomes congested, this class is dropped the most aggressively. Any nonbusiness-related traffic (for example, downloading music in most organizations) could be put into this class.

- **Best Effort class**: This class is the default class. Unless an application has been assigned to another class, it remains in this default class. Most enterprises have hundreds, if not thousands, of applications on their networks; the majority of these applications remain in the Best Effort class.

The QoS Baseline does not mandate that these 11 classes be used; rather, this classification scheme is an example of well-designed traffic classes. Enterprises can have fewer classes, depending on their specific requirements, and can evolve to using more classes as they grow.

Medium Branch Office Design

A typical medium branch office topology, illustrated in Figure 5-26, is similar to the small office topology, except that the WAN edge devices are larger, typically two Cisco 2821 or Cisco 2851 ISRs, and the access switches for LAN connectivity are external stackable switches.

Figure 5-26   *Typical Medium Branch Office Design*

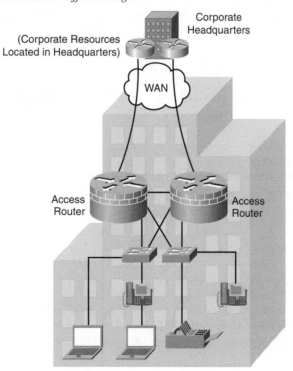

ISR and Switch Connections

To scale up to 100 users, the following options are available:

■ Use a higher port density external access switch

■ Use an ISR module that supports switched access ports; use EtherChannel to provide a redundant connection to the access switches

This design uses the integrated 10/100/1000 interfaces on the ISRs as Layer 3 trunks, providing the flexibility to use various access switches. The stackable Cisco Catalyst 3750 Series switch with an IP Base image or an IP Services image can be used as the access switch, supporting 24 or 48 users per switch. The IP Base image feature set includes advanced QoS, rate limiting, ACLs, and basic static and RIP routing capability. The IP Services image provides a richer set of enterprise-class features, including advanced hardware-based IP unicast and multicast routing. An additional Advanced IP Services license is also available (for example, this license is required for IPv6 routing).

With Cisco StackWise technology, a single 32-Gbps switching unit can be created, using up to nine Cisco Catalyst 3750 Series switches. Cisco StackWise technology uses special stack-interconnect cables and stacking software. The stack behaves as a single switching unit that is managed by a master switch elected from one of the member switches. The master switch automatically creates and updates all the switching and optional routing tables. The number of PoE ports supported depends on the specific access switch selected.

WAN Services

WAN services are typically provided by a private WAN—for example, with dual Frame Relay links.

Network Services

The EIGRP routing protocol is used. High availability across the WAN is provided by dual routers running router redundancy protocols such as Hot Standby Router Protocol (HSRP), Virtual Router Redundancy Protocol (VRRP), and Gateway Load-Balancing Protocol (GLBP) (as described in Chapter 4). QoS mechanisms used include traffic shaping and policing, and the implementation of a scavenger class of traffic (applied on both the switch and the ISR).

Large Branch Office Design

In a typical large branch office design, illustrated in Figure 5-27, dual ISRs are used for redundancy at the WAN edge. Firewall functionality is provided by dual adaptive security appliances (ASA), and dual multilayer switches (stackable or modular) are deployed at the distribution layer.

Figure 5-27   *Typical Large Branch Office Design*

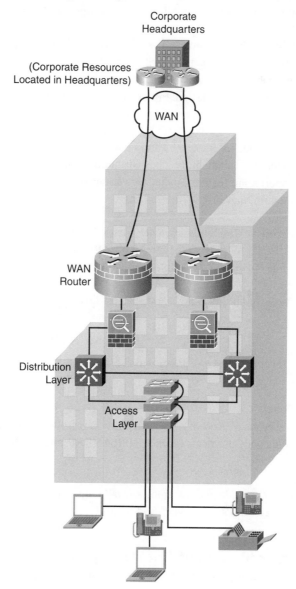

ISR and Switch Connections

In addition to supporting more users, a large office might need higher LAN switching capability if supporting a server farm or DMZ. Support for some of these services requires the use of appliance devices if higher throughput is required. To meet these requirements, a distribution layer is added to the topology by introducing a multilayer switch that provides the required LAN switching capabilities, port density, and flexibility to support additional appliances.

Either a stackable switch (for example, a Cisco Catalyst 3750 Series switch) or a Cisco Catalyst 4500 Series switch could be used at the distribution layer. This LAN topology is highly available, scalable, and manageable. High-availability requirements are met by the link redundancy and device redundancy built into the design. For example, redundant links are used to provide high availability between the distribution and edge layers.

The port density of the stacked switches allows a number of access switches to be connected without compromising high availability. The distribution switches typically run the advanced IOS images, which support more features, including various routing protocols and advanced features such as policy-based routing.

If Cisco Catalyst 3560 or 3750 Series switches are used at the access layer, other Layer 2 security features, such as DHCP snooping, Dynamic Address Resolution Protocol (ARP) Inspection (DAI), and IP Source Guard, can be enabled, providing additional security measures.

The default gateways for all the VLANs at the access layer are on the distribution layer.

WAN Services
WAN services in this typical design are provided by an MPLS network with dual connections.

Network Services
The EIGRP routing protocol is used. High availability across the WAN is provided by dual routers running router redundancy protocols (such as HSRP, VRRP, and GLBP), ASA failover functionality, and object tracking.

QoS mechanisms used include traffic shaping and policing, and the implementation of a scavenger class of traffic (applied on both the switch and the ISR).

Enterprise Teleworker (Branch of One) Design

Organizations are constantly striving to reduce costs, improve employee productivity, and retain valued employees. These goals can be furthered by allowing employees to work from home with quality, function, performance, convenience, and security similar to that available in the office. With a work environment in the residence, employees can optimally manage their work schedules, allowing for higher productivity (less affected by office distractions) and greater job satisfaction (flexibility in schedule). This transparent extension of the enterprise to employee homes is the objective of the Cisco Enterprise Teleworker (or Branch of One) architecture.

Occasional remote users have much lighter application requirements than part-time and full-time teleworkers. They can connect through a wireless hotspot or a guest network at a hotel and have little control over network resiliency and availability.

In contrast, Enterprise teleworkers can be differentiated from other forms of work-at-home or telecommuting scenarios in that the emphasis is on delivering seamless, managed accessibility to the full range of applications and services critical to the operational effectiveness of enterprises, as illustrated in Figure 5-28. The Cisco Enterprise Teleworker architecture is part of the overall secure Cisco Enterprise architecture infrastructure. It companies the capability to integrate and securely manage their remote workers within the corporate network while simultaneously providing a high-quality end-user experience supporting a full range of enterprise applications for the enterprise teleworker.

Figure 5-28 *Comparison of Teleworking Options*

	Occasional Users / Occasional Remote Worker	Part-Time or Full-Time and Day Extenders / Branch of One
E-mail	Yes	Yes
Web-based applications	Yes	Yes
Mission-critical applications	Best effort	Prioritized
Real-time collaboration	Best effort	Prioritized
Voice over IP	Best effort	High quality
Video on demand, Cisco IP/TV	Unlikely	High quality
Videoconferencing	Unlikely	High quality
Remote configuration and management	No	Yes
Integrated security	Basic	Full
Resiliency and availability	No	Yes

The enterprise teleworker typically connects to an ISP through a DSL or cable modem and might use an analog dialup session to back up this connection. The enterprise teleworker solution is implemented with a small ISR, such as the Cisco 871, 876, 877, or 878 ISR, with integrated switch ports, connected behind a broadband modem, as shown in Figure 5-29. This solution uses a transparent, always-on VPN tunnel back to the enterprise.

Figure 5-29 *Teleworker (Branch of One) Architecture*

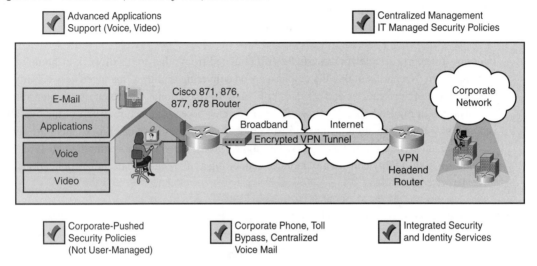

Within this architecture, centralized management means that the enterprise applies security policies, pushes configurations, and periodically tests the connection through the broadband cloud and back to the corporate office to determine the latency, jitter, and packet loss experienced at any time. This solution supports advanced applications such as voice and video as part of the full suite of enterprise services for the end user. For example, a teleworker can access the central-office IP telephone system from home with comparable voice quality and can thereby take advantage of the higher-function IP telephony capabilities instead of using the PSTN.

An alternative solution is an unmanaged VPN approach in which the end user implements a software VPN from a PC across a generic broadband router, access point, or hub appliance. This solution typically cannot support the level of feature integration, QoS, and managed support needed to reliably deliver voice, video, multimedia, and traditional data to the end user, but it might be appropriate for occasional remote users with lighter application requirements.

Summary

In this chapter, you learned about remote connectivity network design with a focus on the following topics:

- Definition of a WAN and the types of WAN interconnections

- Various WAN technologies, including TDM, ISDN, Frame Relay, ATM, MPLS, Metro Ethernet, DSL, cable, wireless, SONET/SDH, DWDM, and dark fiber

- WAN pricing and contract considerations

- WAN design methodology, including the application and technical requirement aspects of WAN design

- WAN bandwidth optimization techniques

- Use of various WAN technologies for remote access, VPNs, WAN backup, and connecting to the Internet as a backup WAN

- Enterprise Edge WAN and MAN architectures and technologies

- Selection of WAN components, including hardware and software

- Enterprise Branch and Enterprise Teleworker design considerations

References

For additional information, refer to the following resources:

- Cisco Systems, Inc., Product Documentation, http://www.cisco.com/univercd/home/home.htm

- Cisco Systems, Inc., *Solution Reference Network Design Guides* home page, http://www.cisco.com/go/srnd/

- Cisco Systems, Inc., *Enterprise QoS Solution Reference Network Design Guide*, http://www.cisco.com/application/pdf/en/us/guest/netsol/ns432/c649/ccmigration_09186a008049b062.pdf

- Cisco Systems, Inc., *Frame Relay* technical overview, http://www.cisco.com/univercd/cc/td/doc/cisintwk/ito_doc/frame.htm

- Cisco Systems, Inc., *MPLS and Tag Switching* technical overview, http://www.cisco.com/univercd/cc/td/doc/cisintwk/ito_doc/mpls_tsw.htm

- Cisco Systems, Inc., *Enterprise Architectures,* http://www.cisco.com/en/US/netsol/ns517/networking_solutions_market_segment_solutions_home.html

- Cisco Systems, Inc., Cisco product index for routers, http://www.cisco.com/en/US/products/hw/routers/index.html

- Cisco Systems, Inc., Cisco product index for switches, http://www.cisco.com/en/US/products/hw/switches/index.html

- Cisco Systems, Inc., Cisco Feature Navigator, http://www.cisco.com/go/fn

- Cisco Systems, Inc., *Cisco IOS Packaging: Introduction*, http://www.cisco.com/en/US/ products/sw/iosswrel/ps5460/index.html

- Cisco Systems, Inc., *Business Ready Branch Solutions for Enterprise and Small Offices— Reference Design Guide*, http://www.cisco.com/application/pdf/en/us/guest/netsol/ns656/ c649/cdccont_0900aecd80488134.pdf

- Cisco Systems, Inc., *LAN Baseline Architecture Branch Office Network Reference Design Guide*, http://www.cisco.com/univercd/cc/td/doc/solution/designex.pdf

- Cisco Systems, Inc., *LAN Baseline Architecture Overview—Branch Office Network*, http:// www.cisco.com/univercd/cc/td/doc/solution/lanovext.pdf

- Cisco Systems, Inc., *Cisco Business Ready Teleworker Architecture*, http://www.cisco.com/ application/pdf/en/us/guest/netsol/ns430/c654/cdccont_0900aecd800df177.pdf

Case Study: ACMC Hospital Network WAN Design

This case study is a continuation of the ACMC Hospital case study introduced in Chapter 2, "Applying a Methodology to Network Design."

Case Study General Instructions

Use the scenarios, information, and parameters provided at each task of the ongoing case study. If you encounter ambiguities, make reasonable assumptions and proceed. For all tasks, use the initial customer scenario and build on the solutions provided thus far. You can use any and all documentation, books, white papers, and so on.

In each step, you act as a network design consultant. Make creative proposals to accomplish the customer's business needs. Justify your ideas when they differ from the provided solutions. Use any design strategies you feel are appropriate. The final goal of each case study is a paper solution.

Appendix A, "Answers to Review Questions and Case Studies," provides a solution for each step based on assumptions made. There is no claim that the provided solution is the best or only solution. Your solution might be more appropriate for the assumptions you made. The provided solution helps you understand the author's reasoning and allows you to compare and contrast your solution.

In this case study, you create a high-level design for the WAN portions of the ACMC Hospital network.

Case Study Additional Information

Figure 5-30 shows the existing WAN links and the planned campus infrastructure.

Figure 5-30 *Case Study ACMC Hospital WAN Links and Planned Campus Infrastructure*

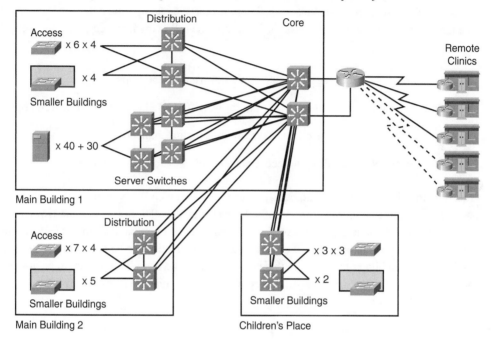

Business Factors

The ACMC Hospital CIO realizes that WAN performance to the remote clinics is poor and that some new applications will require more bandwidth. These applications include programs that allow doctors at the central site to access medical images, such as digital X-rays, stored locally at the clinics. The CIO wants all the remote sites to have the same type of access.

The CIO wants to implement a long-term, cost-effective solution that allows high-bandwidth application deployment on the network and that allows for growth for the next two to five years. The CIO also wants to simplify planning, pricing, and deployment of future applications.

Technical Factors

There is no data about the bandwidth requirements of the new applications. Lab testing would provide better data, but ACMC does not have the time or money for testing. The CIO knows that because TCP adjusts to use the available bandwidth, such that when congestion occurs, there is no way to know how much bandwidth the present applications could ideally use unless extensive lab testing is done.

You discover that your site contact initially supplied you with an out-of-date network diagram. The hospital upgraded the 56 kbps links to 128 kbps a year ago and upgraded the WAN bandwidth at the largest clinic to 256 kbps last month. Therefore, the following is the current state of the WAN links:

- The connection to the largest remote clinic now runs at 256 kbps.

- The connections to two other remote clinics were upgraded from 56 kbps to 128 kbps.

- The two remaining remote clinics have 56-kbps dialup connectivity.

The increased WAN bandwidth you recommend should last for two to five years.

For situations in which you cannot really determine how much WAN bandwidth is needed, one way to proceed is to multiply current traffic levels by a value of 1.5 or 2 per year. However, if the customer does not want to be concerned with needing even more bandwidth in the near future, multiply by bigger numbers. If you expect unknown applications to be added to the network, multiply by even bigger numbers. In this case study, assume that all clinics are to be upgraded to at least T1 access speed. (Pricing structures in many areas might even favor a full T1 over fractional T1 links.)

Case Study Questions

Complete the following steps:

Step 1   Develop a list of relevant information that should be provided in the ACMC WAN Request for Proposal (RFP).

Step 2   ACMC put out an RFP specifying that it requires at least T1 bandwidth at the remote clinics. The responses to the RFP, indicating the technologies currently available to ACMC, are shown in Table 5-8.

Calculate the monthly cost of using each of the technologies shown in Table 5-8 by completing the Monthly Cost column in this table.

Table 5-8 *ACMC RFP Results*

Option	Technology	Speed	Price per Month	Monthly Cost
1	Leased line: T1 at clinics into T3 at central	T1 or T3	$400 for each T1, $8000 for T3	
2	Frame Relay: T1 access at clinics, T3 access at central	T1 or T3	$350 for T1 access, $7000 for T3 access circuit plus CIR in 5-Mbps increments times $75 plus $5 per PVC	

Table 5-8 *ACMC RFP Results (Continued)*

Option	Technology	Speed	Price per Month	Monthly Cost
3	MPLS VPN: T1 access at clinics, T3 access at central	T1 or T3	$500 for T1 access, $8500 for T3 access	
4	High-speed business cable service at clinics T3 Internet at central site	6 Mbps downstream, 768 kbps upstream T3	$90 $4000	

Step 3   Which technology do you recommend that ACMC use? (Using either multilink PPP over multiple T1s or using multilink Frame Relay over multiple T1s are also options.)

NOTE   To simplify this step, budgetary costs are not included for the routers. Make your choice based on capabilities needed, with the understanding that there is an increasing cost for increasing capabilities and options.

Step 4   ACMC mentions that its images might be 100 MB. Transferring 100-MB images over a T1 connection takes more than 8 minutes (because 100 MB * 8 bits per byte / 1.544 Mbps = 518 seconds = 8.6 minutes). Does this information change your recommendation? Why or why not?

Step 5   The CIO indicates that remote site availability is critical to avoid having servers in the remote clinics. What redundancy or backup WAN strategy do you recommend?

Step 6   Assume that the CIO has chosen to deploy multilink PPP over two T1s for simple, reliable service at each remote clinic, with the 6 Mbps cable service as backup. Select an appropriate Cisco router model to use at the central site and at each remote location. Select appropriate switching hardware for each site, remembering that the ISR routers can use integrated switches. Table 5-9 provides the number of switch ports needed at each of the remote clinics. Tables 5-10 and 5-11 provide a condensed version of the product and module information from http://www.cisco.com/.

Table 5-9 *Remote Clinic Switch Port Requirements*

Remote Clinic Site	Number of Switch Ports Needed
1	48
2, 3	24
4, 5	16

Table 5-10 *ISR Routers and Port Capabilities*

Cisco ISR Model	Approx. Mbps of Layer 3 Fast Ethernet or CEF Switching with 64-Byte Packets	LAN Ports	WAN Ports
851	5.12	10/100 four-port switch	10/100 Fast Ethernet
857	5.12	10/100 four-port switch	ADSL
871	12.8	10/100 four-port switch	10/100 Fast Ethernet
876	12.8	10/100 four-port switch	ADSL over ISDN
877	12.8	10/100 four-port switch	ADSL
878	12.8	10/100 four-port switch	G.SHDSL
1801	35.84	10/100 eight-port switch	One Fast Ethernet, ADSL over POTS
1802	35.84	10/100 eight-port switch	One Fast Ethernet, ADSL over ISDN
1803	35.84	10/100 eight-port switch	One Fast Ethernet, G.SHDSL
1811	35.84	10/100 eight-port switch	Two Fast Ethernet
1812	35.84	10/100 eight-port switch	Two Fast Ethernet
1841	38.40	Two Fast Ethernet. Can add four-port switch with HWIC-4ESW.	Can add two HWIC modules: ADSL WAN Interface Card (WIC), G.SHDSL WIC, cable WIC, WIC-1T (one T1), WIC-2T (two T1)
2801	46.08	Two 10/100 Fast Ethernet	Four slots: two slots support HWIC-, WIC-, VIC-, or VWIC-type modules; one slot supports WIC-, VIC-, or VWIC-type modules; one slot supports VIC or VWIC-type modules Can add WIC modules listed for 1841, also HWIC-4T (four T1 HWIC)
2811	61.44	Two 10/100 Fast Ethernet	Four slots: each slot can support HWIC-, WIC-, VIC-, or VWIC-type modules. Can add WIC modules listed for 1841, also HWIC-4T (four T1 HWIC). Plus, one slot supports NM- and NME-type modules Can use NM-1HSSI (T3)

Table 5-10 *ISR Routers and Port Capabilities (Continued)*

Cisco ISR Model	Approx. Mbps of Layer 3 Fast Ethernet or CEF Switching with 64-Byte Packets	LAN Ports	WAN Ports
2821	87.04	Two 10/100 Fast Ethernet	Four slots: each slot can support HWIC-, WIC-, VIC-, or VWIC-type modules; can add WIC modules listed for 1841, also HWIC-4T (four T1 HWIC) Plus, one slot supports NM-, NME-, and NME-X-type modules Can use NM-1HSSI
2851	112.64	Two 10/100 Fast Ethernet	Four slots: each slot can support HWIC-, WIC-, VIC-, or VWIC-type modules. Can add WIC modules listed for 1841, also HWIC-4T (four T1 HWIC). Plus, one slot supports NM-, NME-, NME-X-, NMD-, and NME-XD-type modules Can use NM-1HSSI
3825	179.20	Two Gigabit Ethernet (10/100/1000)	Two NM/NME/NME-X modules or one NMD/NME-XD Four HWIC/WIC/VIC/VWIC slots For relevant NM and WIC/HWICs, see modules listed for 2851
3845	256	Two Gigabit Ethernet (10/100/1000)	Four NM/NME/NME-X modules or two NMD/NME-XDs Four HWIC/WIC/VIC/VWIC slots For relevant NM and WIC/HWICs, see modules listed for 2851

Table 5-11 *Switch Network Modules for Cisco 2800 and 3800 Series Integrated Services Routers*

Module	NME-16ES-1G	NME-16ES-1G-P	NME-X-23ES-1G	NME-X-23ES-1G-P	NME-XD-24ES-1S-P	NME-XD-48ES-2S-P
Limitations	2811 and up only Any 3800	2811 and up only Any 3800	2821 and 2851 only Any 3800	2821 and 2851 only Any 3800	2851 only Any 3800	2851 only Any 3800
Ports	10/100: 16 10/100/1000: 1 Small Form Factor Pluggable (SFP): 0	10/100: 16 10/100/1000: 1 SFP: 0	0/100: 23 10/100/1000: 1 SFP: 0	10/100/1000: 1 10/100: 23 SFP: 0	10/100: 24 10/100/1000: 0 SFP: 1	10/100: 48 10/100/1000: 0 SFP: 2
Powered Switch Ports	0	16	0	24	24	48
IEEE 802.3af POE Support	No	Yes	No	Yes	Yes	Yes

Up to two of the four-port HWICs can be used for switch HWICs in the Cisco 1841 ISR.

Nine-port switch HWICs are also available for Cisco 2800 and 3800 Series ISRs; two of them can be used per 2800 or 3800 router.

Step 7   What design changes would you suggest if the CIO decided that a second router should be used for the backup link at each site?

Review Questions

Answer the following questions, and then refer to Appendix A for the answers.

1. What is the definition of a WAN?

2. What are some typical WAN design objectives?

3. Why are fully meshed networks not always appropriate?

4. What comprises a T1 circuit?

5. Why is ISDN better than analog dialup for data connections?

6. What is an MPLS Forwarding Equivalence Class?

7. How many bits are in the MPLS label field?

8. True or false: Packets sent from Device A to Device B through an MPLS network always take the same path through the network.

9. What is the difference between ADSL and SDSL?

10. Define downstream and upstream.

11. Identify the following key ADSL devices shown in Figure 5-31:

    Layer 3 concentrator

    Layer 2 concentrator or DSLAM

    Splitter

    ADSL CPE

Figure 5-31 *ADSL Devices*

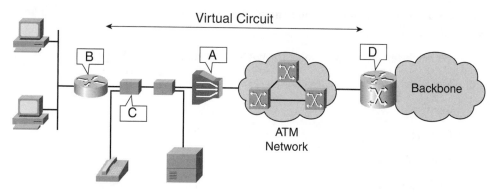

12. What type of cable is used for each of the following?

    ADSL

    VDSL

    Cable

    LRE

13. Which of the following two statements do not describe the operation of cable networks?

    a. The CMTS enables the coax users to connect with either the PSTN or the Internet.

    b. The actual bandwidth for Internet service over a cable TV line is shared 2.5 Mbps on the download path to the subscriber, with about 27 Mbps of shared bandwidth for interactive responses in the other direction.

    c. All cable modems can receive from and send signals to the CMTS and other cable modems on the line.

    d. DOCSIS defines the interface between the cable modem and the CMTS.

14. For what purpose is bridged wireless used?

15. Indicate the frequency and maximum speeds of the following WLAN standards:

    802.11a

    802.11b

    802.11g

16. What is the difference between SONET and SDH?

17. What is Packet over SONET/SDH (POS)?

18. Compare the response time and throughput requirements of a file transfer and an interactive application.

19. Which technologies are suitable for WAN connections over 50 Mbps?

20. Match the terms with their definitions:

    Terms:

    Compression

    Bandwidth

    Response time

    Window size

    Throughput

    Definitions:

    Amount of data transmitted or received per unit time

    Maximum number of frames (or amount of data) the sender can transmit before it must wait for an acknowledgment

Amount of data successfully moved from one place to another in a given time period

Reduction of data size for the purpose of saving transmission time

Time between a user request (such as the entry of a command or keystroke) and the host system's command execution or response delivery

21. What is multilink PPP?

22. What can be done if WAN links are constantly congested?

23. Match each of the following queuing mechanisms with its definition:

Queuing mechanisms:

WFQ

PQ

CQ

CBWFQ

LLQ

Definitions:

Allows sensitive data such as voice to be sent first

Enabled by default on most low-speed serial interfaces (with speeds at or below 2.048 Mbps) on Cisco routers

Establishes up to 16 configurable interface output queues

Reserves a queue for each class

Establishes four interface output queues (high, medium, normal, and low)

24. What is the difference between an overlay VPN and VPDN?

25. What is IPsec?

26. What is the difference between an SP MPLS IP VPN and a self-deployed MPLS network?

27. Describe the four base packages in Cisco IOS Packaging.

28. What is the typical number of users in small, medium, and large branch offices?

29. What is Cisco StackWise technology?

30. Which models of Cisco ISRs would be appropriate for a teleworker?

This chapter discusses IP addressing design and includes the following sections:

- Designing an IP Addressing Plan

- Introduction to IPv6

- Summary

- References

- Case Study: ACMC Hospital IP Addressing Design

- Review Questions

CHAPTER 6

Designing IP Addressing in the Network

This chapter begins with a discussion of the design of an Internet Protocol (IP) version 4 (IPv4) addressing scheme. It continues with an introduction to IP version 6 (IPv6) and a discussion of IPv4-to-IPv6 migration strategies.

> **NOTE** In this chapter, the term *IP* refers to IPv4.

Designing an IP Addressing Plan

This section explores private and public address types, how to determine the size of the network in relation to the addressing plan, and how to plan an IP addressing hierarchy. The section concludes with a discussion of various IP address assignment and name resolution methods.

> **NOTE** Appendix B, "IPv4 Supplement," and Chapter 1, "Network Fundamentals Review," include detailed information about IPv4 addressing. You are encouraged to review any of the material in Appendix B and Chapter 1 that you are not familiar with before reading the rest of this chapter.

Private and Public IPv4 Addresses

Recall from Chapter 1 that the IP address space is divided into public and private spaces. Private addresses are reserved IP addresses that are to be used only internally within a company's network, not on the Internet. Private addresses must therefore be mapped to a company's external registered address when sending anything on the Internet. Public IP addresses are provided for external communication. Figure 6-1 illustrates the use of private and public addresses in a network.

Figure 6-1 *Private and Public Addresses Can Be Used in a Network*

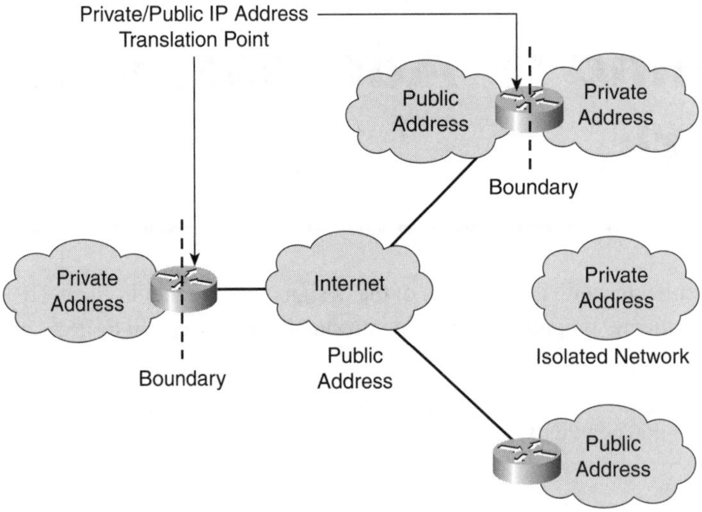

RFC 1918, *Address Allocation for Private Internets*, defines the private IP addresses as follows:

- 10.0.0.0 to 10.255.255.255

- 172.16.0.0 to 172.31.255.255

- 192.168.0.0 to 192.168.255.255

The remaining addresses are public addresses.

Private Versus Public Address Selection Criteria

Very few public IP addresses are currently available, so Internet service providers (ISPs) can assign only a subset of Class C addresses to their customers. Therefore, in most cases, the number of public IP addresses assigned to an organization is inadequate for addressing their entire network.

The solution to this problem is to use private IP addresses within a network and to translate these private addresses to public addresses when Internet connectivity is required. When selecting addresses, the network designer should consider the following questions:

- Are private, public, or both IP address types required?

- How many end systems need only access to the public network? This is the number of end systems that need a limited set of external services (such as e-mail, file transfer, or web browsing) but do not need unrestricted external access. These end systems do not have to be visible to the public network.

■ How many end systems must have access to and be visible to the public network? This is the number of Internet connections and various servers that must be visible to the public network (such as public servers and servers used for e-commerce, such as web servers, database servers, and application servers) and defines the number of required public IP addresses. These end systems require globally unambiguous IP addresses.

■ Where will the boundaries between the private and public IP addresses be, and how will they be implemented?

Interconnecting Private and Public Addresses

According to its needs, an organization can use both public and private addresses. A router or firewall acts as the interface between the network's private and public sections.

When private addresses are used for addressing in a network and this network must be connected to the Internet, Network Address Translation (NAT) or Port Address Translation (PAT) must be used to translate from private to public addresses and vice versa. NAT or PAT is required if accessibility to the public Internet or public visibility is required.

Static NAT is a one-to-one mapping of an unregistered IP address to a registered IP address. *Dynamic NAT* maps an unregistered IP address to a registered IP address from a group of registered IP addresses. *NAT overloading*, or *PAT*, is a form of dynamic NAT that maps multiple unregistered IP addresses to a single registered IP address by using different port numbers. As shown in Figure 6-2, NAT or PAT can be used to translate the following:

■ **One private address to one public address**: Used in cases when servers on the internal network with private IP addresses must be visible from the public network. The translation from the server's private IP address to the public IP address is defined statically.

■ **Many private addresses to one public address**: Used for end systems that require access to the public network but do not have to be visible to the outside world.

■ **Combination**: It is common to see a combination of the previous two techniques deployed throughout networks.

Figure 6-2   *Private to Public Address Translation*

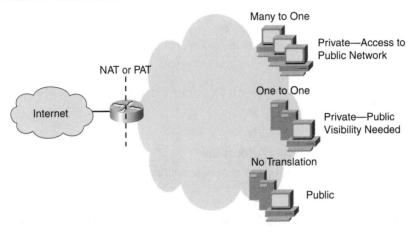

> **NOTE**   As mentioned, the addresses typically used on internal networks are private addresses, and they are translated to public addresses. However, NAT and PAT can be used to translate between any two addresses.

For additional details about NAT and PAT, see Appendix D, "Network Address Translation."

Guidelines for the Use of Private and Public Addresses in an Enterprise Network

As shown in Figure 6-3, the typical enterprise network uses both private and public IP addresses.

Private IP addresses are used throughout the Enterprise Campus, Enterprise Branch, and Enterprise Teleworker modules. The following modules include public addresses:

■   The Internet Connectivity module, where public IP addresses are used for Internet connections and publicly accessible servers.

■   The E-commerce module, where public IP addresses are used for the database, application, and web servers.

■   The Remote Access and virtual private network (VPN) module, the Enterprise Data Center module, and the WAN and metropolitan-area network (MAN) and Site-to-Site VPN module, where public IP addresses are used for certain connections.

Figure 6-3   *Private and Public IP Addresses Are Used in the Enterprise Network*

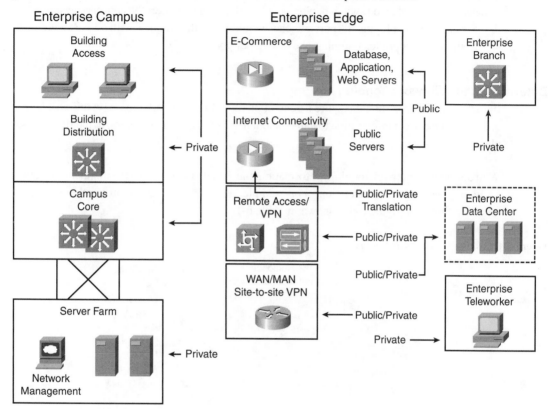

Determining the Size of the Network

The first step in designing an IP addressing plan is determining the size of the network to establish how many IP subnets and how many IP addresses are needed on each subnet. To gather this information, answer the following questions:

- **How many locations does the network consist of?**: The designer must determine the number and type of locations.

- **How many devices in each location need addresses?**: The network designer must determine the number of devices that need to be addressed, including end systems, router interfaces, switches, firewall interfaces, and any other devices.

- **What are the IP addressing requirements for individual locations?**: The designer must collect information about which systems will use dynamic addressing, which will use static addresses, and which systems can use private instead of public addresses.

■ **What subnet size is appropriate?**: Based on the collected information about the number of networks and planned switch deployment, the designer estimates the appropriate subnet size. For example, deploying 48-port switches would mean that subnets with 64 host addresses would be appropriate, assuming one device per port.

Determining the Network Topology

Initially, the designer should acquire a general picture of the network topology; this will help determine the correct information to gather about network size and its relation to the IP addressing plan.

With this general network topology information, the designer determines the number of locations, location types, and their correlations. For example, the network location information for the topology shown in Figure 6-4 is shown in Table 6-1.

Figure 6-4 *Sample Network Topology*

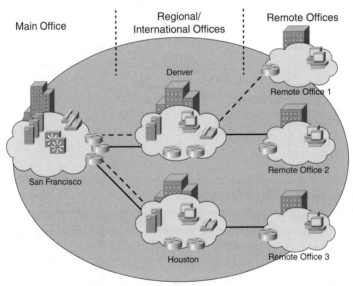

Table 6-1 *Network Location Information for the Topology in Figure 6-4*

Location	Type	Comments
San Francisco	Main office	The central location where the majority of users are located
Denver	Regional office	Connects to the San Francisco main office
Houston	Regional office	Connects to the San Francisco main office

Table 6-1 *Network Location Information for the Topology in Figure 6-4 (Continued)*

Location	Type	Comments
Remote Office 1	Remote office	Connects to the Denver regional office
Remote Office 2	Remote office	Connects to the Denver regional office
Remote Office 3	Remote office	Connects to the Houston regional office

Size of Individual Locations

The network size, in terms of the IP addressing plan, relates to the number of devices and interfaces that need an IP address. To establish the overall network size in a simplistic way, the designer determines the approximate number of workstations, servers, Cisco IP phones, router interfaces, switch management and Layer 3 interfaces, firewall interfaces, and other network devices at each location. This estimate provides the minimum overall number of IP addresses that are needed for the network. Table 6-2 provides the IP address requirements by location for the topology shown in Figure 6-4.

Table 6-2 *IP Addressing Requirements by Location for the Topology in Figure 6-4*

Location	Office Type	Workstations	Servers	IP Phones	Router Interfaces	Switches	Firewall and Other Device Interfaces	Reserve	Total
San Francisco	Main	600	35	600	17	26	12	20%	1290
Denver	Regional	210	7	210	10	4	0	20%	441
Houston	Regional	155	5	155	10	4	0	20%	329
Remote Office 1	Remote	12	1	12	2	1	0	10%	28
Remote Office 2	Remote	15	1	15	3	1	0	10%	35
Remote Office 3	Remote	8	1	8	3	1	0	10%	21
Total		1000	50	1000	45	37	12		2144

Some additional addresses should be reserved to allow for seamless potential network growth. The commonly suggested reserve is 20 percent for main and regional offices, and 10 percent for remote offices; however, this can vary from case to case. The designer should carefully discuss future network growth with the organization's representative to obtain a more precise estimate of the required resources.

Planning the IP Addressing Hierarchy

The IP addressing hierarchy influences network routing. This section describes IP addressing hierarchy and how it reduces routing overhead. This section discusses the issues that influence the IP addressing plan and the routing protocol choice, including summarization, fixed-length subnet masking, variable-length subnet masking, and classful and classless routing protocols.

NOTE   Chapter 7, "Selecting Routing Protocols for the Network," discusses routing protocols in detail.

Hierarchical Addressing

The telephone numbering system is a hierarchical system. For example, the North American Numbering Plan includes the country code, the area code, the local exchange, and the line number.

The telephone architecture has handled *prefix routing*, or routing based only on the prefix part of the address, for many years. For example, a telephone switch in Detroit, Michigan does not have to know how to reach a specific line in Portland, Oregon. It must simply recognize that the call is not local. A long-distance carrier must recognize that area code 503 is for Oregon, but it does not have to know the details of how to reach the specific line in Oregon.

The IP addressing scheme is also hierarchical, and prefix routing is not new in the IP environment either. As in the telephone example, IP routers make hierarchical decisions. Recall that an IP address comprises a prefix part and a host part. A router has to know only how to reach the next hop; it does not have to know the details of how to reach an end node that is not local. Routers use the prefix to determine the path for a destination address that is not local. The host part is used to reach local hosts.

Route Summarization

With route summarization, also referred to as *route aggregation* or *supernetting*, one route in the routing table represents many other routes. Summarizing routes reduces the routing update traffic (which can be important on low-speed links) and reduces the number of routes in the routing table and overall router overhead in the router receiving the routes. In a hierarchical network design, effective use of route summarization can limit the impact of topology changes to the routers in one section of the network.

If the Internet had not adapted route summarization by standardizing on classless interdomain routing (CIDR), it would not have survived.

CIDR

CIDR is a mechanism developed to help alleviate the problem of IP address exhaustion and growth of routing tables. The idea behind CIDR is that blocks of multiple addresses (for example, blocks of Class C address) can be combined, or aggregated, to create a larger (that is, more hosts allowed), classless set of IP addresses. Blocks of Class C network numbers are allocated to each network service provider; organizations using the network service provider for Internet connectivity are allocated subsets of the service provider's address space as required. These multiple Class C addresses can then be summarized in routing tables, resulting in fewer route advertisements. (Note that the CIDR mechanism can be applied to blocks of Class A, B, and C addresses; it is not restricted to Class C.) CIDR is described in RFC 1519, *Classless Inter-Domain Routing (CIDR): An Address Assignment and Aggregation Strategy*.

For summarization to work correctly, the following requirements must be met:

- Multiple IP addresses must share the same leftmost bits.

- Routers must base their routing decisions on a 32-bit IP address and a prefix length of up to 32 bits.

- Routing protocols must carry the prefix length with the 32-bit IP address.

For example, assume that a router has the following networks behind it:

> 192.168.168.0/24
>
> 192.168.169.0/24
>
> 192.168.170.0/24
>
> 192.168.171.0/24
>
> 192.168.172.0/24
>
> 192.168.173.0/24
>
> 192.168.174.0/24
>
> 192.168.175.0/24

Each of these networks could be advertised separately; however, this would mean advertising eight routes. Instead, this router can summarize the eight routes into one route and advertise 192.168.168.0/21. By advertising this one route, the router is saying, "Route packets to me if the destination has the first 21 bits the same as the first 21 bits of 192.168.168.0."

Figure 6-5 illustrates how this summary route is determined. The addresses all have the first 21 bits in common and include all the combinations of the other 3 bits in the network portion of the address; therefore, only the first 21 bits are needed to determine whether the router can route to one of these specific addresses.

Figure 6-5 *Find the Common Bits to Summarize Routes*

192.168.168.0 =	11000000 10101000 10101	000	00000000
192.168.169.0 =	11000000 10101000 10101	001	00000000
192.168.170.0 =	11000000 10101000 10101	010	00000000
192.168.171.0 =	11000000 10101000 10101	011	00000000
192.168.172.0 =	11000000 10101000 10101	100	00000000
192.168.173.0 =	11000000 10101000 10101	101	00000000
192.168.174.0 =	11000000 10101000 10101	110	00000000
192.168.175.0 =	11000000 10101000 10101	111	00000000

Number of Common Bits = 21
Number of Non-Common Network Bits = 3
Number of Host Bits = 8

IP Addressing Hierarchy Criteria

IP addressing hierarchy has an important impact on the routing protocol choice, and vice versa. The decision about how to implement the IP addressing hierarchy is usually based on the following questions:

■ Is hierarchy needed within the IP addressing plan?

■ What are the criteria for dividing the network into route summarization groups?

■ How is route summarization performed, and what is the correlation with routing?

■ Is a hierarchy of route summarization groups required?

■ How many end systems does each route summarization group or subgroup contain?

Benefits of Hierarchical Addressing

A network designer decides how to implement the IP addressing hierarchy based on the network's size, geography, and topology. In large networks, hierarchy within the IP addressing plan is mandatory for a stable network (including stable routing tables). For the following reasons, a planned, hierarchical IP addressing structure, with room for growth, is recommended for networks of all sizes:

■ **Influence of IP addressing on routing**: An IP addressing plan influences the network's overall routing. Before allocating blocks of IP addresses to various parts of the network and assigning IP addresses to devices, consider the criteria for an appropriate and effective IP addressing scheme. Routing stability, service availability, network scalability, and modularity are some crucial and preferred network characteristics and are directly affected by IP address allocation and deployment.

■ **Modular design and scalable solutions**: Whether building a new network or adding a new service on top of an existing infrastructure, a modular design helps to deliver a long-term, scalable solution. IP addressing modularity allows the aggregation of routing information on a hierarchical basis.

■ **Route aggregation**: Route aggregation is used to reduce routing overhead and improve routing stability and scalability. However, to implement route aggregation, a designer must be able to divide a network into contiguous IP address areas and must have a solid understanding of IP address assignment, route aggregation, and hierarchical routing.

Summarization Groups

To reduce the routing overhead in a large network, a multilevel hierarchy might be required. The depth of hierarchy depends on the network size and the size of the highest-level summarization group. Figure 6-6 shows an example of a network hierarchy.

Figure 6-6 *IP Addressing Hierarchy*

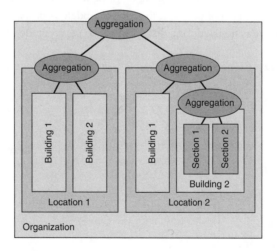

A typical organization has up to three levels of hierarchy:

■ **First level**: Network locations typically represent the first level of hierarchy in enterprise networks. Each location typically represents a group of summarized subnets, known as a *summarization group*.

- **Second level**: A second level of hierarchy can be done within first-level summarization groups. For example, a large location can be divided into smaller summarization groups that represent the buildings or cities within that location. Not all first-level summarization groups require a second level of hierarchy.

- **Third level**: To further minimize the potential routing overhead and instability, a third level of hierarchy can exist within the second-level summarization group. For example, sections or floors within individual buildings can represent the third-level summarization group.

Impact of Poorly Designed IP Addressing

A poorly designed IP addressing scheme usually results in IP addresses that are randomly assigned on an as-needed basis. In this case, the IP addresses are most likely dispersed through the network with no thought as to whether they can be grouped or summarized. A poor design provides no opportunity for dividing the network into contiguous address areas, and therefore no means of implementing route summarization.

Figure 6-7 is a sample network with poorly designed IP addressing; it uses a dynamic routing protocol. Suppose that a link in the network is *flapping* (changing its state from UP to DOWN, and vice versa) ten times per minute. Because dynamic routing is used, the routers that detect the change send routing updates to their neighbors, those neighbors send it to their neighbors, and so on. Because aggregation is not possible, the routing update is propagated throughout the entire network, even if there is no need for a distant router to have detailed knowledge of that link.

Figure 6-7   *A Poorly Designed IP Addressing Scheme Results in Excess Routing Traffic*

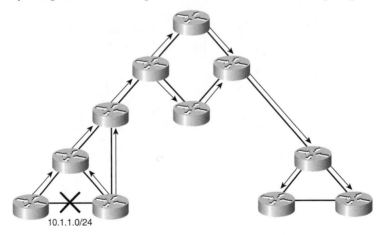

10.1.1.0/24

Impacts of poorly designed IP addressing include the following:

■ **Excess routing traffic consumes bandwidth**: When any route changes, routers send routing updates. Without summarization, more updates are sent, and the routing traffic consumes more bandwidth.

■ **Increased routing table recalculation**: Routing updates require routing table recalculation, which affects the router's performance and ability to forward traffic.

■ **Possibility of routing loops**: When too many routing changes prevent routers from converging with their neighbors, routing loops might occur, which might have global consequences for an organization.

Benefits of Route Aggregation

Implementing route aggregation on border routers between contiguously addressed areas controls routing table size. Figure 6-8 shows an example of implementing route summarization (aggregation) on the area borders in a sample network. If a link within an area fails, routing updates are not propagated to the rest of the network, because only the summarized route is sent to the rest of the network, and it has not changed; the route information about the failed link stays within the area. This reduces bandwidth consumption related to routing overhead and relieves routers from unnecessary routing table recalculation.

Figure 6-8 *A Hierarchical IP Addressing Plan Results in Reduced Routing Traffic*

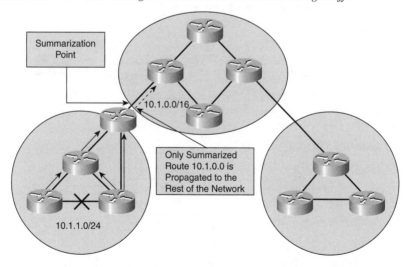

Efficient aggregation of routing advertisements narrows the scope of routing update propagation and significantly decreases the cumulative frequency of routing updates.

Fixed- and Variable-Length Subnet Masks

Another consideration when designing the IP addressing hierarchy is the subnet mask to use—either the same mask for the entire major network or different masks for different parts of the major network.

KEY POINT	A major network is a Class A, B, or C network.
	Fixed-Length Subnet Masking (FLSM) is when all subnet masks in a major network must be the same.
	Variable-Length Subnet Masking (VLSM) is when subnet masks within a major network can be different. In modern networks, VLSM should be used to conserve the IP addresses.

Some routing protocols require FLSM; others allow VLSM.

FLSM requires that all subnets of a major network have the same subnet mask, which therefore results in less efficient address space allocation. For example, in the top network shown in Figure 6-9, network 172.16.0.0/16 is subnetted using FLSM. Each subnet is given a /24 mask. The network is composed of multiple LANs that are connected by point-to-point WAN links. Because FLSM is used, all subnets have the same subnet mask. This is inefficient, because even though only two addresses are needed on the point-to-point links, a /24 subnet mask with 254 available host addresses is used.

Figure 6-9 *Fixed-Length Versus Variable-Length Subnet Mask*

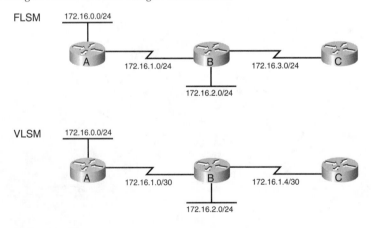

VLSM makes it possible to subnet with different subnet masks and therefore results in more efficient address space allocation. VLSM also provides a greater capability to perform route summarization, because it allows more hierarchical levels within an addressing plan. VLSM requires prefix length information to be explicitly sent with each address advertised in a routing update.

For example, in the lower network shown in Figure 6-9, network 172.16.0.0/16 is subnetted using VLSM. The network is composed of multiple LANs that are connected by point-to-point WAN links. The point-to-point links have a subnet mask of /30, providing only two available host addresses, which is all that is needed on these links. The LANs have a subnet mask of /24 because they have more hosts that require addresses.

Routing Protocol Considerations

To use VLSM, the routing protocol in use must be classless. Classful routing protocols permit only FLSM.

KEY POINT	With classful routing, routing updates *do not* carry the subnet mask. With classless routing, routing updates *do* carry the subnet mask.

Classful Routing Protocols

As illustrated at the top of Figure 6-10, the following rules apply when classful routing protocols are used:

■ The routing updates do not include subnet masks.

■ When a routing update is received and the routing information is about one of the following:

— Routes within the same major network as configured on the receiving interface, the subnet mask configured on the receiving interface is assumed to apply to the received routes also. Therefore, the mask must be the same for all subnets of a major network. In other words, subnetting must be done with FLSM.

— Routes in a different major network than configured on the receiving interface, the default major network mask is assumed to apply to the received routes. Therefore, automatic route summarization is performed across major network (Class A, B, or C) boundaries, and subnetted networks must be contiguous.

Figure 6-10 *Classful Versus Classless Routing Protocols*

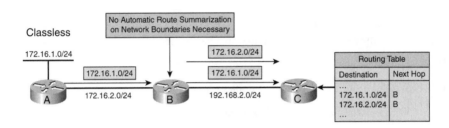

Figure 6-11 illustrates a sample network with a discontiguous 172.16.0.0 network that runs a classful routing protocol. Routers A and C automatically summarize across the major network boundary, so both send routing information about 172.16.0.0 rather than the individual subnets (172.16.1.0/24 and 172.16.2.0/24). Consequently, Router B receives two entries for the major network 172.16.0.0, and it puts both entries into its routing table. Router B therefore might make incorrect routing decisions.

Figure 6-11 *Classful Routing Protocols Do Not Send the Subnet Mask in the Routing Update*

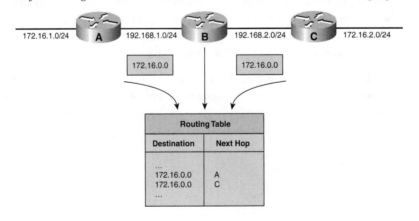

Because of these constraints, classful routing is not often used in modern networks. Routing Information Protocol (RIP) version 1 (RIPv1) is an example of a classful routing protocol.

Classless Routing Protocols

As illustrated in the lower portion of Figure 6-10, the following rules apply when classless routing protocols are used:

- The routing updates include subnet masks.

- VLSM is supported.

- Automatic route summarization at the major network boundary is not required, and route summarization can be manually configured.

- Subnetted networks can be discontiguous.

Consequently, all modern networks should use classless routing. Examples of classless routing protocols include RIP version 2 (RIPv2), Enhanced Interior Gateway Routing Protocol (EIGRP), OSPF, IS-IS, and Border Gateway Protocol (BGP).

> **NOTE**   The classless routing protocols do not all behave the same regarding summarization. For example, RIPv2 and EIGRP automatically summarize at the network boundary by default, but they can be configured not to, and they can be configured to summarize at other address boundaries. Open Shortest Path First (OSPF) and Intermediate System-to-Intermediate System (IS-IS) do not summarize at the network boundary by default; they can be configured to summarize at other address boundaries.

Figure 6-12 illustrates how discontiguous networks are handled by a classless routing protocol. This figure shows the same network as in Figure 6-11, but running a classless routing protocol that does not automatically summarize at the network boundary. In this example, Router B learns about both subnetworks 172.16.1.0/24 and 172.16.2.0/24, one from each interface; routing is performed correctly.

> **NOTE**   Although using discontiguous subnets with classless routing protocols does not pose the routing issues demonstrated in Figure 6-11, contiguous blocks of IP networks should be used whenever possible to promote more efficient summarization.

Figure 6-12 *Classless Routing Protocols Send the Subnet Mask in the Routing Update*

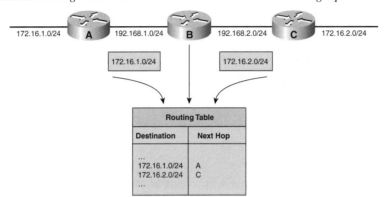

Hierarchical IP Addressing and Summarization Plan Example

Recall that the number of available host addresses on a subnet is calculated by the formula $2^h - 2$, where h is the number of host bits (the number of bits set to 0 in the subnet mask).

The first two columns in Table 6-3 show the location and number of IP addresses required at each location for the sample network shown in Figure 6-4. The third column in this table is the next highest power of 2 from the required number of addresses; this value is used to calculate the required number of host bits, as shown in the fourth column. Assuming that the Class B address 172.16.0.0/16 is used to address this network, the fifth column illustrates sample address blocks allocated to each location.

Table 6-3 *Address Blocks by Location for the Topology in Figure 6-4*

Location	Number of IP Addresses Required	Rounded Power of 2	Number of Host Bits[1]	Address Block Assigned
San Francisco	1290	2048	11	172.16.0.0–172.16.7.255/21
Denver Region		1024	10	172.16.8.0–172.16.11.255/22
Denver Campus	441	512	9	172.16.8.0–172.16.9.255/23
Remote Office 1	28	64	6	172.16.10.0/26
Remote Office 2	35	64	6	172.16.10.64/26
Houston Region		1024	10	172.16.12.0–172.16.15.255/22
Houston Campus	329	512	9	172.16.12.0–172.16.13.255/23
Remote Office 3	21	64	6	172.16.14.0/26

[1] Note that because the largest remote office needs 35 addresses and there is plenty of address space, 64 addresses are allocated to *each* remote office.

For the main campus, 2048 addresses are allocated; 11 host bits are required. This subnet is further divided into smaller subnets supporting floors or wiring closets. For the Denver region, 1024 addresses are allocated; 10 host bits are required. This address block is further divided into smaller subnets supporting buildings, floors, or wiring closets. Similarly, for the Houston region, 1024 addresses are also allocated and further subdivided, as shown in Table 6-3.

Figure 6-13 illustrates one of the links in the Denver region going down and how summarization is performed to reduce routing update traffic.

Figure 6-13   *Hierarchical IP Addressing Plan Example*

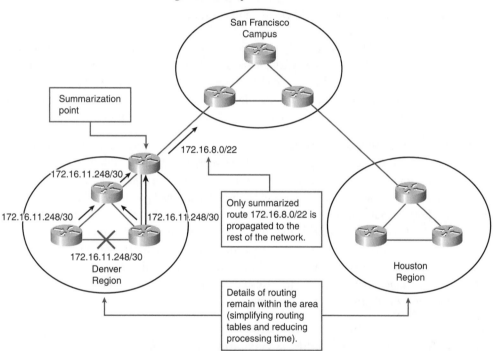

Methods of Assigning IP Addresses

This section discusses methods of assigning IP addresses to end systems and explains their influence on administrative overhead. Address assignment includes assigning an IP address, a default gateway, one or more domain name servers that resolve names to IP addresses, time servers, and so forth. Before selecting the desired IP address assignment method, the following questions should be answered:

■   How many devices need an IP address?

■   Which devices require static IP address assignment?

- Is IP address renumbering expected in the future?

- Is the administrator required to track devices and their IP addresses?

- Do additional parameters (default gateway, name server, and so forth) have to be configured?

- Are there any availability issues?

- Are there any security issues?

Static Versus Dynamic IP Address Assignment Methods

Following are the two basic IP address assignment strategies:

- **Static**: An IP address is statically assigned to a system. The network administrator configures the IP address, default gateway, and name servers manually by entering them into a special file or files on the end system with either a graphical or text interface. Static address assignment is an extra burden for the administrator—especially on large-scale networks—who must configure the address on every end system in the network.

- **Dynamic**: IP addresses are dynamically assigned to the end systems. Dynamic address assignment relieves the administrator of manually assigning an address to every network device. Instead, the administrator must set up a server to assign the addresses. On that server, the administrator defines the address pools and additional parameters that should be sent to the host (default gateway, name servers, time servers, and so forth). On the host, the administrator enables the host to acquire the address dynamically; this is often the default. When IP address reconfiguration is needed, the administrator reconfigures the server, which then performs the host-renumbering task. Examples of available address assignment protocols include Reverse Address Resolution Protocol, Boot Protocol, and DHCP. DHCP is the newest and provides the most features.

When to Use Static or Dynamic Address Assignment

To select either a static or dynamic end system IP address assignment method or a combination of the two, consider the following:

- **Node type**: Network devices such as routers and switches typically have static addresses. End-user devices such as PCs typically have dynamic addresses.

- **The number of end systems**: If there are more than 30 end systems, dynamic address assignment is preferred. Static assignment can be used for smaller networks.

- **Renumbering**: If renumbering is likely to happen and there are many end systems, dynamic address assignment is the best choice. With DHCP, only DHCP server reconfiguration is needed; with static assignment, all hosts must be reconfigured.

- **Address tracking**: If the network policy requires address tracking, the static address assignment method might be easier to implement than the dynamic address assignment method. However, address tracking is also possible with dynamic address assignment with additional DHCP server configuration.

- **Additional parameters**: DHCP is the easiest solution when additional parameters must be configured. The parameters have to be entered only on the DHCP server, which then sends the address and those parameters to the clients.

- **High availability**: Statically assigned IP addresses are always available. Dynamically assigned IP addresses must be acquired from the server; if the server fails, the addresses cannot be acquired. To ensure reliability, a redundant DHCP server is required.

- **Security**: With dynamic IP address assignment, anyone who connects to the network can acquire a valid IP address, in most cases. This might be a security risk. Static IP address assignment poses only a minor security risk.

The use of one address assignment method does not exclude the use of another in a different part of the network.

Guidelines for Assigning IP Addresses in the Enterprise Network

The typical enterprise network uses both static and dynamic address assignment methods. As shown in Figure 6-14, the static IP address assignment method is typically used for campus network infrastructure devices, in the Server Farm and Enterprise Data Center modules, and in the modules of the Enterprise Edge (the E-Commerce, Internet Connectivity, Remote Access and VPN, and WAN and MAN and Site-to-Site VPN modules). Static addresses are required for systems such as servers or network devices, in which the IP address must be known at all times for connectivity, general access, or management.

Figure 6-14 *IP Address Assignment in an Enterprise Network*

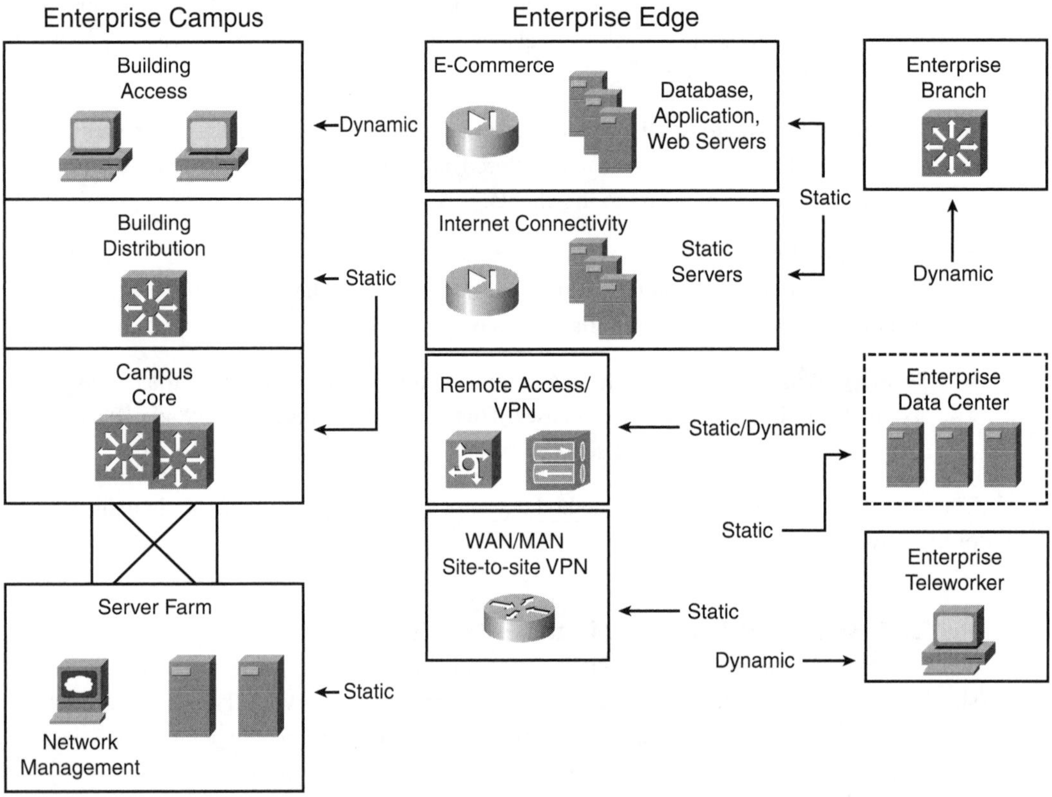

Dynamic IP address assignment is used for assigning IP addresses to end-user devices, including workstations, Cisco IP phones, and mobile devices.

Using DHCP to Assign IP Addresses

DHCP is used to provide dynamic IP address allocation to hosts. DHCP uses a client/server model; the DHCP server can be a Windows server, a UNIX-based server, or a Cisco IOS device. Cisco IOS devices can also be DHCP relay agents and DHCP clients. Figure 6-15 shows the steps that occur when a DHCP client requests an IP address from a DHCP server.

Step 1   The host sends a DHCPDISCOVER broadcast message to locate a DHCP server.

Step 2   A DHCP server offers configuration parameters such as an IP address, a MAC address, a domain name, a default gateway, and a lease for the IP address to the client in a DHCPOFFER unicast message.

Step 3   The client returns a formal request for the offered IP address to the DHCP server in a DHCPREQUEST broadcast message.

Step 4   The DHCP server confirms that the IP address has been allocated to the client by returning a DHCPACK unicast message to the client.

Figure 6-15   *DHCP Operation*

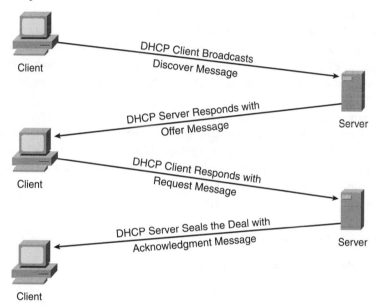

DCHP Relay

A DHCP relay agent is required to forward DCHP messages between clients and servers when they are on different broadcast domains (IP subnets). For example, the DHCP relay agent receives the DHCPDISCOVER message, which is sent as a broadcast, and forwards it to the DHCP server, on another subnet.

A DHCP client might receive offers from multiple DHCP servers and can accept any one of the offers; the client usually accepts the first offer it receives. An offer from the DHCP server is not a guarantee that the IP address will be allocated to the client; however, the server usually reserves the address until the client has had a chance to formally accept the address.

DHCP supports three possible address allocation mechanisms:

- **Manual**: The network administrator assigns an IP address to a specific MAC address. DHCP is used to dispatch the assigned address to the host.

- **Automatic**: DHCP permanently assigns the IP address to a host.

- **Dynamic**: DHCP assigns the IP address to a host for a limited time (called a *lease*) or until the host explicitly releases the address. This mechanism supports automatic address reuse when the host to which the address has been assigned no longer needs the address.

Name Resolution

Names are used to identify different hosts and resources on the network and to provide user-friendly interaction with computers; a name is much easier to remember than an IP address. This section covers the purpose of name resolution, provides information about different available name resolution strategies, and discusses Domain Name System (DNS) name resolution.

Hosts (computers, servers, printers, and so forth) identify themselves to each other using various naming schemes. Each computer on the network can have an assigned name to provide easier communication between devices and among users. Because the IP network layer protocol uses IP addresses to transport datagrams, a name that is used to identify a host must be mapped or resolved into an IP address; this is known as name resolution. To select the desired name resolution method, the following questions should be answered:

- How many hosts require name resolution?

- Are applications that depend on name resolution present?

- Is the network isolated, or is it connected to the Internet?

- If the network is isolated, how frequently are new hosts added, and how frequently do names change?

Static Versus Dynamic Name Resolution

The process of resolving a hostname to an IP address can be either static or dynamic. Following are the differences between these two methods:

- **Static**: With static name-to-IP-address resolution, both the administrative overhead and the configuration are very similar to those of a static address assignment strategy. The network administrator manually defines name-to-IP-address resolutions by entering the name and IP address pairs into the local database (HOSTS file) using either a graphical or text interface. Manual entries create additional work for the administrator; they must be entered on every host and are prone to errors and omissions.

- **Dynamic**: The dynamic name-to-IP-address resolution is similar to the dynamic address assignment strategy. The administrator has to enter the name-to-IP-address resolutions only on a local DNS server rather than on every host. The DNS server then performs the name-to-IP-address resolution. Renumbering and renaming are easier with the dynamic name-to-IP-address resolution method.

When to Use Static or Dynamic Name Resolution

The selection of either a static or dynamic end-system name resolution method depends on the following criteria:

- **The number of hosts**: If there are more than 30 end systems, dynamic name resolution is preferred. Static name resolution is manageable for fewer hosts.

- **Isolated network**: If the network is isolated (it does not have any connections to the Internet) and the number of hosts is small, static name resolution might be appropriate. The dynamic method is also possible; the choice is an administrative decision.

- **Internet connectivity**: When Internet connectivity is available for end users, static name resolution is not an option, and dynamic name resolution using DNS is mandatory.

- **Frequent changes and adding of names**: When dealing with frequent changes and adding names to a network, dynamic name resolution is recommended.

- **Applications depending on name resolution**: If applications that depend on name resolution are used, dynamic name resolution is recommended.

Using DNS for Name Resolution

To resolve symbolic names to actual network addresses, applications use resolver or name resolver programs, which are usually part of the host operating system. An application sends a query to a name resolver that resolves the request with either the local database (HOSTS file) or the DNS server.

When numerous hosts or names must be resolved to IP addresses, statically defined resolutions in HOSTS files are unwieldy to maintain. To ease this process, DNS is used for name resolution. DNS is a client/server mechanism used to access a distributed database providing address-to-name resolution. A DNS server is special software that usually resides on dedicated hardware. DNS servers are organized in a hierarchical structure. A DNS server can query other DNS servers to retrieve partial resolutions for a certain name; for example, one DNS server could resolve cisco.com, and another could resolve www.

To enable DNS name resolution, the network administrator sets up the DNS server, enters information about hostnames and corresponding IP addresses, and configures the hosts to use the DNS server for name resolution.

A recommended practice is to use a DNS server for internal name resolution when there are more than 30 hosts, services, or fully qualified domain names (FQDN) to resolve to IP addresses. An external DNS server is required to provide access to hosts outside the organization.

NOTE An *FQDN* is a complete domain name—for a specific host on the Internet—that contains enough information for it to be converted into a specific IP address. The FQDN consists of a hostname and a domain name. For example, www.cisco.com is the FQDN on the web for the Cisco web server. The host is *www*, the domain is *cisco*, and the top-level domain name is *com*.

Figure 6-16 illustrates the process of resolving an IP address using a DNS server:

Step 1   A user wants to browse www.cisco.com. Because the host does not know that site's IP address, it queries the DNS server.

Step 2   The DNS server responds with the appropriate IP address for www.cisco.com.

Step 3   The host establishes a connection to the appropriate IP address (the www.cisco.com site).

NOTE RFC 2136, *Dynamic Updates in the Domain Name System (DNS UPDATE)*, specifies a technology that helps reduce the administrative overhead of maintaining address-to-name mappings.

Figure 6-16 *Name Resolution with DNS*

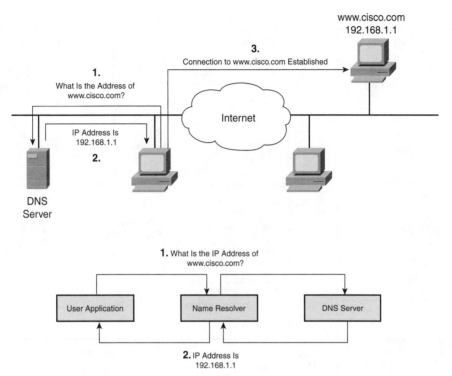

DHCP and DNS Server Location in a Network

As illustrated in Figure 6-17, DHCP and DNS servers can be located at multiple places in the network, depending on the service they support.

Figure 6-17 *Example of Locating DHCP and DNS Servers in a Network*

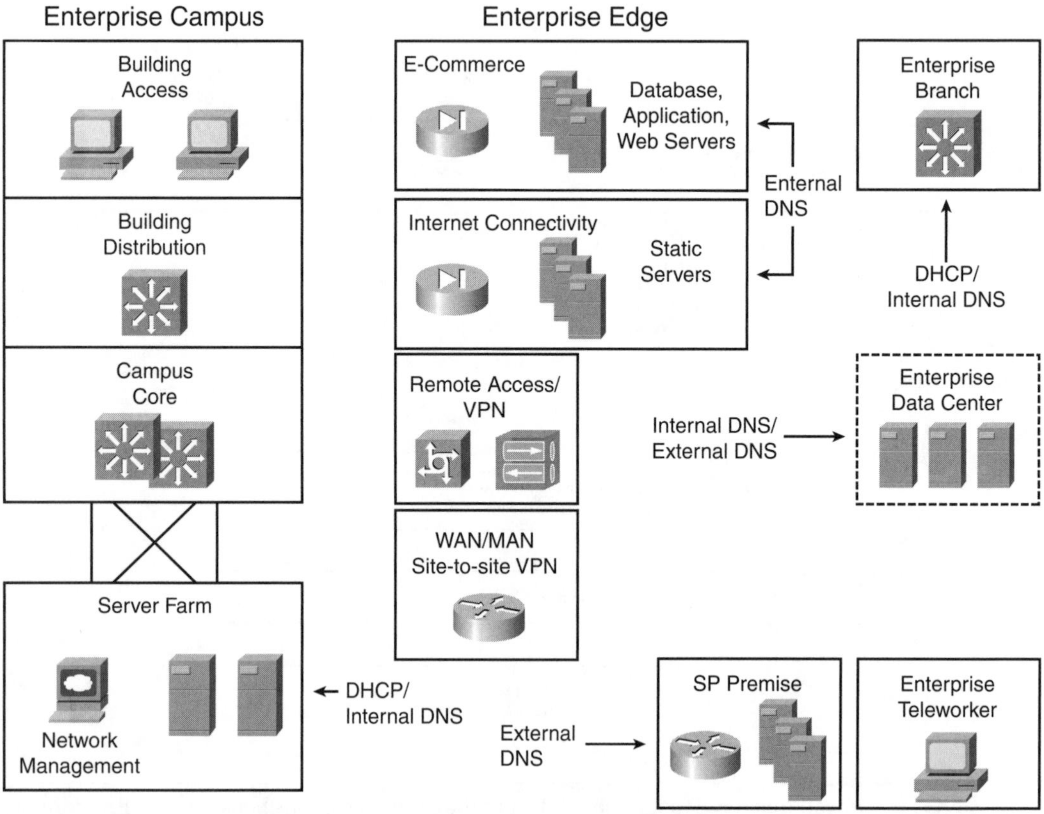

For the Enterprise Campus, DHCP and internal DNS servers should be located in the Server Farm; these servers should be redundant. For remote locations, Cisco routers can provide DHCP and DNS at the Enterprise Edge. External DNS servers should be redundant—for example, at two service provider facilities, or one at a service provider facility and one in a demilitarized zone at the Enterprise Campus or remote data center.

Introduction to IPv6

IPv6 is a technology developed to overcome the limitations of the current standard, IPv4, which allows end systems to communicate and forms the foundation of the Internet as we know it today.

This section on IPv6-specific design considerations provides an overview of IPv6 features and addressing and explains the various IPv6 address types. The address assignment and name resolution strategies for IPv6 are explored. The transition from IPv4 to IPv6 is discussed, and the section concludes with a brief description of the IPv6 routing protocols.

> **NOTE**   RFC 2460, *Internet Protocol, Version 6 (IPv6)*, defines the IPv6 standard.
>
> Information on IPv6 features supported in specific Cisco IOS releases can be found in *Cisco IOS Software Release Specifics for IPv6 Features,* at http://www.cisco.com/univercd/cc/td/doc/product/software/ios123/123cgcr/ipv6_c/ftipv6s.htm.

IPv6 Features

The ability to scale networks for future demands requires a limitless supply of IP addresses and improved mobility; IPv6 combines expanded addressing with a more efficient and feature-rich header to meet these demands. IPv6 satisfies the increasingly complex requirements of hierarchical addressing that IPv4 does not support.

The Cisco IOS supports IPv6 in Release 12.2(2)T and later. The main benefits of IPv6 include the following:

- **Larger address space**: IPv6 addresses are 128 bits, compared to IPv4's 32 bits. This larger addressing space allows more support for addressing hierarchy levels, a much greater number of addressable nodes, and simpler autoconfiguration of addresses.

- **Globally unique IP addresses**: Every node can have a unique global IPv6 address, which eliminates the need for NAT.

- **Site multihoming**: IPv6 allows hosts to have multiple IPv6 addresses and allows networks to have multiple IPv6 prefixes. Consequently, sites can have connections to multiple ISPs without breaking the global routing table.

- **Header format efficiency**: A simplified header with a fixed header size makes processing more efficient.

- **Improved privacy and security**: IPsec is the IETF standard for IP network security, available for both IPv4 and IPv6. Although the functions are essentially identical in both environments, IPsec is mandatory in IPv6. IPv6 also has optional security headers.

- **Flow labeling capability**: A new capability enables the labeling of packets belonging to particular traffic flows for which the sender requests special handling, such as nondefault quality of service (QoS) or real-time service.

■ **Increased mobility and multicast capabilities**: Mobile IPv6 allows an IPv6 node to change its location on an IPv6 network and still maintain its existing connections. With Mobile IPv6, the mobile node is always reachable through one permanent address. A connection is established with a specific permanent address assigned to the mobile node, and the node remains connected no matter how many times it changes locations and addresses.

IPv6 Address Format

Rather than using dotted-decimal format, IPv6 addresses are written as hexadecimal numbers with colons between each set of four hexadecimal digits (which is 16 bits); we like to call this the "coloned hex" format. The format is $x:x:x:x:x:x:x:x$, where x is a 16-bit hexadecimal field. A sample address is as follows:

2035:0001:2BC5:0000:0000:087C:0000:000A

KEY POINT	Fortunately, you can shorten the written form of IPv6 addresses. Leading 0s within each set of four hexadecimal digits can be omitted, and a pair of colons (::) can be used, once within an address, to represent any number of successive 0s.

For example, the previous address can be shortened to the following:

2035:1:2BC5::87C:0:A

An all-0s address can be written as ::.

KEY POINT	A pair of colons (::) can be used only once within an IPv6 address. This is because an address parser identifies the number of missing 0s by separating the two parts and entering 0 until the 128 bits are complete. If two :: notations were to be placed in the address, there would be no way to identify the size of each block of 0s.

Similar to how IPv4 subnet masks can be written as a prefix (for example, /24), IPv6 uses prefixes to indicate the number of bits of network or subnet information.

IPv6 Packet Header

The IPv6 header has 40 octets, in contrast to the 20 octets in the IPv4 header. IPv6 has fewer fields, and the header is 64-bit-aligned to enable fast, efficient, hardware-based processing. The IPv6 address fields are four times larger than in IPv4.

The IPv4 header contains 12 basic header fields, followed by an options field and a data portion (which usually includes a transport layer segment). The basic IPv4 header has a fixed size of 20 octets; the variable-length options field increases the size of the total IPv4 header.

IPv6 contains fields similar to 7 of the 12 IPv4 basic header fields (5 plus the source and destination address fields) but does not require the other fields. The IPv6 header contains the following fields:

- **Version**: A 4-bit field, the same as in IPv4. For IPv6, this field contains the number 6; for IPv4, this field contains the number 4.

- **Traffic class**: An 8-bit field similar to the type of service (ToS) field in IPv4. This field tags the packet with a traffic class that it uses in differentiated services (DiffServ) QoS. These functions are the same for IPv6 and IPv4.

- **Flow label**: This 20-bit field is new in IPv6. It can be used by the source of the packet to tag the packet as being part of a specific flow, allowing multilayer switches and routers to handle traffic on a per-flow basis rather than per-packet, for faster packet-switching performance. This field can also be used to provide QoS.

- **Payload length**: This 16-bit field is similar to the IPv4 total length field.

- **Next header**: The value of this 8-bit field determines the type of information that follows the basic IPv6 header. It can be transport-layer information, such as Transmission Control Protocol (TCP) or User Datagram Protocol (UDP), or it can be an extension header. The next header field is similar to the protocol field of IPv4.

- **Hop limit**: This 8-bit field specifies the maximum number of hops that an IPv6 packet can traverse. Similar to the time to live (TTL) field in IPv4, each router decreases this field by 1. Because there is no checksum in the IPv6 header, an IPv6 router can decrease the field without recomputing the checksum; in IPv4 routers, the recomputation costs processing time. If this field ever reaches 0, a message is sent back to the source of the packet, and the packet is discarded.

- **Source address**: This field has 16 octets (128 bits). It identifies the source of the packet.

- **Destination address**: This field has 16 octets (128 bits). It identifies the destination of the packet.

- **Extension headers**: The extension headers, if any, and the data portion of the packet follow the other eight fields. The number of extension headers is not fixed, so the total length of the extension header chain is variable.

Notice that the IPv6 header does not have a header checksum field. Because link-layer technologies perform checksum and error control and are considered relatively reliable, an IPv6 header checksum is considered redundant. Without the IPv6 header checksum, upper-layer checksums, such as within UDP, are mandatory with IPv6.

IPv6 Address Types

This section covers the various IPv6 address types and their scopes.

IPv6 Address Scope Types

Similar to IPv4, a single source can address datagrams to either one or many destinations at the same time in IPv6.

> **NOTE** RFC 4291, *IPv6 Addressing Architecture*, defines the IPv6 addressing architecture.

Following are the types of IPv6 addresses:

- **Unicast (one-to-one)**: Similar to an IPv4 unicast address, an IPv6 unicast address is for a single source to send data to a single destination. A packet sent to a unicast IPv6 address goes to the interface identified by that address. The IPv6 unicast address space encompasses the entire IPv6 address range, with the exception of the FF00::/8 range (addresses starting with binary 1111 1111), which is used for multicast addresses. The "IPv6 Unicast Addresses" section discusses the different types of IPv6 unicast addresses.

- **Anycast (one-to-nearest)**: An IPv6 anycast address is a new type of address that is assigned to a *set* of interfaces on different devices; an anycast address identifies multiple interfaces. A packet that is sent to an anycast address goes to the closest interface (as determined by the routing protocol being used) identified by the anycast address. Therefore, all nodes with the same anycast address should provide uniform service.

  Anycast addresses are syntactically indistinguishable from global unicast addresses because anycast addresses are allocated from the global unicast address space. Nodes to which the anycast address is assigned must be explicitly configured to recognize the anycast address.

  Anycast addresses must not be used as the source address of an IPv6 packet.

  Examples of when anycast addresses could be used are load balancing, content delivery services, and service location. For example, an anycast address could be assigned to a set of replicated FTP servers. A user in China who wants to retrieve a file would be directed to the Chinese server, whereas a user in the Europe would be directed to the European server.

- **Multicast (one-to-many)**: Similar to IPv4 multicast, an IPv6 multicast address identifies a set of interfaces (in a given scope), typically on different devices. A packet sent to a multicast address is delivered to *all* interfaces identified by the multicast address (in a given scope). IPv6 multicast addresses have a 4-bit scope identifier (ID) to specify how far the multicast packet may travel.

An IPv6 address is valid for a specific scope, which defines the types of applications the address is suitable for.

Interface Identifiers in IPv6 Addresses

In IPv6, a link is a network medium over which network nodes communicate using the link layer. Interface IDs in IPv6 addresses are used to identify a unique interface on a link. They can also be thought of as the "host portion" of an IPv6 address. Interface IDs are required to be unique on a link and can also be unique over a broader scope. When the interface identifier is derived directly from the data link layer address of the interface, the scope of that identifier is assumed to be universal (global). Interface identifiers are always 64 bits and are dynamically created based on the data link layer.

This process is illustrated in Figure 6-18.

Figure 6-18 *EUI-64 Format IPv6 Interface Identifier*

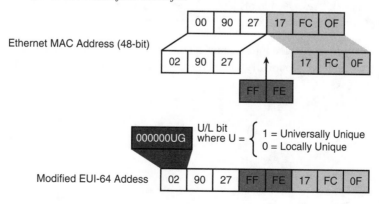

The seventh bit in an IPv6 interface identifier is referred to as the Universal/Local (U/L) bit. This bit identifies whether this interface identifier is locally unique on the link or whether it is universally unique. When the interface identifier is created from an Ethernet MAC address, it is assumed that the MAC address is universally unique and, therefore, that the interface identifier is universally unique. The U/L bit is for future use by upper-layer protocols to uniquely identify a connection, even in the context of a change in the leftmost part of the address. However, this feature is not yet used. The eighth bit in an IPv6 interface identifier, also known as the "G" bit, is the group/individual bit for managing groups.

IPv6 Unicast Addresses

Following are the different unicast addresses that IPv6 supports:

- Global aggregatable address (also called global unicast address)

- Link-local address

- IPv4-compatible IPv6 address

Global aggregatable addresses and link-local addresses are discussed in the next two sections, respectively. IPv4-compatible IPv6 addresses are described in the later "IPv4-to-IPv6 Transition Strategies and Deployments" section.

> **NOTE**   Site-local unicast addresses are another type of IPv6 unicast address; however, the use of site-local addresses was deprecated in September 2004 by RFC 3879, *Deprecating Site Local Addresses*, and future systems must not implement any support for this type of address.
>
> Site-local unicast addresses were similar to private addresses in IPv4 and were used to address a site without having a global prefix. Site-local addresses used the prefix FEC0::/10 (binary 1111 1110 11) with a subnet identifier (a 16-bit field) and an interface identifier (a 64-bit field) concatenated after the prefix. Site-local addresses were considered private addresses to be used to restrict communication to a limited domain.
>
> IPv6 routers must not advertise routes or forward packets that have site-local source or destination addresses, outside the site.

> **KEY POINT**   Every IPv6-enabled interface must contain at least one loopback (::1/128) and one link-local address. Optionally, an interface may have multiple unique local and global addresses.

Global Aggregatable Unicast Addresses

> **KEY POINT** | IPv6 global aggregatable unicast addresses are equivalent to IPv4 unicast addresses.

The structure of global aggregatable unicast addresses enables summarization (aggregation) of routing prefixes so that the number of routing table entries in the global routing table can be reduced. Global unicast addresses used on links are aggregated upward, through organizations, and then to intermediate-level ISPs, and eventually to top-level ISPs. A global unicast address typically consists of a 48-bit global routing prefix, a 16-bit subnet ID, and a 64-bit interface ID (typically in EUI-64 bit format), as illustrated in Figure 6-19.

Figure 6-19 *IPv6 Global Aggregatable Unicast Address Structure*

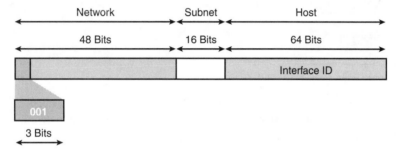

The subnet ID can be used by individual organizations to create their own local addressing hierarchy using subnets. This field allows an organization to use up to 65,536 individual subnets.

A fixed prefix of binary 2000::/3 (binary 001) indicates a global aggregatable IPv6 address; this is the current range of IPv6 global unicast addresses assigned by the Internet Assigned Numbers Authority (IANA). Assignments from this block are registered in the IANA registry, which is available at http://www.iana.org/assignments/ipv6-unicast-address-assignments.

The 64-bit Interface ID field identifies interfaces on a link and therefore must be unique on the link.

> **NOTE** RFC 3587, *IPv6 Global Unicast Address Format*, defines the global unicast address format.

Link-Local Unicast Addresses

A link-local address is useful only in the context of the local link network; its scope limits its relevance to only one link. A link-local address is an IPv6 unicast address that can be automatically configured on any interface by using the link-local prefix FE80::/10 (1111 1110 10) and the 64-bit interface identifier, as shown in Figure 6-20. Link-local addresses are used in the neighbor discovery protocol and the dynamic address assignment process. Dynamic address assignment is discussed in more detail in the next section.

Figure 6-20 *IPv6 Link-Local Unicast Address Structure*

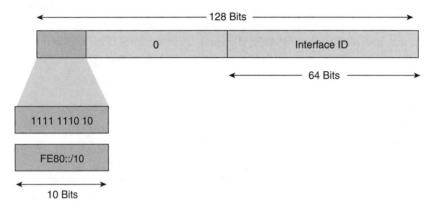

| KEY POINT | A link-local unicast address connects devices on the same local network without requiring globally unique addresses. |

Many routing protocols also use link-local addresses.

When communicating with a link-local address, the outgoing interface must be specified, because every interface is connected to FE80::/10.

An IPv6 router must not forward packets that have either link-local source or destination addresses to other links.

IPv6 Address Assignment Strategies

As with IPv4, IPv6 allows two address assignment strategies: static and dynamic.

Static IPv6 Address Assignment

Static address assignment in IPv6 is the same as in IPv4—the administrator must enter the IPv6 address configuration manually on every device in the network.

Dynamic IPv6 Address Assignment

IPv6 dynamic address assignment strategies allow dynamic assignment of IPv6 addresses, as follows:

- **Link-local address**: The host configures its own link-local address autonomously, using the link-local prefix FE80::0/10 and a 64-bit identifier for the interface, in an EUI-64 format.

- **Stateless autoconfiguration**: A router on the link advertises—either periodically or at the host's request—network information, such as the 64-bit prefix of the local network and its willingness to function as a default router for the link. Hosts can automatically generate their global IPv6 addresses by using the prefix in these router messages; the hosts do not need manual configuration or the help of a device such as a DHCP server. For example, Figure 6-21 shows a host using the prefix advertised by the router as the top 64 bits of its address; the remaining 64 bits contain the host's 48-bit MAC address in an EUI-64 format.

Figure 6-21   *IPv6 Stateless Autoconfiguration Allows a Host to Automatically Configure Its IPv6 Address*

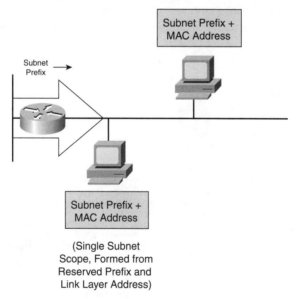

- **Stateful using DHCP for IPv6 (DHCPv6)**: DHCPv6 is an updated version of DHCP for IPv4. DHCPv6 gives the network administrator more control than stateless autoconfiguration and can be used to distribute other information, including the address of the DNS server. DHCPv6 can also be used for automatic domain name registration of hosts using a dynamic DNS server. DHCPv6 uses multicast addresses.

IPv6 Name Resolution

This section discusses IPv6 name resolution strategies and name resolution on a dual-stack (IPv4 and IPv6) host.

Static and Dynamic IPv6 Name Resolution

IPv6 and IPv4 name resolutions are similar. The following two name resolutions are available with IPv6:

■ **Static name resolution**: Accomplished by manual entries in the host's local configuration files.

■ **Dynamic name resolution**: Accomplished using a DNS server that supports IPv6, usually along with IPv4 support. As shown in Figure 6-22, an IPv6-aware application requests the destination hostname's IPv6 address from the DNS server using a request for an A6 record; an *A6 record* is a new DNS feature that contains an address record for an IPv6 host. The task of querying for the address is done with the name resolver, which is usually part of the operating system. The network administrator must set up the appropriate DNS server with IPv6 support and connect it to the IPv6 network with a valid IPv6 address. The hosts must also have IPv6 addresses.

Figure 6-22 *IPv6 Name Resolution*

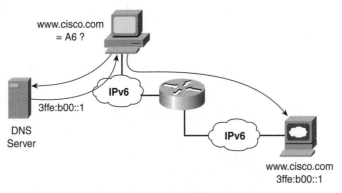

IPv4- and IPv6-Aware Applications and Name Resolution

A dual-stack host has both IPv4 and IPv6 protocol stacks and has a new application program interface (API) defined to support both IPv4 and IPv6 addresses and DNS requests. An application can use both IPv4 and IPv6. An application can be converted to the new API while still using only IPv4.

As shown in Figure 6-23, an IPv6- and IPv4-enabled application chooses which stack to use (the typical default is IPv6) and asks the DNS server for the destination host's address; in this example, it requests the host's IPv6 address. After receiving the response from the DNS server, the application asks the source host to connect to the destination host using IPv6.

Figure 6-23 *Dual-Stack Name Resolution*

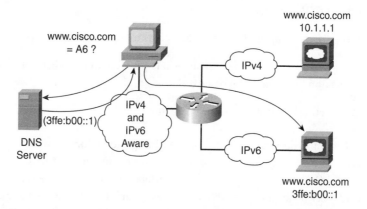

> **NOTE**   Microsoft Windows XP and Windows Server 2003 fully support most aspects of IPv6 with the appropriate service packs installed; Windows Vista supports IPv6.

IPv4-to-IPv6 Transition Strategies and Deployments

IPv4-to-IPv6 migration does not happen automatically. The following sections first explore the differences between IPv4 and IPv6 and then discuss possible transition strategies and deployments.

Differences Between IPv4 and IPv6

Regardless of which protocol is used, the communication between IPv4 and IPv6 domains must be transparent to end users. The major differences to consider between IPv4 and IPv6 include the following:

- IPv4 addresses are 32 bits long, whereas IPv6 addresses are 128 bits long.

- An IPv6 packet header is different from an IPv4 packet header. The IPv6 header is longer and simpler (new fields were added to the IPv6 header, and some old fields were removed).

- IPv6 has no concept of broadcast addresses; instead, it uses multicast addresses.

- Routing protocols must be changed to support native IPv6 routing.

IPv4-to-IPv6 Transition

The transition from IPv4 to IPv6 will take several years because of the high cost of upgrading equipment. In the meantime, IPv4 and IPv6 must coexist. The following are three primary mechanisms for the transition from IPv4 to IPv6:

- **Dual-stack**: Both the IPv4 and the IPv6 stacks run on a system that can communicate with both IPv6 and IPv4 devices.

- **Tunneling**: Uses encapsulation of IPv6 packets to traverse IPv4 networks, and vice versa.

- **Translation**: A mechanism that translates one protocol to the other to facilitate communication between the two networks.

The following sections describe these mechanisms.

In addition, Cisco has designed the IPv6 on the Multiprotocol Label Switching (MPLS) Provider Edge (PE) routers (6PE) feature, which supports smooth integration of IPv6 into MPLS networks. Because the MPLS routers switch packets based on labels rather than address lookups, organizations with an MPLS backbone can scale IPv6 traffic easily and do not need to make costly hardware upgrades.

Dual-Stack Transition Mechanism

As shown in Figure 6-24, a dual-stack node enables both IPv4 and IPv6 stacks. Applications communicate with both IPv4 and IPv6 stacks; the IP version choice is based on name lookup and application preference. This is the most appropriate method for campus and access networks during the transition period, and it is the preferred technique for transitioning to IPv6. A dual-stack approach supports the maximum number of applications. Operating systems that support the IPv6 stack include FreeBSD, Linux, Sun Solaris, and Windows 2000, XP, and Vista.

Figure 6-24 *A Dual-Stack Node Has Both IPv4 and IPv6 Stacks*

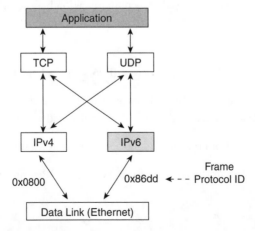

Tunneling Transition Mechanism

The purpose of tunneling is to encapsulate packets of one type in packets of another type. When transitioning to IPv6, tunneling encapsulates IPv6 packets in IPv4 packets, as shown in Figure 6-25.

Figure 6-25 *Tunneling IPv6 Packets Within IPv4 Packets*

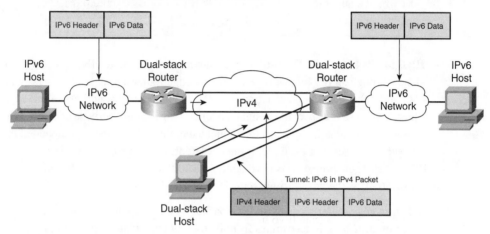

By using overlay tunnels, isolated IPv6 networks can communicate without having to upgrade the IPv4 infrastructure between them. Both routers and hosts can use tunneling. The following different techniques are available for establishing a tunnel:

- **Manually configured**: For a manually configured tunnel, the tunnel source and tunnel destination are manually configured with static IPv4 and IPv6 addresses. Manual tunnels can be configured between border routers or between a border router and a host.

- **Semi-automated**: Semi-automation is achieved by using a tunnel broker that uses a web-based service to create a tunnel. A *tunnel broker* is a server on the IPv4 network that receives tunnel requests from dual-stack clients, configures the tunnel on the tunnel server or router, and associates the tunnel from the client to one of the tunnel servers or routers. A simpler model combines the tunnel broker and server onto one device.

- **Automatic**: Various automatic mechanisms accomplish tunneling, including the following:

  — **IPv4-compatible**: The tunnel is constructed dynamically using an IPv4-compatible IPv6 address (an IPv6 address that consists of 0s in the upper bits and an embedded IPv4 address in the lower 32 bits). Because it does not scale, this mechanism is appropriate only for testing.

NOTE   The format of an IPv4-compatible IPv6 address is 0:0:0:0:0:0:A.B.C.D, or ::A.B.C.D, where A.B.C.D is the IPv4 address in dotted-decimal notation. The entire 128-bit IPv4-compatible IPv6 address is used as a node's IPv6 address, and the IPv4 address that is embedded in the low-order 32 bits is used as the node's IPv4 address. For example, the IPv4 address 192.168.30.1 would convert to the IPv4-compatible IPv6 address 0:0:0:0:0:0:192.168.30.1. Other acceptable representations for this address are ::192.168.30.1 and ::C0A8:1E01.

— **IPv6-to-IPv4 (6-to-4)**: The 6-to-4 tunneling method automatically connects IPv6 islands through an IPv4 network. Each 6-to-4 edge router has an IPv6 address with a /48 prefix that is the concatenation of 2002::/16 and the IPv4 address of the edge router; 2002::/16 is a specially assigned address range for the purpose of 6-to-4. The edge routers automatically build the tunnel using the IPv4 addresses embedded in the IPv6 addresses. For example, if the IPv4 address of an edge router is 192.168.99.1, the prefix of its IPv6 address is 2002:C0A8:6301::/48 because 0xC0A86301 is the hexadecimal representation of 192.168.99.1.

When an edge router receives an IPv6 packet with a destination address in the range of 2002::/16, it determines from its routing table that the packet must traverse the tunnel. The router extracts the IPv4 address embedded in the third to sixth octets, inclusive, in the IPv6 next-hop address. This IPv4 address is the IPv4 address of the 6-to-4 router at the destination site—the router at the other end of the tunnel. The router encapsulates the IPv6 packet in an IPv4 packet with the destination edge router's extracted IPv4 address.

The packet passes through the IPv4 network. The destination edge router unencapsulates the IPv6 packet from the received IPv4 packet and forwards the IPv6 packet to its final destination. A 6-to-4 relay router, which offers traffic forwarding to the IPv6 Internet, is required for reaching a native IPv6 Internet.

— **6over4**: A router connected to a native IPv6 network and with a 6over4-enabled interface can be used to forward IPv6 traffic between 6over4 hosts and native IPv6 hosts. IPv6 multicast addresses are mapped into the IPv4 multicast addresses. The IPv4 network becomes a virtual Ethernet for the IPv6 network; to achieve this, an IPv4 multicast-enabled network is required.

Translation Transition Mechanism

Dual-stack and tunneling techniques manage the interconnection of IPv6 domains. For legacy equipment that will not be upgraded to IPv6 and for some deployment scenarios, techniques are available for connecting IPv4-only nodes to IPv6-only nodes, using translation, an extension of NAT techniques.

As shown in Figure 6-26, an IPv6 node behind a translation device has full connectivity to other IPv6 nodes and uses NAT functionality to communicate with IPv4 devices.

Figure 6-26   *Translation Mechanism*

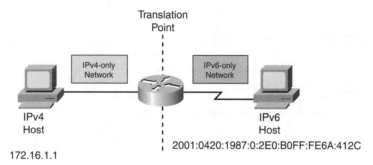

Translation techniques are available for translating IPv4 addresses to IPv6 addresses and vice versa. Similar to current NAT devices, translation is done at either the transport layer or the network layer. NAT-Protocol Translation (NAT-PT) is the main translation technique; the Dual-Stack Transition Mechanism (DSTM) might also be available.

The NAT-PT translation mechanism translates at the network layer between IPv4 and IPv6 addresses and allows native IPv6 hosts and applications to communicate with native IPv4 hosts and applications. An application-level gateway (ALG) translates between the IPv4 and IPv6 DNS requests and responses. NAT-PT is defined in RFC 2766, *Network Address Translation-Protocol Translation (NAT-PT)*.

> **NOTE**   ALGs use a dual-stack approach and enable a host in one domain to send data to another host in the other domain. This method requires that all application servers be converted to IPv6.

The DSTM translation mechanism may be used for dual-stack hosts in an IPv6 domain that have not yet had an IPv4 address assigned to the IPv4 side but that must communicate with IPv4 systems or allow IPv4 applications to run on top of their IPv6 protocol stack. This mechanism requires a dedicated server that dynamically provides a temporary global IPv4 address for the duration of the communication (using DHCPv6) and uses dynamic tunnels to carry the IPv4 traffic within an IPv6 packet through the IPv6 domain.

IPv6 Routing Protocols

The routing protocols available in IPv6 include interior gateway protocols (IGP) for use within an autonomous system and exterior gateway protocols (EGP) for use between autonomous systems.

As with IPv4 CIDR, IPv6 uses the same longest-prefix match routing. Updates to the existing IPv4 routing protocols were necessary for handling longer IPv6 addresses and different header structures. Currently, the following updated routing protocols or draft proposals are available:

- **IGPs:**

    — RIP new generation (RIPng)

    — EIGRP for IPv6

    — OSPF version 3 (OSPFv3)

    — Integrated IS-IS version 6 (IS-ISv6)

- **EGP**: Multiprotocol extensions to BGP version 4 (BGP4+)

RIPng

RIPng is a distance-vector protocol with a limit of 15 hops that uses split-horizon and poison reverse to prevent routing loops. RIPng features include the following:

- RIPng is based on the IPv4 RIPv2 and is similar to RIPv2.

- RIPng uses an IPv6 prefix and a next-hop IPv6 address.

- RIPng uses the multicast address FF02::9, the all-RIP-routers multicast address, as the destination address for RIP updates.

- RIPng uses IPv6 for transport.

- RIPng uses link-local addresses as source addresses.

- RIPng updates are sent on UDP port 521.

> **NOTE** RIPng is defined in RFC 2080, *RIPng for IPv6*.

EIGRP for IPv6

EIGRP for IPv6 is available in Cisco IOS Release 12.4(6)T and later. EIGRP for IPv4 and EIGRP for IPv6 are configured and managed separately; however, the configuration and operation of EIGRP for IPv4 and IPv6 is similar. EIGRP for IPv6 features include the following:

- EIGRP for IPv6 is configured directly on the interfaces over which it runs.

- EIGRP for IPv6 can be configured without the use of a global IPv6 address.

- No **network** commands are used when configuring EIGRP for IPv6.

- EIGRP for IPv6 routes IPv6 prefixes.

NOTE   EIGRP IPv6 is not currently supported on the Cisco 7600 routers or Catalyst 6500 switches.

For more information on this protocol, refer to "Implementing EIGRP for IPv6," available at http://www.cisco.com/.

OSPFv3

OSPFv3 is a new OSPF implementation for IPv6; it has the following features:

- OSPFv3 is similar to OSPF version 2 (OSPFv2) for IPv4; it uses the same mechanisms as OSPFv2, but the internals of the protocols are different.

- OSPFv3 carries IPv6 addresses.

- OSPFv3 uses link-local unicast addresses as source addresses.

- OSPFv3 uses IPv6 for transport.

NOTE   OSPFv3 is defined in RFC 2740, *OSPF for IPv6.*

Integrated IS-IS Version 6

The large address support in integrated IS-IS facilitates the IPv6 address family. IS-ISv6 is the same as IS-IS for IPv4, with the following extensions added for IPv6:

- Two new type-length-values (TLV):

  — IPv6 Reachability

  — IPv6 Interface Address
- New protocol identifier

BGP4+

Multiprotocol extensions for BGP4 enable other protocols to be routed besides IPv4, including IPv6. Additional IPv6-specific extensions incorporated into BGP4+ include the definition of a new identifier for the IPv6 address family.

> **NOTE**   RFC 4760, *Multiprotocol Extensions for BGP-4*, defines multiprotocol extensions to BGP. RFC 2545, *Use of BGP-4 Multiprotocol Extensions for IPv6 Inter-Domain Routing*, defines BGP4+ for IPv6.

Summary

In this chapter, you learned about IPv4 and IPv6 addressing. The following topics were explored:

- Private and public IP addresses, and when to use each

- Determining the network size, including the number and type of locations and the number and type of devices at each location

- Hierarchical addressing, route summarization, and the role of classful and classless routing protocols and fixed-length and variable-length subnet masks

- Static and dynamic (DHCP) address assignment

- Static and dynamic (DNS) name resolution

- Features of IPv6, including its 128-bit addresses

- Types of IPv6 addresses: unicast (one-to-one), anycast (one-to-nearest), and multicast (one-to-many)

- Types of IPv6 unicast addresses: global aggregatable, link-local, and IPv4-compatible

- Types of IPv6 address assignment: static or dynamic, which includes using link-local addresses, stateless autoconfiguration, and stateful using DHCPv6

- Types of IPv6 name resolution: static or dynamic using DNS servers that have IPv6 protocol stack support

- IPv4-to-IPv6 transition strategies, including dual-stack use, tunneling mechanisms, and translation mechanisms

- IPv6 routing protocols, including RIPng, EIGRP for IPv6, OSPFv3, IS-ISv6, and BGP4+

References

For additional information, refer to the following resources:

- Comer, Douglas E. and David L. Stevens. *Internetworking with TCP/IP Volume 1: Principles, Protocols, and Architecture,* Fifth Edition. Englewood Cliffs, New Jersey: Prentice-Hall, 2005.

- Designing Large-Scale IP Internetworks, http://www.cisco.com/univercd/cc/td/doc/cisintwk/idg4/nd2003.htm.

- Subnetting an IP Address Space, http://www.cisco.com/univercd/cc/td/doc/cisintwk/idg4/nd20a.htm.

- DHCP, http://www.cisco.com/univercd/cc/td/doc/product/software/ios124/124cg/hiad_c/ch10/index.htm

- DNS Server Support for NS Records, http://www.cisco.com/en/US/products/ps6350/products_configuration_guide_chapter09186a008045597e.html

- Cisco IOS IPv6 Introduction, http://www.cisco.com/en/US/products/ps6553/products_ios_technology_home.html

- Cisco IP Version 6 Solutions, http://www.cisco.com/univercd/cc/td/doc/cisintwk/intsolns/ipv6_sol/index.htm

- Cisco IPv6 Solutions, http://www.cisco.com/en/US/tech/tk872/technologies_white_paper09186a00802219bc.shtml

- IPv6 Address Space, http://www.iana.org/assignments/ipv6-address-space

Case Study: ACMC Hospital IP Addressing Design

This case study is a continuation of the ACMC Hospital case study introduced in Chapter 2, "Applying a Methodology to Network Design."

Case Study General Instructions

Use the scenarios, information, and parameters provided at each task of the ongoing case study. If you encounter ambiguities, make reasonable assumptions and proceed. For all tasks, use the initial customer scenario and build on the solutions provided thus far. You can use any and all documentation, books, white papers, and so on.

In each step, you act as a network design consultant. Make creative proposals to accomplish the customer's business needs. Justify your ideas when they differ from the provided solutions. Use any design strategies you feel are appropriate. The final goal of each case study is a paper solution.

Appendix A, "Answers to Review Questions and Case Studies," provides a solution for each step based on assumptions made. There is no claim that the provided solution is the best or only solution. Your solution might be more appropriate for the assumptions you made. The provided solution helps you understand the author's reasoning and allows you to compare and contrast your solution.

In this case study, you create an IP addressing design for the ACMC hospital network. Table 6-4 is a review of the switch port counts by location, as derived in the case study for Chapter 4, "Designing Basic Campus and Data Center Networks."

Table 6-4 *Port Counts by Location*

Location	Port Counts	Port Counts with Spares	Comments
Main building 1, per floor	75	150	Six floors
Main building server farm	70	140	Servers will connect with dual network interface cards; this number allows for planned migration of all servers to the server farm
Main building 2, per floor	75	150	Six floors
Children's Place, per floor	60	120	Three floors
Buildings A–D	10 each	20 each	
Buildings E–J	20 each	40 each	
Buildings K–L	40 each	80 each	

Figure 6-27 reviews the planned campus and WAN infrastructure, as determined in the previous case studies.

Figure 6-27 *ACMC Planned Campus and WAN Design*

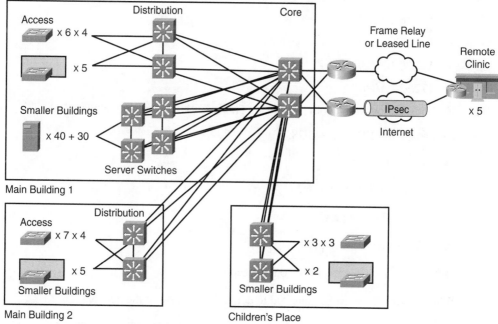

Complete the following steps:

Step 1   Propose a suitable IP addressing plan that takes advantage of good summarization techniques for the ACMC network, including the campus, WAN and backup WAN links, and the remote clinics.

Step 2   Propose possible methods for IP address assignment.

Review Questions

Answer the following questions, and then refer to Appendix A for the answers.

1. Which of the following IPv4 addresses cannot be used in public networks?

   a. 172.167.20.1/24

   b. 192.168.1.200/28

   c. 172.30.100.33/24

   d. 172.32.1.1/16

2. In what situation would both private and public IPv4 addresses be required?

3. For the address 172.17.7.245/28:

   ■ What is the mask?

   ■ What class is the address?

   ■ What is the host part?

   ■ What is the network part?

   ■ How many hosts can reside on this subnet?

4. What information must be collected to determine the size of the network?

5. Approximately how much reserve in the number of network device addresses should be included for future growth purposes?

6. What type of routing protocol can support VLSM?

7. Assume that a router has the following subnets behind it:

   ■ 10.5.16.0/24

   ■ 10.5.17.0/24

   ■ 10.5.18.0/24

   ■ 10.5.19.0/24

   What summary route could the router advertise to represent these four subnets?

8. What are some disadvantages of a poorly designed IP addressing scheme?

9. What are some advantages of a hierarchical IP addressing scheme?

10. What is the difference between classless and classful routing protocols?

11. What are the advantages of using DHCP versus static address assignment?

12. What are the three DHCP address allocation mechanisms?

13. What is the advantage of using dynamic name resolution versus static name resolution?

14. Describe the process used when DNS resolves a URL, such as www.cisco.com.

15. How many bits are in an IPv6 address?

16. How long is the IPv6 packet header?

17. Which are valid ways of writing the following IPv6 address: 2035:0000:134B:0000:0000:088C:0001:004B?

    a. 2035::134B::088C:1:004B

    b. 2035::134B::88C:1:4B

    c. 2035:0:134B::088C:1:004B

    d. 2035::134B:0:0:88C:1:4B

    e. 2035:0:134B:88C:1:4B

18. When a packet is sent to an IPv6 anycast address, where does it go?

19. One-to-many IPv6 addresses are called _____.

20. True or false: Packets with link-local IPv6 source or destination addresses must not be forwarded to the Internet by a router.

21. How many bits are used for the interface ID in an IPv6 unicast address?

22. What IPv6 prefix is used by devices on the same network to communicate?

23. What address assignment strategies are available in IPv6?

24. How does IPv6 stateless autoconfiguration work?

25. What feature allows DNS to support IPv6?

26. Can a host support IPv4 and IPv6 simultaneously?

27. What are three mechanisms for transitioning from IPv4 to IPv6?

28. Describe how 6-to-4 tunneling works.

29. Which IPv6 routing protocols are supported on Cisco routers?

30. What multicast address is used for RIPng?

This chapter discusses IP routing protocols and contains the following sections:

- Routing Protocol Features

- Routing Protocols for the Enterprise

- Routing Protocol Deployment

- Summary

- References

- Case Study: ACMC Hospital Routing Protocol Design

- Review Questions

CHAPTER 7

Selecting Routing Protocols for the Network

This chapter describes considerations for selecting the most appropriate network routing protocol. First, routing protocol features are discussed, followed by a description of various routing protocols appropriate for enterprise use. The chapter discusses why certain protocols are suitable for specific modules in the Enterprise Architecture. It concludes with a description of some advanced routing protocol deployment features, including redistribution, filtering, and summarization.

> **NOTE** Chapter 1, "Network Fundamentals Review," includes introductory information about routers and routing protocols.
>
> For more details about IP routing protocols, see *Authorized Self-Study Guide: Building Scalable Cisco Internetworks (BSCI)*, Third Edition, by Diane Teare and Catherine Paquet, Cisco Press, 2006.

> **NOTE** In this chapter, the term *IP* refers to IP version 4 (IPv4).

Routing Protocol Features

There are many ways to characterize routing protocols, including the following:

- Static versus dynamic routing

- Interior versus exterior routing protocols

- Distance vector versus link-state versus hybrid protocols

- Routing protocol metrics

- Routing protocol convergence

- Flat versus hierarchical routing protocols

The following sections discuss these methods in detail.

Static Versus Dynamic Routing

Whereas static routes are typically configured manually, routing protocols generate dynamic routes. Each method has advantages and disadvantages in specific network scenarios, as discussed in the following sections.

Static Routing

The term static routing denotes the use of manually configured or injected static routes for traffic forwarding purposes. Using a static route might be appropriate in the following circumstances:

■ When it is undesirable to have dynamic routing updates forwarded across slow bandwidth links, such as a dialup link

■ When the administrator needs total control over the routes used by the router

■ When a backup to a dynamically learned route is necessary

■ When it is necessary to reach a network that is accessible by only one path (a stub network)

Configuring and maintaining static routes is time-consuming. Properly implementing static routes requires complete knowledge of the entire network.

Figure 7-1 illustrates a stub network scenario in which the use of static routes is favored over a dynamic routing protocol. The right side of Figure 7-1 shows a stub network with a single entry/exit point over the S0 interface of Router A. On the stub network router (Router A), a static default route is configured so that the S0 link forwards all traffic toward destinations outside the stub network. On Router B, a static route is installed toward the stub network and then is redistributed into the routing protocol so that reachability information for the stub network is available throughout the rest of the network.

Figure 7-1   *Use Static Routes with a Stub Network*

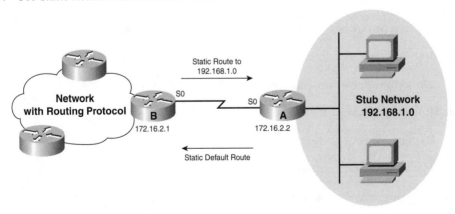

NOTE   Static routes are unidirectional. A static route configured in one direction via one router must have a corresponding static route configured on the adjacent router, in the opposite direction, for the return path. Figure 7-1 includes these two routes.

By using static and default static routes in this scenario, no traffic from a dynamic routing protocol is present on the serial link or in the stub network. In addition, the processor and memory requirements for both routers are lower; in the stub network, a low-end router would suffice. Static routes are therefore appropriate in situations such as with stub networks, hub-and-spoke connections (also called star connections), and dialup environments.

Dynamic Routing

Dynamic routing allows the network to adjust to changes in the topology automatically, without administrator involvement. A static route cannot dynamically respond to changes in the network. If a link fails, the static route is no longer valid if it is configured to use that failed link, so a new static route must be configured. If a new router or new link is added, that information must also be configured on every router in the network. In a very large or unstable network, these changes can lead to considerable work for network administrators. It can also take a long time for every router in the network to receive the correct information. In situations such as these, it might be better to have the routers receive information about networks and links from each other using a dynamic routing protocol. Dynamic routing protocols must do the following:

- Find sources from which routing information can be received (usually neighboring routers)

- Select the best paths toward all reachable destinations, based on received information

- Maintain this routing information

- Have a means of verifying routing information (periodic updates or refreshes)

When using a dynamic routing protocol, the administrator configures the routing protocol on each router. The routers then exchange information about the reachable networks and the state of each network. Routers exchange information only with other routers running the same routing protocol. When the network topology changes, the new information is dynamically propagated throughout the network, and each router updates its routing table to reflect the changes.

Interior Versus Exterior Routing Protocols

An autonomous system (AS), also known as a domain, is a collection of routers that are under a common administration, such as a company's internal network or an Internet service provider's (ISP's) network.

KEY POINT	Because the Internet is based on the AS concept, two types of routing protocols are required:
	■ **Interior gateway protocols (IGP)** are intra-AS (inside an AS) routing protocols. Examples of IGPs include Routing Information Protocol (RIP) version 1 (RIPv1), RIP version 2 (RIPv2), Open Shortest Path First (OSPF), Integrated Intermediate System-to-Intermediate System (IS-IS), and Enhanced Interior Gateway Routing Protocol (EIGRP).
	■ **Exterior gateway protocols (EGP)** are inter-AS (between autonomous systems) routing protocols. Border Gateway Protocol (BGP) is the only widely used EGP protocol on the Internet. BGP version 4 (BGP-4) is considered the acceptable version of BGP on the Internet. It is discussed in the "Border Gateway Protocol" section.

Different types of protocols are required for the following reasons:

■ Inter-AS connections require more options for manual selection of routing characteristics. EGPs should be able to implement various policies.

■ The speed of *convergence* (distribution of routing information) and finding the best path to the destination are crucial for intra-AS routing protocols.

Therefore, EGP routing protocol metrics (used to measure paths to a destination) include more parameters to allow the administrator to influence the selection of certain routing paths. EGPs are slower to converge and more complex to configure. IGPs use less-complicated metrics to ease configuration and speed up the decisions about best routing paths for faster convergence. The "Routing Protocol Metrics" section later in this chapter defines and explains routing protocol metrics.

IGP and EGP Example

Figure 7-2 shows three interconnected autonomous systems (domains). Each AS uses an IGP for intra-AS (intra-domain) routing.

Figure 7-2   *Interior Protocols Are Used Inside and Exterior Protocols Are Used Between Autonomous Systems*

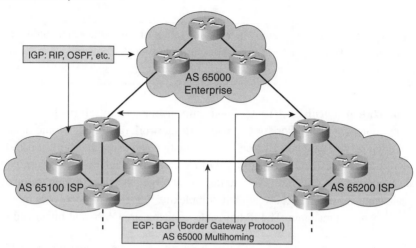

The autonomous systems require some form of interdomain routing to communicate with each other. Static routes are used in simple cases; typically, an EGP is used.

BGP-4 is the dominant EGP currently in use; BGP-4 and its extensions are the only acceptable version of BGP available for use on the public Internet.

Multihoming is when an AS has more than one connection to the Internet (for redundancy or to increase performance). BGP is particularly useful when an AS multihomes to the Internet via multiple ISPs, as illustrated in Figure 7-2. To comply with the contractual requirements from specific ISPs, an administrator uses BGP to apply specific policies—for example, to define traffic exit points, return traffic paths, and levels of quality of service (QoS).

Distance Vector Versus Link-State Versus Hybrid Protocols

There are two main types of routing protocols:

- **Distance vector protocol**: In a distance vector protocol, routing decisions are made on a hop-by-hop basis. Each router relies on its neighbor routers to make the correct routing decisions. The router passes only the results of this decision (its routing table) to its neighbors. Distance vector protocols are typically slower to converge and do not scale well; however, they are easy to implement and maintain. Examples of distance vector protocols include RIPv1, RIPv2, and Interior Gateway Routing Protocol (IGRP).

> **NOTE**   Although they are all distance vector protocols, RIPv1 uses broadcast packets to advertise routes, whereas RIPv2 uses multicast packets.

> **NOTE**   IGRP is no longer supported as of Cisco IOS Release 12.3.

> **NOTE**   A network is converged when routing tables on all routers in the network are synchronized and contain a route to all destination networks. Convergence is discussed in detail in the "Routing Protocol Convergence" section later in this chapter.

- **Link-state protocol**: Each router floods information about itself (its link states) either to all other routers in the network or to a part of the network (area). Each router makes its own routing decision based on all received information and using the shortest path first (SPF) algorithm (also called the *Dijkstra algorithm*), which calculates the shortest path to any destination. Link-state protocols are fast to converge, have less routing traffic overhead, and scale well. However, because of their complexity, link-state protocols are more difficult to implement and maintain. The IP link-state protocols are OSPF and Integrated IS-IS.

> **NOTE**   In the name *link-state*, *link* refers to the interface, and *state* refers to the link's characteristics, such as whether it is up or down.

A third type of protocol also exists: the hybrid interior gateway protocol, which is the Cisco EIGRP. EIGRP has characteristics of both distance vector and link-state protocols; it combines distance vector behavior with some link-state characteristics and some proprietary features. EIGRP is a fast-converging and scalable routing protocol.

> **NOTE**   Cisco uses a variety of terms to characterize EIGRP, including *hybrid, balanced hybrid,* and *advanced distance vector* routing protocol.

Routers running link-state and hybrid protocols use multicast packets to communicate with each other.

KEY POINT   When a network is using a distance vector routing protocol, all the routers periodically send their routing tables, or a portion of their tables, to only their neighboring routers.

In contrast, when a network is using a link-state routing protocol, each of the routers sends the state of its own interfaces (its links) to all other routers, or to all routers in a part of the network known as an area, only when there is a change.

Routers running a hybrid protocol send changed information only when there is a change (similar to link-state protocols), but only to neighboring routers (similar to distance vector protocols).

Table 7-1 summarizes the IP routing protocol types.

Table 7-1 *IP Routing Protocols*

Category	Routing Protocol
Distance vector	RIPv1, RIPv2, IGRP
Link-state	OSPF, Integrated IS-IS
Hybrid	EIGRP

Distance Vector Example

A distance vector router's understanding of the network is based on its neighbor's perspective of the topology; consequently, the distance vector approach is sometimes referred to as routing by rumor. Routers running traditional distance vector protocols periodically send their complete routing tables to all connected neighbors. Convergence might be slow because triggered updates are not typically used (RIPv2 is an exception) and loop detection timers are long. In large networks, running a distance vector protocol might cause routing tables to become enormous and result in a lot of traffic on the links.

> **NOTE**   A distance vector routing protocol's routing-by-rumor behavior and periodic updates might result in inconsistent routing information on routers within a network, which in turn might result in routing loops. Loop-avoidance mechanisms (including hold-down timers, route poisoning, poison reverse, and split horizon) are incorporated into modern distance vector protocols to prevent routing loops; however, these mechanisms result in slower convergence times compared to link-state or hybrid protocols.

> **NOTE**   *Triggered updates* (also called *flash updates* or *gratuitous updates*) are sent only when a change occurs (the link goes down or comes up or link parameters that affect routing, such as bandwidth, change).
>
> Although, as stated, most traditional distance vector protocols do not send triggered updates, the Cisco implementations of all IP distance vector protocols do send triggered updates.

Figure 7-3 shows a sample network that runs a distance vector protocol. In this network, the routing updates are periodic and include the entire routing table.

Figure 7-3 *Distance Vector Routing Periodically Sends the Entire Routing Table*

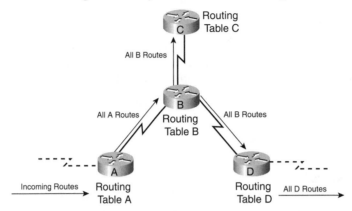

RIPv2, which is a standardized protocol developed from the RIPv1 protocol, is an example of a distance vector protocol. The characteristics of RIPv2 include the following:

■ The hop count is used as the metric for path selection.

■ The maximum allowable hop count is 15.

■ By default, routing updates are sent every 30 seconds (RIPv1 uses broadcast, and RIPv2 uses multicast).

■ RIPv2 supports variable-length subnet masking (VLSM); RIPv1 does not. Chapter 6, "Designing IP Addressing in the Network," describes VLSM.

Link-State Example

Both OSPF and Integrated IS-IS use the Hello protocol for establishing neighbor relationships. Those relationships are stored in a neighbor table (also called an adjacencies database). Each router learns a complete network topology from information shared through these neighbor relationships. That topology is stored in the router's link-state database (LSDB), also called the topology table or topology database. Each router uses this topology and the SPF algorithm to create a shortest-path tree for all reachable destinations. Each router selects the best routes from its SPF tree and places them in its routing table (also called the forwarding database).

Link-State Routing Analogy

You can think of the LSDB as being like a map in a shopping mall. Every map in the mall is the same, just as the LSDB is the same in all routers within an area. The one difference between all the maps in a shopping mall is the "you are here" dot. By looking at this dot, you can determine the best way to get to every store from your current location; the best path to a specific store is different from each location in the mall. Link-state routers function similarly: They each calculate the best way to every network within the area, from their own perspective, using the LSDB.

Figure 7-4 shows a network that uses a link-state protocol. Triggered updates, which include data on the state of only links that have changed, are sent in this network.

Figure 7-4 *Link-State Routing Sends Changed Data Only When There Is a Change*

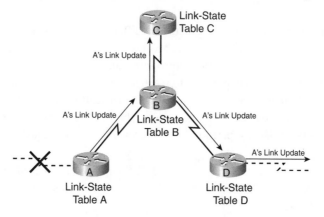

In link-state protocols, the information about connected links (including the subnets on those links) on all routers is flooded throughout the network or to a specific area of the network. Therefore, all routers in the network have detailed knowledge of the entire network. In contrast, routers running a distance vector routing protocol receive knowledge about only the best routes from their neighbors.

After the initial exchange of all link states and on reaching the full (converged) state of operation, almost no periodic updates are sent through the network. (In OSPF, periodic updates are sent every 30 minutes for each specific route, but not at the same time for all routes, reducing the routing traffic volume.) Triggered updates are flooded through the network only when a change in a link state occurs (the link goes down, comes up, or link parameters that affect routing—such as bandwidth—are changed). Only periodic hello messages are sent between neighbors to maintain and verify neighbor relationships.

Most of the control packets used in link-state operations are sent as multicast packets, which might cause problems when deploying link-state protocols in nonbroadcast multiaccess (NBMA) networks, such as with Frame Relay or ATM topologies.

Routing Protocol Metrics

This section introduces routing protocol metrics and compares the metrics used by different routing protocols.

What Is a Routing Metric?

KEY POINT | A *metric* is a value (such as path length) that routing protocols use to measure paths to a destination.

Different routing protocols base their metric on different measurements, including hop count, interface speed, or more-complex metrics. Most routing protocols maintain databases containing all the networks that the routing protocol recognizes and all the paths to each network. If a routing protocol recognizes more than one way to reach a network, it compares the metric for each different path and chooses the path with the lowest metric. If multiple paths have the same metric, a maximum of 16 can be installed in the routing table, and the router can perform load balancing among them. EIGRP can also perform load balancing between unequal-cost paths.

> **NOTE** Before Cisco IOS Release 12.3(2)T, the maximum number of parallel routes (equal-cost paths) supported by IP routing protocols was 6; that maximum was changed to 16 in Cisco IOS Release 12.3(2)T.

Figure 7-5 shows network 172.16.1.0, which is connected to Router A. The parameters for route metric calculation are forwarded in routing protocol updates.

Figure 7-5 *Routing Protocol Metrics Are Passed in Updates*

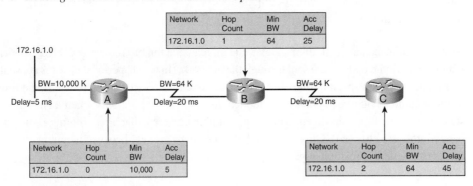

In this case, the EIGRP method of route metric parameters is used, and the minimum bandwidth and cumulative delay influence best path selection (the path with the highest minimum bandwidth and lowest delay is preferred). Figure 7-5 shows the following steps:

Step 1   Router A, which is the originator of the route 172.16.1.0, sends the initial metric values to Router B.

Step 2   Router B takes into account the parameters of its link toward Router A, adjusts the parameters (bandwidth, delay, hop count) appropriately, calculates its metric toward the 172.16.1.0 network, and sends the routing update to Router C.

Step 3   Router C adjusts the parameters again and calculates its metric toward the destination network 172.16.1.0 from those parameters.

Metrics Used by Routing Protocols

Different routing protocols calculate their routing metrics from different parameters and with different formulas. Some use simple metrics (such as RIPv1 and RIPv2), and some use complex metrics (such as EIGRP).

RIPv1 and RIPv2 use only the hop count to determine the best path (the path with the smallest hop count is preferred). Because they do not consider bandwidth, RIPv1 and RIPv2 are not suitable for networks that have significantly different transmission speeds on redundant paths. For networks that use diverse media on redundant paths, routing protocols must account for bandwidth and possibly the delay of the links.

By default EIGRP uses the minimum bandwidth and accumulated delay of the path toward the destination network in its metric calculation. Other parameters (reliability and load) can also be used, but they should be configured only if the consequences are fully understood. If misconfigured, they might affect convergence and cause routing loops.

NOTE   On Cisco routers, the bandwidth and delay metrics can be manually configured and do not necessarily reflect the link's true speed.

These bandwidth and delay metrics should be changed only if the consequences are well understood. For example, a bandwidth change might affect the QoS provided to data. As another example, EIGRP limits the amount of routing protocol traffic it sends to a percentage of the bandwidth value; changing the value could result in either too much bandwidth being used for routing protocol updates or updates not being sent in a timely manner.

EIGRP's minimum bandwidth is the minimum (slowest) bandwidth along the path. An interface's bandwidth is either the default value of the interface or as specified by the **bandwidth** command—this command is usually used on serial interfaces.

> **NOTE** In earlier Cisco IOS releases, the default bandwidth on all serial ports was T1, or 1.544 megabits per second (Mbps). In the latest Cisco IOS releases, the default bandwidth varies with interface type.

EIGRP Metric Calculation

EIGRP calculates the metric by adding weighted values of different link characteristics to a destination network. The formula used is as follows:

Metric = (K1 * bandwidth) + (K2 * bandwidth)/(256 – load) + (K3 * delay)

If K5 does not equal 0, an additional operation is performed:

Metric = Metric * [K5/(reliability + K4)]

The K values in the previous formulas are constants with default values of K1 = K3 = 1 and K2 = K4 = K5 = 0. Therefore, by default, the formula is the following:

Metric = Bandwidth + Delay

The bandwidth used in this formula is calculated using the smallest (slowest) bandwidth along the path between the source and the destination, in kilobits per second (kbps). 10^7 is divided by that value, and the result is multiplied by 256.

The delay used in this formula is the sum of the delays in the path from the source to the destination, in tens of microseconds, multiplied by 256. Figure 7-6 presents a sample network to illustrate the EIGRP metric calculation.

Figure 7-6 *Network for EIGRP Metric Calculation Example*

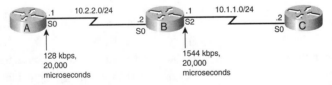

In Figure 7-6, Router B advertises network 10.1.1.0 to Router A. The metric that Router B advertises for 10.1.1.0 is calculated as follows:

■ Bandwidth = (10,000,000/1,544) * 256 = 6476 * 256 = 1,658,031

■ Delay = (20,000/10) * 256 = 2000 * 256 = 512,000

■ Metric = Bandwidth + Delay = 2,170,031

Router A calculates the metric it puts in its routing table for 10.1.1.0 as follows:

■   Bandwidth = (10,000,000/128) * 256 = 20,000,000 (using the minimum bandwidth in the path—in this case, 128 kbps)

■   Delay = ((20,000 + 20,000)/10) * 256 = 1,024,000

■   Metric = Bandwidth + Delay = 21,024,000

The IGRP metric is the EIGRP metric divided by 256 because the metric for EIGRP is a 32-bit number versus the IGRP 24-bit metric; accordingly, EIGRP has additional granularity for route selection.

In the case of link-state protocols (OSPF and IS-IS), a cumulative cost or metric is used (the lowest cost or metric path is selected). OSPF uses cost for path calculation, usually reflecting the link's bandwidth. As a result, the highest accumulated bandwidth (lowest cost) is used to select the best path. The IS-IS interface metric defaults to 10 on Cisco routers; this value can be changed, to reflect different bandwidths, for example.

NOTE   The IS-IS metric is known as the *metric*; the IS-IS specification defines four different types of metrics. All routers support Cost, the default metric. Delay, Expense, and Error are optional metrics. The default Cisco implementation of IS-IS uses Cost only, but the Cisco IOS does allow all four metrics to be set with optional parameters in the **isis metric** command.

BGP uses the AS-path attribute as part of its metric. The length of this attribute is the number of autonomous systems that must be traversed to reach a destination and is usually a factor that influences the path selection. BGP incorporates additional path attributes that can influence routing decisions; these can be manually configured.

Routing Protocol Convergence

Whenever a change occurs in a network's topology, all the routers in that network must learn the new topology. This process is both collaborative and independent; the routers share information with each other, but they must calculate the impact of the topology change independently. Because they must mutually develop an independent agreement on the new topology, they are said to converge on this consensus.

Convergence properties include the speed of propagation of routing information and the calculation of optimal paths. The quicker the convergence, the more optimal the routing protocol is said to be.

KEY POINT	Recall that a network is converged when all routing tables are synchronized and each contains a usable route to each destination network.
	Convergence time is the time it takes for all routers in a network to agree on the current topology. The size of the network, the routing protocol in use, the network design, and numerous configurable timers can affect convergence time. For example, the use of hierarchical addressing and summarization helps localize topology changes, which speeds convergence.

Network convergence must occur whenever a new routing protocol starts and whenever a change takes place in the network. It occurs in both new networks and those that are already operational. Convergence is also important when changes occur in the network.

A network is not completely operable until it has converged. Therefore, short convergence times are required for routing protocols.

RIPv2 Convergence Example

RIPv2 is a distance vector protocol that periodically propagates its routing information. Distance vector protocols use the principle of hold-down to prevent routing loops. Putting a route in hold-down after the route has failed (perhaps due to a link failure) means that if a routing update arrives with the same or a worse metric, the new route is not installed until the hold-down timer expires. Even though the destination might no longer be reachable, a route in hold-down is still used to forward traffic during the entire hold-down period.

Figure 7-7 shows a network running RIPv2; the Ethernet link (Network N) between Routers A and C has failed. The following are the RIPv2 convergence steps:

Step 1   Router C detects the link failure and sends a triggered update to Routers D and B. A triggered update is sent because something happened. In contrast, a periodic update is sent periodically—every 30 seconds, in the case of RIPv1 and RIPv2. The route is *poisoned* (sent with an infinite metric indicating that the route is unreachable) to B and D and is removed from Router C's routing table.

Step 2   Router C sends a request to its neighbors for an alternative path to network N. A broadcast request is used for RIPv1, and a multicast request is used for RIPv2.

Step 3   Router D does not report an alternative path; Router B reports a route with a worse metric.

The route via B is immediately placed in Router C's routing table. Note that Router C does not put Network N in hold-down because Router C knows that the link failed and has already removed the entry from its routing table.

Step 4   Router C advertises the route via B in a periodic update to D.

There is no change to Router D's table because Router D has the route in hold-down.

Step 5   When Router D's hold-down timer expires, the route is added to the table and is propagated to Router E in a periodic update.

Figure 7-7   *RIPv2 Convergence Example*

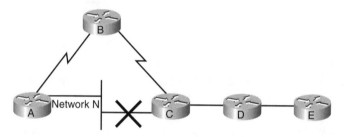

Therefore, the convergence time at Router E is the hold-down time plus one or two update intervals.

> **NOTE**   The default hold-down time is 180 seconds for RIPv1 and RIPv2. This value can be adjusted manually, but this should be done only if necessary and in the entire network to ensure consistency.

Comparison of Routing Protocol Convergence

As shown in Figure 7-8, different routing protocols need different amounts of time to converge in a given network. Although the convergence depends on the network's topology and structure, pure distance vector protocols are slower to converge than link-state protocols. The use of periodic updates and the hold-down mechanism are the main reasons for slow convergence. As a result, the fast-converging protocols should be used when the network's convergence time is crucial.

Figure 7-8 *Routing Protocol Convergence Comparison for the Network Shown in Figure 7-7*

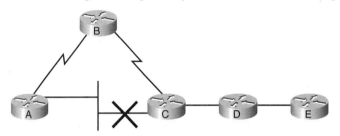

Protocol	Convergence Time to Router E
RIP	Hold-down + 1 or 2 Update Intervals
IGRP	Hold-down +1 or 2 Update Intervals
EIGRP	Matter of Seconds
OSPF	Matter of Seconds

Link-state protocols usually converge much more quickly because they instantly propagate routing updates. Whenever a change occurs in a link's state, a link-state update is flooded through the entire network. There is no need to wait for the hold-down timer to expire or for the next periodic update, as with distance vector protocols.

EIGRP is a special case because it incorporates the distance vector principle of metric propagation (it sends only the best routes to the neighbors). However, it does not have periodic updates, nor does it implement the principle of hold-downs. The most distinct feature of EIGRP is that it stores all feasible backup routes in its topology table. When a backup route exists for a lost destination, the switchover to the best backup route is almost immediate and involves no action from other routers. Therefore, very fast convergence can be achieved with proper EIGRP deployment.

Flat Versus Hierarchical Routing Protocols

> **KEY POINT** Flat routing protocols propagate all routing information throughout the network, whereas hierarchical routing protocols divide large networks into smaller areas.

This section discusses these two types of routing protocols.

Flat Routing Protocols

Flat routing protocols have no means of limiting route propagation in a major network (within a Class A, B, or C network) environment. These protocols are typically classful distance vector protocols.

Recall from Chapter 6 that *classful* means that routing updates do not include subnet masks and that the protocol performs automatic route summarization on major network (class) boundaries. Summarization cannot be done *within* a major network. These protocols support only fixed-length subnet masking (FLSM); they do not support VLSM.

Recall also that distance vector protocols periodically send entire routing tables to neighbors. Distance vector protocols do not scale well because, in a large network, they produce significant volumes of routing information that consume too many network resources (CPU, bandwidth, memory). These resources should be available to the routed traffic (application data and user traffic) instead.

Two examples of flat routing protocols are RIPv1 and RIPv2. Note, however, that RIPv2 is a classless protocol. Figure 7-9 illustrates a flat network and a hierarchical network.

Figure 7-9 *Flat and Hierarchical Networks*

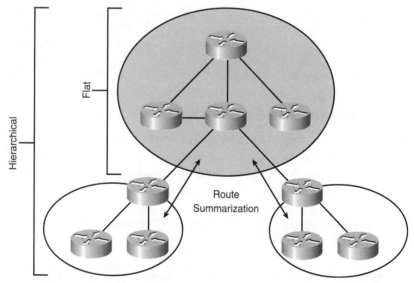

Hierarchical Routing Protocols

To solve the problems associated with flat routing protocols, additional features are implemented in hierarchical routing protocols to support large networks—for example, some support an area-based design.

Hierarchical routing protocols are typically classless link-state protocols. Recall from Chapter 6 that *classless* means that routing updates include subnet masks in their routing updates; therefore, the routing protocol supports VLSM.

Hierarchy is part of the implementation of link-state protocols with the concept of backbone and nonbackbone areas. With link-state protocols such as OSPF and IS-IS, large networks are divided into multiple areas.

Route summarization can be performed manually in hierarchical protocols and is required in most cases. With the help of route summarization, smaller routing updates propagate among areas, resulting in higher scalability. Instabilities in one part of the network are isolated, and convergence is greatly improved. Summarization can be performed on an arbitrary bit boundary within an IP address. Note, however, that OSPF supports summarization on only specific routers called *area border routers* and *autonomous system boundary routers*.

Although it is a classless hybrid protocol, EIGRP is considered a flat routing protocol because it is not area-based. Because EIGRP also supports manual summarization, EIGRP can be used in a hierarchical network design by dividing the network into areas. A hierarchical design is not necessary in EIGRP, but one is recommended for large networks.

NOTE　Although it too is classless and supports manual summarization, RIPv2 is considered a flat protocol. RIPv2 is not recommended for large networks because it is a distance vector protocol.

Routing Protocols for the Enterprise

Routing protocols vary in their support for many features, including VLSM, summarization, scalability, and fast convergence. There is no best protocol—the choice depends on many factors. This section discusses the most common routing protocols for use within the enterprise and evaluates their suitability for given network requirements.

First, the interior routing protocols EIGRP, OSPF, and Integrated IS-IS are discussed, followed by a description of BGP.

NOTE　Integrated IS-IS is not a recommended enterprise protocol for reasons described in this section.

EIGRP

EIGRP is a Cisco-proprietary protocol for routing IPv4; EIGRP can also be configured for routing IP version 6 (IPv6), Internetwork Packet Exchange (IPX), and AppleTalk traffic. EIGRP is an enhanced version of IGRP, which is a pure distance vector protocol. EIGRP, however, is a hybrid routing protocol—it is a distance vector protocol with additional link-state protocol features. EIGRP features include the following:

- Uses triggered updates (EIGRP has no periodic updates).

- Uses a topology table to keep all routes received from its neighbors, not only the best routes.

- Establishes adjacencies with neighboring routers using the Hello protocol.

- Uses multicast, rather than broadcast, for communication.

- Supports VLSM.

- Supports manual route summarization. EIGRP summarizes on major network boundaries by default, but this feature can be turned off, and summarization can be configured at any point in the network.

- Can be used to create hierarchically structured, large networks.

- Supports unequal-cost load balancing.

Routes are propagated in EIGRP in a distance vector manner, from neighbor to neighbor, and only the best routes are sent onward. A router that runs EIGRP does not have a complete view of a network because it sees only the routes it receives from its neighbors. In contrast, with a pure link-state protocol (OSPF and IS-IS), all routers in the same area have identical information and therefore have a complete view of the area and its link states.

Recall that the default EIGRP metric calculation uses the minimum bandwidth and cumulative delay of the path. Other parameters can also be used in this calculation, including worst reliability between source and destination and worst loading on a link between source and destination. Note that the maximum transmission unit and hop count are carried in the EIGRP routing updates but are not used in the metric calculation.

EIGRP Terminology

Some EIGRP-related terms include the following:

- **Neighbor table**: EIGRP routers use hello packets to discover neighbors. When a router discovers and forms an adjacency with a new neighbor, it includes the neighbor's address and the interface through which it can be reached in an entry in the neighbor table. This table is comparable to OSPF's neighbor table (adjacency database); it serves the same purpose, which is to ensure bidirectional communication between each of the directly connected neighbors. EIGRP keeps a neighbor table for each supported network protocol.

■ **Topology table**: When a router dynamically discovers a new neighbor, it sends an update about the routes it knows to its new neighbor and receives the same from the new neighbor. These updates populate the topology table. The topology table contains all destinations advertised by neighboring routers; in other words, each router stores its neighbors' routing tables in its EIGRP topology table. If a neighbor is advertising a destination, it must be using that route to forward packets; this rule must be strictly followed by all distance vector protocols. An EIGRP router maintains a topology table for each network protocol configured.

■ **Advertised distance (AD) and feasible distance (FD)**: EIGRP uses the Diffusing Update Algorithm (DUAL). DUAL uses distance information, known as a *metric* or *cost*, to select efficient loop-free paths. The lowest-cost route is calculated by adding the cost between the next-hop router and the destination—referred to as the *advertised distance*—to the cost between the local router and the next-hop router. The sum of these costs is referred to as the *feasible distance*.

■ **Successor**: A successor, also called a *current successor*, is a neighboring router that has a least-cost path to a destination (the lowest FD) guaranteed not to be part of a routing loop. Successors are offered to the routing table to be used to forward packets. Multiple successors can exist if they have the same FD.

■ **Routing table**: The routing table holds the best routes to each destination and is used to forward packets. Successor routes are offered to the routing table. The router maintains one routing table for each network protocol.

■ **Feasible successor**: Along with keeping least-cost paths, DUAL keeps backup paths to each destination. The next-hop router for a backup path is called the feasible successor. To qualify as a feasible successor, a next-hop router must have an AD less than the FD of the current successor route. In other words, a feasible successor is a neighbor that is closer to the destination, but is not in the least-cost path and, therefore, is not used to forward data. Feasible successors are selected at the same time as successors but are kept only in the topology table. The topology table can maintain multiple feasible successors for a destination.

If the route via the successor becomes invalid because of a topology change or if a neighbor changes the metric, DUAL checks for feasible successors to the destination. If a feasible successor is found, DUAL uses it, thereby avoiding a recomputation of the route. If no suitable feasible successor exists, a recomputation must occur to determine the new successor. Although recomputation is not processor-intensive, it affects convergence time, so it is advantageous to avoid unnecessary recomputations.

EIGRP Characteristics

The characteristics that make EIGRP suitable for deployment in enterprise networks include the following:

- **Fast convergence**: One advantage of EIGRP is its fast-converging DUAL route calculation mechanism. This mechanism allows backup routes (the feasible successors) to be kept in the topology table for use if the primary route fails. Because this process occurs locally on the router, the switchover to a backup route (if one exists) is immediate and does not involve action in any other routers.

- **Improved scalability**: Along with fast convergence, the ability to manually summarize also improves scalability. EIGRP summarizes routes on classful network boundaries by default. Automatic summarization can be turned off, and manual summarization can be configured at any point in the network, improving scalability and network performance because the routing protocol uses fewer resources.

- **Use of VLSM**: Because EIGRP is a classless routing protocol, it sends subnet mask information in its routing updates and therefore supports VLSM.

- **Reduced bandwidth usage**: Because EIGRP does not send periodic routing updates as other distance vector protocols do, it uses less bandwidth—particularly in large networks that have a large number of routes. On the other hand, EIGRP uses the Hello protocol to establish and maintain adjacencies with its neighbors. If many neighbors are reachable over the same physical link, as might be the case in NBMA networks, the Hello protocol might create significant routing traffic overhead. Therefore, the network must be designed appropriately to take advantage of EIGRP's benefits.

- **Multiple network layer protocol support**: EIGRP supports multiple network layer protocols through Protocol-Dependent Modules (PDM). PDMs include support for IPv4, IPv6, IPX, and AppleTalk.

NOTE   EIGRP is a Cisco-proprietary protocol that can pass protocol information only with licensed devices.

OSPF

OSPF is a standardized protocol for routing IPv4, developed in 1988 by the Internet Engineering Task Force to replace RIP in larger, more diverse media networks. In 1998, minor changes in OSPF version 2 (OSPFv2) addressed some of OSPF version 1's problems while maintaining full backward compatibility.

NOTE   OSPFv2 is described in RFC 2328, *OSPF Version 2*.

OSPF was developed for use in large scalable networks in which RIP's inherent limitations failed to satisfy requirements. OSPF is superior to RIP in all aspects, including the following:

■ It converges much faster.

■ It supports VLSM, manual summarization, and hierarchical structures.

■ It has improved metric calculation for best path selection.

■ It does not have hop-count limitations.

At its inception, OSPF supported the largest networks.

OSPF Hierarchical Design

Although OSPF was developed for large networks, its implementation requires proper design and planning; this is especially important for networks with 50 or more routers. The concept of multiple separate areas inside one domain (or AS) was implemented in OSPF to reduce the amount of routing traffic and make networks more scalable.

In OSPF, there must always be one backbone area—area 0—to which all other nonbackbone areas must be directly attached. A router is a member of an OSPF area when at least one of its interfaces operates in that area. Routers that reside on boundaries between the backbone and a nonbackbone area are called *Area Border Routers (ABR)* and have at least one interface in each area. The boundary between the areas is within the ABR itself.

If external routes are propagated into the OSPF AS, the router that redistributes those routes is called an *Autonomous System Boundary Router (ASBR)*. Careful design and correct mapping of areas to the network topology are important because manual summarization of routes can only be performed on ABRs and ASBRs.

Traffic sent from one nonbackbone area to another always crosses the backbone. For example, in Figure 7-10, the Area 1 ABR must forward traffic from Area 1 destined for Area 2 into the backbone. The Area 2 ABR receives the traffic from the backbone and forwards it to the appropriate destination inside Area 2.

> **NOTE**   You might encounter different terminology for the various OSPF tables:
> ■ OSPF neighbor table = adjacency database
> ■ OSPF topology table = OSPF topology database = LSDB
> ■ Routing table = forwarding database

Figure 7-10 *Traffic from OSPF Area 1 to Area 2 Must Go Through the Backbone, Area 0*

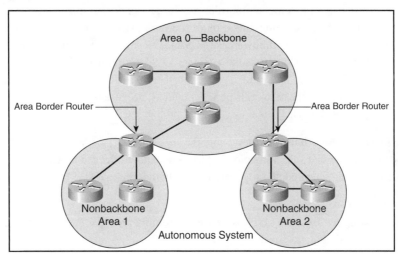

OSPF Characteristics

OSPF is a link-state protocol that has the following characteristics for deployment in enterprise networks:

- **Fast convergence**: OSPF achieves fast convergence times using triggered link-state updates that include one or more link-state advertisements (LSA). LSAs describe the state of links on specific routers and are propagated unchanged within an area. Therefore, all routers in the same area have identical topology tables; each router has a complete view of all links and devices in the area. Depending on their type, LSAs are usually changed by ABRs when they cross into another area.

  When the OSPF topology table is fully populated, the SPF algorithm calculates the shortest paths to the destination networks. Triggered updates and metric calculation based on the cost of a specific link ensure quick selection of the shortest path toward the destination.

  By default, the OSPF link cost value is inversely proportional to the link's bandwidth.

NOTE By default, the cost in Cisco routers is calculated using the formula 100 Mbps / bandwidth in Mbps. For example, a 64-kbps link has a cost of 1562, and a T1 link has a cost of 64. However, this formula is based on a maximum bandwidth of 100 Mbps, which results in a cost of 1. If the network includes faster links, the cost formula can be recalibrated.

- **Very good scalability**: OSPF's multiple area structure provides good scalability. However, OSPF's strict area implementation rules require proper design to support other scalability features such as manual summarization of routes on ABRs and ASBRs, stub areas, totally stubby areas, and not-so-stubby areas (NSSA). The stub, totally stubby, and NSSA features for nonbackbone areas decrease the amount of LSA traffic from the backbone (area 0) into nonbackbone areas (and they are described further in the following sidebar). This allows low-end routers to run in the network's peripheral areas, because fewer LSAs mean smaller OSPF topology tables, less OSPF memory usage, and lower CPU usage in stub area routers.

- **Reduced bandwidth usage**: Along with the area structure, the use of triggered (not periodic) updates and manual summarization reduces the bandwidth used by OSPF by limiting the volume of link-state update propagation. Recall, though, that OSPF does send updates every 30 minutes.

- **VLSM support**: Because OSPF is a classless routing protocol, it supports VLSM to achieve better use of IP address space.

OSPF Area Types

A variety of possible area types exist. The most commonly used are as follows:

- **Standard area**: This default area accepts link updates, route summaries, and external routes.

- **Backbone area (transit area)**: The backbone area, area 0, is the central entity to which all other areas connect to exchange and route information. The OSPF backbone has all the properties of a standard OSPF area.

- **Stub area**: This area does not accept information about routes external to the autonomous system, such as routes from non-OSPF sources. If routers need to route to networks outside the autonomous system, they use a default route, indicated as 0.0.0.0. Stub areas cannot contain ASBRs (except that the ABRs may also be ASBRs). Using a stub area reduces the size of the routing tables inside the area.

- **Totally stubby area**: A totally stubby area is a Cisco-specific feature that further reduces the number of routes in the routing tables inside the area. This area does not accept external autonomous system routes or summary routes from other areas internal to the autonomous system. If a router has to send a packet to a network external to the area, it sends the packet using a default route. Totally stubby areas cannot contain ASBRs (except that the ABRs may also be ASBRs).

- **NSSA**: This area offers benefits similar to those of a stub area. However, NSSAs allow ASBRs, which is against the rules in a stub area. A totally stubby NSSA (although it sounds like a very strange name) is a Cisco-specific feature that further reduces the size of the routing tables inside the NSSA.

Integrated IS-IS

IS-IS was developed by Digital Equipment Corporation (DEC) as the dynamic link-state routing protocol for the Open Systems Interconnection (OSI) protocol suite. The OSI suite uses Connectionless Network Service (CLNS) to provide connectionless delivery of data, and the actual Layer 3 protocol is Connectionless Network Protocol (CLNP). CLNP is the OSI suite solution for connectionless delivery of data, similar to IP in the TCP/IP suite. IS-IS uses CLNS addresses to identify the routers and build the LSDB.

IS-IS was adapted to the IP environment because IP is used on the Internet; this extended version of IS-IS for mixed OSI and IPv4 environments is called *Integrated IS-IS*. Integrated IS-IS tags CLNP routes with information on IP networks and subnets.

> **NOTE** One version of Integrated IS-IS supports IPv6, as described in Chapter 6.

KEY POINT Even if Integrated IS-IS is used only for routing IP (and not CLNP), OSI protocols are used to form the neighbor relationships between the routers; therefore, for Integrated IS-IS to work, CLNS addresses must still be assigned to areas. This proves to be a major disadvantage when implementing Integrated IS-IS, because OSI and CLNS knowledge is not widespread in the enterprise networking community. Therefore, Integrated IS-IS is not recommended as an enterprise routing protocol; it is included here for completeness.

Integrated IS-IS Terminology

ISO specifications call routers *intermediate systems*. Thus, IS-IS is a router-to-router protocol, allowing routers to communicate with other routers.

IS-IS routing takes place at two levels within an AS: Level 1 (L1) and Level 2 (L2). L1 routing occurs within an IS-IS area and is responsible for routing inside an area. All devices in an L1 routing area have the same area address. Routing within an area is accomplished by looking at the locally significant address portion, known as the *system ID*, and choosing the lowest-cost path.

L2 routing occurs between IS-IS areas. L2 routers learn the locations of L1 routing areas and build an interarea routing table. L2 routers use the destination area address to route traffic using the lowest-cost path. Therefore, IS-IS supports two routing levels:

■ L1 builds a common topology of system IDs in the local area and routes traffic within the area using the lowest-cost path.

■ L2 exchanges prefix information (area addresses) between areas and routes traffic to an area using the lowest-cost path.

To support the two routing levels, IS-IS defines three types of routers:

- L1 routers use link-state packets (LSP) to learn about paths within the areas to which they connect (intra-area).

- L2 routers use LSPs to learn about paths among areas (interarea).

- Level 1/Level 2 (L1/L2) routers learn about paths both within and between areas. L1/L2 routers are equivalent to ABRs in OSPF.

The three types of IS-IS routers are shown in Figure 7-11.

Figure 7-11   *Three Types of IS-IS Routers*

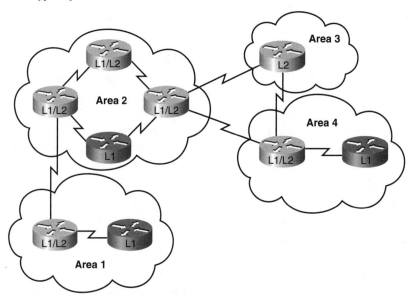

The path of connected L2 and L1/L2 routers is called the *backbone*. All areas and the backbone must be contiguous.

IS-IS area boundaries fall on the links, not within the routers. Each IS-IS router belongs to exactly one area. Neighboring routers learn that they are in the same or different areas and negotiate appropriate adjacencies—L1, L2, or both.

Changing Level 1 routers into Level 1/Level 2 or Level 2 routers can easily expand the Integrated IS-IS backbone. In comparison, in OSPF, entire areas must be renumbered to achieve this.

Integrated IS-IS Characteristics

IS-IS is a popular IP routing protocol in the ISP industry. The simplicity and stability of IS-IS make it robust in large internetworks. Integrated IS-IS characteristics include the following:

- **VLSM support**: As a classless routing protocol, Integrated IS-IS supports VLSM.

- **Fast convergence**: Similar to OSPF, Integrated IS-IS owes its fast convergence characteristics to its link-state operation (including flooding of triggered link-state updates). Another feature that guarantees fast convergence and less CPU usage is the partial route calculation (PRC). Although Integrated IS-IS uses the same algorithm as OSPF for best path calculation, the full SPF calculation is initially performed on network startup only. When IP subnet information changes, only a PRC for the subnet in question runs on routers. This saves router resources and enables faster calculation. A full SPF calculation must be run for each OSPF change.

> **NOTE**   Introduced in Cisco IOS Release 12.0(24)S, the OSPF incremental SPF feature is more efficient than the full SPF algorithm and allows OSPF to converge on a new routing topology more quickly. Information on this feature is available in *OSPF Incremental SPF,* at http://www.cisco.com/en/US/products/ps6350/products_configuration_guide_chapter09186a00804556a5.html.

- **Excellent scalability**: Integrated IS-IS is more scalable and flexible than OSPF; IS-IS backbone area design is not as strict as OSPF, thereby allowing for easy backbone extension.

- **Reduced bandwidth usage**: Triggered updates and the absence of periodic updates ensure that less bandwidth is used for routing information.

Integrated IS-IS offers inherent support for LAN and point-to-point environments only, whereas NBMA point-to-multipoint environment support is not included. In NBMA environments, point-to-point links (subinterfaces) must be established for correct Integrated IS-IS operation.

As mentioned, one disadvantage of Integrated IS-IS is its close association with the OSI world. Because few network administrators have adequate knowledge of OSI addressing and operation, implementation of Integrated IS-IS might be difficult.

Summary of Interior Routing Protocol Features

There is no best or worst routing protocol. The decision about which routing protocol to implement (or whether multiple routing protocols should indeed be implemented in a network) can be made only after you carefully consider the design goals and examine the network's physical topology in detail.

Table 7-2 summarizes some characteristics of IP routing protocols discussed in this chapter. Although they are no longer recommended enterprise protocols, RIPv1, RIPv2, and IGRP are also included in this table for completeness.

Table 7-2 *IP Routing Protocol Comparison*

Feature	RIPv1	RIPv2	IGRP[1]	EIGRP[2]	OSPF	IS-IS
Distance vector	X	X	X	X		
Link-state					X	X
Hierarchical topology required					X	X
Hierarchical topology support				X		
Flat topology support	X	X	X	X		
Classless (and therefore VLSM support)		X		X	X	X
Classful (and therefore no VLSM support)[3]	X		X			
Performs automatic route summarization	X	X	X	X		
Manual route summarization support		X		X	X	X
Multiaccess (LAN) support	X	X	X	X	X	X
Point-to-point support	X	X	X	X	X	X
NBMA point-to-multipoint support				X	X	

[1] IGRP is no longer supported as of Cisco IOS Release 12.3. It is included in this table for completeness.

[2] EIGRP is an advanced distance vector protocol with some characteristics also found in link-state protocols.

[3] Only FLSM is supported, not VLSM, because consistency of the mask is assumed within a classful network.

Selecting an Appropriate Interior Routing Protocol

The selection of a routing protocol is based on the design goals and the physical topology of the network. Both EIGRP and OSPF are recommended as enterprise routing protocols.

When choosing routing protocols, you can use Table 7-3 as a decision table template. Decision tables are discussed in Chapter 2, "Applying a Methodology to Network Design." Additional rows can be added to specify other parameters that might be important in the specific network.

Table 7-3 *Routing Protocol Selection Decision Table Template*

Parameters	OSPF	EIGRP	Required Network Parameters
Size of network (small/medium/large/very large)	Large	Large	
Speed of convergence (very high/high/medium/low)	High	Very high	
Very good scalability (yes/no)	Yes	Yes	
Support for VLSM (yes/no)	Yes	Yes	
Support for mixed vendor devices (yes/no)	Yes	No	
Multiple network layer protocol support (yes/no)	No	Yes	

When to Choose EIGRP

EIGRP is a Cisco-proprietary hybrid protocol that incorporates the best aspects of distance vector and link-state features. EIGRP keeps a topology table, it does not perform periodic route updates, and it does perform triggered updates. It is well suited to almost all environments, including LAN, point-to-point, and NBMA. The EIGRP split-horizon functionality can be disabled in NBMA environments. EIGRP is not suitable for dialup environments because it must maintain its neighbor relationships using periodic hello packets; sending these packets would mean that the dialup connections would have to stay up all the time.

When to Choose OSPF

OSPF is a standards-based link-state protocol that is based on the SPF algorithm for best path calculation. OSPF was initially designed for networks of point-to-point links and was later adapted for operation in LAN and NBMA environments. OSPF can be used on dialup links with the OSPF Demand Circuit feature, which suppresses the Hello protocol.

The OSPF hierarchical area requirements impose design constraints in larger networks. One backbone area is required, and all nonbackbone areas must be directly attached to that backbone area. Expansion of the backbone area can cause design issues because the backbone area must remain contiguous.

Border Gateway Protocol

BGP is an EGP that is primarily used to interconnect autonomous systems. BGP is a successor to EGP, the Exterior Gateway Protocol (note the dual use of the EGP acronym). Because EGP is obsolete, BGP is currently the only EGP in use.

BGP-4 is the latest version of BGP. It is defined in RFC 4271, *A Border Gateway Protocol (BGP-4)*. As noted in this RFC, the classic definition of an AS is "a set of routers under a single technical administration, using an Interior Gateway Protocol (IGP) and common metrics to determine how to route packets within the AS, and using an inter-AS routing protocol to determine how to route packets to other [autonomous systems]."

> **NOTE**   Extensions to BGP-4, known as *BGP4+*, have been defined to support multiple protocols, including IPv6. These multiprotocol extensions to BGP are defined in RFC 2858, *Multiprotocol Extensions for BGP-4*.

KEY POINT | The main goal of BGP is to provide an interdomain routing system that guarantees the loop-free exchange of routing information between autonomous systems. BGP routers exchange information about paths to destination networks.

BGP does not look at speed to determine the best path. Rather, BGP is a policy-based routing protocol that allows an AS to control traffic flow by using multiple BGP attributes.

Routers running BGP exchange network reachability information, called *path vectors* or *attributes*, including a list of the full path of BGP AS numbers that a router should take to reach a destination network. BGP is therefore also called a *path vector routing protocol*. BGP allows a provider to fully use all its bandwidth by manipulating these path attributes. This AS path information is useful in constructing a graph of loop-free autonomous systems. It is used to identify routing policies so that restrictions on routing behavior can be enforced based on the AS path.

> **NOTE**   Attributes can be used within an AS to influence the path that a packet takes within the AS and how the packet gets to a neighboring AS. Some attributes can be used to attempt to influence how a neighboring AS routes its traffic. However, an AS cannot mandate how a neighboring AS routes its traffic.

BGP use in an AS is most appropriate when the effects of BGP are well understood and at least one of the following conditions exists:

- The AS has multiple connections to other autonomous systems.

- The AS allows packets to transit through it to reach other autonomous systems (for example, it is an ISP).

- Routing policy and route selection for traffic entering or leaving the AS must be manipulated.

The use of static routes is recommended for inter-AS routing if none of these requirements exists.

If an enterprise has a policy that requires it to differentiate between its traffic and traffic from its ISP, the enterprise must connect to its ISP using BGP. If, instead, an enterprise is connected to its ISP with a static route, traffic from that enterprise is indistinguishable from traffic from the ISP for policy decision-making purposes.

> **NOTE**   BGP implementation requires considerable knowledge. Improper implementations can cause immense damage, especially when neighbors exchange complete BGP Internet tables (which can have more than 190,000 routes and are growing).

BGP Implementation Example

In Figure 7-12, BGP is used to interconnect multiple autonomous systems. Because of the multiple connections between autonomous systems and the need for path manipulation, the use of static routing is excluded. AS 65000 is multihomed to three ISPs: AS 65500, AS 65250, and AS 64600.

Figure 7-12   *BGP Is Used to Interconnect Autonomous Systems*

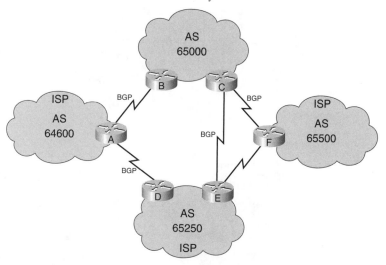

> **NOTE**   The AS designator is a 16-bit number with a range of 1 to 65535. RFC 1930, *Guidelines for Creation, Selection, and Registration of an Autonomous System (AS)*, provides guidelines for the use of AS numbers. A range of AS numbers, 64512 to 65535, is reserved for private use, much like the private IP addresses. All the examples in this book use private AS numbers to avoid publishing AS numbers belonging to an organization.
>
> An organization must use an Internet Assigned Numbers Authority–assigned AS number rather than a private AS number only if it plans to use an EGP, such as BGP, to connect to a public network such as the Internet. On the Internet, ISPs use public AS numbers.

External and Internal BGP

BGP uses TCP to communicate. Any two routers that have formed a TCP connection to exchange BGP routing information—in other words, a BGP connection—are called peers or neighbors. BGP peers can be either internal or external to the AS.

When BGP is running between routers within one AS, it is called *internal BGP (IBGP)*. IBGP is run within an AS to exchange BGP information so that all internal BGP speakers have the same BGP routing information about outside autonomous systems, and so that this information can be passed to other autonomous systems. As long as they can reach each other, routers that run IBGP do not have to be directly connected to each other; static routes or routes learned from an IGP running within the AS provide reachability.

When BGP runs between routers in different autonomous systems, it is called external BGP (EBGP). Routers that run EBGP are usually connected directly to each other. Figure 7-13 illustrates IBGP and EBGP neighbors.

Figure 7-13 *Routers That Have Formed a BGP Connection Are BGP Peers or Neighbors, Either External or Internal*

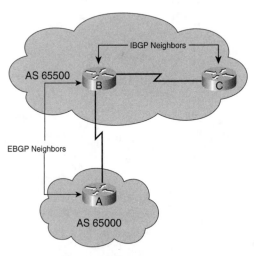

The primary use for IBGP is to carry EBGP (inter-AS) routes through an AS. IBGP can be run on all routers or on specific routers inside the AS.

> **KEY POINT** | All routers in the path between IBGP neighbors within an AS, known as the *transit path*, must also be running BGP. These IBGP sessions must be fully meshed.

IBGP is usually not the only protocol running in the AS; there is usually an IGP running also. Instead of redistributing the entire Internet routing table (learned via EBGP) into the IGP, IBGP carries the EBGP routes across the AS. This is necessary because in most cases the EBGP tables are too large for an IGP to handle. Even if EBGP has a small table, the loss of external routes triggering extensive computations in the IGP should be prevented. Other IBGP uses include the following:

- Applying policy-based routing within an AS using BGP path attributes.

- QoS Policy Propagation on BGP, which uses IBGP to send common QoS parameters (such as Type of Service [ToS]) between routers in a network and results in a synchronized QoS policy.

- Multiprotocol Label Switching (MPLS) virtual private networks (VPN) where the multiprotocol version of BGP is used to carry MPLS VPN information.

Routing Protocol Deployment

This section first describes why certain protocols are suitable for specific modules in the Enterprise Architecture. After that is a discussion of the following advanced routing features: redistribution, filtering, and summarization.

Routing Protocols in the Enterprise Architecture

Recall from Chapter 3, "Structuring and Modularizing the Network," that the modules in the Cisco Enterprise Architecture correspond to places in the network. The choice of routing protocols depends on the network design goals. Therefore, the routing protocol decision should be made only after the network goals and topology are determined. Running multiple routing protocols might be necessary in large enterprise networks, for example, when a network upgrade is performed; the old routing protocol usually coexists with the new one during the transition period.

As discussed in previous sections of this chapter, routing protocols differ in many ways. For example, how routing information is exchanged, convergence times, metrics used for optimal route determination, required amount of processing power and memory, and availability of a routing protocol on various platforms can determine whether a routing protocol is more or less suitable for a network or parts of a network. The following sections explain why certain protocols are suitable for specific modules in the Enterprise Architecture, and the advantages and disadvantages of individual protocols.

Routing in the Campus Core

The Campus Core provides high-speed data transmission between Building Distribution devices. The Campus Core is critical for connectivity and, therefore, incorporates a high level of redundancy using redundant links and load sharing between equal-cost paths. In the event of a link failure, it must immediately converge, adapting quickly to change to provide a seamless transport service.

KEY POINT	EIGRP and OSPF both adapt quickly to changes and have short convergence times. Therefore, they are suitable for use in the Campus Core.

The decision of whether to use EIGRP or OSPF should be based on the underlying physical topology, IP addressing, equipment used, and possible issues related to the routing protocol in a particular situation. Figure 7-14 illustrates routing protocols in the Enterprise Architecture, including those recommended for the Campus Core.

Figure 7-14 *Routing Protocols in the Enterprise Architecture*

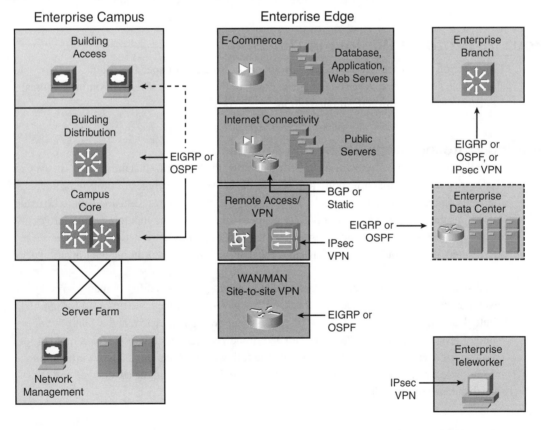

The following are considerations for routing protocol use in the Campus Core:

■ OSPF imposes a strict hierarchical design. OSPF areas should map to the IP addressing plan, which cannot always be achieved.

■ EIGRP restricts vendor selection because it is a Cisco-proprietary protocol. One way to overcome this restriction is to use EIGRP in the Campus Core and other routing protocols in the non-Cisco parts of the network, and redistribute between the protocols.

The following are reasons that other routing protocols are not considered for the Campus Core:

■ Even if routing only IP, IS-IS requires detailed knowledge of the OSI protocol suite for proper configuration, and that knowledge is not widely available.

■ RIP is not recommended as a Campus Core routing protocol because of its periodic transmission of the entire routing table, which results in relatively slow convergence, and because the RIP metric is based on hop count.

■ Using static routing in the Campus Core is not an option because static routing requires administrative intervention for changes and on link failures.

Routing in the Building Distribution Layer

The Building Distribution layer is the intermediate point between the Campus Core and the Building Access layers. In addition to other issues (such as physical media and IP addressing), the choice of routing protocol depends on the routing protocols used in the Campus Core and Building Access.

KEY POINT As a recommended practice, the same routing protocol should be used in all three layers of the Enterprise Campus. If multiple routing protocols must be used, the Building Distribution layer redistributes among them.

Recommended routing protocols in the Building Distribution layer include EIGRP and OSPF.

For example, if EIGRP is the Campus Core routing protocol and RIPv1 is the Building Access layer routing protocol (to support legacy equipment), both routing protocols are used in the Building Distribution devices, with redistribution and filtering.

Routing in the Building Access Layer

The Building Access layer provides local users with access to network resources. The underlying physical topology, IP addressing, and the available processing power and memory in the Building Access layer equipment influence the routing protocol choice. The recommended routing protocols for the Building Access layer are OSPF and EIGRP. Using static routing in the access layer is also a possibility.

Routing in the Enterprise Edge Modules

In the Enterprise Edge modules, the underlying physical topology, IP addressing, and the deployed equipment also drive the choice of routing protocol.

> **KEY POINT** The routing protocols in the Enterprise Edge modules are typically OSPF, EIGRP, BGP, and static routing.

> **NOTE** Routing protocols running in the enterprise edge module are referred to as edge routing protocols.

EIGRP gives an administrator more influence on routing and is suitable for NBMA environments in which there is a split-horizon issue because EIGRP split-horizon can be turned off. When equipment from multiple vendors is part of the overall design, the use of EIGRP is restricted to only where Cisco devices exist.

The limitations of using OSPF as an Enterprise Edge routing protocol are related to its high memory and processing power requirements, which might preclude its use on older routers, and its strict hierarchical design. The high memory and processing power requirements can be reduced using summarization and careful area planning.

OSPF also requires significant configuration expertise. OSPF is appropriate in environments such as LAN, NBMA, and dialup.

The Remote Access and VPN module provides connectivity to corporate networks for remote users via dialup connections and dedicated IPsec VPNs across the Internet. In a dialup environment, static routing is typically used.

Depending on whether multiple exit points exist and on redundancy requirements, either static routes or BGP are used for Internet connectivity. Static routes are used when only one exit point exists; they use less overhead than BGP routing. BGP is used when there are multiple exit points and when multihoming is desired.

Route Redistribution

This section introduces route redistribution and discusses administrative distance and the process used to select the best route. The specifics of route redistribution deployment are described.

Using Route Redistribution

The following are possible reasons why you might need multiple routing protocols running at the same time within your network:

- You are migrating from an older IGP to a new IGP. Multiple redistribution boundaries might exist until the new protocol has displaced the old protocol completely. Running multiple routing protocols during a migration is effectively the same as a network that has multiple routing protocols running as part of its design.

- You want to use another protocol but have to keep the old routing protocol because of the host system's needs. For example, UNIX host-based routers might run only RIP.

- Some departments might not want to upgrade their routers to support a new routing protocol.

- If you have a mixed-vendor environment, you can use the Cisco-proprietary EIGRP routing protocol in the Cisco portion of the network and then use a common standards-based routing protocol, such as OSPF, to communicate with non-Cisco devices.

KEY POINT | When any of these situations arises, Cisco routers allow internetworks using different routing protocols (referred to as *routing domains* or *autonomous systems*) to exchange routing information through a feature called *route redistribution*. This allows, for example, hosts in one part of the network to reach hosts in another part that is running a different routing protocol.

In some cases, the same protocol may be used in multiple different domains or autonomous systems within a network. Multiple instances of the protocol are treated no differently than if they were distinct protocols; redistribution is required to exchange routes between them. Accordingly, redistribution of routes is required when one or both of the following occur:

- Multiple routing protocols are used in the network—for example, RIPv2, EIGRP, and OSPF.

- Multiple routing domains are used in the network—for example, two EIGRP routing processes.

Redistribution occurs on the boundaries between routing protocols and between domains. As shown in Figure 7-15, redistribution occurs on a router with interfaces that participate in multiple routing protocols or routing domains.

Figure 7-15 *Redistribution Occurs on the Boundaries Between Protocols or Domains*

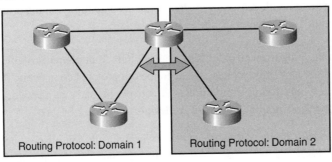

Routing Protocol: Domain 1   Routing Protocol: Domain 2

Administrative Distance

Most routing protocols have metric structures and algorithms that are incompatible with other protocols. It is critical that a network using multiple routing protocols be able to seamlessly exchange route information and be able to select the best path across multiple protocols. Cisco routers use a value called administrative distance to select the best path when they learn of two or more routes to the same destination from different routing protocols.

Administrative distance rates a routing protocol's believability. Cisco has assigned a default administrative distance value to each routing protocol supported on its routers. Each routing protocol is prioritized in order, from most to least believable.

KEY POINT | Administrative distance is a value between 0 and 255. The lower the administrative distance value, the higher the protocol's believability.

Table 7-4 lists the default administrative distance of the protocols supported by Cisco routers.

Table 7-4 *Administrative Distance of Routing Protocols*

Route Source	Default Distance
Connected interface	0
Static route out an interface	0
Static route to a next-hop address	1
EIGRP summary route	5
External BGP	20
Internal EIGRP	90
IGRP[1]	100

Table 7-4 *Administrative Distance of Routing Protocols (Continued)*

Route Source	Default Distance
OSPF	110
Integrated IS-IS	115
RIPv1, RIPv2	120
EGP	140
On-demand routing	160
External EIGRP	170
Internal BGP	200
Unknown	255

[1] IGRP is no longer supported as of Cisco IOS Release 12.3. It is included in this table for completeness.

Selecting the Best Route

Cisco routers use the following two parameters to select the best path when they learn two or more routes to the same destination from different routing protocols:

- **Administrative distance**: As described in the previous section, the administrative distance is used to rate a routing protocol's believability. This criterion is the first thing a router uses to determine which routing protocol to believe if more than one protocol provides route information for the same destination.

- **Routing metric**: The routing metric is a value representing the path between the local router and the destination network, according to the routing protocol being used. This metric is used to determine the routing protocol's "best" path to the destination.

Route Redistribution Direction

Redistribution is often applied between the Campus Core and Enterprise Edge protocols. As shown in Figure 7-16, redistribution is possible in two ways:

- **One-way route redistribution**: Routing information is redistributed from one routing protocol or domain to another, but not vice versa. Static or default routes are required in the opposite direction to provide connectivity.

- **Two-way route redistribution**: Routing information is redistributed from one routing protocol or domain to another, and vice versa. Static or default routes are not required because all routing information is passed between two entities.

Figure 7-16 *Route Redistribution Can Be One-Way or Two-Way*

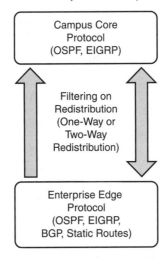

Specific routes can be filtered, and the administrative distance of redistributed routes can be changed in either of these cases to reduce the possibility of routing loops and ensure that traffic is routed optimally.

Route Redistribution Planning

When deciding where and how to use route redistribution, determine the following:

- The routing protocols and domains that will be used in the network

- The routing protocol and domain boundaries (the boundary routers)

- The direction of route redistribution (one-way or two-way)

If route redistribution is not carefully designed, suboptimal routing and routing loops can be introduced into the network when routes are redistributed in a network with redundant paths between dissimilar routing protocols or domains. Route filtering (as described in the "Route Filtering" section of this chapter) helps solve this problem.

Route Redistribution in the Enterprise Architecture

Redistribution is needed in the Building Distribution layer when different routing protocols or domains exist in the Building Access layer and Campus Core. Redistribution might also be needed between the Campus Core and the Enterprise Edge, including to and from WAN module routers, from static or BGP routes in the Internet Connectivity module, and from static routes in the

Remote Access and VPN module. Figure 7-17 shows a sample enterprise network with redistribution points throughout.

Figure 7-17   *Route Redistribution in the Enterprise Architecture*

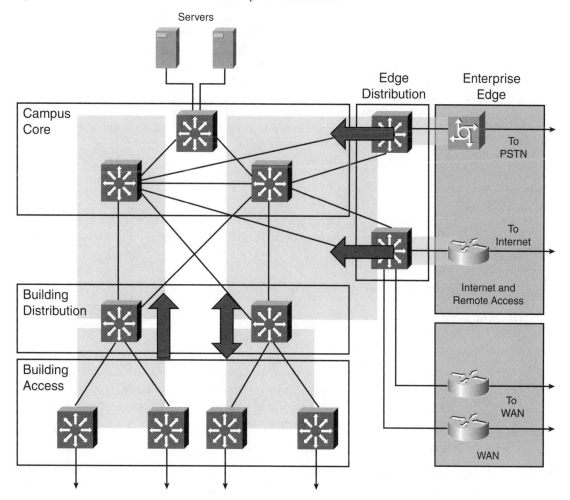

In this example, some remote sites require connectivity to the Server Farm; therefore, one-way redistribution is performed to inject routes from these remote sites into the Campus Core. Some remote sites require connectivity to the entire network; this is provided by two-way redistribution (otherwise, static routes would have to be configured in the Campus Core). The Building Distribution layer propagates only a default route down to the Building Access layer, whereas the Building Access layer advertises its own subnets to the Building Distribution layer.

Redistribution might also be necessary in the Remote Access and VPN and Internet Connectivity modules. For a Remote Access and VPN module with static routing, static routes are injected into the Campus Core routing protocol. In the opposite direction, default routes provide connectivity for remote users.

In an Internet Connectivity module with only one exit point, that exit point is the default route for traffic destined for the Internet and is propagated through the core routing protocol. If multiple exit points toward multiple ISPs exist, BGP provides Internet connectivity, and redistribution can be used.

KEY POINT | Redistribution with BGP requires careful planning. For more details, see *Authorized Self-Study Guide: Building Scalable Cisco Internetworks (BSCI),* Third Edition, by Diane Teare and Catherine Paquet, Cisco Press, 2006.

Route Filtering

As mentioned, route filtering might be required when redistributing routes. Route filtering prevents the advertisement or acceptance of certain routes through the routing domain. Filtering can be configured as follows:

- On a routing domain boundary where redistribution occurs

- Within the routing domain to isolate some parts of the network from other parts

- To limit routing traffic from untrusted external domains

Filtering is used with route redistribution, primarily to prevent suboptimal routing and routing loops that might occur when routes are redistributed at multiple redistribution points. Route filtering is also used to prevent routes about certain networks, such as a private IP address space, from being sent to or received from remote sites.

Redistributing and Filtering with BGP

An enterprise border router running BGP typically announces only the major network (the prefix assigned to the enterprise network) to the external domains, excluding any details about subnets. This is done using the BGP **network** router configuration command, which allows BGP to advertise a network that is already part of its IP routing table.

Alternatively, internal networks could be summarized into one major subnet that covers the assigned public address space and redistributed into BGP. However, redistributing from an IGP into BGP is not recommended, because any change in the IGP routes—for example, if a link goes down—can cause a BGP update, which might result in unstable BGP tables.

If IGP routes are redistributed into BGP, make sure that only local routes—those that originate within the AS—are redistributed. For example, routes learned from other autonomous systems (that were learned by redistributing BGP into the IGP) must not be sent out from the IGP again, because routing loops could result, or the AS could inadvertently become a transit AS. Private IP addresses must not be redistributed, so they should also be filtered. Configuring this filtering can be complex.

In the other direction, either a default route or a default route plus a few other specific routes is passed into an enterprise AS. These can then be redistributed into the IGP running in the AS.

Redistributing all BGP routes into an IGP is not advised, because non-BGP participating routers do not require full Internet routing tables, and IGP protocols are unable to process large numbers of advertised routes. Unnecessary routes should be filtered.

Route Summarization

Chapter 6 explains route summarization (which is also called *route aggregation or supernetting*). In route summarization, a single summary address in the routing table represents a set of routes. Summarization reduces the routing update traffic, the number of routes in the routing table, and the overall router overhead in the router receiving the routes.

The Benefits of Route Summarization

A large flat network is not scalable because routing traffic consumes considerable network resources. When a network change occurs, it is propagated throughout the network, which requires processing time for route recomputation and bandwidth to propagate routing updates.

A network hierarchy can reduce both routing traffic and unnecessary route recomputation. To accomplish this, the network must be divided into areas that enable route summarization. With summarization in place, a *route flap* (a route that goes down and up continuously) that occurs in one network area does not influence routing in other areas. Instabilities are isolated and convergence is improved, thereby reducing the amount of routing traffic, the size of the routing tables, and the required memory and processing power for routing. Summarization is configured manually, or occurs automatically at the major network boundary in some routing protocols.

KEY POINT Recall from Chapter 6 that being able to summarize requires a well-planned underlying IP addressing design.

Recommended Practice: Summarize at the Distribution Layer

It is a recommended practice to configure summarization in a large network from the distribution layers toward the core, as illustrated in Figure 7-18. The distribution layer should summarize all networks on all interfaces toward the Campus Core. WAN connectivity and remote access points should be summarized toward the core. For example, remote subnets could be summarized into major networks, and only those major networks would be advertised to the core.

Figure 7-18 *Summarizing at the Distribution Layer Reduces Routing Traffic*

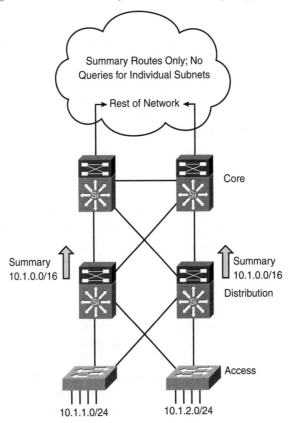

Implementing summarization at the distribution layer optimizes the convergence process. For example, if a link to an access layer device goes down, return traffic to that device is dropped at the distribution layer until the routing protocol converges. Summarizing also limits the number of peers that an EIGRP router must query or the number of LSAs that an OSPF router must process, which also reduces the convergence time.

Core routers that receive two routes for a network install the more-specific route in the routing table. Therefore, summary routes for primary links must use a longer subnet mask.

Recommended Practice: Passive Interfaces for IGP at the Access Layer

Another recommended practice is to limit unnecessary peering across the access layer. In Figure 7-19, the distribution multilayer switches are directly connected to each other and are also interconnected with three access layer switches, each having four VLANs. By default, the distribution layer devices send routing updates and attempt to peer with the remote distribution layer devices across the links from the access switches on every VLAN. Having the distribution switches form neighbor relationships over these 12 access layer connections provides no benefit and wastes resources (including CPU processing time and memory). Therefore, the interfaces on the distribution layer devices toward the access layer devices are configured as passive interfaces under the routing protocol configuration. This suppresses the advertisement of routing updates for that routing protocol on those interfaces.

Figure 7-19 *Limit Unnecessary Peering Across the Access Layer*

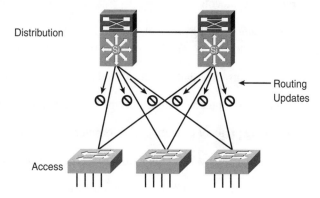

Configuring Passive Interfaces

In a network that has many VLAN interfaces on distribution layer routers, configuring each interface as a passive interface could result in many commands. To ease the configuration burden, Cisco IOS 12.0 introduced the **passive interface default** command, which makes *all* interfaces passive. This command can be used in conjunction with the **no passive interface** {*interface*} command to run the routing protocol on only the interfaces from the distribution layer devices to the core layer devices, minimizing the configuration required.

Summary

In this chapter, you learned about selecting routing protocols for enterprise networks. The following topics were explored:

- Static versus dynamic routing

- Interior versus exterior gateway routing protocols

- Distance vector versus link-state versus hybrid routing protocols

- Routing protocol metrics

- Routing protocol convergence

- Flat versus hierarchical protocols

- EIGRP, a Cisco-proprietary routing protocol that includes a topology table for maintaining all routes received from its neighbors. The best of these routes are put in the routing table.

- OSPF, an open-standard protocol that was developed to overcome the limitations of RIP

- Integrated IS-IS, a routing protocol designed for the OSI protocol suite and adapted for IP

- BGP, an exterior routing protocol primarily used for inter-AS routing

- Route redistribution use in a network running multiple routing protocols

- Route filtering to prevent the advertisement of certain routes through the routing domain

- Route summarization to represent a series of routes by a single summary address

References

For additional information, refer to these resources:

- Cisco Systems, Inc., Designing Large-Scale IP Internetworks, http://www.cisco.com/univercd/cc/td/doc/cisintwk/idg4/nd2003.htm.

- Cisco Systems, Inc., Designing a Campus Network for High Availability, http://www.cisco.com/application/pdf/en/us/guest/netsol/ns432/c649/cdccont_0900aecd801a8a2d.pdf.

- Teare, Diane and Catherine Paquet. *Authorized Self-Study Guide: Building Scalable Cisco Internetworks (BSCI)*, Third Edition. Cisco Press, 2006.

- Comer, Douglas E. and D. L. Stevens. *Internetworking with TCP/IP, Volume 1: Principles, Protocols, and Architecture*, Fifth Edition. Englewood Cliffs, New Jersey: Prentice-Hall, 2005.

Case Study: ACMC Hospital Routing Protocol Design

This case study is a continuation of the ACMC Hospital case study introduced in Chapter 2.

Case Study General Instructions

Use the scenarios, information, and parameters provided at each task of the ongoing case study. If you encounter ambiguities, make reasonable assumptions and proceed. For all tasks, use the initial customer scenario and build on the solutions provided thus far. You can use any and all documentation, books, white papers, and so on.

In each step, you act as a network design consultant. Make creative proposals to accomplish the customer's business needs. Justify your ideas when they differ from the provided solutions. Use any design strategies you feel are appropriate. The final goal of each case study is a paper solution.

Appendix A, "Answers to Review Questions and Case Studies," provides a solution for each step based on assumptions made. There is no claim that the provided solution is the best or only solution. Your solution might be more appropriate for the assumptions you made. The provided solution helps you understand the author's reasoning and allows you to compare and contrast your solution.

In this case study you determine the routing protocol design for the ACMC hospital network. Complete the following steps:

Step 1   Determine a suitable routing protocol or protocols for the ACMC network, and design the protocol hierarchy.

Step 2   What summary routes could be configured in this network?

Review Questions

Answer the following questions, and then see Appendix A for the answers.

1. In what situations could static routing be preferred over dynamic routing?

2. What do dynamic routing protocols do?

3. Which type of routing protocol is used for interconnecting autonomous systems?

4. Do IGPs or EGPs typically converge faster?

5. What is BGP multihoming?

6. How do distance vector and link-state routing protocols differ?

7. What are triggered updates?

8. What parameters do the following routing protocols use in their metric calculation by default?

- RIP

- EIGRP

- OSPF

- BGP

- IS-IS

9. What is convergence?

10. How does the speed of convergence affect the network?

11. What is an advantage of a hierarchical network versus a flat network?

12. A large organization has decided to connect its branch offices to the appropriate regional offices. Each regional office has a minimum of two and a maximum of five branch offices with which it will connect. Each branch office uses low-end routers that will directly connect to their regional office router via a Frame Relay permanent virtual circuit link, effectively creating a hub-and-spoke topology (star network). No physical connections exist between the branch office routers. OSPF is run in the rest of the network, but the routing protocol that runs between the regional office and the branch offices does not need to be OSPF. Select the two best options for use between the regional and branch offices:

- **a.** Deploy EIGRP in both directions.

- **b.** Deploy IS-IS in both directions.

- **c.** Deploy OSPF in both directions.

- **d.** Use static routes in both directions, with a default static route from each branch to the regional office, and static routes on each regional router toward the branch networks.

13. A network consists of links with varying bandwidths. Would RIPv2 be a good routing protocol choice in this network? Why or why not?

14. What are some features of EIGRP that make it an appropriate choice for an enterprise routing protocol?

15. What is an EIGRP feasible successor?

16. Does OSPF support manual route summarization on all routers?

17. What is an OSPF LSA?

18. What is the OSPF metric?

19. For what network layer protocols does Integrated IS-IS provide support?

20. What is the difference between an Integrated IS-IS backbone and an OSPF backbone?

21. Why might Integrated IS-IS be better than OSPF in a very large network?

22. What is the main use of BGP?

23. Which routing protocols are likely to be used in an enterprise Campus Core?

24. Is IS-IS typically a good choice of routing protocol for the Building Distribution layer?

25. What is route redistribution?

26. Which parts of the Enterprise Architecture are likely to implement redistribution?

27. What is route filtering?

28. When is route filtering required?

29. Why does redistributing from an IGP into BGP require caution?

30. What is route summarization, and why would a network need it?

31. What is a passive interface?

This chapter introduces voice design principles and contains the following sections:

- Traditional Voice Architectures and Features

- Integrating Voice Architectures

- Voice Issues and Requirements

- Introduction to Voice Traffic Engineering

- Summary

- References

- Case Study: ACMC Hospital Network Voice Design

- Review Questions

CHAPTER 8

Voice Network Design Considerations

This chapter introduces voice design principles. It begins with an overview of traditional voice architectures and features and continues with a discussion of integrated voice architectures.

This chapter describes how converged voice networks can run the same applications as a telephony network, but in a more cost-effective and scalable manner. It describes voice and data networking concepts and introduces VoIP and IP telephony.

This chapter discusses voice quality issues, coding and compression standards, and bandwidth considerations and requirements when voice traffic is present on a network. Quality of service (QoS) mechanisms available for voice are described, and voice traffic engineering concepts are examined.

Traditional Voice Architectures and Features

This section introduces the traditional telephony infrastructure and explains its major components. It describes analog and digital signaling and the process to convert between the two. PBX and Public Switched Telephone Network (PSTN) switches are described and contrasted. The telephone infrastructure and connections between telephony devices are examined. Telephony signaling mechanisms are described, and PSTN numbering plans are explained.

> **NOTE** We examine traditional telephony in this section to better understand the features and services that must be provided on a converged network.

Analog and Digital Signaling

The human voice generates sound waves; a telephone converts the sound waves into analog signals. However, analog transmission is not particularly efficient. Analog signals must be amplified when they become weak from transmission loss as they travel. However, amplification of analog signals also amplifies noise.

The PSTN is a collection of interconnected voice-oriented public telephone networks, both commercial and government-owned. The PSTN today consists almost entirely of digital technology, except for the final link from the central (local) telephone office to the user. To obtain clear voice connections, the PSTN switches convert analog speech to a digital format and send it over the digital network. At the other end of the connection, the digital signal is converted back to analog and to the normal sound waves that the ear picks up. Digital signals are more immune to noise, and the digital network does not induce any additional noise when amplifying signals.

Signals in digital networks are transmitted over great distances and are coded, regenerated, and decoded without degradation of quality. Repeaters amplify the signal, restore it to its original condition, and send this clean signal to the next network destination.

The Analog-to-Digital Process

Pulse code modulation (PCM) is the process of digitizing analog voice signals. Several steps are involved in converting an analog signal into PCM digital format, as shown in Figure 8-1 and described here:

- **Filtering**: Filters out the signal's nonspeech frequency components. Most of the energy of spoken language ranges from approximately 300 hertz (Hz) to 3400 Hz; this is the 3100 Hz bandwidth, or range, for standard speech. Analog waveforms are put through a voice frequency filter to filter out anything greater than 4000 Hz.

- **Sampling**: Samples the filtered input signal at a constant frequency, using a process called *pulse amplitude modulation (PAM)*. This step uses the original analog signal to modulate the amplitude of a pulse train that has a constant amplitude and frequency. The filtered analog signal is sampled at twice the highest frequency of the analog input signal (4000 Hz); therefore, the signal is sampled 8000 times per second, or every 125 microseconds (Mu-sec).

Sampling Frequency

Analog speech is filtered at 4000 Hz before being sampled. The *Nyquist theorem* states that a signal should be sampled at a rate at least two times the input frequency to obtain a quality representation of the signal. Therefore, the input analog signal is sampled at a rate of 8000 times per second.

- **Digitizing**: Digitizes the samples in preparation for transmission over a telephony network; this is the PCM process. PCM takes the PAM process one step further by encoding each analog sample using binary code words. An analog-to-digital converter is required on the source side, and a digital-to-analog converter is required on the destination side.

Figure 8-1 *Analog-to-Digital Conversion Process*

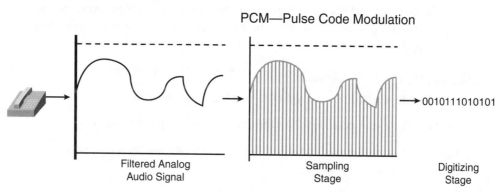

The digitizing process is further divided into the following steps:

- **Quantization and coding**: A process that converts each analog sample value into a discrete value to which a unique digital code word can be assigned. As the input signal sample enters the quantization phase, it is assigned to a quantization interval. All quantization intervals are equally spaced throughout the dynamic range of the input analog signal. Each quantization interval is assigned a discrete binary code word value. The standard word size used is 8 bits, enabling 256 possible quantization intervals.

> **KEY POINT**
> Because the input analog signal is sampled 8000 times per second and each sample is assigned an 8-bit-long code word, the maximum transmission bit rate for telephony systems using PCM is 8000 samples per second * 8 bits per sample, which results in 64,000 bits per second, or 64 kilobits per second (kbps).

- **Companding**: The process of first compressing an analog signal at the source and then expanding (decompressing) this signal back to its original size when it reaches its destination. (Combining the terms *compressing* and *expanding* creates the term *companding*.) During the companding process, input analog signal samples are compressed into logarithmic segments, and each segment is quantified and coded using uniform quantization. The compression process is logarithmic, meaning that the compression increases as the sample signals increase. In other words, larger sample signals are compressed more than smaller sample signals, thereby causing the quantization noise to increase as the sample signal increases. This results in a more accurate value for smaller-amplitude signals and a uniform signal-to-noise ratio across the input range.

Two basic variations of logarithmic companding are commonly used: The a-law companding standard is used in Europe, and Mu-law is used in North America and Japan. The methods are similar—they both use logarithmic compression to achieve linear approximations in 8-bit words—but they are not compatible.

A-law and Mu-law Companding

Following are the similarities between a-law and Mu-law companding:

- Both are linear approximations of a logarithmic input/output relationship.

- Both are implemented using 8-bit code words (256 levels, one for each quantization interval), resulting in a bit rate of 64 kbps.

- Both break a dynamic range into 16 segments: eight positive and eight negative segments. Each segment is twice the length of the preceding one and uses uniform quantization within each segment.

- Both use a similar approach to coding the 8-bit word. The first bit (the most significant bit) identifies polarity; bits 2, 3, and 4 identify the segment, and the final 4 bits quantize the segment.

The differences between a-law and Mu-law include the following:

- Different linear approximations lead to different lengths and slopes.

- The numerical assignment of the bit positions in the 8-bit code word to segments and quantization levels within segments is different.

- A-law provides a greater dynamic range than Mu-law.

- Mu-law provides better signal/distortion performance for low-level signals than a-law.

- A-law requires 13 bits for a uniform PCM equivalent. Mu-law requires 14 bits for a uniform PCM equivalent.

- An international connection should use a-law; Mu-law-to-a-law conversion is the responsibility of the Mu-law country.

This information was adapted from Cisco's *Waveform Coding Techniques* document, available at http://www.cisco.com/warp/public/788/signalling/waveform_coding.html#subrstsix.

Time-Division Multiplexing in PSTN

Time-division multiplexing (TDM) is used in networks that are commonly deployed by telephone companies, including the PSTN. As illustrated in Figure 8-2, TDM is a digital transmission technique for simultaneously carrying multiple signals over a single trunk line by interleaving octets from each signal into different time slots.

Figure 8-2 *Circuit-Switched Networks Use Time-Division Multiplexing*

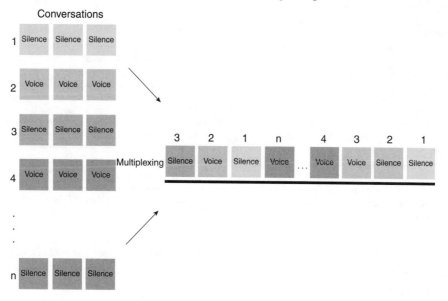

The PSTN allocates a dedicated 64-kbps digital channel for each call. Although TDM cannot allocate bandwidth on demand as packet switching can, TDM's fixed-bandwidth allocation ensures that a channel is never blocked because of competition for bandwidth resources on another channel, and that performance does not degrade because of network congestion.

With time slot allocation, the number of simultaneous calls cannot exceed the number of TDM slots in the trunk. One call always allocates one TDM slot, regardless of whether silence or speech is transmitted. Time slot allocation ensures that connections always have access to a trunk, thereby resulting in low delay. However, because of the allocation method, the overall trunk utilization, also known as *trunk efficiency,* becomes relatively low.

The low trunk efficiency of circuit-switched networks is a major driver for the migration to unified packet-switched networks in which bandwidth is consumed only when there is traffic.

PBXs and the PSTN

This section introduces PBX and PSTN switches and networks.

Differences Between a PBX and a PSTN Switch

As shown in Table 8-1, PBXs and PSTN switches share many similarities, but they also have many differences.

Table 8-1 *PBX and PSTN Switch Comparison*

PBX	PSTN Switch
Used in the private sector	Used in the public sector
Scales to thousands of phones	Scales to hundreds of thousands of phones
Mostly digital	Mostly digital
Uses 64-kbps circuits	Uses 64-kbps circuits
Uses proprietary protocols to control telephones	Uses open-standard protocols between switches and telephones
Interconnects remote branch subsystems and telephones	Interconnects with other PSTN switches, PBXs, and telephones

Both the PBX and PSTN switch systems use 64-kbps circuits; however, the scale is very different. A PSTN switch can support hundreds of thousands of telephones, whereas a PBX can support only several thousand.

KEY POINT | A PSTN switch's primary task is to provide residential telephony. A PBX supports user telephones within a company.

PBX vendors often create proprietary protocols to enable their PBXs to intercommunicate and transparently carry additional features through their voice network. In addition, only the vendor's telephones can be connected to its PBX. This forces enterprise networks to consolidate to one brand of PBX, and the enterprise business customer is restricted to one vendor.

NOTE Many vendors are implementing standards-based signaling protocols that enable interoperability between different vendors' PBXs. The two standards are Q Signaling (QSIG) and Digital Private Network Signaling System (DPNSS), as described in the "Digital Telephony Signaling" section later in this chapter.

Figure 8-3 illustrates the location of and communication between the PSTN and PBXs. PSTN switches connect residential and business users, but PBXs are mainly used for business purposes. PBXs are typically found at corporate locations, whereas PSTN switches are used to build the PSTN network and are located in central offices (CO).

Figure 8-3 *PBXs and the PSTN Interconnect to Facilitate Communication*

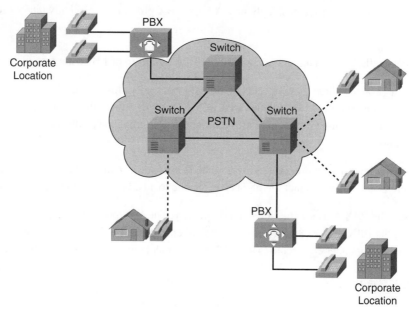

PBX Features

A *PBX* is a business telephone system that provides business features such as call hold, call transfer, call forward, follow-me, call park, conference calls, music on hold, call history, and voice mail. Most of these features are not available in traditional PSTN switches.

A PBX switch often connects to the PSTN through one or more T1 or E1 digital circuits. A PBX supports end-to-end digital transmission, employs PCM switching technology, and supports both analog and digital proprietary telephones.

Recall from Chapter 5, "Designing Remote Connectivity," that the United States, Canada, and Japan use T1. A T1 trunk can carry 24 fixed 64-kbps channels for either voice or data, using PCM signals and TDM, plus additional bits for framing, resulting in an aggregate carrying capacity of 1.544 megabits per second (Mbps). T1 lines originally used copper wire but now also include optical and wireless media.

In Europe, the trunk used to carry a digital transmission is an E1. An E1 trunk can carry up to 31 fixed 64-kbps channels for data and signaling, with another 64-kbps channel reserved for framing, giving an aggregate carrying capacity of 2.048 Mbps.

PBXs support end-to-end digital transmission, use PCM switching technology, and support both analog and digital proprietary telephones. A local PBX provides several advantages for an enterprise:

■ Local calls between telephones within the PBX or group of PBXs are free of charge.

■ Most PBX telephone system users do not call externally, through the T1 or E1 circuits, at the same time. Therefore, companies with a PBX only need the number of external lines to the PSTN to equal the maximum possible number of simultaneous calls, resulting in PSTN cost savings.

■ When adding a new user, changing a voice feature, or moving a user to a different location, there is no need to contact the PSTN carrier; the local administrator can reconfigure the PBX.

However, the PBX adds another level of complexity: The enterprise customer must configure and maintain the PBX. Figure 8-4 illustrates a typical enterprise telephone network that has proprietary telephones connected to the PBX and a trunk between the PBX and the PSTN network.

Figure 8-4 *A PBX Can Reduce the Number of Trunks to the PSTN*

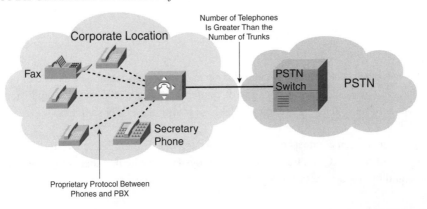

PSTN Switches

The PSTN appears to be a single large network with telephone lines connected. In reality, the PSTN is composed of circuits, switches, signaling devices, and telephones. Many different companies own and operate different systems within the PSTN.

PSTN Features

A PSTN switch's primary role is to connect the calling and called parties. If the two parties are physically connected to the same PSTN switch, the call remains local; otherwise, the PSTN switch forwards the call to the destination switch that owns the called party.

PSTN switches interconnect business PBXs and public and private telephones. Large PSTN switches are located at COs, which provide circuits throughout the telephony network. PSTN switches are deployed in hierarchies to provide resiliency and redundancy to the PSTN network and avoid a single point of failure.

PSTN signaling traditionally supported only basic features such as caller ID and direct inward dialing. Modern PSTN switches now support, on a fee basis, many traditional PBX services, including conferencing, forwarding, call holding, and voice mail.

PSTN Services

Modern PSTN service providers offer competitive services to differentiate themselves and generate additional revenue. These PSTN services include the following:

- **Centrex**: *Centrex* is a set of specialized business solutions (primarily, but not exclusively, for voice service) in which the service provider owns and operates the equipment that provides both call control and service logic functions; therefore, the equipment is located on the service provider's premises.

- **Voice virtual private networks (VPN)**: *Voice VPNs* interconnect corporate voice traffic among multiple locations over the PSTN. PBXs are connected to the PSTN instead of directly over tie trunks. The PSTN service provider provides call routing among locations, and all PBX features are carried transparently across the PSTN.

- **Voice mail**: *Voice mail* is an optional service that lets PSTN customers divert their incoming PSTN calls to a voice mailbox when they are unable to answer their telephones, such as when the line is busy or they are unavailable. Alternatively, all calls can be diverted to the voice mailbox.

- **Call center**: A *call center* is a place of doing business by telephone, combined with a centralized database that uses an automatic call distribution (ACD) system. Call centers require live agents to accept and handle calls.

- **Interactive voice response**: *Interactive voice response (IVR) systems* allow callers to exchange information over the telephone without an intermediary live agent. The caller and the IVR system interact using a combination of spoken messages and dual-tone multifrequency (DTMF) touch-tone telephone pad buttons.

Local Loops, Trunks, and Interswitch Communications

Figure 8-5 illustrates a typical telephone infrastructure and connections between telephony devices.

Figure 8-5 *Local Loops, Trunks, and Interswitch Communication*

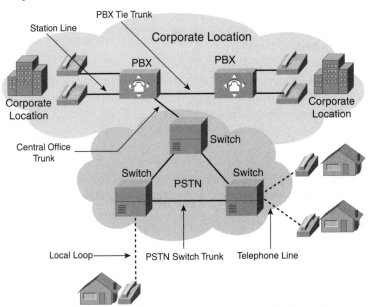

The telephone infrastructure starts with a simple pair of copper wires running to the end user's home or business. This physical cabling is known as a local loop or telephone line; the local loop physically connects the home telephone to the CO PSTN switch. Similarly, the connection between an enterprise PBX and its telephones is called the station line.

A *trunk* is a communication path between two telephony systems. Available trunk types, shown in Figure 8-5, include the following:

- **Tie trunk**: Connects enterprise PBXs without connecting to the PSTN (in other words, not connecting to a phone company's CO). Tie trunks are used, for example, to connect PBXs in different cities so that the enterprise can use the PBX rather than the PSTN for intercity calls between offices and, as a result, save on long-distance toll charges. A connection to the PSTN—via a CO trunk—is still required for off-net calls (to nonoffice numbers).

- **CO trunk**: Connects CO switches to enterprise PBXs. Enterprises connect their PBXs to the PSTN with PBX-to-CO trunks. The telephone service provider is responsible for running CO-to-PBX trunks between its CO and enterprise PBXs; from a service provider point of view, these are *lines* or *business lines*.

- **PSTN switch trunk**: Interconnects CO switches; also called *interoffice trunks*.

As shown in Figure 8-6, another type of trunk, foreign exchange (FX) trunks, are analog interfaces used to interconnect a PBX to telephones, other PBXs, or to the PSTN. FX trunks save on long-distance toll calls; the dial tone from a different toll region is produced via the FX trunk at a reduced tariff.

Figure 8-6 *Foreign Exchange Trunks*

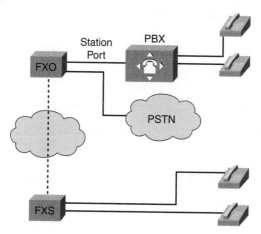

Two types of FX trunk interfaces exist:

- **Foreign Exchange Office (FXO)**: This interface emulates a telephone. It creates an analog connection to a PSTN CO or to a station interface on a PBX. The FXO interface sits on the PSTN or PBX end of the connection and plugs directly into the line side of the PSTN or PBX so that the PSTN or PBX thinks the FXO interface is a telephone. The FXO interface provides either pulse or DTMF digits for outbound dialing. The PBX or PSTN notifies the FXO of an incoming call by sending ringing voltage to the FXO. Likewise, the FXO answers a call by closing the loop to allow current flow. After current is flowing, the FXO interface transports the signal to the Foreign Exchange Station (FXS).

- **FXS**: This interface emulates a PBX. It connects directly to a standard telephone, fax machine, or similar device and supplies line power, ring voltage, and dial tone to the end device. An example of where an FXS is used to emulate a PBX is in locations where there are not physical lines for every telephone.

Telephony Signaling

In a telephony system, a signaling mechanism is required for establishing and disconnecting telephone communications.

Telephony Signaling Types

The following forms of signaling are used when a telephone call is placed via a PBX:

- Between the telephone and PBX

- Between the PBX and PSTN switch

- Between the PSTN switches

- Between two PBXs

At a high level, there are two signaling realms, as shown in Figure 8-7:

- **Local-loop signaling**: Between a PSTN or PBX switch and a subscriber (telephone)

- **Trunk signaling**: Between PSTN switches, between a PSTN switch and a PBX, or between PBX switches

Figure 8-7   *Telephony Signaling Includes Local-Loop and Trunk Signaling*

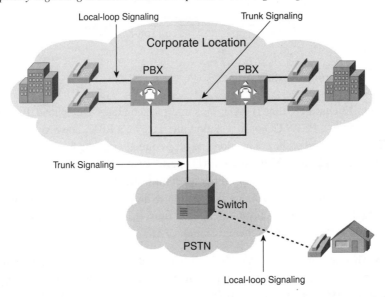

Simple signaling examples include the ringing of the telephone, a dial tone, and a ring-back tone. Following are the three basic categories of signals commonly used in telephone networks:

- **Supervision signaling**: Typically characterized as on-hook, off-hook, and ringing, supervision signaling alerts the CO switch to the state of the telephone on each local loop. Supervision signaling is used, for example, to initiate a telephone call request on a line or trunk and to hold or release an established connection.

- **Address signaling**: Used to pass dialed digits (pulse or DTMF) to a PBX or PSTN switch. These dialed digits provide the switch with a connection path to another telephone or customer premises equipment.

- **Informational signaling**: Includes dial tone, busy tone, reorder tone, and tones indicating that a receiver is off-hook or that no such number exists, such as those used with call progress indicators.

For a telephone call to take place, all three types of signaling occur.

Analog Telephony Signaling

The most common methods of analog local-loop signaling are loop start and ground start. The most common analog trunk signaling method is E&M (derived from a combination of recEive and transMit, and sometimes known as Ear and Mouth). These methods are described as follows:

- **Loop start**: Loop start is the simplest and least intelligent signaling protocol, and the most common form of local-loop signaling. It provides a way to indicate on-hook and off-hook conditions in a voice network. The creation of the electrical loop initiates a call (off-hook), and the opening of the loop terminates the call (on-hook). This type of signaling is not common for PBX signaling because it has a significant drawback in which *glare*—what the telephone industry calls collisions—can occur. Glare occurs when two endpoints try to seize the line at the same time, resulting in the two callers connecting unexpectedly. Because business callers use telephones regularly and the possibility of glare is high, loop-start signaling is acceptable only for residential use.

- **Ground start**: Also called *reverse battery*, ground start is a modification of loop start that provides positive recognition of connects and disconnects (off-hook and on-hook). It uses current-detection mechanisms at each end of the trunk, thereby enabling PBXs to agree which end will seize the trunk before actually doing so, minimizing the effect of glare. Ground start is preferred when there is a high volume of calls; therefore, PBXs typically use this type of signaling.

- **E&M**: E&M is a common trunk signaling technique used between PBXs. In E&M, voice is transmitted over either two- or four-wire circuits, with five types of E&M signaling (Types I, II, III, IV, and V). E&M uses separate paths (or leads) for voice and signaling. The M (Mouth) lead sends the signal, and the E (Ear) lead receives the signal.

Digital Telephony Signaling

On PSTN switches, analog signaling is usually provided through current flow in closed electrical circuits, and digital signaling is provided through channel associated signaling (CAS) or common channel signaling (CCS).

CAS

Many varieties of CAS exist, and they operate over various analog and digital facilities.

KEY POINT	CAS uses defined bits within T1 or E1 channels for signaling; this is *in-band* signaling. Therefore, the signal for call setup and so forth is in the same channel as the voice call.

Examples of CAS signaling include the following:

- **R1 signaling (on T1 facilities)**: Used in North America.

- **R2 signaling (on E1 facilities)**: Used in Europe, Latin America, Australia, and Asia.

- **DTMF signals**: DTMF signals are the "pulses" used within the call path.

CCS

Modern telecommunication networks require more efficient means of signaling, so they are moving toward CCS systems. CCS can have faster connect times than CAS, and it offers the possibility of a number of additional services.

KEY POINT	CCS uses a common link to carry signaling information for several trunks. It differs from CAS signaling because it uses a separate channel for call setup; this is *out-of-band* signaling.

Examples of CCS signaling include the following:

- DPNSS

- Integrated Services Digital Network (ISDN)

- QSIG

- Signaling System 7 (SS7)

The following sections further describe these types of CCS signaling.

DPNSS

DPNSS is an industry-standard interface defined between a PBX and an access network. DPNSS expands the facilities normally available only between extensions on a single PBX to all extensions on PBXs connected in a private network.

ISDN

ISDN provides digital telephony and data transport services. ISDN involves the digitalization of the telephone network, permitting voice, data, text, graphics, music, video, and other source material to be transmitted on the same facility. For example, ISDN enables PBXs to connect over the PSTN and to create voice VPNs by delivering PBX signaling over the network to distant PBXs.

Following are the two ISDN access methods, as illustrated in Figure 8-8:

- **ISDN Basic Rate Interface (BRI)**: Offers two bearer (B) channels and one delta (D) channel (2B+D). The BRI B channel operates at 64 kbps and carries user data and voice. The BRI D channel operates at 16 kbps and carries both control and signaling information. BRI is typically used for residential and small office/home office applications.

- **ISDN Primary Rate Interface (PRI)**: Designed to use T1 or E1 circuits, PRI offers 23 B channels and one D channel (23B+D) in North America and 30 B channels and one D channel (30B+D) in Europe. The PRI B channels operate at 64 kbps and carry user data and voice. The PRI D channel also operates at 64 kbps and carries both control and signaling information. PRI is typically used for enterprise business and voice applications.

Figure 8-8 *ISDN Digital Signaling*

Channel	Capacity	Used For
B	64 kbps	Circuit-Switched Data
D	16 kbps for BRI; 64 kbps for PRI	Signaling Information

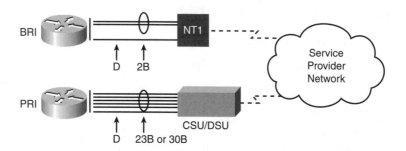

QSIG Digital Signaling

Figure 8-9 illustrates QSIG. QSIG is a peer-to-peer signaling system used in corporate voice networking to provide standardized inter-PBX communications. It is a standards-based mechanism that provides transparent transportation of PBX features across a network.

Figure 8-9   *QSIG*

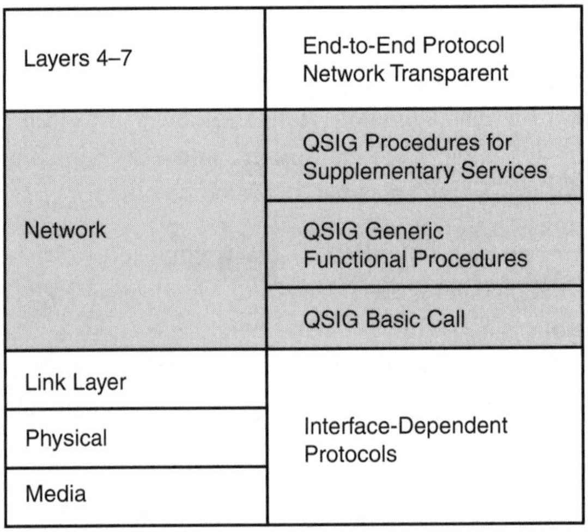

Layers 4–7	End-to-End Protocol Network Transparent
Network	QSIG Procedures for Supplementary Services
	QSIG Generic Functional Procedures
	QSIG Basic Call
Link Layer	Interface-Dependent Protocols
Physical	
Media	

QSIG features include the following:

■ Standards-based protocol that enables interconnection of multivendor equipment

■ Enables inter-PBX basic services, generic feature transparency between PBXs, and supplementary services

■ Interoperability with public and private ISDN

■ Operable in any network configuration and compatible with many PBX-type interfaces

■ No restrictions on private numbering plans

SS7 Digital Signaling

SS7 is an international signaling standard within the PSTN. SS7 defines the architecture, network elements, interfaces, protocols, and management procedures for a network that transports control information between PSTN switches. SS7 works between PSTN switches and replaces per-trunk in-band signaling.

As shown in Figure 8-10, a separate data network within the PSTN implements SS7. SS7 provides call setup and teardown, network management, fault resolution, and traffic management services. The SS7 network is solely for network control. Out-of-band signaling via SS7 provides numerous benefits for internetworking design, including reduced call setup time, bearer capability, and other progress indicators.

Figure 8-10 *SS7 Signaling Is Used Between PSTN Switches*

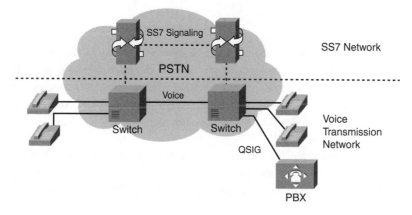

> **KEY POINT** When using SS7, all trunk channels are for voice and data, and the SS7 network carries the associated signaling separately.

PSTN Numbering Plans

PSTN numbering plans are the foundation for routing voice calls through the PSTN network.

International Numbering Plans

For any telephone network to function, a unique address must identify each telephone. Voice addressing relies on a combination of international and national standards, local telephone company practices, and internal customer-specific codes. The International Telecommunications Union Telecommunication Standardization Sector (ITU-T) recommendation E.164 defines the international numbering plan. Each country's national numbering plan must conform to the E.164 recommendation and work in conjunction with the international numbering plan in a hierarchical fashion. PSTN service providers must ensure that their numbering plan aligns with the E.164 recommendation and that their customers' networks conform.

Call Routing

Call routing is closely related to the numbering plan and signaling. Basic routing allows the source telephone to establish a call to the destination telephone. However, most routing is more sophisticated: It enables subscribers to select services or divert calls from one subscriber to another. Routing results from establishing a set of tables or rules within each switch. As each call arrives, the path to the desired destination and the type of services available derive from these tables or rules.

Numbering Plans

Specific numbers within the dialed digits indicate special codes. An *international prefix* is the code dialed before an international number. In most nations, the international prefix is 00. In some nations in Asia, it is 001 (in some cases, alternative codes are available to select a particular international carrier). In North America, the international prefix is 011 (or 01 for special call processing—collect, person-to-person, calling card, and so on).

A *country code* is used to reach a particular telephone system (or special service) for each nation. The initial digit in the country code is a *zone*, which usually relates to a general geographic region (for example, zone 5 is South America and Latin America). Table 8-2 provides examples of country codes and zones.

Table 8-2   *Country Code Examples*

Country Code	Zone	Country
1	1	Canada, United States
1242	1	Bahamas
1787	1	Puerto Rico
1876	1	Jamaica
20	2	Egypt
212	2	Morocco
213	2	Nigeria
30	3	Greece
34	3	Spain
386	3	Slovenia
44	4	United Kingdom
45	4	Denmark

Table 8-2   *Country Code Examples (Continued)*

Country Code	Zone	Country
51	5	Peru
52	5	Mexico
61	6	Australia
63	6	Philippines
679	6	Fiji Islands
7	7	Kazakhstan, Russia
81	8	Japan
86	8	China
886	8	Taiwan
91	9	India
966	9	Saudi Arabia
995	9	Georgia

A *trunk prefix* is the initial digit or digits dialed before the area code (if necessary) and the subscriber number when making a domestic call. The trunk prefix in North America is 1; it is 0 in most other places.

North American Numbering Plan

The North American Numbering Plan (NANP), as illustrated in Figure 8-11, is an example of a PSTN numbering plan. It conforms to the ITU-T recommendation E.164. NANP numbers are ten digits in length and occur in the following format: NXX-NXX-XXXX, where N is any digit 2–9 and X is any digit 0–9. The first three digits identify the numbering plan area and are commonly called the area code. The next three digits are called the CO code; other names for these three digits are prefix, exchange, or simply NXX. The final four digits are called the line number. NANP is also referred to as 1+10 because when a 1 (the trunk prefix) is the first number dialed, a ten-digit number follows to reach another NANP number. This enables the end-office switch to determine whether it should expect a seven- or ten-digit telephone number (although many local calls now require ten-digit, rather than seven-digit, dialing).

Figure 8-11 *North American Numbering Plan Has Ten-Digit Numbers*

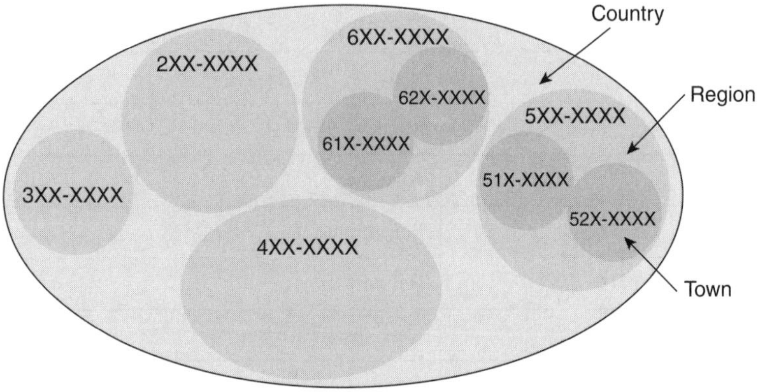

NOTE As telephone numbers in existing area codes are depleted, new area codes are required. One way to add area codes is to split the area covered by an existing area code into two or more areas; one area keeps the existing area code, and the other areas get new area codes.

Another way to add area codes is with overlay area codes, in which the new area code overlays the existing area code, so people within the same geographic area might have different area codes. Existing customers retain their existing area codes and numbers; new customers get the new area code. Overlay area codes can result in two different people living in the same geographic area having the same seven-digit local number, but with two different area codes.

In cities in which overlay area codes are used, everyone must dial ten digits (the area code plus the local number) for local calls.

NOTE A *closed* numbering plan refers to a telephone numbering scheme that has a fixed number of digits, not counting special service codes. The NANP 1+10 is an example, because ten digits are always associated with each national number—three digits of area code followed by seven digits of subscriber number. Australia's numbering plan (with country code 61) is another example of a closed numbering plan.

Figure 8-12 illustrates how the NANP routes telephone calls. In this example, the lower telephone is dialing 212-4321, which is the telephone number of the top-right phone. A PSTN switch forwards the signal as soon as it receives enough digits to send the call to the next switch. The last switch in the path receives all the digits and rings the destination telephone (in this case, the telephone at the top right).

NOTE   The SS7 first determines through out-of-band signaling that there is a path to the destination and that the end station can accept the call, and then it allocates the trunks.

Figure 8-12   *Routing Calls Based on the NANP*

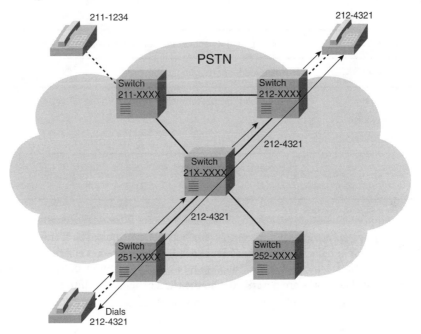

United Kingdom National Numbering Plan

The U.K. national numbering plan is another example of a national PSTN numbering plan conforming to the ITU-T recommendation E.164. Figure 8-13 shows a portion of the U.K. national numbering plan. It supports several geographic numbering options, depending on the population density of the city or area. It also reserves some number ranges for corporate uses.

Figure 8-13 *A Portion of the U.K. National Numbering Plan*

Number Range	Description
(01xxx) xxx xxx	Trunk prefix (national long-distance calling prefix)
(01xxx) xxx xxx	Geographic numbering options—area code and subscriber number
(01x1) xxx xxxxx	
(011x) xxx xxxxx	
(02x) xxxx xxxx	
(01xxx[x]) xxxx[x]	
(05x) xxxx xxxx	Mobile phones, pagers, and personal numbering
(07xxx) xxxxxx	Reserved for corporate numbering
(0800) xxx xxx	Freephone (except for mobile phone)
(0800) xxx xxxx	
(0808) xxx xxxx	
999	Free emergency number
112	

Integrating Voice Architectures

This section discusses integrated voice architecture concepts, components, mechanisms, and issues. Integrated networks are described, and the H.323 standard is introduced. IP telephony is presented and call control and transport protocols are discussed.

Introduction to Integrated Networks

Figure 8-14 illustrates a typical enterprise WAN with separate data and voice networks.

Integrating data, voice, and video in a network enables vendors to introduce new features. The unified communications network model enables distributed call routing, control, and application functions based on industry standards. Enterprises can mix and match equipment from multiple vendors and geographically deploy these systems wherever they are needed.

One means of creating an integrated network is to replace the PBXs' voice tie trunks with IP connections by connecting the PBXs to voice-enabled routers. The voice-enabled routers convert voice traffic to IP packets and direct them over IP data networks. This implementation is called *VoIP*. Figure 8-15 illustrates an integrated network using VoIP over an IP WAN link that carries voice and data at the same time.

Figure 8-14   *Traditional Separate Voice and Data Networks*

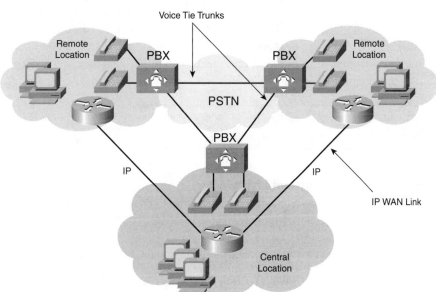

Figure 8-15   *Integrated Voice and Data Traffic in a Converged Network*

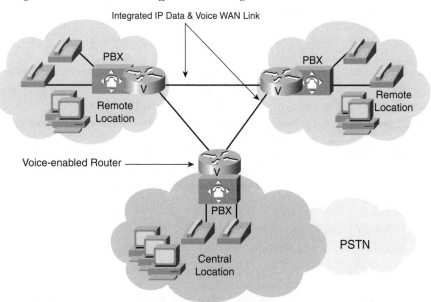

IP telephony, a superset of VoIP, is another implementation. IP phones are used, and the phones *themselves* convert the voice into IP packets. A dedicated network server that runs specialized call processing software replaces the PBX; in Cisco networks, this is the Cisco Unified Communications Manager. IP phones are not connected with telephone cabling. Instead, they send all signals over standard Ethernet. The "Introduction to IP Telephony" section later in this chapter provides details of this solution.

> **NOTE** Earlier names for the Cisco Unified Communications Manager include Cisco CallManager and Cisco Unified CallManager.

Drivers for Integrating Voice and Data Networks

Although a PSTN is effective for carrying voice signals, many business drivers are forcing the need for a new type of network for the following reasons:

- Data has overtaken voice as the primary traffic on many voice networks.

- Companies want to reduce WAN costs by migrating to integrated networks that can efficiently carry any type of data.

- The PSTN architecture was designed and built for voice and is not flexible enough to optimally carry data.

- The PSTN cannot create and deploy features quickly enough.

- Data, voice, and video cannot be integrated on the current PSTN structure.

IP telephony is cost-effective because of the reduced number of tie trunks and higher link efficiency, and because both voice and data networks use the same WAN infrastructure. It is much easier to manage a single network than two separate networks, because doing so requires fewer administrators, a simplified management infrastructure, and lower administrator training costs.

KEY POINT	Whether or not either caller is talking, circuit-switched (classical voice) calls require a dedicated duplex 64-kbps dedicated circuit between the two telephones. During the call, no other party can use the 64-kbps connection, and the company cannot use it for any other purpose.
	Packet-switched networking uses bandwidth only when it is required. This difference is an important benefit of packet-based voice networking.

On an IP network, voice servers and application servers can be located virtually anywhere. The rationale for enterprises to maintain voice servers, as with data application servers, is diminishing over time. As voice moves to IP networks (using the public Internet for inter-enterprise traffic and private intranets for intra-enterprise traffic), service providers might host voice and application servers.

H.323

H.323 is an ITU-T standard for packet-based audio, video, and data communications across IP-based networks.

Introduction to H.323

The ITU-T H.323 standard is a foundation for audio, video, and data communications across IP-based networks, including the Internet. By complying with the H.323 standard, multimedia products and applications from multiple vendors can interoperate, thereby allowing users to communicate without concern for compatibility.

The H.323 standard is broad in scope and includes standalone devices (such as IP telephones and voice gateways), embedded personal computer technology (such as PCs with Microsoft's NetMeeting), and point-to-point and multipoint conferencing. H.323 includes call control (including session setup, monitoring, and termination), multimedia management, bandwidth management, and multicast support in multipoint conferences.

Communications under H.323 are a mix of audio, video, data, and control signals. To establish a voice call, H.323 refers to other standards, including H.225 and H.245. The H.225 standard is based on the Q.931 protocol. It describes call signaling and the Registration, Admission, and Status (RAS) signaling used for H.323 session establishment and packetization between two H.323 devices. For example, the H.225 setup message has information elements that include the calling party number and the called party number. H.245 is a control standard for multimedia communication that describes the messages and procedures used for opening and closing logical channels for audio, video, and data, capability exchange, control, and indications.

An H.323 conference can include endpoints with different capabilities. For example, a terminal with audio-only capabilities can participate in a conference with terminals that have video and data capabilities. An H.323 multimedia terminal can share the data portion of a videoconference with a data-only terminal while sharing voice, video, and data with other H.323 terminals.

H.323 Components

H.323 defines four major components for a network-based communications system: terminals, gateways, gatekeepers, and multipoint control units (MCU).

Terminals

Terminals are client endpoints that provide real-time two-way H.323 communications with other endpoints, such as H.323 terminals, gateways, or MCUs. All terminals must support standard 64-kbps PCM-encoded voice communications; video and data are optional. Examples of H.323 terminals are IP telephones and PCs with Microsoft NetMeeting software.

Gateways

An H.323 *gateway* is an optional element in the voice network; it can be a voice-enabled router or switch. Gateways provide many services, such as translation between H.323 endpoints and non-H.323 devices, which allows H.323 endpoints and non-H.323 devices to communicate. In addition, the gateway also translates between audio, video, and data formats; converts call setup signals and procedures; and converts communication control signals and procedures.

KEY POINT	Gateways are not required between two H.323 terminals because these endpoints can communicate with each other directly.

Terminals use the H.245 and Q.931 protocols to communicate with H.323 gateways. An example of a gateway is a voice-enabled router providing a connection to the PSTN, a PBX, or an analog phone. An interface on a voice gateway that carries voice data is a voice port. A voice port is a physical port on a voice module; this is what makes a router voice-enabled.

A voice module enables connectivity with traditional circuit-switched voice devices and networks. It converts voice into IP packets and vice versa. Specialized processors called *digital signal processors* (DSP) are located on the voice module and perform the coding and compressing of voice data. The following are some of the voice modules available on Cisco voice gateways:

- ISDN PRI on an E1 or T1 voice module

- E1-R2 signaling on an E1 voice module

- T1-CAS signaling on a T1 voice module

- FXS on a low-capacity voice module

- FXO on a low-capacity voice module

- ISDN BRI on a low-capacity voice module

Gatekeepers

KEY POINT An H.323 gatekeeper is another optional element that manages H.323 endpoints. The terminals, gateways, and MCUs managed by a single gatekeeper are known as an *H.323 zone*; there is a one-to-one relationship between a zone and a gatekeeper.

A gatekeeper is typically used in larger, more complex networks; the gatekeeper function can be performed by a Cisco IOS router or by third-party software. A gatekeeper serves as the central point for all calls within its zone and provides call control services to registered H.323 endpoints. All H.323 devices in the zone register with the gatekeeper so that the gatekeeper can perform its basic functions, such as H.323 address translation, admission control, bandwidth control, and zone management. Optionally the gatekeeper provides call control signaling, call authorization, bandwidth management, and call management.

The gatekeeper can balance calls among multiple gateways, either by integrating their addressing into the Domain Name System or via Cisco IOS configuration options. For instance, if a call is routed through a gatekeeper, that gatekeeper can forward the call to a corresponding gateway based on some routing logic. When an H.323 gatekeeper acts as a virtual voice switch, its function is known as *gatekeeper-routed call signaling*.

NOTE   The Cisco Unified Communications Manager does not support the gatekeeper-routed call signaling capability.

The Importance of a Gatekeeper
Figure 8-16 illustrates some different voice design options and emphasizes the importance of a gatekeeper, especially in large voice network designs.

Voice network design depends primarily on the number of voice gateways and, consequentially, the number of logical connections between them. The maximum number of logical connections between voice gateways, and, as a result, the network's complexity, can be calculated by the formula $(N * (N-1))/2$, where N is the number of voice gateways in the system. For example, the maximum number of logical connections between three voice gateways is three, between five voice gateways is ten, and between eight voice gateways is 28. The complexity of the network grows quickly with the number of gateways; adding one more voice gateway to an existing network means reconfiguring all other voice gateways, making network maintenance quite difficult. A solution for this issue is the use of a gatekeeper.

Figure 8-16 *The Importance of a Gatekeeper in Voice Networks*

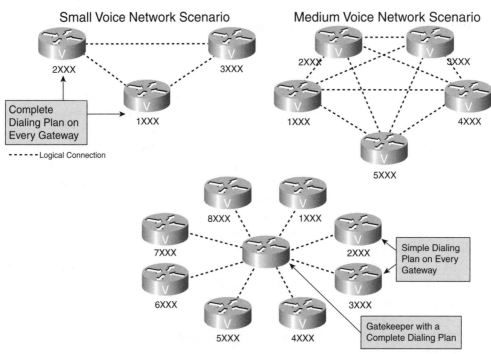

> **KEY POINT** The gatekeeper stores the dialing plan of the entire zone. Gateways only have to register with the gatekeeper; the gatekeeper provides all call control services to the gateways.

Therefore, the configuration of a voice gateway becomes simpler and does not require modification when a new voice gateway is added to the system.

Multipoint Control Units

An MCU is an H.323 endpoint that enables three or more endpoints to participate in a multipoint H.323 conference. An MCU incorporates a multipoint controller (MC) and optionally one or more multipoint processors (MP).

The MC is the conference controller that handles H.245 capability negotiations between the endpoints and controls conference resources. An MC is not a standalone unit and can be located within an endpoint, terminal, gateway, gatekeeper, or MCU.

The MP handles the conference's data streams. It receives multiple streams of multimedia input, switches and mixes the streams, and retransmits the result to the conference members. An MP resides in an MCU.

H.323 Example

Figure 8-17 illustrates the components typically involved in an H.323 call and the interactions between them.

Figure 8-17 *Interactions of H.323 Components*

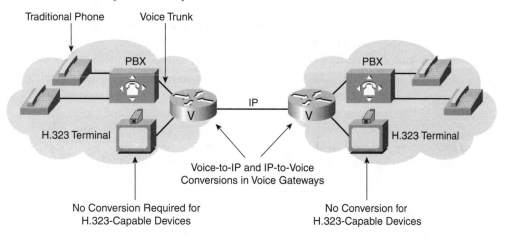

If traditional telephones are used and an IP network must transport calls, a voice gateway is required on both sides of the IP network. In this example, the gateway is a voice-enabled router that performs voice-to-IP and IP-to-voice conversions in DSPs. After the gateway router converts voice into IP packets, it transmits the packets across the IP network. The receiving router performs the same function in the reverse order: It converts IP packets to voice signals and forwards them through the PBX to the destination telephone.

KEY POINT   A voice gateway is not required when H.323-capable devices (terminals) communicate over an IP network; the router forwards IP packets it receives from an H.323 device to the appropriate outgoing interface. A voice gateway is required, however, to convert between an IP network and the PSTN.

Introduction to IP Telephony

IP telephony refers to cost-effective communication services, including voice, fax, and voice-messaging applications, transported via the packet-switched IP network rather than the circuit-switched PSTN.

KEY POINT	VoIP uses voice-enabled routers to convert voice into IP packets and route those packets between corresponding locations. Users do not often notice the implementation of VoIP in the network; they use their traditional phones, connected to a PBX. However, the PBX is not connected to the PSTN or to another PBX, but to a voice-enabled router that is an entry point to VoIP.
	IP telephony replaces traditional phones with IP phones and uses the Cisco Unified Communications Manager, a server for call control and signaling, in place of PBXs. The IP phone itself performs voice-to-IP conversion, and voice-enabled routers are not required within the enterprise network. If connection to the PSTN is required, a voice-enabled router or other gateway must be added where calls are forwarded to the PSTN.

The basic steps for placing an IP telephone call include converting the analog voice signal into a digital format, and compressing and translating the digital signal into IP packets for transmission across the IP network. The process is reversed at the receiving end.

The IP telephony architecture, illustrated in Figure 8-18, includes four distinct components: infrastructure, call processing, applications, and client devices. These components are described as follows:

- **Infrastructure**: The infrastructure is based on data link layer and multilayer switches and voice-enabled routers that interconnect endpoints with the IP and PSTN network. Endpoints attach to the network using switched 10/100 Ethernet ports. Switches may include Power over Ethernet (PoE) ports that sense the presence of IP devices that require inline power, such as Cisco IP phones and wireless access points, and provide that power. Voice-enabled routers perform conversions between the circuit-switched PSTN and IP networks.

- **Call processing**: Cisco Unified Communications Manager is the software-based call-processing component of the Cisco enterprise IP telephony solution. Cisco Unified Communications Manager provides a scalable, distributable, and highly available enterprise IP telephony call processing solution and performs much like the PBX in a traditional telephone network, including providing call setup and processing functions.

  The Cisco Unified Communications Manager can be installed on Cisco MCS 7800 Series server platforms and selected third-party servers.

- **Applications**: Applications provide additional features to the IP telephony infrastructure. Cisco Unity unified messaging (integrating e-mail and voice mail), Cisco Unified MeetingPlace (multimedia conferencing), Cisco Unified IP IVR, and Cisco Unified Contact Center products (including intelligent contact routing, call treatment, network-to-desktop computer telephony integration, and multichannel automatic call distribution) are among the Cisco applications available for IP telephony. The open-source application layer allows third-party companies to develop software that interoperates with Cisco Unified Communications Manager.

- **Client devices**: Client devices are IP telephones and software applications that allow communication across the IP network. Cisco Unified Communications Manager centrally manages the IP telephones through Ethernet connections in the Building Access Layer switches.

Figure 8-18 *IP Telephony Components*

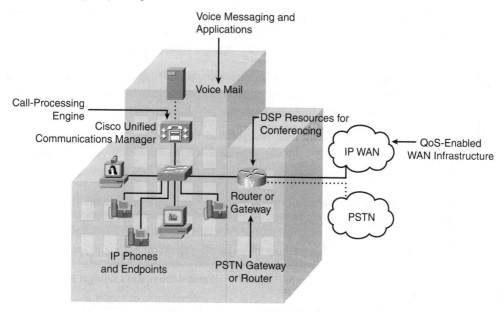

IP Telephony Design Goals

Typical design goals of an IP telephony network are as follows:

- **End-to-end IP telephony**: Using end-to-end IP telephony between sites where IP connectivity is already established. IP telephony can be deployed as an overlaid service that runs on the existing infrastructure.

- **Widely usable IP telephony**: To make IP telephony widely usable, voice quality should be at the same level as in traditional telephony; this is known as *toll quality voice*.

- **Reduced long-distance costs**: Long-distance costs should be lower than with traditional telephony. This can be accomplished by using private IP networks, or possibly the public Internet, to route telephone calls.

- **Cost-effective**: Making IP telephony cost effective depends on using the existing WAN capacity more efficiently and the cost-of upgrading the existing IP network infrastructure to support IP telephony. In some cases, this goal can be accomplished by using the public Internet or private IP networks to route telephone calls.

- **High availability**: To provide high availability, redundant network components can be used and backup power can be provided to all network infrastructure components, including routers, switches, and IP phones.

- **Lower total cost of ownership**: IP telephony should offer lower total cost of ownership and greater flexibility than traditional telephony. Installation costs and operational costs for unified systems are lower than the costs to implement and operate two infrastructures.

- **Enable new applications on top of IP telephony via third-party software**: For example, an intelligent phone used for database information access as an alternative to a PC is likely to be easier to use and less costly to own, operate, and maintain.

- **Improved productivity**: IP telephony should improve the productivity of remote workers, agents, and stay-at-home staff by extending the productivity-enhancing enterprise telephony features such as voice mail and voice conferencing to the remote teleworker.

- **Facilitate data and telephony network consolidation**: Such consolidation can contribute to operational and equipment savings.

The following sections illustrate some sample IP telephony designs.

Single-Site IP Telephony Design

Figure 8-19 illustrates a design model for an IP telephony network within a single campus or site.

Figure 8-19 *Single-Site IP Telephony Design*

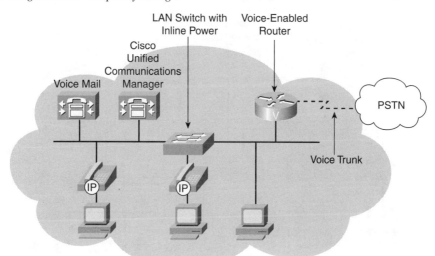

A single-site IP telephony design consists of Cisco Unified Communications Manager, IP telephones, LAN switches with inline power (PoE), applications such as voice mail, and a voice-enabled router, all at the same physical location. The IP telephones are powered through their Ethernet interface via the LAN switch. Gateway trunks are connected to the PSTN so that users can make external calls.

Single-site deployment allows each site to be completely self-contained. All calls to the outside world and remote locations are placed across the PSTN. If an IP WAN is incorporated into the single-site model, it is for data traffic only; no telephony services are provided over the WAN. Therefore, there is no loss of the call processing service or functionality if an IP WAN failure occurs or if the WAN has insufficient bandwidth. The only external requirements are a PSTN carrier and route diversity within the PSTN network. As a recommended practice, use this model for a single campus or a site with fewer than 30,000 lines.

Multisite WAN with Centralized Call Processing Design

Figure 8-20 presents a multisite WAN design model with centralized call processing; Cisco Unified Communications Manager at the central site connects to remote locations through the IP WAN. Remote IP telephones rely on the centralized Cisco Unified Communications Manager to handle their call processing. The IP WAN transports voice traffic between sites and carries call control signaling between the central site and the remote sites. Applications such as voice mail and IVR systems are also centralized, therefore reducing the overall cost of ownership and centralized administration and maintenance.

Figure 8-20 *Multisite WAN with Centralized Call Processing Design*

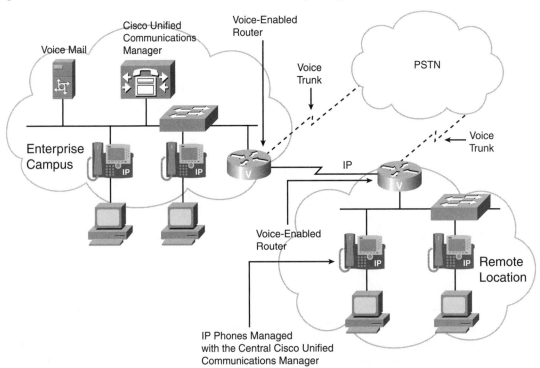

The remote locations require IP connectivity with the Enterprise Campus. IP telephones, powered by a local LAN switch, convert voice into IP packets and send them to the local LAN. The local router forwards the packets to the appropriate destination based on its routing table. In the event of a WAN failure, the voice-enabled routers at the remote sites can provide backup call processing functionality with Cisco Unified Survivable Remote Site Telephony (SRST) services. Cisco Unified SRST extends high-availability IP telephony to branch offices by providing backup call processing functionality on voice-enabled routers.

If an enterprise requires high-quality voice communication over the WAN, the service provider must implement QoS mechanisms. Enterprises and service providers usually sign a service level agreement (SLA) that guarantees bandwidth and latency levels suitable for voice transport.

NOTE The routers are voice-capable to enable voice communication with the outside world through the PSTN.

As a recommended practice, use this model for a main site with many smaller remote sites that connect via a QoS-enabled WAN but that do not require full features and functionality during a WAN outage.

Multisite WAN with Distributed Call Processing Design

Figure 8-21 illustrates a multisite WAN design model with distributed call processing. This model consists of multiple independent sites, each with its own call processing agent and connected to an IP WAN that carries voice traffic between the distributed sites. The IP WAN in this model does not carry call control signaling between the sites because each site has its own call processing agent. Typically, the PSTN serves as a backup connection between the sites in case the IP WAN connection fails or has insufficient available bandwidth for incremental calls.

Figure 8-21 *Multisite WAN with Centralized Call Processing Design*

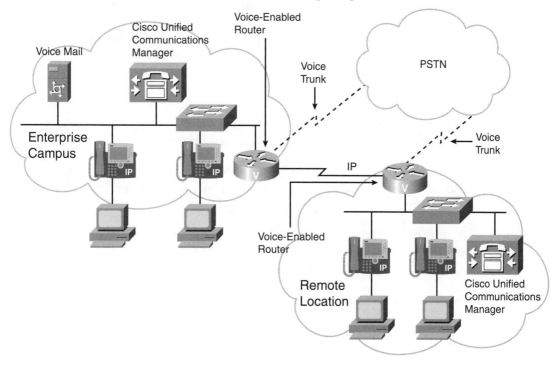

> **NOTE** A site connected only through the PSTN is a standalone site and is not covered by the distributed call processing model.

As a recommended practice, use this model for a large central site with more than 30,000 lines or for a deployment with more than six large sites (more than 30,000 lines total) interconnected via a QoS-enabled WAN.

> **NOTE** IP telephony functionality can be scaled to a small site or branch office with Cisco Unified Communications Manager Express, which is embedded in Cisco IOS software and provides call processing for up to 240 Cisco Unified IP phones. This product offers customers a low-cost, reliable, and feature-rich solution for deployment.

Call Control and Transport Protocols

Voice communication over IP is a mix of call control signals and voice conversations coded and possibly compressed into IP packets. Both reliable (connection-oriented) and so-called "unreliable" (connectionless) transmissions are required for voice communication.

Reliable transmission guarantees sequenced, error-free, flow-controlled transmission of packets. However, because reliable transport is connection-oriented, it can delay transmission and reduce throughput. TCP provides reliable transport in the IP stack, and all voice call control functions make use of it.

The User Datagram Protocol (UDP), which provides best-effort delivery, supplies connectionless transmission in the IP stack and is used for voice conversation transport between two endpoints.

KEY POINT | Control signals and data require reliable transport (using TCP) because the signals and data must be received in the order in which they were sent, and they cannot be lost.

However, voice conversation loses its value with time. If a voice packet is delayed, it loses its relevance to the end user, and retransmitting it is not useful. Therefore, voice conversation uses the more efficient connectionless transport (using UDP).

The following sections detail the protocols used for voice conversation traffic and call control functions.

Voice Conversation Protocols

Because of the time-sensitive nature of voice transport, UDP is the logical choice for carrying voice. However, voice conversation needs more information on a packet-by-packet basis than UDP offers. As shown in Figure 8-22, the Real-Time Transport Protocol (RTP), which runs on top of UDP, carries voice conversation (and video) between two IP endpoints.

Figure 8-22 *VoIP Call Control Protocols Use TCP; Voice Conversation Uses UDP*

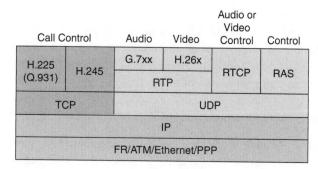

RTP provides the additional packet sequence and time-stamping information needed for voice conversation traffic. RTP uses the sequence information to determine whether the packets are arriving in order, and it uses the time-stamping information to determine the inter-arrival packet time (to determine the variation in delay, called jitter). This information is essential for high-quality VoIP conversations.

Using RTP is important for real-time traffic; however, a few drawbacks exist. The IP/UDP/RTP packet headers are 20, 8, and 12 bytes, respectively, which results in a 40-byte header. This is twice as big as the compressed voice payload (when using the G.729 codec, discussed in the "Voice Coding Standards (Codecs)" section later in this chapter). This large header adds considerable overhead to voice traffic and reduces voice bandwidth efficiency.

NOTE   Large IP/UDP/RTP headers can be compressed by using RTP header compression, called *compressed RTP (cRTP)*. The "Bandwidth Considerations" section of this chapter further describes cRTP.

> **NOTE** Cisco IOS 12.0(7)T introduced the Express RTP Header Compression feature. Before this feature was available, if compression of cRTP was enabled, that function was performed in the process-switching path and slowed down packet transmission. With Express RTP header compression, compression occurs by default in the fast-switched path or the Cisco Express Forwarding–switched path, depending on which switching method is enabled on the interface.

Call Control Functions with H.323

A variety of standards and protocols can be used for call control. H.323 call control functions include signaling for call setup, capability exchange, signaling of commands and indications, and messages to open and describe the content of logical channels. The following H.323 signaling functions provide overall system control:

- **H.225 call signaling channel**: Uses Q.931 to establish a connection between two terminals.

- **H.245 control channel**: A reliable channel carrying control messages that govern voice operation, including capabilities exchange, opening and closing of logical channels, preference requests, flow control messages, and general commands and indications. Capabilities exchange is one of the fundamental capabilities in the ITU-U H.323 recommendation.

- **RAS signaling**: Performs registration, admission, bandwidth change, status, and disengage procedures between endpoints and gatekeepers. The RAS protocol runs on top of UDP/IP and is used only if an H.323 gatekeeper is present.

- **Real-time Transport Control Protocol (RTCP)**: Provides a mechanism for hosts involved in an RTP session to exchange information about monitoring and controlling the session. RTCP monitors quality for such elements as packet counts, packet loss, and inter-arrival jitter.

Figure 8-22 also shows these functions.

Call Control Functions with the Skinny Client Control Protocol

KEY POINT Skinny Client Control Protocol (SCCP) is a Cisco-proprietary terminal control protocol for messaging between IP phones and Cisco Unified Communications Manager, as illustrated in Figure 8-23.

Figure 8-23   *SCCP Call Control*

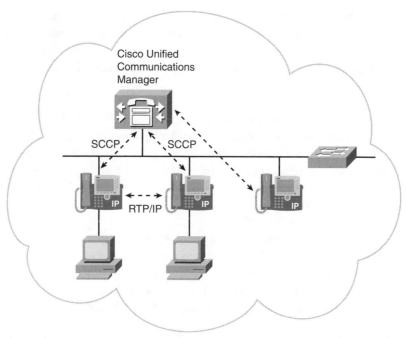

By default, Cisco Unified Communications Manager uses SCCP to signal Cisco IP phones. SCCP is a client/server protocol; Cisco Unified Communications Manager is the server, and the IP phones are the clients. Examples of SCCP clients include the Cisco Unified IP Phone 7900 series phones, such as the Cisco Unified IP Phone 7960 series, the Cisco Unified IP Phone 7970 series, the Cisco Unified IP Phone 7985, and the 802.11b Cisco Unified Wireless IP Phone 7920.

SCCP is a lightweight protocol that uses TCP/IP for efficient communication. Cisco Unified Communications Manager acts as a signaling proxy for the SCCP clients for call events received over other common protocols such as H.323, the session initiation protocol (SIP), and the Media Gateway Control Protocol (MGCP).

SCCP clients register with Cisco Unified Communications Manager to receive their configuration information. After it registers, a Cisco IP phone receives notification of new incoming calls and can make outgoing calls. The SCCP protocol is used for VoIP call signaling and enhanced features such as the Message Waiting Indicator.

Media connections between devices involved in a call, including voice conversations, use RTP.

Call Control Functions with SIP

> **KEY POINT** SIP is the Internet Engineering Task Force (IETF) standard for multimedia conferencing over IP. SIP is an ASCII text-based application-layer control protocol that establishes, maintains, and terminates calls between two or more endpoints. SIP is a peer-to-peer protocol developed as a simple lightweight replacement for H.323.

SIP is defined in RFC 3261, *SIP: Session Initiation Protocol*. SIP performs the signaling and session management functions required in a packet telephony network. Signaling sends call information across network boundaries. Session management controls the attributes of an end-to-end call. SIP requests and responses establish communication among the various components in the network, ultimately creating a conference between two or more endpoints. A SIP network can include the following components:

- **User agent (UA)**: SIP is a peer-to-peer protocol; the peers in a session are called *UAs*. A UA can act as both a UA client (UAC), which initiates calls, and a UA server (UAS), which receives calls. Whether a UA is acting as a UAC or a UAS is defined on a transaction-by-transaction basis; the UA initiating a call acts as a UAC when sending an invitation request, and as a UAS when receiving a goodbye request from the called party.

  A UAS (a server application) notifies the user when it receives a SIP request from a UAC; the UAS then responds on behalf of the user. Cisco Unified Communications Manager can act as both a UAS and a UAC; this functionality is known as a *back-to-back UA*.

- **SIP proxy server**: A SIP proxy server works as an intermediate device that acts as both a server and a client for making requests on behalf of other clients. A SIP proxy server receives SIP requests from a client and interprets and, if necessary, rewrites specific parts of the request message before forwarding it on behalf of the client. Proxy servers provide functions such as authentication, authorization, network access control, call routing, reliable request retransmission, and security.

- **Redirect server**: The redirect server is a UAS that provides the client with information about the next hop or hops that a message should take. For example, if an endpoint has moved, the redirect server might provide an alternative address. The client then contacts the next-hop server directly.

- **Registrar server**: The registrar server processes requests from clients to register their current location; the registrar server puts the information it receives in the requests into the location service for the domain it handles. Redirect or proxy servers often also contain registrar servers.

SIP integrates with other IP services, such as e-mail, web, voice mail, instant messaging, multiparty conferencing, and multimedia collaboration. When used with an IP infrastructure, SIP helps enable rich communications with numerous multivendor devices and media. SIP can set up individual voice or conference calls, videoconferences and point-to-point video-enabled calls, web collaboration and chat sessions, and instant-messaging sessions among any number of SIP-enabled endpoints.

Users in a SIP network are identified by unique SIP addresses, a type of uniform resource identifier (URI) called a *SIP URI*. The format of a SIP URI is similar to that of an e-mail address, typically containing a username and a hostname such as sip:nicholas@sipprovider.com, where sipprovider.com is Nicholas's SIP service provider. Users register their assigned SIP addresses with a registrar server. The registrar server provides this information to the location service (which contains a list of bindings of addresses for contacts) upon request. The basic elements of a SIP system are UAs and proxy servers, as shown in Figure 8-24.

Figure 8-24   *SIP Call Control*

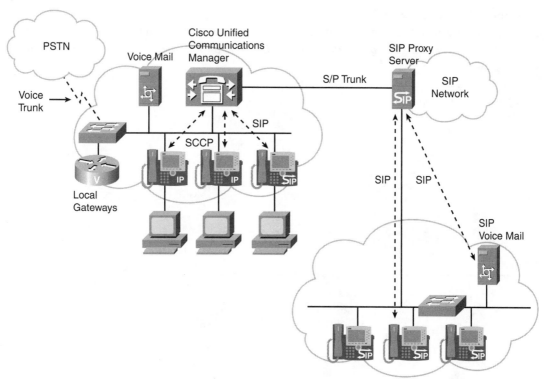

The SIP UA software is implemented in end-user devices and server components to manage the SIP connection. SIP UAs include endpoints such as IP phones, SIP media gateways, conferencing servers, and messaging systems.

SIP UAs communicate with a SIP proxy server. SIP proxy servers, such as the Cisco SIP Proxy Server application, route SIP requests from UAs to their appropriate destinations. SIP proxy servers are typically collocated with a SIP registrar, which maintains a list of contacts for specific users within a specific IP domain.

SIP proxy servers also provide integrated communications with Cisco Unified Communications Manager and enterprise voice gateways. SIP-compliant devices such as IP phones can register directly with Cisco Unified Communications Manager.

NOTE RTP is used to send packetized voice, video, and data in real time between UAs.

Call Control Functions with MGCP

MGCP is a client/server protocol defined in an informational (nonstandard) IETF document, RFC 3435, *Media Gateway Control Protocol (MGCP) Version 1.0.* The components of MGCP are shown in Figure 8-25.

Figure 8-25 *MGCP Control*

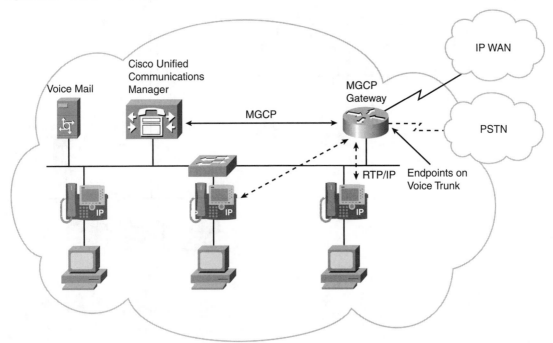

KEY POINT In MGCP, the servers are known as *call agents;* Cisco Unified Communications Manager is an example of a call agent. Call agents control *endpoints*, which are any of the voice ports on a media gateway.

Endpoints communicate over *connections.* A gateway handles translation between audio signals on the endpoints and the packet network. The MGCP call agent knows and controls the state of each individual port on the gateway. MGCP allows complete control of the dial plan from the call agent, including per-port control of connections to the PSTN, legacy PBX, voice-mail systems, plain old telephone service phones, and so forth. The call agent and the gateway communicate using a series of plaintext commands sent over UDP port 2427.

An *endpoint* is a source for call data (using RTP/UDP/IP) that is flowing through the gateway. Examples of endpoints are analog voice ports and channels on a digital trunk on the physical interface between the PSTN and the gateway. Other types of endpoints include logical endpoints.

In an MGCP call, a call agent creates a connection either between an endpoint and the packet network or between two endpoints. When a connection is made to an endpoint, the gateway assigns a connection identifier for that connection.

Voice Issues and Requirements

This section describes issues that might affect voice quality and then introduces various mechanisms that can be used to improve the quality of voice in an integrated network.

Voice Quality Issues

Overall voice quality is a function of many factors, including delay, jitter, packet loss, and echo. This section discusses these factors and ways to minimize them.

Packet Delays

Packet delay can cause voice quality degradation. When designing networks that transport voice, you must understand and account for the network's delay components. Correctly accounting for all potential delays ensures that overall network performance is acceptable.

The generally accepted limit for good quality voice connection delay is 150 milliseconds (ms) one-way. As delays increase, the communication between two people falls out of synch (for example, they speak at the same time or both wait for the other to speak); this condition is called *talker overlap.* The ITU describes network delay for voice applications in recommendation G.114; as shown in Table 8-3, this recommendation defines three bands of one-way delay.

Table 8-3 *ITU G.114 Recommended Delays for One-way Voice Traffic*

Delay	Effect on Voice Quality
0 to 150 ms	Acceptable for most user applications.
151 to 400 ms	Acceptable provided that the organization is aware of the transmission time and its impact on the transmission quality of user applications. Note that this is the expected range for a satellite link.
Longer than 401 ms	Unacceptable for general network planning purposes; however, this limit is exceeded in some exceptional cases.

Voice packets are delayed if the network is congested because of poor network quality, underpowered equipment, congested traffic, or insufficient bandwidth. Delay can be classified into two types: fixed network delay and variable network delay.

Fixed Network Delays

Fixed network delays result from delays in network devices and contribute directly to the overall connection delay. As shown in Figure 8-26, fixed delays have three components: propagation delay, serialization delay, and processing delay.

Figure 8-26 *Fixed Delays Result from Delays in Network Devices*

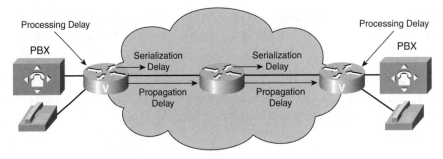

Propagation Delay

KEY POINT *Propagation delay* is the length of time it takes a signal to travel the distance between the sending and receiving endpoints.

This form of delay, which is limited by the speed of light, can be ignored for most designs because it is relatively small compared to other types of delay. A popular estimate of 10 microseconds/mile or 6 microseconds/kilometer is used for estimating propagation delay.

NOTE Propagation delay has a noticeable impact on the overall delay only on satellite links.

Serialization Delay

KEY POINT | *Serialization delay* is the delay encountered when sending a voice or data frame onto the network interface. It is the result of placing bits on the circuit and is directly related to the circuit (link) speed.

The higher the circuit speed, the less time it takes to place the bits on the circuit and the less the serialization delay. Serialization delay is a constant function of link speed and packet size. It is calculated by the following formula:

(packet length)/(bit rate)

A large serialization delay occurs with slow links or large packets. Serialization delay is always predictable; for example, when using a 64-kbps link and 80-byte frame, the delay is exactly 10 ms.

NOTE The previous example is calculated as follows:

- 64 kbps = 64,000 bits/sec * 1 byte/8 bits = 8000 bytes/sec = 8000 bytes/1000 ms = 8 bytes/ms

- Serialization delay = (packet length)/(bit rate) = (80 bytes)/(8 bytes/ms) = 10 ms

NOTE Serialization delay is a factor only for slow-speed links up to 1 Mbps.

Processing Delay

KEY POINT | *Processing delay* is the time the DSP takes to process a block of PCM samples.

Processing delays include the following:

- **Coding, compression, decompression, and decoding delays**: These delays depend on the algorithm used for these functions, which can be performed in either hardware or software. Using specialized hardware such as a DSP dramatically improves the quality and reduces the delay associated with different voice compression schemes.

- **Packetization delay**: This delay results from the process of holding the digital voice samples until enough are collected to fill the packet or cell payload. In some compression schemes, the voice gateway sends partial packets to reduce excessive packetization delay.

Variable Network Delays

Variable network delay is more unpredictable and difficult to calculate than fixed network delay. As shown in Figure 8-27 and described in the following sections, the following three factors contribute to variable network delay: queuing delay, variable packet sizes, and dejitter buffers.

Figure 8-27 *Variable Delays Can Be Unpredictable*

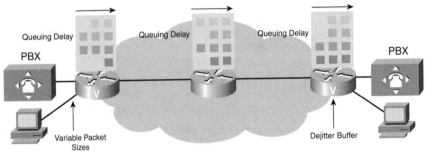

Queuing Delay and Variable Packet Sizes

KEY POINT | Congested output queues on network interfaces are the most common sources of variable delay.

Queuing delay occurs when a voice packet is waiting on the outgoing interface for others to be serviced first. This waiting time is statistically based on the arrival of traffic; the more inputs, the more likely that contention is encountered for the interface. Queuing delay is also based on the size of the packet currently being serviced; larger packets take longer to transmit than do smaller packets. Therefore, a queue that combines large and small packets experiences varying lengths of delay.

Because voice should have absolute priority in the voice gateway queue, a voice frame should wait only for either a data frame that is already being sent or for other voice frames ahead of it. For example, assume that a 1500-byte data packet is queued before the voice packet. The voice packet must wait until the entire data packet is transmitted, which produces a delay in the voice path. If the link is slow (for example, 64 or 128 kbps), the queuing delay might be more than 200 ms and result in an unacceptable voice delay.

Link fragmentation and interleaving (LFI) is a solution for queuing delay situations. With LFI, the voice gateway fragments large packets into smaller equal-sized frames and interleaves them with small voice packets. Therefore, a voice packet does not have to wait until the entire large data packet is sent. LFI reduces and ensures a more predictable voice delay. Configuring LFI fragmentation on a link results in a fixed delay (for example, 10 ms); however, be sure to set the fragment size so that only data packets, not voice packets, become fragmented. Figure 8-28 illustrates the LFI concept.

Figure 8-28   *LFI Ensures That Smaller Packets Do Not Get Stuck Behind Larger Packets*

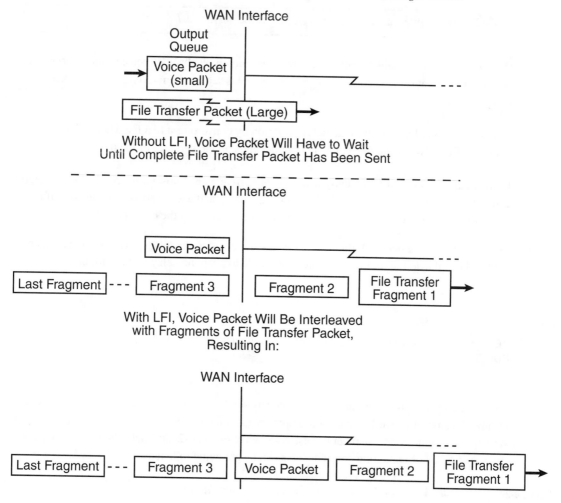

Dejitter Buffers

Because network congestion can occur at any point in a network, interface queues can be filled instantaneously, potentially leading to a difference in delay times between packets from the same voice stream.

KEY POINT | The variable delay between packets is called *jitter*. The next section describes jitter.

Dejitter buffers are used at the *receiving end* to smooth delay variability and allow time for decoding and decompression.

NOTE The dejitter buffer is also referred to as the *playout delay buffer*.

On the first talk spurt, dejitter buffers help provide smooth playback of voice traffic. Setting these buffers too low causes overflows and data loss, whereas setting them too high causes excessive delay.

Dejitter buffers reduce or eliminate delay variation by converting it to a fixed delay. However, dejitter buffers always add delay; the amount depends on the variance of the delay.

Dejitter buffers work most efficiently when packets arrive with almost uniform delay. Various QoS congestion avoidance mechanisms exist to manage delay and avoid network congestion; if there is no variance in delay, dejitter buffers can be disabled, reducing the constant delay.

KEY POINT | When using dejitter buffers, delay is always added to the total delay budget. Therefore, keep the dejitter buffers as small as possible to keep the delay to a minimum.

Jitter

KEY POINT | *Jitter* is a variation in the delay of received packets.

At the sending side, the originating voice gateway sends packets in a continuous stream, spaced evenly. Because of network congestion, improper queuing, or configuration errors, this steady stream can become lumpy; in other words, as shown in Figure 8-29, the delay between each packet can vary instead of remaining constant. This can be annoying to listeners.

Figure 8-29 *Jitter Is the Variation in the Delay of Received Voice Packets*

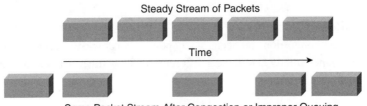

When a voice gateway receives a VoIP audio stream, it must compensate for the jitter it encounters. The mechanism that handles this function is the dejitter buffer (as mentioned previously in the "Dejitter Buffers" section), which must buffer the packets and then play them out in a steady stream to the DSPs, which convert them back to an analog audio stream.

Packet Loss

Packet loss causes voice clipping and skips. Packet loss can occur because of congested links, improper network QoS configuration, poor packet buffer management on the routers, routing problems, and other issues in both the WAN and LAN. If queues become saturated, VoIP packets might be dropped, resulting in effects such as clicks or lost words. Losses occur if the packets are received out of range of the dejitter buffer, in which case the packets are discarded.

The industry-standard codec algorithms used in the Cisco DSP can use interpolation to correct for up to 30 ms of lost voice. The Cisco VoIP technology uses 20-ms samples of voice payload per VoIP packet. Therefore, only a single packet can be lost during any given time for the codec correction algorithms to be effective.

> **KEY POINT** For packet losses as small as one packet, the DSP interpolates the conversation with what it thinks the audio should be, and the packet loss is not audible.

Echo

In a voice telephone call, an echo occurs when callers hear their own words repeated.

> **KEY POINT** An *echo* is the audible leak of the caller's voice into the receive path (the return path).

Echo is a function of delay and magnitude. The echo problem grows with the delay (the later the echo is heard) and the loudness (higher amplitude). When timed properly, an echo can be reassuring to the speaker. But if the echo exceeds approximately 25 milliseconds, it can be distracting and cause breaks in the conversation.

> **KEY POINT** Perceived echo most likely indicates a problem at the *other* end of the call. For example, if a person in Toronto hears an echo when talking to a person in Vancouver, the problem is likely to be at the Vancouver end.

The following voice network elements can affect echo:

■ **Hybrid transformers**: A typical telephone is a two-wire device, whereas trunk connections are four-wire; a hybrid transformer is used to interface between these connections. Hybrid transformers are often prime culprits for signal leakage between analog transmit and receive paths, causing echo. Echo is usually caused by a mismatch in impedance from the four-wire network switch conversion to the two-wire local loop or an impedance mismatch in a PBX.

■ **Telephones**: An analog telephone terminal itself presents a load to the PBX. This load should be matched to the output impedance of the source device (the FXS port). Some (typically inexpensive) telephones are not matched to the FXS port's output impedance and are sources of echo. Headsets are particularly notorious for poor echo performance.

When digital telephones are used, the point of digital-to-analog conversion occurs inside the telephone. Extending the digital transmission segments closer to the actual telephone decreases the potential for echo.

NOTE   The belief that adding voice gateways (routers) to a voice network creates echo is a common misconception. Digital segments of the network do not cause leaks; so, technically, voice gateways cannot be the source of echo. However, adding routers does add delay, which can make a previously imperceptible echo perceptible.

An echo canceller, shown in Figure 8-30, can be placed in the network to improve the quality of telephone conversation. An echo canceller is a component of a voice gateway; it reduces the level of echo leaking from the receive path into the transmit path.

Figure 8-30   *Echo Cancellers Reduce the Echo Level*

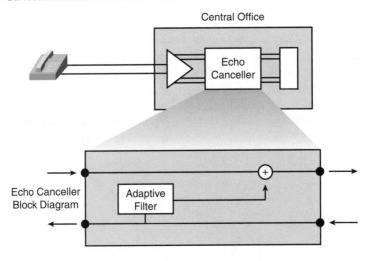

Echo cancellers are built into low-bit-rate codecs and operate on each DSP. By design, echo cancellers are limited by the total amount of time they wait for the reflected speech to be received. This is known as an *echo trail* or *echo cancellation time* and is usually between 16 and 32 milliseconds.

To understand how an echo canceller works, assume that a person in Toronto is talking to a person in Vancouver. When the speech of the person in Toronto hits an impedance mismatch or other echo-causing environment, it bounces back to that person, who can hear the echo several milliseconds after speaking.

Recall that the problem is at the other end of the call (called the *tail circuit*); in this example, the tail circuit is in Vancouver. To remove the echo from the line, the router in Toronto must keep an inverse image of the Toronto person's speech for a certain amount of time. This is called *inverse speech*. The echo canceller in the router listens for sound coming from the person in Vancouver and subtracts the inverse speech of the person in Toronto to remove any echo.

The ITU-T defines an *irritation zone* of echo loudness and echo delay. A short echo (around 15 ms) does not have to be suppressed, whereas longer echo delays require strong echo suppression. Therefore, all networks that produce one-way time delays greater than 16 ms require echo cancellation. It is important to configure the appropriate echo cancellation time. If the echo cancellation time is set too low, callers still hear echo during the phone call. If the configured echo cancellation time is set too high, it takes longer for the echo canceller to converge and eliminate the echo.

Attenuating the signal below the noise level can also eliminate echo.

Voice Coding and Compression

Voice communication over IP relies on voice that is coded and encapsulated into IP packets. This section provides an overview of the various codecs used in voice networks.

NOTE   The term *codec* can have the following two meanings:

- **A coder-decoder**: An integrated circuit device that typically uses PCM to transform analog signals into a digital bit stream and digital signals back into analog signals.

- **A software algorithm**: Used to compress and decompress speech or audio signals in VoIP, Frame Relay, and ATM.

Coding and Compression Algorithms

KEY POINT	A *codec* is a device or software that encodes (and decodes) a signal into digital data stream.

Each codec provides a certain quality of speech. Advances in technology have greatly improved the quality of compressed voice and have resulted in a variety of coding and compression algorithms:

- **PCM**: The toll quality voice expected from the PSTN. PCM runs at 64 kbps and provides no compression, and therefore no opportunity for bandwidth savings.

- **Adaptive Differential Pulse Code Modulation (ADPCM)**: Provides three different levels of compression. Some fidelity is lost as compression increases. Depending on the traffic mix, cost savings generally run at 25 percent for 32-kbps ADPCM, 30 percent for 24-kbps ADPCM, and 35 percent for 16-kbps ADPCM.

- **Low-Delay Code Excited Linear Prediction Compression (LD-CELP)**: This algorithm models the human voice. Depending on the traffic mix, cost savings can be up to 35 percent for 16-kbps LD-CELP.

- **Conjugate Structure Algebraic Code Excited Linear Prediction Compression (CS-ACELP)**: Provides eight times the bandwidth savings over PCM. CS-ACELP is a more recently developed algorithm modeled after the human voice and delivers quality that is comparable to LD-CELP and 32-kbps ADPCM. Cost savings are approximately 40 percent for 8-kbps CS-ACELP.

- **Code Excited Linear Prediction Compression (CELP)**: Provides huge bandwidth savings over PCM. Cost savings can be up to 50 percent for 5.3-kbps CELP.

The following section details voice coding standards based on these algorithms.

Voice Coding Standards (Codecs)

The ITU has defined a series of standards for voice coding and compression:

- **G.711**: Uses the 64-kbps PCM voice coding technique. G.711-encoded voice is already in the correct format for digital voice delivery in the PSTN or through PBXs. Most Cisco implementations use G.711 on LAN links because of its high quality, approaching toll quality.

- **G.726/G.727**: G.726 uses the ADPCM coding at 40, 32, 24, and 16 kbps. ADPCM voice can be interchanged between packet voice and public telephone or PBX networks if the latter has ADPCM capability. G.727 is a specialized version of G.726; it includes the same bandwidths.

- **G.728**: Uses the LD-CELP voice compression, which requires only 16 kbps of bandwidth. LD-CELP voice coding must be transcoded to a PCM-based coding before delivering to the PSTN.

- **G.729**: Uses the CS-ACELP compression, which enables voice to be coded into 8-kbps streams. This standard has various forms, all of which provide speech quality similar to that of 32-kbps ADPCM.

  For example, in G.729a, the basic algorithm was optimized to reduce the computation requirements. In G.729b, voice activity detection (VAD) and comfort noise generation were added. G.729ab provides an optimized version of G.729b requiring less computation.

- **G.723.1**: Uses a dual-rate coder for compressing speech at very low bit rates. Two bit rates are associated with this standard: 5.3 kbps using algebraic code-excited linear prediction (ACELP) and 6.3 kbps using Multipulse Maximum Likelihood Quantization (MPMLQ).

Sound Quality

Each codec provides a certain quality of speech. The perceived quality of transmitted speech depends on a listener's subjective response.

The *mean opinion score* (*MOS*) is a common benchmark used to specify the quality of sound produced by specific codecs. To determine the MOS, a wide range of listeners judge the quality of a voice sample corresponding to a particular codec on a scale of 1 (bad) to 5 (excellent). The scores are averaged to provide the MOS for that sample. Table 8-4 shows the relationship between codecs and MOS scores; notice that MOS decreases with increased codec complexity.

Table 8-4   *Voice Coding and Compression Results*

Algorithm	ITU Standard	Data Rate[1]	MOS Score
PCM	G.711	64 kbps	4.1
ADPCM	G.726/G.727	16/24/32/40 kbps	3.85 or less
LD-CELP	G.728	16 kbps	3.61
CS-ACELP	G.729	8 kbps	3.92
ACELP/MPMLQ	G.723.1	6.3/5.3 kbps	3.9/3.65

[1] Data rates shown are for digitized speech only. In addition to this coded digital stream payload, RTP, UDP, IP, and Layer 2 headers are needed.

KEY POINT   G.729 is the recommended voice codec for most WAN networks (that do not do multiple encodings) because of its relatively low bandwidth requirements and high MOS.

The Perceptual Speech Quality Measurement (PSQM) is a newer, more objective measurement that is overtaking MOS scores as the industry quality measurement of choice for coding algorithms. PSQM is specified in ITU standard P.861. PSQM provides a rating on a scale of 0 to 6.5, where 0 is best and 6.5 is worst. PSQM is implemented in test equipment and monitoring systems. It compares the transmitted speech to the original input to produce a PSQM score for a test voice call over a particular packet network. Some PSQM test equipment converts the 0-to-6.5 scale to a 0-to-5 scale to correlate to MOS.

Codec Complexity, DSPs, and Voice Calls

KEY POINT	A *DSP* is a hardware component that converts information from telephony-based protocols to packet-based protocols (such as IP).

A codec is a technology for compressing and decompressing data; it is implemented in DSPs. Some codec compression techniques require more processing power than others.

KEY POINT	Codec complexity is divided into low, medium, and high complexity. The difference between the complexities of the codecs is the CPU utilization necessary to process the codec algorithm and the number of voice channels that a single DSP can support.

The number of calls supported depends on the DSP and the complexity of the codec used. For example, as illustrated in Table 8-5, the Cisco High-Density Packet Voice/Fax DSP Module (AS54-PVDM2-64) for Cisco voice gateways provides high-density voice connectivity supporting 24 to 64 channels (calls), depending on codec compression complexity.

Table 8-5   *Code Complexity and Calls per DSP on the AS54-PVDM2-64 Voice/Fax DSP Module*

Low Complexity (Maximum 64 Calls)	Medium Complexity (Maximum 32 Calls)	High Complexity (Maximum 24 Calls)
G.711 a-law	G.729a	G.723.1: 5.3/6.3 kbps
G.711 Mu-law	G.729ab	G.723.1a: 5.3/6.3 kbps
Fax Passthrough	G.726: 16/24/32 kbps	G.728
Modem Passthrough	T.38 fax relay	Modem relay
Clear-channel codec	Cisco Fax Relay	Adaptive multirate narrow band: 4.75, 5.15, 5.9, 6.7, 7.4, 7.95, 10.2, and 12.2 kbps, and silence insertion descriptor

Bandwidth Considerations

Bandwidth availability is a key issue to consider when designing voice on IP networks. The amount of bandwidth per call varies greatly, depending on which codec is used and how many voice samples are required per packet. However, the best coding mechanism does not necessarily result in the best voice quality; for example, the better the compression, the worse the voice quality. The designer must decide which is more important: better voice quality or more efficient bandwidth consumption.

Reducing the Amount of Voice Traffic

Two techniques reduce the amount of traffic per voice call and therefore use available bandwidth more efficiently: cRTP and VAD.

Compressed Real-Time Transport Protocol

All voice packets encapsulated into IP consist of two components: the payload, which is the voice sample, and IP/UDP/RTP headers. Although voice samples are compressed by the DSP and can vary in size based on the codec used, the headers are a constant 40 bytes. When compared to the 20 bytes of voice samples in a G.729 call, the headers make up a considerable amount of overhead. As illustrated in Figure 8-31, cRTP compresses the headers to 2 or 4 bytes, thereby offering significant bandwidth savings. cRTP is sometimes referred to as *RTP header compression*. RFC 2508, *Compressing IP/UDP/RTP Headers for Low-Speed Serial Links,* describes cRTP.

Figure 8-31 *RTP Header Compression*

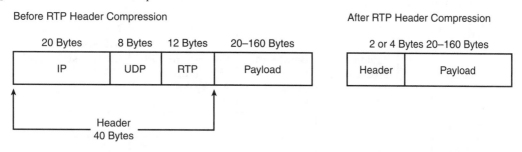

Enabling compression on a low-bandwidth serial link can greatly reduce the network overhead and conserve WAN bandwidth if there is a significant volume of RTP traffic. In general, enable cRTP on slow links up to 768 kbps. However, cRTP is not recommended for higher-speed links because of its high CPU requirements.

> **NOTE**   Because cRTP compresses VoIP calls on a link-by-link basis, all links on the path must be configured for cRTP.

Voice Activity Detection

On average, about 35 percent of calls are silence. In traditional voice networks, all voice calls use a fixed bandwidth of 64 kbps regardless of how much of the conversation is speech and how much is silence. When VoIP is used, this silence is packetized along with the conversation. VAD suppresses packets of silence, so instead of sending IP packets of silence, only IP packets of conversation are sent. Therefore, gateways can interleave data traffic with actual voice conversation traffic, resulting in more effective use of the network bandwidth.

> **NOTE**   In some cases, Cisco recommends disabling VAD, such as when faxes are to be sent through the network. VAD can also degrade the call's perceived quality, because when VAD is enabled, silence is replaced by comfort noise played to the listener by the device at the listener's end of the network. If this causes problems, VAD should be disabled.

Voice Bandwidth Requirements

When building voice networks, one of the most important factors to consider is bandwidth capacity planning. One of the most critical concepts to understand within capacity planning is how much bandwidth is used for each VoIP call.

Table 8-6 presents a selection of codec payload sizes and the required bandwidth without compression and with cRTP. The last column shows the number of uncompressed and compressed calls that can be made on a 512-kbps link.

Table 8-6   *Voice Bandwidth Requirements*

Codec	Payload Size (Bytes)	Bandwidth (kbps)	Bandwidth with cRTP (kbps)	Number of Calls on a 512-kbps Link (No Compression/with cRTP)
G.711 (64 kbps)	160	83	68	6/7
G.726 (32 kbps)	60	57	36	8/14
G.726 (24 kbps)	40	52	29	9/17
G.728 (16 kbps)	40	35	19	14/26
G.729 (8 kbps)	20	26	11	19/46
G.723 (6.3 kbps)	24	18	8	28/64
G.723 (5.3 kbps)	20	17	7	30/73

The following assumptions are made in Table 8-6's bandwidth calculations:

- IP/UDP/RTP headers are 40 bytes.

- RTP header compression can reduce the IP/UDP/RTP headers to 2 or 4 bytes. Table 8-6 uses 2 bytes.

- A Layer 2 header adds 6 bytes.

Table 8-6 uses the following calculations:

- Voice packet size = (Layer 2 header) + (IP/UDP/RTP header) + (voice payload)

- Voice packets per second (pps) = codec bit rate/voice payload size

- Bandwidth per call = voice packet size * voice pps

For example, the following steps illustrate how to calculate the bandwidth required for a G.729 call (8-kbps codec bit rate) with cRTP and default 20 bytes of voice payload:

- Voice packet size (bytes) = (Layer 2 header of 6 bytes) + (compressed IP/UDP/RTP header of 2 bytes) + (voice payload of 20 bytes) = 28 bytes

- Voice packet size (bits) = (28 bytes) * 8 bits per byte = 224 bits

- Voice packets per second = (8-kbps codec bit rate)/(8 bits/byte * 20 bytes) = (8-kbps codec bit rate)/(160 bits) = 50 pps

- Bandwidth per call = voice packet size (224 bits) * 50 pps = 11.2 kbps

Result: The G.729 call with cRTP requires 11.2 kbps of bandwidth. This value is rounded down to 11 in Table 8-6.

A more precise estimate of voice codec bandwidth can be obtained using the Cisco Voice Codec Bandwidth Calculator available at http://tools.cisco.com/Support/VBC/do/CodecCalc1.do.

NOTE You must be a registered user on http://www.cisco.com/ to access this calculator.

Figure 8-32 shows a portion of the results of the Cisco Voice Codec Bandwidth Calculator for the G.729 codec. This calculation uses cRTP and includes 5 percent additional overhead to accommodate the bandwidth required for signaling.

Figure 8-32 *Voice Codec Bandwidth Calculator Partial Output for G.729 Codec*

Codec Information		
Codec Bit Rate	8 kbps	= (Codec Sample Size * 8) / (Codec Sample Interval)
Codec Sample Size	10 bytes	size of each individual codec sample
Codec Sample Interval	10 msec	the time it takes for a single sample
Bandwith Per Call (VoIP)		
Voice Packets Per Second	50	(Codec Bit Rate / Voice Payload Size)
Bandwidth Per Call (RTP Only)	11.6 kbps	(Total Packet Size(bits) + Flag(bits))* (Packets Per Second)
5% Additional Overhead	0.58 kbps	5% additional overhead per call to accomodate bandwidth for signaling (for example: RTCP/H225/H245 messages on H.323 networks).
Bandwith Per Call + 5.0% Additional Overhead	12.18 kbps	Overhead + Bandwidth Per call
Total Bandwith Required (VoIP)		
Bandwidth Used for All Calls (RTP Only)	11.6 kbps	(Bandwidth per Call) * (Number of Calls)
Total Bandwidth (including Overhead)	12.18 kbps	Same as above + 5.0% Overhead
Packet Size Calculation		
Total Packet Size	28 bytes	Excluding Frame Flag
Voice Payload Size	20 bytes	Size of the Codec Samples per packet
Layer2 Overhead	6 bytes	Layer2 Overhead including CRC
Compressed Header	2 bytes	IP/UDP/RTP Compressed header
Frame Flag (7E)	1 byte	Most modern framers can handle a single flag between frames (ie... no beginning flag)

Codec Design Considerations

Although it might seem logical from a bandwidth consumption standpoint to convert all calls to low-bit-rate codecs to save bandwidth and consequently decrease infrastructure costs, the designer should consider both the expected voice quality and the bandwidth consumption when choosing the optimum codec. The designer should also consider the disadvantages of strong voice compression, including signal distortion resulting from multiple encodings. For example, when a G.729 voice signal is tandem-encoded three times, the MOS score drops from 3.92 (very good) to 2.68 (unacceptable). Another drawback is the codec-induced delay with low-bit-rate codecs.

QoS for Voice

IP telephony places strict requirements on IP packet loss, packet delay, and delay variation (jitter). Therefore, QoS mechanisms on Cisco switches and routers are important throughout the network if voice traffic is sharing network resources with data traffic. Redundant devices and network links that provide quick convergence after network failures or topology changes are also important to ensure a highly available infrastructure. The following summarizes the process to determine whether to implement QoS in a network:

Step 1   Determine whether the WAN is congested—for example, whether application users perceive performance degradation.

Step 2   Determine the network goals and objectives, based on the mix of network traffic. The following are some possible objectives:

- Establish a fair distribution of bandwidth allocation across all traffic types

- Grant strict priority to voice traffic at the expense of less-critical traffic

- Customize bandwidth allocation so that network resources are shared among all applications, each having specific bandwidth requirements

Step 3   Analyze the traffic types, and determine how to distinguish them.

Step 4   Review the available QoS mechanisms and determine which approach best addresses the requirements and goals.

Step 5   Configure the routers for the chosen QoS strategy and observe the results.

Figure 8-33 identifies some of the QoS mechanisms available, many of which were introduced in Chapter 4, "Designing Basic Campus and Data Center Networks," and Chapter 5. The specifics of these mechanisms for voice are reviewed here, followed by a discussion of Call Admission Control (CAC). QoS practices in the Building Access Layer are also described. This section concludes with a discussion of AutoQoS.

Figure 8-33 *QoS Mechanism*

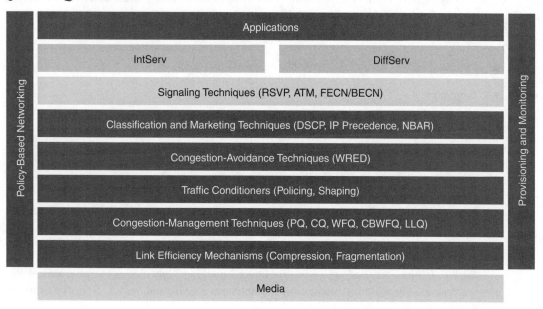

Bandwidth Provisioning

Bandwidth provisioning involves accurately calculating the required bandwidth for all applications, plus the required overhead. CAC should be used to avoid using more bandwidth than has been provisioned.

Signaling Techniques

The Resource Reservation Protocol (RSVP) allows bandwidth and other resources along the routing path to be reserved so that a certain level of quality is provided for delay-sensitive traffic. Other signaling techniques include Frame Relay's Forward Explicit Congestion Notification and Backward Explicit Congestion Notification, and those used with the various ATM adaptation types.

Classification and Marking

Packet *classification* is the process of partitioning traffic into multiple priority levels or classes of service. Information in the frame or packet header is inspected, and the frame's priority is determined. *Marking* is the process of changing the priority or class of service (CoS) setting within a frame or packet to indicate its classification.

Classification is usually performed with access control lists (ACL), QoS class maps, or route maps, using various match criteria. Network-based application recognition, described in Chapter 2, "Applying a Methodology to Network Design," can also be used for classification. Matches can be based on the following criteria:

- Protocol, such as a stateful protocol or a Layer 4 protocol

- Input port

- IP precedence or differentiated services code point (DSCP)

- Ethernet IEEE 802.1p CoS bits

Marking is done at Layer 3 or Layer 2:

- Layer 3 marking changes the IP precedence bits or DSCP values in the IP packet to reflect the result of QoS classification.

- For IEEE 802.1Q frames, the 3 user priority bits in the Tag field—commonly referred to as the *802.1p bits*—are used as CoS bits for Layer 2 marking; eight classes of traffic are possible with these 3 bits. Cisco IP phones, for example, can classify and mark VoIP traffic using the 802.1p bits.

Congestion Avoidance

Recall from Chapter 5 that congestion-avoidance techniques monitor network traffic loads so that congestion can be anticipated and avoided before it becomes problematic. Congestion-avoidance techniques allow packets from streams identified as being eligible for early discard (those with lower priority) to be dropped when the queue is getting full. Congestion-avoidance techniques provide preferential treatment for high priority traffic under congestion situations while maximizing network throughput and capacity utilization and minimizing packet loss and delay.

Weighted random early detection (WRED) is the Cisco implementation of the random early detection (RED) mechanism. WRED extends RED by using the IP Precedence bits in the IP packet header to determine which traffic should be dropped; the drop-selection process is weighted by the IP precedence. Similarly, DSCP-based WRED uses the DSCP value in the IP packet header in the drop-selection process. Distributed WRED (DWRED) is an implementation of WRED for the Versatile Interface Processor (VIP). The DWRED feature is supported only on Cisco 7000 series routers with a Route Switch Processor–based RSP7000 interface processor and Cisco 7500 series routers with a VIP-based VIP2-40 or greater interface processor.

Traffic Policing and Shaping

Traffic shaping and traffic policing, also referred to as committed access rate, are similar mechanisms in that they both inspect traffic and take action based on the various characteristics of that traffic. These characteristics can be based on whether the traffic is over or under a given rate or based on some bits in the IP packet header, such as the DSCP or IP Precedence bits.

Policing either discards the packet or modifies some aspect of it, such as its IP Precedence or CoS bits, when the policing agent determines that the packet meets a given criterion. In comparison, *traffic shaping* attempts to adjust the transmission rate of packets that match a certain criterion. A shaper typically delays excess traffic by using a buffer or queuing mechanism to hold packets and shape the flow when the source's data rate is higher than expected. For example, generic traffic shaping uses a weighted fair queue to delay packets to shape the flow, whereas Frame Relay traffic shaping uses a priority queue, a custom queue, or a FIFO queue, depending on how it is configured.

Congestion Management: Queuing and Scheduling

KEY POINT As noted in Chapter 5, congestion management includes two separate processes: queuing, which separates traffic into various queues or buffers, and scheduling, which decides from which queue traffic is to be sent next.

Queuing is configured on outbound interfaces and is appropriate for cases in which WAN links are occasionally congested.

There are two types of queues: the hardware queue (also called the *transmit queue* or *TxQ*) and software queues. Software queues schedule packets into the hardware queue based on the QoS requirements and include the following types: weighted fair queuing (WFQ), priority queuing (PQ), custom queuing (CQ), class-based WFQ (CBWFQ), and low latency queuing (LLQ).

LLQ adds strict priority queuing to CBWFQ; LLQ is a combination of CBWFQ and PQ. Strict priority queuing allows delay-sensitive data, such as voice, to be dequeued and sent first (before packets in other queues are dequeued), thereby giving the delay-sensitive traffic preferential treatment over other traffic.

KEY POINT | LLQ is the recommended queuing mechanism for voice on IP networks. The voice traffic should be put in the priority queue.

Figure 8-34 illustrates why LLQ is the preferred queuing mechanism for voice transport on integrated networks. The LLQ policing mechanism guarantees bandwidth for voice and gives it priority over other traffic, which is queued based on CBWFQ. LLQ reduces jitter in voice conversations.

Figure 8-34   *With LLQ Voice, Traffic Achieves High Priority*

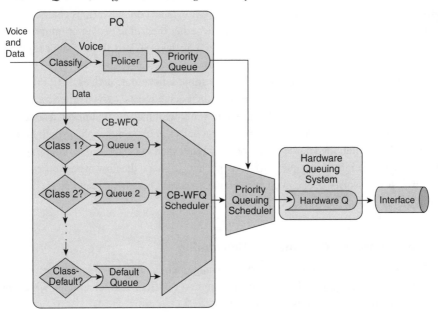

Link Efficiency

Link efficiency techniques, including LFI and compression, can be applied to WAN paths. Recall that LFI prevents small voice packets from being queued behind large data packets, which could lead to unacceptable delays on low-speed links. With LFI, the voice gateway fragments large packets into smaller equal-sized frames and interleaves them with small voice packets so that a voice packet does not have to wait until the entire large data packet is sent. LFI reduces and ensures a more predictable voice delay.

Compression of voice packets includes both header compression and payload compression. cRTP is used to compress large IP/UDP/RTP headers. The various codecs described in the earlier "Voice Coding and Compression" section compress the payload (the voice).

CAC

CAC mechanisms extend the QoS capabilities to protect voice traffic from being negatively affected by other voice traffic by keeping excess voice traffic off the network. The CAC function should be performed during the call setup phase so that if no network resources are available, a message can be sent to the end user, or the call can be rerouted across a different network, such as the PSTN.

CAC is an essential component of any IP telephony system that includes multiple sites connected through an IP WAN. If the provisioned voice bandwidth in the WAN is fully utilized, subsequent calls must be rejected to avoid oversubscribing the WAN, which would cause the quality of all voice calls to degrade. This function is provided by CAC to guarantee good voice quality in a multisite deployment involving an IP WAN.

Location-Based CAC

The location feature in Cisco Unified Communications Manager lets you specify the maximum bandwidth available for calls to and from each location, thereby limiting the number of active calls and preventing the WAN from being oversubscribed.

For example, if a WAN link between two PBXs has only enough bandwidth to carry two VoIP calls, admitting a third call impairs the voice quality of all three calls. The queuing mechanisms that provide policing cause this problem; if packets that exceed the configured or allowable rate are received, they are tail-dropped from the queue. The queuing mechanism cannot distinguish which IP packet belongs to which voice call; any packets that exceed the given arrival rate within a certain period are dropped. As a result, all three calls experience packet loss, and end users perceive clipped speech.

When CAC is implemented, the outgoing voice gateway detects that insufficient network resources are available for a call to proceed. The call is rejected, and the originating gateway must find another means of handling the call. In the absence of any specific configuration, the outgoing gateway provides the calling party with a reorder tone, which might cause the PSTN switch or PBX to announce that "All circuits are busy; please try your call again later." The outgoing voice gateway can be configured for the following scenarios:

■ The call can be rerouted via an alternative packet network path, if such a path exists.

■ The call can be rerouted via the PSTN network path.

■ The call can be returned to the originating TDM switch with the reject cause code.

Figure 8-35 shows examples of a VoIP network with and without CAC.

Figure 8-35 *Call Admission Control Keeps the Quality of Existing Calls*

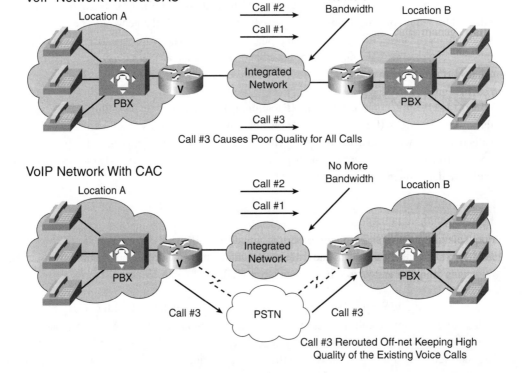

The upper diagram in Figure 8-35 illustrates a VoIP network without CAC. The WAN link between the two PBXs has the bandwidth to carry only two VoIP calls. In this example, admitting the third call impairs the voice quality of all three calls.

The lower example in Figure 8-35 illustrates a VoIP network with CAC. If the outgoing gateway detects that insufficient network resources are available to allow a call to proceed, the gateway automatically reroutes the third call to the PSTN, thereby maintaining the voice quality of the two existing calls.

CAC with RSVP

CAC can be also be implemented with RSVP. Cisco Unified Communications Manager Version 5.0 supports the Cisco RSVP Agent, which enables more efficient use of networks. The Cisco RSVP Agent provides an additional method to achieve CAC besides location-based CAC. RSVP can handle more complex topologies than location-based CAC, which supports only hub-and-spoke network topologies.

RSVP is an industry-standard signaling protocol that enables an application to reserve bandwidth dynamically across an IP network. RSVP, which runs over IP, was first introduced by the IETF in RFC 2205, *Resource ReSerVation Protocol (RSVP)—Version 1 Functional Specification*. Using RSVP, applications request a certain amount of bandwidth for a data flow across a network (for example, a voice call) and receive an indication of the outcome of the reservation based on actual resource availability. RSVP defines signaling messages that are exchanged between the source and destination devices for the data flow and that are processed by intermediate routers along the path. The RSVP signaling messages are encapsulated in IP packets that are routed through the network according to the existing routing protocols.

Not all routers on the path are required to support RSVP; the protocol is designed to operate transparently across RSVP-unaware nodes. On each RSVP-enabled router, the RSVP process intercepts the signaling messages and interacts with the QoS manager for the router interfaces involved in the data flow to "reserve" bandwidth resources. If the available resources anywhere along the path are not sufficient for the data flow, the routers send a signal indicating the failure to the application that originated the reservation request.

For example, a branch office router has a primary link with an LLQ provisioned for ten calls and a backup link that can accommodate two calls. RSVP can be configured on both router interfaces so that the RSVP bandwidth matches the LLQ bandwidth. The call processing agent at the branch can be configured to require RSVP reservations for all calls to or from other branches. Calls are admitted or rejected based on the outcome of the RSVP reservations, which automatically follow the path determined by the routing protocol. Under normal conditions (when the primary link is active), up to ten calls will be admitted; during failure of the primary link, only up to two calls will be admitted.

Policies can typically be set within the call processing agent to determine what to do in the case of a CAC failure. For example, the call could be rejected, rerouted across the PSTN, or sent across the IP WAN as a best-effort call with a different DSCP marking.

Building Access Layer QoS Mechanisms for Voice

To provide high-quality voice and to take advantage of the full voice feature set, QoS mechanisms on Building Access layer switches include the following:

- On 802.1Q trunks, the three 802.1p user priority bits in the Tag field are used as the CoS bits. Layer 2 CoS marking is performed on Layer 2 ports to which IP phones are connected.

- Multiple egress queues provide priority queuing of RTP voice packet streams.

- The ability to classify or reclassify traffic and establish a trust boundary. A *trust boundary* is the point within the network where markings are accepted; any markings made by devices outside the trust boundary can be overwritten at the trust boundary.

   Establishing a trust boundary means that the classification and marking processes can be done once, at the boundary; the rest of the network does not have to repeat the analysis. Ideally, the trust boundary is as close to end devices as possible—or even within the end devices. For example, a Cisco IP phone could be considered a trusted device because it marks voice traffic appropriately. However, a user's PC would not usually be trusted because users could change markings, which they might be tempted to do in an attempt to increase the priority of their traffic.

- Layer 3 awareness and the ability to implement QoS ACLs might be required if certain IP telephony endpoints are used, such as a PC running a software-based IP phone application that cannot benefit from an extended trust boundary.

These mechanisms protect voice from packet loss and delay stemming from oversubscription of aggregate links between switches, which might cause egress interface buffers to become full instantaneously. When voice packets are subject to drops, delay, and jitter, the user-perceivable effects include a clicking sound, harsh-sounding voice, extended periods of silence, and echo.

When deploying voice, it is recommended that two VLANs be enabled in the Building Access Layer switch: a native VLAN for data traffic and a voice VLAN for voice traffic. Note that a voice VLAN in the Cisco IOS software is called an *auxiliary* VLAN under the Catalyst operating system. Separate voice and data VLANs are recommended for the following reasons:

- Configuring RFC 1918 private addressing on phones on the voice (or auxiliary) VLAN conserves addresses and ensures that phones are not accessible directly via public networks. PCs and servers can be addressed with public addresses; however, voice endpoints should be addressed using private addresses.

- QoS trust boundaries can be selectively extended to voice devices without extending the trust boundaries to PCs and other data devices.

- VLAN access control and 802.1p tagging provide protection for voice devices from malicious internal and external network attacks such as worms, denial-of-service attacks, and attempts by data devices to gain access to priority queues via packet tagging.

- Management and QoS configuration are simplified.

NOTE   It is also recommended that Building Access layer switches provide PoE (inline power) for the IP phones.

AutoQoS

The Cisco AutoQoS feature on routers and switches provides a simple, automatic way to enable QoS configurations in conformance with Cisco's best-practice recommendations. Only one command is required; the router or switch then creates configuration commands to perform such things as classifying and marking VoIP traffic and then applying an LLQ queuing strategy on WAN links for that traffic. The configuration created by AutoQoS becomes part of the normal configuration file and therefore can be edited if required. The first phase of AutoQoS, available in various versions of the router Cisco IOS Release 12.3, creates only configurations related to VoIP traffic.

NOTE   The Cisco Feature Navigator tool, available at http://www.cisco.com/go/fn, allows you to quickly find the Cisco IOS and switch Catalyst Operating System Software release required for the features that you want to run on your network. For example, you can use this tool to determine the Cisco IOS release required to run AutoQoS on the routers in your network.

The second phase of AutoQoS is called AutoQoS Enterprise and includes support for all types of data. It configures the router with commands to classify, mark, and handle packets in up to 10 of the 11 QoS Baseline traffic classes (as described in Chapter 5). The Mission-Critical traffic class is the only one not defined, because it is specific to each organization. As with the earlier release, the commands created by AutoQoS Enterprise can be edited if required.

NOTE   Further information on AutoQoS can be found at http://www.cisco.com/en/US/tech/tk543/tk759/tk879/tsd_technology_support_protocol_home.html.

Introduction to Voice Traffic Engineering

This section introduces voice traffic engineering. Voice traffic engineering is the science of selecting the correct number of lines and the proper types of service to accommodate users. From trunks and DSPs to WAN and campus components, detailed capacity planning of all network resources should be considered to minimize degraded voice service in integrated networks.

The bandwidth requirements for voice traffic depend on many factors, including the number of simultaneous voice calls, grade of service required, codec and compression techniques used, signaling protocol used, and network topology. The following sections introduce how to calculate the WAN bandwidth required to support a number of voice calls with a given probability that the call will go through.

Terminology

This section introduces the following terminology used in voice traffic engineering:

■ Blocking probability

■ Grade of Service (GoS)

■ Erlang

■ Centum Call Second (CCS)

■ Busy hour

■ Busy Hour Traffic (BHT)

■ Call Detail Record (CDR)

Blocking Probability and GoS

KEY POINT   The *blocking probability value* describes the calls that cannot be completed because insufficient lines have been provided. For example, a blocking probability value of 0.01 means that 1 percent of calls would be blocked.

GoS is the probability that a voice gateway will block a call while attempting to allocate circuits during the busiest hour. GoS is written as a blocking factor, P*xx*, where *xx* is the percentage of calls that are blocked for a traffic system. For example, traffic facilities that require P01 GoS define a 1 percent probability of callers being blocked.

The number of simultaneous conversations affects the voice traffic. Users vary widely in the number of calls they attempt per hour and the length of time they hold a circuit. Any user's attempts and holding times are independent of the other users' activities. A common method used to determine traffic capacity is to use a call logger to determine the number of simultaneous calls on the network and then determine the probability that exactly *x* simultaneous calls will occur. Voice systems can be provisioned to allow the maximum number of simultaneous conversations that are expected at the busiest time of the day.

Erlang

The Erlang is one of the most common measurements of voice traffic.

> **KEY POINT** One *Erlang* equals one full hour, or 3600 seconds, of telephone conversation.

For example, if a trunk carries 12.35 Erlangs during an hour, an average of a little more than 12 lines (connections) are busy. One Erlang indicates that a single resource is in continuous use. The traffic measurement in Erlangs is used to determine whether a system has too many or too few resources provisioned.

CCS

> **KEY POINT** A CCS represents 1/36th of an Erlang.

> **NOTE** *Centum* means one hundred.

A system port that can handle a continuous one-hour call has a traffic rating of 36 CCSs (or 1 Erlang). Station traffic varies greatly among users, but the typical range is approximately 6 to 12 CCSs per port. If no exact statistical data exists, assume that the average typical trunk traffic is 30 CCSs per port.

For example, one hour of conversation (one Erlang or 36 CCSs) might be ten 6-minute calls or 15 4-minute calls. Receiving 100 calls, with an average length of 6 minutes, in one hour is equivalent to ten Erlangs, or 360 CCSs.

Busy Hour and BHT

> **KEY POINT** The busy hour is the 60-minute period in a given 24-hour period during which the maximum total traffic load occurs. The busy hour is sometimes called the *peak hour*.
>
> The BHT, in Erlangs or CCSs, is the number of hours of traffic transported across a trunk group during the busy hour (the busiest hour of operation).

KEY POINT	To calculate the BHT in Erlangs, multiply the number of calls in the busiest hour by their average duration in seconds, and divide the result by 3600.
	To calculate the BHT in CCSs, multiply the number of calls in the busiest hour by their average duration in seconds, and divide the result by 100.

For example, if you know from your call logger that 350 calls are made on a trunk group in the busiest hour and that the average call duration is 180 seconds, you can calculate the BHT as follows:

- BHT = Average call duration (seconds) * calls per hour/3600

- BHT = 180 * 350/3600

- BHT = 17.5 Erlangs

CDR

A *CDR* is a record containing information about recent system usage, such as the identities of sources (points of origin), the identities of destinations (endpoints), the duration of each call, the amount billed for each call, the total usage time in the billing period, the total free time remaining in the billing period, and the running total charged during the billing period. The format of a CDR varies among telecom providers and call-logging software; some call-logging software allows the user to configure the CDR format.

Erlang Tables

Erlang tables show the amount of traffic potential (the BHT) for specified numbers of circuits for given probabilities of receiving a busy signal (the GoS). The BHT calculation results are stated in CCSs or Erlangs. Erlang tables combine offered traffic (the BHT), number of circuits, and GoS in the following traffic models:

- **Erlang B**: This is the most common traffic model, which is used to calculate how many lines are required if the traffic (in Erlangs) during the busiest hour is known. The model assumes that all blocked calls are cleared immediately.

- **Extended Erlang B**: This model is similar to Erlang B, but it takes into account the additional traffic load caused by blocked callers who immediately try to call again. The retry percentage can be specified.

- **Erlang C**: This model assumes that all blocked calls stay in the system until they can be handled. This model can be applied to the design of call center staffing arrangements in which calls that cannot be answered immediately enter a queue.

> **NOTE**   Erlang tables and calculators can be found at many sites, including
> http://www.erlang.com/.

Erlang B Table

Figure 8-36 shows part of an Erlang B table. The column headings show the GoS, the row headings show the number of circuits (the number of simultaneous connections), and the table cells indicate the BHT in Erlangs for the specified number of circuits with the specified GoS.

Figure 8-36   *An Erlang B Table Is Used to Determine Required Trunk Capacity*

Number of Erlangs Increases with the Increased Blocking Probability

Number of Erlangs Increases with the Number of Simultaneous Connections

GOS= Blocking Probability / Number of Circuits	.003	.005	.01	.02	.03	.05
1	.003	.006	.011	.021	.031	.053
2	.081	.106	.153	.224	.282	.382
3	.289	.349	.456	.603	.716	.900
4	.602	.702	.870	1.093	1.259	1.525
5	.996	1.132	1.361	1.658	1.876	2.219
6	1.447	1.822	1.900	2.278	2.543	2.961
7	1.947	2.158	2.501	2.936	3.250	3.738
8	2.484	2.730	3.128	3.627	3.987	4.543
9	3.053	3.333	3.783	4.345	4.748	5.371
10	3.648	3.961	4.462	5.084	5.530	6.216

Busy Hour Traffic (BHT) in Erlangs

Erlang Examples

Having established the BHT and blocking probability, the required number of circuits can be estimated using the Erlang B traffic model. For example, given BHT = 3.128 Erlangs, blocking = 0.01, and looking at the Erlang table in Figure 8-36, the number of required circuits is eight.

As another example using Figure 8-36, 4.462 Erlangs of traffic is offered for ten circuits (simultaneous connections) with a GoS of P01 (1 percent block probability). 4.462 Erlangs equals approximately 160 CCSs (4.462 * 36). Assuming that there are 20 users in the company, the following steps illustrate how to calculate how long each user can talk:

- BHT = Average call duration (seconds) * calls per hour/3600

- 4.462 = Average call duration (seconds) * 20/3600

- Average call duration = 803 seconds = 13.3 minutes

In another example, six circuits at P05 GoS handle 2.961 Erlangs. 2.961 Erlangs equals approximately 107 CCSs (2.961 * 36). Assuming that the company has ten users, the following illustrates how to calculate how long every user can talk:

- BHT = Average call duration (seconds) * calls per hour/3600

- 2.961 = Average call duration (seconds) * 10/3600

- Average call duration = 1066 seconds = 17.8 minutes

Trunk Capacity Calculation Example

The objective of this example is to determine the number of circuits, or the trunk capacity, required for voice and fax calls between each branch office and an enterprise's headquarters office. The following assumptions apply to this sample network:

- The network design is based on a star topology that connects each branch office directly to the main office.

- There are approximately 15 people per branch office.

- The bidirectional voice and fax call volume totals about 2.5 hours per person per day (in each branch office).

- Approximately 20 percent of the total call volume is between the headquarters and each branch office.

- The busy-hour loading factor is 17 percent. In other words, the BHT is 17% of the total traffic.

- One 64-kbps circuit supports one call.

- The acceptable GoS is P05.

Following are the voice and fax traffic calculations for this example:

- 2.5 hours call volume per user per day * 15 users = 37.5 hours daily call volume per office

- 37.5 hours * 17 percent (busy-hour load) = 6.375 hours of traffic in the busy hour

- 6.375 hours * 60 minutes per hour = 382.5 minutes of traffic per busy hour

- 382.5 minutes per busy hour * 1 Erlang/60 minutes per busy hour = 6.375 Erlangs

- 6.375 Erlangs * 20 percent of traffic to headquarters = 1.275 Erlangs volume proposed

To determine the appropriate number of trunks required to transport the traffic, the next step is to consult the Erlang table, given the desired GoS. This organization chose a P05 GoS. Using the 1.275 Erlangs and GoS = P05, as well as the Erlang B table (in Figure 8-36), four circuits are required for communication between each branch office and the headquarters office.

Off-Net Calls Cost Calculation Example

This example calculates the off-net cost of calls between two locations, New York and London, as shown in Figure 8-37. The PSTN path is used when the transatlantic tie line cannot accept additional on-net calls.

Figure 8-37   *Off-Net Calls Are Sometimes Required*

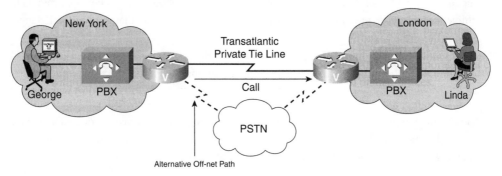

Assume that all calls between these two sites use 64 kbps of bandwidth, which corresponds to one circuit, and that a GoS of .03 is acceptable. How many minutes per month of calls use off-net calling because of the service block on the transatlantic tie line? The transatlantic tie line can simultaneously carry a maximum of ten calls. In the calculation, we assume that a 1-minute call between New York and London costs $.10.

NOTE   The $.10 per minute rate is used here for ease of calculation.

The calculation is as follows:

- According to the Erlang B table in Figure 8-36, 5.53 Erlangs can be offered at P03 and ten circuits.

- At P03, 3 percent of the 5.53 Erlangs of calls are overflowed and sent off-net.

- Therefore, in the peak hour, .03 * 5.53 Erlangs * 60 minutes = 10 overflow minutes.

- Assume that there are two peak hours per day and 21 business days per month. Therefore, 21 days * 2 peak hours per day * 10 overflow minutes = 420 overflow minutes per month.

- 420 overflow minutes per month * $.10 per overflow minute = $42.00.

The calculation shows that 420 minutes per month of off-net calling between New York and London is used, costing $42.00. This cost should be compared to that of adding circuits between New York and London to see whether it is worth adding bandwidth.

Calculating Trunk Capacity or Bandwidth

KEY POINT | The trunk capacity for voice calls can be calculated by the following formula:

Trunk capacity = (number of simultaneous calls to be supported) * (bandwidth required per call)

The first component of this formula, the number of simultaneous calls to be supported, is the number of circuits required for the known amount of traffic, as calculated from the Erlang tables.

NOTE If 100 percent of calls must go through, Erlang tables are not required; instead, the maximum number of simultaneous calls required should be used.

The second component of this formula, the bandwidth required for one call, depends on the codec used and whether cRTP and VAD are used. Earlier in this chapter, the section "Voice Bandwidth Requirements," including Table 8-6, illustrated some bandwidth calculations.

CAUTION Including VAD in bandwidth calculations can result in insufficient bandwidth being provisioned if the calls do not include as much silence as assumed and when features such as music on hold are used.

As an example of calculating the trunk capacity, assume that G.729 compression is used over a PPP connection at 50 pps and cRTP is used. From Table 8-6, each call uses 11 kbps. If five simultaneous calls are to be supported, 5 * 11 = 55 kbps is required for the voice calls.

NOTE The bandwidth for other traffic that will be on the link must also be accounted for.

As another example, based on the Erlang tables, ten circuits are required between two locations to satisfy user demands. VoIP over PPP is used on the link. The G.729 codec, using 50 samples per second, is used. cRTP is not used.

The per-call bandwidth information in Table 8-6 indicates that one voice call without header compression requires 26 kbps of bandwidth. Therefore, 10 * 26 = 260 kbps of bandwidth is required between the two locations, in each direction, to carry ten simultaneous voice calls.

Cisco IP Communications Return on Investment Calculator

The Cisco IP Communications (IPC) Return on Investment (ROI) calculator can be useful for analyzing IP telephony requirements and estimating the cost savings a customer will experience when migrating to IP telephony. The IPC ROI calculator is available at http://www.cisco.com/web/partners/sell/technology/ipc/ipc_calculator.html.

> **NOTE**   You must have a Cisco partner account to access this tool.

Summary

In this chapter, you learned about voice design principles, with a focus on the following topics:

- Analog and digital signaling, including the process to convert between the two

- The features of and similarities and differences between PBXs and PSTN switches

- The connections and signaling between the various devices in a traditional telephony network

- PSTN numbering plans and various PSTN services

- The H.323 standard for packet-based audio, video, and data communications across IP-based networks, including H.323 components

- The concepts of VoIP and IP telephony, including the components and sample design scenarios

- Protocols used to transport all control (signaling) and voice conversation traffic

- Voice quality issues, including delay, jitter, packet loss, and echo

- Voice coding and compression standards

- Bandwidth considerations and requirements for integrated networks

- QoS mechanisms for voice

- Voice traffic engineering to select the correct number of lines and the proper types of service, including the use of Erlang tables to calculate trunk capacity for voice calls.

> **NOTE**   This chapter introduced voice design principles; additional resources, such as voice-related Cisco Press books and documents on http://www.cisco.com/, are required to successfully integrate voice services into a network.

References

For additional information, refer to these resources:

- Echo Analysis for Voice over IP, http://www.cisco.com/en/US/partner/tech/tk652/tk701/technologies_white_paper09186a00800d6b68.shtml.

> **NOTE** You must be a registered user on http://www.cisco.com/ to access this document.

- Cisco IOS Quality of Service Solutions Configuration Guide, Release 12.4, http://www.cisco.com/univercd/cc/td/doc/product/software/ios124/124cg/hqos_c/index.htm.

- Introduction to voice, including telephony signaling documents, http://www.cisco.com/en/US/tech/tk652/tsd_technology_support_category_home.html.

- Traffic Analysis for Voice over IP, http://www.cisco.com/univercd/cc/td/doc/cisintwk/intsolns/voipsol/ta_isd.htm.

- Understanding Delay in Packet Voice Networks, http://www.cisco.com/warp/public/788/voip/delay-details.html.

- Voice Network Signaling and Control, http://www.cisco.com/warp/public/788/signalling/net_signal_control.html.

- Waveform Coding Techniques, http://www.cisco.com/warp/public/788/signalling/waveform_coding.html#subrstsix.

- Erlang tables on Westbay Engineers Limited Home Page, http://www.erlang.com/.

- Szigeti and Hattingh, *End-to-End QoS Network Design: Quality of Service in LANs, WANs, and VPNs*, Indianapolis, Cisco Press, 2004.

- Cisco Unified Communications Manager (CallManager): Introduction, http://www.cisco.com/en/US/products/sw/voicesw/ps556/index.html.

- Cisco Unified Communications SRND Based on Cisco Unified CallManager 5.0, http://www.cisco.com/en/US/products/sw/voicesw/ps556/products_implementation_design_guide_book09186a00806492bb.html.

- Understanding Codecs: Complexity, Hardware Support, MOS, and Negotiation, http://www.cisco.com/en/US/tech/tk1077/technologies_tech_note09186a00800b6710.shtml.

- Davidson, J., and J. Peters. *Voice over IP Fundamentals*. Indianapolis: Cisco Press, 2000.

- Voice Network Signaling and Control, http://www.cisco.com/warp/public/788/signalling/net_signal_control.html.

- Voice over IP—Per-Call Bandwidth Consumption, http://www.cisco.com/warp/customer/788/pkt-voice-general/bwidth_consume.html.

> **NOTE**   You must be a registered user on http://www.cisco.com/ to access this document.

- Cisco IOS Voice Configuration Library, http://www.cisco.com/univercd/cc/td/doc/product/software/ios124/124tcg/vcl.htm.

- High-Density Packet Voice/Fax Digital Signal Processor Module, http://www.cisco.com/en/US/products/hw/univgate/ps501/products_data_sheet0900aecd80458049.html.

- Cisco Voice Codec Bandwidth Calculator, http://tools.cisco.com/Support/VBC/do/CodecCalc1.do.

> **NOTE**   You must be a registered user on http://www.cisco.com/ to access this calculator.

Case Study: ACMC Hospital Network Voice Design

This case study is a continuation of the ACMC Hospital case study introduced in Chapter 2.

Case Study General Instructions

Use the scenarios, information, and parameters provided at each task of the ongoing case study. If you encounter ambiguities, make reasonable assumptions and proceed. For all tasks, use the initial customer scenario and build on the solutions provided thus far.

You can use any and all documentation, books, white papers, and so on. In each step, you act as a network design consultant. Make creative proposals to accomplish the customer's business needs. Justify your ideas when they differ from the provided solutions. Use any design strategies you feel are appropriate. The final goal of each case study is a paper solution.

Appendix A, "Answers to Review Questions and Case Studies," provides a solution for each step based on assumptions made. There is no claim that the provided solution is the best or only solution. Your solution might be more appropriate for the assumptions you made. The provided solution helps you understand the author's reasoning and allows you to compare and contrast your solution.

In this case study you create a high-level voice design for the ACMC Hospital network.

Case Study Additional Information

The ACMC staff wants to replace its PBX and key systems and is eager to achieve cost reduction while providing better service to remote clinics. The replacement system needs to offer at least as many features as the present system. The staff is also very interested in unified voice-mail services for busy doctors and the potential for using phones with web-based menus as part of a quality care system.

Current features include standard PBX features, call conferencing, voice mail, and local calls. Remote clinics currently use some form of key system or remote PBX shelf with limited features. Figure 8-38 summarizes the ACMC design up to this point for your reference.

Figure 8-38 *Case Study ACMC Hospital Current Design*

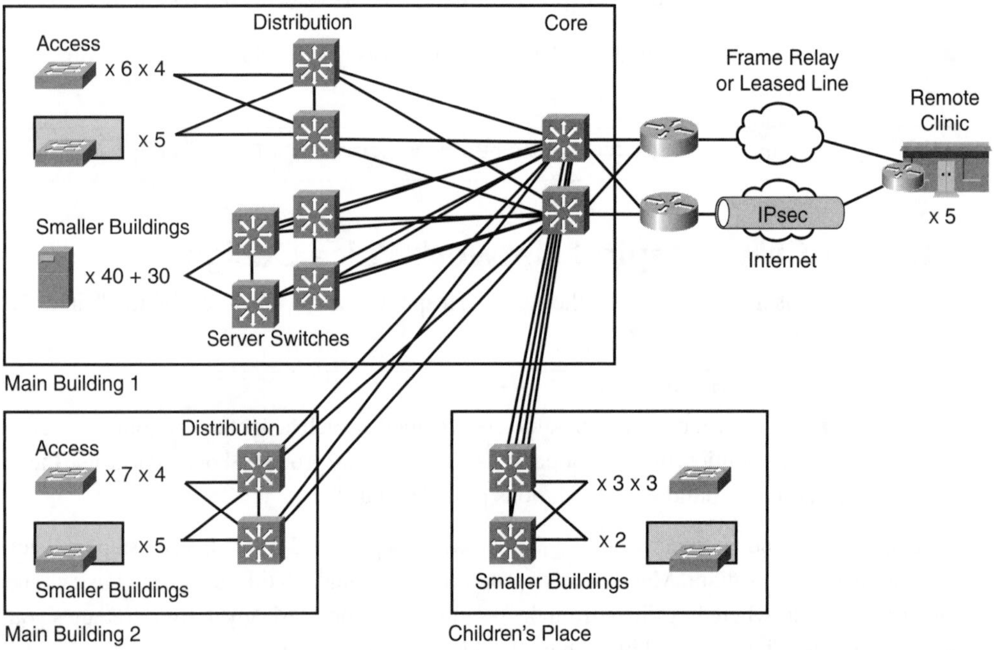

Case Study Questions

Complete the following steps:

Step 1   Based on the design up to this point, what aspects of the infrastructure need to be considered when adding voice?

Step 2   Select the IP telephony design model most appropriate to ACMC, and indicate where you would place the various IP telephony components.

Step 3   Each remote clinic must be able to place local calls without going through the main campus. What devices will be needed at each site? What else must be added to be able to support local conference calls?

Step 4   WAN backup is by IPsec VPN across the Internet. What service characteristics might IPsec or the Internet lack that voice requires? What could be added to your design to remedy this?

Step 5   The ACMC current phone system uses a PBX at each clinic, with phone trunks to the main campus PBX. The Director of Telephony just had a call study done and is convinced she has sufficient capacity. Table 8-7 summarizes the number of calls currently supported for each remote site.

Table 8-7 *ACMC Call Study Results*

Remote Clinic	Number of Calls on the Trunk to the Main Campus
1	8
2, 3, 4, 5	4

Estimate how much WAN bandwidth each ACMC site would need if the G.711 and G.729 codecs were used. Assume that with the required call parameters, a G.729 call uses about 25 kbps and a G.711 call uses about 92 kbps. Is there enough bandwidth in the ACMC WAN?

Review Questions

Answer the following questions, and then refer to Appendix A for the answers.

1. What steps are involved in converting analog signals to digital signals?

2. What is pulse amplitude modulation?

3. What is pulse code modulation?

4. Match the following terms with their definitions:

   Terms:

   - Filtering

   - Quantization

   - Companding

   - Logarithmic compression

Definitions:

- Converting an analog sample to a digital code word

- Compression increases as the sample signal increases

- Removing nonspeech components

- Compressing and expanding signals

5.   What is TDM?

6.   What are some differences between a PBX and a PSTN switch?

7.   What are some of the call features provided by PBXs?

8.   How does having a PBX save on communication costs?

9.   Match the following terms with their definitions:

Terms:

- Local loop

- Station line

- Trunk

- Tie trunk

- CO trunk

- PSTN switch trunk

Definitions:

- Connects CO switches to PBXs

- Physical cabling

- Communication path between two telephony systems

- Connects PBXs

- Interconnects CO switches

- Communication between PBX and business telephone

10.   What is the difference between local-loop and trunk signaling?

11.   What is the difference between channel associated signaling (CAS) and common channel signaling (CCS)?

12. Which signaling method allows standardized communication between PBXs?

13. Which signaling method is used between PSTN switches?

14. Describe how a telephone call is routed from location A to location B through the PSTN using the NANP.

15. Match the following terms with each part of the following telephone number used to call someone in North America:

Telephone Number: 1-416-555-1212

Terms:

- Area code
- Zone
- Trunk prefix
- Country code
- Line number
- Prefix

16. What is the difference between VoIP and IP telephony?

17. What role does an H.323 terminal play in voice networks?

18. What is the difference between an H.323 gateway and an H.323 gatekeeper?

19. What is a voice port?

20. What does Cisco Unified Communications Manager do?

21. What are the four components of IP telephony architecture?

22. How does IP telephony lower costs?

23. Describe the difference between a multisite WAN design model with distributed call processing and a multisite WAN design model with centralized call processing.

24. Match the protocols with their descriptions:

Protocols:

- H.323
- SCCP
- SIP
- MGCP

Descriptions:

- A Cisco-proprietary terminal control protocol used for messaging between IP phones and Cisco Unified Communications Manager

- A client/server protocol in which call agents control endpoints

- An IETF standard for multimedia conferencing over IP

- An ITU-T standard for packet-based audio, video, and data communications across IP-based networks

25. Complete the following sentence:

    Dejitter buffers are used on _____ of the network to smooth out delay variability.

    a. The originating side

    b. The receiving side

    c. All sides

26. What is the generally acceptable one-way delay limit for good-quality voice?

27. Match the following terms with their definitions:

    Terms:

    - Processing delay

    - Propagation delay

    - Jitter

    - Echo

    Definitions:

    - Variation in the delay of received packets

    - Audible leak of the caller's voice into the receive (return) path

    - Length of time it takes a signal to travel the distance between the sending and receiving endpoints

    - Time the DSP takes to process a block of PCM samples

28. What is link fragmentation and interleaving (LFI)?

29. Is a voice packet loss always audible?

30. Match each of the following coding standards with a data rate or rates that it supports:

Coding standards:

- G.711

- G.729

- G.726

- G.723.1

- G.728

Data rates:

- 5.3 kbps

- 64 kbps

- 24 kbps

- 8 kbps

- 16 kbps

31. Which of the following ITU voice coding standards results in the highest mean opinion score (MOS): G.711, G.723.1, G.726, G.728, or G.729?

32. What is the difference between low-, medium-, and high-complexity codecs?

33. What protocols are used to transport voice conversation traffic?

34. Match the following terms with their definitions:

Terms:

- H.225 channel

- H.245 channel

- RAS

- RTCP

Definitions:

- Used only if a gatekeeper is present

- Uses Q.931 to establish a connection between two terminals

- Used by hosts communicating with RTP to monitor the session

- Carries control messages that govern voice operation

35. What does voice activity detection do?

36. What does compressed RTP do?

37. Which of these codecs have relatively more IP header overhead compared to the payload? Arrange them in descending order.

- G.729

- G.711

- G.728

38. Which queuing mechanism is recommended for most VoIP designs?

39. What is the purpose of the Call Admission Control (CAC) mechanisms?

40. Describe how CAC with RSVP works.

41. True or false: When deploying voice, it is recommended that the data and voice traffic from a user travel on the same VLAN.

42. How many centum call seconds (CCS) equals five Erlangs?

43. What does a GoS of P05 mean?

44. If your call logger says that 290 calls are made on a trunk group in the busiest hour and the average call duration is 180 seconds, what is the busy hour traffic (in Erlangs)?

This chapter describes wireless network design principles and includes the following sections:

CHAPTER 9

Wireless Network Design Considerations

The goal of this chapter is to introduce the Cisco Unified Wireless Network (UWN) architecture and to discuss wireless design principles. The chapter starts with an introduction to wireless technologies. Then the Cisco UWN is described. The chapter concludes with an exploration of considerations for designing Cisco UWNs in enterprise environments.

Introduction to Wireless Technology

> **NOTE** As noted in the introduction to this book, we assume that you understand the wireless networking material in the Cisco Press title *Building Cisco Multilayer Switched Networks (BCMSN) (Authorized Self-Study Guide), 4th Edition,* ISBN 1-58705-273-3. This section includes some material from that book as an introduction to wireless technology. Refer to that Cisco Press BCMSN title for more detailed information.

A wireless communication system uses radio frequency (RF) energy to transmit data from one point to another, through the air; the term *signal* is used to refer to this RF energy. The data to be transmitted is first modulated onto a carrier and then sent; receivers demodulate the signal and process the data.

There are many different types of wireless network technologies, each providing a defined coverage area. Figure 9-1 illustrates the following wireless technologies, along with a description of how the coverage areas are used:

■ **Personal-area network (PAN)**: A PAN typically covers a person's personal workspace.

■ **Local-area network**: Wireless LANs (WLAN) are designed to be enterprise-based networks that allow the use of complete suites of enterprise applications, without wires.

■ **Metropolitan-area network (MAN)**: Wireless MANs are deployed inside a metropolitan area, allowing wireless connectivity throughout an urban area.

■ **Wide-area network**: Wireless WANs are typically slower but offer more coverage, such as across rural areas.

Figure 9-1 *Wireless Technologies*

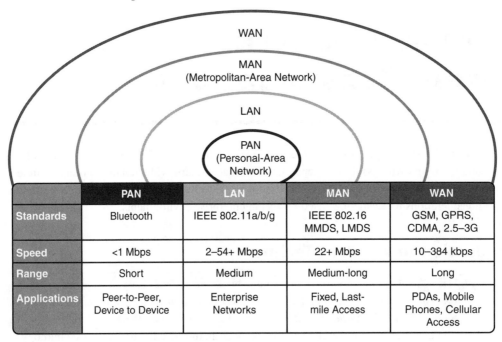

MMDS = Multichannel multipoint distribution service
LMDS = Local multipoint distribution service
GSM = Global system for mobile communications
GPRS = General packet radio service
CDMA = Code division multiple access

KEY POINT | The Cisco Aironet wireless products, Cisco's brand of wireless devices, are considered to be WLAN products—not PAN, MAN, or WAN—and are the focus of this chapter.

WLANs replace the Layer 1 transmission medium of a traditional wired network (usually Category 5 cable) with radio transmission over the air. WLANs can plug into a wired network and function as an overlay to wired LANs, or they can be deployed as a standalone LAN where wired networking is not feasible. A computer with a wireless network interface card (NIC) connects to the wired LAN through an access point (AP). Properly deployed WLANs can provide instant access to the network from anywhere in a facility so that users can roam without losing their network connection.

WLANs use spread-spectrum RF signals on the three unlicensed bands: 900 MHz, 2.4 GHz, and 5 GHz. The 900 MHz and 2.4 GHz bands are referred to as the *industrial, scientific, and medical bands*, and the 5 GHz band is commonly referred to as the *Unlicensed National Information Infrastructure (UNII) band*.

RF Theory

Radio frequencies are high-frequency AC signals radiated into the air via an antenna, creating radio waves. Radio waves propagate away from the antenna in a straight line in all directions at once, just as light from a light bulb does. And, just as more light bulbs spread around a room provide better overall lighting, more antennas spread around a room provide stronger RF signals for mobile clients.

Phenomena Affecting RF

When radio waves hit a wall, door, or any other obstruction, the signal is attenuated, or weakened, which might result in reduced throughput. The following natural phenomena affect RF signals, as illustrated in Figure 9-2:

- **Reflection**: Occurs when the RF signal bounces off objects such as metal or glass surfaces.

- **Refraction**: Occurs when the RF signal passes through objects such as glass surfaces and changes direction.

- **Absorption**: Occurs when an object, such as a wall or furniture, absorbs the RF signal.

- **Scattering**: Occurs when an RF wave strikes an uneven surface and reflects in many directions. Scattering also occurs when an RF wave travels through a medium that consists of objects that are much smaller than the signal's wavelength, such as heavy dust.

- **Diffraction**: Occurs when an RF wave strikes sharp edges, such as external corners of buildings, which bend the signal.

- **Multipath**: Occurs when an RF signal has more than one path between the sender and receiver. The multiple signals at the receiver might result in a distorted, low-quality signal.

Figure 9-2 *RF Phenomena*

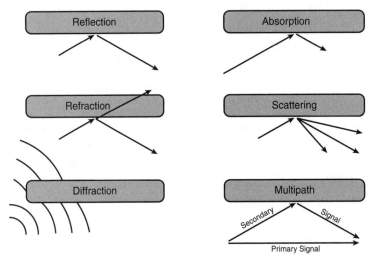

Consider all these phenomena when designing, implementing, and troubleshooting WLANs.

RF Math

KEY
POINT

RF *gain* is an increase in the RF signal amplitude or strength. Two common sources of gain are amplifiers and antennas.

RF *loss* is a decrease in the RF signal strength. Losses affect WLAN design and are part of our everyday world. For example, the cables and connections between the AP and the antenna cause loss.

WLANs transmit signals just as radio stations do to reach their listeners. The transmit power levels for WLANs are in milliwatts (mW), whereas for radio stations the power levels are in megawatts (MW).

The following are some units of measure used in RF calculations:

■ **Decibel (dB)**: The difference or ratio between two signal levels. dBs are used to measure relative gains or losses in an RF system and to describe the effect of system devices on signal strength. The dB is named after Alexander Graham Bell.

■ **dB milliwatt (dBm)**: A signal strength or power level. Zero dBm is defined as 1 mW of power into a terminating load such as an antenna or power meter. Small signals, those below 1 mW, are therefore negative numbers (such as –80 dBm); WLAN signals are in the range of –60 dBm to –80 dBm.

- **dB watt (dBw):** A signal strength or power level. Zero dBw is defined as 1 watt (W) of power; 1 W is one ampere (A) of current at 1 volt (V).

- **dB isotropic (dBi):** The gain a given antenna has over a theoretical isotropic (point source) antenna. Unfortunately, an isotropic antenna cannot be made in the real world, but it is useful for calculating theoretical system operating margins.

The formula used for calculating losses, gains, and power for WLANs is too complex for most people to solve without a calculator. Gains or losses in decibels are summed and then converted into an absolute power in milliwatts or watts.

The following formula calculates the transmit power:

$$\text{Transmit Power (dBm)} = 10 * \log_{10}[\text{Transmit Power (mW)}]$$

Table 9-1 indicates how various gains and losses relate to power levels; it is useful for WLAN calculations.

Table 9-1 *dBm-to-milliwatt Conversion Table*

dBm	mW		dBm	mW
−3	.5		10	10
0	1		20	100
3	2		30	1,000 or 1 watt
6	4		40	10,000 or 10 watts
9	8		50	100,000 or 100 watts
12	16		100	1,000,000 or 1000 watts

Notice in Table 9-1 that RF math is easier when the following key points are considered:

- Every gain of 3 dBm means that the power is doubled. A loss of 3 dBm means that the power is cut in half.

- A gain of 10 dBm means that the power increases by a factor of 10. A loss of 10 dBm means that the power decreases by a factor of 10.

To calculate the power increase or decrease for a given dBm, factor the given number into a sum of 3dBm and 10dBm, and then convert using these rules. For example, a 9 dBm loss is equivalent to −3dBm + −3dBm + −3dBm. The following illustrates how to calculate the power level that a 200 mW signal decreases to when it experiences a 9 dBm loss.

- 200 mW –3dBm = 100 mW

- 100 mW –3dBm = 50 mW

- 50 mW –3dBm = 25 mW

Therefore, the 200 mW signal decreases to 25 mW with a 9dBm loss.

Gain

Although it is probably obvious how losses affect WLAN design, it might seem that higher gains are always better (providing more power at greater distances). However, standards bodies such as the FCC and European Telecommunications Standards Institute (ETSI) regulate the amount of power radiating from an antenna. That power is called the *effective isotropic radiated power (EIRP)* and is calculated using the following formula:

EIRP (dBm) = Transmit Radio Power (dBm) – cable loss (dB) – antenna gain (dBi)

Antennas

Antennas used in WLANs come in many shapes and sizes, depending on the differing RF characteristics desired. The physical dimensions of an antenna directly relate to the frequency at which the antenna transmits or receives radio waves. As the gain increases, the coverage area becomes more focused. High-gain antennas provide longer coverage areas than low-gain antennas at the same input power level. As frequency increases, the wavelength and the antennas become smaller. Antennas can be categorized into one of the three following types:

- **Omnidirectional**: These antennas are the most widely used today but are not always the best solution. The radiant energy is shaped like a doughnut; consequently, the transmit signal is weak or absent directly under the AP (in the "hole" of the doughnut).

- **Semidirectional**: These antennas offer the capability to direct and apply gain to the signal. The radiant energy is in a cowbell shape.

- **Highly directional**: These antennas are intended for highly directed signals that must travel a long distance. The radiant energy is in a telescope shape.

Agencies and Standards Groups

Some of the agencies and standards groups related to WLANs are as follows:

- **Institute of Electrical and Electronic Engineers** (http://www.ieee.org/): Creates and maintains operational standards.

- **European Telecommunications Standards Institute** (http://www.etsi.org/): Chartered to produce common standards in Europe.

- **Wi-Fi Alliance** (http://www.wi-fi.com/): Promotes and tests for WLAN interoperability.

- **WLAN Association** (http://www.wlana.org/): Educates and raises consumer awareness about WLANs.

- **FCC** (http://www.fcc.gov/): Regulates United States interstate and international communications by radio, television, wire, satellite, and cable.

- **Canadian Radio-Television and Telecommunications Commission** (http://www.crtc.gc.ca/): Regulates Canada's broadcasting and telecommunications systems.

IEEE 802.11 Operational Standards

In September 1999 the IEEE ratified the IEEE 802.11a standard (5 GHz at 54 Mbps) and the IEEE 802.11b standard (2.4 GHz at 11 Mbps). In June 2003, the IEEE ratified the 802.11g standard (2.4 GHz at 54 Mbps); this standard is backward-compatible with 802.11b systems, because both use the same 2.4-GHz bandwidth. The following are the existing IEEE 802.11 standards for wireless communication:

- **802.11a**: 54 Mbps at 5 GHz, ratified in 1999

- **802.11b**: 11 Mbps 2.4 GHz, ratified in 1999

- **802.11d**: World mode, ratified in 2001

- **802.11e**: Quality of service, ratified in 2005

- **802.11F**: Inter-Access Point Protocol, withdrawn in 2006

- **802.11g**: 54 Mbps at 2.4 GHz, higher data rate than 802.11b, ratified in 2003

- **802.11h**: Dynamic frequency selection and transmit power control mechanisms, ratified in 2003

- **802.11i**: Authentication and security, ratified in 2005

- **802.11j**: Additional Japanese frequencies, ratified in 2005

- **802.11k**: Radio resource management draft, planned to be ratified in 2007

- **802.11n**: High-throughput draft, planned to be ratified in 2007

IEEE 802.11b/g Standards in the 2.4 GHz Band

The 2.4 GHz band used for 802.11b/g has multiple channels, each 22 MHz wide. In North America, 11 channels are defined, as illustrated in Figure 9-3. The top of the figure shows the channel's center frequency (which is the frequency by which the channel is known); the lower numbers show the channel's starting frequency. In North America, the 2.4 GHz band has three nonoverlapping channels: channels 1, 6, and 11.

Figure 9-3   *2.4 GHz Channels in North America*

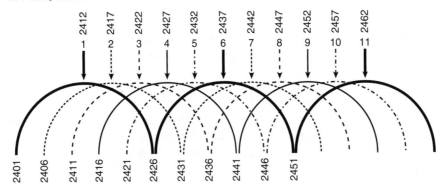

Careful channel placement eliminates overlapping cells on the same channel so that aggregate WLAN throughput is maximized. This concept is similar to the placement of FM radio stations throughout the country; two radio stations in the same geographic area are never on the same channel.

Therefore, three APs, using the three nonoverlapping channels, could operate in the same area without sharing the medium. For example, an AP on channel 1 does not have any frequencies in common with an AP on channel 6 or with an AP on channel 11. Therefore, there is no degradation in throughput when three APs are in the same area if they are each on a nonoverlapping channel. Figure 9-4 illustrates how 802.11b/g cells can be placed so that no adjacent channels overlap.

Figure 9-4   *2.4 GHz Channel Placement*

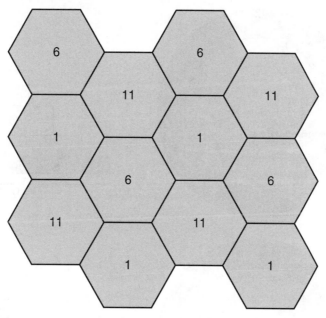

No two adjacent cells use the same channel.

Different countries allow different channels and transmit power levels.

> **NOTE**   802.11g is backward-compatible with 802.11b. The 802.11g specification uses orthogonal frequency division multiplexing (OFDM) modulation for 802.11g data rates and complementary code keying modulation for 802.11b data rates.
>
> Multipath interference is more of an issue with 802.11b. Some Cisco APs reduce multipath interference by providing multiple antennas; this feature is called *antenna diversity.* The device selects the antenna from which the best signal is received. For example, a typical Linksys wireless router has two "rubber duck" antennas. However, only one antenna is used at a time—the one that experiences the least multipath distortion of the signal.

The 802.11g data rates are 54, 48, 36, 24, 18, 12, 9, and 6 Mbps. The 802.11b data rates are 11, 5.5, 2, and 1 Mbps. Figure 9-5 compares the 2.4 GHz common data rates and ranges for 802.11b/g.

Figure 9-5 *2.4 GHz 802.11b/g Common Data Rate and Range Comparison*

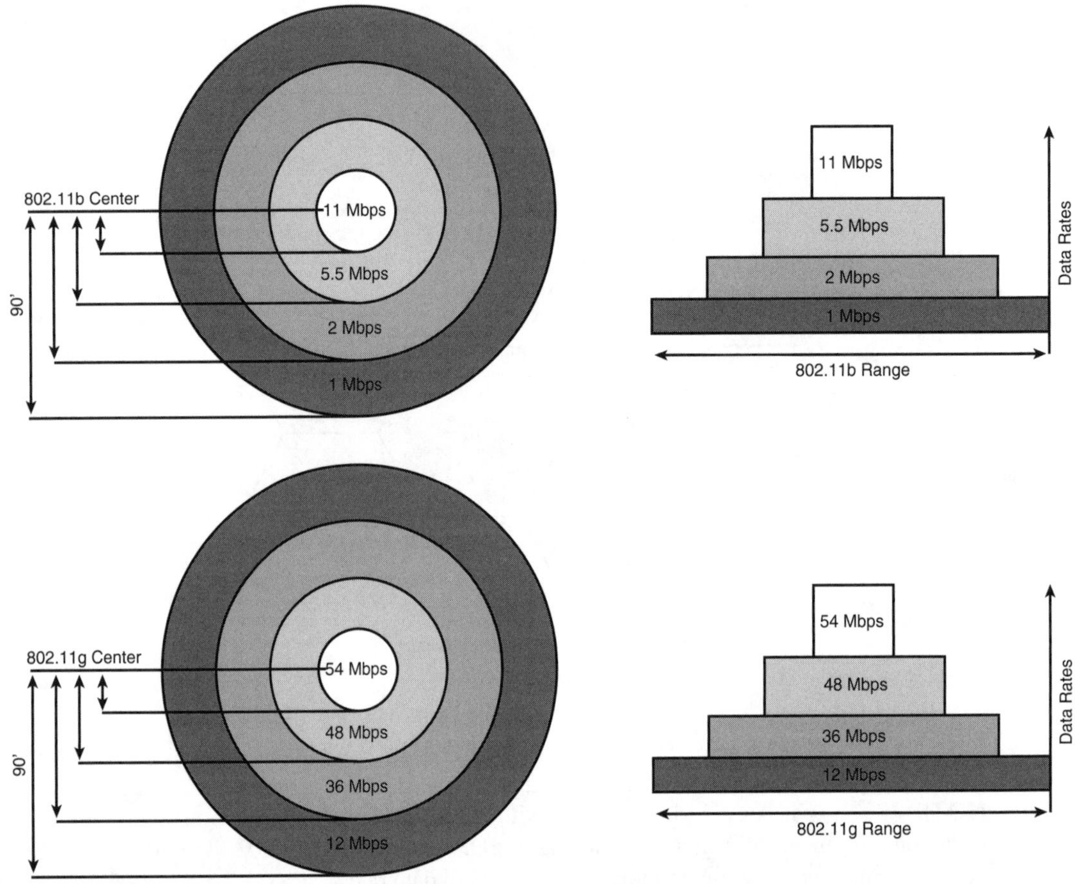

NOTE Higher data rates require more complex modulation than lower data rates. A greater signal-to-noise ratio is required to receive a signal with more complex modulation. Therefore, higher data rates can be received only at shorter distances, because signal strength decreases with distance while the noise floor (level) stays constant. At greater distances, the signal-to-noise ratio is lower than it is at shorter distances.

802.11a Standard in the 5-GHz Band

KEY POINT 802.11a and 802.11b/g are incompatible because they use different frequencies. 802.11a requires a different radio and antenna than 802.11b/g.

The 5 GHz UNII band can be divided into multiple channels, depending on the regulations that vary by country. The U.S. now has three separate 100 MHz–wide bands known as the *lower, middle,* and *upper* bands. Within each of these three bands are four nonoverlapping channels. In the U.S., the FCC specifies that the lower band is for indoor use, the middle band is for indoor and outdoor use, and the upper band is for outdoor use. Figure 9-6 illustrates the nonoverlapping 802.11a channels.

Figure 9-6 *5 GHz 802.11a Nonoverlapping Channels*

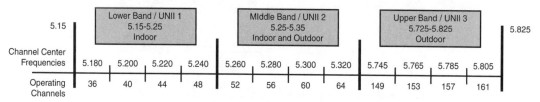

802.11a uses the same OFDM modulation and supports the same data rates as 802.11g. Figure 9-7 shows the 802.11a common data rates and ranges.

Figure 9-7 *5 GHz 802.11a Common Data Rates and Ranges*

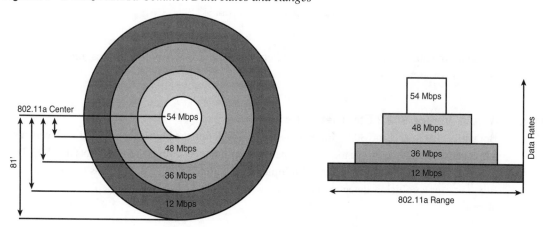

802.11a channel placement is easier to deploy than 802.11b/g, because 802.11a has 12 nonoverlapping channels that can provide a simpler channel reuse schema. However, the nonoverlapping channels for 802.11a (as shown in Figure 9-6) are close enough to each other that some clients might experience interference from adjacent channels (called *side-band* or *side-channel interference*). As a result, the recommendation for 802.11a is that neighboring cells not be placed on neighboring channels (in other words, neighboring channels are skipped) to reduce interference. Figure 9-8 illustrates 802.11a channel placement.

Figure 9-8 *5 GHz Channel Placement*

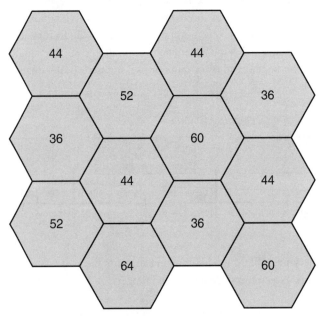

No two adjacent cells use the same channel.

Note that the 802.11a coverage area is smaller than the 802.11b/g coverage area, requiring more APs on a per-area basis.

802.11 WLANs Versus 802.3 Ethernet LANs

Both 802.11 WLANs and 802.3 Ethernet wired LANs define the physical and data link layers, use MAC addresses, and support the same upper-layer protocols. Both 802.11 WLANs and 802.3 Ethernet LANs use the Carrier Sense Multiple Access protocol to control access to the media. Ethernet uses a collision-detection algorithm, whereas 802.11 WLANs use a collision-avoidance algorithm.

KEY POINT | 802.11 uses the same frequency for both transmitting and receiving. Therefore, 802.11 is half duplex (also called *simplex*).

All the computers on the WLAN share the bandwidth. It is for this reason that collision detection is not possible on WLANs. A sending station cannot receive at the same time it is transmitting and therefore cannot detect whether another station is transmitting at the same time. Instead, devices avoid collisions by using request-to-send and clear-to-send messages.

WLAN Topologies

Cisco wireless products support the following three topologies:

- **Wireless client access**: For mobile user connectivity

- **Wireless bridging**: To interconnect LANs that are physically separated—for example, in different buildings

- **Wireless mesh networking**: To provide both client access and a dynamic, redundant connection between buildings

WLAN Components

Client devices use wireless NICs or adapters to connect to a wireless network in either ad hoc (peer-to-peer) mode or infrastructure mode using APs. Cisco APs can be either autonomous or lightweight.

> **NOTE**   Autonomous APs used to be called *thick*, *fat*, or *decentralized* APs, whereas lightweight APs were called *thin* or *centralized* APs.

These components are described in the following sections.

Cisco-Compatible WLAN Clients

The Cisco Compatible Extensions (CCX) program for WLAN client devices allows vendors of WLAN client devices or adapters to ensure interoperability with the Cisco WLAN infrastructure and take advantage of Cisco innovations. Wireless client products are submitted to an independent lab for rigorous testing; passing this testing process allows the devices to be marketed as Cisco Compatible client devices. There are four versions of the Cisco Compatible specification, versions 1 through 4. Each version builds on its predecessors; with a few exceptions, every feature that must be supported in one version must also be supported in each subsequent version.

Autonomous APs

KEY POINT | An autonomous AP has a local configuration and requires local management, which might make consistent configurations difficult and add to the cost of network management.

Cisco's core WLAN feature set includes autonomous APs and the CiscoWorks Wireless LAN Solutions Engine (WLSE) management appliance.

CiscoWorks WLSE is a turnkey and scalable management platform for managing hundreds to thousands of Cisco Aironet autonomous APs and wireless bridges. Autonomous APs may also be configured with CiscoWorks WLSE Express, a complete WLAN management solution with an integrated authentication, authorization, and accounting (AAA) server for small to medium-sized enterprise facilities or branch offices using Cisco Aironet autonomous APs and wireless bridges.

Lightweight APs

KEY POINT | A lightweight AP receives control and configuration from a WLAN controller (WLC) to which it is associated. This provides a single point of management and reduces the security concern of a stolen AP.

The WLCs and lightweight APs communicate over any Layer 2 (Ethernet) or Layer 3 (IP) infrastructure using the Lightweight AP Protocol (LWAPP) to support automation of numerous WLAN configuration and management functions. WLCs are responsible for centralized systemwide WLAN management functions, such as security policies, intrusion prevention, RF management, quality of service (QoS), and mobility.

KEY POINT | The Cisco advanced WLAN feature set includes lightweight APs, WLCs, and the Wireless Control System (WCS) management application. These components are the basis for the Cisco UWN.

A Cisco wireless location appliance may be added to track the location of wireless devices.

AP Power

One issue for WLANs is that power might not be available where APs need to be located. Two solutions to this issue are Power over Ethernet (PoE) and power injectors. PoE, or inline power, provides operating current to a device, such as an AP, from an Ethernet port, over the Category 5 cable.

> **NOTE**   The IEEE 802.3af standard defines PoE. In addition, some Cisco devices support a prestandard proprietary method of powering devices over Ethernet. An optional power classification feature allows switches to recognize powered devices and identify their power requirements.

A midspan power injector is a standalone unit that adds PoE capability to existing networking equipment. The power injector is inserted into the LAN between the Ethernet switch and the device requiring power, such as an AP.

WLAN Operation

> **KEY POINT**   The coverage area of an AP is called the Basic Service Set (BSS); other names for the BSS are *microcell* and *cell*. The identifier of the BSS is called the BSS identifier (BSSID).

If a single cell does not provide enough coverage, any number of cells can be added to extend the range to an extended service area (ESA). It is recommended that the ESA cells have 10 to 15 percent overlap to allow remote users to roam without losing RF connections. If VoIP is implemented in the wireless network, it is recommended that the ESA cells have a 15 to 20 percent overlap. As discussed earlier, bordering cells should be set to different nonoverlapping channels for best performance.

> **KEY POINT**   A Service Set Identifier (SSID) is an identifier or name of a WLAN.

An SSID on an AP and on an associated client must match exactly. APs broadcast their SSIDs in a beacon, announcing their available services; clients associate with a specific SSID or learn the available SSIDs from the beacon and choose one with which to associate.

APs can be configured not to broadcast a particular SSID, but the SSID is still sent in the header of all the packets sent and thus is discoverable by wireless survey tools. Therefore, configuring the AP not to broadcast an SSID is not considered a strong security mechanism by itself. This feature should be combined with some of the stronger mechanisms discussed in the next section.

> **KEY POINT**   *Roaming* occurs when a wireless client moves from being associated to one AP to another AP—from one cell to another cell—within the same SSID. Roaming is explored in the "Mobility in a Cisco Unified Wireless Network" section later in this chapter.

APs can have up to 16 SSIDs; VLANs are extended to the wireless network by mapping VLANs to SSIDs.

WLAN Security

WLAN security includes the following:

- **Authentication**: Ensures that only legitimate clients access the network via trusted APs.

- **Encryption**: Ensures the confidentiality of transmitted data.

- **Intrusion detection and intrusion protection**: Monitors, detects, and mitigates unauthorized access and attacks against the network.

Initially, basic 802.11 WLAN security was provided via Wired Equivalent Privacy (WEP) authentication and encryption, using static keys. With static WEP, the encryption keys must match on both the client and the access point. Unfortunately, the keys are relatively easy to compromise, so static WEP is no longer considered secure.

While the 802.11 committee was developing a more robust standard security solution, vendors incorporated the IEEE 802.1X Extensible Authentication Protocol (EAP) to authenticate users via a RADIUS authentication server such as Cisco Secure Access Control Server (ACS) and to enforce security policies for them. Basing the authentication transaction on users, rather than on machine credentials, reduces the risk of security compromise from lost or stolen equipment. 802.1X authentication also permits flexible credentials to be used for client authentication, including passwords, one-time tokens, public key infrastructure (PKI) certificates, and device IDs.

When 802.1X is used for wireless client authentication, dynamic encryption keys can be distributed to each user, each time that user authenticates on the network. The Wi-Fi Alliance also introduced Wi-Fi Protected Access (WPA) to enhance encryption and protect against all known WEP key vulnerabilities. WPA includes the Temporal Key Integrity Protocol (TKIP) to provide per-packet keying that protects the WEP key from exploits that seek to derive the key using packet comparison, and a message integrity check (MIC) to protect against packet replay. MIC protects the wireless system from *inductive attacks* that seek to induce the system to send either key data or a predictable response that can be compared to known data to derive the WEP key.

In late 2001, Cisco implemented a prestandard version of TKIP and MIC now called Cisco Key Integrity Protocol and Cisco Message Integrity Check, respectively. Cisco devices also now support the standard TKIP and MIC.

The IEEE 802.11i standard now encompasses a number of security improvements, including those implemented in WPA. 802.1X authentication is still used; however, 802.11i specifies the use of the Advanced Encryption Standard (AES). AES is a stronger security algorithm than WEP, but it is more CPU-intensive and therefore requires updated hardware to run AES encryption while maintaining comparable throughput. The Wi-Fi Alliance–interoperable implementation of 802.11i with AES is called WPA2.

> **NOTE**   WPA and WPA2 can also use a preshared key (PSK) instead of 802.1X when a RADIUS server is not available—for example, for home users. A PSK is similar to a password. Before communication starts, the same password is put on both devices (it is preshared) and the devices authenticate each other using the key.

Table 9-2 summarizes the WLAN security evolution.

Table 9-2   *Evolution of WLAN Security*

Initial	WEP: No strong authentication, static keys, first-generation encryption, not scalable
Interim	802.1X and WPA: Strong, user-based authentication, dynamic keys, improved encryption
Present	Wireless intrusion detection system (IDS): Identify and protect against attacks 802.1X, 802.11i/WPA2: Strong, user-based authentication, dynamic key management, AES encryption
Future	Improvements to hashing algorithms and key management in conjunction with AES

The Cisco Unified Wireless Network

This section introduces the Cisco UWN. The fundamental architectural concepts are discussed first, followed by an introduction to the protocols and devices that make up the UWN. *Mobility*, the capability of wireless client devices to move to new locations while remaining connected, is explored. The section concludes with a discussion of managing wireless radio resources.

The Cisco UWN Architecture

In a traditional WLAN, each AP operates as a separate autonomous node configured with SSID, RF channel, RF power settings, and so forth. Scaling to large contiguous, coordinated WLANs and adding higher-level applications is challenging with these autonomous APs. For example, if an autonomous AP hears a nearby AP operating on the same channel, the autonomous AP has no way of determining whether the adjacent AP is part of the same network or a neighboring network. Some form of centralized coordination is needed to allow multiple APs to operate across rooms and floors.

Cisco UWN Elements

The Cisco UWN architectural elements allow a WLAN to operate as an intelligent information network and to support advanced mobility services. Beginning with a base of client devices, each element provides additional capabilities needed as networks evolve and grow, interconnecting with the elements above and below it to create a unified, secure, end-to-end enterprise-class WLAN solution. The five interconnected elements of the Cisco UWN architecture are as follows:

- **Client devices**: With more than 90 percent of shipping client devices certified as Cisco Compatible under the CCX program, almost any client device that is selected will support the Cisco UWN advanced features.

- **Lightweight APs**: Dynamically configured APs provide ubiquitous network access in all environments. Enhanced productivity is supported through plug-and-play with the LWAPP used between the APs and the Cisco WLCs. Cisco APs are a proven platform with a large installed base and market share leadership. All Cisco lightweight APs support mobility services, such as fast secure roaming for voice, and location services for real-time network visibility.

- **Network unification**: Integration of wired and wireless networks is critical for unified network control, scalability, security, and reliability. Seamless functionality is provided through wireless integration into all major switching and routing platforms.

- **Network management**: The same level of security, scalability, reliability, ease of deployment, and management for WLANs as wired LANs is provided through network management systems such as the Cisco WCS, which helps visualize and secure the airspace. The Cisco wireless location appliance provides location services.

- **Mobility services**: Unified mobility services include advanced security threat detection and mitigation, voice services, location services, and guest access.

Benefits of the Cisco UWN architecture include ease of deployment and upgrades, reliable connectivity through dynamic RF management, optimized per-user performance through user load balancing, guest networking, Layer 2 and 3 roaming, embedded wireless IDS, location services, voice over IP support, lowered total cost of ownership, and wired and wireless unification.

The Cisco WCS is an optional Windows or Linux server-based network management component that works in conjunction with Cisco Aironet lightweight APs and Cisco WLCs. With Cisco WCS, network administrators have a single solution for RF prediction, policy provisioning, network optimization, troubleshooting, user tracking, security monitoring, and WLAN systems management. The Cisco WCS includes tools for WLAN planning and design, RF management, basic location tracking, intrusion prevention systems, and WLAN systems configuration, monitoring, and management.

The Cisco wireless location appliance integrates with Cisco WCS for enhanced physical location tracking of many wireless devices to within a few meters. This appliance also records historical location information that can be used for location trending, rapid problem resolution, and RF capacity management.

An enterprise network can start with client devices, lightweight APs, and WLCs. As the enterprise's wireless networking requirements grow, additional elements, such as the Cisco WCS and the Cisco wireless location appliance, can be incorporated into the network.

Cisco UWN Lightweight AP and WLC Operation

An autonomous AP acts as an 802.1Q translational bridge and is responsible for putting the wireless client RF traffic into the appropriate local VLAN on the wired network, as illustrated in Figure 9-9.

Figure 9-9 *An Autonomous Access Point Bridges and Puts Traffic into VLANs*

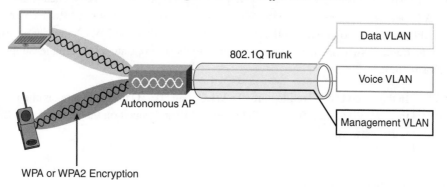

KEY POINT | In contrast, the Cisco UWN architecture centralizes WLAN configuration and control on a WLC; the APs are *lightweight*, meaning that they cannot act independently of a WLC. The lightweight APs and WLCs communicate using LWAPP, and the WLCs are responsible for putting the wireless client traffic into the appropriate VLAN.

Figure 9-10 shows an example of this architecture.

Figure 9-10 *Cisco UWN Includes Lightweight APs and WLCs*

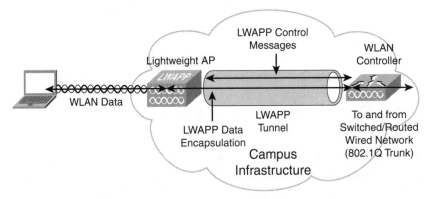

It is a recommended enterprise practice that the connection between client device and APs be both authenticated and encrypted, as described in the next section. When a WLAN client sends a packet as an RF signal, it is received by a lightweight AP, decrypted if necessary, encapsulated with an LWAPP header, and forwarded to the WLC. From the perspective of the AP, the controller is an LWAPP tunnel endpoint with an IP address. At the controller, the LWAPP header is stripped off, and the frame is switched from the controller onto the appropriate VLAN in the campus infrastructure.

KEY POINT | In the Cisco UWN architecture, the WLC is an 802.1Q bridge that takes client traffic from the LWAPP tunnel (from the lightweight AP) and puts it on the appropriate VLAN in the wired network.

Figure 9-11 illustrates this process.

Figure 9-11 *In the UWN, the WLC Bridges and Puts Traffic into VLANs*

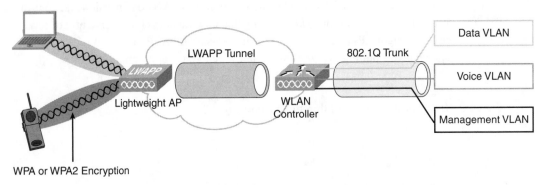

NOTE   If you move a statically addressed AP to a different IP subnet, it cannot forward traffic, because it will not be able to form a LWAPP tunnel with the WLC.

When a client on the wired network sends a packet to a WLAN client, the packet first goes into the WLC, which encapsulates it with an LWAPP header and forwards it to the appropriate AP. The AP strips off the LWAPP header, encrypts the frame if necessary, and then bridges the frame onto the RF medium.

Consequently, much of the traditional WLAN functionality has moved from autonomous APs to a centralized WLC under the Cisco UWN architecture. LWAPP splits the MAC functions of an AP between the WLC and the lightweight AP. The lightweight APs handle only real-time MAC functionality, leaving the WLC to process all the non-real-time MAC functionality. This split-MAC functionality allows the APs to be deployed in a zero-touch fashion such that individual configuration of APs is not required.

Although Cisco WLCs always connect to 802.1Q trunks on a switch or a router, Cisco lightweight APs do not understand VLAN tagging and so should be connected only to untagged access ports on a neighbor switch. Table 9-3 summarizes the lightweight AP and WLC MAC functions within the Cisco UWN.

Table 9-3 *UWN Lightweight AP and WLC MAC Functions*

Lightweight AP MAC Functions	WLC MAC Functions
802.11: Beacons, probe response	802.11 MAC management: Association requests and actions
802.11 Control: Packet acknowledgment and transmission	802.11e Resource reservation
802.11e: Frame queuing and packet prioritization	802.11i Authentication and key management
802.11i: MAC layer data encryption/decryption	

Cisco UWN Wireless Authentication and Encryption

The Cisco UWN provides full support for WPA and WPA2 with its building blocks of 802.1X EAP mutual authentication and TKIP or AES encryption.

802.1X EAP is recommended in the Cisco UWN architecture. The client device, called the EAP supplicant, communicates with the Cisco WLC, which acts as the EAP authenticator. The WLC communicates with an authentication server such as Cisco Secure ACS; this server is also a RADIUS server. Figure 9-12 illustrates this process.

Figure 9-12 *UWN Wireless Authentication and Encryption*

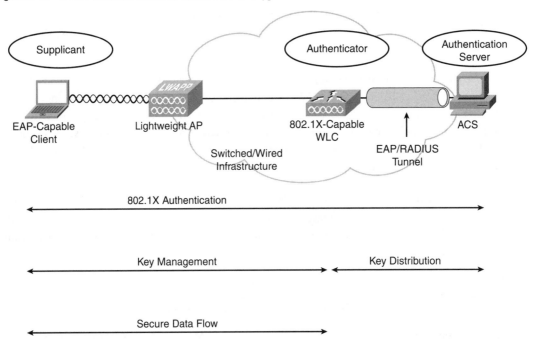

After the wireless client associates to the AP, the AP blocks the client from gaining access to anything on the network, except the authentication server, until the client has logged in and authenticated. The client (the supplicant) supplies network login credentials such as a user ID and password to the authenticator (the WLC). The supplicant, the authenticator, and the authentication server participate in the authentication process. If the authentication process succeeds, the authenticator allows network access to the supplicant through the appropriate port. The WLC tells the lightweight AP which dynamic interface (as described in the "WLC Interfaces" section later in this chapter) and policies to use for the client.

After mutual authentication has been successfully completed, the client and RADIUS server each derive the same encryption key, which is used to encrypt all data exchanged between the client and the WLC. Using a secure channel on the wired LAN, the RADIUS server sends the key to WLC, which stores and uses it when communicating with the client. The result is per-user, per-session encryption keys, with the length of a session determined by a policy defined on the RADIUS server. When a session expires or the client roams from one AP to another, a reauthentication occurs and generates a new session key. The reauthentication is transparent to the user.

Several 802.1X authentication types exist, each providing a different approach to authentication while relying on the same framework and EAP for communication between a client and the authentication server. Cisco UWN EAP support includes the following types:

- **EAP-Transport Layer Security (EAP-TLS)**: EAP-TLS is an Internet Engineering Task Force (IETF) open standard that is well supported among wireless vendors but rarely deployed. It uses PKI to secure communications to the RADIUS server using TLS and digital certificates; it requires certificates on both the server and client.

- **EAP-Tunneled TLS (EAP-TTLS)**: EAP-TTLS was codeveloped by Funk Software and Certicom. It is widely supported across platforms and offers very good security. EAP-TTLS uses PKI certificates only on the RADIUS authentication server. The authentication of the client is done with a username and password.

- **Protected Extensible Authentication Protocol (PEAP)**: PEAP was a joint proposal by Cisco Systems, Microsoft, and RSA Security as an open standard. Authentication of the client is done using PEAP-Generic Token Card (GTC) or PEAP-Microsoft Challenge Handshake Authentication Protocol version 2 (MSCHAPv2). PEAP-MSCHAPv2 is the most common version and is widely available in products and widely deployed. It is similar in design to EAP-TTLS but requires a PKI certificate only on the server to create a secure TLS tunnel to protect user authentication. PEAP-GTC allows more generic authentication to a number of databases, such as Novell Directory Services.

- **Cisco Lightweight Extensible Authentication Protocol (LEAP)**: LEAP is an early proprietary EAP method and is supported in the CCX program. It is vulnerable to dictionary attack.

- **Cisco EAP-Flexible Authentication via Secure Tunneling (EAP-FAST)**: EAP-FAST is a proposal by Cisco Systems to fix the weaknesses of LEAP; it is supported in the CCX program. EAP-FAST uses a protected access credential (PAC) and optionally uses server certificates. EAP-FAST has three phases. Phase 0 is an optional phase where the PAC can be provisioned manually or dynamically. In Phase 1, the client and the AAA server use the PAC to establish TLS tunnel. In Phase 2, the client sends user information across the tunnel.

Each EAP type has advantages and disadvantages. Trade-offs exist between the security provided, manageability, operating systems supported, client devices supported, client software and authentication messaging overhead, certificate requirements, user ease of use, and WLAN infrastructure device support. When selecting an EAP type to use, considerations include the type of security mechanism used for the security credentials, the user authentication database, the client operating systems in use, the available client supplicants, the type of user login needed, and whether RADIUS or AAA servers are used.

LWAPP Fundamentals

LWAPP is an IETF draft protocol that defines the control messaging for setup and path authentication and runtime operations between APs and WLCs. LWAPP also defines the tunneling mechanism for data traffic. The LWAPP tunnel uses Layer 2 or Layer 3 transport.

KEY POINT	LWAPP defines how the lightweight APs communicate with the WLC.
	LWAPP data messages encapsulate and forward data frames from and to wireless clients. LWAPP control messages are management messages exchanged between a WLC and the APs.
	LWAPP control messages are encrypted. LWAPP-encapsulated data messages, containing client data, are not encrypted.

One WLC can manage and operate a large number of lightweight APs and can coordinate and collate information across a large wireless network and even across a WAN. The WLC supplies both configuration information and firmware updates to the lightweight APs, if needed.

Layer 2 LWAPP Architecture

LWAPP communication between the AP and the WLC can be in native Layer 2 Ethernet frames. This is known as *Layer 2 LWAPP transport mode* and is illustrated in Figure 9-13.

Figure 9-13 *Layer 2 LWAPP Architecture*

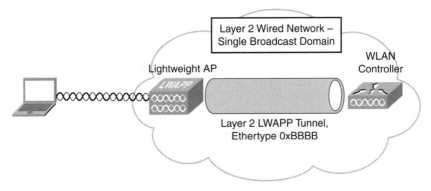

With this configuration, the APs do not require IP addresses. However, a WLC is needed on every subnet where there are APs, because all LWAPP communication between the AP and WLC is in Ethernet-encapsulated frames, not IP packets. As a result, Layer 2 LWAPP mode is not scalable and might not be suitable in most deployments across routed boundaries.

Although Layer 2 LWAPP transport mode was used earlier by some vendors, many current products do not support this mode because of its lack of scalability and flexibility. Layer 2 LWAPP transport mode is now considered deprecated in Cisco's implementation of LWAPP, and most Cisco APs do not support it.

Layer 3 LWAPP Architecture

LWAPP control and data packets can also be carried over the IP network, encapsulated in User Datagram Protocol (UDP) segments. This is called Layer 3 *LWAPP transport mode* and is illustrated in Figure 9-14.

Figure 9-14 *Layer 3 LWAPP Architecture*

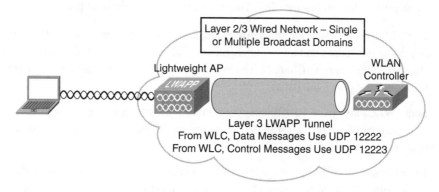

With Layer 3 LWAPP, APs require IP addresses. The LWAPP tunnel uses the IP address of the AP and the IP address of the AP manager interface on the WLC as tunnel endpoints.

> **NOTE** The various WLC interfaces, including AP-manager interfaces, are described in the "WLC Interfaces" section on the next page.

Cisco lightweight APs by default get an IP address via the Dynamic Host Configuration Protocol (DHCP). On the AP, both LWAPP control and data messages use an ephemeral (short-lived) UDP port number derived from a hash of the AP MAC address. On the WLC, LWAPP data messages always use UDP port 12222, and LWAPP control messages always use UDP port 12223. This allows APs to communicate with a WLC across subnets, as long as the UDP ports are not filtered by a firewall.

Because Layer 3 LWAPP transport mode is more flexible and scalable than Layer 2 LWAPP mode, most current products support Layer 3 LWAPP mode, and it is the recommended mode of LWAPP operation.

WLAN Controllers

> **KEY POINT** Despite being called a *wireless* LAN controller, a WLC is connected to the *wired* LAN and to the lightweight APs by *wires*. The WLC does not have *any* wireless connections.

WLC Terminology

The following are three important WLC terms:

- **Ports**: A WLC port is a *physical* connection on the WLC that connects to its neighboring switch in the wired campus infrastructure. Each WLC port is by default an 802.1Q VLAN trunk port; the WLC forwards information received from the WLANs, via the APs, over a trunk port to the campus network. There may be multiple physical ports on a WLC.

  Some Cisco WLCs support link aggregation (LAG), which is based on the IEEE 802.3ad port aggregation standard and allows aggregation of all the ports on a WLC into a single port-channel, called an EtherChannel. The WLC uses LAG to dynamically manage traffic load balancing and port redundancy.

  Some WLCs also have a 10/100 copper service port, which is reserved for out-of-band management of the WLC, for system recovery and maintenance. Use of the service port is optional.

- **Interfaces**: A WLC interface is a logical connection on the WLC that maps to a VLAN on the wired network. There are several kinds of WLC interfaces, as detailed in the next section.

  An interface has multiple parameters associated with it, including IP address, default gateway (for the IP subnet), primary physical port, secondary physical port, VLAN tag, and DHCP server.

  When LAG is not used, each interface is mapped to at least one primary physical port and an optional secondary port. Multiple interfaces can be mapped to a single WLC port. When LAG is used, the system dynamically maps the interfaces to the aggregated port-channel. A WLC can have static and dynamic interfaces, as detailed in the next section.

- **WLANs**: A WLAN is a logical entity that maps an SSID to an interface on the WLC. A WLAN is configured with security, QoS, radio policies, and other wireless network parameters. Up to 16 WLANs can be configured per WLC.

WLC Interfaces

The following interfaces might be present on a WLC:

- **Management interface**: A mandatory static interface, configured at setup time. The management interface is the default interface for in-band management of the WLC and for connectivity to enterprise services such as AAA servers. If the service port is in use, the management interface must be on a different subnet than the service port. The management interface is also used for Layer 2 communications between the WLC and the APs. The management interface is the only in-band interface IP address on the WLC that can be consistently pinged from the APs.

- **AP-manager interface**: A static interface, configured at setup time, an AP-manager interface is mandatory when using Layer 3 LWAPP transport mode. A WLC uses one or more AP-manager interfaces for all Layer 3 communications between the WLC and the lightweight APs after the APs discover the controller. The AP-manager IP address is used as the tunnel source for LWAPP packets from the WLC to the AP, and as the tunnel destination for LWAPP packets from the AP to the WLC. Each AP-manager interface must have a unique IP address, which is usually (but not necessarily) on the same subnet as the management interface.

- **Virtual interface**: A mandatory static interface, configured at setup time. The virtual interface supports mobility management, DHCP relay, and embedded Layer 3 security such as guest web authentication and virtual private network (VPN) termination. The virtual interface must be configured with an unassigned and unused gateway IP address; a typical virtual interface address is 1.1.1.1. The virtual interface address cannot be pinged and should not exist in any routing table in the network. If multiple WLCs are configured in a mobility group (which is described in the "Mobility Groups" section later in this chapter), the virtual interface IP address must be the same on all WLCs to allow seamless roaming.

- **Service-port interface**: An optional static interface, configured at setup time. The service-port interface is statically mapped by the system to the physical service port. The service-port interface must have an IP address on a different subnet from the management, AP-manager, and any dynamic interfaces. The service-port interface can obtain an IP address via DHCP, or it can be assigned a static IP address, but a default gateway cannot be assigned to the service-port interface. Static routes can be defined in the WLC for remote network access to the service-port. The service-port interface is typically reserved for out-of-band management in the event of a network failure. It is also the only port active when the controller is in boot mode. The physical service port is a copper 10/100 Ethernet port and is not capable of carrying 802.1Q tags, so it must be connected to an access port on the neighboring switch.

- **Dynamic interfaces**: Dynamic interfaces are created by the network administrator and are for carrying the WLAN client data traffic into different VLANs; thus, they are analogous to VLANs for WLAN client devices. The WLC supports up to 512 dynamic interface instances. Each dynamic interface must be assigned to a unique IP subnet and VLAN and acts as a DHCP relay for wireless clients associated to WLANs mapped to the interface.

Table 9-4 summarizes the WLC interfaces.

Table 9-4   *WLC Interfaces*

Interface	Static or Dynamic	Number of Interfaces	Use	802.1Q VLAN support
Management	Static	1 per WLC	In-band management	Native VLAN
AP-manager	Static	1 or more (1 per port)	Layer 3 LWAPP	Native VLAN
Virtual	Static	1 per mobility group	• Mobility • DHCP relay • Layer 3 security	No
Service-port	Static	1 (optional)	Out-of-band management	No
Dynamic	Dynamic	0 or more (1 per VLAN)	WLAN client data	Yes, VLANs

Figure 9-15 illustrates the relationships among WLANs, interfaces, and ports on a WLC. Interfaces must be assigned to a port for connectivity to the enterprise network. Multiple WLANs can be assigned to an interface. Multiple interfaces can be assigned to the same port, but an interface can be assigned to only one port. The service-port interface is associated only with the physical service port. The virtual interface is not associated with any port. The AP-manager interface and the management interface can be in the same subnet.

WLC Platforms

A variety of Cisco WLC platforms are available—as standalone appliances or integrated on a module within another device—to support a range of APs. The WLC appliances connect to the wired network over an 802.1Q trunk; the integrated controllers support Layer 2 connections internally and can use Layer 2 or Layer 3 connections to the wired network.

Figure 9-15   *WLC WLANs, Interfaces, and Ports*

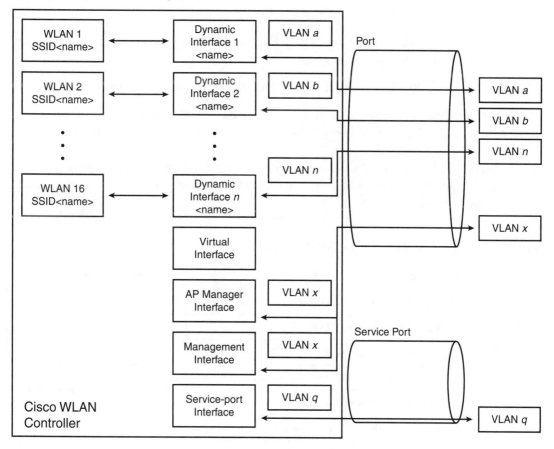

The Cisco 2000 Series WLC manages up to six lightweight APs. The Cisco WLC module (WLCM) for Cisco 2800 and 3800 series Integrated Services Routers (ISR) also manages up to six Cisco lightweight APs.

The Cisco Catalyst 3750G Integrated WLC integrates WLC functions into the Cisco Catalyst 3750G Series switches. The following two models are supported:

■ The Cisco Catalyst WS-C3750G-24WS-S25, with 24 10/100/1000 PoE ports, two small form-factor pluggable (SFP) transceiver-based Gigabit Ethernet ports, and an integrated Cisco WLC supporting up to 25 Cisco lightweight APs

■ The Cisco Catalyst WS-C3750G-24WS-S50, with 24 10/100/1000 PoE ports, two SFP transceiver-based Gigabit Ethernet ports, and an integrated Cisco WLC supporting up to 50 Cisco lightweight APs

The Cisco 4400 Series WLCs are designed for medium-to-large enterprise facilities. The Cisco 4400 Series is available in the following two models:

■ The Cisco 4402 WLC with two Gigabit Ethernet ports comes in configurations that support 12, 25, and 50 lightweight APs

■ The Cisco 4404 WLC with four Gigabit Ethernet ports supports 100 lightweight APs

The Cisco Catalyst 6500 Series Wireless Services Module (WiSM) supports up to 300 lightweight APs. These WLCs and the number of APs supported on them are detailed in Table 9-5.

> **NOTE** The number of APs supported might change as products are updated, products are replaced, and other products become available. Refer to http://www.cisco.com/ for the latest product information.

Table 9-5 *Cisco WLCs and the Number of APs Supported on Them*

Name/Part Number	Number of APs Supported
Cisco WLC Appliance: AIR-WLC2006-K9	6
Cisco WLCM for ISRs: NM-AIR-WLC6-K9	6
Cisco Catalyst 3750G Integrated WLC: WS-C3750G-24WS-S25	25
Cisco Catalyst 3750G Integrated WLC: WS-C3750G-24WS-S50	50
Cisco WLC Appliance: AIR-WLC4402-12-K9	12
Cisco WLC Appliance: AIR-WLC4402-25-K9	25
Cisco WLC Appliance: AIR-WLC4402-50-K9	50
Cisco WLC Appliance: AIR-WLC4404-100-K9	100
Cisco Catalyst 6500 Series WiSM	Up to 300

Access Point Support Scalability

KEY POINT Cisco 440x-based WLC platforms normally support no more than 48 APs per port. This limitation applies to the 440x WLC appliances (4402, 4404), the Cisco Catalyst 3750G Integrated WLCs, and the Cisco Catalyst 6500 Series WiSM.

There are two ways to scale beyond 48 APs on these WLCs:

■ **Use multiple AP-manager interfaces**: With this option, supported only on 440x appliance WLCs, the LWAPP algorithm load-balances APs across the AP-manager interfaces.

- **Use LAG**: This option is supported on the 440x appliance controllers. It is the default and only option on the Cisco Catalyst 3750G Integrated WLCs and the Cisco Catalyst 6500 Series WiSM. With LAG enabled, one AP-manager interface load-balances traffic across one EtherChannel interface.

The 440x appliance controllers can use LAG or multiple AP-manager interfaces. With LAG enabled, the logical port on a Cisco 4402 controller supports up to 50 APs, and the logical port on a Cisco 4404 controller supports up to 100 APs. The following sections detail these two options.

Multiple AP-Manager Interfaces

As shown in Figure 9-16, two or more AP-manager interfaces can be created on a 440x appliance controller. Each AP-manager interface is mapped to a different physical port. All AP-manager IP addresses are included in the LWAPP Discovery Response message from a WLC to an AP, along with information about how many APs are currently using each AP-manager IP address. The AP selects an AP-manager IP address to use for the LWAPP Join Request, preferring the least-loaded AP-manager interface. Therefore, the AP load is dynamically distributed across the multiple AP-manager interfaces.

Figure 9-16 *Using Multiple AP-Manager Interfaces to Increase the Number of APs Supported*

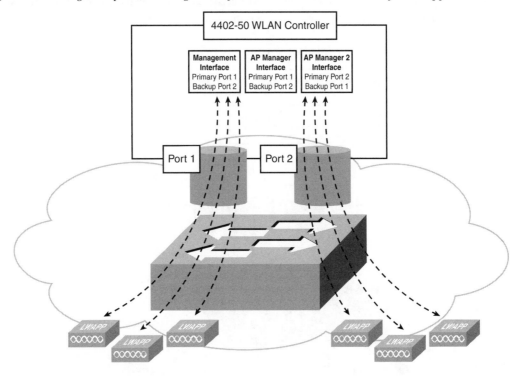

Multiple AP-manager interfaces can exist on the same VLAN and IP subnet, or they can be configured on different VLANs and IP subnets. Cisco recommends that you configure all AP-manager interfaces on the same VLAN and IP subnet. One advantage of using the multiple AP-manager interface solution is that the WLC platform can be connected to more than one neighbor device.

Using multiple AP-manager interfaces affects port and WLC redundancy engineering. For example, the 4402-50 WLC supports a maximum of 50 APs and has two ports. To support the maximum number of APs, you have to create two AP-manager interfaces. A problem arises, though, if you want to support port redundancy. For example, consider if the first static AP-manager is assigned port 1 as its primary port and port 2 as its secondary port, and the second AP-manager interface is assigned port 2 as its primary port and port 1 as its secondary port. If either port fails, the WLC would try to support 50 APs on a port that supports only 48 APs. In this situation, two APs will be unable to communicate with the WLC and will be forced to look for an alternative WLC.

LAG with a Single AP-Manager Interface

As illustrated in Figure 9-17, when LAG is enabled, the WLC dynamically manages port redundancy and transparently load-balances APs across an EtherChannel interface. The 48-APs-per-port limitation does not apply when LAG is enabled.

Figure 9-17 *Using LAG to Increase the Number of APs Supported*

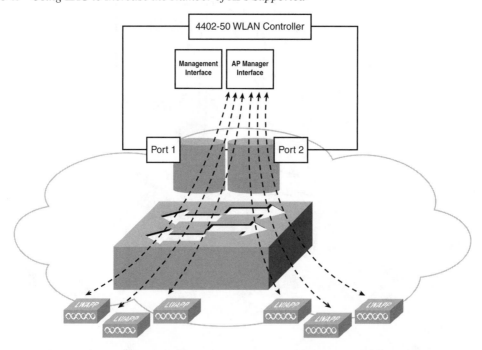

Using LAG simplifies controller configuration, because primary and secondary ports for each interface do not need to be configured. If any controller port fails, traffic is automatically migrated to one of the other ports. As long as at least one controller port is functioning, the system continues to operate, APs remain connected to the network, and wireless clients can continue to send and receive data.

One limitation with LAG is that the WLC platform supports only one LAG group per controller. There is only one logical port; all the physical ports, excluding the service port, are included in the EtherChannel bundle. Therefore, packets may be forwarded out of the same port on which they were received, and a WLC in LAG mode cannot be connected to more than one neighbor device.

KEY POINT | When possible, Cisco recommends using LAG to support AP scaling, rather than using multiple AP-manager interfaces.

Lightweight APs

The available Cisco lightweight APs and their features are detailed in Table 9-6.

Table 9-6   *Cisco Lightweight AP Features*

Feature	1000 Series	1100 Series (Currently 1121)	1130AG Series	1200 Series (Currently 1231)	1230 Series	1240 Series	1300 Series	1500 Series
Lightweight, or both autonomous and lightweight	Light-weight	Both	Both	Both	Both	Both	Both (light-weight in AP mode)	Light-weight
External antenna supported	Yes	No	No	Yes	Yes	Yes	Yes	Yes
Outdoor install supported	No	No	No	No	No	No	Yes	Yes
REAP/ H-REAP supported[1]	REAP	No	H-REAP	No	No	H-REAP	No	No
Dual radio	Yes	No (b/g only)	Yes	Yes	Yes	Yes	No (b/g only)	Yes
Power (watts)	13	6	15	15	14	15	N/A	N/A

continues

Table 9-6 *Cisco Lightweight AP Features (Continued)*

Feature	1000 Series	1100 Series (Currently 1121)	1130AG Series	1200 Series (Currently 1231)	1230 Series	1240 Series	1300 Series	1500 Series
Memory (MBytes)	16	16	32	16	16	32	16	16
WLANs/ radio supported	16	8	8	—	8	8	8	16

[1] Remote edge AP (REAP) and hybrid REAP (H-REAP) are described in the "Design Considerations for Branch Office Wireless Networks" section later in this chapter.

AP models with the most memory support the most feature flexibility.

> **NOTE** The AP features supported might change as products are updated, products are replaced, and other products become available. Refer to http://www.cisco.com/ for the latest product information.

> **NOTE** If an AP is being used in a PoE configuration, the power drawn from the power sourcing equipment is higher than the maximum power required at the AP; the amount depends on the length of the interconnecting cable. Refer to the product data sheets at http://www.cisco.com/ for specific power requirements.

Lightweight AP Discovery and Join Process

As mentioned earlier, lightweight APs are deployed in a "zero-touch" fashion and are not configured directly. After a lightweight AP is physically installed and connected to an access port on infrastructure switch, the AP goes through a WLC discovery and join process using an exchange of LWAPP messages.

LWAPP WLC Discovery Process

The following are the LWAPP WLC discovery process steps:

Step 1   The AP issues a DHCPDISCOVER request to obtain an IP address, unless it has a static IP address configured.

Step 2   If the AP supports Layer 2 LWAPP transport mode, the AP broadcasts an LWAPP Discovery message in a Layer 2 LWAPP frame. Any WLC connected to the network configured to operate in Layer 2 LWAPP transport mode responds with a Layer 2 LWAPP Discovery Response.

Step 3   If Step 2 fails or if the AP does not support Layer 2 LWAPP transport mode, the AP attempts a Layer 3 LWAPP WLC discovery, as described in the next section.

Step 4   If Step 3 fails, the AP resets and returns to Step 1.

Layer 3 LWAPP transport mode is the most commonly used mode because it is more flexible and scalable than Layer 2 LWAPP transport mode. All Cisco WLC platforms and lightweight APs support Layer 3 LWAPP transport mode.

Layer 3 LWAPP Discovery Algorithm

The Layer 3 LWAPP WLC discovery algorithm is used by a lightweight AP to build a list of possible WLCs with which it can connect; this is called a *controller list*. After building the controller list, the AP selects a WLC and attempts to join with that WLC. A lightweight AP has the following mechanisms available to discover WLCs:

- The AP broadcasts a Layer 3 LWAPP Discovery message on the local IP subnet.

- If over-the-air provisioning is enabled on a WLC, APs joined to the WLC advertise their known WLCs in neighbor messages that are sent over the RF. New APs attempting to discover WLCs receive these messages and unicast LWAPP Discovery Requests to these WLCs.

- The AP maintains previously learned WLC IP addresses locally in nonvolatile RAM. The AP sends a unicast LWAPP Discovery Request to each of these WLC IP addresses.

- DHCP servers can be programmed to return WLC IP addresses in the vendor-specific "Option 43" in DHCPOFFER messages to Cisco lightweight APs. The AP sends a unicast LWAPP Discovery message to each WLC listed in the DHCP option 43 information.

- The AP attempts to resolve the DNS name "CISCO-LWAPP-CONTROLLER.localdomain." If the AP can resolve this name to one or more IP addresses, the AP sends a unicast LWAPP Discovery message to the resolved IP addresses.

Each of the WLCs receiving the LWAPP Discovery message replies with a unicast LWAPP Discovery Response message to the AP. The AP compiles a list of candidate controllers.

LWAPP WLC Selection

The LWAPP discovery and selection process is important, because it provides a mechanism for network administers to manage which AP is joined to which WLC. WLCs embed important information in the LWAPP Discovery Response: the controller sysName, the controller type, the controller AP capacity and its current AP load, the Master Controller status, and AP-manager IP addresses.

The AP selects a WLC to which it sends an LWAPP Join Request from the candidate WLC list based on the embedded information in the LWAPP Discovery Response, as follows:

Step 1   If the AP has previously been configured with a primary, secondary, or tertiary controller, the AP examines the controller sysName field (from the LWAPP Discovery Responses), attempting to find the WLC configured as primary. If the AP finds a matching sysName, it sequentially tries to join the primary, secondary, and tertiary controllers.

Step 2   If no primary, secondary, or tertiary controllers have been configured for an AP, if these controllers cannot be found in the candidate list, or if the LWAPP joins to those controllers have failed, the AP then looks at the Master Controller status field in the LWAPP Discovery Responses from the candidate WLCs. If a WLC is configured as a Master Controller, the AP sends an LWAPP Join Request to that WLC.

Step 3   If the AP is unsuccessful at joining a WLC based on the criteria in Steps 1 and 2, it attempts to join the WLC that has the most capacity for AP associations.

When a WLC receives an LWAPP Join Request, the WLC validates the AP and then sends an LWAPP Join Response to the AP. The AP validates the WLC to complete the discovery and join process. The validation on both the AP and WLC is a mutual authentication mechanism, after which an encryption key derivation process is initiated. The encryption key is used to secure future LWAPP control messages. LWAPP-encapsulated data messages containing client data are not encrypted.

Lightweight AP and WLC Control Messages

After a lightweight AP has joined a WLC, the two devices send control messages to each other.

The AP downloads firmware from the WLC if its running code version does not match the WLC; the AP always matches its code revision to the WLC.

The WLC then provisions the AP with the appropriate SSID, security, QoS, and other parameters that have been configured on the WLC. At this point, the AP is ready to serve WLAN clients.

The WLC periodically queries the APs joined to it for statistics, in LWAPP control messages. These statistics are used for dynamic radio resource management (RRM), alarming, reporting, and other tasks.

The AP periodically (every 30 seconds) sends an LWAPP heartbeat control message to the WLC. The WLC responds to the heartbeat with an LWAPP acknowledgment. If a heartbeat acknowledgment from the controller is missed, the AP resends the heartbeat up to five times at 1-

second intervals. If no acknowledgment is received after five retries, the AP declares the controller unreachable, releases and renews its IP address, and looks for a new controller.

> **NOTE**   The heartbeat mechanism is used to support controller redundancy designs, as discussed in the "Controller Redundancy Design" section later in this chapter.

Access Point Modes

Lightweight APs can be configured to operate in the following modes, depending on their intended usage:

- **Local mode**: The default mode of operation. When an AP is placed into local mode, it spends 60 ms on channels on which it does not operate, every 180 seconds. During this time, the AP performs noise floor (level) and interference measurements and scans for IDS events and rogue APs.

- **Remote edge AP (REAP) mode**: REAP mode enables an AP to reside across a WAN link and still be able to communicate with the WLC and provide the functionality of a regular lightweight AP. Currently, REAP mode is supported only on the Cisco Aironet 1030 Lightweight APs. Hybrid REAP (H-REAP) is supported on the Cisco Aironet 1130 and 1240 AG Series Lightweight APs. REAP and H-REAP are described further in the later "Design Considerations for Branch Office Wireless Networks" section.

- **Monitor mode**: In monitor mode, the radio on the lightweight AP is set to receive only, so the AP does not serve clients. The AP acts as a dedicated sensor for location-based services, rogue AP detection, and IDS. When an AP is in monitor mode, it continuously cycles through all configured channels, listening to each channel for approximately 60 ms. In this mode, an AP can also send packets to a rogue AP to deauthenticate end users.

- **Rogue detector mode**: APs that operate in rogue detector mode monitor for the presence of rogue APs on a trusted *wired* network. They do not use their RF (the radio is turned off). An AP in rogue detector mode receives periodic rogue AP reports from the WLC (including a list of rogue client MAC addresses) and sniffs all Address Resolution Protocol (ARP) packets. The rogue detector AP can be connected to a trunk port to monitor all VLANs in the network because a rogue AP could be connected to any VLAN. If a match occurs between a MAC address in an ARP packet and a MAC address in the rogue AP report, the rogue AP to which those clients are connected is known to be on the wired network, so the rogue detector AP generates a rogue AP alert to the WLC. The AP does not restrict the rogue AP; it only alerts the WLC.

- **Sniffer mode**: A lightweight AP that operates in sniffer mode functions as a protocol sniffer at a remote site; the AP is put into promiscuous mode. It captures and forwards all the packets (including time stamps, information on signal strength, packet size, and so forth) on a particular channel to a remote PC running AiroPeek, a third-party network analyzer software that supports decoding of wireless data packets. The AiroPeek software analyzes the packets it receives and provides the same information as it does when capturing packets using a wireless card. Sniffer mode should be enabled only when AiroPeek is running.

> **NOTE**   AiroPeek information is available at http://www.wildpackets.com/products/.

- **Bridge mode**: The bridge mode feature on the Cisco Aironet 1030 Series (for indoor usage) and 1500 Series APs (for outdoor mesh usage) provides cost-effective, high-bandwidth, wireless bridging connectivity. Applications supported are point-to-point bridging, point-to-multipoint bridging, point-to-point wireless access with integrated wireless backhaul, and point-to-multipoint wireless access with integrated wireless backhaul.

Additional information on selecting an AP based on the intended use is covered in the "Designing Wireless Networks with Lightweight Access Points and Wireless LAN Controllers" section later in this chapter.

Mobility in a Cisco Unified Wireless Network

This section covers how mobility is supported in a Cisco UWN deployment.

> **KEY POINT**   One significant benefit of wireless networks—and a key reason they are deployed—is mobility. This is the capability of end devices to move to new locations and remain networked without reassociation and DHCP delays.

> **KEY POINT**   Roaming occurs when a wireless client moves its association from one AP and reassociates to another AP, within the same SSID.

In a low-quality roaming experience, mobility involves a new association with a new AP, a new IP address (via DHCP), and possibly reestablishing security credentials. These steps take time, so clients might lose network connectivity or other services; for example, voice calls could be dropped.

A high-quality roaming experience should be seamless to the client and preserve the security context and associations. For a high-quality roaming experience, a WLAN client must be able to maintain its association seamlessly from one AP to another securely and with as little latency as possible. The roaming event is triggered on signal quality, not proximity to an AP. When the signal quality for a client drops as a result of movement, the client device roams to another AP.

Mobility introduces challenges in a network implementation. Roaming must be supported when the wireless client roams from one AP to another, whether both APs are joined to the same WLC (intracontroller) or to different WLCs (intercontroller). Depending on the application, the Cisco UWN might have to support Layer 2 or Layer 3 roaming. These scenarios are described in the following sections.

Intracontroller Roaming

KEY POINT | Intracontroller roaming is roaming between APs joined to the same WLC.

When a wireless client associates to an AP and authenticates through a WLC, the WLC places an entry for that client in its client database. This entry includes the MAC and IP addresses of the client, security context and associations, QoS context, WLAN, and associated AP. The WLC uses this information to forward frames and manage traffic to and from the wireless client.

When the wireless client moves its association from one AP to another on the same WLC, as illustrated in Figure 9-18, the WLC simply updates the client database with the new associated AP. If necessary, new security context and associations are established as well. With intracontroller roaming, an IP address refresh is not needed.

When WLAN clients roam, they are always reauthenticated by the system in some way, to protect against client spoofing. When wireless clients support pairwise master key (PMK) caching, as defined in the 802.11i and WPA2 specifications, Cisco WLCs support full, secure roaming and rekeying without reauthenticating the client with the server in the back end. This is true for both Layer 2 and Layer 3 intracontroller and intercontroller roaming. The proactive caching (before the client roaming event) of the PMK that is derived during a client 802.1 x/EAP authentication at the AP is called *proactive key caching (PKC)*. Although no special client-side software is required to support roaming, PKC requires client-side supplicant support.

Cisco Centralized Key Management (CCKM) is an earlier Cisco standard (supported by Cisco Compatible clients) to provide fast, secure roaming. The principal mechanism for accelerating roaming is the same as PKC, by using a cached PMK, but the implementation is slightly different, and the two mechanisms are not compatible.

Figure 9-18 *Intracontroller Roaming Is Roaming Between APs on the Same WLC*

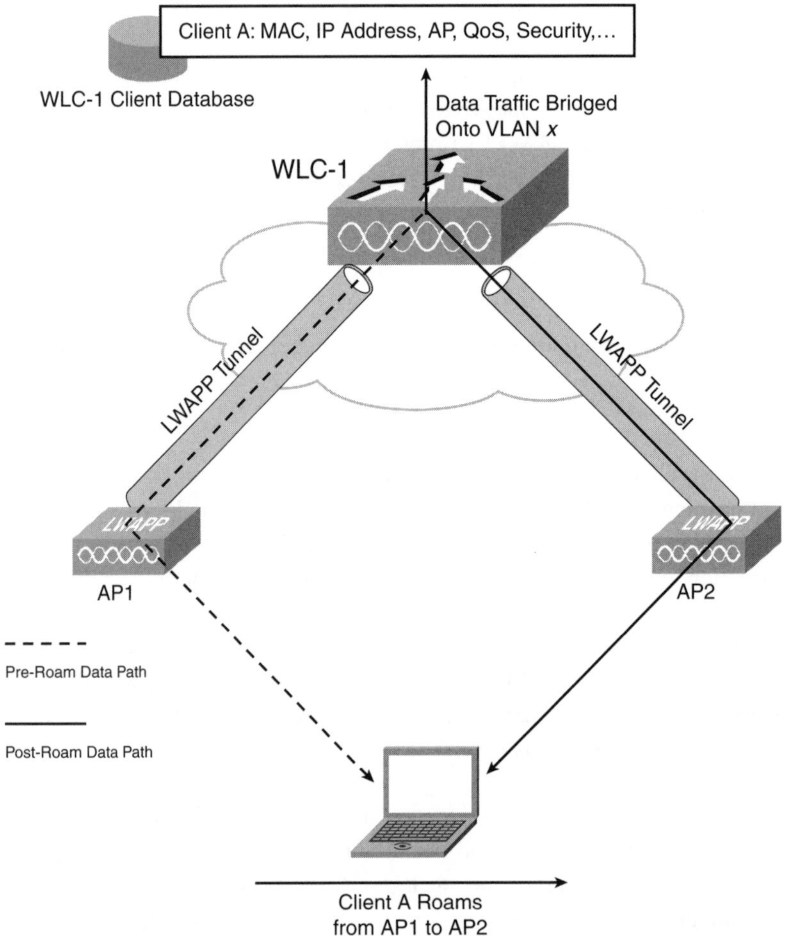

Client A: MAC, IP Address, AP, QoS, Security,...

WLC-1 Client Database

Data Traffic Bridged
Onto VLAN *x*

WLC-1

LWAPP Tunnel

LWAPP Tunnel

AP1

AP2

Pre-Roam Data Path

Post-Roam Data Path

Client A Roams
from AP1 to AP2

Intercontroller Roaming at Layer 2

KEY POINT Intercontroller roaming occurs when a client roams from an AP joined to one WLC to an AP joined to a different WLC. Intercontroller roaming can be at Layer 2 or Layer 3.

Figure 9-19 illustrates an intercontroller Layer 2 roam.

Figure 9-19 *Layer 2 Intercontroller Roaming*

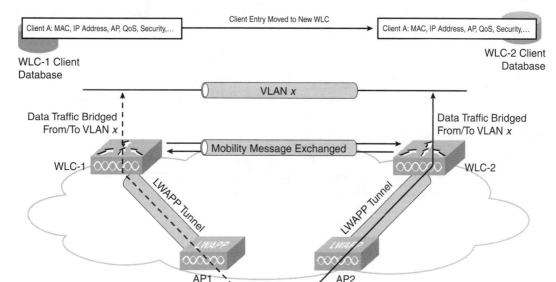

<table>
<tr><td style="border:1px solid black; padding:2px;">
KEY POINT
</td><td>
A Layer 2 intercontroller roam occurs when the client traffic is bridged to the same IP subnet (and thus the same VLAN) through the LAN interfaces on both WLCs.

When the client reassociates to an AP connected to a new WLC, the new WLC exchanges mobility messages with the original WLC, and the client database entry is moved to the new WLC.
</td></tr>
</table>

New security context and associations are established if necessary, and the client database entry is updated for the new AP. With Layer 2 intercontroller roaming, an IP address refresh is not needed. This process is transparent to the end user.

> **NOTE**   Both forms of intercontroller roaming require the controllers to be in the same mobility group, as described in the "Mobility Groups" section later in this chapter.

Intercontroller Roaming at Layer 3

KEY POINT | Layer 3 intercontroller roaming occurs when the client associates to an AP on a different WLC and the traffic is bridged to a different subnet.

When the client roams at Layer 3 and reassociates to an AP connected to a new WLC, the new WLC exchanges mobility messages with the original WLC, as shown in Figure 9-20.

Figure 9-20 *Layer 3 Intercontroller Roaming*

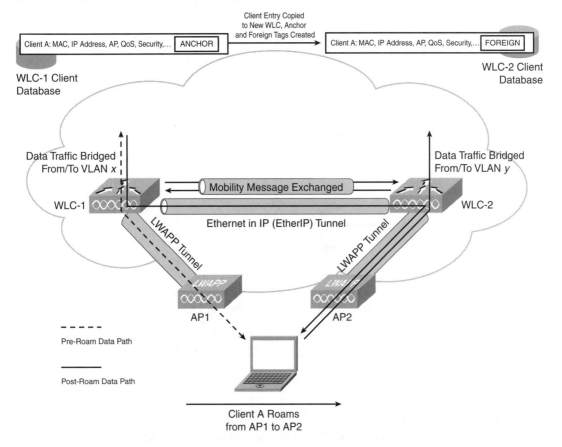

KEY POINT | With Layer 3 roaming, instead of *moving* the client entry to the new WLC's client database, the original WLC marks the entry for the client in its own client database with an Anchor entry and *copies* the database entry to the new WLC's client database, where it is marked with a Foreign entry.

Security credentials and context are reestablished if necessary. The roam is still transparent to the wireless client, which maintains its original IP address, even though the new WLC uses a different subnet.

After a Layer 3 roam, the data transferred to and from the wireless client might flow in an asymmetric traffic path. The Foreign WLC forwards traffic from the client to the network directly into the network. Traffic to the client arrives at the Anchor WLC, which forwards the traffic to the Foreign WLC in an Ethernet in IP (EtherIP) tunnel. The Foreign WLC then forwards the data to the client.

If a wireless client roams to a new Foreign WLC, the client database entry is moved from the original Foreign WLC to the new Foreign WLC, but the original Anchor WLC is always maintained.

Mobility Groups

> **KEY POINT** A set of WLCs in a network can be configured as a mobility group, which allows them to dynamically share important information among them, including the context and state of client devices, and WLC loading information.

With this information, the network can support intercontroller roaming, AP load balancing, and controller redundancy. A mobility group also supports forwarding of data traffic through EtherIP tunnels for intercontroller roaming.

Each WLC in a mobility group is configured with a list of the other members of the mobility group. Each WLC device builds a neighbor relationship with every other member of the group. When client data is forwarded between members of a mobility group to support Layer 3 roaming, the packets are carried over an EtherIP tunnel.

A mobility group can include up to 24 WLCs. The number of APs supported in a mobility group is a maximum of 3600 and is bounded by the number of controllers and controller types in the mobility group. For example, a mobility group made up of 24 4404-100 WLC devices will support up to 2400 APs, because each 4404-100 supports up to 100 APs per WLC (thus, 24 * 100 = 2400 APs per group). A mobility group made up of 12 4402-25 and 12 4402-50 WLC devices supports up to 900 APs, because each 4402-25 supports up to 25 APs, and each 4402-50 supports up to 50 APs, (thus, [12 * 25] + [12 * 50] = 300 + 600 = 900 APs per group) and so on. A WiSM controller module counts as two controllers in a mobility group, so a maximum of 12 WiSM modules can be supported in a single mobility group.

Typically, WLCs should be placed in the same mobility group when an intercontroller roam is possible. If there is no possibility of a roaming event occurring, it might make sense to not put

WLCs in the same mobility group. For example, suppose that you have deployed two separate WLCs in two buildings, with each WLC managing the APs in its building. If the buildings are separated by a large parking area with no RF coverage, a WLAN client won't roam from an AP in one building to an AP in the other building. These WLCs therefore do not need to be members of the same mobility group.

As a recommended practice, redundant WLCs should be in the same mobility group. When an AP joins a WLC, it learns the IP addresses of the other WLCs in the mobility group from its joined WLC. These addresses are remembered and used the next time the AP goes through the LWAPP discovery process. To support mobility, the following requirements must be met:

■ There must be IP connectivity between the management interfaces of all WLC devices; verify by pinging between them.

■ The WLCs need unrestricted access through any firewalls or access control lists (ACL) to use UDP port 16666 (unencrypted) or UDP port 16667 (encrypted) for message exchange between them.

■ All WLCs in the mobility group must be configured to use the same LWAPP transport mode: either Layer 2 or Layer 3.

■ All WLCs must be configured with the same mobility group name; the mobility group name is case-sensitive.

■ All WLCs must be configured to use the same virtual interface IP address.

■ Each WLC must be manually configured with the MAC address and IP address of all the other mobility group members.

Mobility Group Ping Tests

Controllers belonging to the same mobility group communicate with each other by sending control information over well-known UDP port 16666 and exchanging data traffic through an EtherIP tunnel. Because UDP and EtherIP are not reliable transport mechanisms, there is no guarantee that a mobility control packet or data packet will be delivered to a mobility peer. Mobility packets might be lost in transit due to a firewall filtering the UDP port or EtherIP packets or due to routing issues.

Cisco WLC software Release 4.1 and later enables you to test the mobility communication environment by performing two mobility ping tests:

■ **mping**: This test runs over mobility UDP port 16666 and tests mobility UDP control packet communication between two controllers over the management interface.

■ **eping**: This test runs over EtherIP and tests mobility EtherIP data packet communication between two controllers over the management interface.

Only one mobility ping test per controller can be run at a time. Note that these ping tests are not Internet Control Message Protocol–based; the term *ping* is used to indicate an echo request and an echo reply message.

The information in this sidebar was derived from http://www.cisco.com/en/US/products/ps6366/ products_configuration_guide_chapter09186a008082d712.html#wp1102312.

Recommended Practices for Supporting Roaming

This section outlines some recommended practices to support roaming. When designing roaming support in the network, try to minimize intercontroller roaming. When intercontroller roaming is necessary, design the network to support a round-trip time (RTT) of less than 10 ms between controllers. Strive to use Layer 2 intercontroller roaming, maintaining traffic on the same subnet, for more efficiency.

Because roaming WLAN clients are always reauthenticated by the system in some way, use client-side supplicants that support key caching (PKC or CCKM) to speed up and secure the roaming process. PKC or CCKM enables WLAN clients to quickly roam between APs. The WLC caches session credentials (security keys) derived for a client session and uses them for reauthentication and rekeying when a client roams within the mobility group. Caching this information rather than forcing the client to do a full authentication reduces the authentication time and therefore the total time required for roaming. This can enhance application transparency because the impact of roaming is reduced and less likely to affect either the application or the user.

NOTE   Either PKC or CCKM should be implemented to assist in seamless Layer 3 roaming.

For example, if a PMK for a given WLAN client is already present at an AP when presented by the associating client, full 802.1X/EAP authentication is not required. Instead, the WLAN client uses a WPA four-way handshake process to securely derive a new session encryption key (called the *pairwise transient key*) for communication with that AP. The distribution of these cached PMKs to APs is greatly simplified in the Cisco UWN deployment: The PMK is cached in the controller and is made available to all APs that connect to that controller and between all controllers that belong to that controller's mobility group, in advance of a client roaming event.

Client roaming capabilities vary by vendor, driver, and supplicant. The client must match both AP security (PMK or CCKM) and SSID.

Radio Resource Management and RF Groups

This section provides a brief overview of Cisco RRM and RF groups.

Radio Resource Management

KEY POINT | Real-time RF management is a foundation of the Cisco UWN solution.

Key RF challenges in managing a wireless environment include the following:

- Limited nonoverlapping channels

- The physical characteristics of RF propagation

- Contention for the medium

- The transient nature of RF environments

AP capacity is affected by the applications being run over the wireless network. For example, a recommended practice is to support approximately seven to eight voice calls over a WLAN (VoWLAN) (depending on the codec used), or about 20 data devices, because all clients must share the available bandwidth. The most common response to strained network capacity is to add more APs. However, wireless is a fixed resource. For example, only three channels can be used without causing interference between APs when using 802.11 b/g. To minimize cochannel interference, channels 1, 6, and 11 are usually the only ones used in medium- to high-density enterprise deployments. Adding more 802.1 b/g APs using only three channels with too much RF power can actually decrease RF performance. This situation can be somewhat improved by managing 802.11b/g RF power or using 802.11a, which provides significantly more channels than 802.11 b/g. Some enterprise designs reserve 802.1a for VoWLAN support.

The user experience in a wireless network is dependent on radio propagation and other building characteristics affecting connection speeds and error rates. The RF environment is transient; an office looks dramatically different at 10 a.m., when hundreds of people are walking around contending for network resources, than at 3 a.m., when doors are closed, no people are present, and neighboring offices are not generating RF interference. Wireless and RF propagation issues directly affect the QoS delivered to users.

KEY POINT | RRM continuously analyzes the existing RF environment and automatically adjusts the AP power and channel configurations to help mitigate cochannel interference, signal coverage problems, and so on. RRM also reduces the need to perform exhaustive site surveys, increases system capacity, and provides automated self-healing functionality to compensate for RF dead zones and AP failures.

The Cisco WLC uses dynamic RRM algorithms to create an environment that is completely self-configuring, self-optimizing, and self-healing, via the following specific RRM functions:

- **Radio resource monitoring**: Cisco lightweight APs are designed to monitor all channels. The AP goes "off-channel" for a period no greater than 60 ms to listen to channels on which it is not operating. Packets collected during this time are sent to the WLC, where they are analyzed to detect rogue APs (whether or not SSIDs are broadcast), rogue clients, ad-hoc clients, and interfering APs.

- **Dynamic channel assignment**: WLCs dynamically allocate AP channel assignments to avoid conflict and minimize cochannel interference between adjacent APs. To avoid wasting scarce RF resources, channels are reused where there is no conflict.

- **Interference detection and avoidance**: *Interference* is defined as any 802.11 traffic that is not part of the WLAN, including a rogue AP, a Bluetooth device, or a neighboring WLAN. Cisco lightweight APs constantly scan all channels, looking for major sources of interference. If the interference reaches a predefined threshold (the default is 10 percent), a trap message is sent to the Cisco WCS. When there is interference, the WLC attempts to rearrange channel assignments to increase system performance.

- **Dynamic transmit power control**: The Cisco WLC dynamically controls AP transmit power based on real-time WLAN conditions. In normal instances, power can be kept low to gain extra capacity and reduce interference. The Cisco WLC attempts to balance APs such that they see their neighbors at –65 dBm (a number based on best-practices experience). If a failed AP is detected, power can be automatically increased on surrounding APs to fill the gap created by the loss in coverage.

- **Coverage hole detection and correction**: Coverage holes are areas where clients cannot receive a signal from the wireless network. If clients on an AP are detected at low received signal strength indicator levels, Cisco lightweight APs send a coverage hole alarm to the Cisco WCS. This alarm indicates the existence of an area where clients are continually getting poor signal coverage without having a viable location to roam to. The Cisco WLC might also adjust AP power levels to correct the detected hole.

- **Client and network load balancing**: WLAN capacity is effective only if clients can be load-balanced in such a way that they take advantage of this capacity. The Cisco WLC provides a centralized view of client loads on all APs that can influence where new clients attach to the network. The Cisco UWN can be configured to proactively "herd" existing clients to new APs to improve WLAN performance, resulting in a smooth distribution of capacity across the network.

RF Grouping

<table>
<tr>
<td>**KEY POINT**</td>
<td>An *RF group* is a cluster of WLC devices that coordinate their dynamic RRM calculations on a per 802.11 physical layer (PHY) type. Clustering WLCs into RF groups allows the dynamic RRM algorithms to scale beyond a single WLC and span building floors, buildings, and even campuses.</td>
</tr>
</table>

An RF domain exists for each 802.11 PHY type. RF groups are formed with the following process, as shown in Figure 9-21:

1. Lightweight APs periodically send neighbor messages over the air that include the WLC IP address and a hashed MIC derived from the time stamp, the AP's BSSID, and a shared secret. WLCs are configured with an RF domain name parameter; this parameter is pushed down to all the APs joined to the WLC and is used by the APs as the shared secret for generating the hashed MIC in the neighbor messages.

2. APs sharing the same secret can validate messages from each other via the MIC. When APs on different WLCs hear validated neighbor messages at a signal strength of –80 dBm or stronger, they inform their WLCs; the WLCs dynamically form an RF group.

3. The members or controllers of an RF group elect an RF group leader to maintain a "master" power and channel scheme for the RF group. The RF group leader analyzes real-time radio data collected by the system and calculates the master power and channel plan. The RRM algorithms try to optimize at a signal strength of –65 dBm between all APs and to avoid 802.11 cochannel interference and contention as well as non-802.11 interference. The RRM algorithms employ dampening calculations to minimize systemwide dynamic changes. The end result is dynamically calculated, near-optimal power and channel planning that is responsive to an always-changing RF environment.

The RF group leader and members exchange RRM messages at a specified updated interval, 600 seconds by default. Between update intervals, the RF group leader sends keepalive messages to each of the RF group members and collects real-time RF data. These messages use UDP port 12214 for 802.11b/g and UDP port 12115 for 802.11a; therefore, these UDP ports must not be restricted by firewalls or filters between RF group members.

Figure 9-21 *RF Group Formation*

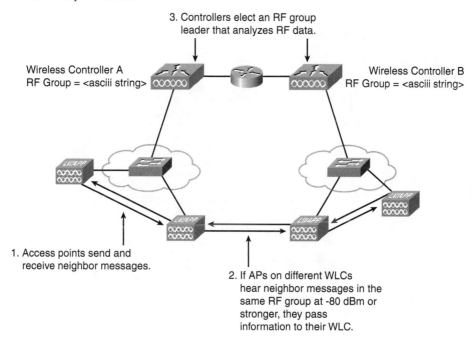

3. Controllers elect an RF group
leader that analyzes RF data.

Wireless Controller A
RF Group = <asciii string>

Wireless Controller B
RF Group = <asciii string>

1. Access points send and
receive neighbor messages.

2. If APs on different WLCs
hear neighbor messages in the
same RF group at -80 dBm or
stronger, they pass
information to their WLC.

AP Self-Healing

AP self-healing is another benefit of RRM. An AP is determined to be lost when the neighbor APs no longer see RF neighbor messages at –65 dBm from the AP. Lost neighbor APs are reported to the WLC. RRM automatically increases power levels and adjusts channel selection on surrounding APs to fill the gap created by the loss in coverage.

It is important to note that the system must be designed and installed with a greater AP density than is otherwise required to support self-healing capabilities. Specifically, APs must be placed so that the system has at least one power level available to step up to if RF self-healing is triggered. AP self-healing works only for APs configured to be in the same RF Group.

Cisco UWN Review

Figure 9-22 reviews the key concepts of the Cisco UWN design.

Figure 9-22 *Cisco UWN*

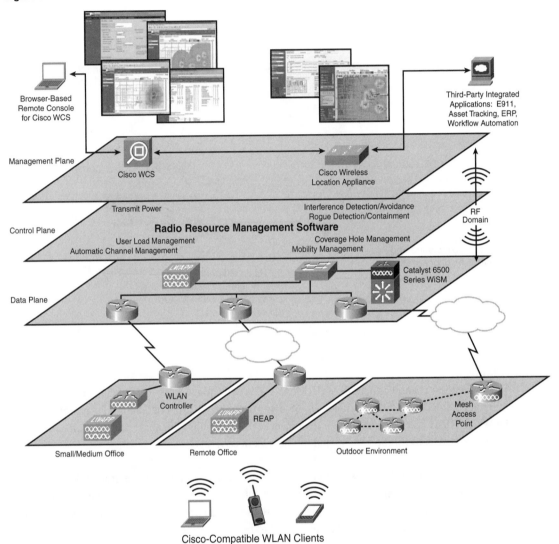

Cisco client devices or Cisco Compatible client devices are at the foundation of the UWN, connected to Cisco lightweight APs. The APs connect to Cisco WLCs.

In small and medium office environments, the WLCs are controller appliances. In larger enterprise offices, integrated controllers such as the Cisco WiSM or the Catalyst 3750G Integrated WLC switch could be used. Remote offices use REAP or H-REAP for connectivity to the enterprise network. Outdoor environments can be supported with mesh WLAN solutions.

At the control plane in the Cisco UWN is the RRM, which detects and adapts to changes in the air space in real time. These adjustments create the optimal topology for wireless networking.

Above the control plane is the management plane, which may contain the Cisco WCS and a Cisco wireless location appliance. The Cisco wireless location appliance can integrate with third-party applications such as asset tracking, enhanced 911 (E911), enterprise resource planning (ERP), and workflow automation.

Designing Wireless Networks with Lightweight Access Points and Wireless LAN Controllers

This section discusses design considerations for using lightweight APs and WLCs in various scenarios. RF site surveys and their importance in the design process are introduced first. Controller redundancy design is described, followed by considerations for WLAN design for guest services, outdoor wireless networks, campus wireless networks, and branch wireless networks.

RF Site Survey

This section reviews the reasons that an RF site survey is used in wireless network design, and the process to conduct such a survey. An RF site survey is the first step in the design and deployment of a wireless network, and the most important step to ensure desired operation. A site survey is a process by which the surveyor studies the facility to understand the RF characteristics in the environment, plans and reviews RF coverage areas, checks for RF interference, and determines the appropriate placement of wireless infrastructure devices.

In a wireless network, issues that can prevent the RF signal from reaching all parts of the facility include multipath distortion, hidden node problems, and near/far issues. To address these issues, the regions where these issues occur must be found. A site survey helps by defining the contours of RF coverage in a particular facility, discovering regions where multipath distortion can occur and areas where RF interference is high, and finding solutions to eliminate such issues.

Although the WCS can detect RF interference and optimize around it, it cannot analyze the RF interference to provide the information necessary to identify and locate the source. A spectrum analysis tool, such as Cognio Spectrum Expert, can classify the interference, determine its impact on the network, and enable the administrator to physically locate the source of interference and take action.

NOTE   Information on Cognio Spectrum Expert is available at http://www.cognio.com/.

A site survey that determines the RF coverage area in a facility also helps to determine the number of wireless infrastructure devices required and where they should be deployed such that an organization's business requirements are met.

RF Site Survey Process

Typical steps in an RF site survey process include the following:

Step 1   **Define customer requirements**: This includes the number and type of wireless devices to support, the sites where such devices will be located, and the service levels expected. Peak requirements, such as support for conference rooms, should also be identified. APs should be placed to support the locations and numbers of WLAN clients.

Step 2   **Identify coverage areas and user density**: Obtain a facility diagram, and visually inspect the facility to identify the potential RF obstacles. Identify areas that might have a large number of users, such as conference rooms, and the areas that are not used as heavily, such as stairwells.

Step 3   **Determine preliminary AP locations**: AP location information includes the availability of power, wired network access, cell coverage and overlap, channel selection, and mounting locations and antenna type.

Step 4   **Perform the actual survey**: The actual survey verifies the AP locations. Be sure to use the same AP model for the survey that is in use or will be used in the network. During the survey, relocate APs as needed, and retest.

Step 5   **Document the findings**: Record the locations and log signal readings and data rates at the outer boundaries of the WLAN.

These steps are expanded on in the following sections.

Define the Customer Requirements

As part of defining the customer requirements, the following questions should be asked:

1. What type and number of wireless devices need to be supported? Here are some considerations:

    a. Is existing WLAN or RF equipment in place? Existing WLAN equipment will need to be integrated, and the impact of existing RF devices should be mitigated.

    b. Will the WLAN be used only for data, or will wireless phones also be supported? If wireless phones will be used, the wireless network needs to be built with better receive signal strength to support the required QoS.

    c. Are there peak periods to support? For example, use of wireless services in a conference room will peak during meetings.

2. Will users be stationary or on the move while using the WLAN? If users are mobile, high-quality hand-offs during client roaming are required.

3. Where should wireless coverage be supported? How many buildings, floors, and areas should be supported? Are outdoor bridged links needed?

4. What level of support should be provided? What level of redundancy and self-healing is needed in the wireless infrastructure?

The answers to these questions are important to defining the scope of the wireless infrastructure design.

Identify Coverage Areas and User Density

Part of the site survey report should include a floor plan showing coverage areas and areas that the customer has defined as no-coverage areas. A sample floor plan is shown in Figure 9-23. The floor plan provides the customer, installer, and troubleshooter with some indication of what coverage each AP should be providing. The expected density of the wireless devices, which might be one or two per office and 20 or more per conference room, should be identified.

Figure 9-23   *Identify Coverage Areas on a Floor Plan*

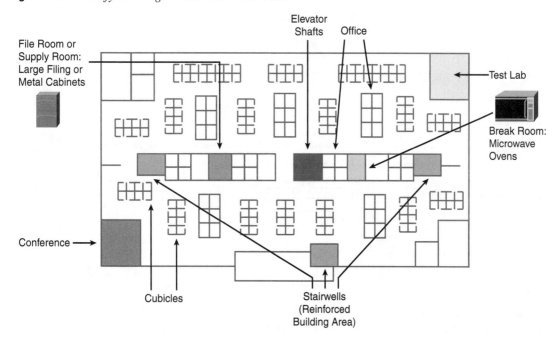

KEY	In general, an AP can support approximately seven to eight wireless phones or about 20
POINT	data-only devices.

The facility should be visually inspected to identify potential issues, such as metal racks, elevator shafts, stairwells, and microwave equipment.

Determine Preliminary AP Locations

The next step in the RF site survey process is to identify preliminary AP locations based on the planned coverage area and user density. This step can be supported with several tools. For example, you can import real floor plans and assign RF characteristics to building components in the Cisco WCS to increase design accuracy. WCS has a planning mode feature that estimates how many APs are needed for a given floor in a building, based on the floor plan; an example is provided in Figure 9-24. When predicting range and coverage, the planning mode feature takes into account the following:

■ Protocol in use: 802.11b/g or 802.11a

■ Coverage or capacity

■ Throughput required

■ Number of square feet

Figure 9-24 *Preliminary AP Locations Are Based on the Floor Plan*

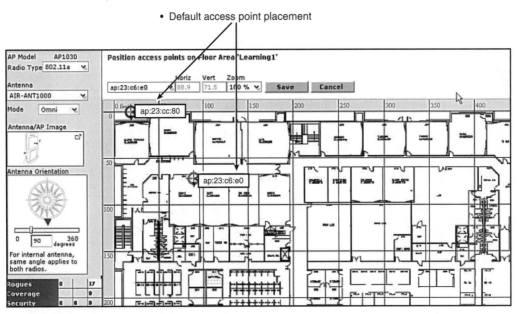

NOTE Recall that, after implementation, the Cisco UWN can adjust power and channels so that APs create the least amount of interference with each other.

The WCS can be used to estimate the quantity and preliminary locations of APs at the start of a site survey. This approach is most successful in simple carpeted office environments that are less RF-challenging than other environments, such as warehouses.

The Cisco WCS also provides an integrated RF prediction tool that can be used to visualize the detailed WLAN design, including lightweight AP placement, configuration, and performance/coverage estimates. Graphical heat maps, as illustrated in Figure 9-25, help IT staff visualize anticipated WLAN behavior for easier planning and faster rollout. A heat map diagrammatically represents signal strength—the warmer the color, the stronger the signal.

Figure 9-25 *Heat Maps Help Visualize Coverage*

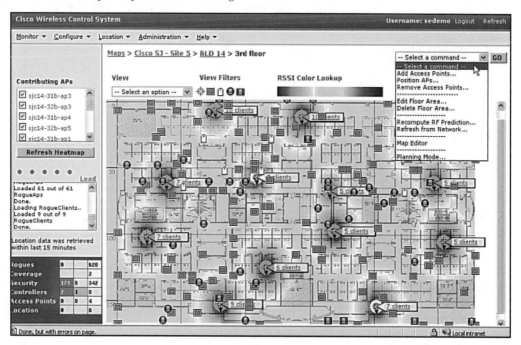

NOTE   The accuracy of this heat map greatly depends on the effort spent adjusting RF loss characteristics of building components such as walls, solid doors, and stairways.

Perform the Actual Survey

The next step in the process is to conduct the actual survey to determine the coverage based on the planned AP locations. The process to determine the coverage characteristics of an enterprise office site includes the following:

1. Measure the radius of the coverage area for a given data rate.

2. Move from the corner to the edge of the coverage area, and measure the data rate.

3. Determine the coverage range behind stairwells, offices, supply rooms, cubicles, and so on.

4. With as many APs as available, build the planned wireless coverage.

5. Establish nonoverlapping channels as often as possible to reduce contention.

6. Repeat this process until all the required coverage areas are set up.

A tool, such as AirMagnet Survey PRO, can be used to perform a manual site survey; results include the following:

- Signal strength

- Noise level

- Signal-to-noise ratio

- Channel interference

- Data rate

- Retry rate

- Loss rate

NOTE AirMagnet Survey PRO information is available at http://www.airmagnet.com/.

A free tool available for Cisco 802.11a/b/g client cards is the Cisco Aironet Site Survey Utility. The following information is provided by the tool:

- AP IP and MAC address

- Channel

- Signal strength

- Noise level

- Signal-to-noise ratio

- Link speed

NOTE Information about the Aironet Site Survey Utility is available at http://www.cisco.com/en/US/products/hw/wireless/ps4555/products_installation_and_configuration_guide_chapter09186a0080796b85.html.

Coverage holes are areas where clients cannot receive a signal from the wireless network. When deploying a network, there is a trade-off between the cost of the initial network deployment and the percentage of coverage hole areas. A reasonable goal for launch is to have between 2 and 10 percent coverage holes; in other words, between two and ten test locations out of 100 random test locations might receive marginal service. After launch, RRM identifies these coverage areas and reports them to the WCS, allowing the network manager to correct the holes, based on user demand.

Document the Findings

After completing the site survey, the final step in the process is to document the findings. A proper site survey report provides detailed information that includes customer requirements, AP coverage, interference sources, equipment placement, power considerations, and wiring requirements. The site survey documentation serves as a guide for the wireless network design, and for the installation and verification of the wireless communication infrastructure. The site survey report should also contain a list of the parts that will be needed, including the following:

- The total number of APs, and a recommendation that a spare be kept on hand in case of emergency

- The total number and type of antennas required and how they will be mounted

- Any proposed accessories and network components

The site survey report should include diagrams showing the facility, AP locations and coverage, and proposed cable runs. Covered areas, as well as those not needing coverage, should be indicated. Whenever possible, include photographs of the planned AP location or proposed antenna installation to make it very clear how and where the equipment should be installed. The tools and methods used for the site survey should be described.

If wireless voice support is required, the site survey methodology needs to be enhanced to plan for voice coverage and capacity. For example, wireless data is less susceptible to disruption than wireless voice when it comes to cell overlap, RF noise, and packet delay. Therefore, surveying for wireless voice coverage requires more effort and time than for data-only coverage at the same site.

> **NOTE** Further discussion of site surveys to support voice over WLANs is available in *Design Principles for Voice over WLAN* at http://www.cisco.com/en/US/netsol/ns340/ns394/ns348/networking_solutions_white_paper0900aecd804f1a46.shtml.

Controller Redundancy Design

Recall that the AP discovery and join decision process first looks for a defined primary, secondary, or tertiary WLC (as specified by the controller's sysName). An AP's second choice is to join a

WLC configured as a master controller. This is typically used only on initial AP deployment to find an initial controller, at which time the AP should be configured with its deterministic controllers.

The last choice in the AP join decision algorithm is to try to dynamically choose a WLC based on the greatest availability for AP associations. Using this process, WLCs can support either dynamic or deterministic redundancy.

Dynamic Controller Redundancy

The LWAPP protocol supports dynamic controller load balancing and redundancy. In the controller LWAPP Discovery Response, the WLC embeds information about its current AP load (defined as the number of APs joined to it at the time), its AP capacity, and the number of wireless clients connected to the controller.

With dynamic load balancing, an AP attempts to join the least-loaded controller, defined as the controller with the greatest available AP capacity. Dynamic load balancing works best when the controllers are clustered in a centralized design.

This dynamic load balancing can also be the basis for a dynamic controller redundancy scheme. Recall that when an AP misses a heartbeat acknowledgment from a WLC, the AP resends the heartbeat messages up to five times at 1-second intervals. If no acknowledgment is received after five retries, the AP declares the controller unreachable, releases and renews its IP address, and looks for a new controller. The advantages of dynamic controller redundancy are that it is easy to deploy and configure, and that APs dynamically load-balance across WLCs. Disadvantages include the following:

- More intercontroller roaming

- More operational challenges because of the unpredictability of traffic patterns

- Longer failover times (than with deterministic redundancy)

With dynamic load balancing, the APs can join controllers in no particular order or sequence, which might be acceptable if there are not many roaming clients. However, if many clients are roaming, many intercontroller roaming events can have a potential impact on aggregate network performance.

Traffic patterns from wireless clients are unpredictable, making it difficult to implement stateful security mechanisms in the infrastructure and take advantage of some other security features in Cisco switches. For example, if the APs are enabled sequentially with dynamic redundancy, the network can develop a "salt and pepper" AP design, where adjacent APs are joined to different controllers, as shown in Figure 9-26. Every odd-numbered AP is joined to WLC1, and every even-numbered AP is joined to WLC2. In theory, this design provides for dynamic traffic load-balancing across WLCs and coverage redundancy in the event of a WLC failure. However, in actual practice, this type of design can result in a large number of intercontroller roaming events and therefore generally is not widely recommended or deployed.

Figure 9-26   *Dynamic WLC Redundancy May Result in a "Salt and Pepper" Design*

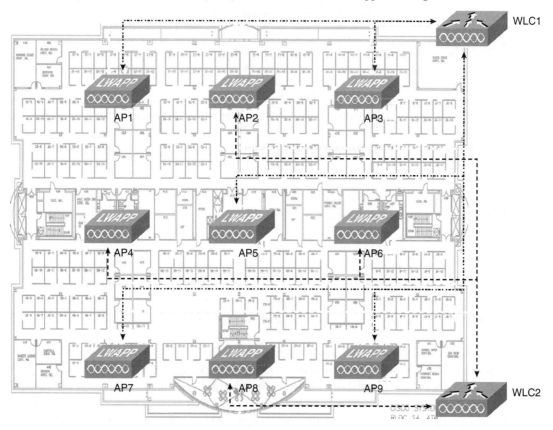

> **NOTE**   LAG supports dynamic controller redundancy.

Deterministic Controller Redundancy

With deterministic controller redundancy, the network administrator statically configures a primary, a secondary, and, optionally, a tertiary controller. Advantages of using deterministic controller redundancy include the following:

■ Predictability (easier operational management)

■ Higher network stability

■ More flexible and powerful redundancy design options

■ Faster failover times

■ Fallback option in the case of failover

When an AP determines, from missed heartbeat acknowledgments, that its primary controller is unreachable, it attempts to join the secondary controller. If the AP fails to join the secondary controller, it attempts to join the tertiary controller. If the primary, secondary, and tertiary controllers are not available, the AP resorts to the dynamic LWAPP algorithms to connect to the least-loaded available controller.

KEY POINT | Failover to a defined secondary or tertiary controller is more rapid than dynamic failover to the least-loaded controller.

With this process, the network administrator can deterministically predict the results of an AP reassociation, resulting in easier operational management of the WLAN. The network can be designed for WLC infrastructure redundancy, and extra capacity on the secondary and tertiary controllers can be provisioned to be available in the event of catastrophic WLC failures.

WLCs have a configurable parameter for AP fallback. When the WLC AP fallback option is enabled, APs return to their primary controllers when the primary controller comes back online after a failover event. This feature is enabled by default, and some administrators choose to leave the AP fallback default value in place. However, when an AP falls back to its primary controller, there is a brief window of time, usually approximately 30 seconds, during which service to wireless clients is interrupted because the APs are rejoining the primary WLC. Also, if connectivity to the primary WLC has become unstable for some reason, the AP might "flap" back and forth between a primary and the backup WLCs. Many WLAN administrators prefer to disable the AP fallback option and move the APs back to the primary WLC in a controlled manner, during a scheduled service window.

A disadvantage of deterministic controller redundancy is that it requires more upfront planning and configuration. The configuration of primary, secondary, and tertiary WLCs can be performed somewhat laboriously on each AP, or more easily using templates with the Cisco WCS.

Figure 9-27 shows three APs configured with primary, secondary, and tertiary WLCs. If WLC-B fails, its attached AP connects to WLC-C. If WLC-A fails while WLC-B is down, its APs connect to WLC-C.

Figure 9-27 *Deterministic WLC Redundancy*

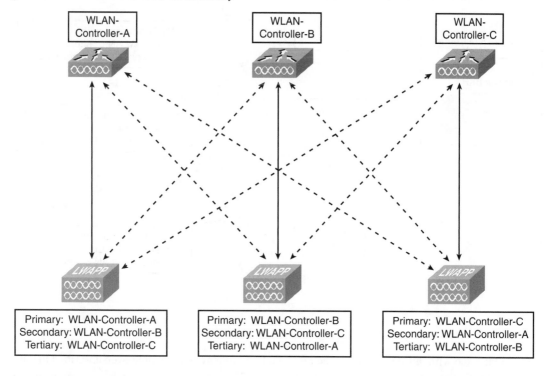

<table>
<tr><td>Primary: WLAN-Controller-A
Secondary: WLAN-Controller-B
Tertiary: WLAN-Controller-C</td><td>Primary: WLAN-Controller-B
Secondary: WLAN-Controller-C
Tertiary: WLAN-Controller-A</td><td>Primary: WLAN-Controller-C
Secondary: WLAN-Controller-A
Tertiary: WLAN-Controller-B</td></tr>
</table>

KEY POINT Cisco recommends using deterministic controller redundancy with predefined primary, secondary, and tertiary controllers, rather than using dynamic controller redundancy.

Deterministic Redundancy Options

There are three options for the design of deterministic controller redundancy, as described in the following sections.

N + 1 Redundancy Design

KEY POINT | In an N + 1 configuration, the one redundant controller in a network operations center (NOC) or data center acts as a backup for multiple other WLCs.

This scenario is illustrated in Figure 9-28. Each AP is configured with a WLC as primary; all APs are configured with the one redundant controller as secondary.

Figure 9-28 *N + 1 Deterministic WLC Redundancy*

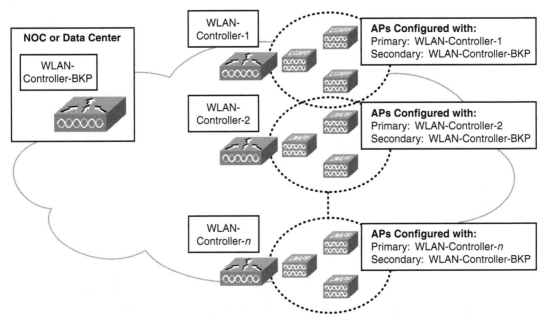

One issue with this design is that the redundant controller could become oversubscribed in the unlikely event of multiple primary WLC failures. When a WLC has reached the maximum number of joined APs, it does not accept any more LWAPP Join requests. Consequently, if the backup WLC becomes oversubscribed, some APs might not be able to join with a WLC. Therefore, when designing an N + 1 redundant solution, you should assess the risks of multiple WLC failures and the consequences of an oversubscribed backup WLC.

N + N Redundancy Design

KEY POINT | In an N + N redundancy configuration, N controllers back up N controllers.

For example, Figure 9-29 has two controllers. Some of the APs are configured with controller A as primary and controller B as secondary; the other APs are configured to use controller B as primary and controller A as secondary.

Figure 9-29 *N + N Deterministic WLC Redundancy*

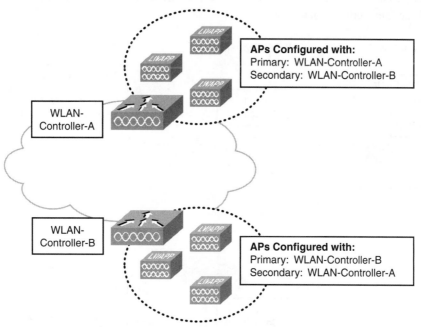

In this design, the AP capacity across both controllers should be balanced. APs should also be logically grouped on controllers to minimize intercontroller roaming events. For example, in a four-floor building with two redundant controllers, the APs on floors 1 and 2 could be configured to use one controller as primary and the APs on floors 3 and 4 could be configured to use the other controller as primary. Enough excess capacity must be provisioned on each controller to handle a failover situation.

N + N +1 Redundancy Design

KEY POINT In an N + N + 1 redundancy configuration, N controllers back up N controllers as secondary, and one additional controller backs up all N controllers as tertiary.

For example, in Figure 9-30 some of the APs are configured with controller A as primary and controller B as secondary; the other APs are configured with controller B as primary and controller A as secondary. All the APs are configured to use the same backup controller as tertiary. Typically, the primary and secondary controllers are placed at the network distribution level, and the single tertiary controller is placed in a NOC or data center. Multiple distribution blocks can be configured with the same tertiary controller.

Figure 9-30 *N + N + 1 Deterministic WLC Redundancy*

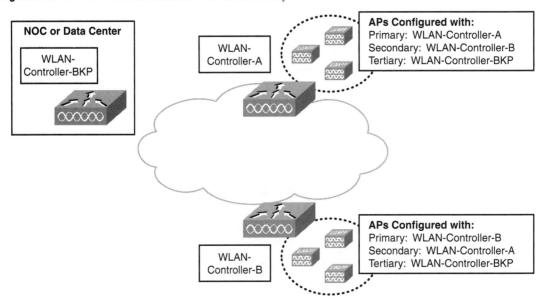

When selecting a redundancy option, consider the risks of WLC failure and the service level agreement (SLA) required to be maintained by the WLAN. The higher the SLA, the more robust redundancy scheme your designed solution should provide.

Design Considerations for Guest Services in Wireless Networks

Providing wireless guest services with traditional autonomous APs poses significant challenges. To maintain internal corporate network security, guest traffic must be restricted to the appropriate subnet and VLAN; these guest VLANs must extend throughout the infrastructure to reach every location where guest access is required. Reconfiguring of the access switches that serve conference rooms, offices, and cubicles to selectively adjust VLANs for guest access can involve many network staff hours.

The Cisco UWN supports simplified configuration and deployment of guest access for customers, vendors, and partners through deployment of lightweight APs. In a basic scenario, WLCs centralize the configuration and management of the APs and segregate internal user traffic from guest user traffic with VLANs. With this architecture, VLAN and subnet configuration occurs only at the wired network where the controller is connected, as shown in Figure 9-31. The result is a dramatic reduction in time to configure the network.

Figure 9-31   *Supporting Basic Guest Access*

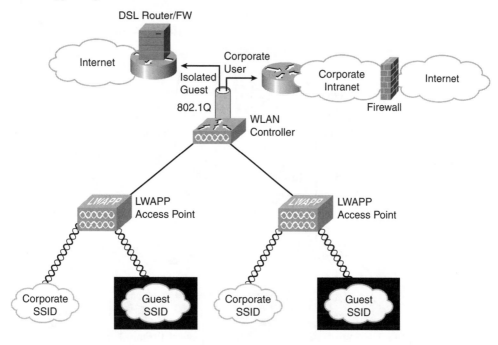

If the guest network SSID is the only one broadcast, unauthorized users might make fewer attempts to access the internal private WLANs. To increase security, the Cisco UWN ensures that all clients gain access within the number of attempts specified by the administrator. Should a client fail to gain access within that limit, it is automatically excluded (blocked from access) until the administrator-set timer expires.

In this scenario, however, traffic isolation is provided by VLANs, only up to the switch to which the controller is connected. For many enterprises, guest traffic isolation via a VLAN may not provide a sufficient level of security.

In such cases, the Cisco UWN can provide path isolation using a Layer 2 (EtherIP) tunnel to direct all guest traffic to a WLC dedicated to guest services (called the *anchor WLC*) in a demilitarized zone (DMZ), a secured network zone between the private (inside) network and a public (outside) network. EtherIP tunnels logically segment and transport the guest traffic between Edge and Anchor WLCs, whereas other traffic (for example, employee traffic) is still locally bridged on the corresponding VLAN. This scenario is illustrated in Figure 9-32.

Figure 9-32 *Guest Access Path Isolation Using an EtherIP Tunnel*

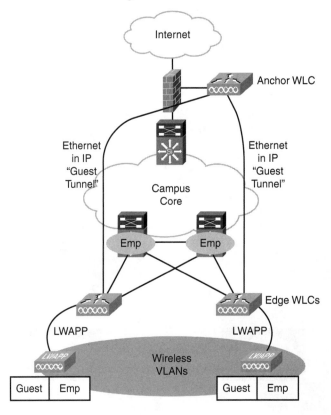

The guest VLANs do not need to be defined on the switches connected to the edge controllers; the original Ethernet frame from the guest client is maintained across the LWAPP and EtherIP tunnels to the anchor WLC. This WLC applies the appropriate policies before Internet access is granted. Corporate wireless use policies are managed by the WLCs internal to the enterprise.

NOTE   EtherIP tunnels are supported across all Cisco WLCs. The 2006 WLC, however, cannot anchor the EtherIP connections.

Path isolation allows the guest traffic to be separated and differentiated from the corporate internal traffic and to be securely transported across the internal network infrastructure.

Design Considerations for Outdoor Wireless Networks

Traditional outdoor wireless deployment options include point-to-point or point-to-multipoint bridging between buildings. Outdoor wireless mesh is a relatively new option in which the APs are connected in a mesh with many redundant connections between nodes. Figure 9-33 illustrates these options.

Figure 9-33   *Outdoor Wireless Options*

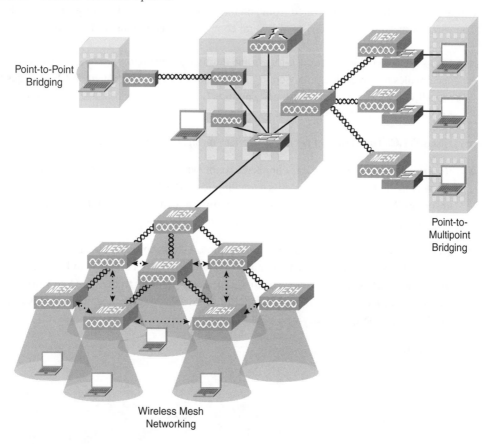

Mesh APs discover each other automatically and select the best path through the mesh for maximizing system capacity and minimizing latency. APs continuously communicate with other nodes in the mesh, evaluating the potential of each link to improve performance. If a link degrades, the AP determines whether a better path exists and routes traffic through a more optimal node. A mesh network eliminates the need to wire every AP in the network, making it easier and more cost-effective to extend the network's reach. It is easy to connect an existing indoor wired or wireless network with the outdoor mesh network so that users can roam from one area to another without reconnecting. Perhaps more importantly, administrators can set up one access policy that works across all environments, increasing security and making the systemwide network infrastructure more manageable.

Wireless Mesh Components

A mesh network consists of two or more indoor or outdoor Cisco LWAPP-enabled mesh APs, communicating with each other over one or more wireless hops (using 802.11a) to join multiple LANs or to extend IEEE 802.11b/g wireless coverage. Cisco LWAPP-enabled mesh APs are configured, monitored, and operated from and through any Cisco WLC deployed in the network. The wireless mesh solution consists of several components, as illustrated in Figure 9-34:

- **Cisco WCS**: WCS includes easy-to-use and intuitive software for wireless mesh management and enables networkwide policy configuration and device management. WCS provides the overall view of the wireless mesh and supports Simple Network Management Protocol and Syslog.

- **Cisco WLC**: The WLC connects the wireless mesh APs to the wired network.

- **Rooftop APs (RAP)**: A RAP is connected to the wired network and serves as the root or gateway to the wired network. As its name implies, a RAP is typically located on a rooftop or tower. A RAP uses wireless 802.11a to communicate with up to 32 neighboring poletop mesh APs (MAP).

- **Poletop MAPs**: The poletop MAPs are the remote APs that provide 802.11b/g wireless client access. MAPs are typically located on top of a pole such as a lamppost and connect through a separate 802.11a wireless interface to a RAP as the gateway to the wired network. MAPs require AC or DC power and might support PoE. MAPs typically also have an Ethernet port for connecting peripheral devices, such as a camera.

Figure 9-34 *Outdoor Wireless Mesh Components*

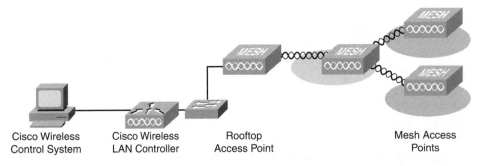

| Cisco Wireless Control System | Cisco Wireless LAN Controller | Rooftop Access Point | Mesh Access Points |

MAP-to-RAP Connectivity

The outdoor component of the Cisco wireless mesh networking solution is based on the Cisco Aironet 1500 Series, an outdoor Wi-Fi (802.11/a/b/g) mesh AP using Cisco's patent-pending Adaptive Wireless Path Protocol. The 1500 series uses a two-radio design where the radios have dedicated roles. One radio provides local access for client devices, and the second radio provides the wireless backhaul for network connectivity. The network's overall throughput is controlled by topology and path considerations in the mesh network.

During bootup, an AP tries to become a RAP if it is connected to the wired network. If a RAP loses its wired network connection, it attempts to become a MAP and searches for an appropriate RAP. By default, the backhaul interface (to the MAPs) on the RAP uses the 802.11a 5 GHz radio and is set to a speed of 18 Mbps. A RAP is the parent node to any bridging or mesh network and connects a bridge or mesh network to the wired network. By default, only one RAP can exist for any bridged or mesh network. A mesh algorithm enables APs to find the least-cost path back to the controller or RAP to minimize latency and maximize usable bandwidth. The algorithm takes into account total hop count and throughput at each hop to determine the best path back to a RAP.

> **KEY POINT** | MAPs do not have any wired connectivity to a WLC. MAPs can be completely wireless, supporting clients that are communicating with other MAPs or RAPs, or they can be wired and serve as a bridge to a remote wired network.

MAPs are typically installed in places where a wired connection cannot be provided, but power can be made available. The MAP provides IEEE 802.11b/g client access via the 2.4 GHz radio and connects wirelessly to the RAP via the 802.11a backhaul radio. MAPs can connect back to a RAP using one or multiple hops, thereby providing a broader coverage area than a typical wireless bridge device. Figure 9-35 illustrates a sample deployment.

Figure 9-35 *Sample MAP-to-RAP Connectivity*

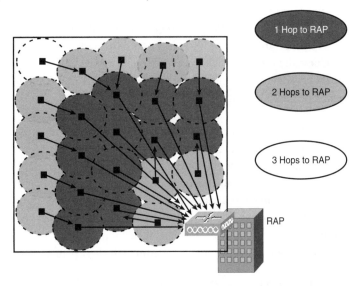

Mesh Design Recommendations

Figure 9-36 illustrates the throughput in a mesh network. Notice that each hop reduces the throughput by half because the data has to be re-sent across the same half-duplex network. The MAP connection back to the RAP can support eight hops on a 1500 Series AP, although Cisco recommends four or fewer hops for best performance because each hop can add 1 to 3 ms of latency.

Figure 9-36 *Wireless Mesh Throughput*

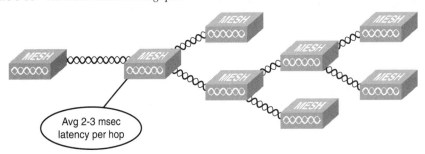

HOPS	One	Two	Three	Four
Throughput	~10 Mbps	~5 Mbps	~3 Mbps	up to 1 Mbps

RAPs can connect up to 32 MAPs. Cisco recommends connecting only 20 to 25 MAPs to a RAP; a maximum of 20 MAPs provides the best performance.

Design Considerations for Campus Wireless Networks

This section reviews design considerations for enterprise campus wireless networks.

Common Wireless Design Questions

To develop an enterprise campus wireless network design, the following questions need to be answered:

- **How many APs are needed?** Sufficient APs to provide RF coverage, with the required features to support the wireless clients, are needed. Different APs have different features, including internal or external antenna, single or dual radios, and number of devices supported. Optimally, deploy more APs than indicated by the client density requirements to allow for overdeployment and to ensure seamless coverage and future higher capacity. For example, a few extra APs can be used to cover unforeseen coverage holes or as spares. The Cisco UWN compensates for RF overlap.

- **Where should the APs be located?** The APs should be located where WLAN clients will be located. APs should be placed in central locations that can cover several walled offices or cubicle areas. APs typically are not as effective deployed in a wiring closet as when placed close to users. An AP deployed in a meeting room can support peak wireless requirements during a meeting better than an AP in an adjacent hallway that might also be used for day-to-day office requirements.

- **How will the APs receive power?** PoE is typically used to minimize power cabling requirements for APs, especially those mounted on ceilings. Traditional power sources can also be used.

- **How many WLCs will be needed?** The number of APs that a controller can support varies depending on the selected controller. Enough controllers to support the required number of APs and provide redundancy as dictated by the location's reliability requirements should be provisioned. Higher redundancy is needed for mission-critical applications and voice over wireless.

- **Where should the WLCs be located?** WLCs should be located in a secure area such as a wiring closet or data center. Placing WLCs in multiple wiring closets improves reliability in the event of a power loss to one wiring closet.

KEY POINT | Remember, a WLC is connected to the wired LAN and to the lightweight APs by wires. The WLC does not have any wireless connections.

Controller Placement Design

WLCs in the enterprise campus can be placed in the distribution layer or centralized in the core layer. As much as possible, controllers should be placed to minimize intercontroller roaming and traffic flow latency over the wireless media. LWAPP tunneling separates the physical controller placement from the subnets so that the WLCs can be positioned where they are connected, secured, and powered, and where traffic flows work well. As noted earlier, controllers should be deployed using deterministic redundancy to avoid unnecessary intercontroller roaming that results from dynamic redundancy.

Although distributed controller deployment might work well with existing networks or focused wireless coverage areas, the general recommendation from Cisco is to use a centralized design for controller placement to minimize operational complexity and support. However, the decision should be based on the design's capability to support the current network and policies as well as future growth plans.

Figure 9-37 illustrates a distributed WLC design with the APs in the access layer and WLCs in the distribution layer. The distributed WLC design can easily support coverage areas that are isolated by building and where mobility between buildings is not implemented.

Figure 9-37 *Sample Distributed WLCs Design*

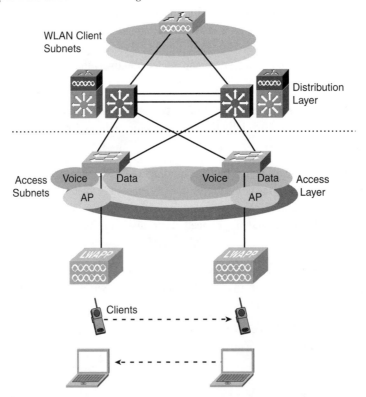

Figure 9-38 illustrates a centralized WLC design with the APs in the access layer and WLCs in a service block in the core layer. The centralized WLC design provides simplified management with fewer endpoints and fewer locations to manage for issues such as high availability, routing, and power needs. A centralized WLC design also supports the most efficient mobility.

Figure 9-38 *Sample Centralized WLCs Design*

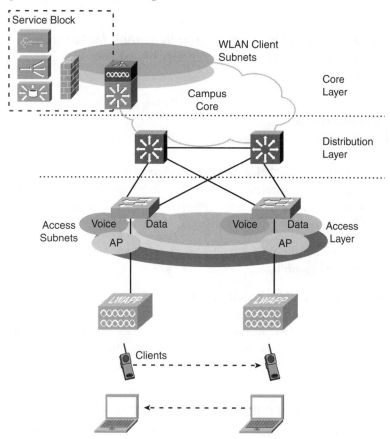

Campus Controller Options

Depending on the size of the campus and whether integration with Layer 3 infrastructure devices is desired, one of two categories of WLCs is typically deployed in the enterprise campus.

Appliance controllers from the Cisco 4400 Series can be used to support from 6 to 100 APs. These controllers can support from 40 to 2000 wireless devices, depending on the mix of data and voice clients. Layer 3 routing would need to be supported on another platform, not on the 4400 WLC. Recall that WLC appliances connect to the enterprise network over an 802.1Q trunk.

Controllers integrated in Layer 3 devices such as the Cisco Catalyst 3750G Switch with integrated WLC (for small to medium deployments or an individual building) or the Cisco Catalyst WiSM (for medium to large deployments) support a centralized design and control 25 to 300 APs. In this case, Layer 3 routing can be supported on the same platform. Recall that the integrated controllers support Layer 2 connections internally and can use Layer 2 or Layer 3 connections to the wired enterprise network.

Design Considerations for Branch Office Wireless Networks

This section reviews design considerations for branch wireless network design, including REAP and H-REAP.

Branch Office Considerations

The following are several key design considerations for branch office wireless networks:

- **How many APs are needed, and what are their requirements?** Recall that, generally, an AP can support 7 to 8 wireless phones or 20 or more data-only devices. Ports must be available on the local switch to connect the APs to the wired network. Power to the APs, either through PoE or traditional power cabling, is also required.

- **What is the cost of the WLC?** It might not be economically feasible for small sites to implement local controllers.

- **What are the bandwidth requirements?** Sufficient bandwidth to support the required wireless traffic is needed. If a centralized controller supports branch office APs, the RTT latency between the APs and the WLC should not exceed 200 ms, and only REAPs or H-REAPs should be used, as discussed in the upcoming "REAP" and "Hybrid REAP" sections.

Local MAC

Recall that in a typical LWAPP deployment, the AP MAC functions are split between the lightweight AP and the WLC. LWAPP also supports a local MAC feature in which the full 802.11 functionality is on the lightweight AP; this solution might be appropriate for branch wireless deployments.

With local MAC, the AP provides the MAC management support for association requests and actions. Local MAC allows for the decoupling of the data plane from the control path by terminating all client traffic at the AP's wired port. This allows direct wireless access to resources local to the AP and provides link resiliency because wireless service persists if the LWAPP control path (between the AP and the controller) goes down. This functionality is particularly useful in small remote and branch offices across WAN links where only few APs are needed and the cost of a local controller is not justified. Table 9-7 summarizes the lightweight AP and WLC MAC functions with the local MAC feature; compare this to Table 9-3.

Table 9-7 *Local MAC Lightweight AP and WLC MAC Functions*

Lightweight AP MAC Functions	WLC MAC Functions
802.11: Beacons, probe response	802.11 Proxy association requests and actions
802.11 Control: Packet acknowledgment and transmission	802.11e Resource reservation
802.11e: Frame queuing and packet prioritization	802.11i Authentication and key management
802.11i: MAC layer data encryption/decryption	
802.11 MAC management: Association requests and actions	

REAP

Connecting lightweight APs to a WLC over a WAN is not recommended unless a REAP or H-REAP is used.

KEY POINT | A *REAP* is a lightweight AP designed to be controlled across WAN links. The LWAPP controller timers are extended on a REAP.

The Cisco 1030 series APs are Cisco first-generation REAP devices (versus the second-generation H-REAP devices described in the next section). REAP capabilities allow a lightweight AP to be deployed remotely from the WLC, to extend wireless management and control support to branch office and small retail locations.

The 1030 series AP is a superset of the 1010 and 1020 APs that can operate as a campus access point or as a REAP device and that delivers the same LAN security, performance, and RF management capabilities as the campus 1010 and 1020 APs. The 1030 AP can operate via most standard WAN technologies, including T1, Frame Relay, and so forth, enabling IT managers to centrally control SSIDs, security parameters, and software loads for unified, enterprise-wide WLAN services.

With a REAP, all control traffic is LWAPP-encapsulated and sent to a Cisco WLC, as it is with other APs. With a REAP, however, client data traffic is not LWAPP-encapsulated, but is locally bridged onto the WAN.

All management control and RF management are available when the WAN link is up and connectivity is available to a Cisco WLC. The REAP continues to provide connectivity to local wireless clients and local network resources if the WAN goes down.

First-generation REAP devices do have a few limitations (which are addressed by H-REAP devices):

- The Cisco 1030 series AP does not support 802.1Q trunking. All WLANs terminate on a single local VLAN/subnet.

- With connectivity to the controller, the Cisco 1030 series APs support multiple (up to 16) WLANs. During a WAN outage, the AP goes into standalone mode, and all WLANs except the first WLAN configured on the AP, WLAN 1, are disabled and unavailable. Therefore, multiple WLANs are not recommended.

- With REAP devices, only Layer 2 security using WEP or WPA-PSK is supported in standalone mode. Layer 3 security polices are not supported on REAP devices.

- REAPs and clients require a routable IP address, but the embedded Cisco WLC DHCP server is not supported; a local DHCP server must provide IP addresses locally. Network address translation (NAT) is also not supported.

Hybrid REAP

An H-REAP is another option for branch office and remote office deployments. An H-REAP is an enhancement to a REAP that enables customers to configure and control two or three APs in a branch or remote office from the corporate office through a WAN link without deploying a controller in each office. The H-REAPs can switch client data traffic locally and perform client authentication locally when their connection to the controller is lost. When they are connected to the controller, they can also send traffic back to the controller.

An H-REAP supports simultaneous tunneling and local switching. Local switching bridges traffic onto local VLANs, whereas central switching tunnels traffic to a WLC. An H-REAP provides more security options than a REAP for the remote site:

- **Standalone mode**: When the H-REAP cannot reach the WLC, it goes into standalone mode and performs its own client authentication; WPA-PSK and WPA2-PSK are supported in standalone mode.

- **Connected mode**: When the H-REAP can reach the controller, it is in a connected state and gets help from the controller to complete client authentication. In connected mode, an H-REAP supports many client authentication protocols, including WPA-PSK, WPA2-PSK, VPNs, Layer 2 Tunneling Protocol, 802.1X EAP, and web authentication.

An H-REAP is more delay-sensitive than a REAP; round-trip latency must not exceed 200 ms between the AP and the controller, and LWAPP control packets must be prioritized over all other traffic. An H-REAP supports a one-to-one NAT configuration. It also supports port address translation for all features except true multicast. Multicast is supported across NAT boundaries when configured by using the Unicast option.

An H-REAP can be deployed with a static IP address or it can obtain its IP address via DHCP. The DHCP server must be available locally and must be able to provide the IP address for the H-REAP at bootup.

H-REAP is supported on all the LWAPP WLCs, but only on the 1130AG and 1240AG APs. Figure 9-39 illustrates a typical H-REAP deployment. H-REAP APs should be connected using trunk ports to support switched VLANs.

Figure 9-39 *H-REAP Allows APs to Be Remote from the WLC*

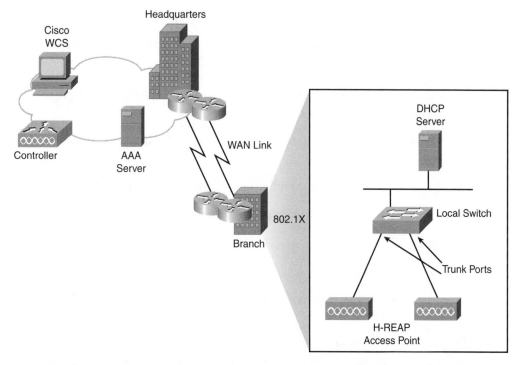

> **NOTE**   Although H-REAP functionality is limited to three units per site in Cisco UWN code version 4.0, an increase to six units might be available in a maintenance release. Refer to http://www.cisco.com/ documentation for the latest features and limitations of H-REAP.

Branch Office WLAN Controller Options

Depending on the size of the branch and whether integration with Layer 3 infrastructure devices is desired, one of two categories of WLCs is typically deployed in a branch office.

Appliance controllers such as the Cisco 2006 and the Cisco 4400 Series are often used to support six to 25 APs (although versions of the 4400 that support more APs are available). For example, the 4402-12 and 4402-25 could be used in a branch office to support 12 or 25 APs, respectively. These appliance controllers can support from 40 to 500 wireless devices, depending on the mix of data and voice clients. Depending on redundancy requirements, one or two routers would be needed for WAN connectivity to the enterprise network.

Controllers integrated in Layer 3 devices, such as the WLCM for ISRs or the integrated WLC for the Cisco Catalyst 3750G switch, also support six to 25 APs. WAN redundancy can be supported with another router or a pair of these devices.

Summary

In this chapter, you learned about the Cisco UWN architecture and wireless design principles. The following topics were explored:

■ An introduction to RF theory, including phenomena affecting RF signals, RF signal calculations, and types of RF antennas

■ The 802.11 standards, including the 802.11a/b/g half-duplex standards for wireless communication

■ WLAN components, including the differences between autonomous and lightweight APs

■ WLAN security, including authentication and encryption

■ The Cisco UWN, including lightweight APs, WLCs, and the WCS management application

■ LWAPP operation between the lightweight APs and WLCs, in Layer 2 or Layer 3 mode

■ The terminology related to and operation of WLCs, including how lightweight APs discover and join with WLCs

■ Mobility, the capability of end devices to move to new locations and remain networked, and roaming, when a wireless client moves its association from one AP and reassociates to another AP within the same SSID

■ The real-time RRM in the Cisco UWN, which continuously analyzes the existing RF environment and automatically adjusts the AP power and channel configurations

■ The RF site survey process and its importance in the design process

■ Controller redundancy design, both dynamic and the recommended deterministic redundancy with predefined primary, secondary, and tertiary controllers

■ Design considerations for using lightweight APs and WLCs in various scenarios, including for guest services, outdoor wireless networks, campus wireless networks, and branch wireless networks

References

For additional information, see the following resources:

■ Cisco Systems, Inc., Enterprise Mobility 3.0 Design Guide, http://www.cisco.com/univercd/cc/td/doc/solution/emblty30.pdf

■ Cisco Systems, Inc., Cisco UWN home page, http://www.cisco.com/go/unifiedwireless/

■ Cisco Systems, Inc., Cisco Wireless LAN Controller Configuration Guide, Release 4.0, http://www.cisco.com/en/US/products/ps6366/products_configuration_guide_book09186a008082d572.html

■ Cisco Systems, Inc., Cisco Wireless LAN Controller Configuration Guide, Release 4.1, http://www.cisco.com/en/US/products/ps6366/products_configuration_guide_chapter09186a 008082d712.html#wp1102312

■ Cisco Systems, Inc., Deploying Cisco 440X Series Wireless LAN Controllers, http://www.cisco.com/en/US/products/ps6366/prod_technical_reference09186a00806cfa96.html

■ Cisco Systems, Inc., Cisco Compatible Client Devices, http://www.cisco.com/web/partners/pr46/pr147/partners_pgm_partners_0900aecd800a7907.html

■ Cisco Systems, Inc., Cisco Wireless Control System home page, http://www.cisco.com/en/US/products/ps6305/index.html

■ Cisco Systems, Inc., Cisco Outdoor Wireless Network Solution home page, http://www.cisco.com/en/US/netsol/ns621/networking_solutions_package.html

■ Cisco Systems, Inc., Achieving Business Goals and Enhancing Customer Relationships with a Secure Guest Access Wi-Fi Network, http://www.cisco.com/en/US/products/ps6366/products_white_paper0900aecd8047180a.shtml

■ Cisco Systems, Inc., Cisco 4400 Series Wireless LAN Controllers, Cisco Centralized Wireless LAN Software Release 3.0, http://www.cisco.com/en/US/products/ps6366/prod_bulletin0900aecd802d2742.html

■ Cisco Systems, Inc., *Radio Resource Management Under Unified Wireless Networks*, http://www.cisco.com/en/US/tech/tk722/tk809/technologies_design_guide09186a0080 72c759tech_note09186a008072c759.shtml

Case Study: ACMC Hospital UWN Considerations

This case study is a continuation of the ACMC Hospital case study introduced in Chapter 2, "Applying a Methodology to Network Design."

Case Study General Instructions

Use the scenarios, information, and parameters provided at each task of the ongoing case study. If you encounter ambiguities, make reasonable assumptions and proceed. For all tasks, use the initial customer scenario and build on the solutions provided thus far.

You can use all documentation, books, white papers, and so on. In each step, you act as a network design consultant. Make creative proposals to accomplish the customer's business needs. Justify your ideas when they differ from the provided solutions. Use any design strategies you feel are appropriate. The final goal of each case study is a paper solution.

Appendix A, "Answers to Review Questions and Case Studies," provides a solution for each step based on assumptions made. There is no claim that the provided solution is the best or only solution. Your solution might be more appropriate for the assumptions you made. The provided solution helps you understand the author's reasoning and allows you to compare and contrast your solution.

In this case study you develop a high-level UWN design for the ACMC hospital network. A site survey is customarily required to determine RF propagation characteristics, select AP locations and antennas, look for interference (possibly a major factor in hospitals), and so forth. Hospitals also might have areas where radio signals would interfere with critical equipment; such areas must be protected from wireless AP signals. These specific hospital details are outside the scope of this book, but obviously they would have to be considered in a real hospital.

Assume that the site survey has been done, the results of which are summarized in Table 9-8. No sources of interference or RF prohibitions were discovered. For this design, assume that the wireless devices can be supported by the existing Ethernet ports. Notice that wireless coverage in the cafeteria on floor 1 of Main Building 1 has been added. The required ports in the remote clinics have also been added. The ACMC CIO has indicated no desire to implement any outdoor wireless support at this time.

Table 9-8 *ACMC Hospital RF Site Survey Results*

Building	Port Counts	Access Point Requirements	Total Number of APs Required
Main Building 1	150 per floor, 7 floors (plus server farm)	8 per floor, 7 floors (including the cafeteria) 4 in the server farm (for administrator convenience)	60
Main Building 2	150 per floor, 7 floors	8 per floor, 7 floors	56
Children's Place	120 per floor, 3 floors	6 per floor	18
Buildings A–D	20	1 per building, 4 buildings	4
Buildings E–J	40	2 per building, 6 buildings	12
Buildings K–L	80	4 per building, 2 buildings	8
Remote clinic 1	48	3	3
Remote clinics 2, 3	24	1 per building, 2 buildings	2
Remote clinics 4, 5	16	1 per building, 2 buildings	2
Total			165

Complete the following steps:

Step 1   Determine where to place controllers, how many of them to use, and which models to use. How will LWAPP WLC discovery be done? Justify your choices.

Step 2   The hospital wants to separate wireless traffic based on its three staff organizations: Financial, Medical, and Support. The intent is to enforce compliance with the U.S. Health Insurance Portability and Accountability Act (HIPAA) by allowing staff to authenticate to only the appropriate SSID based on the type of access they need. How does this affect your wireless design? What could you do to enforce the HIPAA access restrictions?

> **Step 3**   What IP addressing scheme will you use to support the WLANs? How will you modify or extend the IP addressing scheme to the various wireless groups?
>
> **Step 4**   What will your mobility group(s) be?
>
> **Step 5**   How will wireless for the remote clinics be handled?
>
> **Step 6**   How will secure guest wireless access be supported?

Review Questions

Answer the following questions, and then see Appendix A for the answers.

1. A client with a wireless NIC connects to the wired network through what type of device?

2. Describe the following natural phenomena that might affect RF signals:

   - Reflection

   - Refraction

   - Absorption

   - Scattering

   - Diffraction

   - Multipath

3. Fill in the blanks in the following sentences:

   Every gain of 3 dBm means that the power is _____. A loss of 3 dBm means that the power is _____.

   A gain of 10 dBm means that the power _____ by a factor of _____. A loss of 10 dBm means that the power _____ by a factor of _____.

4. If a 100 mW signal experiences a 9 dBm loss, what is the resulting signal level?

5. True or false: High-gain antennas provide longer coverage areas than low-gain antennas at the same input power level.

6. At what frequency do the 802.11a, 802.11b, and 802.11g standards operate?

7. What are the nonoverlapping 2.4 GHz channels used in North America?

8. True or false: As the distance from the AP increases, the data rate also increases.

9. Is 802.11a compatible with 802.11g?

10. For a given area, does 802.11a require more or fewer APs than 802.11b/g to provide coverage?

11. Is 802.11 communication full-duplex or half-duplex?

12. What is the difference between an autonomous AP and a lightweight AP?

13. What is an SSID?

14. Describe how WLAN authentication and encryption are provided in 802.11i.

15. What are the five elements of the Cisco UWN?

16. Which devices and applications comprise the Cisco UWN?

17. In the Cisco UWN, which device is responsible for putting the wireless client traffic into the appropriate VLAN?

18. Describe the split-MAC functionality of the UWN architecture.

19. Describe how 802.1X works within the Cisco UWN.

20. How does LWAPP work?

21. How is the WLC connected to an AP?

22. Define the following WLC terms:

■ Port

■ Interface

■ WLAN

23. How many AP-manager interfaces can a WLC have? What is the AP-manager interface used for?

24. Describe the relationships between WLANs, interfaces, and ports on a WLC.

25. How many APs can each of the following WLCs support?

■ 2000 Series

■ WLCM for ISRs

■ Catalyst 3750G Integrated WLC WS-C3750G-24WS-S25

■ Catalyst 3750G Integrated WLC WS-C3750G-24WS-S50

■ 4402 WLC AIR-WLC4402-12-K9

■ 4404 WLC AIR-WLC4404-100-K9

■ Catalyst 6500 Series WiSM

26. How does LAG allow more than 48 APs to be supported on each port of the 440x-based WLC platforms?

27. How does a lightweight AP select which WLC to join?

28. What does an AP in rogue detector mode do?

29. What is mobility? What is roaming? What are intracontroller and intercontroller roaming?

30. How are client entries in the WLC client database handled in Layer 3 and Layer 2 intercontroller roaming?

31. What is the recommended limit on the number of voice calls and the number of data devices that can be supported over a WLAN?

32. What does radio resource management do?

33. List the five typical steps in an RF site survey process.

34. What does the administrator have to configure to support deterministic WLC redundancy?

35. How can secure guest WLAN services be provided in a network?

36. What components comprise a Cisco wireless mesh network?

37. What is the local MAC LWAPP feature?

38. What is a REAP? What is an H-REAP?

This chapter discusses network security solutions and contains the following sections:

CHAPTER 10

Evaluating Security Solutions for the Network

Network security is one of the essential network services; it spans the entire network and it must be addressed within each modular block. Modularity ensures that the network designer can focus on a security problem within a particular network module and integrate a particular solution into a global security solution. A modular approach simplifies the design and ensures that a security breach in one of the network modules remains isolated so that it does not affect the entire network.

This chapter starts by describing network security, including threats and risks, and network security policies. The Cisco Self-Defending Network strategy for designing network security is explored. The chapter concludes with a discussion of Cisco network security solutions for enterprise networks.

> **NOTE** Wireless local-area network (WLAN) security is covered in Chapter 9, "Wireless Network Design Considerations."

Network Security

The scope of a network security solution is determined by organizational requirements and by potential threats to the organization. To create a secure network, the threats against which the network has to be protected must be determined. This section discusses the rationale for network security, including various threats and risks. Creating a network security policy is key to understanding and implementing security; network security policies and processes are discussed, and using risk assessment to create a security policy is explained.

The Need for Network Security

In the distant past, networks were designed to be open, and network security was largely a matter of physical security. As networks become increasingly interconnected and data flows more freely, security services become critical. In the commercial world, connectivity is no longer optional; the possible risks of providing connectivity do not outweigh its benefits, including revenue generation. Therefore, security services must provide adequate protection to allow organizations to conduct business in a relatively open environment.

Secure networks are required not only to defend against attacks and prevent unauthorized access; legislation, industry regulations, and company policies might also require secure networks to keep data private and ensure that it is not misused.

Network Security Requirements

Network security should include the following requirements:

- Prevent external hackers from getting access to the network

- Allow only authorized users into the network

- Prevent those inside the network from executing deliberate or inadvertent attacks

- Provide different levels of access for different types of users

- Protect data from misuse and corruption

- Comply with security legislation, industry standards, and company policies

To be truly effective, network security must meet these requirements in a way that is transparent to users, easy to administer, and does not disrupt business.

Security Legislation Examples

Security legislation and industry standards might define how data has to be handled, how to make sure that private information is protected, and what kind of information can be public. Based on legislative mandates and industry directives, organizations might have to protect customer records and privacy and even encrypt data to help ensure that the network is secure. Some examples of laws and directives influencing network security include the following:

- **The U.S. Gramm-Leach-Bliley Act of 1999 (GLBA)**: Information that many individuals would consider private—including bank balances and account numbers—is regularly bought and sold by banks, credit card companies, and other financial institutions. The GLBA, which is also known as the Financial Services Modernization Act of 1999, provides limited privacy protections against the sale of private financial information and codifies protections against *pretexting*, the practice of obtaining personal information through false pretenses.

- **The U.S. Health Insurance Portability and Accountability Act (HIPAA)**: HIPAA is U.S. federal legislation that was passed into law in August 1996. The overall purpose of the act is to enable better access to health insurance, reduce fraud and abuse, and lower the overall cost of health care in the United States. The HIPAA security regulations apply to protected health information that is electronically maintained or used in an electronic transmission. Thousands of U.S. organizations must comply with the HIPAA security rule.

- **European Union data protection Directive 95/46/EC**: This directive requires that European Union member states protect people's privacy rights when processing personal data, and that the flow of personal data between member states must not be restricted or prohibited because of these privacy rights.

- **The U.S. Sarbanes-Oxley Act of 2002 (SOX)**: This U.S. Federal law, passed in response to a number of major corporate scandals, is also known as the Public Company Accounting Reform and Investor Protection Act. SOX establishes new or enhanced auditing and financial standards for all U.S. public company boards, management, and public accounting firms. The act contains 11 sections, ranging from additional corporate board responsibilities to criminal penalties, and requires the U.S. Securities and Exchange Commission to implement rulings on requirements to comply with the new law.

- **Payment Card Industry (PCI) Data Security Standard (DSS)**: The PCI DSS was developed to ensure safe handling of sensitive payment information, such as the storage and transfer of credit card information. The PCI DSS is the umbrella program for other programs, such as the Visa Cardholder Information Security program and MasterCard Site Data Protection program.

- **The Canadian Personal Information Protection and Electronic Documents Act (PIPEDA)**: This act establishes rules for managing personal information by organizations involved in commercial activities. It aims to strike a balance between an individual's right to the protection of personal information and the need of organizations to obtain and handle such information for legitimate business purposes.

Terminology Related to Security

This section defines some terms related to security used throughout the rest of the chapter.

Most of us equate hacking with malicious activities. In fact, *hacking* really means to work diligently on a computer system until it performs optimally. The popular use of the term *hacking* is more related to *cracking*, which is defined as the act of unlawfully accessing a network infrastructure to perform unethical activities. But for the purposes of this book, the widely accepted term *hacking* denotes malicious activities directed at networks and systems.

A *virus* is a program that triggers a damaging outcome. Viruses often disguise themselves as executables with clever filenames like "You won." Viruses can be delivered via an e-mail or a website; a virus requires a human action, such as opening an e-mail attachment, to be activated. A *worm* is a virus that can self-duplicate. A worm might also be able to scan a network and infect neighboring workstations.

A *Trojan horse* pretends to be an inoffensive application when in fact it might contain a destructive payload. An example of a Trojan horse is an attachment that, after being opened, shows a picture of a cute puppy, but in the background, the code is reading the e-mail addresses of the user's address book and forwarding those addresses to a hacker's repository for future spam use.

Attacks are becoming more complex. *Malware* is a generic term that describes malicious software such as viruses and Trojan horses. *Combo malware* is a hybrid menace that combines destructive components of different threats. A worm that carries a viral payload is an example of combo malware.

Spam is unsolicited, unwanted e-mail. Spam might contain viruses or other threats, or point to infected or dangerous websites.

Spyware is a program that gathers information without the user's knowledge or consent and sends it back to the hacker. For example, spyware could log keystrokes, upload information (such as all addresses in the victim's address book), or download a program (known as a *zombie*) that waits for further instructions from the hacker.

Phishing e-mails try to convince the victim to release personal information; the e-mail appears to come from a legitimate source, and it directs the victim to website that looks legitimate. When the victim enters his or her information (such as usernames and passwords) on the counterfeit website, it is sent to the hacker.

Spear phishing is a very targeted phishing attack. For example, a hacker sends an e-mail that appears to be from a company's Human Resources department, asking all employees to confirm their banking information, or they won't get paid. If any employees reply with their information, the hacker may use it to gain access to their bank accounts.

Social engineering is the practice of obtaining confidential information by manipulating legitimate users. Examples include the following:

- **Getting physical access**: A hacker might get confidential information and passwords by having physical access to the organization. For example, the hacker might visit an organization and see passwords that are insecurely posted in an office or cubicle.

- **Using a psychological approach**: A hacker might exploit human nature to obtain access to confidential information. For example, a hacker might send an e-mail or call and ask for passwords, pretending that the information is required to maintain the victim's account.

Threats and Risks

Designing a secure network requires an understanding of the types of attacks that can compromise system security and their associated risks. The threats to network security can be classified into the following three categories:

- **Reconnaissance**: *Reconnaissance* is the active gathering of information about an enemy or target; the idea is to learn as much as possible about the target and the involved systems. In the network security area, reconnaissance is usually the prelude to a more focused attack against a particular target.

- **Gaining unauthorized system access**: After information about the target system is known, the next step is gaining access to the system by exploiting the system or using social engineering techniques.

- **Denial of service (DoS)**: Even if direct access to a system is not possible, another type of threat is DoS. A DoS attack is used to make systems unusable by overloading their resources such as CPU or bandwidth. When multiple sources conduct a DoS attack, it is called a *distributed DoS* (DDoS) attack.

To provide adequate protection of network resources, the network procedures and technologies need to address the following security risks:

- **Confidentiality of data**: Confidentiality should ensure that only authorized users can view sensitive information, to prevent theft, legal liabilities, and damage to the organization.

- **Integrity of data**: Integrity should ensure that only authorized users can change sensitive information and guarantee the authenticity of data.

- **System and data availability**: Availability should ensure uninterrupted access to important computing resources to prevent business disruption and loss of productivity.

Given the broad range of potential threats, everything in the network is a potential target. Hosts are typically the preferred target for worms and viruses. For example, host files could be corrupted in an attack, and the compromised host could be used to launch attacks against other hosts, creating a *botnet*. However, other high-value targets include the following:

- Network infrastructure devices, including routers and switches

- Support services, such as Dynamic Host Configuration Protocol (DHCP) and Domain Name System servers

- Endpoints, including IP phones, management stations, and user endpoints (such as PCs and laptops)

- Network infrastructure, including the network capacity or bandwidth

- Security devices, including firewalls, intrusion detection systems (IDS), and intrusion prevention systems (IPS)

The various threats and risks are described further in the following sections.

Threat: Reconnaissance Attacks

Reconnaissance attacks aim to discover information about a network, including the following:

- Active targets

- Network services that are running

- Operating system platform

- Trust relationships

- File permissions

- User account information

A common technique to find active targets such as networking devices and user endpoints is *port scanning*, in which data is sent to various TCP and User Datagram Protocol (UDP) ports on a device and the response from the device is evaluated.

To avoid reconnaissance attacks, a network should be tested to see how much it would reveal if attacked. The following are some examples of port-scanning tools:

- **Network Mapper (Nmap)**: Nmap is a free open-source utility for network exploration or security auditing. It was designed to rapidly scan large networks; it also maps single hosts.

- **NetStumbler**: NetStumbler is a tool for Microsoft Windows that facilitates detection of WLANs using the IEEE 802.11b, 802.11a, and 802.11g WLAN standards. A trimmed-down version of the tool called MiniStumbler is available for Windows CE.

- **SuperScan**: SuperScan is a popular Windows port-scanning tool with high scanning speed, host detection, extensive banner grabbing, and Windows host enumeration capability.

- **Kismet**: Kismet is an 802.11 Layer 2 wireless network detector, sniffer, and IDS that can sniff 802.11b, 802.11a, and 802.11g traffic. It identifies networks by passively collecting packets and detecting standard named networks, detecting hidden networks, and inferring the presence of *nonbeaconing networks* (networks that do not advertise themselves) via data traffic.

Port-scanning tools are designed to scan large networks and determine which hosts are up and the services they offer. The tools support a large number of scanning techniques, such as UDP, TCP connect (open), TCP SYN (half open), FTP proxy (bounce attack), Internet Control Message Protocol (ICMP) (ping sweep), FIN, ACK sweep, Xmas Tree (which sets the FIN, PSH, and URG flags and therefore appears to light up the packet like a Christmas tree), SYN sweep, IP Protocol, and Null scans. After TCP or UDP ports are discovered using one of the scan methods, version detection communicates with those ports to try to determine more about what is actually running.

Other tools, called *vulnerability scanners*, help find known vulnerabilities in a network. The tools use either passive scanning (by analyzing network traffic) or active testing (by sending packets through the network). The following are examples of vulnerability scanning tools:

- **Nessus**: Nessus is an open-source product designed to automate the testing and discovery of known security problems. A Windows graphical front end is available, although the core Nessus product requires Linux or UNIX to run.

■ **Microsoft Baseline Security Analyzer (MBSA)**: Although it's not a true vulnerability scanner, companies that rely primarily on Microsoft Windows products can use the freely available MBSA. MBSA scans the system and identifies whether any patches are missing for products such as the Windows operating systems, Internet Information Server, SQL Server, Exchange Server, Internet Explorer, Windows Media Player, and Microsoft Office products. MBSA also identifies missing or weak passwords and other common security issues.

■ **Security Administrator's Integrated Network Tool (SAINT)**: SAINT is a commercial vulnerability assessment tool that runs exclusively on UNIX.

The following are some sites where published vulnerability information is available:

■ CERT Coordination Center (CERT/CC): http://www.cert.org/certcc.html

■ MITRE Common Vulnerabilities and Exposures: http://www.cve.mitre.org/

■ Microsoft Security Bulletin Summaries and Webcasts: http://www.microsoft.com/technet/security/bulletin/summary.mspx

■ Cisco Security Notices: http://www.cisco.com/en/US/products/products_security_advisories_listing.html

Threat: Gaining Unauthorized Access to Systems

There are many ways that hackers gain access to systems. One often-seen threat is the knowledge of usernames and passwords by unauthorized persons. For example, known vulnerabilities in operating systems or services could be exploited, usernames and passwords could be captured or cracked, or the default administrative or service accounts might be accessible. It might be possible to decrypt or crack passwords from a system password file or by capturing passwords when they are being transmitted over the network. If a hacker gains access to a sufficiently privileged account, that person might gain access to all files on the system and might also be able to exploit other systems based on the user trust relationships across systems.

Another way that hackers gain access to a system is through various methods of social engineering. As mentioned, this could include exploiting human nature and gaining physical access to an organization. The impact of gaining system access could include exposure or compromise of sensitive data or machines, and the execution of arbitrary commands on the system.

Threat: DoS

DoS attacks attempt to compromise the availability of a network, host, or application. DoS and DDoS attacks are considered a major risk because they can easily interrupt business processes and cause significant loss. DoS attacks are relatively simple to conduct, even by an unskilled attacker.

Two methods of causing a DoS attack are by sending malformed data and by sending a large quantity of data. A successful DoS attack is usually the consequence of one of the following failures:

- The incapability of a network, host, or application to handle an enormous quantity of data, which renders the system unresponsive or brings it to a halt. The difficulty of defending against such an attack lies in the difficulty of distinguishing legitimate data from attack data.

- The failure of a host or application to handle an unexpected condition, such as maliciously formatted input data, an unexpected interaction of system components, or simple resource exhaustion.

Figure 10-1 depicts potential availability threats to network resources that an attacker might exploit. In this network, an attacker might do the following if adequate protection is not in place:

- Flood the Internet connection with random traffic in an attempt to consume as much bandwidth as possible. This can deny service to legitimate users of that connection.

- Flood a public server with an enormous number of connection requests, thereby rendering the server unresponsive to legitimate users.

Figure 10-1 *Availability Threats Can Deny Service to Network Users*

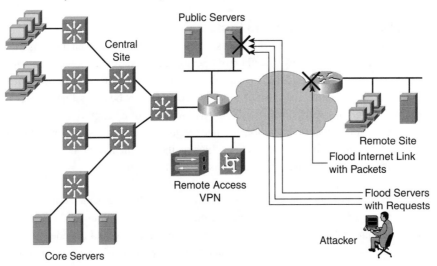

Most DoS attacks rely on spoofing and flooding techniques. The impact of DoS attacks can be managed in the following ways:

- Use DHCP snooping to verify DHCP transactions and protect against rogue DHCP servers. DHCP snooping filters DHCP packets; it prevents a rogue DHCP server from handing out IP addresses on a network by blocking all replies to a DHCP request from an interface (port) unless that port is allowed to reply. DHCP snooping also builds and maintains a DHCP-snooping binding table, which includes MAC address and IP address information for DHCP clients on untrusted interfaces.

■ Use Dynamic Address Resolution Protocol (ARP) Inspection (DAI) to intercept all ARP requests and replies on untrusted interfaces (ports), and use the DHCP-snooping binding table information to verify that ARP packets have valid IP-to-MAC address bindings.

■ Implement unicast reverse path forwarding checks to verify if the source IP address is reachable so that packets from malformed or forged source IP addresses are prevented from entering the network.

■ Implement access control lists (ACL) to filter traffic.

■ Rate-limit traffic such as incoming ARP and DHCP requests.

Risk: Integrity Violations and Confidentiality Breaches

Key security risks are integrity violations and confidentiality breaches.

> **KEY POINT** | Integrity violations can occur when an attacker attempts to *change* sensitive data without proper authorization.

An example of an integrity violation is when an attacker obtains permission to write to sensitive data and then changes or deletes it. The owner of the data might not detect such a change until it is too late, perhaps when the change has already resulted in tangible loss. Because of the difficulty of detecting changes and the possible cascading consequences of late detection, many businesses treat integrity violations as the most serious threat to their business.

> **KEY POINT** | Confidentiality breaches can occur when an attacker attempts to *read* sensitive data without proper authorization.

Confidentiality attacks can be extremely difficult to detect because the attacker can copy sensitive data without the owner's knowledge and without leaving a trace.

The risks of both integrity violations and confidentiality breaches are usually managed by enforcing access control in various ways, including the following:

■ Limiting access to network resources using network access control, such as physical separation of networks, restrictive firewalls, and VLANs.

■ Limiting access to files and objects using operating system-based access controls, such as UNIX host security and Windows domain security.

- Limiting users' access to data by using application-level controls, such as different user profiles for different roles.

- Using cryptography to protect data outside the application. Examples include encryption to provide confidentiality, and secure fingerprints or digital signatures to provide data authenticity and integrity. (These methods are described in the later "Secure Connectivity" section.)

Figure 10-2 illustrates potential confidentiality and integrity risks to network resources that an outside attacker might exploit. In this sample network, an attacker might do the following if adequate protection is not in place:

- Access an internal server and copy confidential data (a confidentiality breach)

- Deface (change) the corporate web page (an integrity breach)

- Intercept data sent over the Internet between a branch office and the central site, and change or read it in transit (a confidentiality or integrity breach)

Figure 10-2 *Integrity and Confidentiality Threats*

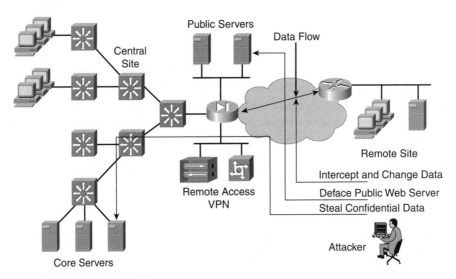

Network Security Policy and Process

Network security is an integral part of the system life cycle, as illustrated in Figure 10-3.

Figure 10-3 *Network Security in the System Life Cycle*

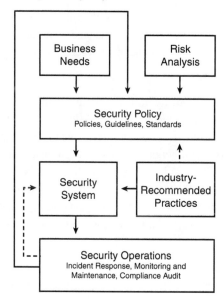

Network security is a continuous process, built around a security policy. Business needs (organizational requirements) and risk analysis are inputs to the development of a security policy. Regardless of the security implications, business needs must come first; if the business cannot function because of security constraints, the organization will have a major problem.

The following are the key areas to consider when designing a secure network:

- **Business needs**: What the organization wants to do with the network

- **Risk analysis**: The risk-versus-cost balance

- **Security policy**: The policies, standards, and guidelines that address business needs and risk

- **Industry-recommended practices**: The reliable, well-understood, and recommended security practices in the industry

- **Security operations**: The process for incident response, monitoring, maintenance, and compliance auditing of the system

Security Policy

> **KEY POINT** | A *security policy* is a set of objectives, the rules of behavior for users and administrators, and the requirements for system and management that collectively are designed to ensure the security of computer systems in an organization.

A very good introduction to security policies and the components that should be in a security policy is available in RFC 2196, *Site Security Handbook*. This RFC is a guide to developing computer security policies and procedures for sites that have systems on the Internet. The purpose of the handbook is to provide practical guidance to administrators trying to secure their information and services. The subjects covered include policy content and formation, a broad range of technical system and network security topics, and security incident response. This RFC defines a security policy as "a formal statement of the rules by which people who are given access to an organization's technology and information assets must abide."

The Need for a Security Policy

The main purpose of a security policy is to inform users, staff, and managers of the requirements and their responsibilities for protecting technology and information assets. The policy specifies the mechanisms through which these requirements are met. A security policy sets the framework for the security implementation, including the following:

- Defines organizational assets and how to use them

- Defines and communicates roles

- Helps determine the tools and procedures necessary to implement the policy

- Defines how to identify and handle security incidents

Some questions you might need to ask when developing a security policy include the following:

- What data and assets will be covered by the security policy?

- Under what conditions is communication allowed between networked hosts?

- How will implementation of the policies be verified?

- How will policy violations be detected?

- What is the impact of a policy violation?

- What actions are required if a policy is violated?

Another purpose of a security policy is to provide a baseline of the current security situation from which to acquire, configure, and audit computer systems and networks for compliance with the policy. The policy defines behaviors that are allowed and those that are not allowed and informs users of their responsibilities and the ramifications of asset misuse. Attempting to use security tools in the absence of at least an implied security policy is meaningless.

As part of developing a security policy, you should perform a risk assessment and cost-benefit analysis, including considering the latest attack techniques. Remember that the security system must be designed to accommodate the goals of the business, not hinder them.

Risk Assessment and Management

KEY POINT | Network security employs risk management to reduce risk to acceptable levels. It is important to note that risks are not *eliminated* by network security; they are reduced to levels acceptable to the organization.

An organization defines an acceptable level of risk based on such factors as the following:

- The value of the organization's data

- The expectation of loss in the event of compromise

- The severity and probability of risks

The weighting of these factors is called *risk assessment*, which is a continuously recurring procedure of knowing the following factors:

- What assets to protect

- The value of the assets

- The cost of expected loss (including financial loss) that would result from a security incident

- The probability that an attack could be directed against the assets

- The ability to control or minimize the risk through the security design and policy

Figure 10-4 summarizes these factors into three aspects of risk assessment: probability, control, and severity.

Figure 10-4 *Risk Assessment Includes Probability, Control, and Severity*

Risk assessment results in the development of a network security policy, which documents the level of risk and suggests the methods of managing the risk to an acceptable level. The network security policy describes risk management measures as they relate to potential threats. It does not usually consider security implementation details; rather, it provides a more general security philosophy that directs the implementation of security mechanisms.

KEY POINT
Risk assessment defines threats, their probability, and their severity.

A *network security policy* enumerates risks that are relevant to the network and how those risks will be managed.

A *network security design* implements the security policy.

Because the severity and probability of risks change daily, risk management and the consequent building of the security policy must be a continuous process. A good example is the use of cryptography to provide confidentiality through encryption. A company's encryption algorithm and the length of the encryption key might have to be reconsidered if a relatively inexpensive and exceptionally fast code-cracking computer, which allows decryption of high-value secrets, becomes available. In this case, the organization must choose a stronger algorithm to provide protection against the new threat.

KEY POINT
The cost of security should not exceed the cost of potential security incidents.

A security designer must evaluate the severity of a particular risk, including the damage a successful attack could cause. However, it is often difficult to associate a value with an asset. For example, consider the following:

- A large hospital system's medical database, in which disastrous consequences result if confidentiality is breached

- A corporation's public web page, which, if defaced (an integrity violation), can become a public-relations nightmare even though it might not result in any serious confidentiality breach

Evaluating potential damage is also difficult, but it is possible to some degree for most scenarios. In the commercial world, it is common practice to build systems that have just enough security to bring down potential losses to the desired level. Alternatively, organizations that have higher security requirements, such as legislative mandates, might want to implement stronger measures than might appear to be economically necessary, to mitigate potential unforeseen risks.

Risk Index

An organization can use a risk index to compare risks for potential threats. As illustrated in Table 10-1, a risk index is based on the following factors:

- The probability of risk (in other words, the likelihood that compromise will occur)

- The severity of loss in the event of compromise of an asset

- The ability to control or manage the risk

Table 10-1 *Risk Index Calculation*

Risk	Probability (P) (Value Between 1 and 3)	Severity (S) (Value Between 1 and 3)	Control (Value Between 1 and 3)	Risk Index (P*S)/C (Value Between 1 and 9)
1				
2				

All risks are identified in the first column. For each risk, each of the three factors is assigned a value between 1 (lowest) and 3 (highest). For example, for severity, a risk with high severity produces the greatest impact on user groups or particular environments and may even affect an entire site. Moderate-severity risks critically affect user environments or have some effect on an entire site (and mitigating the attack is a reasonably attainable scenario). Low-severity risks have a minor impact on user environments (and typically can be easily mitigated).

The risk index is calculated by dividing the product of the probability and severity factors by the control factor, resulting in this formula:

Risk index = (probability factor * severity factor) / (control factor)

NOTE   You might decide to include more levels (for example, using values between 1 and 5) to further differentiate risks.

Therefore, higher risk indices indicate risks that will have a more severe impact if they occur, that are more likely to occur, and that are less easy to control or manage. Risks with a higher risk index therefore require constant monitoring.

Stakeholders and subject matter experts should be involved in building the risk index matrix. The security policy should identify and outline a plan of activities to manage or control each risk and the actions to take if a security incident occurs. Table 10-2 shows sample risk index calculations.

Table 10-2 *Sample Risk Index Calculations*

Risk	Probability (P) (Value Between 1 and 3)	Severity (S) (Value Between 1 and 3)	Control (Value Between 1 and 3)	Risk Index (P*S)/C (Value Between 1 and 9)
Breach of confidentiality of customer database	1	3	2	1.5
DDoS attack against an e-commerce server sustained for more than 1 hour	2	2	1	4

Documenting the Security Policy

Figure 10-5 illustrates a sample security policy and how it can be divided into multiple documents that are applicable to the network segments.

Figure 10-5 *Network Security Policy Documents*

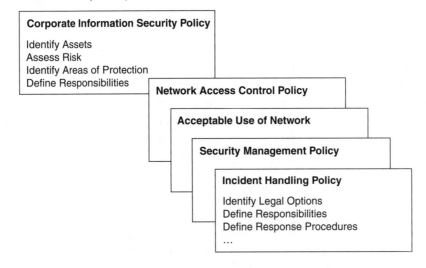

A general document describes the overall risk-management policy, identifies the corporation's assets, and identifies where protection must be applied. It also documents how risk management responsibility is distributed throughout the enterprise. Other documents, such as the following, might address more specific areas of risk management:

- A general *Network Access Control Policy* documents how data is categorized (such as confidential, internal, and top-secret) and what general access control principles are implemented in the networks.

- An *Acceptable Use of Network* document is usually written in easy-to-understand language and distributed to end users. This document informs users about their risk-management roles and responsibilities and should be as explicit as possible to avoid ambiguity or misunderstanding.

- A *Security Management Policy* defines how to perform secure computer infrastructure management.

- An *Incident Handling Policy* documents, the procedures to be used to ensure the reliable and acceptable handling of emergency situations.

Numerous other areas can be covered in separate documents, depending on the organization's requirements. The security policy should have the acceptance and support of all levels of employees in the organization. Therefore, representatives of all key stakeholders and affected management should be involved in creating and revising the security policy.

Network Security Process

A security policy should be considered a living document, continuously updated as technology and organizational requirements change. As shown in Figure 10-6, a process consisting of the following four steps helps maintain the security policy:

- **Secure**: A security solution is implemented to stop or prevent unauthorized access or activities and to protect information and assets. Securing the network might include implementing filtering and stateful inspection, identity authentication, encryption, virtual private networks (VPN), vulnerability patching, and other countermeasures to implement the security policy.

- **Monitor**: Monitoring the security solution is required to detect violations of the security policy; monitoring might include system auditing, real-time intrusion detection and response, and content-based detection and response.

- **Test**: The effectiveness of the security policy and the implemented security solution is validated by regular system auditing and assessment, and vulnerability scanning. Any applications installed and patches applied to software must be verified against the security policy.

- **Improve**: The information gathered from monitoring and testing the security solution, including event and data analysis and reporting, is used to make improvements to the security implementation. The security policy might have to be adjusted as new security vulnerabilities and risks are identified, and as network security intelligence improves.

Figure 10-6 *Network Security Is a Continuous Process*

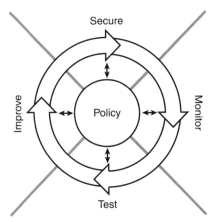

Security is becoming more and more an embedded part of the network. Security services such as firewalls, IPSs, Secure Sockets Layer (SSL), and IP security (IPsec) might now reside within the network infrastructure. SSL enables a secure path between a web browser and router resources. Recall from Chapter 5, "Designing Remote Connectivity," that IPsec is both a tunnel encapsulation protocol and a security protocol.

KEY POINT Integrating security within a network design is more manageable than adding security components after the network is implemented. Accordingly, it is now a recommended practice to integrate security when designing a network.

However, an integrated security and network design requires coordination not only between the network and security teams, but also with the rest of the IT organization—including, for example, the security policy and desktop operations teams.

The Cisco Self-Defending Network

This section introduces the Cisco Self-Defending Network and describes how it can be used to design a secure network.

The Cisco Self-Defending Network Framework

To mitigate and prevent information theft, organizations must implement precautions such as establishing formal organizational security policies, enforcing access rights to authenticated users, and securing the transport of data and voice communications. Security must be fully integrated into all aspects of the network to proactively recognize potential suspicious activity, identify threats, react adaptively, and facilitate a coordinated response to attacks. Cisco has defined the Self-Defending Network to take advantage of the intelligence in network resources and to protect organizations by identifying, preventing, and adapting to threats from both internal and external sources.

The Self-Defending Network's integrated network security incorporates the following three critical elements, as illustrated in Figure 10-7:

- **Trust and identity management**: To protect critical assets by allowing access based on privilege level

- **Threat defense**: To minimize and mitigate outbreaks

- **Secure connectivity**: To ensure privacy and confidentiality of communications

Figure 10-7   *Cisco Self-Defending Network*

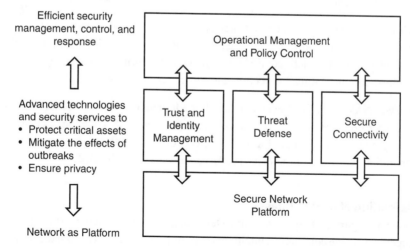

These three elements are explored in detail starting in the upcoming "Trust and Identity Management" section.

Secure Network Platform

The Cisco Self-Defending Network is based on a secure network platform that is a strong, secure, flexible base from which the self-defending network solution is built. With security integrated into the very fabric of the network, security becomes an integral and fundamental network feature. Advanced technologies and security services use the secure network platform to provide the critical elements of security—where and when they are needed. These elements are controlled by security policies and security management applications providing efficient security management, control, and response.

Because the network touches all parts of the infrastructure, it is the ideal location to implement core and advanced security services. The nucleus of secure network infrastructure solutions include adaptive security appliances (ASA) and routers and switches with security integrated and embedded both in and between them, as follows:

- **Routers**: Routers such as Cisco Integrated Services Routers (ISR) incorporate Cisco IOS firewall, IPS, IPsec VPN (including Cisco Easy VPN and Dynamic Multipoint VPN [DMVPN]), and SSL VPN services into the routing infrastructure, in addition to features that protect the router if it should be the target of an attack. New security features can be deployed on existing routers using updated Cisco IOS software. Routers can also participate in the Network Admission Control (NAC) process. NAC is a multivendor effort that admits endpoints to the network only after they have demonstrated their compatibility with various network security policies.

- **Cisco Catalyst switches**: Cisco Catalyst switches incorporate firewall, IPS, SSL VPN, IPsec VPN, DDoS and man-in-the-middle attack mitigation, and virtualization services allowing unique policies for each security zone. Integrated security services modules are available for high-performance threat protection and secure connectivity.

- **Cisco ASAs**: Cisco ASAs consolidate all the foundation security technologies (including high-performance firewall, IPS, network antivirus, and IPsec and SSL VPNs) in a single easily managed unified platform. Device consolidation reduces the overall deployment and operations costs and complexity. ASAs can also be NAC-enabled.

Cisco Self-Defending Network Phases

As shown in Figure 10-8, the Cisco Self-Defending Network contains three characteristic phases that together provide continuous, intelligent, future-proofed security, from the network through to the application layer:

- **Integrated security**: Security defense technologies are incorporated across all network elements, including routing, switching, wireless, and security platforms so that every point in the network can defend itself. These security features include firewalls, VPNs, and trust and identity capabilities. An example is the use of the Cisco Security Agent, which provides endpoint server and desktop protection against new and emerging threats stemming from malicious network activity.

- **Collaborative security systems**: The secure network components work together as a security system that adheres to and responds to an organization's security policies. An example of this collaborative characteristic is NAC, implemented in devices from multiple vendors.

- **Adaptive threat defense**: The secure network uses several tools to defend against new security threats and changing network conditions. Application awareness defends against security threats entering the network from within Internet-enabled applications. Behavioral recognition defends against worms, viruses, spyware, DDoS attacks, and other threats. Network control intelligently monitors and manages the security infrastructure and provides tools for IT managers to audit, control, and correlate.

Figure 10-8 *Cisco Self-Defending Network Phases*

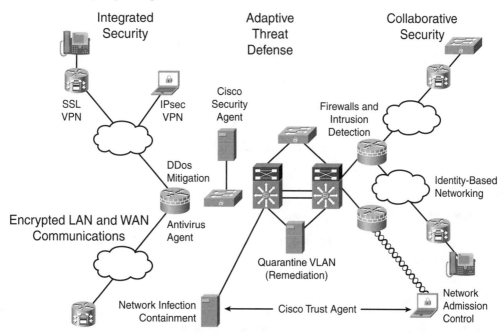

The Cisco Self-Defending Network products can be deployed independently of one another or as part of a solution that links multiple products.

Trust and Identity Management

This section discusses the trust and identity management element of the Cisco Self-Defending Network.

> **KEY POINT** | Businesses need to effectively and securely manage *who* and *what* can access the network, as well as *when*, *where*, and *how* that access can occur.

Trust and identity management is critical for organizations. It underpins the creation of any secure network or system by providing or denying access to business applications and networked resources based on a user's specific privileges and rights.

Trust and identity management solutions provide secure network access and admission at any point in the network and isolate and control infected or unpatched devices that attempt to access the network. The three aspects of trust and identity management are trust, identity, and access control, as shown in Figure 10-9 and described in the following sections.

Figure 10-9 *Trust and Identity Management*

Trust

Trust is the root of security.

> **KEY POINT** | Trust defines the relationship in which two or more network entities are allowed to communicate. Security policy decisions are based on trust.

Trusted entities are allowed to communicate freely; communication with untrusted entities needs to be carefully managed and controlled because of its higher risk.

> **KEY POINT** | Trust and risk are opposites; security is used to limit risk by enforcing limitations on trust relationships.

Trust relationships might be explicitly defined or informally implied. Trust relationships can be inherited—for example, if a user is granted certain privileges on one system, another similar system might extend the same privileges. However granted, trust and privileges are sometimes abused.

Domains of Trust

To segment a network into parts, based on similar policy and concerns, *domains of trust* are established. The required system security in a network can vary in terms of importance to the business and the likelihood of being attacked. Consistent security controls should be applied within a segment, and trust relationships should be defined between segments. Segments can have different trust models, depending on the security needed.

Figure 10-10 illustrates two domains of trust examples. Case 1 includes internal and external portions of a network in the domain on the far left; the security policy within that domain will not be consistent, though. In contrast, Case 2 includes four domains, each with unique security requirements, and is therefore a better division into domains of trust.

Figure 10-10   *Domains of Trust*

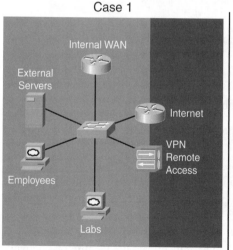
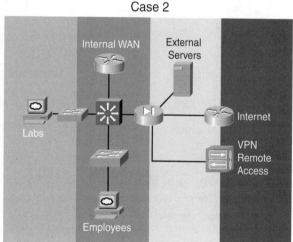

Gradient of Trust

The gradient of trust determines the trust level between domains, which can be minor to extreme, and determines the extent of security safeguards and attention to monitoring required. The trust relationship between segments should be controlled at defined points, using some form of network firewall or access control, as illustrated in the examples in Figure 10-11. Mastering domains of trust is a key component of good network security design.

Figure 10-11 *Domains and Gradients of Trust*

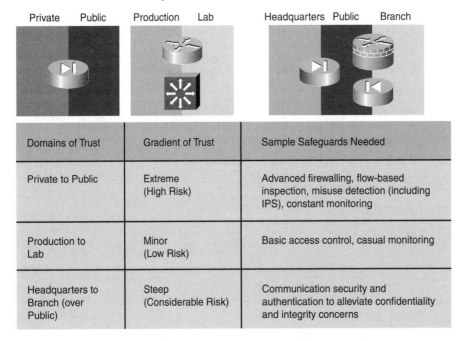

Domains of Trust	Gradient of Trust	Sample Safeguards Needed
Private to Public	Extreme (High Risk)	Advanced firewalling, flow-based inspection, misuse detection (including IPS), constant monitoring
Production to Lab	Minor (Low Risk)	Basic access control, casual monitoring
Headquarters to Branch (over Public)	Steep (Considerable Risk)	Communication security and authentication to alleviate confidentiality and integrity concerns

Identity

Identity defines the parties in a trust relationship.

> **KEY POINT**
>
> The identity is the *who* of a trust relationship.
>
> The identity of a network entity is verified by credentials.

The identity can be individuals, devices, organizations, or all three. Using identities properly enables effective risk mitigation and the ability to apply policy and access control in a granular and accurate manner.

Credentials are elements of information used to verify or authenticate the identity of a network entity. It is important to separate the concept of identification, in which a subject *presents* its identity, from authentication, in which a subject *proves* its identity. For example, to log on to a resource, a user might be identified by a username and authenticated by a secret password.

The most common identity credentials are passwords, tokens, and certificates. Passwords and tokens are described in the next sections; certificates are described in the later "Encryption Fundamentals" section.

KEY POINT | Authentication, or the proving of identity, is traditionally based on one (or more) of the following three proofs:

- **Something the subject knows**: This usually involves knowledge of a unique secret, which the authenticating parties usually share. To a user, this secret appears as a classic password, a personal identification number, or a private cryptographic key.

- **Something the subject has**: This usually involves physical possession of an item that is unique to the subject. Examples include password token cards, Smartcards, and hardware keys.

- **Something the subject is**: This involves verifying a subject's unique physical characteristic, such as a fingerprint, retina pattern, voice, or face.

Passwords

Passwords demonstrate the authentication attribute "something the subject knows" and can be used to authenticate an authorized user to network resources. Passwords correlate an authorized user with network resources.

Passwords can be a problem in secure environments because users try to do what is easiest for them. Password policies and procedures must be created and enforced if password authentication is used as a credible security measure. These password policies and procedures should specify the use of strong, nondictionary passwords that are changed often. They should clearly state that passwords should never be shared and never posted where they can be easily found (such as on a monitor or wall or hidden under a keyboard).

Implementing Strong Password Policies

A dictionary attack is when a hacker tries to guess a user's password (to gain network access) by using every "word" in a dictionary of common passwords or possible combinations of passwords. A dictionary attack relies on the fact that a password is often a common word, name, or concatenation of words or names with a minor modification such as a trailing digit or two.

Instructing users to select strong passwords is one of the most effective means to mitigate the possibility of a successful dictionary attack. On a Windows host, it is possible to implement password complexity rules to force users to choose strong passwords, which are more difficult for hackers to determine. Some characteristics of a strong password include the following:

- It is a minimum of ten characters

- It is a mixture of uppercase and lowercase letters

- It contains at least one numeric character (0–9) or nonalphanumeric character (for example, !#@&)

- It has at least one special character within the password—not at the beginning or end

- It is not a form of the user's name or user ID

- It is a word that is not found in a dictionary (domestic or foreign)

The following are two examples of strong passwords and how they were derived (and therefore how they can be remembered):

- 4yosc10cP!, from "For your own safety, choose ten-character password!"

- cnw84Fri*YAD, from "Cannot wait for Friday."

The information in this sidebar was derived from http://www.cisco.com/en/US/products/hw/wireless/ps430/prod_bulletin09186a00801cc901.html.

Tokens

Many trusted systems require two-factor authentication.

KEY POINT | *Two-factor* (or *strong*) *authentication* is where a subject provides at least two types of proof of identity.

With two-factor authentication, the compromise of one factor does not lead to the compromise of the system. An example is an access control system based on a token and a password, as illustrated in Figure 10-12. A password might become known, but it is useless without the token. Conversely, if the token is stolen, the thief cannot use it without the password.

Figure 10-12   *Strong Authentication with a Token*

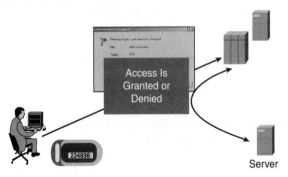

A token can be a physical device or software application that generates a one-time authentication password or number. An example of a token is a keychain-sized device that shows—one at a time in a predefined order—a one-time password (OTP) on its small LCD, for approximately one minute. The token is synchronized with a token server that has the same predefined list of passwords for that user. At any given time, the user has only one valid password. For example, this technology could be used by an organization that needs to deploy remote-access services to its network over the Internet. The organization has implemented remote-access VPN technology and requires proper user authentication before users enter the protected network. The organization has had poor experiences enforcing password updates and wants to deploy a very secure, yet simple, system. Using OTP generators for remote users could be the ideal solution because they are secure and simple to use.

Access Control

Trust and identity management is also supported by access control.

> **KEY POINT** | *Access control* is the ability to enforce a policy that states which entities (such as users, servers, and applications) can access which network resources.

> **NOTE**   Access control also indirectly helps ensure confidentiality and integrity of sensitive data by limiting access to the data. In contrast, authorization mechanisms limit the access of an entity to resources based on subject identity.

Network access control mechanisms are classified in the following ways:

■ **Authentication mechanisms**, which establish the subject's identity.

■ **Authorization mechanisms**, which define what a subject can do in a network and thus limit access to a network. The granularity of access, such as read-only or write, may also be defined.

■ **Accounting mechanisms**, such as an audit trail, which provides evidence and accounting of the subject's actions, and real-time monitoring, which provides security services such as intrusion detection.

Authentication, authorization, and accounting (AAA) are network security services that provide a framework through which access control to a network is defined.

Trust and Identity Management Technologies

Some of the many technologies used for trust and identity management include the following:

■ **ACLs**: Lists maintained by network devices such as routers, switches, and firewalls to control access through the device. An example is an ACL on a router that specifies which clients, based on their IP addresses, can connect to a critical server in the data center.

- **Firewall**: A device designed to permit or deny network traffic based on certain characteristics, such as source address, destination address, protocol, port number, and application. The firewall enforces the access and authorization policy in the network by specifying which connections are permitted or denied between security perimeters.

- **NAC**: A set of technologies and solutions that uses the network infrastructure to enforce security policy compliance on all devices trying to access network computing resources, thereby limiting damage from emerging security threats.

- **IEEE 802.1X**: An IEEE standard for media-level access control, providing the ability to permit or deny network connectivity, control VLAN access, and apply traffic policy based on user or device identity.

- **Cisco Identity-Based Networking Services (IBNS)**: An integrated solution combining several Cisco products that offer authentication, access control, and user policies to secure network connectivity and resources.

The following sections provide more information about some of these technologies.

Firewall Filtering Using ACLs

Figure 10-13 illustrates the use of a network firewall to control (or filter) access; this is a common network authorization implementation. An enterprise network is usually divided into separate security domains (also called *perimeters* or *zones*)—such as the untrusted Internet zone, the trusted Enterprise Campus zone, public and semipublic server zones, and so forth—to allow a network firewall to control all traffic that passes between the perimeters. Because all traffic must pass through the network firewall, it enforces the network's access and authorization policy effectively by specifying which connections are permitted or denied between security zones.

Figure 10-13 *A Firewall Can Filter Network Sessions*

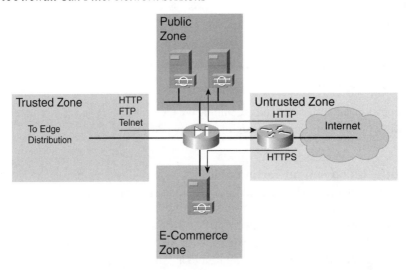

> **NOTE**   Security domains that are connected to a leg of a firewall and that contain one or more servers are also called *demilitarized zones (DMZ)*. The purpose of a DMZ network is to contain an attacker who has compromised a host so that the firewall again filters all access from the compromised host. This allows the enforcement of an extremely strict connection policy that denies all connections from public servers by default and prevents connectivity to hosts outside the DMZ network. If multiple hosts are located in the same DMZ, LAN switch-based security access control mechanisms such as private VLANs can also effectively restrict communications among such hosts.

For example, the policy for the Internet interface of the firewall in Figure 10-13 is as follows:

- From the Internet, HTTP traffic is permitted to the public web servers, and the public web servers can reply.

- HTTP secured by SSL (HTTPS) traffic from the Internet is permitted to the e-commerce server, and response HTTPS traffic from the e-commerce server is allowed.

- HTTP, FTP, and Telnet traffic initiated from the internal network to the Internet, and responses to this traffic, are allowed.

NAC Framework and Cisco NAC Appliance

NAC allows network access only to compliant and trusted wired or wireless endpoint devices, such as PCs, laptops, servers, and personal digital assistants (PDA), and it can restrict the access of noncompliant devices. Two NAC options are available: the NAC framework and the NAC appliance.

The NAC framework is an industrywide initiative led by Cisco that uses the network infrastructure and third-party software to enforce security policy compliance on all endpoints. The NAC framework is sold through NAC-enabled products, providing an integrated solution that leverages Cisco network products and other vendor products.

The Cisco NAC appliance is a turnkey solution, sold as either a virtual or integrated appliance, to control network access based on user authentication and to provide wired and wireless endpoint compliance with built-in device remediation. The Cisco NAC appliance identifies whether networked devices, such as laptops and PDAs, are compliant with the network security policies. It repairs any vulnerability before permitting the device to access the network.

For example, a Cisco router can act as a network access device (NAD) that intercepts attempts to connect from local or remote users. A Cisco trust agent, installed on a user's laptop, provides the NAD with pertinent information, such as the version of antivirus software running and the patch level of the laptop's operating system. The NAD passes this information to a policy server, which decides whether network access will be granted to the laptop; devices not granted access might be quarantined until they meet the NAC standards.

IEEE 802.1x and IBNS

Recall from Chapter 9 that IEEE 802.1X is an open standards–based protocol for authenticating network clients (or ports) based on a user ID or on the device. 802.1X runs between end devices or users (called *supplicants*) trying to connect to ports, and an Ethernet device, such as a Cisco Catalyst switch or Cisco wireless access point (AP) (called the *authenticator*). Authentication and authorization are achieved with back-end communication to an *authentication server* such as Cisco Secure Access Control Server (ACS).

The Cisco IBNS solution supports identity authentication and secure network connectivity, dynamic provisioning of VLANs on a per-user basis, guest VLANs, and 802.1X port security. Figure 10-14 illustrates the IBNS solution. When the Cisco Catalyst switch (the authenticator) detects that a user (the supplicant) is attempting to connect to the network, the authenticator initiates an Extensible Authentication Protocol over LAN (EAPoL) session, asking the supplicant to provide credentials. The supplicant sends its credentials to the authenticator. The switch (the authenticator) passes the user ID and password to an authentication server using RADIUS.

Figure 10-14 *Cisco IBNS Provides Enhancements and Extensions to 802.1X*

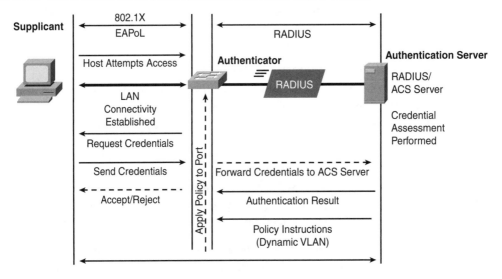

The authentication server determines whether the user ID and password are valid. It also notes the port to which the user is connected, and the MAC address of the user's device. If the user ID and password are valid, the authentication server sends a message to the authenticator to allow the user to connect to the network on a specific VLAN, and the user accesses the physical LAN services. If the user ID and password are not valid, the server sends a message to the switch to block the port to which the user is connected.

Identity and Access Control Deployment

Figure 10-15 illustrates examples of where authentication can take place in the Cisco Enterprise Architectures, including the following locations:

■ Dialup access points, where any subject can establish a dialup connection to the network; authentication is necessary to distinguish between trusted and untrusted subjects.

■ WAN and VPN infrastructures, where network devices authenticate each other on WAN or VPN links, thereby mitigating the risk of infrastructure compromise or misconfiguration. WAN peer authentication usually involves PPP mechanisms and routing protocol authentication. In a VPN, authentication is embedded in the VPN security protocols—most often IPsec and Internet Key Exchange (IKE).

■ LAN access, where a network device (switch) authenticates the user, typically with IEEE 802.1X, before allowing access to the switched network.

■ Wireless access, where only an authenticated user can establish an association with a wireless AP using IEEE 802.1X.

■ Firewall authentication, where users must prove their identity when entering a critical network that is protected by a firewall.

Figure 10-15 *Trust and Identity Management*

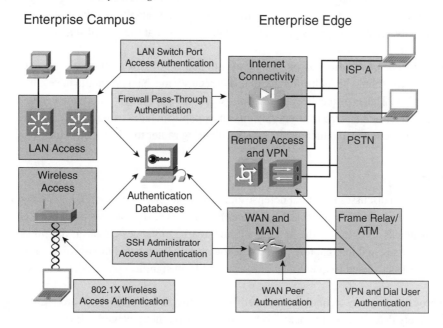

> **NOTE** Secure Shell (SSH) supports secure Telnet access between applications and router resources.

Authentication validation should be deployed as close to the network edge as possible, with strong authentication required for access from external and untrusted networks.

Access controls to enforce policy are deployed at various locations:

- Source-specific rules (to any destination) should be applied as close to the source as possible.

- Destination-specific rules (from any source) should be applied as close to the destination as possible.

- Mixed rules, using combinations of specific sources and destinations, should be applied as close to the source as possible.

The *principle of least privilege* should be followed. This principle is based on the practice by which each subject is given only the minimal rights that are necessary (access permissions) to perform the subject's tasks. For example, if a user needs to access a particular web server, the firewall should allow that user to access only the specified web server. In reality, however, enterprises often introduce lenient rules that allow subjects greater access than they require, which can result in deliberate or accidental confidentiality and integrity breaches. Highly distributed rules afford greater granularity and overall performance scalability at the cost of management complexity. Centralized rules provide easier management at the cost of scalability.

The *principle of defense in depth* should also be followed. This principle suggests that security mechanisms should be fault-tolerant; that is, a security mechanism should have a backup security mechanism. This is also called the *belt-and-suspenders approach*—both the belt and suspenders are used to ensure that the trousers stay up. An example includes using a dedicated firewall to limit access to a resource and then using a packet-filtering router to add another line of defense.

Threat Defense

This section discusses the threat defense element of the Cisco Self-Defending Network. Network security must protect a business from increasing threats such as access breaches, "Day Zero" worm attacks and viruses (the first day of the threat), DoS attacks, man-in-the-middle attacks, Trojan horses, and internal threats. Threats today, both known and unknown, continue to become more destructive and frequent than in the past and can significantly affect business profitability.

Appropriate security technologies and advanced networking intelligence are required to effectively defend against attacks. To be most effective, these technologies must be implemented throughout the network, rather than just in specific products or technologies, because an attack can start anywhere and instantly spread across all network resources.

The Cisco Threat Defense System enhances security in an existing network infrastructure, adds comprehensive security on the endpoints (both server and desktops), and adds dedicated security technologies to networking devices and appliances, proactively defending the business, applications, users, and network and protecting businesses from operation disruption, lost revenue, and loss of reputation. The Cisco Threat Defense System comprises several critical technologies and products, enabling security integrated in routers, switches, and appliances—including firewalls, network-based IPS sensors and detection instrumentation, and traffic isolation techniques. The Cisco Security Agent provides endpoint protection. These technologies and products are described in later sections, after a discussion of physical security.

Physical Security

Physical security is critical to the successful implementation of network security and can significantly influence the strength of the total security design. This section discusses various aspects of physical security and provides guidelines for its successful inclusion in the overall security policy.

Physical Threats

KEY POINT | Physical security is an often-overlooked aspect of network security design; most of the protection is implemented inside network devices. However, physical access to the device or the communications medium can compromise security.

Consider the following potential physical threats:

- A network device does not always enforce all its security settings when an attacker accesses the hardware directly (for example, it might allow console access, memory probing, and installation of unreliable software).

- Access to the physical communication medium (such as unrestricted access to a switch port, unrestricted wireless network access, or access to the telecommunications infrastructure) could allow an attacker to impersonate trusted systems and view, intercept, and change data that is flowing in a network.

- An attacker might use physically destructive attacks against devices and networks (such as physical force, attacks on the power network, or electromagnetic surveillance and attacks).

- An attacker might steal a device such as a home office router or laptop computer and use it to access the corporate network.

A good security policy must anticipate possible physical attacks and assess their relevance in terms of possible loss, probability, and simplicity of attack. Figure 10-16 illustrates possible physical breaches of network security. In this sample network, an attacker might do the following:

■ Break into the computing center, obtain physical access to a firewall, and then compromise its physical connections to bypass it, or access the console port on some routers or switches and alter their security settings.

■ Obtain physical access to the copper media of the corporate WAN or the public switched telephone network (PSTN), and intercept all communications. The attacker could read and change sensitive data that is not protected by cryptography.

■ Steal a device, such as a small office/home office (SOHO) router or laptop, and use it to access the corporate network.

Figure 10-16 *Physical Security Is Often Overlooked*

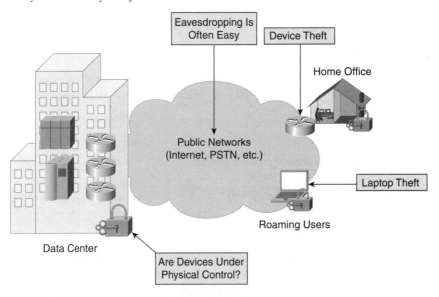

Physical Security Guidelines

The traditional method of managing the risk of physical compromise is to deploy physical access controls using techniques such as locks or alarms. It is also important to identify how a physical security breach might interact with network security mechanisms. For example, there could be a significant risk if an attacker physically accesses a switch port located in a corporate building and from there has unrestricted access to the corporate network. If, during the development of the security policy, it were incorrectly assumed that only legitimate users could obtain such access, the attacker would be able to connect to the network without authentication and thus bypass network access control.

SOHO Wireless Routers

Another risk related to physical security is if users bring their personal SOHO wireless routers to work and connect them to the corporate LAN. Unfortunately, the default settings on many SOHO wireless routers do not have any network security. Therefore, anyone within range of the wireless router (whether inside or outside the building) would be able to associate with it and would be connected to the inside of the corporate network, behind the protected perimeter. This threat can be mitigated by enforcing IEEE 802.1X or other port-based security policies on the corporate campus network.

A security designer must identify the consequences of device theft on network security. For example, if a laptop computer is stolen from a roaming user, does it contain cryptographic keys that enable the attacker to connect to the enterprise network while impersonating a legitimate user? Moreover, does the network administrator have some scalable means of revoking such credentials that the attacker could obtain through physical theft?

Sometimes a significant portion of the network infrastructure is beyond the enterprise's physical control, and physical controls cannot be enforced at the media access level. For example, many enterprises rely on the fact that the physical infrastructure of the service provider's Frame Relay network is well protected, despite the fact that access to its wire conduits might be obtained easily. To protect communications over such networks, cryptography could be used. Cryptography provides confidentiality, protects the integrity of communication over unsafe networks, and is fully under the enterprise's control. For example, an enterprise that simultaneously transmits sensitive and nonsensitive data over a Frame Relay network could use IPsec protection for the sensitive traffic and send the other traffic unencrypted.

Another example is a government intelligence agency concerned about the theft of laptops that might contain extremely sensitive data. To manage this risk, the agency deploys robust file encryption software on the laptops; this software decrypts sensitive files only on special request. Sensitive information is therefore hidden from a potential thief, who could otherwise read raw data from the laptop's disk.

Infrastructure Protection

> **KEY POINT** | Infrastructure protection consists of the measures taken to minimize the risks and threats to which the network elements are exposed so as to preserve the integrity and availability of the network as a transport entity.

To meet business needs, it is critical to utilize security features and services to protect the infrastructure so that network devices are not accessed or altered in an unauthorized manner and so that end-to-end network transport and integrated services are available.

Deploying recommended practices and security policy enforcement to harden network devices helps secure the network foundation by protecting network elements and the integrity of their interactions. Cisco has enhanced the Cisco IOS software security features and services for both network elements and infrastructure, to improve the availability of the network elements and the network.

> **NOTE** *Device hardening* is limiting information provided by devices to only the information necessary to support business needs. For example, if it is not necessary for a device to respond to pings, that function should be turned off so that the device will not provide information to hackers.

Secure network infrastructure solutions include ASAs and routers and switches with integrated security.

Infrastructure Protection Deployment Locations

Infrastructure protection practices should be deployed on all network infrastructure devices throughout the network, especially at strategic perimeter points, to control ingress and egress traffic.

Different mechanisms might be available on different platforms, but typically equivalent functions are available on similar devices. More-advanced mechanisms might be available only on higher-end devices.

Recommended Practices for Infrastructure Protection

The following are some recommended practices for infrastructure protection:

■ Allow only SSH, instead of Telnet, to access devices.

■ Enable AAA and role-based access control (using RADIUS or TACACS+) for access to the command-line interface (CLI) and privileged mode access on all devices.

- Collect and archive syslog messages (event notification messages) from network devices on a syslog server.

- When using Simple Network Management Protocol (SNMP), use SNMP version 3 (SNMPv3) and its authentication and privacy features.

- Disable unused services on network devices, including using the following commands on Cisco IOS devices:
  no service tcp-small-servers
  no service udp-small-servers

> **NOTE**   When the minor TCP/IP servers are disabled using the **no service tcp-small-servers** command, and a packet trying to access the Echo, Discard, Chargen, and Daytime ports is received, the Cisco IOS software sends a TCP RESET packet to the sender and discards the original incoming packet. When the minor UDP servers are disabled using the **no service udp-small-servers** command and a packet trying to access Echo, Discard, and Chargen ports is received, the Cisco IOS software sends an "ICMP port unreachable" message to the sender and discards the original incoming packet. These servers are disabled by default.

- Use SSH FTP and Secure Copy (SCP) to move Cisco IOS images and configuration files; avoid using FTP and Trivial File Transfer Protocol (TFTP) when possible.

- Install ACLs on the virtual terminal lines to limit access to management and CLI services.

- Enable protocol authentication in the control plane where it is available. Examples include enabling routing protocol authentication in both Interior Gateway Protocols (IGP) and Exterior Gateway Protocols (EGP), such as in Enhanced Interior Gateway Routing Protocol (EIGRP), Open Shortest Path First (OSPF), and Border Gateway Protocol. These routing protocols support Message Digest 5 (MD5) authentication. Other protocols, such as Hot Standby Router Protocol (HSRP) and VLAN Trunking Protocol (VTP), also support authentication.

- Consider using the one-step router lockdown feature in the Cisco Router and Security Device Manager (SDM) to help ensure that all nonessential services in Cisco IOS software are shut off before the Cisco router is connected to the public Internet or a WAN.

SDM

The SDM one-step router lockdown tool might shut off services that it considers nonessential yet prove to be essential in your own enterprise. SDM allows the administrator to view summary information about the suggested changes before the changes are applied. Specific changes can be unchecked as required, and links in the tool to Cisco's website describe the nature of the suggested changes in greater detail.

AutoSecure

You might also consider using the Cisco IOS AutoSecure feature when using the command-line interface. AutoSecure is an interactive script that is more granular in its settings than the one-step router lockdown tool in SDM.

■ Perimeter routers should implement ingress traffic filtering to prohibit DoS attacks, which use forged IP addresses to propagate from the Internet. RFC 2827, *Network Ingress Filtering: Defeating Denial of Service Attacks which employ IP Source Address Spoofing,* specifies current Internet best practices for ingress traffic filtering.

■ All switches should be configured to support bridge protocol data unit guard and root guard, and the VTP mode should be set to transparent.

■ More-advanced protection mechanisms, such as DAI and DHCP snooping, might be available only on higher-end switches. When supported, infrastructure devices should consider implementing control plane policing (CoPP) to manage the traffic flow of control plane packets on Cisco IOS routers and switches to limit reconnaissance and DoS attacks.

Threat Detection and Mitigation

Threat detection and mitigation technologies provide early detection and notification of unpredicted malicious traffic or behavior. The goals of these technologies include the following:

■ Detecting, notifying, and helping stop events or traffic that are unauthorized and unpredictable

■ Helping preserve the network's availability, particularly against unknown or unforeseen attacks

Threat Detection and Mitigation Technologies

The following are some of the threat detection and mitigation technologies available:

■ Network-based intrusion prevention systems (NIPS), such as the ASA, IPS appliances, and Cisco IOS IPS

■ Host-based intrusion prevention systems (HIPS), such as Cisco Security Agent

■ NetFlow

■ Syslog

■ Event-correlation systems, such as Cisco Security Monitoring, Analysis, and Response System (MARS)

■ Cisco Traffic Anomaly Detector Module

These threat detection and mitigation technologies provide many network security functions, including the following:

- **Endpoint protection**: Viruses and worms frequently create network congestion as a byproduct of rapid propagation and infection of endpoints. The Cisco Security Agent therefore becomes a first-order dampener of the effects of virus and worm propagation. A second and equally compelling reason for deploying Cisco Security Agent is that it establishes a presence on endpoints that can be used to establish a feedback loop between the endpoint and the network, resulting in a network that rapidly adapts to emerging threats. In addition, antivirus software allows hosts to detect and remove infections based on patterns.

- **Infection containment**: The Cisco ASA 5500 Series ASAs, Cisco PIX 500 Series Security Appliances, Cisco Catalyst 6500 Series Firewall Services Module (FWSM), and the firewall feature set in Cisco IOS software protect the network perimeter and create islands of security on the internal network. Strong network admission policies are important but are not a cure-all and therefore do not eliminate the need to continue monitoring devices after they enter a network. Determined attackers can evade just about any admission check, and the network cannot always rely on, or trust, an infected element to turn itself in. Compliant devices might also become infected through a variety of ways when on a network (for example, a universal serial bus key with infected content could infect another device). To help protect the network further, the Cisco Self-Defending Network is designed to extend the security checks performed by NAC at the time of network admission for the duration of the network connection. The Cisco Self-Defending Network also relies on other network elements, including other endpoints, to detect when another endpoint is no longer trustworthy.

- **Inline intrusion and anomaly detection**: An important area of ongoing security development is network intrusion detection systems (NIDS). One of the first Cisco innovations in this area was to integrate an NIDS into Cisco router and switch platforms. NIPSs with inline filtering capabilities provide even more protection. NIPSs provide a mechanism to remove unwanted traffic with fine-grained programmable classification engines. Examples of these devices are the Cisco IPS 4200 Series Sensors, the Cisco Catalyst 6500 Series IDS Module (IDSM-2), and the Cisco IOS IPS, which quickly identify, analyze, and stop malevolent traffic. The Cisco Traffic Anomaly Detector XT and Guard XT appliances and the Cisco Catalyst 6500/Cisco 7600 Traffic Anomaly Detector Module and Anomaly Guard Module are further examples of capabilities that help ensure business continuity in the event of DDoS attacks.

- **Application security and anti-X defense**: Over the past several years, a number of new application-layer network products have emerged to help protect against new classes of threats that were not adequately addressed by classic firewall and NIDS products, including viruses and worms, e-mail-based spam, phishing, and spyware, web services abuse, IP telephony abuse, and unauthorized peer-to-peer activity. Packet- and content-inspection security services on firewalls and IPS appliances help deal with these types of threats and misuse. This convergence brings granular traffic-inspection services to critical network security enforcement points, containing malicious traffic before it can be propagated across the network.

> **NOTE**   *Anti-X services* refers to unified antivirus, antispyware, file blocking, antispam, antiphishing, URL blocking and filtering, and content filtering. For example, the Content Security and Control security services module (CSC-SSM) for the Cisco ASA 5500 Series provides a comprehensive set of anti-X services.

Threat Detection and Mitigation Solution Deployment Locations

Threat detection and mitigation solutions can be deployed throughout the network, as illustrated in Figure 10-17.

Figure 10-17   *Threat Detection and Mitigation Solution Deployment Locations*

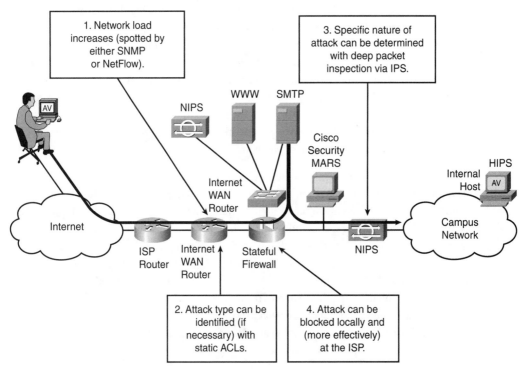

In this example, the perimeter Internet WAN router is the first line of defense in a worm attack. A network management station detects an increase in network load through SNMP or NetFlow events from the perimeter router.

Specific ACLs can be applied on this router to identify the attack type. NIPSs can use deep packet examination to determine the specific nature of the attack. HIPSs are typically implemented in software, whereas NIPSs are typically appliances or software features in a network device. Both IPS implementations use inline signature-based attack detection. HIPSs can also be used to provide host policy enforcement and verification.

A stateful firewall can be used to block the attack locally, until the Internet service provider (ISP) shuts down the attack. A key element of a successful threat detection and mitigation system is understanding when to look at which information from sources such as NetFlow, Syslog, SNMP traps, changes in SNMP values and thresholds, and Remote Monitoring (RMON).

A good security information manager such as Cisco Security MARS helps aggregate this data and present it in a useful format.

Secure Connectivity

This section discusses the secure connectivity element of the Cisco Self-Defending Network.

KEY POINT | Secure connectivity relies on privacy and data integrity.

Ensuring the privacy and integrity of all information is vital to today's businesses. Increased network connectivity results in increased exposure. As organizations adopt the use of the Internet for intranet, extranet, and teleworker connectivity—such as broadband always-on connections—maintaining security, data integrity, and privacy across these connections is a paramount requirement. LAN connections, traditionally considered trusted networks, now also require higher levels of security. In fact, internal threats are said to be ten times more financially damaging than external threats. Preserving the confidentiality and integrity of the data and applications that traverse the wired or wireless LAN needs to be an important part of business decisions.

The Cisco secure connectivity systems use encryption and authentication capabilities to provide secure transport across untrusted networks. To protect data, voice, and video applications over wired and wireless media, Cisco offers IPsec, SSL, SSH, and Multiprotocol Label Switching–based VPN technologies in addition to extensive security capabilities incorporated into Cisco wireless and IP telephony solutions to help ensure the privacy of IP communications.

Encryption Fundamentals

KEY POINT | Cryptography provides confidentiality through encryption, which is the process of disguising a message to hide its original content.

With encryption, plain text (the readable message) is converted into ciphertext (the unreadable, disguised message); decryption at the destination reverses this process. Figure 10-18 illustrates this process.

Figure 10-18   *Encryption Protects Data Confidentiality*

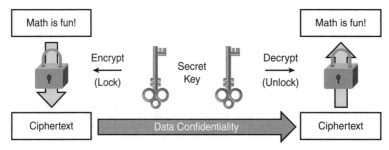

The purpose of encryption is to guarantee confidentiality; only authorized entities can encrypt and decrypt data. With most modern algorithms, successful encryption and decryption require knowledge of the appropriate cryptographic keys. A sample use of data encryption is when the IPsec encryption algorithm is used to hide the payload of IP packets.

Encryption Keys

KEY POINT | For encryption and decryption to work, devices need keys. The sender needs a key to lock (encrypt) the message, and the receiver needs a key to unlock (decrypt) the message.

Two secure ways to ensure that the receiving device has the correct key are the use of shared secrets and the Public Key Infrastructure (PKI).

With shared secrets, both sides know the same key. The encryption key can either be identical to the decryption key or just need a simple transformation to create the decryption key. The keys represent a shared secret between two or more parties that can be used to maintain a private information link. The key is carried out-of-band to the remote side; for example, one user might telephone the other to tell him or her what the key is. Although this is the easiest mechanism, it has some inherent security concerns. Because the keys are potentially subject to discovery, they need to be changed often and kept secure during distribution and while in service. Reliably selecting, distributing, and maintaining shared keys without error or discovery can be difficult.

PKI uses asymmetric keys, in which the encryption key is different from the decryption key. Most PKI systems rely on certificates to establish a party's identity and its public key; certificates are issued by a centralized certificate authority (CA) computer whose legitimacy is trusted. Each unique pair of public and private keys is related but not identical.

KEY POINT	Data encrypted with a public key can be decrypted only with the corresponding private key, and data that is encrypted with a private key can be decrypted only with the corresponding public key.
	In PKI, data encrypted with the public key cannot be decrypted with the public key.

Parties that need to encrypt their communications exchange their public keys (contained in certificates) but do not disclose their private keys. The sending party uses the receiving party's public key to encrypt the message data and forwards the ciphertext (the encrypted data) to the receiving party. The receiving party then decrypts the ciphertext with its private key. PKI encryption is widely used in e-commerce sites.

VPN Protocols

IPsec and SSL are the two common VPN protocols. IPsec VPNs are built directly on the IP layer using protocol 50, the Encapsulating Security Payload, to encrypt traffic. IPsec VPNs use the IKE protocol to exchange keys; IKE normally uses PKI certificates. IPsec requires both communicating endpoints to run software that understands IPsec. Most routers and security appliances currently support high-speed IPsec.

SSL VPNs are built on top of the TCP layer using port 443, the HTTPS port. SSL VPNs are used extensively to provide confidentiality for web traffic and are supported by all major browsers.

Transmission Confidentiality: Ensuring Privacy

Transmission confidentiality protects data as it is transported over unsafe networks. When connecting trusted and untrusted networks (for example, when connecting a corporate network to the Internet), data can be transmitted among trusted subjects over untrusted networks. Untrusted networks do not allow implementation of classic access control mechanisms, because a corporation does not have control over users and network resources in the untrusted network. Therefore, the transmitted data must be protected to ensure that no one in the untrusted network can view it (violate its confidentiality) or change it (violate its integrity). Modern network security relies on cryptography to provide confidentiality and integrity for transmitted data.

The network shown in Figure 10-19 shows a connection of two sites over an untrusted network, the Internet. To provide data confidentiality, a VPN technology that supports encryption creates a secured point-to-point association of the sites over the Internet. All packets that leave one site are encrypted, forwarded through the untrusted network, and decrypted by a device on the remote site. Anyone who eavesdrops on the untrusted network should not be able to decrypt the packet payloads to read sensitive data.

Figure 10-19   *Transmission Confidentiality Provided by Encryption*

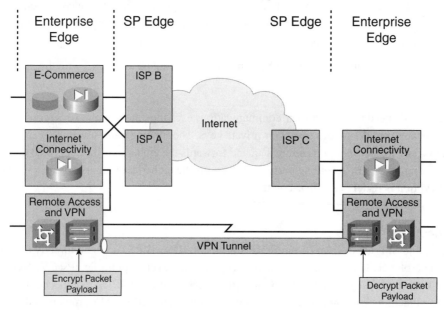

Transmission Confidentiality Guidelines

Following are some specific cryptography guidelines to consider when designing and implementing a solution for transmission confidentiality:

■ Cryptography can become a performance bottleneck, and careful analysis is required to determine where data should be protected. In general, if confidential or sensitive data travels over a network where an attacker could easily intercept communications (such as a network outside of the organization's physical control or a network where device compromises are likely), communications must be protected as the security policy defines.

■ Modern cryptography algorithms can now be exported, although some might still be subject to controls, depending on legal regulations. Use the strongest available cryptography to provide sufficient protection. Be cautious, however; some cryptographic algorithms allow you to specify extremely long key lengths, which, at some point, do not provide worthwhile confidentiality improvements over shorter keys.

■ Use only well-known cryptographic algorithms, because only well-known algorithms that have been tested and analyzed are considered trustworthy. Examples of well-known algorithms are Triple Data Encryption Standard (3DES), Advanced Encryption Standard (AES), and Rivest Cipher 4 (RC4). In general, do not trust any algorithms that claim to represent a security breakthrough; these are often extremely weak and easily broken.

> **NOTE** The data encryption standard (DES) uses a 56-bit key. 3DES encrypts the data three times, with up to three different keys.

■ Do not forget that encryption provides only confidentiality, and most organizations consider data integrity and authenticity equally important security elements. If possible, use both confidentiality- and integrity-guaranteeing cryptographic algorithms.

For example, to lower communication costs, a health insurance company decides to connect some of its branch offices to its headquarters over the Internet. The company must protect patient record confidentiality; because attackers on the Internet can intercept communications, the company implements a VPN using the strongest possible encryption algorithms to guarantee data confidentiality. In the event of interception, it is unlikely that the attacker can decrypt messages that are protected with modern cryptographic algorithms such as 3DES, AES, or RC4.

Maintaining Data Integrity

Cryptography also provides data integrity mechanisms to protect data in transit over untrusted networks. Cryptographic protocols, such as secure fingerprints and digital signatures, can detect any integrity violation of sensitive data.

> **KEY POINT** Secure fingerprints attach a cryptographically strong checksum to data. This checksum is generated and verified using a secret key that only authorized subjects know.

By verifying the checksum of received data, an authorized subject can verify data integrity. For example, a method of secure fingerprints known as a Hash-Based Message Authentication Code (HMAC) is implemented in the IPsec standard to provide packet integrity and authenticity in IP networks. The HMAC method is very fast and is suitable for real-time traffic protection (for both integrity and authentication).

> **KEY POINT** Digital signing of data uses a cryptography method that attaches a digital signature to sensitive data. This signature is generated using a unique signature generation key that is known only to the signer, not to anyone else. Other parties use the signer's signature verification key to verify the signature.

The cryptography behind digital signing guarantees the data's authenticity and the fact that the data has not been modified since it was signed. In the financial world, digital signatures also provide nonrepudiation of transactions, in which a subject can prove to a third party that a transaction has indeed occurred. Digital signature protocols are based on public-key cryptography and, because of their performance limitations, are not used for bulk protection.

Figure 10-20 illustrates a connection between two network sites over the Internet. To provide data integrity, a VPN that supports secure fingerprinting is used to create a secured point-to-point association over the Internet. All packets that leave one site are imprinted with a secure digital fingerprint (similar to a very strong checksum) that uniquely identifies the data at the sender's side. The packets are forwarded onto the untrusted network, and a device on the remote site verifies the secure fingerprint to ensure that no one has tampered with the packet. Anyone who eavesdrops on the untrusted network should not be able to change the packet payloads; therefore, they should not be able to change sensitive data without being detected.

Figure 10-20 *Secure Fingerprints Ensure Data Integrity*

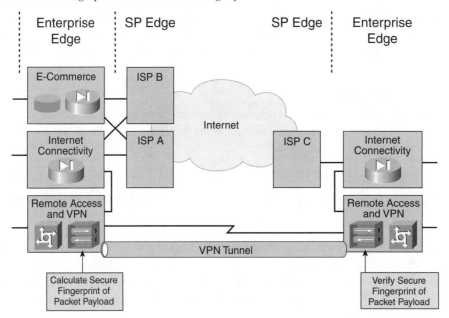

Transmission Integrity Guidelines

Following are some guidelines for using data integrity cryptography mechanisms, which are similar to those for confidentiality mechanisms:

■ Carefully evaluate the need for integrity and enforce only where justified by potential threats.

- Use the strongest available mechanisms for integrity, but take the performance effects into account.

- Use only established and well-known cryptographic algorithms.

For example, consider an organization that must transmit stock market data over the Internet. Confidentiality is not its main concern; rather, its primary risk lies in the possibility of an attacker changing data in transit and presenting false stock market data to the organization. Because e-mail is the organization's preferred data exchange application, it decides to implement digital signatures of all e-mail messages when exchanging data among partners over the Internet.

Security Management

This section provides an overview of security management.

KEY POINT | A secured network must be managed securely.

Security management applications and technologies are used to monitor and control the network, including performing the following tasks:

- Collecting, analyzing, and presenting network data to network managers. The tools used should allow for centrally storing and analyzing audit results, including logs and traps. In addition to logging using the syslog protocol, IDSs can be used to provide automatic correlation and in-depth visibility into complex security events, saving administrators a considerable amount of time.

- Structured deployment and provisioning of security policies on security devices.

- Maintaining consistency and change control of policies.

- Providing roles-based access control and accounts for all activities, and implementing change control and monitoring to prevent accidental damage.

Organizations must audit changes made and ensure that new versions of device configurations and device software are installed according to corporate policies.

Security implementation is only as good as the security policies being implemented. The biggest risk to security in a properly planned network architecture is an error in the security policy. Network management personnel must be aware of the security policies and defined operational procedures so that they can respond to an incident quickly, reliably, and appropriately.

Cisco Security Management Technologies

The Cisco Security Management Suite is a framework of products and technologies designed for scalable policy administration and enforcement for the Cisco Self-Defending Network. This integrated solution can simplify and automate the tasks associated with security management operations, including configuration, monitoring, analysis, and response. The key components of this suite include the following:

- **Cisco Security Manager**: Cisco Security Manager is a powerful but easy-to-use solution for configuring firewall, VPN, and IPS policies on Cisco security appliances, firewalls, routers, and switch modules. Using a GUI, Cisco Security Manager allows security policies to be easily configured per device, per device group, or globally.

- **Cisco Security MARS**: Cisco Security MARS is an appliance-based solution that allows network and security administrators to monitor, identify, isolate, and counter security threats. Cisco Security MARS obtains network intelligence by understanding the topology and device configurations from routers, switches, NetFlow, IPS, firewalls, and other network devices and by profiling network traffic. The integrated network discovery in the system builds a topology map containing device configuration and current security policies that enables Cisco Security MARS to model packet flows through the network. Because the appliance does not operate inline and makes minimal use of existing software agents, there is minimal impact on network or system performance.

These products are built on an architecture that facilitates integration with other security management tools, such as the following:

- **Cisco SDM**: Cisco SDM is a web-based device-management tool for Cisco routers that can improve the productivity of network managers; simplify router deployments for integrated services such as dynamic routing, WAN access, WLAN, firewall, VPN, SSL VPN, IPS, and quality of service (QoS); and help troubleshoot complex network and VPN connectivity issues. Cisco SDM supports a wide range of Cisco IOS Software releases and is available free of charge on Cisco router models from Cisco 830 Series Routers to Cisco 7301 Routers.

- **Cisco Adaptive Security Device Manager (ASDM)**: Cisco ASDM provides security management and monitoring services for the Cisco ASA 5500 Series Adaptive Security Appliances, Cisco PIX 500 Series Security Appliances (running Cisco PIX Security Appliance Software Release 7.0 or later) and the Cisco Catalyst 6500 Series Firewall Services Modules (FWSM version 3.1 or later) through an intuitive, easy-to-use web-based management interface. Cisco ASDM accelerates security appliance deployment with intelligent wizards, robust administration tools, and versatile monitoring services.

- **Cisco Intrusion Prevention System Device Manager (IDM)**: Cisco IDM is a web-based Java application that allows configuration and management of IPS sensors. The web server software for Cisco IDM resides on the sensor and is accessed through Netscape or Internet Explorer web browsers with SSL. The whole range of IPS v5.0-capable platforms can be managed using Cisco IDM.

- **CiscoWorks Management Center for Cisco Security Agents**: Using Management Center for Cisco Security Agents (a component of the CiscoWorks VPN/Security Management Solution), network devices are assembled into specified groups, and then security policies are attached to those groups. All configuration is done through the web-based user interface and then is deployed to the agents. The Management Center for Cisco Security Agents software is installed on a system that maintains all policy and host groups. The administration user interface is accessed securely using SSL from any device on the network that can connect to the server and run a web browser. The web-based interface is used to deploy policies from the Management Center for Cisco Security Agents software to agents across the network.

- **Cisco Secure Access Control Server**: Cisco Secure ACS provides identity-based services that provide centralized control for role-based access to all Cisco devices and security management applications, including Cisco IOS routers, VPNs, firewalls, dialup and DSL connections, cable access solutions, storage, content, VoIP connections, Cisco wireless solutions, and Cisco Catalyst switches.

Network Security Solutions

This section discusses how security is integrated in Cisco network devices and describes designing network security solutions for enterprise networks.

Integrated Security Within Network Devices

The section explains the security features integrated in Cisco network devices. To design and implement a secure network, it is necessary to integrate security in every part of the network environment. Cisco network devices supporting integrated security include the following:

- Cisco IOS routers

- Security appliances, including

  — VPN concentrators

  — Cisco PIX security appliances

  — ASAs

- IPSs

- Catalyst services modules

- Endpoint security solutions

The following sections describe these devices.

Cisco IOS Router Security

Devices based on Cisco IOS software incorporate various security features to create an integrated and scalable network.

The Cisco IOS Firewall is a security-specific option for Cisco IOS software that provides integrated network security with robust stateful firewall functionality for network perimeters. The Cisco IOS Firewall gives enterprises and small and medium businesses a very cost-effective option, in terms of both initial capital investment and continuing administrative costs. The Cisco IOS Firewalls help businesses guarantee network uptime and security by protecting customer networks from network and application layer attacks, viruses, and worms, and providing effective control of application traffic flowing through the network. The Cisco IOS Firewall offers sophisticated security and policy-enforcement services for connections within an organization (intranet) and between partner networks (extranets), as well as for securing Internet connectivity for teleworker and branch offices.

The Cisco IOS IPS is an inline, deep packet inspection–based feature that enables Cisco IOS software to effectively mitigate a wide range of network attacks. As a core facet of the Cisco Self-Defending Network, the Cisco IOS IPS enables the network to defend itself with the intelligence to accurately identify, classify, and stop or block malicious or damaging traffic in real time. The Cisco IOS IPS operates by loading a set of attack signatures on the router. To assist users in signature selection, Cisco provides prebuilt signature definition files that contain high-fidelity signatures based on the memory available on a router. Registered users on http://www.cisco.com/ with a Cisco service agreement can download the latest version of these files and the complete set of Cisco IPS signatures in Cisco IOS IPS signature definition files. The Cisco IOS IPS complements the Cisco IOS Firewall and VPN solutions for superior threat protection at all entry points into the network.

The Cisco IOS IPsec functionality provides network data encryption at the IP packet level, resulting in a robust, standards-based security solution. IPsec provides data confidentiality, data authentication, and antireplay services, and it is the only way to implement secure VPNs. Organizations combine IPsec with other Cisco IOS software functionality to build scalable, robust, and secure QoS-aware VPNs.

The Cisco IOS software trust and identity services include core technologies that enable network traffic security: AAA, PKI, SSH, SSL, and 802.1X. The Cisco IOS AAA is an architectural framework for configuring a set of three independent security functions in a consistent manner, providing a modular way to perform authentication, authorization, and accounting services on a router or access server. PKI provides strong and robust authentication, authorization, confidentiality, and nonrepudiation for e-business and e-commerce applications.

Cisco ISRs support the following additional options to enhance network security:

- **Built-in VPN acceleration**: The built-in, hardware-based encryption acceleration offloads the VPN processes to provide increased VPN throughput with minimal impact on the router CPU.

- **Secure voice**: Packet voice digital signal processor (DSP) modules (PVDM) for the DSP slots in ISRs provide conferencing, transcoding, and secure voice features. The Secure Real-Time Transport Protocol encrypts the voice payload, leaving the header in cleartext to support QoS and other features.

- **High-performance advanced integration module (AIM)**: The VPN and encryption AIMs are used for aggregation-type applications, such as DMVPNs, in which large numbers of remote VPN tunnels are required. The VPN and encryption AIMs support 3DES and AES and boost router encryption and compression performance.

- **Cisco IDS Network Module for the Cisco 2600, 2800, 3600, 3700, and 3800 Routers**: The Cisco IDS Network Module (NM-CIDS) includes innovative technologies, including correlation and validation tools, which take preventive actions on a broader range of threats and greatly reduce the risk of dropping legitimate traffic.

- **Cisco 2600/2800/3600/3700/3800 Series Content Engine Module**: The Cisco Content Engine Network Module provides a router-integrated application and content networking system. Available configurations include a 40-GB hard disk or an 80-GB internal hard disk.

- **Cisco Network Analysis Module (NAM)**: The Cisco NAM analyzes traffic flows for applications, hosts, conversations, and IP-based services such as QoS and VoIP. It also collects exported NetFlow data to provide broad application-level visibility.

NOTE   Although the 2600, 3600, and 3700 routers are not ISRs, they do support the IDS network module and Content Engine Network Module.

NOTE   For a complete list of supported modules, refer to *Cisco Integrated Services Routers— 1800/2800/3800 Series At-a-Glance,* available at http://www.cisco.com/warp/public/765/tools/ quickreference/isr.pdf.

Security Appliances

This section introduces Cisco security appliances.

VPN Concentrators

The Cisco VPN 3000 Series concentrators are remote-access VPN devices that provide enterprises with IPsec- and SSL-based VPN connectivity. The centralized architecture provides ease of management and implementation in deployments that require detailed access controls for numerous deployment scenarios with diverse user communities, including mobile workers, telecommuters, and extranet users.

Cisco PIX Security Appliances

The Cisco PIX 500 Series security appliances deliver rich application and protocol inspection, robust user and application policy enforcement, multivector attack protection, and secure connectivity services in cost-effective, easy-to-deploy solutions. Ranging from the compact, plug-and-play desktop Cisco PIX 501 security appliance for SOHOs to the modular gigabit Cisco PIX 535 security appliance with superior investment protection for enterprise and service-provider environments, Cisco PIX 500 Series security appliances provide comprehensive security, performance, and reliability for network environments of all sizes.

ASAs

The Cisco ASA 5500 Series ASAs are high-performance, multifunction security appliances delivering converged firewall, IPS, network antivirus, and VPN services. As a key component of the Cisco Self-Defending Network, these appliances provide proactive threat mitigation that stops attacks before they spread through the network, control network activity and application traffic, and deliver flexible VPN connectivity while remaining cost-effective and easy to manage.

Compared to the Cisco PIX security appliances, the ASAs offer additional services, such as IPS functionality, adaptive threat defense capabilities, application security, Anti-X defenses, integration with Cisco WebVPN Services modules, and AIMs to enhance the appliance's processing capabilities.

IPSs

The Cisco IPS solution combines passive IDS with inline IPS. The Cisco IPS appliances offer comprehensive proactive protection of the network through their capability to collaborate with other network security resources. These appliances support multivector threat identification to protect the network from policy violations, vulnerability exploitations, and anomalous activity through detailed inspection of traffic in Layers 2 through 7.

Cisco IPS 4200 Series sensors offer significant network protection by helping detect, classify, and stop threats, including worms, spyware, adware, network viruses, and application abuse. Using Cisco IPS Sensor Software Version 5.1, the Cisco IPS solution combines inline IPS with innovative technologies that improve accuracy so that more threats can be stopped without the risk of dropping legitimate network traffic. This software includes enhanced detection capabilities and improved scalability, resiliency, and performance features.

The available sensors support bandwidths up to 1 gigabit per second (Gbps) and include the following:

■   The Cisco IPS 4215 sensor accurately investigates and protects up to 65 Mbps of traffic and is suitable for multiple T1/E1 and T3 environments.

■   The Cisco IPS 4240 sensor, at 250 Mbps, can be deployed to provide protection in switched environments with multiple T3 subnets. With the support of multiple 10/100/1000 interfaces, it can also be deployed on partially utilized gigabit links or fully saturated full-duplex 100-Mbps environments.

■   The Cisco 4240-DC sensor is based on the IPS 4240 sensor but supports DC power. The IPS 4240-DC is Network Equipment Building System (NEBS)–compliant and can be deployed in environments that have specific requirements pertaining to NEBS Level 3 compliance.

NOTE   *NEBS* is a set of standards for telecommunications equipment that specifies the equipment's operation with respect to a variety of environmental factors such as temperature, humidity, and vibration.

■   The Cisco IPS 4255 sensor delivers 500 Mbps of performance. It can be used to protect partially utilized gigabit subnets and traffic traversing switches being used to aggregate traffic from many subnets.

■   The Cisco IPS 4260 sensor delivers 1 Gbps of protection performance. It can be used to protect both gigabit subnets and aggregated traffic traversing switches from multiple subnets. This purpose-built device supports both copper and fiber environments, providing deployment flexibility.

Catalyst Services Modules

The following are various security-related modules for the Cisco Catalyst 6500 Series switching platform (and some are also for the Cisco 7600 Series routers):

■   **Cisco Catalyst 6500 Series FWSM**: The Cisco FWSM is a high-speed, integrated firewall module for Cisco Catalyst 6500 Series switches and Cisco 7600 Series routers. Up to four Cisco FWSMs can be installed in a single chassis, providing scalability up to 20 Gbps per chassis. The Cisco FWSM includes many advanced features, such as multiple security contexts at both the routed level and in bridging mode, helping reduce cost and operational complexity while managing multiple firewalls from the same management platform.

■ **Cisco Catalyst 6500 Series Intrusion Detection System Services module 2 (IDSM-2)**: The Cisco IDSM-2 is part of the Cisco IPS that works in concert with the other components to efficiently protect the data infrastructure. It supports both inline (IPS) mode and passive operation (IDS). Up to 500 Mbps of IDS and IPS inspection provides high-speed packet examination and allows for protection of a wider variety of networks and traffic.

■ **Cisco Catalyst 6500 Series SSL Services module**: The Cisco SSL Services module is an integrated services module for the Cisco Catalyst 6500 Series switches and Cisco 7600 Series routers. It offloads processor-intensive tasks related to securing traffic with SSL, increases the number of secure connections supported by a website, and reduces the operational complexity of high-performance web server farms. Up to four Cisco SSL Services modules can be installed in each chassis.

■ **Cisco IPsec VPN Shared Port Adapter (SPA)**: The Cisco IPsec VPN SPA delivers scalable and cost-effective VPN performance for Cisco Catalyst 6500 Series switches and Cisco 7600 Series routers. Using the Cisco Services SPA Carrier-400, each slot of the Cisco Catalyst 6500 switch or Cisco 7600 router can support up to two Cisco IPsec VPN SPAs. Although the Cisco IPsec VPN SPA does not have physical WAN or LAN interfaces, it takes advantage of the breadth of LAN and WAN interfaces of each of the platforms.

■ **Cisco Catalyst 6500/Cisco 7600 Traffic Anomaly Detector module**: The Cisco Traffic Anomaly Detector module uses behavioral analysis and attack recognition technology to proactively detect and identify all types of online assaults. By constantly monitoring traffic destined for a protected device, such as a web or e-commerce server, the Cisco Traffic Anomaly Detector module compiles detailed profiles that indicate how individual devices behave under normal operating conditions. If the Cisco Traffic Anomaly Detector module detects any per-flow deviations from the profile, it considers the anomalous behavior a potential attack and responds based on user preference—by sending an operator alert to initiate a manual response, by notifying a management system, or by launching the Cisco Anomaly Guard Module to immediately begin mitigation services.

■ **Cisco Catalyst 6500/Cisco 7600 Anomaly Guard module**: A single Cisco Anomaly Guard module allows the platform to process attack traffic at gigabit-per-second line rates. The Cisco Anomaly Guard module employs a unique on-demand deployment model, diverting and scrubbing only traffic addressed to targeted devices or zones without affecting other traffic. Within the module, integrated multiple layers of defense enable it to identify and block malicious attack traffic while allowing legitimate transactions to continue flowing to their original destinations.

- **Cisco Catalyst 6500 Series NAM**: The Cisco NAM provides visibility into all layers of network traffic by using Remote Monitoring 2 and other advanced management information bases. The Cisco NAM accesses the built-in Remote Monitoring (mini-RMON) features of the Cisco Catalyst 6500 Series switches and Cisco 7600 Series routers to provide port-level traffic statistics at the MAC (data link) layer. It also delivers the intelligence required to analyze traffic flows for applications, hosts, conversations, and network-based services, such as QoS and VoIP.

Endpoint Security Solutions

Cisco also has security solutions for endpoint security: the Cisco Security Agent and the Management Center for Cisco Security Agents. The Cisco Security Agent software integrates endpoint server and desktop computers into the Cisco Self-Defending Network. The Cisco Security Agent provides the following services for endpoints:

- Spyware and adware protection

- Protection against buffer overflows

- Distributed firewall capabilities

- Malicious mobile code protection

- Operating system integrity assurance

- Application inventory

- Audit log consolidation

The Cisco Security Agent identifies and prevents malicious behavior, eliminating known and unknown ("Day Zero") network threats. The Cisco Security Agent aggregates and extends multiple endpoint security functions by providing intrusion prevention and distributed firewall capabilities in addition to malicious mobile code protection, system integrity assurance, and audit log consolidation. All these capabilities are based on deploying Cisco Security Agents throughout the network and configuring and managing the agents through the Management Center for Cisco Security Agents. The Cisco Security Agent also provides important endpoint information to the Cisco Security MARS to enhance threat identification and investigation across the network. The Cisco Security Agent integrates with Cisco NAC and NAC Appliances with trusted QoS to improve the delivery of mission-critical traffic when the network is under a heavy load.

As discussed earlier, the Management Center for Cisco Security Agents provides all management functions for all agents in a centralized manner. Its role-based web browser access makes it easy for administrators to create agent software distribution packages, create or modify security policies, monitor alerts, or generate reports. The Management Center ships with more than 20 fully configured default policies, making it easy for administrators to deploy thousands of agents across the enterprise. It also allows customers to deploy agents in IDS mode, in which alerts are generated for suspicious activities, but traffic is not blocked.

Securing the Enterprise Network

Securing the enterprise network involves deploying technologies that support identity and access control, threat defense and infrastructure protection, and security management. This section reviews the locations at which security devices and solutions might be deployed within the Enterprise network of a sample organization.

Deploying Security in the Enterprise Campus

Consider an organization that has experienced several incidents in which laptop users on the campus network have brought in viruses from home, some users have attempted to intercept network traffic, and some interns have tried to hack the network infrastructure. To manage the risks, the organization implements identity and access control solutions, threat detection and mitigation solutions, infrastructure protection, and security management. Figure 10-21 illustrates where various security technologies might be deployed within the Enterprise Campus.

Figure 10-21 *Security in the Enterprise Campus*

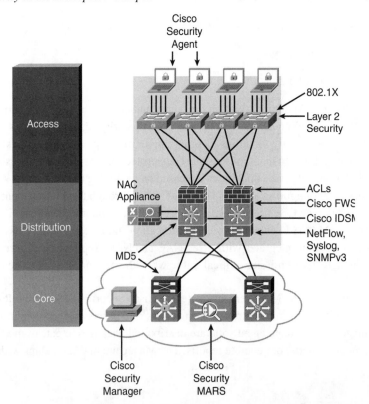

Identity and access control technologies include the following:

- 802.1X port security and/or NAC for user endpoints

- NAC appliances

- ACLs on Cisco IOS devices

- Firewalls (for example, Cisco FWSM) provide stateful inspection and application inspection

Threat detection and mitigation technologies include the following:

- NetFlow

- Syslog

- SNMPv3

- HIPS (for example, the Cisco Security Agent)

- NIPS

- Cisco Security MARS

- Cisco Security Manager

Infrastructure protection technologies include the following:

- AAA

- SSH

- SNMPv3

- IGP or EGP MD5 routing protocol security

- Layer 2 security features

Security management technologies include Cisco Security MARS and Cisco Security Manager.

Deploying Security in the Enterprise Data Center

The organization's data center hosts servers for the main campus network and branch offices. These servers contain the enterprise's most sensitive information and are available to a large number of users. Network performance is a critically important issue, which sometimes limits the choice of protection mechanisms. Some specific risks in the data center include direct compromise of exposed applications and unauthorized access to data, and compromise of other hosts from compromised servers in this module.

To provide security, the organization implements identity and access control solutions, threat detection and mitigation solutions, infrastructure protection, and security management. Figure 10-22 illustrates where various security technologies might be deployed within the Enterprise Data Center.

Figure 10-22 *Security in the Enterprise Data Center*

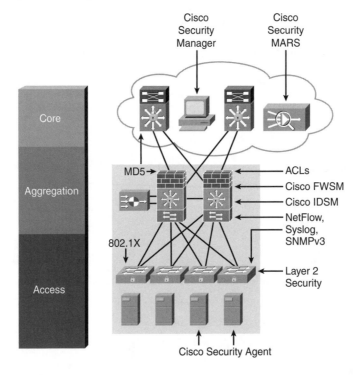

Identity and access control technologies include the following:

- 802.1X port security

- ACLs on Cisco IOS devices

- Firewalls (for example, Cisco FWSM)

Threat detection and mitigation technologies include the following:

- NetFlow

- Syslog

- SNMPv3

- HIPS (for example, the Cisco Security Agent)

- IDS (for example, the Cisco IDSM-2)

- NIPS

- Cisco Security MARS

- Cisco Security Manager

Infrastructure protection technologies include the following:

- AAA

- SSH

- SNMPv3

- IGP or EGP MD5 routing protocol security

- Layer 2 security features

Security management technologies include Cisco Security MARS and Cisco Security Manager.

Deploying Security in the Enterprise Edge

The enterprise edge modules provide WAN connectivity among various parts of the enterprise network. Security is important whenever data is transferred between locations. For example, some specific risks in the WAN module include the following:

- Data transmission confidentiality and integrity violations, in which an attacker who obtains physical access to the network media or to a service provider WAN switch can intercept WAN traffic and might eavesdrop or change data in transit.

- Accidental or deliberate misconfiguration of the WAN network, which can result in the interconnection of different enterprises. Some WAN protocols might establish automatic peering, and unwanted connectivity could become possible.

To provide security, the organization implements identity and access control solutions, threat detection and mitigation solutions, infrastructure protection, and security management. Figure 10-23 illustrates where various security technologies might be deployed within the Enterprise Edge.

Figure 10-23 *Security in the Enterprise Edge*

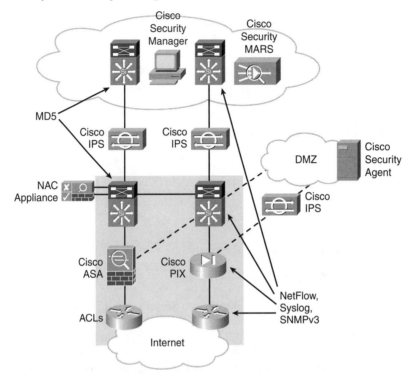

Identity and access control technologies include the following:

- ACLs on Cisco IOS devices

- Firewalls (such as Cisco PIX Security appliances)

- IPsec or SSL VPNs

- NAC appliances

- ASA appliances

Threat detection and mitigation technologies include the following:

- NetFlow

- Syslog

- SNMPv3

- HIPS (for example, the Cisco Security Agent)

- NIPS

- Cisco Security MARS

- Cisco Security Manager

Infrastructure protection technologies include the following:

- AAA

- SSH

- SNMPv3

- IGP or EGP MD5 routing protocol security

Security management technologies include Cisco Security MARS and Cisco Security Manager.

Summary

In this chapter, you learned about security design principles with a focus on the following topics:

- The need for network security, including business and legal requirements

- The threats to network security, including reconnaissance, unauthorized access, and DoS

- Security risks, including a breach of data confidentiality or integrity, and system and data availability interruptions

- Network security policies and process

- Calculating risk indices

- The Cisco Self-Defending Network, including three critical elements: trust and identity management, threat defense, and secure connectivity

- Security management

- How security is integrated in Cisco network devices

- How security solutions are deployed in the Enterprise network

References

For additional information, refer to the following resources:

- Cisco Systems, Inc., Security: Introduction, http://www.cisco.com/en/US/products/hw/vpndevc/index.html

- Cisco Systems, Inc., Infrastructure Protection on Cisco IOS Software-Based Platforms, http://www.cisco.com/application/pdf/en/us/guest/products/ps1838/c1244/cdccont_0900aecd804ac831.pdf

- Cisco Systems, Inc., Security: Support Resources, http://www.cisco.com/en/US/products/hw/vpndevc/tsd_products_support_category_home.html

- Cisco Systems, Inc., Cisco Router and Security Device Manager: Introduction, http://www.cisco.com/en/US/products/sw/secursw/ps5318/index.html

- Cisco Systems, Inc., Cisco Adaptive Security Device Manager: Introduction, http://www.cisco.com/en/US/products/ps6121/index.html

- Cisco Systems, Inc., Cisco Intrusion Prevention System: Introduction, http://www.cisco.com/en/US/products/sw/secursw/ps2113/index.html

- Cisco Systems, Inc., CiscoWorks Management Center for Cisco Security Agents: Introduction, http://www.cisco.com/en/US/products/sw/cscowork/ps5212/index.html

- Cisco Systems, Inc., Cisco Secure Access Control Server for Windows: Introduction, http://www.cisco.com/en/US/products/sw/secursw/ps2086/index.html

- Cisco Systems, Inc., Cisco Security Management Suite: Introduction, http://www.cisco.com/en/US/netsol/ns647/networking_solutions_sub_solution_home.html

- Cisco Systems, Inc., Cisco Security Manager: Introduction, http://www.cisco.com/en/US/products/ps6498/index.html

- Cisco Systems, Inc., Cisco Security Monitoring, Analysis and Response System: Introduction, http://www.cisco.com/en/US/products/ps6241/index.html

- Cisco Systems, Inc., Cisco IOS Firewall: Introduction, http://www.cisco.com/en/US/products/sw/secursw/ps1018/index.html

- Cisco Systems, Inc., Cisco IOS Intrusion Prevention System (IPS): Introduction, http://www.cisco.com/en/US/products/ps6634/products_ios_protocol_group_home.html

- Cisco Systems, Inc., Cisco IOS IPsec: Introduction, http://www.cisco.com/en/US/products/ps6635/products_ios_protocol_group_home.html

- Cisco Systems, Inc., Cisco IOS Trust and Identity: Introduction, http://www.cisco.com/en/US/products/ps6638/products_ios_protocol_group_home.html

- Cisco Systems, Inc., Cisco Intrusion Prevention System: Introduction, http://www.cisco.com/en/US/products/sw/secursw/ps2113/index.html

- Cisco Systems, Inc., Cisco Integrated Services Routers—1800/2800/3800 Series, at-a-Glance, http://www.cisco.com/warp/public/765/tools/quickreference/isr.pdf

- Cisco Systems, Inc., Security Solutions for Large Enterprises, http://www.cisco.com/en/US/netsol/ns340/ns394/ns171/ns413/networking_solutions_package.html

- Cisco Systems, Inc., Cisco Security Center, http://tools.cisco.com/security/center/home.x

Case Study 10-1: ACMC Hospital Network Security Design

This case study is a continuation of the ACMC Hospital case study introduced in Chapter 2, "Applying a Methodology to Network Design."

Case Study General Instructions

Use the scenarios, information, and parameters provided at each task of the ongoing case study. If you encounter ambiguities, make reasonable assumptions and proceed. For all tasks, use the initial customer scenario and build on the solutions provided thus far. You can use any and all documentation, books, white papers, and so on.

In each step, you act as a network design consultant. Make creative proposals to accomplish the customer's business needs. Justify your ideas when they differ from the provided solutions. Use any design strategies you feel are appropriate. The final goal of each case study is a paper solution.

Appendix A, "Answers to Review Questions and Case Studies," provides a solution for each step based on assumptions made. There is no claim that the provided solution is the best or only solution. Your solution might be more appropriate for the assumptions you made. The provided solution helps you understand the author's reasoning and allows you to compare and contrast your solution.

In this case study, you create a high-level security design for the ACMC Hospital network. Figure 10-24 summarizes the design thus far.

Figure 10-24 *ACMC Hospital Network Design*

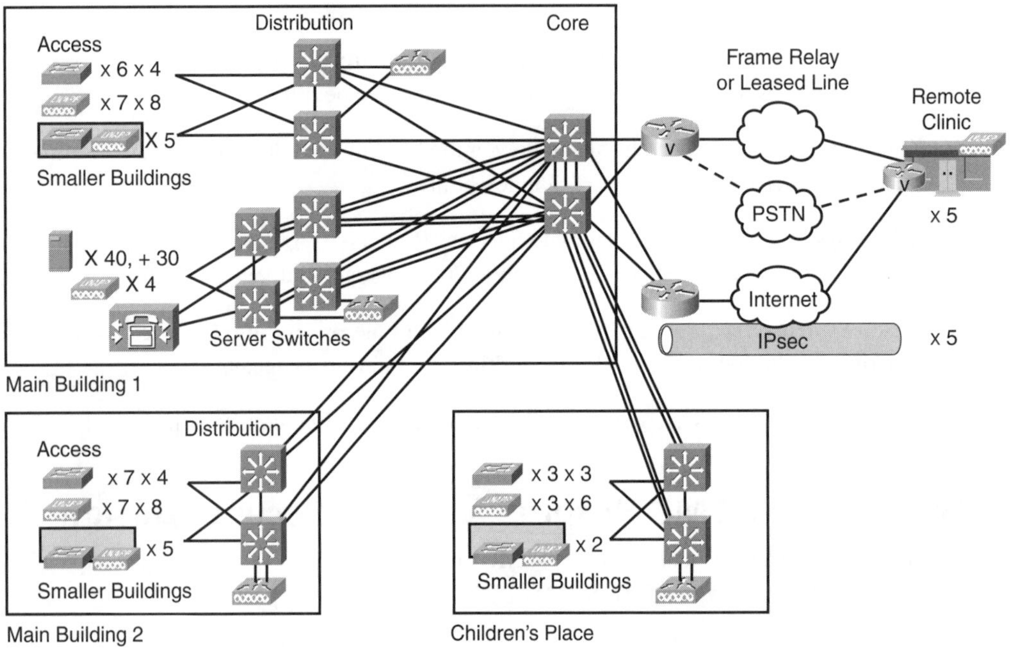

Case Study Questions

Complete the following steps:

Step 1   Identify key business security requirements, risks, and threats about which ACMC should be concerned.

Step 2   Design the Enterprise Edge modules for ACMC (E-commerce, Internet Connectivity, Remote Access and VPN, and WAN and MAN and Site-to-Site VPN). Determine how they should connect to the rest of the ACMC Hospital network. The design can use a consolidated approach in which devices are shared between modules.

Step 3   Design the security for remote clinics, using the Internet with VPN for backup access.

Step 4   Determine suitable IP subnetting for the Internet, DMZ, and VPN.

Step 5   Which Cisco security products and features would you recommend in the Enterprise Campus and the data center or server switches?

Step 6   Identify some of the other security considerations, products, and features that should be part of deployment and where they should be used. For example, how should you handle infrastructure protection?

Case Study 10-2: ACMC Hospital Network—Connecting More Hospitals

This case study is a continuation of ACMC Hospital Case Study 10-1.

Case Study General Instructions

Use the scenarios, information, and parameters provided at each task of the ongoing case study. If you encounter ambiguities, make reasonable assumptions and proceed. For all tasks, use the initial customer scenario and build on the solutions provided thus far.

You can use any and all documentation, books, white papers, and so on. In each step, you act as a network design consultant. Make creative proposals to accomplish the customer's business needs. Justify your ideas when they differ from the provided solutions. Use any design strategies you feel are appropriate. The final goal of each case study is a paper solution.

Appendix A provides a solution for each step based on assumptions made. There is no claim that the provided solution is the best or only solution. Your solution might be more appropriate for the assumptions you made. The provided solution helps you understand the author's reasoning and allows you to compare and contrast your solution.

In this case study, you expand the ACMC hospital network as it merges with two other hospitals. The government of the state in which ACMC operates wants to improve patient service by networking hospitals; the network will be called MedNet. The legislature hopes to leverage large-city medical expertise for telemedicine at smaller locations. Short-term TDM circuits are funded; MedNet will move to Metro Ethernet service after terms for provider construction and contract are agreed on. Clinics will be associated with and connected via county hospitals.

Case Study Questions

Complete the following steps:

Step 1   Hospital Omega is a nearby hospital that has been having financial difficulties. It is facing large licensing and application development costs to bring its financial and other applications up to date. To cut costs and stabilize finances, Hospital Omega will merge with ACMC. All data services will move to the ACMC data center and gradually migrate to the modern applications that ACMC already has in place. The Hospital Omega network was deployed between seven and ten years ago, and in many cases, the equipment vendors no longer exist. The following are some details about Hospital Omega:

- Hospital Omega does not use DHCP.

- Hospital Omega consists of one building of ten floors, with fewer than 250 computers per floor.

- Hospital Omega uses static routes.

- The Hospital Omega network is flat and Layer 2 switched. The switching equipment is from a third-party vendor and is seven and ten years old.

- The Hospital Omega network uses old copper and fiber cabling that was added by various people in a random manner over the years. For any given closet, about 50 percent of the cable (copper or fiber) goes to unknown locations and is of unknown quality.

- Servers are scattered around the building in random closets near the department that originally installed them.

- Hospital Omega accesses the Internet via the University Research Group.

Figure 10-25 shows the Hospital Omega network.

Figure 10-25 *Hospital Omega Network*

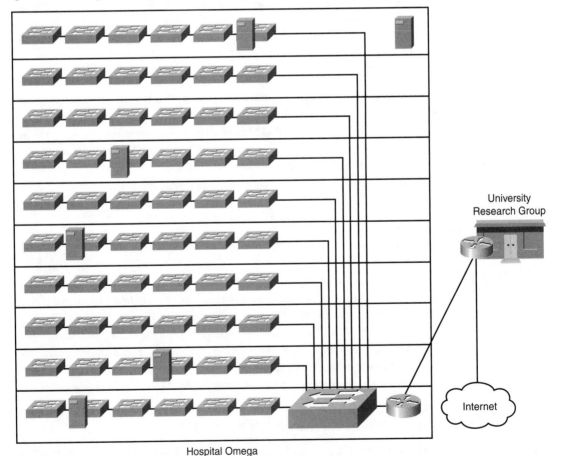

Hospital Omega

The CIO wants a design to modernize the Hospital Omega network and allow robust access to the ACMC data center. Identify any issues you have with this merger and what design you would propose to the CIO.

Step 2   What is the key security issue for the Hospital Omega network? How could this issue be resolved?

Step 3   Hospital Beta is another nearby hospital. ACMC and Hospital Beta overlap in several areas of medical expertise and feel that pooling talent and facilities should lead to better depth of medical expertise and better patient care. Sharing financial and other applications should also reduce overhead costs. The following are some details about Hospital Beta:

- Hospital Beta uses DHCP.

- Hospital Beta consists of four buildings, each with four large floors (with fewer than 250 Ethernet users and ports each). Each floor uses eight 24-port Cisco Catalyst 3560 switches in intermediate distribution frame closets, with dual uplinks to the distribution layer switches. The data center and Internet complex is on one floor of one of the four buildings.

- Each building uses two Cisco Catalyst 6506 switches at the distribution layer. The switches are dual-homed via single-mode fiber at 10 Gbps to the core switches.

- The two Cisco Catalyst 6506 core switches are interconnected with 10-Gbps links and have dual connections to two Cisco Catalyst 4948 switches for the servers.

- The campus network is based on high-speed Layer 3 Cisco switches.

- Wireless is supported using Cisco WLAN controllers (WLC).

- The hospital has a DMZ, dual firewalls in each of two layers, IPS monitoring for the DMZ, and so forth.

- Cisco IP telephony is in place.

- Hospital Beta has a connection to the University Research Group.

Figure 10-26 shows the Hospital Beta network.

Figure 10-26 *Hospital Beta Network*

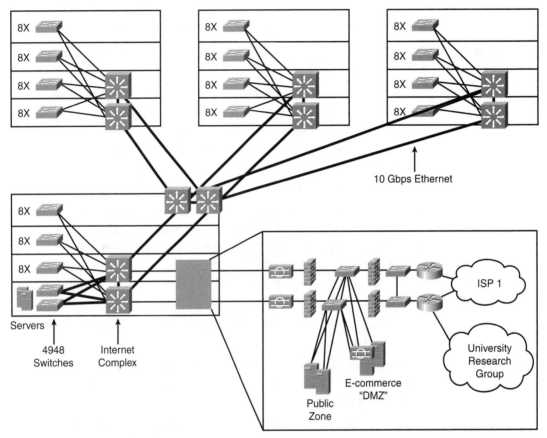

The CIO wants a design to standardize the Hospital Beta network and allow robust access to the ACMC data center. Identify any issues you have with this merger and what design you would propose to the CIO.

Step 4   The CIO wants to consolidate servers in the ACMC data center. What issues need to be examined before proceeding with such a migration?

Step 5   Suppose that inexpensive Metro Ethernet is available between ACMC and Hospital Beta. How does this change your answer to the question in the previous step?

Step 6   Hospital Beta already has deployed a Cisco Unified Communications Manager, IP phones, voice gateways, and so forth. Should the Cisco Unified Communications Manager and Cisco Unity servers be moved to the ACMC data center? Why or why not? If not, how should they interact with a Cisco Unified Communications Manager on the ACMC campus?

Step 7   Should the WLCs at Hospital Beta be moved to the ACMC campus?

Step 8   Hospital Omega uses static routes on its one Internet router. Hospital Beta uses the Intermediate System-to-Intermediate System (IS-IS) routing protocol. Make a recommendation for overall routing protocol and routing design for the merged networks.

Step 9   The CIO at ACMC is concerned about HIPAA compliance and general security. She and you agree on running all Internet connectivity through ACMC and Hospital Beta. Assume that firewalls, firewall rules, DMZs, and properly configured IPsec VPN access are all in place. What additional steps can be taken to improve security in the combined ACMC-Omega-Beta network?

Step 10   Hospital Omega is paying a large amount per phone for Centrex service. The CIO urgently wants to cut costs by moving to IP phones for Hospital Omega. The return on investment for doing this indicates that it would pay for itself in less than a year. The CIO has asked you for technical comments on doing this; what do you tell her?

Step 11   ACMC has been assigned address block 10.1.0.0 /16. Could ACMC re-address within 10.1.0.0 /16? Assuming that it could, provide a revised addressing scheme that includes appropriate addressing for Hospital Beta and Hospital Omega. What are the summarized routes that each hospital should be advertising to the others?

Review Questions

Answer the following questions, and then refer to Appendix A for the answers:

1.   List some laws that might influence network security.

2.   What is the difference between a virus and a worm?

3.   Why might a hacker launch a reconnaissance attack?

4.   What is a denial-of-service (DoS) attack?

5.   How do Dynamic ARP Inspection (DAI) and DHCP snooping interact?

6. Match the terms with the definitions:

    Terms:

    - Integrity violation

    - Confidentiality breach

    - Availability threat

    Definitions:

    - The result of a network's incapability to handle an enormous quantity of data

    - An attacker changes sensitive data

    - Can be very difficult to detect

7. How are risk assessment and security policy related?

8. Using levels 1 through 3 to quantify risk factors, calculate the risk index for a risk with the following parameters:

    - The probability of risk = level 2

    - The severity of loss = level 1

    - The ability to control or manage the risk = level 2

9. What are some components of a typical security policy?

10. What are the components of the process that helps maintain a security policy?

11. Match the terms with the definitions:

    Terms:

    - Trust and identity management

    - Threat defense

    - Secure connectivity

    Definitions:

    - To protect critical assets by allowing access based on privilege level

    - To ensure privacy and confidentiality of communications

    - To minimize and mitigate outbreaks

12. What are the three phases of the Cisco Self-Defending Network?

13. What is the difference between *trust* and *identity*?

14. Match the terms with the definitions:

Terms:

- Identification

- Authentication

- Domains of trust

- Trust

- Password

- Token

Definitions:

- Something the subject *knows*

- Parts of the network with similar security policy

- A subject *presents* its identity

- A subject *proves* its identity

- A physical device or software application

- The basis of security policy decisions

15. What are the three proofs on which authentication is based?

16. What is the difference between authentication and authorization?

17. Describe how NAC works.

18. In IEEE 802.1X, what are the supplicant and the authenticator?

19. What is the principle of least privilege?

20. How can a network security mechanism manage the risk of stolen laptops?

21. Match the following Cisco technologies with the security functions they provide. There might be more than one technology for each function.

Technologies:

- ASA

- FWSM

- IDS module

- IPS sensor

- Cisco Traffic Anomaly Guard

- Cisco IOS IPS

- PIX

- Cisco Traffic Anomaly Detector

- Content Security and Control Security Services module

- Cisco IOS Firewall

- Cisco Security Agent

Security functions:

- Endpoint protection

- Infection containment

- Inline intrusion and anomaly detection

- Application security and Anti-X defense

22. Which two of the following attacks can be prevented using a firewall for network filtering?

   a. An attacker who has a legitimate account on a UNIX server uses locally available tools to obtain administrator privileges.

   b. An attacker attempts to connect to an organization's sensitive, nonpublic server from the Internet.

   c. An attacker steals a bank ATM to obtain its cryptographic keys.

   d. An attacker maps a company's network using network management tools.

   e. An attacker decrypts a sensitive e-mail message that was sent freely over the Internet.

23. Complete this sentence: Cryptography provides confidentiality through _____.

24. True or false: Cryptography can affect network performance.

25. Data is encrypted with a public key in a PKI system. Which key is required to decrypt the data?

26. Provide some examples of cryptographic mechanisms that ensure data integrity.

27. Match the security management tools with their functions:

Tools:

- Cisco Security Manager
- Cisco Security MARS
- Cisco SDM
- Cisco ASDM
- Cisco IDM
- CiscoWorks Management Center for Cisco Security Agents
- Cisco Secure ACS

Functions:

- Configures firewall, VPN, and IPS policies
- Centralized control for role-based access to all Cisco devices and security management applications
- Web-based application for IPS sensors
- Security management and monitoring for ASA and PIX
- Appliance-based solution that models packet flows through the network
- Assembles network devices into groups to which security policies are attached
- Web-based device-management tool for Cisco routers

28. What functionality does the Cisco IOS IPS provide?

29. What is the Cisco Catalyst 6500 Series FWSM?

Answers to Review Questions and Case Studies

This appendix provides internetworking expert solutions (listed by chapter) to the review questions and case study questions in each chapter. A solution is provided for each case study task based on assumptions made. There is no claim that the provided solution is the best or only solution. Your solution might be more appropriate for the assumptions you made. The provided solution enables you to understand the author's reasoning and offers a means of comparing and contrasting your solution.

Chapter 2

Case Study Answers

1. The following table summarizes ACMC's requirements.

Requirement	Comments
Structural cabling	
High availability, redundancy	
Higher campus speeds, at least Gigabit Ethernet core	Medical image files are very large
Higher WAN speeds	
More uniform WAN	
IPsec virtual private network for teleworkers	Although this is not a stated requirement, it would be useful and is common in today's networks
Designated server farm, improved "data center" area	
Wireless for WoWs	
Network management capabilities	
DHCP	
Scalable IP addressing scheme	
QoS-capable equipment	To allow for future delay-sensitive applications (such as IP telephony) without replacing network equipment

2. The following table summarizes information missing from the scenario and the related assumptions that we made (obviously, your assumptions may be different).

Missing Item	Comments and Assumptions
Bandwidth utilization	There is no bandwidth utilization data, because much of the equipment is not manageable. There are many 100-Mbps trunks between switches. The servers are on 100-Mbps ports. A version of a network analysis tool is available. It indicates that some uplinks have 80% to 100% utilization. Therefore, assume that there is congestion.
Are there any plans for IP telephony? Video? Videoconferencing? Multimedia?	All of these are possible in the two-to-five-year time frame.
What are the security requirements?	HIPAA compliance is a big driver, so the hospital needs "good security."
Is there wireless already on site? Are there any plans for wireless? Have any specific wireless requirements been identified, especially related to security?	Several departments have wireless "experiments," but the hospital suspects they are not adequately secured. The network team has not had time to investigate the use of wireless.
What are the QoS requirements?	The hospital is currently using VoD for some training and continuing education. IP multicast might reduce bandwidth used and make more efficient use of servers. Future IP telephony, video, and so forth will add further QoS requirements.
Are there any security cameras in the hospital?	There are no cameras yet, but the hospital already has coax cable in place.
Are there any mobility requirements for staff?	Yes, secure mobile access is a real need. However, ACMC recognizes that its network has other problems that need to be corrected before this can be done.
Is there any information about the application WAN requirements or usage?	There is no data because of the unmanageable equipment and lack of time.
What current network management tools are in place?	An older tool called Ethereal is the only tool in place (the current version is Wireshark).
Does ACMC headquarters have Internet access today? Do the remote WAN sites require Internet access?	Internet access requirements are not yet clear.
What are the future plans for a server farm? Will the servers be consolidated to one location? Where will that be?	Assume that the servers will all move to the server room in Main Building #1.
What type of WAN is currently in use?	The three existing 56-kbps circuits are point-to-point links.

Missing Item	Comments and Assumptions
Is there a WAN backup?	There is no WAN backup today.
Are there any technical constraints for WAN availability at the remote clinics?	Frame Relay and Multiprotocol Label Switching are also available to the remote clinics.
What is the budget available for the upgrade?	The budget is not clear; assume approximately $500,000.
Who is responsible for the network?	Mr. Jones is the network architect, and Ms. Smith is the MIS manager.
Are there any business constraints, such as policies and goals? What is the criticality of applications?	Medical imaging is identified as the most critical application.

3. The following are the major design areas to be addressed:

Step 1 Identify the relevant network applications, their logical connectivity requirements, and the services required as part of the initial design.

Step 2 Divide the network into modules.

Step 3 Identify the scope of the design to decide which modules are to be redesigned.

Step 4 Identify design alternatives for each module, including the following:

a. **Redesign the campus LAN**: The current campus LAN is shared and interconnects three buildings. Because there is no redundancy, the designer needs to entirely redesign the campus, including the placement of servers.

b. **Redesign the IP addressing scheme**: The flat addressing scheme and static routes are not desirable features in a scalable growing network. New hierarchical addressing is required.

c. **Introduce a new routing protocol**: The hospital is aware of the drawbacks of static routes. The designer should implement a dynamic routing protocol that is more scalable and that better fits the planned hierarchical addressing scheme.

d. **Upgrade the WAN links**: The upgrade of the WAN links is essential because, according to the company, the current bandwidth seems insufficient. The introduction of new applications along with the existing applications will result in a higher load on the WAN links.

After the design is complete, the implementation will be planned, and the design will be implemented.

Answers to Review Questions

1. The Cisco vision for an intelligent information network includes the following:

   - Integration of networked resources and information assets that have been largely unlinked

   - Intelligence across multiple products and infrastructure layers

   - Active participation of the network in the delivery of services and applications

2. Evolving to an intelligent information network consists of three phases in which functionality can be added to the infrastructure as required:

   - **Phase 1: Integrated transport**: Everything (data, voice, and video) consolidates onto an IP network for secure network convergence.

   - **Phase 2: Integrated services**: When the network infrastructure is converged, IT resources can be pooled and shared, or virtualized, to flexibly address the organization's changing needs.

   - **Phase 3: Integrated applications**: This phase focuses on making the network application-aware so that it can optimize application performance and more efficiently deliver networked applications to users.

3. The SONA framework defines the following three layers:

   - **Networked Infrastructure layer**: Where all the IT resources interconnect across a converged network foundation. The objective of this layer is to provide connectivity, anywhere and anytime.

   - **Interactive Services layer**: Includes both application networking services and infrastructure services. This layer enables efficient allocation of resources to applications and business processes delivered through the networked infrastructure.

   - **Application layer**: Includes business applications and collaboration applications. The objective of this layer is to meet business requirements and achieve efficiencies by leveraging the Interactive Services layer.

4. The benefits of SONA include the following:

   - **Functionality**: Supports the organizational requirements.

   - **Scalability**: Supports growth and expansion of organizational tasks by separating functions and products into layers.

   - **Availability**: Provides the necessary services, reliably, anywhere, anytime.

- **Performance**: Provides the desired responsiveness, throughput, and utilization on a per-application basis through the network infrastructure and services.

- **Manageability**: Provides control, performance monitoring, and fault detection.

- **Efficiency**: Provides the required network services and infrastructure with reasonable operational costs and appropriate capital investment on a migration path to a more intelligent network, through step-by-step network services growth.

- **Security**: Provides for an effective balance between usability and security while protecting information assets and infrastructure from inside and outside threats.

5. Answer:

    a. 5

    b. 4

    c. 2

    d. 1

    e. 3

    f. 6

6. The initial design verification is performed during the PPDIOO Implement phase.

7. The three basic steps of the design methodology are as follows:

    Step 1   Identify customer requirements.

    Step 2   Characterize the existing network and sites.

    Step 3   Design the network topology and solutions, which includes the following:

    - Possibly building a pilot or prototype network

    - Creating a detailed design document

8. When the design is complete, the design implementation process is executed; this process includes the following steps:

    Step 1   Plan the implementation.

    Step 2   Implement and verify the design.

    Step 3   Monitor and optionally redesign.

9. Some determinants of the scope of a design project are as follows:

   ■ Whether the design is for a new network or is a modification of an existing network

   ■ Whether the design is for an entire enterprise network, a subset of the network, or simply a single segment or module

   ■ Whether the design addresses a single function or the network's entire functionality

   ■ The OSI protocol layers involved

10. The steps involved in gathering network requirements include identifying the following:

    ■ Planned applications and network services

    ■ Organizational goals

    ■ Organizational constraints

    ■ Technical goals

    ■ Technical constraints

11. C

12. Typical goals include the following:

    ■ Increased revenue

    ■ Shorter development cycles

    ■ Improved customer support

    ■ Open the organization's information infrastructure

13. A

14. Typical organizational constraints include the following:

    ■ Budget

    ■ Availability of personnel

    ■ Policies

    ■ Schedule

15. The new network design is often driven by the introduction of new network applications; the implementation time frames for new applications are often tightly connected and therefore influence the available time for network design.

16. B

17. If parts of the network have insufficient bandwidth and the bandwidth cannot be increased because of technical constraints, the situation must be resolved by other means.

18. Traffic analysis provides information about the applications and protocols used in the network and might reveal any shortcomings in the network.

19. Site contact information should include the following:

    ■ Site location, name, address, shipping address

    ■ Site contact's name and all the possible ways to reach that person (phone, cell phone, pager, e-mail address, and so forth)

    ■ Site owner

    ■ Hours of operation

    ■ Access procedures, including those for security, safety, and union or labor

    ■ Specific location of equipment

20. False. The auditing process might require minor (temporary) changes in the network.

21. CiscoWorks and many third-party tools such as WhatsUp Professional, SNMPc, Cacti, NetMRI, NetVoyant, AirMagnet Survey PRO, AiroPeek, and so on can be used for network assessment.

22. A

23. D

24. An Ethernet segment is considered saturated at 40 percent network utilization, whereas a WAN link is not considered saturated until 70 percent network utilization.

25. A

26. False. Network characterization typically takes from one to many weeks of effort, depending on the network's size and complexity, the experience of the network engineer, the quality of the documentation and communication, the efficiency of the tools, and so forth.

27. A, C, and F

28. B

29. The following types of tools can be used during the network design process:

    ■ Network modeling tools

    ■ Strategic analysis tools

    ■ Decision tables

    ■ Simulation and verification tools or services

30. A pilot network tests and verifies the design before the network is launched, or is a subset of the existing network in which the design is tested. A prototype network tests and verifies a redesign in an isolated network before it is applied to the existing network.

31. A typical final design document includes the following sections:

    ■ Introduction

    ■ Design requirements

    ■ Existing network infrastructure

    ■ Design

    ■ Proof of concept

    ■ Implementation plan

    ■ Appendixes

32. The documentation of each step in the implementation plan should contain

    ■ A description of the step

    ■ References to design documents

    ■ Detailed implementation guidelines

    ■ Detailed rollback guidelines in case of failure

    ■ Estimated time needed for implementation

33. The designer is involved in the implementation phase to assist in the design verification and to take remedial actions, if necessary.

34. A network redesign might be required if troubleshooting problems becomes too frequent or even impossible to manage. Hopefully this scenario can be avoided if all previous design steps have been completed properly.

Chapter 3

Case Study Answers

1. The following figure shows the location of each of the Cisco Enterprise Architecture modules for the existing ACMC network.

Cisco Enterprise Architecture Modules in the Existing ACMC Hospital Network

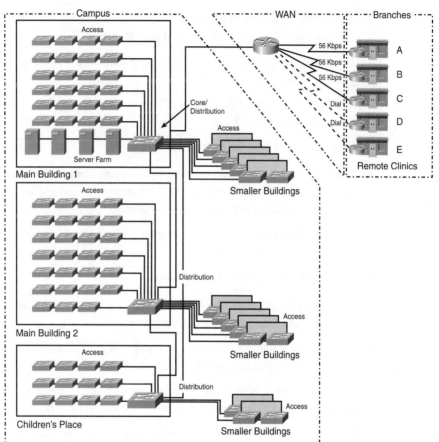

2. The following are some considerations for each of the functional areas and modules.

■ Enterprise Campus Building Access layer:

— Each building has a Building Access layer.

— This layer supports important services such as broadcast suppression, protocol filtering, network access, IP multicast, and QoS; Layer 2 functions such as VLANs and spanning tree are also provided by this layer.

— For high availability, the access layer switches could be dual-attached to the distribution layer switches.

— In the future, this layer could provide PoE and auxiliary VLANs to support voice services if required.

- Enterprise Campus Building Distribution layer:

  — Each of the three main buildings has a Building Distribution layer, which could be combined with the Campus Core in Main Building 1.

  — This layer aggregates access networks using multilayer switching and performs routing, QoS, and access control.

  — Redundancy and load balancing with both the Building Access and Campus Core layers are recommended.

- Campus Core layer of the Enterprise Campus:

  — This layer provides redundant and fast-converging connectivity between buildings and with the Server Farm and Enterprise Edge modules, routing and switching traffic as fast as possible from one module to another.

  — This layer uses multilayer switches for high-throughput functions with added routing, QoS, and security features.

- Enterprise Campus Server Farm module:

  — This layer contains internal e-mail and corporate servers that provide application, file, print, e-mail, and DNS services to internal users.

  — Because access to these servers is vital, as a best practice they should be connected to two different switches, enabling full redundancy and load sharing.

  — To provide high reliability and availability for servers, the Server Farm module switches should be cross-connected with the Campus Core layer switches.

  — This layer also supports network management services for the enterprise.

- Enterprise Edge modules:

  — Current network requirements indicate that only the WAN and MAN and Site-to-Site VPN module of the Enterprise Edge is required; this module provides reliable WAN connectivity. In the figure in the answer to Step 1, this module is labeled "WAN."

  — This module supports traditional, circuit-switched, and more advanced media. All Cisco devices that support these WAN technologies, in addition to routing, access control, and QoS mechanisms, can be used in this module.

  — Although security is not as critical when all links are enterprise-owned, it should be considered in the network design.

- Service Provider modules:

  — The Frame Relay/ATM module covers all WAN technologies for *permanent* connectivity with remote locations; although it is not explicitly shown in the figure in the answer to Step 1, this module represents the 56-kbps connections to the remote clinics.

  — The PSTN module (also not shown in the figure in the answer to Step 1) represents the dialup infrastructure for accessing the enterprise network using ISDN, analog, and wireless telephony (cellular) technologies.

- Enterprise Data Center:

  — This module is not indicated in the current network requirements.

- Enterprise Teleworker:

  — This module is not indicated in the current network requirements.

- Enterprise Branch:

  — This module is used for the remote clinics.

  — This module allows branch office users to connect to the central site to access company information. Therefore, it benefits from high-speed Internet access, VPN connectivity to corporate intranets, videoconferencing, and economical PSTN-quality voice and fax calls over the managed IP networks.

  — The Enterprise Branch module typically uses a simplified version of the Campus Infrastructure module design.

3. An Internet Connectivity module, an E-commerce module, a Remote Access and VPN module, and a possibly an Enterprise Teleworker module will be added to the network design. The following figure shows the addition of these modules.

New Requirements Incorporated into the ACMC Hospital Network

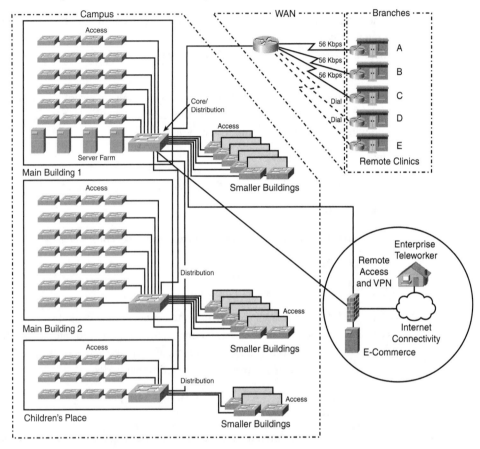

The following are some considerations for each of these modules.

■ Enterprise Edge E-commerce module:

— This module provides scalability, security, and high availability within the overall e-commerce network design. Devices in this module include various servers (Web, application, database), firewalls or firewall routers, NIDS appliances, and multilayer switches with IDS modules.

■ Enterprise Edge Internet Connectivity module:

— This module provides internal users with Internet connectivity and access to information published on the enterprise's public servers, such as HTTP and FTP servers.

— This module accepts VPN traffic from remote users and forwards it to the Remote Access and VPN module, where VPN termination takes place.

— Devices in this module include SMTP mail servers, DNS servers, public servers (FTP and HTTP), firewalls or firewall routers, and edge routers.

■ Enterprise Edge Remote Access and VPN module:

— This module terminates VPN and dial-in and uses the Internet Connectivity module to initiate VPN connections to remote sites.

— Devices in this module include dial-in access concentrators, ASAs, firewalls, and NIDS appliances.

■ Enterprise Teleworker:

— This module provides people in geographically dispersed locations, such as home offices or hotels, with highly secure access to central-site applications and network services.

4. The following details how these services are relevant to the design:

■ Security services should support the Internet Connectivity, E-commerce, and Remote Access and VPN modules. Firewalls and IDS might be appropriate.

■ Voice services are not immediately applicable.

■ Wireless services are not immediately applicable.

■ Some basic network management tools are appropriate.

■ High availability is applicable in the campus and is possibly needed in the WAN.

■ There is no indication that QoS is currently needed.

■ Some possible use of IP multicast has been indicated by the customer; therefore, the infrastructure should support IP multicast.

5. Each circled R in the following figure indicates where redundancy is appropriate in the network.

Redundancy Within the Existing ACMC Hospital Network

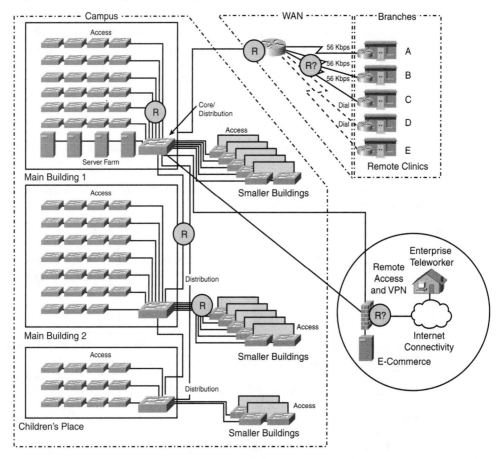

Redundancy in the Enterprise Campus is most critical in the Campus Core layer, followed by the Building Distribution layer. The Building Access layer itself is seldom redundant, but redundant uplinks to the Building Distribution layer are common.

The WAN router could be made redundant, but the value versus the cost of doing this depends on the actual WAN technology in use, which is why redundancy is indicated with an R? in the figure. One common approach is to provide backup WAN links with site-to-site IPsec VPN. If the network has a Remote Access and VPN module anyway, using it for WAN backup should add minimal cost.

Some components within the E-commerce module could be made redundant, depending on the results of a cost-benefit-risk analysis considering the criticality of the e-commerce services, the monetary value to ACMC, the costs of downtime, and the costs of redundancy.

If teleworker access is required for productivity rather than convenience, redundancy should be considered within that module. Similarly, the Internet Connectivity module might require redundancy, depending on how critical Internet access is for ACMC.

Answers to Review Questions

1. **Access layer**: Devices A, B, E, and F

    Distribution layer: Devices A, B, D, and F

    Core layer: Device C

2. The role of each layer in the hierarchical network model is as follows:

    ■ The access layer provides local and remote workgroup or user access to the network.

    ■ The distribution layer provides policy-based connectivity.

    ■ The core (or backbone) layer provides high-speed transport.

3. False. The layers do not need to be implemented as distinct physical entities. The layers are defined to aid successful network design and to represent functionality that must exist in a network; the actual manner in which the layers are implemented depends on the needs of the network that is being designed. Each layer can be implemented in routers or switches, represented by physical media, or combined in a single device. A particular layer can be omitted, but hierarchy should be maintained for optimum performance.

4. A and B

5. Some multilayer switch features that are useful to the access layer include the following:

    ■ Routing between broadcast domains (including VLANs)

    ■ Access to remote offices using various wide-area technologies

    ■ Route propagation

    ■ Packet filtering

    ■ Authentication and security

    ■ Quality of service (QoS)

    ■ Dial-on-demand routing (DDR) and static routing

6. The distribution layer provides media translation.

7. The distribution layer can redistribute between bandwidth-intensive access-layer routing protocols and optimized core routing protocols. Redistribution allows the access and core layers to share routing information.

8. A, B, and F

9. Because core devices are responsible for accommodating failures by rerouting traffic and responding quickly to network topology changes, and because performance for routing in the core with a multilayer switch incurs no cost, most implementations have multilayer switching in the core layer. The core layer can therefore more readily implement scalable protocols and technologies, alternate paths, and load balancing.

10. The six functional areas are as follows:

    ■ Enterprise Campus

    ■ Enterprise Edge

    ■ Service Provider

    ■ Enterprise Branch

    ■ Enterprise Data Center

    ■ Enterprise Teleworker

11. The Enterprise Campus functional area includes the Campus Infrastructure module and, typically, a Server Farm module.

    The Campus Infrastructure module consists of several buildings connected across a Campus Core. The Campus Infrastructure module includes three layers:

    ■ The Building Access layer

    ■ The Building Distribution layer

    ■ The Campus Core layer

12. The Enterprise Edge functional area is composed of the following four modules:

    ■ E-commerce module

    ■ Internet Connectivity module

    ■ Remote Access and VPN module

    ■ WAN and MAN and Site-to-Site VPN module

13. The modules within the Service Provider functional area include

- Internet Service Provider module

- PSTN module

- Frame Relay/ATM module

14. The Frame Relay/ATM module covers all WAN technologies for permanent connectivity with remote locations, including wireless bridging.

15. This architecture allows network designers to focus on a selected module and its functions. Designers can describe each network application and service on a per-module basis and validate each as part of the complete enterprise network design.

Modularizing to small subsets of the overall network simplifies the network design and often reduces the network's cost and complexity.

16. The Campus Core layer interconnects the Building Distribution layer with the Server Farm and Enterprise Edge modules.

17. Answer:

- **E-commerce module**: Web servers, firewalls, NIDS appliances

- **Internet Connectivity module**: SMTP mail servers, firewalls, Public FTP servers, DNS servers

- **Remote Access and VPN module**: ASAs, NIDS appliances, firewalls

18. The modules in the Service Provider functional area are not implemented by the enterprise itself. However, they are necessary for enabling communication with other networks, using a variety of WAN technologies, and with ISPs.

19. The Enterprise Branch module typically uses a simplified version of the Campus Infrastructure module design.

20. The Enterprise Data Center module has an architecture similar to the campus Server Farm module.

21. The Enterprise Teleworker module provides people in geographically dispersed locations, such as home offices or hotels, with highly secure access to central-site applications and network services. The Enterprise Teleworker module supports a small office with one to several employees or a telecommuter's home office.

22. The SONA interactive services layer includes both <u>application networking</u> services and <u>infrastructure</u> services.

23. Enterprises often overlook the Server Farm module from a security perspective. Given the high degree of access most employees have to these servers, they often become the primary goal of internally originated attacks. Simply relying on effective passwords does not provide a comprehensive attack mitigation strategy. Using host-based and network-based intrusion prevention systems (IPS) and intrusion detection systems (IDS), private VLANs, and access control provides a much more comprehensive attack response.

24. High availability from end to end is possible only when <u>redundancy</u> is deployed throughout the internetwork.

25. Redundant routes do the following:

    ■ Minimize the effect of link failures

    ■ Minimize the effect of an internetworking device failure

    ■ Allow load balancing to take place when all routes are up

26. A

27. True

28. The following components are required for IP telephony:

    ■ IP phones (replacing traditional phones) to perform voice-to-IP conversion

    ■ Switches, typically with inline power (for the IP phones)

    ■ Call-processing manager, a server for call control and signaling

    ■ Voice gateway, also called a *voice-enabled router* or *voice-enabled switch*, to provide voice services such as voice-to-IP coding and compression, PSTN access, IP packet routing, backup call processing, and voice services.

29. The Building Access layer is where IP phones and end-user computers are attached to Layer 2 switches. Switches might provide power to the IP phones and provide QoS packet classification and marking, which is essential for proper voice packet manipulation through the network.

30. When evaluating the existing data infrastructure for IP telephony, consider the following:

    ■ Performance

    ■ Availability

    ■ Features

    ■ Capacity

    ■ Power

31. The main components of a centralized WLAN deployment are as follows:

- **End-user devices**: A PC, or other end-user device, uses a wireless network interface card (NIC) to connect to an access point (AP) using radio waves.

- **Wireless APs**: APs are shared devices that function similar to a hub. Cisco APs can be either lightweight or autonomous. In a centralized environment, a lightweight AP receives control and configuration from a WLAN controller (WLC) with which it is associated.

- **WLC**: A WLC provides management and support for wireless services such as roaming.

- **Existing switched and routed wired network**: The wireless APs connect to the wired enterprise network.

32. A Cisco Wide-Area Application Engine (WAE) appliance provides high-performance global LAN-like access to enterprise applications and data. WAEs use either WAAS or ACNS software. WAEs help consolidate storage, servers, and so forth in the corporate data center, with only low-cost, easy-to-maintain network appliances in distant offices.

33. A network management agent is software on a managed device that collects and stores management information.

34. The manager first sends a Get Request message to request the specific MIB variable from the agent. Then Get Next Request messages are used to retrieve the next object instance from a table or list.

35. An SNMPv2 manager sends a GetBulk message to request a list of data. This SNMPv2 message reduces repetitive requests and replies, thereby improving performance when retrieving large amounts of data.

36. Each object in a MIB has a unique identifier that network management applications use to identify and to retrieve the value of the specific object. The MIB structure is a tree-like structure in which similar objects are grouped under the same branch of the MIB tree. For example, different interface counters are grouped under the MIB tree's interfaces branch.

37. Vendors can obtain their own branch of the MIB subtree and create custom managed objects under that branch. Private definitions of managed objects must be compiled into the NMS before they can be used; the results are outputs that are more descriptive, with variables and events that can be referred to by name.

38. The following are the RMON1 groups:

- Statistics

- History

- Alarm

- Host

- Host Top N

- Matrix

- Filters

- Packet Capture

- Events

- TokenRing

39. RMON2 adds the following RMON groups:

- Protocol Directory

- Protocol Distribution

- Address Mapping

- Network Layer Host

- Network Layer Matrix

- Application Layer Host

- Application Layer Matrix

- User History Collection

- Probe Configuration

40. Without RMON, a MIB could be used to check each device's network performance. However, doing so would require a large amount of bandwidth for management traffic. By using RMON, the managed device itself (via its RMON agent) collects and stores the data that would otherwise be retrieved from the MIB frequently.

41. A network flow is a unidirectional sequence of packets between source and destination endpoints. Network flows are highly granular; flow endpoints are identified by both IP address and transport layer application port numbers. NetFlow also identifies the flows by IP protocol type, ToS, and the input interface identifier.

42. NetFlow's information-gathering benefits include greater detail of data collected, time-stamping of the data, support for various data per interface, and greater scalability to a large number of interfaces. NetFlow's performance impact is much lower than that of RMON, and external probes are not required.

43. CDP works at the data link layer.

44. If CDP frames are being received, the Frame Relay connection (the data link layer) is running. Because ping does not work, the problem is likely with the IP addresses configured on the interfaces. CDP shows the IP addresses configured on neighboring devices; thus, CDP information can be used to determine where the IP addressing problem resides.

45. Syslog defines the following severity levels:

- Emergency (level 0, which is the highest level)

- Alert (level 1)

- Critical (level 2)

- Error (level 3)

- Warning (level 4)

- Notice (level 5)

- Informational (level 6)

- Debugging (level 7)

46. The severity level of the first message is 5, a notice. The severity level of the second message is 3, an error.

Chapter 4

Case Study Answers

1. The following figure illustrates the recommended Campus design; this figure includes the Campus Core, Building Distribution, and Building Access layers, and the Server Farm.

Case Study: Campus Proposed Design

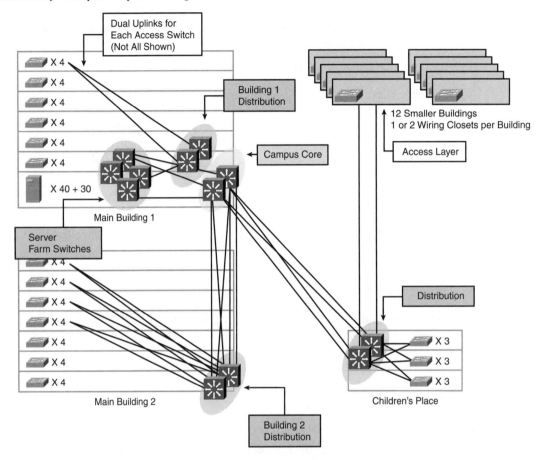

For the Campus Core, two switches are used for high availability.

Putting the Campus Core switches in Main Building 1 with the servers is ideal because a lot of network traffic generally flows to the Server Farm. Alternatively, the switches could be split between the two main buildings for geographic diversity. The exact location of the switches within the building depends on space, where the fiber terminates, and so on.

A redundant pair of Building Distribution switches is used in each building for high availability.

Dual uplinks from each Building Distribution switch to each Campus Core switch are used, again for high availability.

Assume that four Server Farm switches are used.

Each Campus Core switch needs two ports for the uplinks to each Building Distribution switch. Thus, the core switches each need 20 ports (four ports for the Building Distribution switches in each of the three buildings plus eight ports for the four Server Farm switches). More ports are required if more than four Server Farm switches are used.

1-Gbps, Gigabit EtherChannel, or 10-Gbps links are used between the Building Distribution and Campus Core. Note that using N-way EtherChannel multiplies the number of ports needed by N. For example, four Gigabit EtherChannel uplinks would mean that 64 ports (4×16) are needed.

Dual power supplies in the switches should be considered for high availability. Another option that would further increase the availability is to include dual supervisors in each switch, route processing in the supervisors, or dual supervisors with route processing modules in each switch.

2. As shown in the figure in the answer to Step 1, Building Distribution switches are used in the three main buildings. Separate core switches and distribution switches are used in Main Building 1 because the three buildings and the Server Farm connect here. Combining the core and distribution layers in Main Building 1 is an alternative design.

    As noted, a redundant pair of Building Distribution switches is used in each building for high availability. Dual uplinks from each Building Distribution switch to each Campus Core switch are used, again for high availability.

    Building Distribution switches are not required on each floor because not enough aggregation is required.

    Layer 3 switching is used between the Campus Core and the Building Distribution layers.

    The port counts from the Building Access switch uplinks are as follows:

    ■   Main Building 1: 6 floors × 4 access switches per floor = 24 access switches (not including the Server Farm switches.)

    ■   Main Building 2: 7 floors × 4 access switches per floor = 28 access switches

    ■   Children's Place: 3 floors × 3 access switches per floor = 9 access switches

    Dual power supplies in the Building Distribution switches should be considered for high availability. Dual supervisors in each switch, route processing in the supervisors, or dual supervisors with route processing modules in each switch could also be considered.

3. As shown in the figure in the answer to Step 1, a Building Access layer switch is used in every wiring closet; these switches are all dual-homed to the Building Distribution layer switches. Layer 3 switching is used between the Building Distribution and Building Access layers.

Each of the main buildings requires 150 ports per floor (75 people per floor × 2 for spares); the Server Farm requires 140 ports (70 ports × 2 for spares). Dividing the number of ports by four closets results in about 38 ports per closet required; rounding up this value results in recommending a 48-port switch at the Building Access layer. The same switch should be used in all wiring closets for simplicity and commonality.

The Children's Place has 120 ports per floor (60 people per floor × 2). Dividing the number of ports by three closets results in 40 ports per closet; therefore, a 48-port switch is also used here.

The port counts for the other buildings are as follows:

- Buildings A through D each have ten people and therefore 20 ports; a 24-port switch is used.

- Buildings E through J each have 20 people and therefore 40 ports; one 48-port switch or two 24-port switches are used.

- Buildings K through L each have 40 people and therefore 80 ports; one 96-port switch, two 48-port switches, or four 24-port switches are used. Choosing which combination to use depends on where local cabling terminates. One big switch is easiest to manage.

If there is sufficient fiber, the Building Access switches in the 12 smaller buildings can be dual-homed to one of the three pairs of Building Distribution layer switches, connecting to whichever main Building Distribution layer switch the fiber goes to. If there is not enough fiber, consider adding more. A less-preferable alternative is to dual-home a primary access layer switch in each of the smaller buildings to the Building Distribution layer switches and daisy-chain the other access layer switches through that primary switch.

The following table provides the resulting Building Access layer port counts by location.

Building Access Layer Port Counts by Location

Location	Port Counts	Port Counts with Spares	Comments
Main Building 1, per floor	75	150	Six floors
Main Building Server Farm	70	140	Servers will connect with dual NICs; these numbers allow for planned migration of all servers to the Server Farm
Main Building 2, per floor	75	150	Seven floors
Children's Place, per floor	60	120	Three floors

Building Access Layer Port Counts by Location (Continued)

Location	Port Counts	Port Counts with Spares	Comments
Buildings A–D	10 each	20 each	
Buildings E–J	20 each	40 each	
Buildings K–L	40 each	80 each	

4. Recall that five of the smaller buildings are connected to Main Building 1, five are connected to Main Building 2, and two are connected to the Children's Place.

Assume that the Building Access layer switches will connect to the Building Distribution layer switches via gigabit uplinks.

For the two main buildings, each Building Distribution switch requires 24 or 28 connections to the Building Access layer switches plus five uplinks to the remote buildings, resulting in 29 to 33 ports. (This value would be multiplied by N for N-way EtherChannel.)

For the Children's Place, each Building Distribution switch requires nine connections to the Building Access switches plus two uplinks to the remote buildings, resulting in a total of 11 ports. A 12-port distribution switch will suffice, but 16 or 24 ports allows for growth.

Assume that all uplinks in the buildings are MM fiber with distances of less than 550 m, and that SM fiber is used between buildings.

> **NOTE**   The "Transceivers, Module Connectors, and Cables Specifications" section of the "Catalyst 6500 Series Switch Installation Guide" (http://www.cisco.com/en/US/partner/products/hw/switches/ps708/products_installation_guide_chapter09186a008020e0ae.html#wp1078681) provides specifications for the maximum distances for each transceiver or fiber type.

5. Three options are considered:

- Connect the servers directly to the Campus Core switches.

- Connect the servers directly to the Building Distribution switches.

- Implement separate server switches (either two larger ones or multiple smaller ones).

The third option is preferred because it keeps any server link failures and STP requirements far from the Layer 3 core.

If, for cost reasons, separate server switches are not used, the servers should be connected to the Building Distribution switches rather than directly to the Campus Core switches, and a trunk should be used between the two distribution switches to allow traffic to return to the server VLAN.

Recall that the Server Farm requires 140 ports. Four 48-port switches are initially used for the server switches, allowing for expansion as servers are consolidated into the Server Farm and as the number of servers grows.

Dual power supplies in the switches should be considered, for high availability. Dual supervisors in each switch, route processing in the supervisors, or dual supervisors with route processing modules in each switch could also be considered.

6. Power supply sizing needs to be considered.

   Although not currently required, Power over Ethernet (PoE) might be needed in the future.

7. Using the links provided, the following switches were chosen (at the time this book was published; your results may be different):

   - Cisco Catalyst 6500 or 4500 Series switches for the Campus Core and Building Distribution layers. These switches are usually recommended for use in the Campus Core and Building Distribution layers in medium to large enterprises.

   - Cisco Catalyst 3560 switches for the Building Access layer.

   - Cisco Catalyst 6500, 4500, 4948, 3750, or 3560 models for Server Farm switches. (Note that only the first two of these allow dual power supplies in the chassis.)

   The following table shows one solution.

Case Study: One Solution for Switch Models

Layer	Location	Number of Ports	Switch Model	Quantity
Campus Core	Main Building 1	20 (for distribution layer termination)	WS-C4507R, power supply, supervisor V, 4 of WS-X4306-GB-T	2
Building Distribution	Main Building 1	29	WS-C4507R, power supply, supervisor V, 1 of WS-X4448-GB-SFP	2
Building Distribution	Main Building 2	33	WS-C4507R, power supply, supervisor V, 1 of WS-X4448-GB-SFP	2
Building Distribution	Children's Place	11	C3750G-24TS	2

Case Study: One Solution for Switch Models (Continued)

Layer	Location	Number of Ports	Switch Model	Quantity
Server Farm	Main Building 1	Servers are dual-NIC connected; current total is 170 ports	C4948-E	4
Building Access	Main Buildings 1 and 2 and Children's Place	up to 40 each	C3560G-48TS-S	$61 = ([6 \times 4] + [7 \times 4] + [3 \times 3])$
Building Access	Buildings A–D	20	C3560G-24TS-S	4 (1 per building)
Building Access	Buildings E–J	40	C3560G-48TS-S	6 (1 per building)
Building Access	Buildings K–L	80	C3560G-48TS-S	4 (2 per building)

NOTE   Using 10 Gbps for the links between the Campus Core and the Building Distribution or Server Farm would increase performance but would also increase cost.

8.   Your results depend on the specific switch you chose to configure.

9.   The following table is a sample BOM.

Case Study: Sample BOM

Part Number	Description	Unit Price	Qty	Extended Price
WS-C4507R	Catalyst 4500 Chassis (7-Slot), Fan, No Power Supply, Redundant Supervisor Capable	$10,000	6	$60,000
PWR-C45-1400AC	Catalyst 4500 1400W AC Power Supply (Data Only)	$1500	6	$9000
WS-X4516	Catalyst 4500 Supervisor V (2 GE), Console (RJ-45)	$16,500	6	$99,000
S4KL3E-12220EWA	Cisco IOS Enhanced Layer 3 Catalyst 4500 Supervisor 4/5 (OSPF, EIGRP, IS-IS)	$10,000	6	$60,000
WS-X4306-GB-T	Catalyst 4500 6-Port 10/100/1000 PoE or SFP	$3500	8	$28,000

continues

Case Study: Sample BOM (Continued)

Part Number	Description	Unit Price	Qty	Extended Price
WS-X4448-GB-SFP	Catalyst 4500 48-Port 1000BSE-X (SFP)	$16,500	4	$66,000
	Generic SFP (20 + 29 + 33 = 82)	$400	82	$32,800
WS-C3750G-24TS-S1U	Catalyst 3750 24 10/100/1000 + 4 SFP Standard Multilayer; 1RU	$7000	2	$14,000
	Generic SFP	$400	8	$3200
WS-C4948-E	Catalyst 4948, ES software, 48-Port 10/100/1000 + 4 SFP, 1 AC power supply	$14,500	4	$58,000
	Generic SFP	$400	16	$6400
WS-C3560G-48TS-S	Catalyst 3560 48 10/100/1000T + 4 SFP Standard Image	$8000	71	$568,000
	Generic SFP (2 per switch)	$400	142	$56,800
WS-C3560G-24TS-S	Catalyst 3560 24 10/100/1000T + 4 SFP Standard Image	$4800	4	$19,200
	Generic SFP (2 per switch)	$400	8	$3200
Total list price				$1,083,600

Answers to Review Questions

1. You should consider the following three characteristics when designing the campus network:

    ■ Network application characteristics

    ■ Environmental characteristics (including network geography and transmission media)

    ■ Infrastructure device characteristics

2. Security and high availability are the most important network requirements for client–Enterprise Edge application communication.

3. Examples of applications that would be appropriate to reside in a Server Farm include the following:

    ■ Organizational mail servers (such as Microsoft Exchange)

    ■ Common file servers (such as Microsoft and Sun)

    ■ Common database servers for organizational applications (such as Oracle)

4. An intrabuilding structure should be chosen for the design.

5. Answer:

   ■ The interbuilding structure is for high-speed connectivity between individual campus buildings, typically a few hundred meters to a few kilometers apart. Companies might deploy their own medium, which is typically MM or SM fiber.

   ■ The distant remote building structure is for connecting buildings farther apart than a few kilometers. QoS and filtering might be required to allow optimal use of the bandwidth. Connectivity can be via an organization's own medium (including SM fiber), but it could also be via public service providers, using traditional WAN links or Metro Ethernet.

6. The conventional 80/20 rule underlies traditional network design models. The 80/20 rule says that 80 percent of the traffic is local to the LAN segment and 20 percent leaves the segment.

   Client–Server Farm applications apply the 20/80 rule, where only 20 percent of the traffic remains on the local LAN segment, and 80 percent leaves the segment to reach centralized servers, the Internet, and so on.

7. MM optical cable is recommended.

8. The specifications are compared in the following table.

Transmission Media Types Bandwidth and Range Characteristics

Parameter	Copper Twisted Pair	MM Fiber	SM Fiber	Wireless
Distance (range)	Up to 100 meters	Up to 2 kilometers (km) (Fast Ethernet) Up to 550 m (Gigabit Ethernet) Up to 300 m (10 Gigabit Ethernet)	Up to 10 km (Fast Ethernet) Up to 5 km (Gigabit Ethernet) Up to 80 km (10 Gigabit Ethernet)	Up to 500 m at 1 Mbps
Bandwidth	Up to 10 Gbps	Up to 10 Gbps	Up to 10 Gbps or higher	Up to 54 Mbps[1]

[1] Wireless is half-duplex, so effective bandwidth will be no more than half of this rate.

9. The following table indicates the IEEE 802.11 wireless standard characteristics.

IEEE 802.11 Wireless Standards

Standard	Frequency Band	Maximum Bandwidth
802.11a	5 GHz	54 Mbps
802.11b	2.4 GHz	11 Mbps
802.11g	2.4 GHz	54 Mbps

10. The difference between data link layer and multilayer switching is the type of information that is used inside the frame to determine the correct output interface. Data link layer switching forwards frames based on data link layer information (the MAC address), whereas multilayer switching forwards frames based on network layer information (such as IP address). Multilayer switching is hardware-based switching and routing integrated into a single platform.

11. A *network flow* is a unidirectional sequence of packets between a source and a destination. Flows can be very specific. For example, a network flow can be identified by source and destination IP addresses, protocol numbers, and port numbers, as well as the interface on which the packet enters the switch.

12. Videoconferencing, corporate communications, distance learning, distribution of software, stock quotes, and news are some applications that take advantage of IP multicast traffic to deliver source traffic to multiple receivers.

13. CGMP should be enabled on the LAN switches, assuming that they are Cisco switches. CGMP is used between switches and routers. The routers tell each of their directly connected switches about IGMP registrations that were received from hosts through the switch—in other words, from hosts accessible through the switch. The switch then forwards the multicast traffic only to ports that those requesting hosts are on, rather than flooding the data to all ports. Switches, including non-Cisco switches, can alternatively use IGMP snooping to eavesdrop on the IGMP messages sent between routers and hosts to learn similar information.

14. The Protocol-Independent Multicast (PIM) protocol is used by routers that are forwarding multicast packets. The *protocol-independent* part of the name indicates that PIM is independent of the unicast routing protocol (for example, EIGRP or OSPF) running in the network. PIM uses the normal routing table, populated by the unicast routing protocol, in its multicast routing calculations.

15. Many networks or individual network elements are oversubscribed; it is easy to create scenarios in which congestion potentially occurs and that therefore require some form of QoS. The sum of the bandwidths on all ports on a switch where end devices are connected is usually greater than that of the uplink port; when the access ports are fully used, congestion on the uplink port is unavoidable. Uplinks from the Building Access layer to the Building

Distribution layer, or from the Building Distribution layer to the Campus Core layer, most often require QoS. Depending on traffic flow and uplink oversubscription, bandwidth is managed with QoS mechanisms on the Building Access, Building Distribution, or even Campus Core switches.

16. The Campus Core layer and Server Farm module typically have both high availability and high performance requirements.

17. One solution is to simply provide sufficient bandwidth on the link. However, an alternative is to implement a QoS mechanism to classify, mark, and police the traffic on the Building Distribution switch.

18. A multilayer switch should be used as the Building Distribution layer in the basement to route between the VLANs, route to the WANs, and take advantage of the intelligent network services, such as QoS and traffic filtering, which must be supported at the distribution layer.

19. The recommended best practices related to managing VLANs and STP in the Building Access layer include the following:

     ■ Limit VLANs to a single wiring closet whenever possible.

     ■ Avoid using STP if possible.

     ■ If STP is required, use RPVST+.

20. The Building Distribution layer of the Campus Infrastructure module aggregates the Building Access layer, segments workgroups, and isolates segments from failures and broadcast storms. This layer implements many policies based on access lists and QoS settings.

21. As a recommended practice, deploy a dedicated Campus Core layer to connect three or more buildings in the Enterprise Campus, or four or more pairs of Building Distribution switches in a very large campus.

     Campus Core switches are typically multilayer switches.

     Using a Campus Core makes scaling the network easier. For example, with a Campus Core, new Building Distribution switches only need connectivity to the core rather than full-mesh connectivity to all other distribution switches.

22. A multilayer switched backbone with redundant devices and redundant links to the Campus Core from each Building Distribution layer switch is recommended.

23. The optional Edge Distribution module connects the Campus Core with the Enterprise Edge modules. The Edge Distribution multilayer switches filter and route traffic into the Campus Core, aggregate Enterprise Edge connectivity, and provide advanced services.

24. The company should create a Server Farm to host the centralized servers. Because of probable high traffic load, the servers should be Gigabit Ethernet–attached to the Server Farm switches. Intelligent multilayer switches should be used to provide scalability, availability, responsiveness, throughput, and security for the mission-critical applications, as required.

25. The Enterprise Data *service*-centric model evolved from a *server*-centric data center model as follows:

    ■ The deployment of virtual machine software that breaks the one-to-one relationship between applications and the server hardware and operating system on which they run. Virtual machine software allows multiple applications to run on a single server, independent of each other and of the underlying operating system.

    ■ The removal of storage from the server, consolidating it in storage pools. Networked storage allows for easier management, provisioning, and improved utilization and consistent recovery practices.

    ■ The creation of pools of one-way, two-way, or four-way servers that can be pooled and provisioned on demand.

    ■ The consolidation of I/O resources so that the I/O can be pooled and provisioned on demand for connectivity to other servers, storage, and LAN pools.

26. The following is the correct order of the phases:

    ■ Consolidation

    ■ Virtualization

    ■ Automation

27. The Data Center Aggregation (distribution) layer aggregates the uplinks from the access layer to the Data Center Core layer and is the critical point for control and application services.

28. When determining whether to implement a Core layer within a Data Center design, you should consider the following:

    ■ **10-Gigabit Ethernet density**: Without a Data Center Core, will there be enough 10-Gigabit Ethernet ports on the Campus Core switch pair to support both the campus Building Distribution layer and the Data Center Aggregation layer?

    ■ **Administrative domains and policies**: Separate campus and data center cores help isolate the campus Building Distribution layers from Data Center Aggregation layers for troubleshooting, maintenance, administration, and implementation of policies (using QoS and ACLs).

    ■ **Anticipation of future development**: The impact that could result from implementing a separate Data Center Core layer at a later date might make it worthwhile to install it at the beginning.

Chapter 5

Case Study Answers

1. The RFP should include the following items:

   - The number of sites and the minimum bandwidth required to each site

   - The service level that should be guaranteed (that the provider will deliver) under the SLA

   - The mean time to repair (MTTR) that is acceptable under the SLA

   - The level of packet loss, latency, and jitter that is acceptable under the SLA

   - How the SLA parameters will be measured

   - Any penalties for SLA noncompliance

2. The monthly cost calculations are shown in the last column of the following table.

ACMC RFP Results

Option	Technology	Speed	Price per Month	Monthly Cost
1	Leased line: T1 at clinics into T3 at central	T1 or T3	$400 for each T1, $8000 for the T3	5 * $400 = $2000 1 * $8000 = $8000 Total = $10,000 per month
2	Frame Relay: T1 access at clinics, T3 access at central	T1 or T3	$350 for T1 access, $7000 for T3 access circuit plus CIR in 5-Mbps increments times $75 plus $5 per PVC	5 * $350 = $1750 1 * $7000 = $7000 5 * 1.544/5 * $75 = $115.80 5 * $5 = $25 Total = $8890.80 per month
3	MPLS VPN: T1 access at clinics, T3 access at central	T1 or T3	$500 for T1 access, $8500 for T3 access	5 * $500 = $2500 1 * $8500 = $8500 Total = $11,000 per month

continues

ACMC RFP Results (Continued)

Option	Technology	Speed	Price per Month	Monthly Cost
4	High-speed business cable service at clinics	6 Mbps downstream, 768 kbps upstream	$90	5 * $90 = $450 1 * $4000 = $4000 Total = $4450 per month
	T3 Internet at central site	T3	$4000	

3. In the ACMC area, the total cost of the Frame Relay connections is less expensive than for leased lines; the MPLS VPN is the most expensive.

   The cable connection is quite competitive on price but does not provide the same bandwidth upstream. This would be an issue (as it would be with asymmetric DSL) because moving images from the remote offices to the central office is limited to the 768-kbps upstream speed. An alternative would be to store the images at the main hospital if cable technology is used.

   Because ACMC does not know how much bandwidth will be needed in the future, being able to add more bandwidth as needed is attractive. Including multilink PPP on T1 leased lines or multilink Frame Relay over multiple T1 access circuits would allow for some bandwidth growth.

   T1 Frame Relay at the remote clinics into T3 at the central site is recommended. This approach should provide guaranteed bandwidth with a good SLA at a reasonable price. Assuming that the carrier supports it, multilink Frame Relay could be used to add bandwidth up to 6 Mbps in the future.

   NOTE   This answer is, of course, very subjective; there is no *right* answer. Costs might cause some customers to rethink their requirements. For example, for some customers, cost is more important than the terms of an SLA. Some customers might prefer a specific technology for other reasons. For example, leased-line T1 connections could also be used in this case, with pricing about 12% higher than Frame Relay.

4. This calculation suggests that more bandwidth would be useful as soon as it becomes affordable. One way to approach convincing administrators of the need for more bandwidth is to arrange a lab demonstration of how long it will take the image to display using various bandwidth links and then present the costs of each solution.

The medical images could be automatically uploaded and stored centrally. For example, some imaging applications allow a doctor to mark images for transfer and view them later when they become available locally. Until a higher-speed connection (such as Metro Ethernet) becomes available, ACMC will have to use the current WAN technologies along with software that is smart about WAN usage.

5. IPsec VPNs over the Internet, via a cable connection, is an attractive lower-cost approach for backup links. However, this option probably has a lower SLA level; ACMC must decide whether the SLA level is acceptable or will compromise application availability. The following figure illustrates the recommended WAN and WAN backup solution.

Case Study: ACMC Hospital Recommended WAN Solution

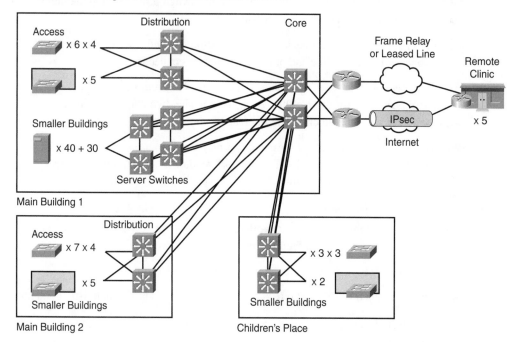

6. Considering the available ISRs results in the following:

   ■ The Cisco 870, 1800, 2800, and 3800 Series routers can handle the necessary traffic levels.

   ■ The 870 router does not support serial ports.

- The 1841 router supports Fast Ethernet and a two-port serial WIC and a cable modem connection.

- All the 2800 Series models except the 2801 router can be used with high-speed serial interface (HSSI) T3 links. All the 2800 Series models support the four-port high-speed T1 HWIC. The 3800 Series routers could also be used.

To allow for growth, using the 2800 Series routers at remote sites, with four T1 HWIC serial ports and a cable WIC, is recommended. If cost is an issue, use the 1841 router; however, this option is limited to two T1 ports.

At each remote site, use an external switch with the 2800 Series router, or use the 3800 Series with switching network modules. Using an external switch provides more flexibility if you are considering adding a backup router later.

Use a 2821 router or 3800 Series model at the central site with two T3 links (using NM-1 HSSI): one for the leased line and one for the Internet connection.

7. An 870 router could be used for a cable connection at each remote site. A 2800 Series router would still be needed for the T1 links. At the central site, two 2800 Series models could be used: one for T3 and the other for the Internet T3 connection.

With two routers at the remote clinics, it makes more sense to use an external switch with two uplinks than to use an integrated switch network module in a 3800 Series router.

Answers to Review Questions

1. A WAN is a data communications network that covers a relatively broad geographic area and typically uses the transmission facilities provided by service providers.

2. The following are typical objectives of an effective WAN design:

   - A well-designed WAN must reflect the organization's goals, characteristics, and policies.

   - The selected technology should be sufficient for current and, to some extent, future application requirements.

   - The associated costs of investment and usage should stay within the budget limits.

3. The key rationale for creating a fully meshed network is to provide a high level of redundancy; however, a fully meshed topology is not scalable to large packet-switched networks. Key issues include the following:

   - The large number of virtual circuits required (one for every connection between routers)

   - Problems associated with the requirement for large numbers of packet and broadcast replications

- The configuration complexity for routers in the absence of multicast support in nonbroadcast environments

4. A T1 circuit is made up of 24 channels each at 64 kbps, resulting in a bandwidth of 1.544 Mbps.

5. Connectivity over ISDN offers the network designer increased bandwidth, reduced call setup time, reduced latency, and lower signal-to-noise ratios compared to analog dialup.

6. An MPLS FEC is a grouping of packets; packets that belong to the same FEC receive the same treatment in the network. Various parameters, including source or destination IP address or port numbers, IP protocol, IP precedence, or Layer 2 circuit identifier can determine FEC.

7. An MPLS label is a 32-bit field placed between a packet's data link layer and its IP header.

8. False. Packets sent between the same endpoints can belong to different FECs and therefore can can flow through different network paths.

9. With ADSL, traffic moves upstream and downstream at different speeds. ADSL also allows PSTN telephony services concurrently on the same line.

    With SDSL, traffic in either direction travels at the same speed over a single copper twisted pair. However, unlike ADSL, SDSL does not allow PSTN telephony services concurrently on the same line.

10. Downstream refers to data that travels from the Internet to the end-user computer.

    Upstream refers to data that travels from the end-user computer to the Internet.

11. D is the Layer 3 concentrator.

    A is the Layer 2 concentrator or DSLAM.

    C is the splitter.

    B is the ADSL CPE.

12. Answer:

    - **ADSL**: copper twisted pair

    - **VDSL**: copper twisted pair

    - **Cable**: coaxial cable

    - **LRE**: copper twisted pair

13. B and C

14. Bridged wireless is designed to connect two or more networks, which are typically located in different buildings, at high data rates for data-intensive line-of-sight applications.

15. Answer:

    - **802.11a**: Up to 54 Mbps in the 5-GHz band

    - **802.11b**: Up to 11 Mbps in the 2.4-GHz band

    - **802.11g**: Up to 54 Mbps in the 2.4-GHz band

16. SONET is an ANSI specification. SDH is the SONET-equivalent specification proposed by the ITU. Whereas European carriers use SDH widely, North American and Asia/Pacific Rim carriers use SONET more frequently.

17. POS sends native IP packets directly over SONET/SDH frames.

18. A file transfer is a high-volume traffic application and therefore typically has high throughput requirements, but it is typically not susceptible to response time delays. Interactive applications are typically low-volume and therefore have low throughput requirements. However, interactivity involves users, and users have very stringent response time requirements.

19. Technologies suitable for WAN connections over 50 Mbps include Fast Ethernet, Gigabit Ethernet, 10 Gigabit Ethernet, ATM over SONET/SDH, and POS.

20. Answer:

    - **Compression**: Reduction of data size for the purpose of saving transmission time

    - **Bandwidth**: Amount of data transmitted or received per unit time

    - **Response time**: Time between a user request (such as the entry of a command or keystroke) and the host system's command execution or response delivery

    - **Window size**: Maximum number of frames (or amount of data) the sender can transmit before it must wait for an acknowledgment

    - **Throughput**: Amount of data successfully moved from one place to another in a given time period

21. Multilink PPP (MLP) logically connects multiple links between two systems, as needed, to provide extra bandwidth. The bandwidth of two or more physical communication links, such as analog modems, ISDN, and other analog or digital links, are logically aggregated, resulting in an increase in overall throughput.

22. If WAN links are constantly congested, either greater bandwidth or compression is required. QoS mechanisms, including queuing, do not relieve constant congestion. If WAN links are never congested, queuing is unnecessary.

23.   Answer:

- **WFQ**: Enabled by default on most low-speed serial interfaces (with speeds at or below 2.048 Mbps) on Cisco routers

- **PQ**: Establishes four interface output queues (high, medium, normal, and low)

- **CQ**: Establishes up to 16 configurable interface output queues

- **CBWFQ**: Reserves a queue for each class

- **LLQ**: Allows sensitive data such as voice to be sent first

24.   With overlay VPNs, the provider's infrastructure provides virtual point-to-point links between customer sites. From a Layer 3 perspective, the provider network is invisible. The provider is not aware of customer routing and does not have any information about customer routes.

With VPDNs, the customers use a provider's dial-in infrastructure for their private dialup connections. The ISP agrees to forward the company's traffic from the ISP's POP to a company-run home gateway. Network configuration and security remain in the client's control.

25.   IPsec is both a tunnel encapsulation protocol and a security protocol. IPsec provides security for the transmission of sensitive information over unprotected networks (such as the Internet) by encrypting the tunnel's data. IPsec acts as the network layer in tunneling or transport mode and protects and authenticates IP packets between participating IPsec devices.

26.   An SP MPLS IP VPN allows any-to-any connections (any branch can be networked to any branch) with comprehensive QoS for voice and video traffic. The secure, reliable connectivity and relatively lower carrier fees inherent in this technology make a network-based IP VPN a good choice for businesses looking to use a managed service solution to connect branches, remote offices, teleworkers, and remote call agents.

Self-deployed MPLS is a network segmentation technique that allows enterprises to logically segment the network. Self-deployed MPLS is typically reserved for very large enterprises or a service provider willing to make a significant investment in network equipment and training, and for those that have an IT staff that is comfortable with a high degree of technical complexity.

27.   The four Cisco IOS Packaging packages that have been designed to satisfy the requirements in base service categories are as follows:

- **IP Base**: Supports IP data

- **IP Voice**: Supports converged voice and data

- **Advanced Security**: Provides security and VPN

- **Enterprise Base**: Provides enterprise Layer 3 protocols and IBM support

28. Branch offices can be categorized based on the number of users:

    ■ **Small office**: Up to 50 users

    ■ **Medium office**: Between 50 and 100 users

    ■ **Large office**: Between 100 and 200 users

29. With Cisco StackWise technology, a single 32-Gbps switching unit can be created, using up to nine Cisco Catalyst 3750 Series Switches. Cisco StackWise technology uses special stack-interconnect cables and stacking software. The stack behaves as a single switching unit that is managed by a master switch elected from one of the member switches. The master switch automatically creates and updates all the switching and optional routing tables.

30. The enterprise teleworker solution could be implemented with a small ISR such as the Cisco 871, 876, 877, or 878 ISR with integrated switch ports, connected behind a broadband modem.

Chapter 6

Case Study Answers

1. The following details from previous case study answers help determine the IP addressing requirements:

    ■ Each of the main buildings has 150 ports per floor; the server farm has 140 ports. Thus, approximately $7 \times 150 = 1050$ ports are required for each building, including the server farm. Each wiring closet has a 48-port switch.

    ■ The Children's Place has 120 ports per floor on three floors. Thus, a total of $3 \times 120 = 360$ ports are required. Each of the three wiring closets has a 48-port switch.

    ■ Buildings A through D each have one 24-port switch.

    ■ Buildings E through J each have one 48-port switch (or two 24-port switches).

    ■ Buildings K through L each have one switch with 96 ports, two 48-port switches, or four 24-port switches.

    ■ Connections between the access and distribution, between the distribution and core, and between the WAN routers and core are all Layer 3 point-to-point connections; therefore, a subnet mask of /30 is appropriate for all these connections.

    ■ Allocating the addressing for the WAN connections from a single prefix allows summarization; allowing room for expansion to more remote sites is appropriate.

Recall that five of the small buildings are connected to Main Building 1, five are connected to Main Building 2, and two are connected to the Children's Place. For addressing purposes, assume that Buildings A through E connect to Main Building 1, Buildings F through J to Main Building 2, and Buildings K through L to the Children's Place. If the actual connectivity is different, the building numbers in the addressing plan could easily be altered.

The total number of required addresses fits easily into a Class B address (which provides up to 65,534 hosts). Subnetting a private network such as 172.16.0.0/16 is therefore an option. However, using the private Class A network 10.0.0.0/8 results in much simpler subnetting (the entire second and third octets can be used, and subnetting within an octet can be minimized). Because using the Class A network 10.0.0.0 has the most advantages, it is chosen for this example. The drawback of selecting any particular network is that if ACMC ever merges with another organization using that same network, the network will have to be re-addressed. Because you cannot predict the future, this will not be a concern in your address selection.

A simple approach is to use the second octet to distinguish the building or site, and the third octet for the floor number; the resulting /24 subnet mask keeps the addressing simple. The addresses within the /24 subnets in the main buildings are divided into four /26 subnets, one for each of the access switches (closets).

Another option would be to treat Buildings A through L and the remote clinics as "floors" of a fictitious building; this approach would be less wasteful of address space. However, network 10.0.0.0 has so much address space that you do not need to add this complication.

The /30 subnets that interconnect locations are allocated from the 10.*building_number*.255.0/24 network. For the connections to the small buildings and remote sites, addressing from the small building or remote site block is used so that the connection summarizes within the building or remote site address block to which it connects. If redundant links are used, twice as many addresses are required; more than enough addresses are available in this block.

For the links between the access and distribution Layer 3 devices in each of the main buildings, there are 29 to 33 uplink ports on each of the two distribution switches (multiplied by N if N-way EtherChannel is configured). Five of these are for the connections to the remote buildings; therefore, up to $28 \times 2 = 56$ subnets with a /30 subnet mask are required for the connections to the access switches (closets). In Main Building 1, the 10.1.255.0/24 subnet is further subnetted to a /30 mask, providing 64 blocks each with two host addresses, which is more than enough for the required 56 uplinks. Similarly, in Main Building 2, the 10.16.255.0/24 subnet is further subnetted.

For the links between the access and distribution Layer 3 devices in Children's Place, there are 11 uplink ports on each of the two distribution switches. Two of these are for the connections to the remote buildings; therefore, $9 \times 2 = 18$ subnets with a /30 subnet mask are required for the closet switches. The 10.32.255.0/24 subnet is further subnetted to a /30 mask, providing 64 blocks each with two host addresses, which is more than enough for the required 18 uplinks.

Each of the two core switches has six distribution switches, four server switches, and possibly two WAN routers connected to it. Thus, there are a total of 24 uplinks to core. One option for addressing these links is to use /30 blocks from the building range for each of the two main buildings and the Children's Place. If this was done in Main Building 1, all the /30 blocks will be used. Another approach is to allocate addresses for all distribution and WAN router connections to the core from a separate subnet—for example, 10.1.253.0/24. This is a more scalable solution.

The following table details the addressing plan.

ACMC Hospital Proposed IP Address Assignments

Location	IP Address Block	IP Address Details
Main Building 1	10.1.0.0 /16	Third octet = floor number, with /24 subnet mask Fourth octet divided into four blocks, using a /26 subnet mask (with addresses in multiples of 64), one per access switch (closet) Treat server farm as a separate "floor," floor 8 10.1.253.0 /24 is subnetted to /30 for all distribution and WAN router connections to the core 10.1.255.0 /24 is subnetted to /30 for the links between the access and distribution devices
Building A	10.2.0.0 /16	
Building B	10.3.0.0 /16	
Building C	10.4.0.0 /16	
Building D	10.5.0.0 /16	
Building E	10.6.0.0 /16	
Reserved	10.7.0.0 /16 through 10.15.0.0 /16	Allow room for growth within a block that can be summarized to 10.0.0.0/12
Main Building 2	10.16.0.0 /16	Third octet = floor number, with /24 subnet mask Fourth octet divided into four blocks, using a /26 subnet mask (with addresses in multiples of 64), one per access switch (closet) 10.16.255.0 /24 is subnetted to /30 for the links between the access and distribution devices
Building F	10.17.0.0 /16	
Building G	10.18.0.0 /16	

ACMC Hospital Proposed IP Address Assignments (Continued)

Location	IP Address Block	IP Address Details
Building H	10.19.0.0 /16	
Building I	10.20.0.0 /16	
Building J	10.21.0.0 /16	
Reserved	10.22.0.0 /16 through 10.31.0.0 /16	Allow room for growth within a block that can be summarized to 10.16.0.0/12
Children's Place	10.32.0.0 /16	Third octet = floor number, with /24 subnet mask Fourth octet divided into four blocks, using a /26 subnet mask (with addresses in multiples of 64), one per access switch (closet); the last one is not used 10.32.255.0 /24 is subnetted to /30 for the links between the access and distribution devices
Building K	10.33.0.0 /16	
Building L	10.34.0.0 /16	
Reserved	10.35.0.0 /16 through 10.47.0.0 /16	Allow room for growth within a block that can be summarized to 10.32.0.0/12
Remote site 1	10.48.0.0 /16	
Remote site 2	10.49.0.0 /16	
Remote site 3	10.50.0.0 /16	
Remote site 4	10.51.0.0 /16	
Remote site 5	10.52.0.0 /16	
Reserved	10.53.0.0 /16 through 10.63.0.0 /16	For expansion, to allow room for growth within a block that can be summarized to 10.48.0.0/12
Future space	10.64.0.0 /16 through 10.255.0.0 /16	Unused space

2. A combination of DHCP and static IP address assignment is suitable for the ACMC Hospital, as follows:

■ Static IP addresses for network devices, management ports, WAN links, and so forth.

- DHCP for the devices in the access layer. A router in each site could be the DHCP server for the site.

- Remote clinics could use local DHCP with the router as the DHCP server. Alternatively, a DHCP server in the central site could be used, but if the WAN failed, the remote clinics would lose their connection to that central site DHCP server.

Answers to Review Questions

1. B and C

2. Both private and public IPv4 addresses might be required in a network that requires Internet connectivity but that does not require all its end systems to be publicly accessible.

3. Answer:

   - The mask is 255.255.255.240.

   - The address is a Class B address.

   - The host part is binary 0101 (decimal 5).

   - The network part is 172.17.7.binary 1111xxxx (decimal 172.17.7.240).

   - $2^4 - 2 = 14$ hosts can reside on this subnet.

4. Information that must be collected to determine the size of the network includes the number and type of locations, the number of devices in each location (such as workstations, router interfaces, and so on) that need addresses and their addressing requirements, and the size of the subnet required.

5. The commonly suggested reserve in the number of network device addresses is 20 percent for main and regional offices and 10 percent for remote offices. Depending on the circumstances, more reserve might be required.

6. Classless routing protocols support VLSM.

7. The router could advertise the 10.5.16.0/22 summary route to represent these four subnets.

8. Some disadvantages of a poorly designed IP addressing scheme include the following:

   - Excess routing traffic, which consumes bandwidth

   - Increased routing table recalculation

   - The possibility of routing loops

9. A hierarchical IP addressing scheme supports route summarization, which reduces routing overhead and the bandwidth required for routing traffic.

10. With classful routing, routing updates do not carry the subnet mask; with classless routing, routing updates carry the subnet mask.

11. DHCP relieves the administrator of the task of manually assigning an address to every device and makes it easier to reconfigure addresses.

12. DHCP supports three possible address allocation mechanisms:

    ■ **Manual**: The network administrator assigns the IP address to a specific MAC address. DHCP is used to dispatch the assigned address to the host.

    ■ **Automatic**: DHCP assigns a permanent IPv4 address to a host.

    ■ **Dynamic**: DHCP assigns an IP address to a host for a limited time (called a *lease*) or until the host explicitly releases the address. This mechanism allows automatic address reuse when the host to which it has been assigned no longer needs the address.

13. Dynamic name resolution reduces administrative overhead.

14. Answer:

    Step 1   A user wants to browse www.cisco.com. The host queries the DNS server because it does not know that site's IP address.

    Step 2   The DNS server responds with the appropriate IP address for www.cisco.com.

    Step 3   The host establishes the connection to the appropriate IP address (the www.cisco.com site).

15. An IPv6 address has 128 bits.

16. The IPv6 packet header is 40 octets, or 320 bits.

17. C and D

18. A packet that is sent to an anycast address goes to the *closest* interface (as determined by the routing protocol being used) identified by the anycast address.

19. One-to-many IPv6 addresses are called <u>multicast</u>.

20. True

21. 64 bits are used for the interface ID in an IPv6 unicast address.

22. FE80::/10, the prefix for link-local addresses, is used by devices on the same network to communicate.

23. IPv6 address assignment can be done with static addresses, link-local addresses, stateless autoconfiguration, and DHCPv6.

24.   A router on the link advertises—either periodically or at the host's request—network information, such as the 64-bit prefix of the local network and its willingness to function as a default router for the link. Hosts can automatically generate their global IPv6 addresses by using the prefix in these router messages; the hosts do not need manual configuration or the help of a device such as a DHCP server.

25.   The A6 record, which is an address record for an IPv6 host, allows DNS to support IPv6.

26.   Yes; this is called a *dual-stack host*.

27.   Dual stack, tunneling, and translation are three mechanisms for transitioning from IPv4 to IPv6.

28.   The 6-to-4 tunneling method automatically connects IPv6 islands through an IPv4 network. Each 6-to-4 edge router has an IPv6 address with a /48 prefix, which is the concatenation of 2002::/16 and the IPv4 address of the edge router; 2002::/16 is a specially assigned address range for the purpose of 6-to-4. The edge routers automatically build the tunnel using the IPv4 addresses that are embedded in the IPv6 addresses.

When the edge router receives an IPv6 packet with a destination address in the range of 2002::/16, it determines from its routing table that the packet must traverse the tunnel. The router extracts the IPv4 address embedded in the third to sixth octets, inclusive, in the IPv6 next-hop address. This IPv4 address is the IPv4 address of the 6-to-4 router at the destination site—the router at the other end of the tunnel. The router encapsulates the IPv6 packet in an IPv4 packet with the destination edge router's extracted IPv4 address.

The packet passes through the IPv4 network. The destination edge router unencapsulates the IPv6 packet from the received IPv4 packet and forwards the IPv6 packet to its final destination. A 6-to-4 relay router, which offers traffic forwarding to the IPv6 Internet, is required for reaching a native IPv6 Internet.

29.   Cisco routers support the following:

- RIPng

- EIGRP for IPv6

- OSPFv3

- IS-ISv6

- BGP4+

30.   RIPng uses the multicast address FF02::9, the all-RIP-routers multicast address, as the destination address for RIP updates.

Chapter 7

Case Study Answers

1. Either EIGRP or OSPF is recommended. Both are fast to converge, send triggered updates, can be used to create hierarchical networks, and support manual summarization and VLSM.

    Route summarization should be implemented. The IP addressing scheme proposed in the case study solution for Chapter 6 was designed to easily allow summarization.

    If desired, static routes could be used for the connections to the remote clinics. If a WAN backup is provided by an IPsec VPN connection over the Internet, a static route for 10.0.0.0 /8 through the IPsec tunnel might be needed, assuming that the default route points toward the Internet.

2. As detailed in the case study solution for Chapter 6, the proposed IP addressing scheme was designed to easily allow summarization. The summary routes are as follows:

    ■ In Main Building 1: 10.0.0.0/12

    ■ In Main Building 2: 10.16.0.0/12

    ■ In the Children's Place: 10.32.0.0/12

    ■ In the remote clinics: 10.48.0.0/12

    The following figure shows the summary routes at OSPF area boundaries. If EIGRP is used, the same summary routes could be used at similar boundary points within the network.

Summarization Routes for the ACMC Hospital Network

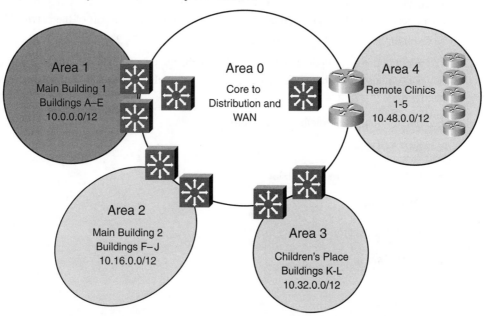

Answers to Review Questions

1. Static routing might be preferred over dynamic routing in the following situations:

   ■ For slow links, such as dialup links

   ■ When the administrator needs control over the routes used

   ■ For a backup to a dynamically learned route

   ■ For stub networks

2. Dynamic routing protocols do the following:

   ■ Find sources from which routing information can be received (usually neighboring routers)

   ■ Select best paths toward all reachable destinations, based on received information

   ■ Maintain this routing information

   ■ Have a means of verifying routing information (periodic updates or refreshes)

3. Exterior gateway protocols (EGP) are used to interconnect autonomous systems.

4. IGPs typically converge faster than EGPs

5. BGP multihoming is when an AS has more than one connection to the Internet.

6. When a network is using a distance vector routing protocol, all the routers periodically send their routing tables (or a portion of their tables) to only their neighboring routers. In contrast, when a network is using a link-state routing protocol, each of the routers sends the state of its own interfaces (its links) to all other routers (or to all routers in a part of the network known as an area) only when there is a change.

7. Triggered updates are updates sent only when a change occurs. For example, the link goes down or comes up, or there is a change in a link parameter that affects routing (such as bandwidth).

8. The default metric parameters are as follows:

   ■ **RIP**: Hop count

   ■ **EIGRP**: Bandwidth and delay

   ■ **OSPF**: Cost

   ■ **BGP**: Path vector, including the AS-path

   ■ **IS-IS**: Metric

9. A network is converged when routing tables on all routers in the network are synchronized and contain a usable route to each destination network. Convergence time is the time it takes for all routers in a network to agree on the current topology.

10. A network is not completely operable until the network has converged. Therefore, short convergence times are required for routing protocols.

11. Advantages of hierarchical networks include the capability to summarize, resulting in less routing traffic overhead, better scalability, isolation of network instabilities, and faster convergence time.

12. C and D

13. No. RIPv2 would not be a good choice because it uses only hop count as its metric. It does not take the links' bandwidth into account.

14. The following are some EIGRP features that make it an appropriate enterprise routing protocol:

    ■ Fast convergence using the DUAL algorithm

    ■ Improved scalability with manual summarization

    ■ Use of VLSM

    ■ Reduced bandwidth usage with triggered updates

    ■ Multiple network layer protocol support

15. An EIGRP feasible successor is a neighbor that is closer to the destination, but is not in the least-cost path and therefore is not used to forward data. In other words, a feasible successor is a backup route to the destination.

16. No. Manual route summarization is supported only on Area Border Routers (ABR) and Autonomous System Boundary Routers (ASBR).

17. An OSPF link-state advertisement (LSA) describes the state of links on specific routers and is propagated, unchanged, within an area.

18. The OSPF metric is Cost, which by default is inversely proportional to the link's bandwidth.

19. Integrated IS-IS can route IPv4 and CLNP. A version of Integrated IS-IS also supports IPv6.

20. In Integrated IS-IS, the path of connected Level 2 (L2) and Level 1/Level 2 (L1/L2) routers is called the backbone. All areas and the backbone must be contiguous. IS-IS area boundaries fall on the links, not within the routers.

    An OSPF network is separated into multiple areas. There must always be one backbone area—area 0—to which all other nonbackbone areas must be directly attached. A router is a member of an OSPF area when at least one of its interfaces operates in that area. Routers that reside on boundaries between the backbone and a nonbackbone area are called Area Border Routers (ABR) and have at least one interface in each area. The boundary between the areas is in the ABR itself.

21. In a very large network, Integrated IS-IS might be better than OSPF because its partial route calculation (PRC) provides faster convergence, and because it allows easier extension of the backbone.

22. BGP is an EGP that is primarily used to interconnect autonomous systems. The main goal of BGP is to provide an interdomain routing system that guarantees the loop-free exchange of routing information between autonomous systems. BGP routers exchange information about paths to destination networks.

23. EIGRP and OSPF are likely to be used in an enterprise Campus Core.

24. No. IS-IS requires detailed knowledge of the OSI protocol suite for proper configuration, even if only routing IP. As a recommended practice, the same routing protocol should be used in all three layers of the Enterprise Campus; therefore, the recommended routing protocols in the Building Distribution layer include EIGRP and OSPF.

25. Cisco routers allow internetworks using different routing protocols (referred to as *routing domains* or *autonomous systems*) to exchange routing information through a feature called route redistribution. This allows, for example, hosts in one part of the network to reach hosts in another part that is running a different routing protocol.

26. Redistribution is needed in the Building Distribution layer when different routing protocols or domains exist in the Building Access layer and Campus Core. Redistribution might also be needed between the Campus Core and the Enterprise Edge, including to and from WAN module routers, from static or BGP routes in the Internet Connectivity module, and from static routes in the Remote Access and VPN module.

27. Route filtering prevents the advertisement or acceptance of certain routes through the routing domain.

28. Filtering is used primarily with route redistribution to prevent suboptimal routing and routing loops that might occur when routes are redistributed at multiple redistribution points. Route filtering is also used to prevent routes about certain networks, such as private IP address spaces, from being sent to or received from remote sites.

29. Redistributing from an IGP into BGP is not recommended because any change in the IGP routes—for example, if a link goes down—can cause a BGP update, which might result in unstable BGP tables. If IGP routes are redistributed into BGP, make sure that only local routes—those that originate within the AS—are redistributed. For example, routes learned from other autonomous systems (that were learned by redistributing BGP into the IGP) must not be sent out from the IGP again, because routing loops could result, or the AS could inadvertently become a transit AS.

30. In route summarization (also called route aggregation or supernetting), a single summary address in the routing table represents a set of routes. Summarization reduces the routing update traffic, the number of routes in the routing table, and the overall router overhead in the router receiving the routes.

31. Configuring interfaces on a router as passive interfaces under the routing protocol configuration suppresses the advertisement of routing updates for that routing protocol on those interfaces.

Chapter 8

Case Study Answers

1. The following are some of the infrastructure aspects that should be considered:

    ■ Switches and power supplies that support PoE should be recommended.

    ■ The available building wiring closet power, cooling, and space need to be reviewed.

    ■ QoS mechanisms should be considered, including in the Campus switches and on the WANs. CAC might be required for calls from the clinics to the main campus. cRTP and LFI can also be considered.

    ■ The current cabling infrastructure and configuration need to be reviewed, including the use of the correct category of cable and the duplex configuration.

2. The most appropriate design is multisite WAN with centralized call processing. This model potentially reduces costs and simplifies administration. The Cisco Unified Communications Manager should be placed in the server farm. SRST and local PSTN connections should be used for survivability at the remote clinics.

    The following figure shows the voice transport features in the design.

Case Study: ACMC Hospital Network Voice Design

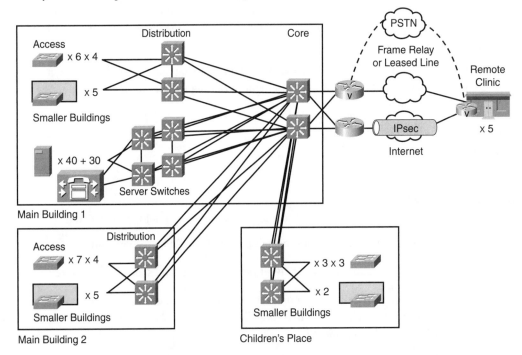

3. Voice gateways, with DSP resources, connected to the PSTN must be included at the remote clinics.

4. The Internet is a best-effort network that does not support any SLA; packet loss, high latency, and high jitter might occur, implying poor-quality voice if the IPsec VPN is used for VoIP.

   To remedy this situation, the dial plan design could route calls via the PSTN if the WAN fails or exhibits poor QoS. Another alternative would be to add a second Frame Relay or WAN link instead of IPsec VPN or Internet for backup. Although this would add cost, it would also make the network more robust overall.

5. The following table shows the calculations and results.

ACMC Call Study Results

Remote Clinic	Number of Calls on the Trunk to the Main Campus	G.711 Bandwidth (kbps)	G.729 Bandwidth (kbps)
1	8	8 * 92 = 736	8 * 25 = 200
2, 3, 4, 5	4	4 * 92 = 368	4 * 25 = 100
	Totals	1104	300

With G.729, bandwidth should not be a problem. With G.711, the voice traffic might consume a significant portion of the bandwidth on the two T1 links at each of the remote clinics.

Answers to Review Questions

1. Several steps are involved in converting an analog signal into PCM digital format, including the following:

   - **Filtering**: Filters out the signal's nonspeech frequency components.

   - **Sampling**: Samples the filtered input signal at a constant sampling frequency.

   - **Digitizing**: Digitizes the samples in preparation for transmission over a telephony network; this is the PCM process.

2. PAM uses the original analog signal to modulate the amplitude of a pulse train that has a constant amplitude and frequency.

3. The process of digitizing analog voice signals is called pulse code modulation. PCM takes the PAM process one step further by encoding each analog sample using binary code words.

4. Answer:

   - **Filtering**: Removing nonspeech components

   - **Quantization**: Converting an analog sample to a digital code word

   - **Companding**: Compressing and expanding signals

   - **Logarithmic compression**: Compression increases as the sample signal increases

5. TDM is a digital transmission technique for carrying multiple signals simultaneously over a single trunk line by interleaving bits of each signal into different time slots.

6. Answer:

   - A PBX is used in the private sector, whereas a PSTN is used in the public sector.

   - A PBX scales to thousands of phones, whereas a PSTN scales to hundreds of thousands of phones.

   - A PBX uses proprietary protocols to control phones, whereas a PSTN uses open-standard protocols between switches and phones.

7. A PBX provides many call features, including call hold, call transfer, call forward, follow me, call park, conference calling, music on hold, call history, and voice mail.

8. Enterprises install PBXs because the number of telephones is usually greater than the number of simultaneous calls to the PSTN network. Only a small percentage of telephones are active at one time. Companies with a PBX need only the number of external lines (to the PSTN) equal to the maximum possible number of simultaneous calls. Local calls between telephones within the PBX or group of PBXs are free of charge.

9. Answer:

    - **Local loop**: Physical cabling

    - **Station line**: Communication between PBX and business telephone

    - **Trunk**: Communication path between two telephony systems

    - **Tie trunk**: Connects PBXs

    - **CO trunk**: Connects CO switches to PBXs

    - **PSTN switch trunk**: Interconnects CO switches

10. Local-loop signaling is between a PSTN or PBX switch and a subscriber (telephone). Trunk signaling is between PSTN switches, between a PSTN switch and a PBX, or between PBX switches.

11. CAS uses defined bits within T1 or E1 channels for signaling; this is in-band signaling. Therefore, the signal for call setup and so forth is in the same channel as the voice call.

    CCS uses a common link to carry signaling information for several trunks. It differs from CAS signaling because it uses a separate channel for call setup; this is out-of-band signaling.

12. QSIG allows standardized communication between PBXs.

13. SS7 is the signaling method used between PSTN switches.

14. The phone at location A dials the phone number of location B. A PSTN switch forwards the signal as soon as it receives enough digits to send the call to the next switch. The last switch in the series receives all the digits and rings the destination telephone.

15. Answer:

    - Area code: 416

    - Zone: 1

    - Trunk prefix: 1

    - Country code: 1

    - Line number: 1212

    - Prefix: 555

16. VoIP uses voice-enabled routers to convert voice into IP packets and route the packets between locations.

     With IP telephony, IP phones themselves convert voice into IP packets. A dedicated network server that runs specialized software replaces the PBX. IP telephony implementations do not use telephone cabling; instead, they send all signals over standard Ethernet.

17. Terminals are client endpoints that provide real-time, two-way H.323 communications with other endpoints, such as H.323 terminals, gateways, or MCUs.

18. An H.323 gateway is an optional element in the voice network and can be a voice-enabled router or switch. Gateways provide many services, such as translating between H.323 endpoints and non-H.323 devices, which allows H.323 endpoints and non-H.323 endpoints to communicate.

     An H.323 gatekeeper is another optional H.323 element that manages H.323 endpoints. A gatekeeper is typically used in larger, more complex networks. The gatekeeper provides call control services to registered H.323 endpoints within its zone.

19. A voice port is an interface on a voice gateway that carries voice data. It is a physical port on a voice module; a voice port is what makes a router voice-enabled.

20. Cisco Unified Communications Manager is the software-based call-processing component of the Cisco enterprise IP telephony solution. Cisco Unified Communications Manager provides a scalable, distributable, and highly available enterprise IP telephony call processing solution. It performs much like a PBX in a traditional telephone network, including call setup and processing functions.

21. The IP telephony architecture includes four distinct components: infrastructure, call processing, applications, and client devices.

22. IP telephony lowers costs in the following ways:

     ■ **Reduced long-distance costs**: Long-distance costs should be lower than with traditional telephony. This can be accomplished by using the public Internet or private IP networks to route telephone calls.

     ■ **Lower total cost of ownership**: IP telephony should offer lower total cost of ownership and greater flexibility than traditional telephony. Installation costs and operational costs for unified systems are lower than the cost to implement and operate two infrastructures.

     ■ **Cost-effective**: Making IP telephony cost-effective depends on using the existing WAN capacity more efficiently and the cost of upgrading the existing IP network infrastructure to support IP telephony. In some cases, this can be accomplished by using the public Internet or private IP networks to route telephone calls.

23. In a multisite WAN design model with centralized call processing, Cisco Unified Communications Manager at the central site connects to remote locations through the IP WAN. Remote IP telephones rely on the centralized Cisco Unified Communications Manager to handle their call processing. The IP WAN is used to transport voice traffic between sites and to carry call control signaling between the central site and the remote sites. Applications such as voice mail and IVR systems are also centralized, thereby reducing the overall cost of ownership and centralized administration and maintenance.

    In a multisite WAN design model with distributed call processing, each independent site has its own call processing agent and is connected to an IP WAN that carries voice traffic between the distributed sites. The IP WAN in this model does not carry call control signaling between the sites because each site has its own call processing agent.

24. Answer:

    - **H.323**: An ITU-T standard for packet-based audio, video, and data communications across IP-based networks

    - **SCCP**: A Cisco-proprietary terminal control protocol used for messaging between IP phones and Cisco Unified Communications Manager

    - **SIP**: An IETF standard for multimedia conferencing over IP

    - **MGCP**: A client/server protocol in which call agents control endpoints

25. B. Dejitter buffers are used on the receiving side of the network to smooth out delay variability.

26. The generally acceptable one-way delay limit for good-quality voice is 150 ms.

27. Answer:

    - **Processing delay**: Time the DSP takes to process a block of PCM samples

    - **Propagation delay**: Length of time it takes a signal to travel the distance between the sending and receiving endpoints

    - **Jitter**: Variation in the delay of received packets

    - **Echo**: Audible leak of the caller's voice into the receive (return) path

28. LFI is a solution for queuing delay situations. With LFI, the voice gateway fragments large packets into smaller equal-sized frames and interleaves them with small voice packets. Consequently, a large voice packet does not have to wait until the entire data packet is sent. LFI reduces and ensures a more predictable voice delay.

29. No. For packet losses as small as one packet, the DSP interpolates the conversation with what it thinks the audio should be, and the packet loss is not audible.

30. Answer:

- **G.711**: 64 kbps

- **G.729**: 8 kbps

- **G.726**: 24 kbps and 16 kbps

- **G.723.1**: 5.3 kbps

- **G.728**: 16 kbps

31. G.711, with a MOS of 4.1.

32. Codec complexity is divided into low, medium, and high complexity. The difference between the complexities of the codecs is the CPU utilization necessary to process the codec algorithm and the number of voice channels that a single DSP can support.

33. RTP, UDP, and IP are used to transport voice conversation traffic.

34. Answer:

- **H.225 channel**: Uses Q.931 to establish a connection between two terminals

- **H.245 channel**: Carries control messages that govern voice operation

- **RAS**: Used only if a gatekeeper is present

- **RTCP**: Used by hosts communicating with RTP to monitor the session

35. VAD suppresses packets of silence.

36. cRTP offers significant bandwidth savings by compressing the IP/UDP/RTP headers from 40 bytes to 2 or 4 bytes. cRTP is sometimes referred to as RTP header compression.

37. Answer:

- **G.729**: 1 (8 kbps)

- **G.711**: 3 (64 kbps)

- **G.728**: 2 (16 kbps)

G.729 has the most compression of the payload, but the IP header is a constant 40 bytes. Therefore, G.729 has more IP overhead relative to its payload.

38. LLQ, which is a combination of CBWFQ and PQ, is recommended. Strict priority queuing allows delay-sensitive data, such as voice, to be dequeued and sent first (before packets in other queues are dequeued), giving the delay-sensitive traffic preferential treatment over other traffic.

39.   CAC protects voice traffic from being negatively affected by other voice traffic and keeps excess voice traffic off the network.

40.   Using RSVP, applications request a certain amount of bandwidth for a voice call across a network and receive an indication of the outcome of the reservation based on actual resource availability. The call processing agent at a location can be configured to require RSVP reservations for all calls to or from other locations. Calls are admitted or rejected based on the outcome of the RSVP reservations, which automatically follow the path determined by the routing protocol. Policies can typically be set within the call processing agent to determine what to do in the case of a CAC failure. For example, the call could be rejected, rerouted across the PSTN, or sent across the IP WAN as a best-effort call with a different DSCP marking.

41.   False. When deploying voice, it is recommended that two VLANs be enabled in the Building Access Layer switch: a native VLAN for data traffic and a voice VLAN for voice traffic.

42.   1 Erlang = 36 CCSs. Therefore, five Erlangs = 5 * 36 = 180 CCSs.

43.   A GoS of P05 means that there is a 5% probability that a call will be blocked.

44.   The calculation is as follows:

- BHT = Average call duration (seconds) * calls per hour/3600

- BHT = 180 * 290/3600

- BHT = 14.5 Erlangs

Chapter 9

Case Study Answers

1.   Answer:

> **NOTE**   Because WLC redundancy requirements were not addressed in the case study, the customer should be asked whether redundancy is required.

There are many possibilities for selection and placement of the WLCs. One option is to use 4404 WLCs with LAG, supporting up to 100 APs on each WLC. This solution allows a distributed approach, with one controller in each Main Building and in the Children's Place. These three controllers would provide enough capacity such that any two could support all 165 APs if one of the WLCs fails. If more redundancy is required, another 4404 WLC could be added. These WLCs would be connected at the distribution layer in each building.

Another option is to use a WiSM in Building 1's distribution switch (if a Catalyst 6500 is used); for redundancy, another WiSM could be added in another distribution switch.

If remote clinic 1 has enough users to justify having a WLCM in its ISR, wireless support would be available at the clinic if the WAN link failed.

Wireless control traffic should be prioritized on the WAN.

WCS could be added to centralize controller management.

The LWAPP WLC discovery process would be at Layer 3 because it is more flexible and scalable than Layer 2 LWAPP transport mode and better reflects the mostly Layer 3 network design.

The following figure shows the wireless transport features in the design.

ACMC Hospital Network with Wireless Features

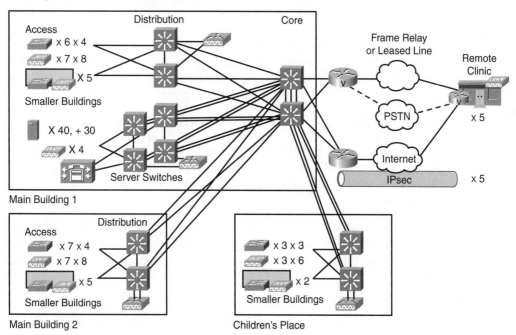

2. Each SSID represents a WLAN that can be mapped to a VLAN. Therefore, SSIDs representing WLANs should be added to the controllers; these should be mapped to VLANs representing each of the staff organizations. The VLANs are separate subnets at the distribution layer, to which appropriate access can be provided—for example, by using ACLs to control which servers each such subnet (user group) can reach.

3. The WLANs represent VLANs or subnets attached to the network at the distribution switch(es). Because the VLANs are separated by the Layer 3 core, each building needs distinct subnets for the VLANs, which should be part of the relevant building's address block.

   The number of users per WLAN/VLAN determines the addressing space required, and thus the subnet mask to use. Although the number of wired users is limited by the number of physical ports available, some assumptions must be made to determine the number of wireless users. Assuming a maximum of 500 users per VLAN for addressing purposes provides plenty of room for growth or flexibility, because there are currently 500 staff members. With this assumption at least 9 host bits are required, resulting in a /23 prefix.

   The following are two of the many IP addressing options available:

   - Use blocks of /23. For example, in Building 1 use 10.1.24.0/23 (addresses 10.1.24.0 through 10.1.25.255) for one VLAN, 10.1.26.0/23 (addresses 10.1.26.0 through 10.1.27.255) for another, and 10.1.28.0/23 (addresses 10.1.28.0 through 10.1.29.255) for the third.

   - Use blocks of /22, providing 1022 addresses per VLAN, for further flexibility. For example, in Building 1 use 10.1.24.0/22 (addresses 10.1.24.0 through 10.1.27.255) for one VLAN, 10.1.28.0/22 (addresses 10.1.28.0 through 10.1.31.255) for another, and 10.1.32.0/22 (addresses 10.1.32.0 through 10.1.35.255) for the third.

4. With just three or four controllers, all of them should be in one mobility group.

5. The remote clinics will be supported by one of the central controllers—for example, the one in Building 1. Use H-REAPs in the remote clinics so that client data traffic can be switched locally and client authentication can be performed locally when the connection to the controller is lost.

6. To support secure guest access, locate a WLC in the DMZ (as discussed in Chapter 10, "Evaluating Security Solutions for the Network") to be an anchor for the guest WLAN. For example, a 4402 WLC could be used for this purpose; recall that a 2206 WLC cannot be used as an anchor.

   A separate guest DMZ would be the best place for this WLC, to protect the DMZ servers from being attacked by hospital guest users. The guest WLAN also requires a separate IP subnet.

Answers to Review Questions

1. A client with a wireless NIC connects to the wired network through an AP.

2. Answer:

   - **Reflection**: Occurs when the RF signal bounces off objects such as metal or glass surfaces.

- **Refraction**: Occurs when the RF signal passes through objects such as glass surfaces and changes direction.

- **Absorption**: Occurs when the RF signal is absorbed by an object such as a wall or furniture.

- **Scattering**: Occurs when an RF wave strikes an uneven surface and is reflected in many directions. Scattering also occurs when an RF wave travels through a medium that consists of objects that are much smaller than the signal's wavelength, such as heavy dust.

- **Diffraction**: Occurs when an RF wave strikes sharp edges, such as external corners of buildings, which bend the signal.

- **Multipath**: Occurs when an RF signal has more than one path between the sender and receiver. The multiple signals at the receiver might result in a distorted, low-quality signal.

3. Every gain of 3 dBm means that the power is <u>doubled</u>. A loss of 3 dBm means that the power is <u>cut in half</u>.

    A gain of 10 dBm means that the power <u>increases</u> by a factor of <u>10</u>. A loss of 10 dBm means that the power <u>decreases</u> by a factor of <u>10</u>.

4. To calculate the level that a 100 mW signal will decrease to when it experiences a 9 dBm loss, do the following:

    100 mW –3dBm = 50 mW

    50 mW –3dBm = 25 mW

    25 mW –3dBm = 12.5 mW

    Therefore, the 100 mW signal will decrease to 12.5 mW when it experiences a 9-dBm loss.

5. True

6. 802.11a operates at 5 GHz. 802.11b and 802.11g operate at 2.4 GHz.

7. The 2.4 GHz band has three nonoverlapping channels in North America: channels 1, 6, and 11.

8. False

9. No. 802.11a and 802.11b/g are not compatible because they use different frequencies. 802.11a requires a different radio and antenna than 802.11b/g.

10. The 802.11a coverage area is smaller than the 802.11b/g coverage area, so more APs are required on a per-area basis for 802.11a.

11. 802.11 uses the same frequency for both transmitting and receiving; therefore, 802.11 is half-duplex (sometimes called *simplex*).

12. An autonomous AP has a local configuration and requires local management, whereas a lightweight AP receives control and configuration from a WLC to which it is associated.

13. An SSID is the identifier or name of a WLAN.

14. The IEEE 802.11i standard uses 802.1X for authentication and AES for encryption. AES is a stronger security algorithm than WEP, but it is more CPU-intensive and therefore requires updated hardware to run AES encryption while maintaining comparable throughput.

15. The five elements of the Cisco UWN are

    ■ Client devices

    ■ Lightweight APs

    ■ Network unification

    ■ Network management

    ■ Mobility services

16. The Cisco UWN includes lightweight APs, WLCs, and optionally the WCS management application and the Cisco wireless location appliance.

17. The WLCs are responsible for putting the wireless client traffic into the appropriate VLAN.

18. Much of the traditional WLAN functionality has moved from autonomous APs to a centralized WLC under the Cisco UWN architecture. LWAPP splits the MAC functions of an AP between the WLC and the lightweight AP. The lightweight APs handle only real-time MAC functionality, leaving all the non-real-time MAC functionality to be processed by the WLC. This split-MAC functionality allows the APs to be deployed in a zero-touch fashion such that individual configuration of APs is not required.

19. The client device, called the EAP supplicant, communicates with the Cisco WLC, which acts as the EAP authenticator. The WLC communicates with an authentication server such as Cisco Secure ACS; this server is also a RADIUS server. The client (the supplicant) supplies network login credentials such as a user ID and password to the authenticator (the WLC). The supplicant, the authenticator, and the authentication server participate in the authentication process. If the authentication process succeeds, the authenticator allows network access to the supplicant through the appropriate port. The WLC tells the lightweight AP which dynamic interface and policies to use for the client.

20. Lightweight APs communicate with WLCs using LWAPP; LWAPP also defines the tunneling mechanism for wireless client data. LWAPP data messages encapsulate and forward data frames from and to wireless clients. LWAPP control messages are management messages exchanged between a WLC and the APs. LWAPP control messages are encrypted. LWAPP-encapsulated data messages, containing client data, are not encrypted.

The LWAPP tunnel uses Layer 2 or Layer 3 transport; Layer 3 is recommended.

21. Despite being called a *wireless* LAN controller, a WLC is connected to the *wired* LAN and to the lightweight APs by *wires*. The WLC does not have *any* wireless connections.

22. Answer:

- **Port**: A WLC port is a physical connection on the WLC that connects to its neighboring switch in the wired campus infrastructure. Each WLC port is by default an 802.1Q VLAN trunk port; the WLC forwards information received from the WLANs, via the APs, over a trunk port to the campus network. A WLC may have multiple physical ports.

- **Interface**: A WLC interface is a logical connection on the WLC that maps to a VLAN on the wired network. The types of WLC interfaces include management interface, AP-manager interface, virtual interface, service-port interface, and dynamic interface.

- **WLAN**: A WLAN is a logical entity that maps an SSID to an interface on the WLC.

23. A WLC has one or more AP-manager interfaces that are used for all Layer 3 communications between the WLC and the lightweight APs after the APs discover the controller. There can be one AP-manager interface per port. The AP-manager IP address is used as the tunnel source for LWAPP packets from the WLC to the AP, and as the tunnel destination for LWAPP packets from the AP to the WLC.

24. Interfaces must be assigned to a port for connectivity to the enterprise network. Multiple WLANs can be assigned to an interface. Multiple interfaces can be assigned to the same port, but an interface can be assigned to only one port. The service-port interface is associated only with the physical service port. The virtual interface is not associated with any port. The AP-manager interface and the management interface can be in the same subnet.

25. The number of APs that each WLC supports is as follows:

- 2000 Series: 6

- WLCM for ISRs: 6

- Catalyst 3750G Integrated WLC WS-C3750G-24WS-S25: 25

- Catalyst 3750G Integrated WLC WS-C3750G-24WS-S50: 50

- 4402 WLC AIR-WLC4402-12-K9: 12

- 4404 WLC AIR-WLC4404-100-K9: 100

- Catalyst 6500 Series WiSM: 300

26. When LAG is enabled, the WLC dynamically manages port redundancy, and one AP-manager interface transparently load-balances APs across an EtherChannel interface. The 48 APs per port limitation does not apply when LAG is enabled. Primary and secondary ports for each interface do not need to be configured. If any of the controller ports fail, traffic is automatically migrated to one of the other ports. As long as at least one controller port is functioning, the system continues to operate, APs remain connected to the network, and wireless clients can continue to send and receive data.

27. The AP selects a WLC to which it sends an LWAPP Join Request from the candidate WLC list, as follows:

    Step 1   If the AP has previously been configured with a primary, secondary, or tertiary controller, the AP attempts to find the WLC configured as its primary. If the AP finds a matching sysName, it sequentially tries to join the primary, secondary, and tertiary controllers.

    Step 2   If no primary, secondary, or tertiary controllers have been configured for an AP, if these controllers cannot be found in the candidate list, or if the LWAPP joins to those controllers have failed, the AP then looks for a WLC configured as a master controller.

    Step 3   Otherwise, the AP attempts to join the WLC that has the most capacity for AP associations.

28. APs that operate in rogue detector mode monitor for the presence of rogue APs on a trusted *wired* network. Their radio is turned off. An AP in rogue detector mode receives periodic rogue AP reports from the WLC (including a list of rogue client MAC addresses) and sniffs all ARP packets. If a match occurs between a MAC address in an ARP packet and a MAC address in the rogue AP report, the rogue AP to which those clients are connected is known to be on the wired network, so the rogue detector AP generates a rogue AP alert to the WLC. The AP does not restrict the rogue AP; it only alerts the WLC.

29. Mobility is the capability of end devices to move to new locations and remain networked without reassociation. Roaming occurs when a wireless client moves its association from one AP and reassociates to another AP, within the same SSID.

    Intracontroller roaming is roaming between APs associated to the same WLC. Intercontroller roaming occurs when a client roams from an AP joined to one WLC to an AP joined to a different WLC. Intercontroller roaming can be at Layer 2 or Layer 3.

30. When a client reassociates to an AP connected to a new WLC with a Layer 2 roam, the new WLC exchanges mobility messages with the original WLC, and the client database entry is *moved* to the new WLC.

With Layer 3 roaming, instead of *moving* the client entry to the new WLC's client database, the original WLC marks the entry for the client in its own client database with an Anchor entry and *copies* the database entry to the new WLC's client database, where it is marked with a Foreign entry.

31. A recommended practice is to support approximately seven to eight voice calls (depending on the codec used) or about 20 data devices over a WLAN.

32. RRM continuously analyzes the existing RF environment and automatically adjusts the AP power and channel configurations to help mitigate cochannel interference, signal coverage problems, and so on.

33. Typical steps in an RF site survey process include the following:

    Step 1   Define customer requirements.

    Step 2   Identify coverage areas and user density.

    Step 3   Determine preliminary AP locations.

    Step 4   Perform the actual survey.

    Step 5   Document the findings.

34. With deterministic controller redundancy, the network administrator statically configures a primary, a secondary, and optionally a tertiary controller.

35. The Cisco UWN can provide path isolation using a Layer 2 (EtherIP) tunnel to direct all guest traffic to a WLC dedicated to guest services (called the *Anchor WLC*) in a *DMZ*—a secured network zone between the private (inside) network and a public (outside) network. EtherIP tunnels logically segment and transport the guest traffic between Edge and Anchor WLCs, whereas other traffic (for example, employee traffic) is still locally bridged on the corresponding VLAN. The original Ethernet frame from the guest client is maintained across the LWAPP and EtherIP tunnels to the anchor WLC.

36. A mesh network consists of two or more indoor or outdoor Cisco LWAPP-enabled mesh APs, communicating with each other over one or more wireless hops (using 802.11a) to join multiple LANs or to extend IEEE 802.11b/g wireless coverage. The APs include a RAP, connected to the wired network, and poletop MAPs. The network also includes WLCs, and optionally the Cisco WCS.

37. With the local MAC feature, the full 802.11 functionality is on the lightweight AP; this solution might be appropriate for branch wireless deployments.

38.   A REAP is a lightweight AP designed to be controlled across WAN links. An H-REAP is an enhancement to a REAP that enables customers to configure and control two or three APs in a branch or remote office from the corporate office through a WAN link without deploying a controller in each office.

Chapter 10

Case Study 10-1 Answers

1.   As mentioned in Chapter 2, a key business security requirement is that the hospital must comply with the U.S. Health Insurance Portability and Accountability Act (HIPAA). HIPAA is about patient confidentiality and the costs of failing to provide adequate security and confidentiality. Threats to network security include the following:

- Reconnaissance, usually the prelude to a more focused attack

- Gaining unauthorized system access

- DoS, including from worms, viruses, and patch management issues

These threats to network security could result in the following risks for ACMC:

- Breach of data confidentiality, including patient records

- Breach of data integrity; for example, if patient records were altered, the results could be life-threatening

- Denial of availability of systems or data, which could also be life-threatening

2.   The following figure illustrates one possible design, in which a single firewall (for example, a Cisco PIX Security Appliance) or a single ASA is used. The Internet router is needed to connect to the T3 link, so the PIX Security appliance or ASA goes between the router and the core switches. An ASA would be used if ACMC wants to use SSL VPNs; ACMC has not mentioned this feature, but asking about it would be a good idea.

With a suitable PIX Security appliance model, VLANs can be trunked to the core switches. VLANs can then be used to separate the public zone (for public servers) and the E-commerce zone (the DMZ). The firewall also secures outbound Internet traffic from ACMC (providing Internet access for the main campus).

ACMC Single Firewall Design

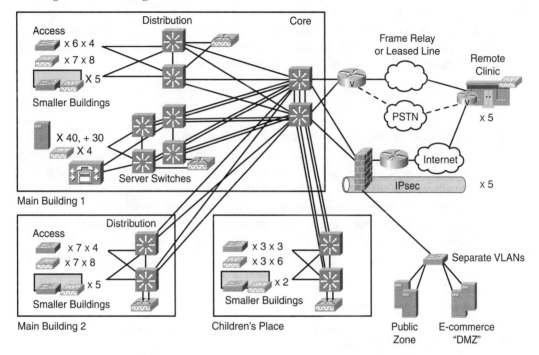

The firewall could terminate IPsec tunnels or pass them through to one or both of the core switches; the device terminating the IPsec tunnels should be equipped with hardware IPsec encryption acceleration. Router-to-router GRE tunnels could be used with IPsec security to allow dynamic routing across the Internet. Additions to the design could include the following:

■ Adding an IPS behind the firewall.

■ Adding another IPS outside the firewall, but it would be subject to many alarms.

■ Using a Cisco Catalyst 6500 Series switch with a FlexWAN module and FWSM installed instead of a separate Internet router. (A FlexWAN module holds WAN port adapters to provide WAN connectivity from the switch.)

■ Using IPsec to encrypt the Frame Relay or leased-line link. Some medical organizations use this approach for enhanced HIPAA confidentiality. Others reason that Frame Relay or leased lines are generally secure. Banks or government, judiciary, and law enforcement agencies might use encryption on such links.

- Some sites, usually larger sites, prefer a "firewall sandwich" approach, in which two firewalls are used with one or more switches in between. The idea is to provide defense-in-depth in case the outer firewall should somehow be compromised. Some security personnel use this approach with firewalls from two vendors to avoid common failure modes; however, support becomes more complex.

- Client VPNs can easily be terminated at the firewall or IPsec router to add remote access for doctors or other users.

Another consideration is Internet redundancy. If Internet access or e-commerce availability is sufficiently important, ACMC should consider links to two different ISPs. The following figure illustrates this redundant design using redundant firewalls or ASAs and DMZ functions. IPS devices and IDS devices are also included in this design. This approach increases availability. However, it is also more costly, increases the number of devices to manage, and increases routing complexity, including the mechanism to fail over from one ISP to another. Many organizations now consider e-commerce and other functions, including e-mail, sufficiently important for such a design to be worth the increase in complexity and cost.

ACMC Redundant Firewall Design

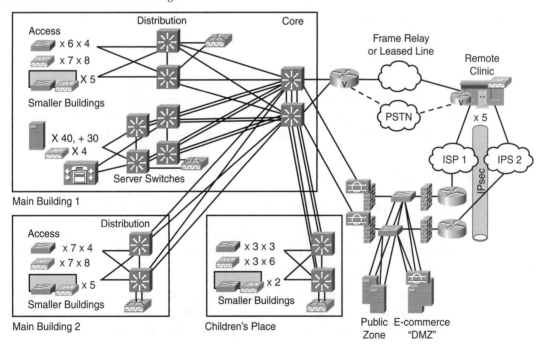

3. To secure the remote clinics, the Cisco IOS Firewall and Cisco IOS IPS features in the ISRs should be used. IPsec VPN acceleration can be used for high-performance secure connectivity on the backup links across the Internet. VPN split tunneling is used so that the remote Internet traffic does not have to go across an IPsec tunnel and then back out to the Internet from the main campus. Using NAC and Cisco Security Agents should be considered to increase security. URL filtering could improve security for remote users.

4. Assuming that the redundant firewall design is chosen, IP addressing could be done as follows:

    ■ Use the 10.7.0.0/16 block, which is one of the reserved blocks. This is far more address space than needed, so there is plenty of room for growth.

    ■ Use 10.7.1.0/28 for the VLAN that connects the two inside firewalls to the core switches (for a total of four connected devices).

    ■ Two VLANs are between the firewall pairs: one for the Public zone and one for the E-commerce DMZ. Use 10.7.2.0/24 and 10.7.3.0/24 for these, providing lots of room for additional servers in each zone.

    ■ Use 10.7.1.16/28 for the connections from the outer firewalls to the routers. These should be connected through switches in a common VLAN to allow for redundancy (using HSRP, Virtual Router Redundancy Protocol, or Gateway Load Balancing Protocol).

    ■ The addresses from the routers to the ISPs will be provided by the ISPs.

    ■ If using a GRE tunnel with IPsec to each remote clinic, a subnet is required for each tunnel. For example, use the 10.7.1.32/30, 10.7.1.36/30, 10.7.1.40/30, 10.7.1.44/30, and 10.7.1.48/30 subnets, reserving the other /30 subnets for future tunnels. Alternatively, /30 subnets from a block allocated for WAN subnets could be used for each remote site.

    ■ If remote VPN client access is allowed, a block of addresses is required for the VPN client pool. For example, 10.7.4.0 /24 could be allocated.

5. The following Cisco products and features could be deployed:

    ■ IPS for intrusion protection in the campus, particularly for traffic going to or from the servers

    ■ Cisco Security MARS for event correlation

    ■ NetFlow, Network-Based Application Recognition, and syslog for monitoring and event detection

    ■ Cisco NAC appliance for quarantine or patch enforcement, and identity-based access control

- 802.1X for identity-based networking

- Endpoint protection (including Cisco Security Agents, antivirus, and so forth)

- ACLs on VLANs to limit the information to which outsiders and selected staff have access

- Cisco Traffic Anomaly Detector module

- Cisco Security Management suite

6. Other security products, features, and considerations include the following:

- Physical protection of devices, including protecting from physical access and theft

- Cisco IOS security features

- Infrastructure hardening measures, such as using ACLs to limit Telnet connections (if they are used), using SSH instead of Telnet, using ACLs on SNMP and web devices, using SNMPv3, using SCP instead of FTP or TFTP, and so forth

- Layer 2 security measures, such as out-of-band device management, DHCP snooping, DAI, controlling trunking and native VLANs on access ports, and so forth

- Layer 3 (control plane) security, such as using MD5 routing protocol authentication

Case Study 10-2 Answers

1. The flat Layer 2 network is one issue. Some stability could be added to the network with Layer 3 switching.

   The hospital does not use DHCP; adding it could be a time-consuming but worthwhile process.

   Another issue is the hospital's older equipment, which should be modernized.

   The old cabling is another issue that needs to be addressed. Random testing of 10 to 20 percent of the cabling should be conducted to get a feel for its condition. If the cabling is substandard, the hospital will need to be rewired; ensure that the new cabling is done to standard.

   Redundancy should be added to improve network robustness.

   The servers should be moved into a controlled environment.

2. The main security issue is a lack of any security devices such as firewalls on the connection to external entities (the university and the Internet).

   Adding a firewall or using Cisco IOS Firewall software could resolve this issue.

3. The Hospital Beta network appears to be advanced and secure. The fact that Hospital Beta has much greater network speed might be an issue in the merger.

4. The WAN bandwidth between Hospital Beta and ACMC would need to be substantial if all servers were relocated to ACMC; Metro Ethernet might or might not provide enough bandwidth. For example, if the servers and users use most of the bandwidth in the 10-Gbps core, relocating the servers is not recommended.

5. Without knowing the details of bandwidth usage, a 100-Mbps or 1-Gbps Metro Ethernet connection might or might not be sufficient.

6. Moving the Hospital Beta Cisco Unified Communications Manager means the two hospitals need to be connected robustly—for example, with dual Metro Ethernet or fiber connections from two providers over diverse paths. In the short term, leaving the Cisco Unified Communications Manager where it is would be much simpler and less likely to result in a disruption of this critical service.

   Standalone Cisco Unified Communications Manager systems offer survivability advantages. Removing a Cisco Unified Communications Manager might eventually lower licensing and support costs, but trading the survivability for small savings might not be a good idea.

   The two Cisco Unified Communications Manager systems can communicate via H.323.

7. This issue is similar to the one considered in the previous step. Although there might be some slight savings on support costs, Hospital Beta would lose wireless connectivity if the inter-hospital link experienced problems.

8. Either EIGRP or OSPF should be used, as it is for ACMC. The address block from each hospital should be summarized.

9. IDS monitoring of traffic between hospitals could be added in case a weakness at one leads to an attack on another.

   NetFlow or anomaly detection could be deployed to look for odd traffic flows.

   Internal firewalling should be considered on the links between hospitals and in the path to servers. Only users who require access (as specified in the security policy) should be granted access to patient financial or medical records.

10. Until the infrastructure at Hospital Omega is fixed, it would be unwise to deploy IP telephony. The quality of calls would likely be poor and subject to failures. A better plan would be to conduct pilot testing and ramp up staff skills on IP telephony during the infrastructure mitigation project, and then rapidly deploy IP telephony after the infrastructure is updated.

11. Two options exist:

- Re-address using the 10.1.0.0 /16 block.

- Use network address translation (NAT) to translate all inbound traffic from other hospitals and to translate outbound ACMC traffic going to other hospitals.

The two-way NAT would be complex and would create troubleshooting and scalability challenges. Therefore, readdressing is the preferred alternative. There is not a lot of room to fit in all the required addresses, but it can be done.

When the original addressing scheme for the ACMC Hospital was created (in Chapter 6), the wireless LANs were not taken into account. Since that time (in Chapter 9), three WLANs represented by VLANs or subnets were added in each building. We assumed that we needed blocks of /22, providing 1022 addresses per VLAN, for these WLANs. Assuming that the same WLAN coverage will be provided in the other hospitals, three VLANs are required in each building, resulting in a total of 21 VLANs required. Rounding up to the nearest power of 2, 32 subnets must be reserved for the WLANs. Creating subnets with a /22 mask from the 10.1.0.0/16 address space requires using 6 bits of subnetting, which means that $2^6 = 64$ such subnets could be created. The resulting subnets are 10.1.0.0/22, 10.1.4.0/22, 10.1.8.0/22, and so forth. Reserve the upper 32 subnets for the WLANs: 10.1.128.0/22, 10.1.132.0/22, 10.1.136.0/22, and so forth.

Many /24 subnets are needed for the hospital buildings, so the lower 32 /22 subnets are further subnetted to /24. A few of these will be further subnetted to /30 for point-to-point subnets.

The following three tables (for ACMC, Hospital Beta, and Hospital Omega, respectively) provide the revised addressing scheme for the combined three hospitals. The summarized routes are also provided in these tables.

ACMC Hospital Revised IP Address Assignments

Location	IP Address Block	IP Address Details
Main Building 1 WLANs	10.1.128.0/22 10.1.132.0/22 10.1.136.0/22	10.1.140.0/22 reserved for future use
Main Building 1 VLANs	10.1.0.0/24 = floor 0 10.1.1.0/24 = floor 1 10.1.2.0/24 = floor 2 and so forth, through to 10.1.7.0/24 = floor 7	Treat server farm as a separate "floor," floor 0. Divide fourth octet into four blocks, using a /26 subnet mask (with addresses in multiples of 64), one per access switch (closet) 10.1.15.0/24 is subnetted to /30 for all distribution and WAN router connections to the core and for the links between the access and distribution devices

ACMC Hospital Revised IP Address Assignments (Continued)

Location	IP Address Block	IP Address Details
Building A	10.1.8.0/24	
Building B	10.1.9.0/24	
Building C	10.1.10.0/24	
Building D	10.1.11.0/24	
Building E	10.1.12.0/24	
Reserved	10.1.13.0/24 through 10.1.14.0/24	Allow room for growth within a block that can be summarized to 10.1.0.0/20
Main Building 2 WLANs	10.1.144.0/22 10.1.148.0/22 10.1.152.0/22	10.1.156.0/22 reserved for future use
Main Building 2 VLANs	10.1.16.0/24 = floor 1 10.1.17.0/24 = floor 2 and so forth, through to 10.1.22.0/24 = floor 7	Divide fourth octet into four blocks, using a /26 subnet mask (with addresses in multiples of 64), one per access switch (closet) 10.1.31.0/24 is subnetted to /30 for the links between the access and distribution devices
Building F	10.1.23.0/24	
Building G	10.1.24.0/24	
Building H	10.1.25.0/24	
Building I	10.1.26.0/24	
Building J	10.1.27.0/24	
Reserved	10.1.28.0/24 through 10.1.30.0/24	Allow room for growth within a block that can be summarized to 10.1.16.0/20
Children's Place WLANs	10.1.160.0/22 10.1.164.0/22 10.1.168.0/22	10.1.172.0/22 reserved for future use
Children's Place VLANs	10.1.32.0/24 = floor 1 10.1.33.0/24 = floor 2 10.1.34.0/24 = floor 3	Divide fourth octet into four blocks, using a /26 subnet mask (with addresses in multiples of 64), one per access switch (closet); the last one is not used 10.1.39.0/24 is subnetted to /30 for the links between the access and distribution devices
Building K	10.1.35.0/24	

continues

ACMC Hospital Revised IP Address Assignments (Continued)

Building L	10.1.36.0/24	
Reserved	10.1.37.0/24 through 10.1.38.0/24	Allow room for growth within a block that can be summarized to 10.1.32.0/21
Remote site 1	10.1.40.0/24	
Remote site 2	10.1.41.0/24	
Remote site 3	10.1.42.0/24	
Remote site 4	10.1.43.0/24	
Remote site 5	10.1.44.0/24	
WAN and firewall links	10.1.48.0/24	10.1.48.0/24 is subnetted to /30 for these links
Reserved	10.1.50.0/24 through 10.1.63.0/24	Allow room for growth within a block that can be summarized to 10.1.0.0/18

Hospital Beta Revised IP Address Assignments

Location	IP Address Block	IP Address Details
Building 1 WLANs	10.1.176.0/22 10.1.180.0/22 10.1.184.0/22	10.1.188.0/22 reserved for future use
Building 1 VLANs	10.1.64.0/24 = floor 1 10.1.65.0/24 = floor 2 10.1.66.0/24 = floor 3 10.1.67.0/24 = floor 4	Divide fourth octet into four blocks, using a /26 subnet mask (with addresses in multiples of 64), one per access switch (closet) 10.1.68.0/24 is subnetted to /30 for all distribution and WAN router connections to the core and for the links between the access and distribution devices
Reserved	10.1.69.0/24 through 10.1.71.0/24	Allow room for growth within a block that can be summarized to 10.1.64.0/21
Building 2 WLANs	10.1.192.0/22 10.1.196.0/22 10.1.200.0/22	10.1.204.0/22 reserved for future use

Hospital Beta Revised IP Address Assignments (Continued)

Location	IP Address Block	IP Address Details
Building 2 VLANs	10.1.72.0/24 = floor 1 10.1.73.0/24 = floor 2 10.1.74.0/24 = floor 3 10.1.75.0/24 = floor 4	Divide fourth octet into four blocks, using a /26 subnet mask (with addresses in multiples of 64), one per access switch (closet) 10.1.76.0/24 is subnetted to /30 for the links between the access and distribution devices
Reserved	10.1.77.0/24 through 10.1.79.0/24	Allow room for growth within a block that can be summarized to 10.1.72.0/21
Building 3 WLANs	10.1.208.0/22 10.1.212.0/22 10.1.216.0/22	10.1.220.0/22 reserved for future use
Building 3 VLANs	10.1.80.0/24 = floor 1 10.1.81.0/24 = floor 2 10.1.82.0/24 = floor 3 10.1.83.0/24 = floor 4	Divide fourth octet into four blocks, using a /26 subnet mask (with addresses in multiples of 64), one per access switch (closet); the last one is not used 10.1.84.0/24 is subnetted to /30 for the links between the access and distribution devices
Reserved	10.1.85.0/24 through 10.1.87.0/24	Allow room for growth within a block that can be summarized to 10.1.80.0/21
Building 4 WLANs	10.1.224.0/22 10.1.228.0/22 10.1.232.0/22	10.1.236.0/22 reserved for future use
Building 4 VLANs	10.1.88.0/24 = floor 1 10.1.89.0/24 = floor 2 10.1.90.0/24 = floor 3 10.1.91.0/24 = floor 4	Divide fourth octet into four blocks, using a /26 subnet mask (with addresses in multiples of 64), one per access switch (closet); the last one is not used 10.1.92.0/24 is subnetted to /30 for the links between the access and distribution devices
WAN and firewall links	10.1.93.0/24	10.1.93.0/24 is subnetted to /30 for these links
Reserved	10.1.94.0/24 through 10.1.95.0/24	Allow room for growth within a block that can be summarized to 10.1.88.0/21

Hospital Omega Revised IP Address Assignments

Location	IP Address Block	IP Address Details
WLANs	10.1.240.0/22 10.1.244.0/22 10.1.248.0/22	10.1.252.0/22 reserved for future use
VLANs	10.1.96.0/24 = floor 1 10.1.97.0/24 = floor 2 and so forth, through to 10.1.105.0/24 = floor 3	Divide fourth octet into four blocks, using a /26 subnet mask (with addresses in multiples of 64), one per access switch (closet) 10.1.111.0/24 is subnetted to /30 for all distribution and WAN router connections to the core and for the links between the access and distribution devices
Reserved	10.1.106.0/24 through 10.1.110.0/24	Allow room for growth within a block that can be summarized to 10.1.96.0/20

Answers to Review Questions

1. Some examples of laws and directives influencing network security include the following:

    ■ The U.S. Gramm-Leach-Bliley Act of 1999 (GLBA): Provides limited privacy protections against the sale of private financial information.

    ■ The U.S. Health Insurance Portability and Accountability Act (HIPAA): Aims to enable better access to health insurance, reduce fraud and abuse, and lower the overall cost of health care in the United States.

    ■ European Union Data Protection Directive 95/46/EC: Aims to protect people's privacy rights when their personal data is processed.

    ■ The U.S. Sarbanes-Oxley Act of 2002 (SOX): Aims to establishe new or enhanced auditing and financial standards for all United States public company boards, management, and public accounting firms.

    ■ Payment Card Industry (PCI) Data Security Standard (DSS): Aims to ensure safe handling of sensitive payment information, such as storage and transfer of credit card information.

    ■ The Canadian Personal Information Protection and Electronic Documents Act (PIPEDA): Establishes rules for the management of personal information by organizations involved in commercial activities.

2. A *virus* is a program that triggers a damaging outcome. A *worm* is a virus that can self-duplicate.

3. Reconnaissance is usually the prelude to a more focused attack against a particular target. For example, it can be used to determine which active targets, network services, and so forth are running.

4. A DoS attack attempts to compromise the availability of a network, host, or application. Two methods of causing a DoS attack are by sending malformed data and by sending a large quantity of data.

5. DHCP snooping filters DHCP packets; it prevents a rogue DHCP server from handing out IP addresses on a network by blocking all replies to a DHCP request from an interface (port) unless that port is allowed to reply. DCHP snooping also builds and maintains a DHCP-snooping binding table, which includes MAC address and IP address information for DHCP clients on untrusted interfaces. DAI intercepts all ARP requests and replies on untrusted interfaces and uses the DHCP-snooping binding table information to verify that ARP packets have valid IP-to-MAC address bindings.

6. Answer:

    ■ **Integrity violation**: An attacker changes sensitive data

    ■ **Confidentiality breach**: Can be very difficult to detect

    ■ **Availability threat**: The result of a network's incapability to handle an enormous quantity of data

7. Risk assessment defines threats, their probability, and their severity. A network security policy enumerates risks relevant to the network and determines how to manage those risks. A network security design implements the security policy.

8. The risk index is calculated by dividing the product of the probability and severity factors by the control factor, resulting in this formula:

    Risk index = (probability factor * severity factor) / (control factor)

    For this example:

    Risk index = (2 * 1) / (2) = 1

9. A general document describes the overall risk management policy, identifies the corporation's assets, identifies where protection must be applied, and documents how risk management responsibility is distributed throughout the enterprise. Other documents might include a general Network Access Control policy, an Acceptable Use of Network policy, a Security Management policy, and an Incident Handling policy.

10. A process consisting of the following four steps helps maintain the security policy:

   Step 1   Secure

   Step 2   Monitor

   Step 3   Test

   Step 4   Improve

11. Answer:

   - **Trust and identity management**: To protect critical assets by allowing access based on privilege level

   - **Threat defense**: To minimize and mitigate outbreaks

   - **Secure connectivity**: To ensure privacy and confidentiality of communications

12. The Cisco Self-Defending Network contains three characteristic phases: integrated security, collaborative security systems, and adaptive threat defense.

13. Trust defines the relationship in which two or more network entities are allowed to communicate. The identity is the *who* of a trust relationship. The identity of a network entity is verified by credentials.

14. Answer:

   - **Identification**: A subject *presents* its identity

   - **Authentication**: A subject *proves* its identity

   - **Domains of trust**: Parts of the network with similar security policy

   - **Trust**: The basis of security policy decisions

   - **Password**: Something the subject *knows*

   - **Token**: A physical device or software application

15. Authentication is traditionally based on one of the following three proofs:

   - Something the subject knows

   - Something the subject has

   - Something the subject is

16. Authentication is used to establish the subject's identity. Authorization is used to limit the subject's access to a network.

17. NAC allows network access only to wired or wireless endpoint devices that are compliant with the network security policies, and can restrict the access of noncompliant devices.

Two NAC options are available: the NAC framework or the NAC appliance. If an endpoint device is noncompliant, the Cisco NAC appliance repairs any vulnerability before permitting the device to access the network.

18. The supplicant is an 802.1X end device or user who is trying to connect to a port. The authenticator is an Ethernet device to which a supplicant is trying to connect.

19. The principle of least privilege is based on the practice by which each subject is given only the minimal rights that are necessary to perform his or her tasks.

20. This risk is managed by not keeping encryption keys on the laptop and by having the ability to revoke credentials.

21. Answer:

- **Endpoint protection**: Cisco Security Agent

- **Infection containment**: ASA, PIX, FWSM, Cisco IOS Firewall

- **Inline intrusion and anomaly detection**: IPS sensor, IDS module, Cisco IOS IPS, Cisco Traffic Anomaly Detector, Cisco Traffic Anomaly Guard

- **Application security and Anti-X defense**: Content Security and Control Security Services module

22. B and D

23. Cryptography provides confidentiality through <u>encryption</u>.

24. True

25. Data encrypted with a public key can be decrypted only with the corresponding private key. Data encrypted with a private key can be decrypted only with the corresponding public key.

26. Digital signatures and secure fingerprints are examples of cryptographic mechanisms that ensure data integrity. Secure fingerprints attach a cryptographically strong checksum to data. This checksum is generated and verified using a secret key that only authorized subjects know.

Digital signing of data uses a cryptography method that attaches a digital signature to sensitive data. This signature is generated using a unique signature generation key that is known only to the signer, not to anyone else. Other parties use the signer's signature verification key to verify the signature.

27. Answer:

- **Cisco Security Manager**: Configures firewall, VPN, and IPS policies

- **Cisco Security MARS**: Appliance-based solution that models packet flows through the network

- **Cisco SDM**: Web-based device-management tool for Cisco routers

- **Cisco ASDM**: Security management and monitoring for ASA and PIX

- **Cisco IDM**: Web-based application for IPS sensors

- **CiscoWorks Management Center for Cisco Security Agents**: Assembles network devices into groups to which security policies are attached

- **Cisco Secure ACS**: Centralized control for role-based access to all Cisco devices and security management applications

28. The Cisco IOS IPS is an inline, deep packet inspection–based feature that enables Cisco IOS software to effectively mitigate a wide range of network attacks. The Cisco IOS IPS enables the network to defend itself with the intelligence to accurately identify, classify, and stop or block malicious or damaging traffic in real time by loading a set of attack signatures on the router.

29. The Cisco Catalyst 6500 Series Firewall Services Module (FWSM) is a high-speed, integrated firewall module for Cisco Catalyst 6500 Series switches and Cisco 7600 Series routers.

This appendix contains job aids and supplementary information that cover the following topics:

- IPv4 Addresses and Subnetting Job Aid

- Decimal-to-Binary Conversion Chart

- IPv4 Addressing Review

- IPv4 Access Lists

IPv4 Supplement

This Internet Protocol Version 4 (IPv4) supplement provides job aids and supplementary information intended for your use when working with IPv4 addresses.

> **NOTE** In this appendix, the term *IP* refers to IPv4.

This appendix includes an IP addressing and subnetting job aid and a decimal-to-binary conversion chart. The information in the sections "IPv4 Addressing Review" and "IPv4 Access Lists" should serve as a review of the fundamentals of IP addressing and of the concepts and configuration of access lists, respectively.

IPv4 Addresses and Subnetting Job Aid

Figure B-1 is a job aid to help you with various aspects of IP addressing, including how to distinguish address classes, the number of subnets and hosts available with various subnet masks, and how to interpret IP addresses.

Figure B-1 *IP Addresses and Subnetting Job Aid*

Class	Net Host	First Octet	Standard Mask Binary
A	N.H.H.H	1–126	1111 1111 0000 0000 0000 0000 0000 0000
B	N.N.H.H	128–191	1111 1111 1111 1111 0000 0000 0000 0000
C	N.N.N.H	192–223	1111 1111 1111 1111 1111 1111 0000 0000

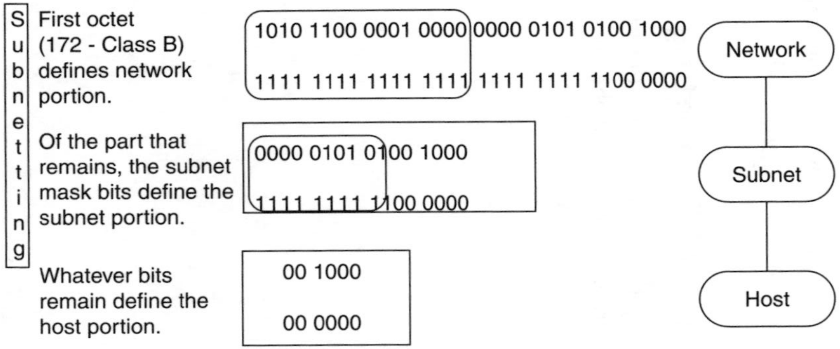

Subnet Bits	Subnet Mask	Number of Subnets	Number of Hosts
Class B			
1	255.255.128.0	2	32766
2	255.255.192.0	4	16382
3	255.255.224.0	8	8190
4	255.255.240.0	16	4094
5	255.255.248.0	32	2046
6	255.255.252.0	64	1022
7	255.255.254.0	128	510
8	255.255.255.0	256	254
9	255.255.255.128	512	126
10	255.255.255.192	1024	62
11	255.255.255.224	2048	30
12	255.255.255.240	4096	14
13	255.255.255.248	8192	6
14	255.255.255.252	16384	2
Class C			
1	255.255.255.128	2	126
2	255.255.255.192	4	62
3	255.255.255.224	8	30
4	255.255.255.240	16	14
5	255.255.255.248	32	6
6	255.255.255.252	64	2

Address 172.16.5.72   1010 1100 0001 0000 | 0000 0101 0100 1000

Subnet mask 255.255.255.192   1111 1111 1111 1111 | 1111 1111 1100 0000

Network

Subnet

Host

S
u First octet
b (172 - Class B)
n defines network
e portion.
t
t Of the part that
i remains, the subnet
n mask bits define the
g subnet portion.

0000 0101 0100 1000
1111 1111 1100 0000

Whatever bits remain define the host portion.

00 1000
00 0000

Decimal-to-Binary Conversion Chart

Table B-1 can be used to convert from decimal to binary and from binary to decimal.

Table B-1   *Decimal-to-Binary Conversion Chart*

Decimal	Binary	Decimal	Binary	Decimal	Binary
0	00000000	22	00010110	44	00101100
1	00000001	23	00010111	45	00101101
2	00000010	24	00011000	46	00101110
3	00000011	25	00011001	47	00101111
4	00000100	26	00011010	48	00110000
5	00000101	27	00011011	49	00110001
6	00000110	28	00011100	50	00110010
7	00000111	29	00011101	51	00110011
8	00001000	30	00011110	52	00110100
9	00001001	31	00011111	53	00110101
10	00001010	32	00100000	54	00110110
11	00001011	33	00100001	55	00110111
12	00001100	34	00100010	56	00111000
13	00001101	35	00100011	57	00111001
14	00001110	36	00100100	58	00111010
15	00001111	37	00100101	59	00111011
16	00010000	38	00100110	60	00111100
17	00010001	39	00100111	61	00111101
18	00010010	40	00101000	62	00111110
19	00010011	41	00101001	63	00111111
20	00010100	42	00101010	64	01000000
21	00010101	43	00101011	65	01000001

continues

Table B-1 *Decimal-to-Binary Conversion Chart (Continued)*

Decimal	Binary	Decimal	Binary	Decimal	Binary
66	01000010	92	01011100	118	01110110
67	01000011	93	01011101	119	01110111
68	01000100	94	01011110	120	01111000
69	01000101	95	01011111	121	01111001
70	01000110	96	01100000	122	01111010
71	01000111	97	01100001	123	01111011
72	01001000	98	01100010	124	01111100
73	01001001	99	01100011	125	01111101
74	01001010	100	01100100	126	01111110
75	01001011	101	01100101	127	01111111
76	01001100	102	01100110	128	10000000
77	01001101	103	01100111	129	10000001
78	01001110	104	01101000	130	10000010
79	01001111	105	01101001	131	10000011
80	01010000	106	01101010	132	10000100
81	01010001	107	01101011	133	10000101
82	01010010	108	01101100	134	10000110
83	01010011	109	01101101	135	10000111
84	01010100	110	01101110	136	10001000
85	01010101	111	01101111	137	10001001
86	01010110	112	01110000	138	10001010
87	01010111	113	01110001	139	10001011
88	01011000	114	01110010	140	10001100
89	01011001	115	01110011	141	10001101
90	01011010	116	01110100	142	10001110
91	01011011	117	01110101	143	10001111

Table B-1   *Decimal-to-Binary Conversion Chart (Continued)*

Decimal	Binary	Decimal	Binary	Decimal	Binary
144	10010000	170	10101010	196	11000100
145	10010001	171	10101011	197	11000101
146	10010010	172	10101100	198	11000110
147	10010011	173	10101101	199	11000111
148	10010100	174	10101110	200	11001000
149	10010101	175	10101111	201	11001001
150	10010110	176	10110000	202	11001010
151	10010111	177	10110001	203	11001011
152	10011000	178	10110010	204	11001100
153	10011001	179	10110011	205	11001101
154	10011010	180	10110100	206	11001110
155	10011011	181	10110101	207	11001111
156	10011100	182	10110110	208	11010000
157	10011101	183	10110111	209	11010001
158	10011110	184	10111000	210	11010010
159	10011111	185	10111001	211	11010011
160	10100000	186	10111010	212	11010100
161	10100001	187	10111011	213	11010101
162	10100010	188	10111100	214	11010110
163	10100011	189	10111101	215	11010111
164	10100100	190	10111110	216	11011000
165	10100101	191	10111111	217	11011001
166	10100110	192	11000000	218	11011010
167	10100111	193	11000001	219	11011011
168	10101000	194	11000010	220	11011100
169	10101001	195	11000011	221	11011101

continues

Table B-1 *Decimal-to-Binary Conversion Chart (Continued)*

Decimal	Binary	Decimal	Binary	Decimal	Binary
222	11011110	234	11101010	246	11110110
223	11011111	235	11101011	247	11110111
224	11100000	236	11101100	248	11111000
225	11100001	237	11101101	249	11111001
226	11100010	238	11101110	250	11111010
227	11100011	239	11101111	251	11111011
228	11100100	240	11110000	252	11111100
229	11100101	241	11110001	253	11111101
230	11100110	242	11110010	254	11111110
231	11100111	243	11110011	255	11111111
232	11101000	244	11110100		
233	11101001	245	11110101		

IPv4 Addressing Review

This section reviews the basics of IPv4 addresses:

■ Converting IP addresses between decimal and binary

■ Determining an IP address class

■ Private addresses

■ Extending an IP classful address using subnet masks

■ Calculating a subnet mask

■ Calculating the networks for a subnet mask

■ Using prefixes to represent a subnet mask

Converting IP Addresses Between Decimal and Binary

An *IP address* is a 32-bit, two-level hierarchical number. It is hierarchical because the first portion of the address represents the network, and the second portion of the address represents the node (or host).

The 32 bits are grouped into four octets, with 8 bits per octet. The value of each octet ranges from 0 to 255 decimal, or 00000000 to 11111111 binary. IP addresses are usually written in dotted-decimal notation, which means that each octet is written in decimal notation and dots are placed between the octets. Figure B-2 shows how you convert an octet of an IP address in binary to decimal notation.

Figure B-2   *Converting an Octet of an IP Address from Binary to Decimal*

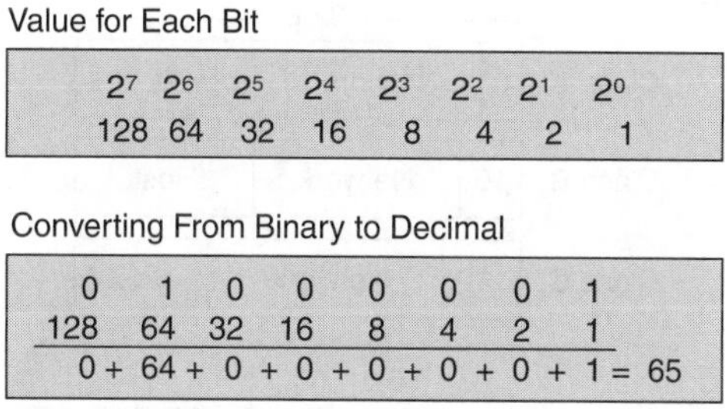

Value for Each Bit

2^7	2^6	2^5	2^4	2^3	2^2	2^1	2^0
128	64	32	16	8	4	2	1

Converting From Binary to Decimal

0	1	0	0	0	0	0	1
128	64	32	16	8	4	2	1

0 + 64 + 0 + 0 + 0 + 0 + 0 + 1 = 65

It is important that you understand how this conversion is done because it is used when calculating subnet masks, a topic discussed later in this section.

Figure B-3 shows three examples of converting IP addresses between binary and decimal.

Figure B-3   *Converting IP Addresses Between Binary and Decimal*

Binary
Address: 00001010.00000001.00010111.00010011

Decimal
Address: 10 . 1 . 23 . 19

Binary
Address: 10101100.00010010.01000001.10101010

Decimal
Address: 172 . 18 . 65 . 170

Binary
Address: 11000000.10101000.00001110.00000110

Decimal
Address: 192 . 168 . 14 . 6

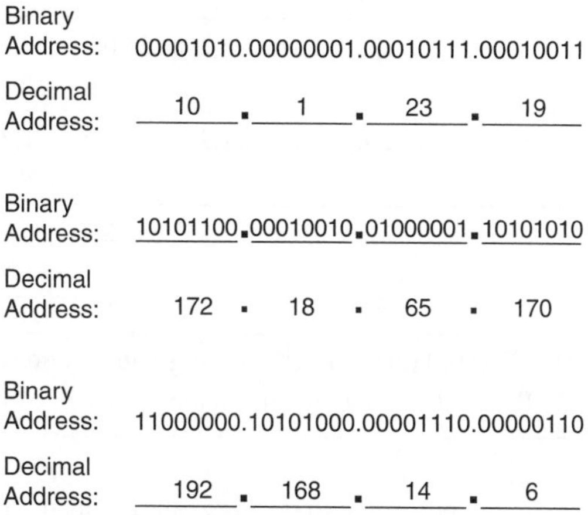

Now that you understand the decimal-to-binary and binary-to-decimal conversion processes, use the following sections to review address classes and the uses of subnet masks.

Determining an IP Address Class

To accommodate large and small networks, the 32-bit IP addresses are segregated into Classes A through E. The first few bits of the first octet determine the class of an address; this then determines how many network bits and host bits are in the address. Figure B-4 illustrates the bits for Class A, B, and C addresses. Each address class allows for a certain number of network addresses and a certain number of host addresses within a network. Table B-2 shows the address format, the address range, the number of networks, and the number of hosts for each of the classes. (Note that Class D and E addresses are used for purposes other than addressing hosts.)

Figure B-4 *Determining an IP Address Class from the First Few Bits of an Address*

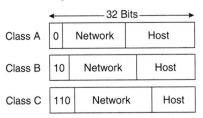

Table B-2 *IP Address Classes*

Class	Format (N = Network Number, H = Host Number)	Address Range	Number of Networks	Number of Hosts
A	N.H.H.H	1.0.0.0 to 126.0.0.0	126 ($2^7 - 2$ that are reserved)	16,777,214
B	N.N.H.H	128.0.0.0 to 191.255.0.0	16,386 (2^{14})	65,532
C	N.N.N.H	192.0.0.0 to 223.255.255.0	Approximately 2 million (2^{21})	254
D	—	224.0.0.0 to 239.255.255.255	Reserved for multicast addresses	—
E	—	240.0.0.0 to 254.255.255.255	Reserved for research	—

NOTE   The network 127.0.0.0 (any address starting with decimal 127) is reserved for loopback. Network 0.0.0.0 is also reserved and cannot be used to address devices.

Using classes to denote which portion of the address represents the network number and which portion represents the node or host address is called classful addressing. Several issues must be addressed with classful addressing. First, the number of available Class A, B, and C addresses is finite. Another problem is that not all classes are useful for a midsize organization, as illustrated in Table B-2. As can be expected, the Class B range best accommodates a majority of today's organizational network topologies. Subnet masks, as described in the later "Extending an IP Classful Address Using Subnet Masks" section, were introduced to maximize the use of the IP addresses an organization receives, regardless of the class.

Private Addresses

Private addresses are reserved IPv4 addresses to be used only internally within a company's network. These private addresses are not to be used on the Internet, so they must be mapped to a company's external registered address when the company sends anything to a recipient on the Internet.

KEY POINT

IPv4 Private Addresses

Requests For Comments (RFC) 1918, *Address Allocation for Private Internets*, has set aside the following IPv4 address space for private use:

- **Class A network**—10.0.0.0 to 10.255.255.255
- **Class B network**—172.16.0.0 to 172.31.255.255
- **Class C network**—192.168.0.0 to 192.168.255.255

NOTE   RFCs are available at http://www.rfc-editor.org/rfcsearch.html.

NOTE   The examples in this book use only private addressing.

Extending an IP Classful Address Using Subnet Masks

RFC 950, *Internet Standard Subnetting Procedure*, was written to address the IP address shortage. It proposed a procedure, called *subnet masking*, for dividing Class A, B, and C addresses into smaller pieces, thereby increasing the number of possible networks.

A subnet mask is a 32-bit value that identifies which address bits represent network bits and which represent host bits. In other words, the router does not determine the network portion of the address by looking at the value of the first octet; rather, it looks at the subnet mask that is associated with the address. In this way, subnet masks let you extend the usage of an IP address. This is one way of making an IP address a three-level hierarchy, as shown in Figure B-5.

Figure B-5   *A Subnet Mask Determines How an IP Address Is Interpreted*

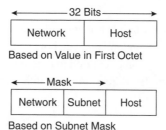

To create a subnet mask for an address, use a binary 1 for each bit that you want to represent the network or subnet portion of the address, and use a binary 0 for each bit that you want to represent the node portion of the address. Note that the 1s in the mask are contiguous. The default subnet masks for Class A, B, and C addresses are as shown Table B-3.

Table B-3 *IP Address Default Subnet Masks*

Class	Default Mask in Binary	Default Mask in Decimal
A	11111111.00000000.00000000.00000000	255.0.0.0
B	11111111.11111111.00000000.00000000	255.255.0.0
C	11111111.11111111.11111111.00000000	255.255.255.0

Calculating a Subnet Mask

When contiguous 1s are added to the default mask, making the all-1s field in the mask longer, the definition of the network part of an IP address is extended to include subnets. Adding bits to the network part of an address decreases the number of bits in the host part. Thus, creating additional networks (subnets) is done at the expense of the number of host devices that can occupy each network segment.

The number of subnetworks created is calculated by the formula 2^s, where s is the number of bits by which the default mask was extended.

> **NOTE** Subnet 0 (where all the subnet bits are 0) must be explicitly allowed using the **ip subnet-zero** global configuration command in Cisco IOS releases before 12.0. In Cisco IOS Release 12.0 and later, this command is enabled by default.

The number of hosts available is calculated by the formula $2^h - 2$, where h is the number of bits in the host portion. In the host counting range, the all-0s bit pattern is reserved as the subnet identifier (sometimes called *the wire*), and the all-1s bit pattern is reserved as a directed broadcast address, to reach all hosts on that subnet.

Because subnet masks extend the number of network addresses you can use by using bits from the host portion, you do not want to randomly decide how many additional bits to use for the network portion. Instead, you want to do some research to determine how many network addresses you need to derive from your given IP address. For example, suppose you have the IP address

172.16.0.0, and you want to configure the network shown in Figure B-6. To establish your subnet mask, do the following:

Step 1   Determine the number of networks (subnets) needed. Figure B-6, for example, has five networks.

Figure B-6   *Network Used in the Subnet Mask Example*

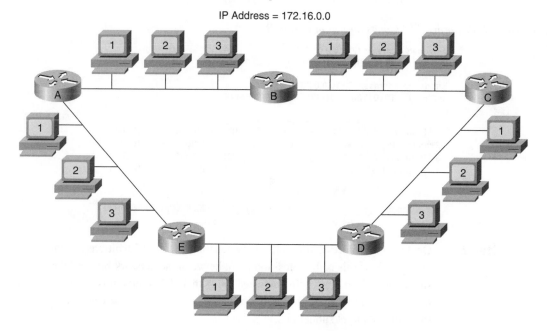

IP Address = 172.16.0.0

Step 2   Determine how many nodes per subnet must be defined. This example has five nodes (two routers and three workstations) on each subnet.

Step 3   Determine future network and node requirements. For example, assume 100 percent growth.

Step 4   Given the information gathered in Steps 1 to 3, determine the total number of subnets required. For this example, ten subnets are required. Refer to the earlier section "IPv4 Addresses and Subnetting Job Aid" to select the appropriate subnet mask value that can accommodate 10 networks.

No mask accommodates exactly 10 subnets. Depending on your network growth trends, you might select 4 subnet bits, resulting in a subnet mask of 255.255.240.0. The binary representation of this subnet mask is as follows:

11111111.11111111.11110000.00000000

The additional 4 subnet bits would give you $2^4 = 16$ subnets.

Calculating the Networks for a Subnet Mask

Refer to Figure B-6. After you identify your subnet mask, you must calculate the ten subnetted network addresses to use with 172.16.0.0 255.255.240.0. One way to do this is as follows:

Step 1   Write the subnetted address in binary format, as shown at the top of Figure B-7. If necessary, use the decimal-to-binary conversion chart provided in Table B-1.

Figure B-7   *Calculating the Subnets Shown in Figure B-6*

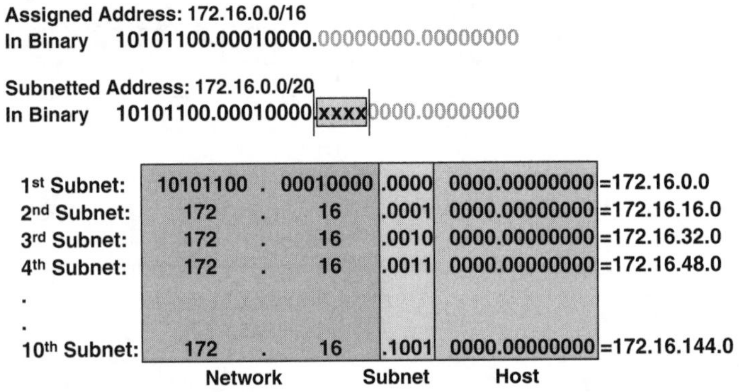

Step 2   On the binary address, draw a line between the 16th and 17th bits, as shown in Figure B-7; this is the transition point between the network bits and the subnet bits. Then draw a line between the 20th and 21st bits; this is the transition point between the subnet bits and the host bits. Now you can focus on the target subnet bits.

Step 3   Historically, it was recommended that you begin choosing subnets from highest (from the leftmost bit) to lowest, so that you could leave bits available in case you need more host bits later on. However, this strategy does not allow you to adequately summarize subnet addresses, so the present recommendation is to choose subnets from lowest to highest (right to left).

When you calculate the subnet address, all host bits are set to 0. To convert back to decimal, it is important to note that you must always convert an entire octet, 8 bits. For the first subnet, your subnet bits are 0000, and the rest of the octet (all host bits) is 0000.

If necessary, use the decimal-to-binary conversion chart provided in Table B-1, and locate this first subnet number. The first subnet number is 00000000, or decimal 0.

Step 4   (Optional) List each subnet in binary form to reduce the number of errors. This way, you will not forget where you left off in your subnet address selection.

Step 5   Calculate the second-lowest subnet number. In this case, it is 0001. When combined with the next 4 bits (the host bits) of 0000, this is subnet binary 00010000, or decimal 16.

Step 6   Continue calculating subnet numbers until you have as many as you need— in this case, 10 subnets, as shown in Figure B-7.

Using Prefixes to Represent a Subnet Mask

As discussed, subnet masks identify the number of bits in an address that represent the network, subnet, and host portions of the address. Another way of indicating this information is to use a *prefix*. A prefix is a slash (/) followed by a numeric value that is the number of bits in the network and subnet portion of the address. In other words, it is the number of contiguous 1s in the subnet mask. For example, assume you are using a subnet mask of 255.255.255.0. The binary representation of this mask is 11111111.11111111.11111111.00000000, which is 24 1s followed by eight 0s. Thus, the prefix is /24, for the 24 bits of network and subnet information, the number of 1s in the mask.

Table B-4 shows some examples of the different ways you can represent a prefix and subnet mask.

Table B-4 *Representing Subnet Masks*

IP Address/Prefix	Subnet Mask in Decimal	Subnet Mask in Binary
192.168.112.0/21	255.255.248.0	11111111.11111111.11111000.00000000
172.16.0.0/16	255.255.0.0	11111111.11111111.00000000.00000000
10.1.1.0/27	255.255.255.224	11111111.11111111.11111111.11100000

It is important to know how to write subnet masks and prefixes because Cisco routers use both, as shown in Example B-1. You will typically be asked to input a subnet mask when configuring an IP address, but the output generated using **show** commands typically displays an IP address with a prefix.

Example B-1 *Examples of Subnet Mask and Prefix Use on Cisco Routers*

```
p1r3#show run
<Output Omitted>
interface Ethernet0
 ip address 10.64.4.1 255.255.255.0
```

continues

Example B-1 *Examples of Subnet Mask and Prefix Use on Cisco Routers (Continued)*

```
!
interface Serial0
 ip address 10.1.3.2 255.255.255.0
<Output Omitted>

p1r3#show interface ethernet0
Ethernet0 is administratively down, line protocol is down
  Hardware is Lance, address is 00e0.b05a.d504 (bia 00e0.b05a.d504)
  Internet address is 10.64.4.1/24
<Output Omitted>

p1r3#show interface serial0
Serial0 is down, line protocol is down
  Hardware is HD64570
  Internet address is 10.1.3.2/24
<Output Omitted>
```

IPv4 Access Lists

This section reviews IPv4 access lists. It includes the following topics:

- IP access list overview

- IP standard access lists

- IP extended access lists

- Restricting virtual terminal access

- Verifying access list configuration

IP Access List Overview

Packet filtering helps control packet movement through the network, as shown in Figure B-8. Such control can help limit network traffic and restrict network use by certain users or devices. To permit packets to cross or deny packets from crossing specified router interfaces, Cisco provides access lists. An IP access list is a sequential collection of permit and deny conditions that apply to IP addresses or upper-layer IP protocols.

Figure B-8 *Access Lists Control Packet Movement Through a Network*

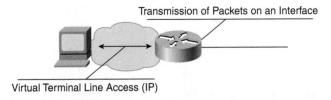

Transmission of Packets on an Interface

Virtual Terminal Line Access (IP)

Table B-5 shows the available types of IP access lists on a Cisco router and their access list numbers. Named access lists are also available for IP.

Table B-5 *IP Access List Numbers*

Type of Access List	Range of Access List Numbers
IP standard	1 to 99 or from 1300 to 1999
IP extended	100 to 199 or from 2000 to 2699

This section covers IP standard and extended access lists. For information on other types of access lists, refer to the technical documentation on the Cisco website at http://www.cisco.com.

> **WARNING**   Cisco IOS Release 10.3 introduced substantial additions to IP access lists. These extensions are backward compatible. Migrating from older releases to the Cisco IOS Release 10.3 or a later image will convert your access lists automatically. However, previous releases are not upwardly compatible with these changes. Therefore, if you save an access list with the Cisco IOS Release 10.3 or a later image and then use older software, the resulting access list will not be interpreted correctly. This incompatibility can cause security problems. Save your old configuration file before booting Cisco IOS Release 10.3 (or later) images in case you need to revert to an earlier version.

IP Standard Access Lists

Standard access lists permit or deny packets based only on the packet's source IP address, as shown in Figure B-9. The access list number range for standard IP access lists is 1 to 99 or from 1300 to 1999. Standard access lists are easier to configure than their more robust counterparts, extended access lists.

Figure B-9 *Standard IP Access Lists Filter Based Only on the Source Address*

A standard access list is a sequential collection of permit and deny conditions that apply to source IP addresses. The router tests addresses against the conditions in an access list one by one. The first match determines whether the router accepts or rejects the packet. Because the router stops testing conditions after the first match, the order of the conditions is critical. If no conditions match, the router rejects the packet.

Figure B-10 shows the processing of inbound standard access lists. After receiving a packet, the router checks the packet's source address against the access list. If the access list permits the address, the router exits the access list and continues to process the packet. If the access list denies the address, the router discards the packet and returns an Internet Control Message Protocol (ICMP) administratively prohibited message.

Figure B-10 *Inbound Standard IP Access List Processing*

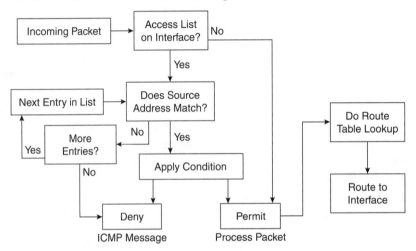

Note that the action taken if no more entries are found in the access list is to deny the packet; this illustrates an important rule to remember when creating access lists. For example, consider what will happen if you create a list that simply denies traffic that you do not want to let into your network, and you configure this on an interface. If you forget about this rule, *all* of your traffic is denied—the traffic explicitly denied by your list, and the rest of the traffic that is implicitly denied because the access list is applied to the interface.

KEY POINT

Implicit deny any at the End of the Access List

The last entry in an access list is known as an *implicit deny any*. All traffic not explicitly permitted is implicitly denied.

KEY POINT

Order Is Important When Configuring Access Lists

When configuring access lists, order is important. Make sure that you list the entries in order from specific to general. For example, if you want to deny a specific host address and permit all other addresses, make sure that your entry about the specific host appears first.

Figure B-11 illustrates the processing of outbound standard IP access lists. After receiving and routing a packet to a controlled interface, the router checks the packet's source address against the access list. If the access list permits the address, the router transmits the packet. If the access list denies the address, the router discards the packet and returns an ICMP administratively prohibited message.

Figure B-11 *Outbound Standard IP Access List Processing*

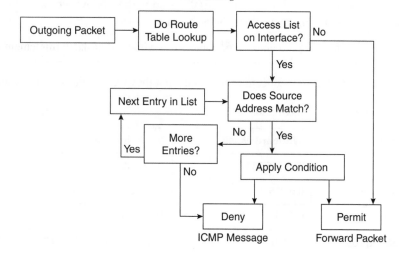

Wildcard Masks

Both standard and extended IP access lists use a wildcard mask. Like an IP address, a *wildcard mask* is a 32-bit quantity written in dotted-decimal format. The wildcard mask tells the router which bits of the address to use in comparisons.

KEY POINT | **Wildcard Mask Used to Interpret the IP Address**

Address bits corresponding to wildcard mask bits set to 1 are ignored in comparisons; address bits corresponding to wildcard mask bits set to 0 are used in comparisons.

An alternative way to think of the wildcard mask is as follows. If a 0 bit appears in the wildcard mask, the corresponding bit location in the access list address and the same bit location in the packet address must match (both must be 0 or both must be 1). If a 1 bit appears in the wildcard mask, the corresponding bit location in the packet matches (whether it is 0 or 1), and that bit location in the access list address is ignored. For this reason, bits set to 1 in the wildcard mask are sometimes called *don't care bits*.

Remember that the order of the access list statements is important because the access list is not processed further after a match is found.

Wildcard Masks

The concept of a wildcard mask is similar to the wildcard character used in DOS-based computers. For example, to delete all files on your computer that begin with the letter *f*, you would enter this:

delete f*.*

The * character is the wildcard; any files that start with f, followed by any other characters, and then a dot, and then any other characters, are deleted.

Instead of using wildcard characters, routers use wildcard masks to implement this concept.

Examples of addresses and wildcard masks, and what they match, are shown in Table B-6.

Table B-6   *Access List Wildcard Mask Examples*

Address	Wildcard Mask	What It Matches
0.0.0.0	255.255.255.255	Any address
172.16.0.0/16	0.0.255.255	Any host on network 172.16.0.0
172.16.7.11/16	0.0.0.0	Host address 172.16.7.11
255.255.255.255	0.0.0.0	Local broadcast address 255.255.255.255
172.16.8.0/21	0.0.7.255	Any host on subnet 172.16.8.0/21

Access List Configuration Tasks

Whether you are creating a standard or extended access list, you need to complete the following two tasks:

Step 1   Create an access list in global configuration mode by specifying an access list number and access conditions.

Define a standard IP access list using a source address and wildcard, as shown later in this section.

Define an extended access list using source and destination addresses, as well as optional protocol-type information for finer granularity of control, as discussed in the "IP Extended Access Lists" section later in this appendix.

Step 2   Apply the access list in interface configuration mode to interfaces (or in line configuration mode to terminal lines).

After creating an access list, you can apply it to one or more interfaces. Access lists can be applied either outbound or inbound on interfaces.

IP Standard Access List Configuration

Use the **access-list** *access-list-number* {**permit** | **deny**} {*source* [*source-wildcard*] | **any**} [**log**] global configuration command to create an entry in a standard access list, as detailed in Table B-7.

Table B-7   *Standard IP* **access-list** *Command Description*

Parameter	Description
access-list-number	Identifies the list to which the entry belongs. A number from 1 to 99 or from 1300 to 1999.
permit	**deny**	Indicates whether this entry allows or blocks traffic from the specified address.
source	Identifies the source IP address.
source-wildcard	(Optional) Identifies which bits in the address field must match. A 1 in any bit position indicates don't care bits, and a 0 in any bit position indicates that the bit must strictly match. If this field is omitted, the wildcard mask 0.0.0.0 is assumed.
any	Use this keyword as an abbreviation for a source and source wildcard of 0.0.0.0 255.255.255.255.
log	(Optional) Causes an informational logging message about the packet that matches the entry to be sent to the console. Exercise caution when using this keyword, because it consumes CPU cycles.

When a packet does not match any of the configured lines in an access list, the packet is denied by default because there is an invisible line at the end of the access list that is equivalent to **deny any**. (**deny any** is the same as denying an address of 0.0.0.0 with a wildcard mask of 255.255.255.255.)

The keyword **host** can also be used in an access list. It causes the address that immediately follows it to be treated as if it were specified with a mask of 0.0.0.0. For example, configuring **host 10.1.1.1** in an access list is equivalent to configuring **10.1.1.1 0.0.0.0**.

Use the **ip access-group** *access-list-number* {**in** | **out**} interface configuration command to link an existing access list to an interface, as shown in Table B-8. Each interface can have both an inbound and an outbound IP access list.

Table B-8   **ip access-group** *Command Description*

Parameter	Description
access-list-number	Indicates the number of the access list to be linked to this interface.
in	**out**	Processes packets arriving on or leaving from this interface. The default is **out**.

Eliminate the entire list by entering the **no access-list** *access-list-number* global configuration command. Remove an access list from an interface with the **no ip access-group** *access-list-number* {**in** | **out**} interface configuration command.

Implicit Wildcard Masks

Implicit, or default, wildcard masks reduce typing and simplify configuration, but you must take care when relying on the default mask.

The access list line shown in Example B-2 is an example of a specific host configuration. For standard access lists, if no wildcard mask is specified, the wildcard mask is assumed to be 0.0.0.0. The implicit mask makes it easier to enter a large number of individual addresses.

Example B-2 *Standard Access List Using the Default Wildcard Mask*

```
access-list 1 permit 172.16.5.17
```

Example B-3 shows common errors found in access list lines.

Example B-3 *Common Errors Found in Access Lists*

```
access-list 1 permit 0.0.0.0
access-list 2 permit 172.16.0.0
access-list 3 deny any
access-list 3 deny 0.0.0.0 255.255.255.255
```

The first list in Example B-3—**permit 0.0.0.0**—would exactly match the address 0.0.0.0 and then permit it. Because you would never receive a packet from 0.0.0.0, this list would prevent all traffic from getting through (because of the implicit **deny any** at the end of the list).

The second list in Example B-3—**permit 172.16.0.0**—is probably a configuration error. The intention was probably 172.16.0.0 0.0.255.255. The exact address 172.16.0.0 refers to the network and would never be assigned to a host. As a result, nothing would get through with this list, again because of the implicit **deny any** at the end of the list. To filter networks or subnets, use an explicit wildcard mask.

The next two lines in Example B-3—**deny any** and **deny 0.0.0.0 255.255.255.255**—are unnecessary to configure because they duplicate the function of the implicit deny that occurs when a packet fails to match all the configured lines in an access list. Although they are not necessary, you might want to add one of these entries for record-keeping purposes.

Configuration Principles

The following general principles help ensure that the access lists you create have the intended results:

- Top-down processing

  — Organize your access list so that more specific references in a network or subnet appear before more general ones.

  — Place more frequently occurring conditions before less-frequent conditions.

- Implicit **deny any**

  — Unless you end your access list with an explicit **permit any**, it denies all traffic that fails to match any of the access list lines by default.

- New lines added to the end

  — Subsequent additions are always added to the end of the access list.

  — You cannot selectively add or remove lines when using numbered access lists, but you can when using named access lists for IP (a feature that is available in Cisco IOS Release 11.2 and later).

> **NOTE**   Cisco IOS Release 12.2(14)S introduced a feature called IP Access List Entry Sequence Numbering that allows network administrators to apply sequence numbers to **permit** or **deny** statements in a named IP access list and also reorder, add, or remove such statements. Prior to this feature, network administrators could only add access list entries to the end of an access list (which is the case for numbered access lists), meaning that if statements need to be added anywhere except the end of the access list, the entire access list must be reconfigured.

- An undefined access list equals **permit any**

  — If you apply an access list with the **ip access-group** command to an interface before any access list lines have been created, the result is **permit any**. However, the list is live, so if you enter only one line, it goes from a **permit any** to a **deny** *most* (because of the implicit **deny any**) as soon as you press **Enter**. For this reason, you should create your access list before applying it to an interface.

Standard Access List Example

Figure B-12 shows a sample network, and Example B-4 shows the configuration on Router X in that figure.

Figure B-12 *Network Used for the Standard IP Access List Example*

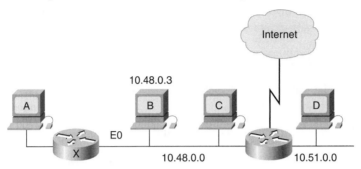

Example B-4 *Standard Access List Configuration of Router X in Figure B-12*

```
Router(config)#access-list 2 permit 10.48.0.3
Router(config)#access-list 2 deny 10.48.0.0 0.0.255.255
Router(config)#access-list 2 permit 10.0.0.0 0.255.255.255
Router(config)#!(Note: all other access implicitly denied)
Router(config)#interface ethernet 0
Router(config-if)#ip access-group 2 in
```

Consider which devices can communicate with Host A in this example:

■ Host B can communicate with Host A. It is permitted by the first line of the access list, which uses an implicit host mask.

■ Host C cannot communicate with Host A. Host C is in the subnet that is denied by the second line in the access list.

■ Host D can communicate with Host A. Host D is on a subnet that is explicitly permitted by the third line of the access list.

■ Users on the Internet cannot communicate with Host A. Users outside this network are not explicitly permitted, so they are denied by default with the implicit **deny any** at the end of the access list.

Location of Standard Access Lists

Access list location can be more of an art than a science. Consider the network in Figure B-13 and the access list configuration in Example B-5 to illustrate some general guidelines. If the policy goal is to deny Host Z access to Host V on another network, and not to change any other access policy, determine on which interface of which router this access list should be configured.

Figure B-13 *Location of the Standard IP Access List Example*

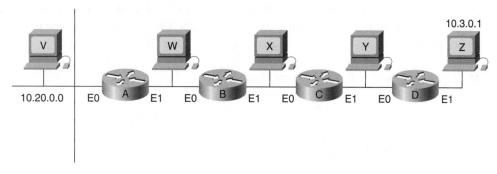

Example B-5 *Standard Access List to Be Configured on a Router in Figure B-13*

```
access-list 3 deny 10.3.0.1
access-list 3 permit any
```

The access list should be placed on Router A because a standard access list can specify only a source address. No hosts beyond the point in the path where the traffic is denied can connect.

The access list could be configured as an outbound list on E0 of Router A. However, it would most likely be configured as an inbound list on E1 so that packets to be denied would not have to be routed through Router A first.

Consider the effect of placing the access list on other routers:

- **Router B**—Host Z could not connect with Host W (and Host V).

- **Router C**—Host Z could not connect with Hosts W and X (and Host V).

- **Router D**—Host Z could not connect with Hosts W, X, and Y (and Host V).

KEY POINT | **Place Standard Access Lists Close to the Destination**

For standard access lists, the rule is to place them as close to the *destination* as possible to exercise the most control. Note, however, that this means that traffic is routed through the network, only to be denied close to its destination.

IP Extended Access Lists

Standard access lists offer quick configuration and low overhead in limiting traffic based on source addresses in a network. *Extended access lists* provide a higher degree of control by enabling filtering based on the source and destination addresses, transport layer protocol, and application port number. These features make it possible to limit traffic based on the uses of the network.

Extended Access List Processing

As shown in Figure B-14, every condition tested in a line of an extended access list must match for the line of the access list to match and for the permit or deny condition to be applied. As soon as one parameter or condition fails, the next line in the access list is compared.

Figure B-14 *Extended IP Access List Processing Flow*

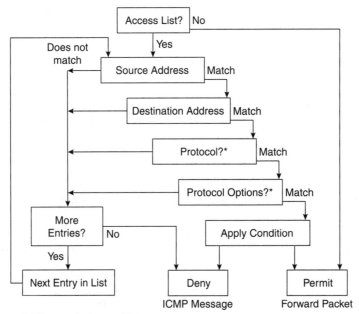

The extended access list checks source address, destination address, and protocol. Depending on the configured protocol, more protocol-dependent options might be tested. For example, a Transmission Control Protocol (TCP) port might be checked, which allows routers to filter at the application layer.

Extended IP Access List Configuration

Use the **access-list** *access-list-number* {**permit** | **deny**} *protocol* {*source source-wildcard* | **any**} {*destination destination-wildcard* | **any**} [*protocol-specific-options*] [**log**] global configuration command to create an entry in an extended-traffic filter list. Table B-9 describes this command.

Table B-9 *Extended IP* **access-list** *Command Description*

Parameter	Description
access-list-number	Identifies the list to which the entry belongs (a number from 100 to 199 or from 2000 to 2699).
permit | **deny**	Indicates whether this entry allows or blocks traffic.
protocol	**ip, tcp, udp, icmp, igmp, gre, eigrp, ospf, nos, ipinip, pim,** or a number from 0 to 255. To match any Internet protocol, use the keyword **ip**. As shown later in this section, some protocols allow more options that are supported by an alternative syntax for this command.
source and *destination*	Identifies the source and destination IP addresses.
source-wildcard and *destination-wildcard*	Identifies which bits in the address field must match. A 1 in any bit position indicates don't care bits, and a 0 in any bit position indicates that the bit must strictly match.
any	Use this keyword as an abbreviation for a source and source wildcard or destination and destination wildcard of 0.0.0.0 255.255.255.255.
log	(Optional) Causes informational logging messages about a packet that matches the entry to be sent to the console. Exercise caution when using this keyword, because it consumes CPU cycles.

The wildcard masks in an extended access list operate the same way as they do in standard access lists. The keyword **any** in either the source or the destination position matches any address and is equivalent to configuring an address of 0.0.0.0 with a wildcard mask of 255.255.255.255. Example B-6 shows an example of an extended access list.

Example B-6 *Use of the Keyword* **any**

```
access-list 101 permit ip  0.0.0.0  255.255.255.255  0.0.0.0  255.255.255.255
! (alternative configuration)
access-list 101 permit ip any any
```

The keyword **host** can be used in either the source or the destination position. It causes the address that immediately follows it to be treated as if it were specified with a mask of 0.0.0.0. Example B-7 shows an example.

Example B-7 *Use of the Keyword* **host**

```
access-list 101 permit ip  0.0.0.0  255.255.255.255  172.16.5.17  0.0.0.0
! (alternative configuration)
access-list 101 permit ip any host 172.16.5.17
```

Use the **access-list** *access-list-number* {**permit** | **deny**} **icmp** {*source source-wildcard* | **any**} {*destination destination-wildcard* | **any**} [*icmp-type* [*icmp-code*] | *icmp-message*] global configuration command to filter ICMP traffic. The protocol keyword **icmp** indicates that an alternative syntax is being used for this command and that protocol-specific options are available, as described in Table B-10.

Table B-10   *Extended IP* **access-list icmp** *Command Description*

Parameter	Description
access-list-number	Identifies the list to which the entry belongs (a number from 100 to 199 or from 2000 to 2699).
permit	**deny**	Indicates whether this entry allows or blocks traffic.
source and *destination*	Identifies the source and destination IP addresses.
source-wildcard and *destination-wildcard*	Identifies which bits in the address field must match. A 1 in any bit position indicates don't care bits, and a 0 in any bit position indicates that the bit must strictly match.
any	Use this keyword as an abbreviation for a source and source wildcard or destination and destination wildcard of 0.0.0.0 255.255.255.255.
icmp-type	(Optional) Packets can be filtered by ICMP message type. The type is a number from 0 to 255.
icmp-code	(Optional) Packets that have been filtered by ICMP message type can also be filtered by ICMP message code. The code is a number from 0 to 255.
icmp-message	(Optional) Packets can be filtered by a symbolic name representing an ICMP message type or a combination of ICMP message type and ICMP message code. These names are listed in Table B-11.

Cisco IOS Release 10.3 and later versions provide symbolic names that make configuring and reading complex access lists easier. With symbolic names, it is no longer critical to understand the meaning of the ICMP message type and code (for example, message 8 and message 0 can be used to filter the **ping** command). Instead, the configuration can use symbolic names, as shown in Table B-11. For example, the **echo** and **echo-reply** symbolic names can be used to filter the **ping** command. (You can use the Cisco IOS context-sensitive help feature by entering **?** when entering the **access-list** command to verify the available names and proper command syntax.)

Table B-11   *ICMP Message and Type Names*

Administratively-prohibited	Dod-host-prohibited	Echo-reply
Alternate-address	Dod-net-prohibited	General-parameter-problem
Conversion-error	Echo	Host-isolated

Table B-11 *ICMP Message and Type Names (Continued)*

Host-precedence-unreachable	Net-tos-redirect	Redirect
Host-redirect	Net-tos-unreachable	Router-advertisement
Host-tos-redirect	Net-unreachable	Router-solicitation
Host-tos-unreachable	Network-unknown	Source-quench
Host-unknown	No-room-for-option	Source-route-failed
Host-unreachable	Option-missing	Time-exceeded
Information-reply	Packet-too-big	Timestamp-reply
Information-request	Parameter-problem	Timestamp-request
Mask-reply	Port-unreachable	Traceroute
Mask-request	Precedence-unreachable	TTL-exceeded
Mobile-redirect	Protocol-unreachable	Unreachable
Net-redirect	Reassembly-timeout	

Use the **access-list** *access-list-number* {**permit** | **deny**} **tcp** {*source source-wildcard* | **any**} [*operator source-port* | *source-port*] {*destination destination-wildcard* | **any**} [*operator destination-port* | *destination-port*] [**established**] global configuration command to filter TCP traffic. The protocol keyword **tcp** indicates that an alternative syntax is being used for this command and that protocol-specific options are available, as described in Table B-12.

Table B-12 *Extended IP **access-list tcp** Command Description*

Parameter	Description
access-list-number	Identifies the list to which the entry belongs (a number from 100 to 199 or from 2000 to 2699).
permit	**deny**	Indicates whether this entry allows or blocks traffic.
source and *destination*	Identifies the source and destination IP addresses.
source-wildcard and *destination-wildcard*	Identifies which bits in the address field must match. A 1 in any bit position indicates don't care bits, and a 0 in any bit position indicates that the bit must strictly match.
any	Use this keyword as an abbreviation for a source and source wildcard or destination and destination wildcard of 0.0.0.0 255.255.255.255.
operator	(Optional) A qualifying condition. Can be **lt**, **gt**, **eq**, or **neq**.

continues

Table B-12 *Extended IP* **access-list tcp** *Command Description (Continued)*

Parameter	Description
source-port and *destination-port*	(Optional) A decimal number from 0 to 65535 or a name that represents a TCP port number.
established	(Optional) A match occurs if the TCP segment has the ACK or RST bits set. Use this if you want a Telnet or other activity to be established in one direction only.

established Keyword in Extended Access Lists

When a TCP session is started between two devices, the first segment that is sent has the synchronize (SYN) code bit set but does not have the acknowledge (ACK) code bit set in the segment header, because it is not acknowledging any other segments. All subsequent segments sent do have the ACK code bit set, because they are acknowledging previous segments sent by the other device. This is how a router can distinguish between a segment from a device that is attempting to *start* a TCP session and a segment of an ongoing *established* session. The RST code bit is set when an established session is being terminated.

When you configure the **established** keyword in a TCP extended access list, it indicates that that access list statement should match only TCP segments in which the ACK or RST code bit is set. In other words, only segments that are part of an established session are matched; segments that are attempting to start a session do not match the access list statement.

Table B-13 lists TCP port names that can be used instead of port numbers. You can find the port numbers corresponding to these protocols by entering a **?** in place of a port number or by looking at the port numbers on http://www.iana.org/numbers.html.

Table B-13 *TCP Port Names*

Bgp	Hostname	Syslog
Chargen	Irc	Tacacs-ds
Daytime	Klogin	Talk
Discard	Kshell	Telnet
Domain	Lpd	Time
Echo	Nntp	Uucp
Finger	Pop2	Whois
Ftp control	Pop3	www
Ftp-data	Smtp	
Gopher	Sunrpc	

Other port numbers can be found at http://www.iana.org/numbers.html. A partial list of the assigned TCP port numbers is shown in Table B-14.

Table B-14 *Some Reserved TCP Port Numbers*

Port Number (Decimal)	Keyword	Description
7	ECHO	Echo
9	DISCARD	Discard
13	DAYTIME	Daytime
19	CHARGEN	Character generator
20	FTP-DATA	File Transfer Protocol (data)
21	FTP-CONTROL	File Transfer Protocol
23	TELNET	Terminal connection
25	SMTP	Simple Mail Transfer Protocol
37	TIME	Time of day
43	WHOIS	Who is
53	DOMAIN	Domain name server
79	FINGER	Finger
80	WWW	World Wide Web HTTP
101	HOSTNAME	NIC host name server

Use the **access-list** *access-list-number* {**permit** | **deny**} **udp** {*source source-wildcard* | **any**} [*operator source-port* | *source-port*] {*destination destination-wildcard* | **any**} [*operator destination-port* | *destination-port*] global configuration command to filter User Datagram Protocol (UDP) traffic. The protocol keyword **udp** indicates that an alternative syntax is being used for this command and that protocol-specific options are available, as described in Table B-15.

Table B-15 *Extended IP* **access-list udp** *Command Description*

Parameter	Description
access-list-number	Identifies the list to which the entry belongs (a number from 100 to 199 or from 2000 to 2699).
permit	**deny**	Indicates whether this entry allows or blocks traffic.
source and *destination*	Identifies the source and destination IP addresses.

continues

Table B-15 *Extended IP* **access-list udp** *Command Description (Continued)*

Parameter	Description
source-wildcard and *destination-wildcard*	Identifies which bits in the address field must match. A 1 in any bit position indicates don't care bits, and a 0 in any bit position indicates that the bit must strictly match.
any	Use this keyword as an abbreviation for a source and source wildcard or destination and destination wildcard of 0.0.0.0 255.255.255.255.
operator	(Optional) A qualifying condition. Can be **lt**, **gt**, **eq**, or **neq**.
source-port and *destination-port*	(Optional) A decimal number from 0 to 65535 or a name that represents a UDP port number.

Table B-16 lists UDP port names that can be used instead of port numbers. You can find port numbers corresponding to these protocols by entering a **?** in place of a port number or by looking at www.iana.org/numbers.html.

Table B-16 *UDP Port Names*

Biff	Nameserver	Syslog
Bootpc	NetBios-dgm	Tacacs-ds
Bootps	NetBios-ns	Talk
Discard	Ntp	Tftp
Dns	Rip	Time
Dnsix	Snmp	Whois
Echo	Snmptrap	Xdmcp
Mobile-ip	Sunrpc	

Other port numbers can be found at http://www.iana.org/numbers.html. A partial list of the assigned UDP port numbers is shown in Table B-17.

Table B-17 *Some Reserved UDP Port Numbers*

Port Number (Decimal)	Keyword	Description
7	ECHO	Echo
9	DISCARD	Discard
37	TIME	Time of day
42	NAMESERVER	Host name server

Table B-17   *Some Reserved UDP Port Numbers (Continued)*

Port Number (Decimal)	Keyword	Description
43	WHOIS	Who is
53	DNS	Domain name server
67	BOOTPS	Bootstrap protocol server
68	BOOTPC	Bootstrap protocol client
69	TFTP	Trivial File Transfer Protocol
123	NTP	Network Time Protocol
137	NetBios-ns	NetBIOS name service
138	NetBios-dgm	NetBIOS datagram service
161	SNMP	SNMP
162	SNMPTrap	SNMP traps
520	RIP	RIP

Extended Access List Examples

In Figure B-15, router A's interface Ethernet 1 is part of a Class B subnet with the address 172.22.3.0, router A's interface Serial 0 is connected to the Internet, and the e-mail server's address is 172.22.1.2. The access list configuration applied to router A is shown in Example B-8.

Figure B-15   *Network Used for the Extended IP Access List Example*

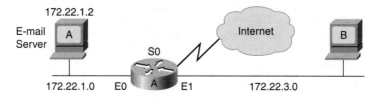

Example B-8   *Configuration on Router A in Figure B-15*

```
access-list 104 permit tcp any 172.22.0.0 0.0.255.255 established
access-list 104 permit tcp any host 172.22.1.2 eq smtp
access-list 104 permit udp any any eq dns
access-list 104 permit icmp any any echo
access-list 104 permit icmp any any echo-reply
!
interface serial 0
ip access-group 104 in
```

In Example B-8, access list 104 is applied inbound on Router A's Serial 0 interface. The keyword **established** is used only for the TCP protocol to indicate an established connection. A match occurs if the TCP segment has the ACK or RST bits set, which indicate that the packet belongs to an existing connection. If the session is not already established (the ACK bit is not set and the SYN bit is set), this means that someone on the Internet is attempting to initialize a session, in which case the packet is denied. This configuration also permits Simple Mail Transfer Protocol (SMTP) traffic from any address to the e-mail server. UDP domain name server packets and ICMP echo and echo-reply packets are also permitted from any address to any other address.

Another example is shown in Figure B-16. Example B-9 shows the access list configuration applied to router A.

Figure B-16 *Extended IP Access List Example with Many Servers*

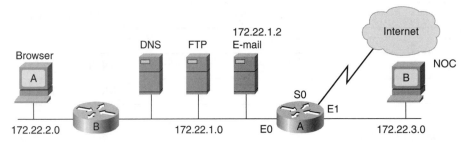

Example B-9 *Configuration on Router A in Figure B-16*

```
access-list 118 permit tcp any 172.22.0.0  0.0.255.255 eq www established
access-list 118 permit tcp any host 172.22.1.2 eq smtp
access-list 118 permit udp any any eq dns
access-list 118 permit udp 172.22.3.0  0.0.0.255 172.22.1.0 0.0.0.255 eq snmp
access-list 118 deny icmp any 172.22.0.0  0.0.255.255 echo
access-list 118 permit icmp any any echo-reply
!
interface ethernet 0
ip access-group 118 out
```

In Example B-9, access list 118 is applied outbound on router A's Ethernet 0 interface. With the configuration shown in Example B-9, *replies* to queries from the Client A browser (or any other host on the corporate network) to the Internet are allowed back into the corporate network (because they are established sessions). Browser queries *from* external sources are not explicitly allowed and are discarded by the implicit **deny any** at the end of the access list.

The access list in Example B-9 also allows e-mail (SMTP) to be delivered exclusively to the mail server. The name server is permitted to resolve DNS requests. The 172.22.1.0 subnet is controlled by the network management group located at the NOC server (Client B), so network-management queries (Simple Network Management Protocol [SNMP]) will be allowed to reach these devices in the server farm. Attempts to ping the corporate network from the outside or from subnet 172.22.3.0 will fail because the access list blocks the echo requests. However, replies to echo requests generated from within the corporate network are allowed to reenter the network.

Location of Extended Access Lists

Because extended access lists can filter on more than a source address, location is no longer the constraint it was when considering the location of a standard access list. Policy decisions and goals are frequently the driving forces behind extended access list placement.

If your goal is to minimize traffic congestion and maximize performance, you might want to push the access lists close to the source to minimize cross-network traffic and administratively prohibited ICMP messages. If your goal is to maintain tight control over access lists as part of your network security strategy, you might want them to be more centrally located. Notice how changing network goals affects access list configuration.

Here are some things to consider when placing extended access lists:

- Minimize distance traveled by traffic that will be denied (and ICMP unreachable messages).

- Keep denied traffic off the backbone.

- Select the router to receive CPU overhead from access lists.

- Consider the number of interfaces affected.

- Consider access list management and security.

- Consider network growth impacts on access list maintenance.

Restricting Virtual Terminal Access

This section discusses how you can use standard access lists to limit virtual terminal access. Standard and extended access lists block packets from going *through* the router. They are not designed to block packets that originate within the router. An outbound Telnet extended access list does not prevent router-initiated Telnet sessions by default.

For security purposes, users can be denied virtual terminal (vty) access to the router, or they can be permitted vty access to the router but denied access to destinations from that router. Restricting vty access is less of a traffic-control mechanism than one technique for increasing network security.

Because vty access is accomplished using the Telnet protocol, there is only one type of vty access list.

How to Control vty Access

Just as a router has physical ports or interfaces such as Ethernet 0 and Ethernet 1, it also has virtual ports. These virtual ports are called virtual terminal lines. By default, there are five such virtual terminal lines, numbered vty 0 to 4, as shown in Figure B-17.

Figure B-17   *A Router Has Five Virtual Terminal Lines (Virtual Ports) by Default*

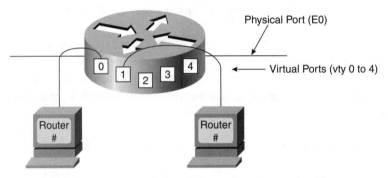

You should set identical restrictions on all virtual terminal lines, because you cannot control on which virtual terminal line a user will connect.

> **NOTE**   Some experts recommend that you configure one of the vty terminal lines differently than the others. This gives you a *back door* into the router.

Virtual Terminal Line Access Configuration

Use the **line vty** {*vty-number* | *vty-range*} global configuration command to place the router in line configuration mode, as described in Table B-18.

Table B-18   **line vty** *Command Description*

Parameter	Description
vty-number	Indicates the number of the vty line to be configured
vty-range	Indicates the range of vty lines to which the configuration applies

Use the **access-class** *access-list-number* {**in** | **out**} line configuration command to link an existing access list to a terminal line or range of lines, as described in Table B-19.

Table B-19   **access-class** *Command Description*

Parameter	Description
access-list-number	Indicates the number of the standard access list to be linked to a terminal line. This is a decimal number from 1 to 99 or from 1300 to 1999.
in	Prevents the router from receiving incoming connections *from* the addresses defined in the access list.
out	Prevents someone from initiating a Telnet *to* the addresses defined in the access list.

NOTE   When you use the **out** keyword in the **access-class** command, the addresses in the specified standard access list are treated as *destination* addresses, rather than as source addresses.

In Example B-10, any device on network 192.168.55.0 is permitted to establish a virtual terminal (Telnet) session with the router. Of course, the user must know the appropriate passwords for entering user mode and privileged mode.

Example B-10   *Configuration to Restrict Telnet Access to a Router*

```
access-list 12 permit 192.168.55.0 0.0.0.255
!
line vty 0 4
access-class 12 in
```

Notice that in this example, identical restrictions have been set on all virtual terminal lines (0 to 4), because you cannot control on which virtual terminal line a user will connect. Note that the implicit **deny any** still applies to this alternative application of access lists.

Verifying Access List Configuration

Use the **show access-lists** [*access-list-number* | *name*] privileged EXEC command to display access lists from all protocols, as described in Table B-20. If no parameters are specified, all access lists are displayed.

Table B-20   **show access-lists** *Command Description*

Parameter	Description
access-list-number	(Optional) Number of the access list to display.
name	(Optional) Name of the access list to display.

The system counts how many packets match each line of an access list; the counters are displayed by the **show access-lists** command.

Example B-11 illustrates sample output from the **show access-lists** command. In this example, the first line of the access list has been matched three times, and the last line has been matched 629 times. The second line has not been matched.

Example B-11   *Output of the* **show access-lists** *Command*

```
p1r1#show access-lists
Extended IP access list 100
    deny tcp host 10.1.1.2 host 10.1.1.1 eq telnet (3 matches)
    deny tcp host 10.1.2.2 host 10.1.2.1 eq telnet
    permit ip any any (629 matches)
```

Use the **show ip access-list** [*access-list-number | name*] EXEC command to display IP access lists, as described in Table B-21. If no parameters are specified, all IP access lists are displayed.

Table B-21   **show ip access-list** *Command Description*

Parameter	Description
access-list-number	(Optional) Number of the IP access list to display.
name	(Optional) Name of the IP access list to display.

Use the **clear access-list counters** [*access-list-number | name*] EXEC command to clear the counters for the number of matches in an extended access list, as described in Table B-22. If no parameters are specified, the counters are cleared for all access lists.

Table B-22   **clear access-list counters** *Command Description*

Parameter	Description
access-list-number	(Optional) Number of the access list for which to clear the counters.
name	(Optional) Name of the access list for which to clear the counters.

Use the **show line** [*line-number*] EXEC command to display information about terminal lines. The *line-number* is optional and indicates the absolute line number of the line for which you want to list parameters. If a line number is not specified, all lines are displayed.

This appendix contains information on the Open System Interconnection (OSI) reference model. It includes the following sections:

- Characteristics of the OSI Layers

- Protocols

- OSI Model and Communication Between Systems

- OSI Model's Physical Layer

- OSI Model's Data Link Layer

- OSI Model's Network Layer

- OSI Model's Transport Layer

- OSI Model's Session Layer

- OSI Model's Presentation Layer

- OSI Model's Application Layer

- Information Formats

Open System Interconnection (OSI) Reference Model

The Open System Interconnection (OSI) reference model describes how information from a software application in one computer moves through a network medium to a software application in another computer. The OSI reference model is a conceptual model that is composed of seven layers, each specifying particular network functions. The International Organization for Standardization (ISO) developed the model in 1984. It is now considered the primary architectural model for intercomputer communications. The OSI model divides the tasks involved with moving information between networked computers into seven smaller, more-manageable task groups. A task or group of tasks is assigned to each of the seven OSI layers. Each layer is reasonably self-contained so that the tasks assigned to each can be implemented independently. This enables the solutions offered by one layer to be updated without adversely affecting the other layers. The following list details the OSI reference model's seven layers:

- **Layer 7**—Application layer

- **Layer 6**—Presentation layer

- **Layer 5**—Session layer

- **Layer 4**—Transport layer

- **Layer 3**—Network layer

- **Layer 2**—Data link layer

- **Layer 1**—Physical layer

Figure C-1 illustrates the seven-layer OSI reference model.

Figure C-1 *OSI Reference Model Contains Seven Independent Layers*

7	Application
6	Presentation
5	Session
4	Transport
3	Network
2	Data link
1	Physical

Characteristics of the OSI Layers

The OSI reference model's seven layers can be divided into two categories: upper layers and lower layers.

The upper layers contend with application issues and are generally only implemented in software. The highest layer, the application layer, is closest to the end user. Both users and application layer processes interact with software applications that contain a communications component. The term *upper layer* is sometimes used to refer to any layer above another layer in the OSI model.

Terminology: Upper Layers

Generally speaking, the term *upper layers* is often used to refer to Layers 5, 6, and 7; however, this terminology is relative.

The OSI model's *lower layers* handle data transport issues. The physical layer and the data link layer are implemented in hardware and software. The other lower layers are generally only implemented in software. The lowest layer, which is the physical layer, is closest to the physical network medium (for example, the network cabling) and is responsible for actually placing information on the medium.

Terminology: Lower Layers

Generally speaking, the term *lower layers* is often used to refer to Layers 1 through 4; however, this terminology is relative.

Figure C-2 illustrates the division between the upper and lower OSI layers.

Figure C-2 *Two Sets of Layers Comprise the OSI Layers*

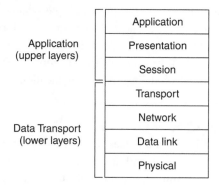

Protocols

Although the OSI model provides a conceptual framework for communication between computers, the model itself is not a method of communication. Actual communication is made possible through communication protocols. In the context of data networking, a *protocol* is a formal set of rules and conventions that governs how computers exchange information over a network medium. A protocol implements the functions of one or more OSI layers. A wide variety of communication protocols exist, but they all tend to fall into one of the following groups: LAN protocols, WAN protocols, network protocols, or routing protocols. *LAN protocols* operate at the physical and data link layers of the OSI model and define communication over the various LAN media. *WAN protocols* operate at the lowest three layers of the OSI model and define communication over the various wide-area media. *Routing protocols* are network layer protocols that are responsible for path determination and traffic switching. Finally, *network protocols* are the various upper-layer protocols that exist in a given protocol suite.

Many *protocol suites* specify various protocols defined in the seven OSI layers. Protocol suites are also known as *protocol stacks*.

OSI Model and Communication Between Systems

When information is transferred from a software application in one computer system to a software application in another computer system, it must pass through each of the OSI layers. For example, if a software application in System A has information to transmit to a software application in System B, the application program in System A passes its information to System A's application layer (Layer 7). Next, the application layer passes the information to the presentation layer (Layer 6), which relays the data to the session layer (Layer 5), and so on, down to the physical layer (Layer 1). At the physical layer, the information is placed on the physical network medium and sent across the medium to System B. System B's physical layer removes the information from the physical medium. Its physical layer then passes the information up to the data link layer (Layer 2), which passes it to the network layer (Layer 3), and so on, until it reaches System B's application layer (Layer 7). Finally, System B's application layer passes the information to the recipient application program to complete the communication process.

Interaction Between OSI Model Layers

A given OSI layer generally communicates with three other OSI layers: the layer directly above it, the layer directly below it, and its peer layer in other networked computer systems. For example, System A's data link layer communicates with System A's network layer, System A's physical layer, and System B's data link layer. Figure C-3 illustrates this interaction example.

Figure C-3   *OSI Model Layer Communicates with Three Other Layers*

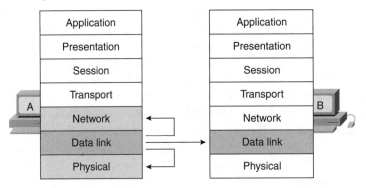

OSI Layer Services

One OSI layer communicates with another layer to make use of the services provided by that other layer. The services provided by adjacent layers help a given OSI layer communicate with its peer layer in other computer systems. Layer services involve three basic elements: the service user, the service provider, and the service access point (SAP).

In this context, the *service user* is the OSI layer that requests services from an adjacent OSI layer. The *service provider* is the OSI layer that provides services to service users. OSI layers can provide services to multiple service users. The *SAP* is a conceptual location at which one OSI layer can request the services of another OSI layer.

Figure C-4 illustrates how these three elements interact at the network and data link layers.

Figure C-4 *Service Users, Service Providers, and SAPs Interact at the Network and Data Link Layers*

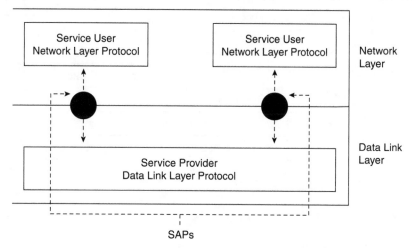

OSI Model Layers and Information Exchange

The seven OSI layers use various forms of control information to communicate with their peer layers in other computer systems. This control information consists of specific requests and instructions that are exchanged between peer OSI layers.

Control information typically takes one of two forms: headers and trailers. *Headers* are prepended to data that has been passed down from upper layers. *Trailers* are appended to data that has been passed down from upper layers. An OSI layer is not required to attach a header or trailer to data from upper layers.

Depending on the layer that analyzes the information unit, headers, trailers, and data are relative concepts. An information unit, for example, consists of a Layer 3 header and data at the network layer. At the data link layer, however, all the information passed down by the network layer (the Layer 3 header and the data) is treated as data.

In other words, the data portion of an information unit at a given OSI layer can potentially contain headers, trailers, and data from all the higher layers. This is known as *encapsulation*. Figure C-5 illustrates how the header and data from one layer are encapsulated to become the data of the next lowest layer.

Figure C-5 *Headers and Data Are Encapsulated During Information Exchange*

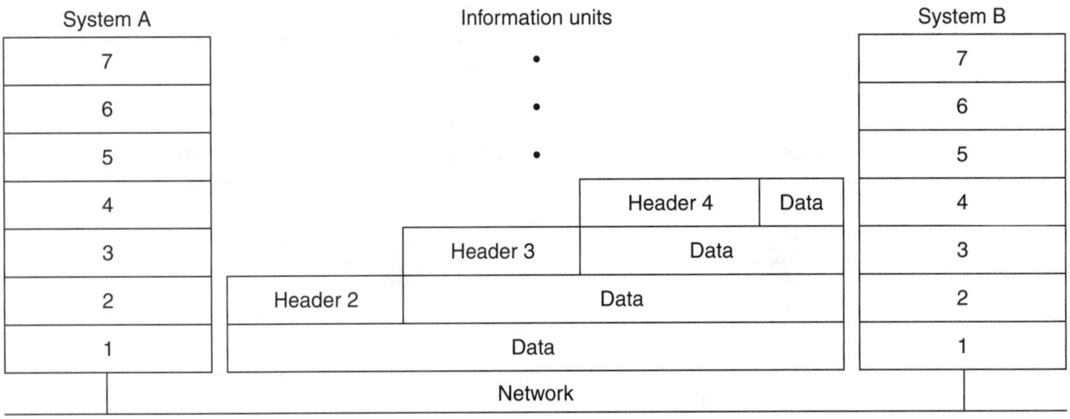

Information Exchange Process

The information exchange process occurs between peer OSI layers. Each layer in the source system adds control information to data, and each layer in the destination system analyzes and removes the control information from that data.

For example, if System A sends data from a software application to System B, the data is passed to System A's application layer. System A's application layer then communicates any control information required by System B's application layer by prepending a header to the data. The resulting information unit (a header and the data) is passed to the presentation layer, which prepends its own header that contains control information intended for System B's presentation layer.

The information unit grows in size as each layer prepends its own header, which contains control information to be used by its peer layer in System B. At the physical layer, the entire information unit is placed on the network medium (in some cases a trailer will also be appended; for simplicity, this example assumes that only headers will be prepended).

System B's physical layer receives the information unit and passes it to the data link layer. Next, System B's data link layer reads the control information contained in the header that was prepended by System A's data link layer. Next, the data link layer removes the header and passes the remainder of the information unit to the network layer. Each layer performs the same actions: the layer reads the header from its peer layer, strips it off, and passes the remaining information unit to the next highest layer. After the application layer performs these actions, the data is passed to System B's recipient software application in exactly the form in which it was transmitted by the application in System A.

OSI Model's Physical Layer

The *physical layer* defines the electrical, mechanical, procedural, and functional specifications for activating, maintaining, and deactivating the physical link between communicating network systems. Physical layer specifications define characteristics such as voltage levels, timing of voltage changes, physical data rates, maximum transmission distances, and physical connectors. Physical layer implementations can be categorized as either LAN or WAN specifications. Figure C-6 illustrates some common LAN and WAN physical layer implementations.

Figure C-6   *Physical Layer Implementations Can Be LAN or WAN Specifications*

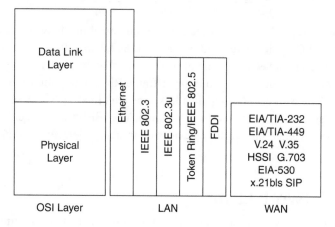

Physical Layer Implementations

OSI Model's Data Link Layer

The *data link layer* reliably transits data across a physical network link. Different data link layer specifications define different network and protocol characteristics, including physical addressing, network topology, error notification, frame sequencing, and flow control. Physical addressing (as opposed to network addressing) defines how devices are addressed at the data link layer. A network topology consists of the data link layer specifications that often define how devices are to be connected physically, such as in a bus or ring topology. Error notification alerts upper-layer protocols that a transmission error has occurred, and the sequencing of data frames reorders frames that are transmitted out of sequence. Finally, flow control moderates data transmission so that the receiving device is not overwhelmed with more traffic than it can handle at one time.

The Institute of Electrical and Electronics Engineers (IEEE) has subdivided the LAN data link layer into two sublayers: Logical Link Control (LLC) and Media Access Control (MAC), as illustrated in Figure C-7.

Figure C-7 *LAN Data Link Layer Contains Two Sublayers*

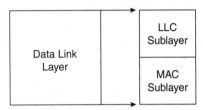

The data link layer's LLC sublayer manages communications between devices over a single network link. LLC, which is defined in the IEEE 802.2 specification, supports both connectionless and connection-oriented services used by higher-layer protocols. IEEE 802.2 defines a number of fields in data link layer frames that enable multiple higher-layer protocols to share a single physical data link. The data link layer's MAC sublayer manages protocol access to the physical network medium. The IEEE MAC specification defines MAC addresses, thereby enabling multiple devices to uniquely identify each other at the data link layer.

OSI Model's Network Layer

The *network layer* provides routing and related functions that enable multiple data links to be combined into an internetwork. This is accomplished by the logical addressing (as opposed to the physical addressing) of devices. The network layer supports both connection-oriented and connectionless service from higher-layer protocols. Routing protocols, routed protocols, and other types of protocols are implemented at the network layer.

Some common routing protocols include Border Gateway Protocol (BGP), which is an Internet interdomain routing protocol; Open Shortest Path First (OSPF), which is a link-state, interior gateway protocol developed for use in Transmission Control Protocol/Internet Protocol (TCP/IP) networks; and Routing Information Protocol (RIP), which is a TCP/IP routing protocol that uses hop count as its metric.

OSI Model's Transport Layer

The *transport layer* implements optional, reliable internetwork data transport services that are transparent to upper layers. Transport layer functions can include flow control, multiplexing, virtual circuit management, and error checking and recovery.

Flow control manages data transmission between devices so that the transmitting device does not send more data than the receiving device can process. Multiplexing enables the transmission of data from several applications to a single physical link. The transport layer establishes, maintains, and terminates virtual circuits. Error checking involves creating various mechanisms for detecting transmission errors, while error recovery involves taking an action, such as requesting that data be retransmitted, to resolve any errors.

Some transport layer implementations include *TCP*, which is the protocol in the TCP/IP suite that provides reliable transmission of data, and *OSI transport protocols*, which are a series of transport protocols in the OSI protocol suite.

OSI Model's Session Layer

The *session layer* establishes, manages, and terminates communication sessions between presentation layer entities. Communication sessions consist of service requests and service responses that occur between applications that are located in different devices. Protocols that are implemented at the session layer coordinate these requests. Some examples of session layer implementations include Zone Information Protocol (ZIP), which is the AppleTalk protocol that coordinates the name binding process; and Session Control Protocol (SCP), which is the DECnet Phase IV session layer protocol.

OSI Model's Presentation Layer

The *presentation layer* provides a variety of coding and conversion functions that are applied to application layer data. These functions ensure that information sent from one system's application layer is readable by another system's application layer. Some examples of presentation layer coding and conversion schemes include common data representation formats, conversion of character representation formats, common data compression schemes, and common data encryption schemes.

Common data representation formats, or the use of standard image, sound, and video formats, enable different computer systems to interchange application data. Conversion schemes are used to exchange information with systems by using different text and data representations, such as extended binary coded decimal interchange code (EBCDIC) and American Standard Code for Information Interchange (ASCII). Standard data compression schemes enable data that is compressed at the source device to be properly decompressed at the destination. Standard data encryption schemes enable data that is encrypted at the source device to be properly deciphered at the destination.

Presentation layer implementations are not typically associated with a particular protocol stack. Some well-known standards for video include QuickTime and Motion Picture Experts Group (MPEG). *QuickTime* is an Apple Computer specification for video and audio, and *MPEG* is a standard for video compression and coding.

Among the well-known graphic image formats are Graphics Interchange Format (GIF) and Joint Photographic Experts Group (JPEG). *GIF* is a standard for compressing and coding graphic images. *JPEG* is another compression and coding standard for graphic images.

OSI Model's Application Layer

The *application layer* is the OSI layer that is closest to the end user; this means that both the OSI application layer and the user interact directly with the software application.

This layer interacts with software applications that implement a communicating component. Such application programs fall outside the scope of the OSI model. Application layer functions typically include identifying communication partners, determining resource availability, and synchronizing communication.

When identifying communication partners, the application layer determines the identity and availability of communication partners for an application that has data to transmit. When determining resource availability, the application layer must decide whether sufficient network resources for the requested communication exist. In synchronizing communication, the application layer manages all communication between applications. Some examples of application layer implementations include TCP/IP applications and OSI applications. TCP/IP applications are protocols, such as Telnet, File Transfer Protocol (FTP), and Simple Mail Transfer Protocol (SMTP) that exist in the TCP/IP protocol suite. *OSI applications* are protocols, such as File Transfer, Access, and Management (FTAM), Virtual Terminal Protocol (VTP), and Common Management Information Protocol (CMIP) that exist in the OSI protocol suite.

Information Formats

The data and control information that is transmitted through internetworks takes various forms. The terms used to refer to these information formats are not used consistently in the internetworking industry, but are sometimes used interchangeably. Common information formats include the following:

- Frames

- Datagrams

- Packets

- Segments

- Messages

- Cells

- Data units

A *frame* is an information unit whose source and destination are data link layer entities. A frame is composed of the data link layer header (and possibly a trailer) and upper-layer data. The header and trailer contain control information that is intended for the destination system's data link layer entity. The data link layer header and trailer encapsulate data from upper-layer entities. Figure C-8 illustrates the basic components of a data link layer frame.

Figure C-8 *Data from Upper-Layer Entities Comprises the Data Link Layer Frame*

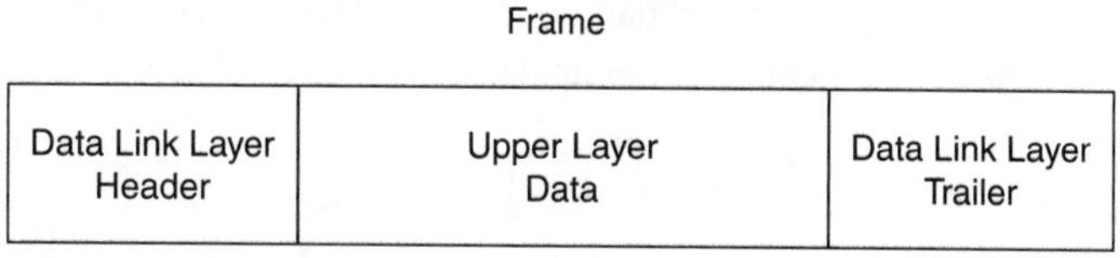

Frame

Data Link Layer Header	Upper Layer Data	Data Link Layer Trailer

The term *datagram* refers to an information unit whose source and destination are network layer entities. If a datagram needs to be sent across a network that can only handle a certain amount of data at a time, the datagram can be fragmented into multiple packets and then reassembled at the destination. Thus, a datagram is a unit of data, whereas a packet is what physically goes on the network. If no fragmentation is required, a packet is a datagram. The two terms are often used interchangeably.

A datagram or packet is composed of the network layer header (and possibly a trailer) and upper-layer data. The header and trailer contain control information that is intended for the destination system's network layer entity. The network layer header and trailer encapsulate data from upper-layer entities. Figure C-9 illustrates the basic components of a network layer datagram or packet.

Figure C-9 *Three Basic Components Comprise a Network Layer Datagram or Packet*

Datagram or Packet

Network Layer Header	Upper Layer Data	Network Layer Trailer

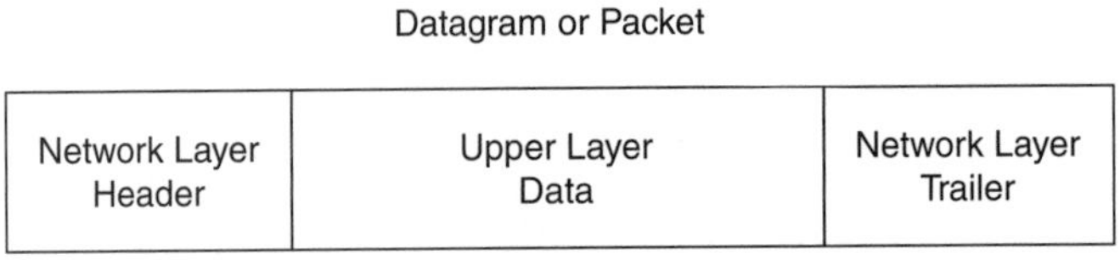

The term *segment* refers to an information unit whose source and destination are transport layer entities.

A *message* is an information unit whose source and destination entities exist above the network layer (often in the application layer).

A *cell* is an information unit of a fixed size whose source and destination are data link layer entities. Cells are used in switched environments such as Asynchronous Transfer Mode (ATM) networks. A cell is composed of the header and payload. The header contains control information that is intended for the destination data link layer entity; an ATM cell header is 5 bytes long. The payload contains upper-layer data that is encapsulated in the cell header; an ATM cell payload is 48 bytes long.

The length of the header and the payload fields are always exactly the same for each cell. Figure C-10 depicts an ATM cell's components.

Figure C-10 *Two Components Comprise an ATM Cell*

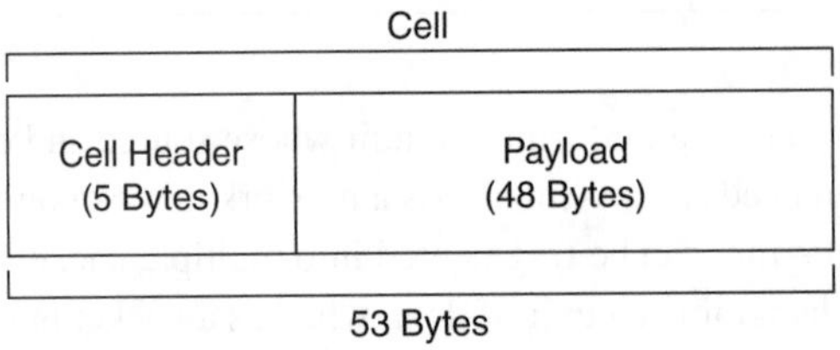

Cell

Cell Header (5 Bytes)	Payload (48 Bytes)

53 Bytes

Data unit is a generic term that refers to a variety of information units. Some common data units include service data units (SDU), protocol data units (PDU), and bridge protocol data units (BPDU). *SDUs* are information units from upper-layer protocols that define a service request to a lower-layer protocol. *PDU* is OSI terminology for describing the data unit at a given layer; for example, the Layer 3 PDU is also known as a packet, and the Layer 4 PDU is also known as a segment. *BPDUs* are used as hello messages by the spanning-tree algorithm.

This appendix contains information about Cisco Network Address Translation (NAT) and Port Address Translation (PAT) and includes the following sections:

- Why Use NAT?

- NAT Terminology

- NAT and PAT Operation

- Configuring NAT and PAT

- Verifying NAT and PAT

- Implementation Considerations

Network Address Translation

IP address depletion is a key problem facing the Internet. To help maximize the use of registered IP addresses, Cisco IOS Release 11.2 and later versions include software that implements Network Address Translation and Port Address Translation. This feature, which is the Cisco implementation of RFC 3022, *Traditional IP Network Address Translator (Traditional NAT)*, provides a method for using the same IP addresses in multiple internal stub networks, thereby reducing the need for registered IP addresses.

Why Use NAT?

NAT is used in the following situations:

- **When you want to connect to the Internet, but not all hosts have globally unique IP addresses**: NAT technology enables private IP internetworks that use nonregistered IP addresses to connect to the Internet. A NAT router is placed on the border of a stub domain (referred to as the *inside network*) and a public network, such as the Internet (referred to as the *outside* network). The NAT router translates the internal local addresses into globally unique IP addresses before sending packets to the outside network.

  NAT takes advantage of the fact that relatively few hosts in a stub domain communicate outside of the domain at any given time. As a result, only a subset of the IP addresses in a stub domain must be translated into globally unique IP addresses when outside communication is necessary.

- **When you need to modify your internal addresses because you are changing Internet service providers (ISP)**: NAT can be used to translate the appropriate addresses. This enables you to change addresses incrementally, without changing hosts or routers other than those that border stub domains.

NAT Terminology

NAT uses the terms *inside* and *outside,* and *local* and *global*, as shown in Figure D-1 and defined in Table D-1.

Figure D-1   *Network Address Translation Is Used to Translate Addresses Between the Inside and Outside Networks*

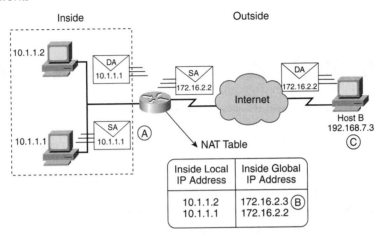

> **NOTE**   Recall that the IP addresses shown in the examples in this book are private addresses. In practice, public addresses would be used on the Internet.

Table D-1   *NAT Terminology*

Term	Definition
Inside local IP address (A)	The IP address assigned to a host on the inside network. The address is typically an RFC 1918 (*Address Allocation for Private Internet Space*) address.
Inside global IP address (B)	A globally unique IP address (typically assigned by an ISP) that represents one or more inside local IP addresses to the outside world.
Outside global IP address (C)	The IP address assigned to a host on the outside network by its owner. The address is globally unique.
Outside local IP address (not shown)	The IP address of an outside host as it appears to the inside network. The address is typically allocated from address space that is routable on the inside, usually from the RFC 1918 address space.
Simple translation entry	A translation entry that maps one IP address to another. The NAT table in Figure D-1 shows this type of entry.
Extended translation entry (not shown)	A translation entry that maps one IP address and port pair to another.

> **NOTE** The terms *inside*, *outside*, *local*, and *global* in Table D-1 are *relative* references in the end-to-end transmission path between devices, depending on the viewpoint of the end station. For example, an *inside local* address from a sender's point of view is an *outside local* address from a receiver's point of view.

NAT and PAT Operation

NAT can be used to perform several functions, including the following:

- **Static address translation**: Establishes a one-to-one mapping between inside local and global addresses.

- **Dynamic source address translation**: Establishes a dynamic mapping between the inside local and global addresses by associating the local addresses to be translated with a pool of addresses from which to allocate global addresses. The router creates translations as needed.

- **Address overloading**: Can conserve addresses in the inside global address pool by allowing source ports in TCP connections or User Datagram Protocol (UDP) conversations to be translated. When different inside local addresses map to the same inside global address, TCP or UDP port numbers are used to distinguish between them. Address overloading is also known as PAT.

The following sections describe the operation of these NAT functions.

> **NOTE** NAT also supports TCP load distribution and handles overlapping network addressing; these features are not described in this appendix.

Translating Inside Local Addresses

Figure D-2 illustrates NAT operation when NAT is used to translate addresses from inside a network.

Figure D-2 *Translating Inside Local Addresses*

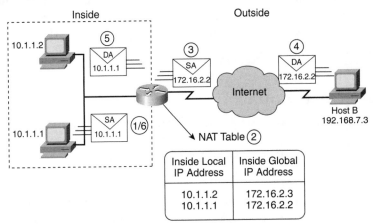

The following describes this process of translating inside local addresses:

Step 1   The user at Host 10.1.1.1 opens a connection to Host B.

Step 2   The first packet that the router receives from Host 10.1.1.1 causes the router
to check its NAT table.

If a translation is found because it has been statically configured, the router
continues to Step 3.

If no translation is found, the router determines that address 10.1.1.1 must
be translated. The router allocates a new address and sets up a translation
of the inside local address 10.1.1.1 to an inside global address from the
dynamic address pool. This type of translation entry is referred to as a
simple entry.

Step 3   In the packet's source IP address field, the router replaces Host 10.1.1.1's
inside local IP address with the selected inside global address (172.16.2.2)
and forwards the packet.

Step 4   Host B receives the packet and responds to Host 10.1.1.1 using the inside
global IP address 172.16.2.2.

Step 5   When the router receives the packet with the inside global IP address
172.16.2.2, the router uses the inside global address as a reference to
perform a NAT table lookup. The router then changes the packet's
destination address field to Host 10.1.1.1's inside local address and
forwards the packet to Host 10.1.1.1.

Step 6   Host 10.1.1.1 receives the packet and continues the conversation. For each packet, the router performs Steps 2 through 5.

Overloading Inside Global Addresses

Figure D-3 illustrates NAT operation when a single inside global address simultaneously represents multiple inside local addresses; overloading addresses is also known as PAT.

Figure D-3   *PAT: Overloading Inside Global Addresses*

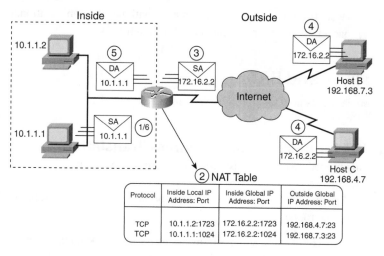

The following describes the process of overloading inside global addresses, as depicted in Figure D-3:

Step 1   The user at Host 10.1.1.1 opens a connection to Host B.

Step 2   The first packet the router receives from Host 10.1.1.1 causes the router to check its NAT table.

If no translation is found, the router determines that address 10.1.1.1 must be translated. The router allocates a new address and sets up a translation of the inside local address 10.1.1.1 to an inside global address (172.16.2.2). If overloading is enabled and another translation is active, the router reuses the global address from that translation and uses the port number to distinguish it from the other translation entry. This type of entry is called an *extended entry.*

Step 3   In the packet's source IP address field, the router replaces Host 10.1.1.1's inside local IP address with the selected inside global address (172.16.2.2) and forwards the packet.

Step 4   Host B receives the packet and responds to Host 10.1.1.1 using the inside global IP address 172.16.2.2.

Step 5   When the router receives the packet with the inside global IP address 172.16.2.2, the router uses the inside global address and port number and the outside address and port number as references to perform a NAT table lookup. The router then changes the packet's destination IP address field to Host 10.1.1.1's inside local address and forwards the packet to Host 10.1.1.1.

Host 10.1.1.1 receives the packet and continues the conversation. For each packet, the router performs Steps 2 through 5.

Configuring NAT and PAT

This section describes how to configure NAT and PAT.

Configuring NAT for Basic Local IP Address Translation

The following procedure enables basic local IP address translation:

Step 1   At a minimum, IP routing and appropriate IP addresses must be configured on the router.

Step 2   To perform static address translations for inside local addresses, define the addresses using the following command:

```
Router(config)#ip nat inside source static local-ip global-ip
```

Step 3   To perform dynamic translations, do the following:

a. Configure a standard IP access list to identify the inside network addresses that will be translated.

```
Router(config)#access-list access-list-number permit source [source-
wildcard]
```

b. Configure an IP NAT pool that defines the global addresses to which the inside local addresses will be translated, using the following command:

```
Router(config)#ip nat pool name start-ip end-ip {netmask netmask |
  prefix-length prefix-length}
```

This command defines a pool of contiguous addresses from the start address to the end address, using the netmask or prefix length. These addresses are allocated as needed.

c. Configure the translation to use the access list and the IP NAT pool, using the following command:

```
Router(config)#ip nat inside source list access-list-number pool name
```

Step 4   Enable NAT on at least one inside and one outside interface using the following command:

```
Router(config-if)#ip nat {inside ¦ outside}
```

Step 5   Only packets moving between inside and outside interfaces are translated. For example, if a packet is received on an inside interface but is not destined for an outside interface, it is not translated.

Example D-1 shows a sample configuration of basic inside local address translation. This example uses a pool of addresses named net-172 to translate inside local addresses 10.1.1.x to inside global addresses 172.16.2.x.

Example D-1   *Example of Basic Inside Local Address Translation*

```
ip nat pool net-172 172.16.2.1 172.16.2.254 netmask 255.255.255.0
ip nat inside source list 1 pool net-172
!
interface Serial0
  ip address 172.30.232.182 255.255.255.240
  ip nat outside
!
interface Ethernet0
  ip address 10.1.1.254 255.255.255.0
  ip nat inside
!
access-list 1 permit 10.1.1.0 0.0.0.255
```

Configuring Inside Global Address Overloading or PAT

The following procedure configures inside global address overloading:

Step 1   At a minimum, IP routing and appropriate IP addresses must be configured on the router.

Step 2   Configure dynamic address translation, as described in the "Configuring NAT for Basic Local IP Address Translation" section earlier in this appendix.

When you define the mapping between the access list and the IP NAT pool, add the **overload** keyword to the command:

```
Router(config)#ip nat inside source list access-list-number pool name
  overload
```

Alternatively, the address of an interface on the router can be used as the address to which the inside local addresses will be translated, using the following command:

```
Router(config)#ip nat inside source list access-list-number interface
  interface-name overload
```

Step 3   Enable NAT on the appropriate interfaces with the following command:

```
Router(config-if)#ip nat {inside ¦ outside}
```

Example D-2 shows a sample configuration of inside global address overloading. This example uses a pool of addresses named net-172 to translate inside local addresses 10.1.1.x to inside global addresses 172.16.2.x. Inside global addresses are overloaded.

Example D-2   *Example of Inside Global Address Overloading*

```
ip nat pool net-172 172.16.2.1 172.16.2.254 netmask 255.255.255.0
ip nat inside source list 1 pool net-172 overload
!
interface Serial0
  ip address 172.30.232.182 255.255.255.240
  ip nat outside
!
interface Ethernet0
  ip address 10.1.1.254 255.255.255.0
  ip nat inside
!
access-list 1 permit 10.1.1.0 0.0.0.255
```

Verifying NAT and PAT

This section lists **show**, **clear**, and **debug** commands used to verify NAT and PAT operation.

show Commands

Table D-2 identifies **show** commands used to verify NAT operation.

Table D-2   **show** *Commands to Verify NAT Operation*

Command	Description
show ip nat translations [verbose]	Shows active translations
show ip nat statistics	Shows translation statistics

Example D-3 shows sample output from when basic IP address translation is configured.

Example D-3   *Sample Verification Output for Basic IP Address Translation*

```
router#show ip nat translation
Pro  Inside global      Inside local      Outside local      Outside global
---    172.16.2.2         10.1.1.1           ---                ---
---    172.16.2.3         10.1.1.2           ---                ---
```

Example D-4 shows sample output from when IP address translation with overloading is configured.

Example D-4 *Sample Verification Output for IP Address Translation with Overloading*

```
router#show ip nat translation
Pro  Inside global      Inside local      Outside local       Outside global
udp  172.16.2.2:1220     10.1.1.1:1220     172.30.2.132:53     172.30.2.132:53
tcp  172.16.2.2:11012    10.1.1.2:11012    172.30.1.220:23     172.30.1.220:23
tcp  172.16.2.2:1067     10.1.1.1:1067     172.30.1.161:23     172.30.1.161:23
```

Clearing NAT Translation Entries

To clear a dynamic translation entry, use the commands shown in Table D-3.

Table D-3 *Commands to Clear NAT Translation Entries*

Command	Description
clear ip nat translation*	Clears all dynamic translation entries.
clear ip nat translation inside *global-ip local-ip* [**outside** *local-ip global-ip*]	Clears a simple dynamic translation entry that contains an inside translation or both an inside and outside translation.
clear ip nat translation outside *local-ip global-ip*	Clears a simple dynamic translation entry that contains an outside translation.
clear ip nat translation *protocol* **inside** *global-ip global-port local-ip local-port* [**outside** *local-ip local-port global-ip global-port*]	Clears an extended dynamic entry (in its various forms).

Examples D-5 and D-6 provide two sample outputs using the **clear ip nat translation** commands.

Example D-5 *Clearing NAT Translation Example 1*

```
router#show ip nat translation
Pro  Inside global      Inside local      Outside local       Outside global
udp  172.16.2.2:1220     10.1.1.1:1220     172.30.2.132:53     172.30.2.132:53
tcp  172.16.2.2:11012    10.1.1.2:11012    172.30.1.220:23     172.30.1.220:23
tcp  172.16.2.2:1067     10.1.1.1:1067     172.30.1.161:23     172.30.1.161:23
router#clear ip nat translation *
router#show ip nat translation
router#
```

Example D-6 *Clearing NAT Translation Example 2*

```
router#show ip nat translation
Pro  Inside global       Inside local      Outside local       Outside global
udp  172.16.2.2:1220     10.1.1.1:1220     172.30.2.132:53     172.30.2.132:53
tcp  172.16.2.2:11012    10.1.1.2:11012    172.30.1.220:23     172.30.1.220:23
tcp  172.16.2.2:1067     10.1.1.1:1067     172.30.1.161:23     172.30.1.161:23
router#clear ip nat translation udp inside 172.16.2.2 1220 10.1.1.1 1220 outside
  172.30.2.132 53 172.30.2.132 53
router#show ip nat translation
Pro  Inside global       Inside local      Outside local       Outside global
tcp  172.16.2.2:11012    10.1.1.2:11012    172.30.1.220:23     172.30.1.220:23
tcp  172.16.2.2:1067     10.1.1.1:1067     172.30.1.161:23     172.30.1.161:23
```

Troubleshooting NAT

To view NAT operation, use the **debug ip nat** [**list** | **detailed**] command, which displays a line of output for each packet that is translated. Example D-7 shows sample output using the **debug ip nat** command.

Example D-7 *Tracing NAT Operations with* **debug ip nat**

```
router#debug ip nat
NAT:  s=10.1.1.1->172.16.2.2, d=172.30.2.132       [6825]
NAT:  s=172.30.2.132,        d=172.16.2.2->10.1.1.1  [21852]
NAT:  s=10.1.1.1->172.16.2.2, d=172.30.1.161       [6826]
NAT*: s=172.30.1.161,        d=172.16.2.2->10.1.1.1  [23311]
NAT*: s=10.1.1.1->172.16.2.2, d=172.30.1.161       [6827]
NAT*: s=10.1.1.1->172.16.2.2, d=172.30.1.161       [6828]
NAT*: s=172.30.1.161,        d=172.16.2.2->10.1.1.1  [23313]
NAT*: s=172.30.1.161,        d=172.16.2.2->10.1.1.1  [23325]
```

As an example of the meaning of the output in Example D-7, consider the fourth line of output:

- The asterisk next to NAT indicates that the translation is occurring in the fast path. The first packet in a conversation always goes through the slow path (that is, it is process-switched). The remaining packets go through the fast path if a cache entry exists.

- s=172.30.1.161 is the source address.

- d=172.16.2.2 is the destination address.

- 172.16.2.2->10.1.1.1 indicates that the address was translated.

- The value in brackets is the IP identification number. It might be useful for troubleshooting because it correlates with other packet traces, such as from protocol analyzers.

Implementation Considerations

Some things to consider before implementing NAT include the following:

■ Translation introduces delays into the switching paths.

■ NAT makes some applications that use IP addresses difficult or impossible to use. For example, public web pages that have links expressed using local IP addresses rather than DNS names are not usable by outside hosts.

■ NAT hides the hosts' real identity.

■ All packets that need to be translated must go through the NAT router, which might place limitations on the network design.

> **NOTE** Further information on NAT and PAT is available from the *Network Address Translation (NAT) Introduction* page at http://www.cisco.com/en/US/tech/tk648/tk361/tk438/tsd_technology_support_sub-protocol_home.html.

Acronyms and Abbreviations

This element lists abbreviations, acronyms, and initialisms used in this book and in the internetworking industry. Many of these acronyms and other terms are also described in the Cisco Internetworking Terms and Acronyms resource, available at http://www.cisco.com/univercd/cc/td/doc/cisintwk/ita/.

Acronym	Expanded Term
mu-sec	Microsecond
1RU	One rack unit
3DES	Triple Data Encryption Standard
3G	Third-generation
6PE	IPv6 on the MPLS PE routers
6-to-4	IPv6 to IPv4 tunnel
AAA	Authentication, authorization, and accounting
ABR	Area border router
AC	Alternating current
ACD	Automatic call distribution
ACELP	Algebraic code-excited linear prediction
ACL	Access Control List
ACNS	Application and Content Networking System
ACS	Access Control Server
AD	Advertised distance
ADPCM	Adaptive Differential Pulse Code Modulation
ADSL	Asymmetric DSL
AES	Advanced Encryption Standard
AIM	Advanced integration module
ALG	Application level gateway
AMR-NB	Adaptive Multi-Rate Narrow Band
ANS	Application Networking Services

Acronym	Expanded Term
ANSI	American National Standards Institute
AON	Application-Oriented Networking
AP	Access point
API	Application programming interface
APS	Automatic protection switching
ARCnet	Attached Resource Computer Network
ARP	Address Resolution Protocol
AS	Autonomous system
ASA	Adaptive Security Appliance
ASBR	Autonomous system boundary router
ASDM	Adaptive Security Device Manager
ASIC	Application-specific integrated circuit
ATM	Asynchronous Transfer Mode
AWPP	Adaptive Wireless Path Protocol
B	Bearer
BASc	Bachelor's degree in applied science
BCMSN	Building Cisco Multilayer Switched Networks
BECN	Backward explicit congestion notification
BER	Bit error rate
BGP	Border Gateway Protocol
BGP-4	BGP Version 4
BGP4+	Multiprotocol extensions to BGP version 4
BHT	Busy-hour traffic
BIA	Burned-in address
BOM	Bill of Materials
BOOTP	Bootstrap Protocol
BPDU	Bridge protocol data unit
BRI	Basic Rate Interface
BSCI	Building Scalable Cisco Internetworks
BSS	Basic Service Set
BSSID	Basic Service Set Identifier
CA	Collision Avoidance Certificate authority
CAC	Call admission control

Acronym	Expanded Term
CAM	Content-addressable memory
CAR	Committed access rate
CAS	Channel associated signaling
CatOS	Catalyst operating system
CATV	Cable TV
CBC-DES	Cipher-block chaining data encryption standard
CBWFQ	Class-based weighted fair queuing
CCDA	Cisco Certified Design Associate
CCDP	Cisco Certified Design Professional
CCIE	Cisco Certified Internet Expert
CCITT	Consultative Committee for International Telegraph and Telephone
CCK	Complementary Code Keying
CCKM	Cisco Centralized Key Management
CCNA	Cisco Certified Network Associate
CCNP	Cisco Certified Network Professional
CCS	Common channel signaling Centum Call Second
CCSI	Cisco Certified Systems Instructor
CCX	Cisco-Compatible Extensions
CD	Collision Detection
CDMA	Code Division Multiple Access
CDP	Cisco Discovery Protocol
CEF	Cisco Express Forwarding
CELP	Code Excited Linear Prediction Compression
CGMP	Cisco Group Management Protocol
CIDR	Classless interdomain routing
CIR	Committed information rate
CISP	Cardholder Information Security Program
CKIP	Cisco Key Integrity Protocol
CLI	Command-line interface
CLNP	Connectionless Network Protocol
CLNS	Connectionless Network Service
CMIC	Cisco Message Integrity Check

Acronym	Expanded Term
CMTS	Cable Modem Termination System
CNS	Cisco Network Service
CO	Central office
CoPP	Control plane policing
CoS	Class of service
CPE	Customer Premises Equipment
CQ	Custom queuing
CRTC	Canadian Radio-television and Telecommunications Commission
cRTP	RTP header compression, or compressed RTP
CS-ACELP	Conjugate Structure Algebraic Code Excited Linear Prediction Compression
CSC-SSM	Content Security and Control Security Services Module
CSMA	Carrier sense multiple access
CSMA/CD	Carrier sense multiple access collision detect
CST	Common Spanning Tree
CTI	Computer telephony integration
CTS	Clear to send
D	Delta
DAI	Dynamic ARP Inspection
dB	Decibel
dBi	dB isotropic
dBm	dB milliwatt
dBw	dB watt
DDoS	Distributed denial of service
DDR	Dial-on-demand routing
DEC	Digital Equipment Corporation
DES	Digital Encryption Standard
DESGN	Designing for Cisco Internetwork Solutions
DHCP	Dynamic Host Configuration Protocol
DHCPv6	DHCP for IPv6
DID	Direct Inward Dialing
DiffServ	Differentiated Services
DMVPN	Dynamic Multipoint VPN

Acronym	Expanded Term
DMZ	Demilitarized zone
DNS	Domain Name Service, or Domain Name System
DOCSIS	Data Over Cable Service Interface Specification
DoS	Denial of service
DPNSS	Digital Private Network Signaling System
DRED	Distributed random early detection
DS0	Digital signal level 0
DSCP	Differentiated Services Code Point
DSL	Digital subscriber line
DSLAM	DSL access multiplexer
DSP	Digital signal processor
DSS	Data Security Standard
DSTM	Dual-Stack Transition Mechanism
DSU	Data service unit
DTMF	Dual-tone multifrequency
DTP	Dynamic Trunking Protocol
DUAL	Diffusing Update Algorithm
DWDM	Dense Wavelength Division Multiplexing
E	Ear
E&M	recEive and transMit; sometimes also known as Ear and Mouth
E911	Enhanced 911
EAP	Extensible Authentication Protocol
EAP-FAST	EAP Flexible Authentication via Secure Tunneling
EAPoL	Extensible Authentication Protocol over LAN
EAP-TLS	EAP Transport Layer Security
EAP-TTLS	EAP Tunneled Transport Layer Security
EBGP	External BGP
ECN	Explicit congestion notification
EGP	Exterior Gateway Protocol
EIGRP	Enhanced Interior Gateway Routing Protocol
EIRP	Effective Isotropic Radiated Power
ERP	Enterprise resource planning

Acronym	Expanded Term
ES	End system
ESA	Extended service area
ESP	Encapsulating Security Payload
EtherIP	Ethernet in IP
ETSI	European Telecommunications Standards Institute
EUI-64	Extended universal identifier 64-bit
FCC	Federal Communications Commission
FCIP	Fiber Channel over IP
FD	Feasible distance
FDM	Frequency division multiplexing
FEC	Forwarding Equivalence Class
FECN	Forward Explicit Congestion Notification
FIB	Forwarding Information Base
FICON	Fiber Connection
FLSM	Fixed-Length Subnet Masking
FQDN	Fully qualified domain name
FRR	Fast reroute
FRTS	Frame Relay Traffic Shaping
FS	Feasible successor
FWSM	Firewall Services Module
FX	Foreign exchange
FXO	Foreign Exchange Office
FXS	Foreign Exchange Station
Gbps	Gigabits per second
GE	Gigabit Ethernet
GLBA	U.S. Gramm-Leach-Bliley Act of 1999
GLBP	Gateway Load-Balancing Protocol
GoS	Grade of Service
GPRS	General Packet Radio Service
GPS	Global positioning system
GRE	Generic Routing Encapsulation
GSM	Global System for Mobile

Acronym	Expanded Term
GSS	Global Site Selector
GTC	Generic Token Card
GTS	Generic Traffic Shaping
HDLC	High-Level Data Link Control
HDSL	High-data-rate DSL
HDSL-2	Second generation of HDSL
HIDS	Host-based intrusion detection system
HIPAA	Health Insurance Portability and Accountability Act
HIPS	Host-based intrusion prevention system
HMAC	Hash-based Message Authentication Code
HMAC-MD5	Hash-based Message Authentication Code Message Digest 5
HMAC-SHA	Hash-based Message Authentication Code Secure Hash Algorithm
H-REAP	Hybrid Remote Edge AP
HSRP	Hot Standby Router Protocol
HSSI	High-speed serial interface
HTTPS	HTTP secured by SSL
HVAC	Heating, ventilation, and air conditioning
HWIC	High-speed WAN interface card
Hz	Hertz
IANA	Internet Assigned Numbers Authority
IAPP	Inter-Access Point Protocol
IBGP	Internal BGP
IBNS	Identity-Based Networking Services
ICMP	Internet Control Message Protocol
ID	Identifier
IDF	Intermediate distribution frame
IDM	Cisco Intrusion Prevention System Device Manager
IDS	Intrusion Detection System
IDSL	ISDN DSL
IEEE	Institute of Electrical and Electronics Engineers
IETF	Internet Engineering Task Force
IGMP	Internet Group Management Protocol

Acronym	Expanded Term
IGP	Interior gateway protocol
IGRP	Interior Gateway Routing Protocol
IIS	Internet Information Server
IKE	Internet Key Exchange
IPC	IP Communications
IPCC	IP Contact Center
IPFIX	IP Flow Information Export
IPS	Intrusion Prevention System
IPsec	Internet Protocol Security
IP/TV	Internet Protocol Television
IPv4	IP version 4
IPv6	IP version 6
IPX	Internetwork Packet Exchange
IS	Intermediate system
ISDN	Integrated Services Digital Network
IS-IS	Intermediate System-to-Intermediate System
IS-ISv6	IS-IS version 6
ISL	Inter-switch link
ISM	Industrial, Scientific, and Medical
ISP	Internet service provider
ISR	Integrated Services Router
ISSU	In-Service Software Upgrade
IVR	Interactive voice response
kbps	Kilobits per second
kHz	Kilohertz
km	Kilometer
L1	Level 1
L1/L2	Level 1/Level 2
L2	Layer 2 Level 2
L2F	Layer 2 Forwarding
L2TP	Layer 2 Tunneling Protocol

Acronym	Expanded Term
LAC	L2TP Access Concentrator
LACP	Link Aggregation Control Protocol
LAG	Link aggregation
LAPB	Link Access Procedure Balanced
LBS	Location-based services
LD-CELP	Low-Delay Code Excited Linear Prediction Compression
LDP	Label Distribution Protocol
LEAP	Cisco Lightweight Extensible Authentication Protocol
LFI	Link Fragmentation and Interleaving
LLC	Logical Link Control
LLQ	Low latency queuing
LNS	L2TP Network Server
LRE	Long-Reach Ethernet
LSA	Link-state advertisement
LSDB	Link-state database
LSP	Label Switched Path Link-state packet
LSR	Label Switched Router
LSU	Link-state update
LWAPP	Lightweight AP Protocol
LZS	Lempel-Ziv Stack
M	Mouth
MAN	Metropolitan-area network
MAP	Mesh AP
MARS	Cisco Security Monitoring, Analysis, and Response System
MASc	Master's degree in applied science
Mbps	Megabits per second
MBSA	Microsoft Baseline Security Analyzer
MC	Multipoint controller
MCU	Multipoint control unit
MD5	Message Digest 5
MDS	Multilayer Directors and Fabric Switches

Acronym	Expanded Term
MGCP	Media Gateway Control Protocol
MHz	Megahertz
MIC	Message Integrity Check
MIR	Minimum information rate
MISTP	Multiple-Instance STP
MLP	Multilink Point-to-Point Protocol
MLS	Multilayer switching
MLSP	Multilayer Switching Protocol
MLS-RP	MLS Route Processor
MLS-SE	MLS Switching Engine
MM	Multimode
MoH	Music on hold
MOS	Mean opinion score
MP	Multilink Protocol Multipoint processor
MP3	MPEG-1 Audio Layer 3
MPCC	Microsoft Point-to-Point Compression
MPEG	Moving Picture Experts Group
MPLS	Multiprotocol Label Switching
MPMLQ	Multipulse Maximum Likelihood Quantization
MPPP	Multilink Point-to-Point Protocol
MRTG	Multi-Router Traffic Grapher
ms	Milliseconds
MSB	Most significant bit
MSCHAPv2	Microsoft Challenge Handshake Authentication Protocol version 2
MTBF	Mean time between failures
MTTR	Mean time to repair
MTU	Maximum transmission unit
mW	Milliwatt
MW	Megawatt
MWI	Message Waiting Indicator

Acronym	Expanded Term
NAC	Network Admission Control
NAD	Network Access Device
NAM	Network Analysis Module
NANP	North American Numbering Plan
NAP	Network Access Provider
NAS	Network Attached Storage Network Access Server
NAT	Network Address Translation
NAT-PT	NAT Protocol Translation
NBAR	Network-based application recognition
NBMA	Nonbroadcast multiaccess
NDS	Novell Directory Services
NEBS	Network Equipment Building System
NFC	NetFlow Collection Engine
NIC	Network interface card
NIDS	Network Intrusion Detection System
NIPS	Network-based intrusion prevention systems
NMS	Network management system
NOC	Network operations center
NPA	Numbering Plan Area
NSF	Nonstop Forwarding
NSP	Network Service Provider
NSSA	Not-so-stubby area
NTP	Network Time Protocol
OC	Optical carrier
ODR	On-Demand Routing
OFDM	Orthogonal Frequency Division Multiplexing
ONS	Optical Networking Solutions
OS	Operating system
OSI	Open Systems Interconnection
OSPF	Open Shortest Path First
OSPFv2	OSPF version 2

Acronym	Expanded Term
OSPFv3	OSPF version 3
OTAP	Over-the-Air Provisioning
OTP	One-time password
OUI	Organizational Unique Identifier
PAC	Protected Access Credential
PAgP	Port Aggregation Protocol
PAM	Pulse amplitude modulation
PAN	Personal-area network
PAT	Port Address Translation
PCI	Payment Card Industry
PCM	Pulse code modulation
PDA	Personal digital assistant
PDM	Protocol-Dependent Module
PDU	Protocol data unit
PE	Provider Edge
PEAP	Protected Extensible Authentication Protocol
PHY	Physical layer
PIM	Protocol-Independent Multicast
PIN	Personal identification number
PIPEDA	Canadian Personal Information Protection and Electronic Documents Act
PKC	Proactive Key Caching
PKI	Public key infrastructure
PMK	Pair-wise Master Key
PoE	Power over Ethernet
POP	Point of presence
POP3	Post Office Protocol version 3
POS	Packet over SONET/SDH
POTS	Plain old telephone service
PPDIOO	Prepare, Plan, Design, Implement, Operate, Optimize
PPPoA	PPP over ATM
PPPoE	PPP over Ethernet
pps	Packets per second

Acronym	Expanded Term
PPTP	Point-to-Point Tunneling Protocol
PQ	Priority queuing
PRC	Partial Route Calculation
PSK	Preshared key
PSQM	Perceptual Speech Quality Measurement
PSTN	Public switched telephone network
PTK	Pairwise Transient Key
PVC	Permanent virtual circuit
PVDM	Packet voice DSP module
PVST	Per-VLAN spanning tree
QoS	Quality of service
QPPB	QoS Policy Propagation on BGP
QSIG	Q Signaling
RAP	Rooftop AP
RARP	Reverse Address Resolution Protocol
RAS	Registration, Admission, and Status
RC4	Rivest Cipher 4
RDMA	Remote Data Memory Access
RDP	Router Discovery Protocol
REAP	Remote edge AP
RED	Random early detection
RF	Radio Frequency
RFI	Request for Information
RFP	Request for Proposal
RIP	Routing information protocol
RIPng	RIP new generation
RIPv1	Routing Information Protocol version 1
RIPv2	Routing Information Protocol version 2
RME	Resource Manager Essentials
RMON	Remote Monitoring
RMON2	Remote Monitoring 2
ROI	Return on Investment

Acronym	Expanded Term
RP	Rendezvous point
RPF	Reverse Path Forwarding
RPVST+	Rapid Per-VLAN Spanning Tree Plus, or RSTP with Per-VLAN Spanning Tree Plus
RRM	Radio resource management
RSP	Route Switch Processor
RSSI	Received signal strength indicator
RSTP	Rapid Spanning Tree Protocol
RSVP	Resource Reservation Protocol
RTCP	Real-time Transport Control Protocol
RTP	Real-time Transport Protocol
RTS	Request to send
RTT	Round-trip time
SAA	Service assurance agent
SAINT	Security Administrator's Integrated Network Tool
SAN	Storage area network
SCCP	Skinny Client Control Protocol
SCP	Secure Copy
SDF	Signature definition file
SDH	Synchronous Digital Hierarchy
SDM	Security Device Manager
SDP	Site Data Protection
SDSL	Symmetric DSL
SEC	U.S. Securities and Exchange Commission
SFP	Small Form Factor Pluggable
SFS	Server Fabric Switching
SFTP	SSH FTP
SIP	Session Initiation Protocol
SLA	Service level agreement
SM	Single-mode
SMDS	Switched Multimegabit Data Services
SMI	Structure of Management Information
SMTP	Simple Mail Transfer Protocol

Acronym	Expanded Term
SNA	Systems Network Architecture
SNAP	Subnetwork access protocol
SNMP	Simple Network Management Protocol
SNMPv1	SNMP version 1
SNMPv2	SNMP version 2
SNMPv3	SNMP version 3
SNR	Signal-to-noise ratio
SOA	Service-oriented architecture
SOHO	Small office, home office
SONA	Service-Oriented Network Architecture
SOX	U.S. Sarbanes-Oxley Act of 2002
SP	Service provider
SPA	Shared Port Adapter
SPF	Shortest path first
SRST	Survivable Remote Site Telephony
SRTP	Secure Real-Time Transport Protocol
SS7	Signaling System 7
SSH	Secure Shell
SSID	Service Set Identifier
SSL	Secure Sockets Layer
SSO	Stateful Switchover
STAC	Stacker
STP	Spanning Tree Protocol
SVC	Switched virtual circuit
TCO	Total cost of ownership
TDM	Time-division multiplexing
TDMA	Time division multiple access
TKIP	Temporal Key Integrity Protocol
TLV	Type, length, value
ToS	Type of service
TTL	Time to live

Acronym	Expanded Term
UA	User agent
UAC	UA client
UAS	UA server
uBR	Universal Broadband Router
UDLD	Unidirectional Link Detection
UDP	User Datagram Protocol
U/L	Universal/Local
UMTS	Universal Mobile Telephone Service
UNII	Unlicensed National Information Infrastructure
URI	Uniform Resource Identifier
uRPF	Unicast Reverse Path Forwarding
USB	Universal Serial Bus
UTP	Unshielded twisted-pair
UWN	Unified Wireless Network
V	Volt
v9	Version 9
VACM	View-based Access Control Model
VAD	Voice activity detection
VC	Virtual circuit
VDSL	Very-high-data-rate DSL
VIP	Versatile Interface Processor
VLSM	Variable-length subnet mask
VMPS	VLAN Membership Policy Server
VMS	VPN/Security Management Solution
VoATM	Voice over ATM
VoD	Video on demand
VoFR	Voice over Frame Relay
VoIP	Voice over IP
VoWLAN	Voice calls over a WLAN
VPDN	Virtual private dialup network
VPN	Virtual Private Network
VRRP	Virtual Router Redundancy Protocol
VTP	VLAN Trunking Protocol

Acronym	Expanded Term
W	Watt
WAAS	Wide-Area Application Services
WAE	Wide-Area Application Engine
WAFS	Wide-Area File Services
WAP	Wireless access point
WCS	Wireless Control System
WEP	Wired Equivalent Privacy
WFA	Wi-Fi Alliance
WFQ	Weighted fair queuing
WIC	WAN interface card
WiSM	Wireless Services Module
WLAN	Wireless LAN
WLANA	WLAN Association
WLC	WLAN controller
WLCM	Cisco WLC module
WLSE	Wireless LAN Solutions Engine
WoW	Workstation on wheels
WPA	Wi-Fi Protected Access
WRED	Weighted random early detection

Index

J -K -L

N

X - Y - Z